THE CANADIAN CRIMINAL JUSTICE SYSTEM

An Issues Approach to the Administration of Justice

Edited by
Nick Larsen

Canadian Scholars' Press Inc.   Toronto   1995

The Canadian Criminal Justice System

First published in 1995 by
Canadian Scholars' Press Inc.
180 Bloor St. W., Ste. 402,
Toronto, Ontario M5S 2V6

Canadian Cataloguing in Publication Data

Includes bibliographical references.
ISBN 1-55130-046-X

1. Criminal Justice, Administration of - Canada. 2. Criminal Justice, Administration of - Social Aspects - Canada. I. Larsen, Nick, 1948-.

HV9960.C2C3 1995 364.971 C94-931095-6

Cover design by Brad Horning

Printed and bound in Canada

Dedication

This book is dedicated to J.T.L.

acknowledgements

I wish to express my appreciation to several people who have contributed to the successful completion of this book. I would first like to thank the staff at Canadian Scholars' Press for undertaking to publish this collection of readings on relatively short notice. In particular, I would like to acknowledge the assistance of Brad Lambertus, who as managing editor, ensured that the project was kept on track and took care of all the necessary administrative details in an efficient and expedient fashion. I would also like to thank the contributors of the articles contained in this volume, and would especially like to acknowledge the efforts of Catherine Crow for taking time to write a completely new article for this collection during one of her busiest periods. Finally, I would like to thank the many people who provided encouragement and helpful suggestions during the selection of the articles. These people are too numerous to name, but I would especially like to thank Rick Linden of the Department of Sociology at the University of Manitoba and Brian Burtch and Simon Verdun-Jones of the School of Criminology at Simon Fraser University.

Contents

Young People and the Law

Aboriginal Justice

Future Directions in Criminal Justice

PREFACE

This edited collection is intended to provide students of criminal justice with an up-to-date collection of articles dealing with many of the most important issues affecting the current operation of the Canadian criminal justice system. Several criteria were used in selecting the specific articles for inclusion in this book. First, it was decided that, wherever possible, the articles would involve current empirical research under five years old. Although there are several exceptions to this criteria, older articles were included only if they dealt with significant issues and more recent research was unavailable on a given topic.

Although the collection is organized following the standard outline of the criminal justice system as it is covered in most criminal justice texts, the articles were selected around five main themes: 1) the lack of coordination in the criminal justice system; 2) the overly lenient sentences handed down by the criminal courts; 3) the recruitment of women and visible minorities in the criminal justice system and their experiences once employed; 4) young offenders and the youth justice system; and 5) Aboriginal justice. In addition, several articles were included which do not deal with these issues, but address important issues of a highly topical nature, including police burnout, AIDS in prisons, plea bargaining and the right to legal representation. Finally, two articles were selected which deal with the future of criminal justice. It should be noted that the manner in which the various articles intersect the issues is discussed in detail in the Introduction which follows.

A final selection criterion centres on the intended purpose of this book, which is to accompany a main text in criminal justice. Thus, the articles were selected so as to provide in-depth discussions of specialized, controversial topics, rather than detailed discussions about the operation of the criminal justice system, which are normally covered in lectures and/or a main text. In this respect, the articles were also selected with a view to providing the basis for presentations and/or debates in seminars and tutorials. However, in the final analysis, individual instructors will be the best judges of how to use this collection in their own classes.

Introduction

Many people argue that the Canadian criminal justice system appears to be in a state of crisis. Certainly, anyone following the current media coverage of crime and criminal justice issues could quite reasonably conclude that crime and disorder are rampant in Canadian society, and that the criminal justice system is virtually powerless to protect the Canadian public. There are almost daily reports of drive-by shootings, rapes, pre-teen crack dealers and other sensational crimes. Indeed, these reports have become so routine that they are often pushed off the front pages of major Canadian newspapers by coverage of the war in Bosnia or rising unemployment rates. At the same time, there are equally disturbing reports outlining how the police are unable to cope with crime which is spiralling out of control because of inadequate laws, unresponsive politicians and the leniency of the courts. In these accounts, the police and correctional personnel are depicted as dedicated professionals striving to protect society, only to have the courts acquit offenders on technicalities and/or impose completely inadequate sentences. The already lenient sentences are further diluted by the activities of the National Parole Board, whose members insist on releasing dangerous criminals back into society, where they invariably commit violent crimes against innocent citizens.

All of the above scenarios were documented in the pages of Canada's print media during a thirty day period in early 1994. Although many of the sensational headlines were loosely based on factual events, the articles which accompanied the headlines frequently made little attempt to provide balanced discussions of the issues. Although a few people did attempt to place Canada's "crime problem" into a more realistic perspective, their calls for a reasoned approach to the question of crime control have largely been ignored. Most of the editorial positions have generally followed the lead of a recent *Maclean's* editorial which called for a drastic crackdown on crime, albeit without suggesting many concrete approaches to be implemented.[1] Nevertheless, it appears clear that Canadians are frightened by what they perceive as escalating crime rates, and many people are demanding that the government do something about the problem before it reaches the proportions evident in the United States. It is also clear that many people feel that this "problem" can be solved by ever tougher measures against crime. Politicians have reacted to the public outcry by promising swift and decisive action. The proposed solutions range from toughening the National Parole Act and Young Offenders Act, through to the establishment of "boot camps" based on the training model used by the US Marine Corps. Any suggestions that these proposals are unlikely to work are dismissed as examples of the "left-wing, bleeding heart rhetoric" which created the crime problem in the first place.

The above discussion can be situated firmly within what is generally referred to as the "functionalist" or "consensus" approach to criminal justice. Briefly, the functionalist/consensus model argues that there is general agreement in society over norms and values, and that the laws are necessary to protect all of us from the activities of a few antisocial elements. The consensus model also argues that the criminal justice system operates fairly and can be trusted to administer justice in an unbiased fashion against all individuals and groups. Thus, we need not fear that the demanded crackdown will unfairly target certain minority groups. The proponents of the consensus model further argue that there are sufficient procedural safeguards in place to preclude wrongful conviction in the unlikely event that innocent people are drawn into the criminal justice process.

These two stipulations form the basis for a significant point of disagreement by the critical approach to criminal justice. The critical model starts from the basic assumption that there is much less consensus than is assumed by the consensus theorists, and that criminal legislation primarily reflects the interests of certain elite groups, who use the law to maintain their version of "social order".[2] The critical perspective further argues that the criminal justice system is not unbiased and that there are systematic biases insofar as the groups and/or types of crimes that are targeted by the system. More specifically, the critical theorists argue that the crimes committed by the capitalist elites rarely attract as much attention as the "street" crimes committed by the lower classes, even though they are often more harmful. In terms of the media debate discussed above, the critical theorists would argue that the sensational headlines are part of the attempt by elite groups to focus attention on lower class street crimes, and away from the crimes committed by elites (e.g. pollution, false advertising, etc.). Since the media are largely controlled (either through direct ownership or through advertising revenues) by capitalist elites, the selective reporting of sensational street crimes can be seen as part of an overall strategy by capitalist elites to impose their version of social order on society, and to ensure their continued dominance of the political and economic order.[3]

In addition to their macro-level focus on the capitalist elite's control and influence over the broad priorities of the legal and criminal justice systems, the critical theorists also argue that the day-to-day operation of the criminal justice system is rife with inequities and discrimination. They point out that minority groups such as blacks and aboriginals are routinely discriminated against at all levels of the system. From a critical perspective, the apparent over-representation of certain minority groups in criminal justice statistics is more a function of the increased attention paid to these groups by the police than it is because they commit proportionately more crimes. The critical theorists argue that the proposed crackdown would almost certainly target minority groups to a greater extent than other groups, and some critical theorists would characterize it as part of a more general strategy of social control aimed at subjugating certain minorities. This contention is supported by the debate surrounding the recent wave of murders in Ontario. It is interesting that because several of the suspects in the murders are black, some commentators have implied that the "black community" needs to take responsibility for the crimes committed by its members. This has caused at least one prominent black community leader to rhetorically question why the "white community" is never asked to assume responsibility for crimes committed by whites. The point is well taken, and many critical theorists would argue that the attempt to blame the entire black community for crimes committed by a very small minority of its members represents an attempt to stigmatize the community, and thereby justify repressive action against blacks generally.[4]

Another major concern of the critical perspective centres on the inadequate representation of women and visible minorities within police departments and other criminal justice agencies. Critical theorists argue that the selection criteria for these agencies are culturally biased and that the agencies discriminate, either intentionally or unintentionally, against women and other minorities. For example, until recently, the height and weight requirements for most police forces routinely excluded many ethnic groups. Similarly, many aptitude tests are oriented toward white middle-class values and experiences, and thus other groups are at a disadvantage when taking such tests. Many critical theorists argue that it is impossible to justify these requirements on the basis that they constitute legitimate employment-related requirements. Indeed, critical theorists argue that the opposite is true since the criminal justice system deals increasingly with women and minorities. Since white middle-class males will be less able to relate to these groups, it is likely that the administration of justice will suffer as a direct consequence of the failure to ensure that women and minorities are adequately represented in the system.[5]

This problem is accentuated by the even greater imbalance which exists within the upper ranks of the police and other criminal justice agencies, where women and other minorities are even less well represented than they are in the ranks. Although officials frequently argue that women and minorities often lack the seniority for promotion to higher rank, many critical theorists argue that this is not the real reason, since the "seniority system" is often breached in the case of white males. In any event, critical theorists point out that minorities have been employed in criminal justice agencies long enough to attain the needed seniority, but are often passed over in favour of white males.[6] It is further argued that the exclusion of women and other minorities from management positions ensures that the Canadian criminal justice system will continue to reflect the values held primarily by white middle-class males.

The above brief synopses of the consensus and critical approaches to criminal justice in Canada clearly represent over-generalized and, to some extent, ideological positions. Nevertheless, neither position can be dismissed out of hand, and it is important to assess the degree to which each accurately depicts the state of Canadian criminal justice. In this respect, it is important to note that crime rates have remained relatively stable over the past several years and violent crime has even shown a slight decline in some years.[7] Thus, the sensational headlines depicting ever-increasing crime rates appear to represent a media wave more than an actual crime wave. Similarly, the critical contention that police over-attention to minority groups is responsible for their over-representation in crime statistics appears borne out by recent research on aboriginal justice. This research found that, although aboriginal persons were drastically over-represented in correctional institutions, they actually commit less serious crime than whites.[8] On the other side of the argument, consensus theorists argue that many of the inequities are more apparent than real, and that in any case, the criminal justice system has taken positive steps to rectify the problem areas.[9] In addition, media polls indicate that the public is indeed concerned about crime and the apparent inability of the criminal justice system to deal with it effectively. Consensus theorists argue that this demonstrated public concern provides evidence of a consensus of values which cannot be ignored, regardless of the degree to which it is precipitated by media coverage.

While it is outside the scope of this introduction to conduct a detailed analysis of all the evidence supporting and refuting both sides of the debate, there is little doubt that the Canadian criminal justice system is characterized by several controversial issues which detract from its effectiveness. Many of the articles in this reader deal with these issues and the remainder of this introduction will conduct a brief overview of how the articles relate to the issues.

Lack of Coordination

One of the major debates in Canadian criminal justice centres on the degree to which the Canadian criminal justice system can be considered a true system. The classic definition of a unitary system involves several criteria, including common goals, a common underlying philosophy and a centralized decision-making authority. Although the Canadian criminal justice system meets some of these criteria to some degree, there are significant departures which negatively affect the overall coordination of the system. For example, although the different components of the criminal justice system likely all share the common goals of crime control and the protection of society, there are significant disagreements over the best strategies for accomplishing these goals. Further, in terms of overall decision-making authority, the system is fragmented along political, legal and functional lines. In the political/legal arena, there are a federal system, ten provincial systems and two territorial systems. There is no centralized decision-making hierarchy, and the fragmentation is compounded by the fact that the delineation of jurisdiction and responsibilities between the federal and provincial systems is not always clear. Further, the different components often fail to consult with each other on a regular basis, and this often leads to needless (and expensive) duplication of efforts.[10]

The lack of administrative coordination is accentuated by the fact that the different functional components, i.e. the police, courts and corrections, frequently adhere to different philosophical orientations. The police generally adhere to a crime control orientation, which elevates the repression of crime to the top of their list of priorities. The courts, on the other hand, are entrusted with protecting the rights of defendants, and thus usually operate within a due process philosophy which enforces a strong distinction between "factual" guilt and "legal" guilt. This often creates resentment and conflict with the police, who cannot understand why the courts are willing to acquit guilty people on what appear to them as meaningless "technicalities".

Finally, the correctional systems have a mandate to rehabilitate offenders, and thus subscribe to a treatment oriented approach. This approach assumes that offenders are "sick" and that the best strategy is to treat the problems that caused their antisocial behaviour. Several operational aspects of this treatment mentality, and especially the activities of the National Parole Board, create conflict with the police and courts who feel that the "rehabilitative" interests of offenders unfairly take precedence over the security interests of the public. Many of these factors, and specifically the issues of coordination and public input, are discussed in greater detail by Boyell and Connidis in their article "A Social Systems Approach to Criminal Justice."

Overly Lenient Treatment of Criminals

One of the most persistent themes in the media debate over crime control involves the alleged overly lenient treatment of offenders. Indeed, a recent much publicized caning of an American teenager in Singapore precipitated a rash of letters to the editor in major Canadian newspapers supporting the action and calling for the introduction of similar practices in Canada.[11] There are really three separate issues involved in the debate over punishment. First, many people argue that criminals are not dealt with harshly enough by the criminal justice system and thus feel free to continue their criminal activities without fear of punishment. A second issue centres on the belief that the National Parole Board routinely releases dangerous offenders, who then commit further violent offences while on parole. Indeed, the Head of the National Parole Board has recently been fired by the federal government, and a Parole Board member from the Prairie Region is facing possible disciplinary action over a recent series of violent crimes committed by parolees. And finally, a recent much publicized series of crimes committed by juveniles has precipitated an intense debate over the perceived inadequacy of the Young Offenders Act. (This issue will be discussed separately later in this introduction.)

In assessing these issues, it is important to note that Mandel, in his article, "The Great Repression: Criminal Punishment in the Nineteen-Eighties," argues that instead of becoming more lenient, Canada is actually becoming more repressive. He points out that Canada has incarcerated an ever-increasing proportion of the population since the end of the Second World War. This increased use of incarceration has not appeared to affect crime rates and certainly calls into question the contention that harsher penalties will deter crime. With respect to the issue of the Parole Board releasing dangerous criminals, Menzies et al. in "Risky Business: Classification in the Carceral Enterprise," discuss many of the problems inherent in attempting to identify dangerous people and then translate the assessment of danger-ousness into predictions of risk. Essentially, there are few accurate tech-niques for predicting dangerousness, and unless we wish to deny parole to all violent offenders, it is inevitable that mistakes will occur. Ratner, in "Bilateral Legitimation: The Parole Pendulum," takes the argument a step further and discusses some of the potential aftereffects that restricting parole might exert on future crime rates. He also argues that increased punitiveness is unlikely to be effective unless crime and crime control are placed into a larger societal framework which sees the exploitation of the capitalist system as a true cause of crime.

Women and Visible Minorities in the Justice System

Another major issue which is generating controversy involves the cur-rent emphasis on increasing the numbers of women and visible minorities in criminal justice agencies. The criticism which has been levelled at criminal justice agencies has prompted them to attempt to remedy the historical lack of participation by these groups. There are several side issues involved in this debate. For example, how sincere and/or successful are criminal justice agencies at the stated goal of increasing the representation of these groups? In this respect, Jain's article, "The Recruitment and Selection of Visible Minorities in Canadian Police Organizations, 1985-1987," discusses the success of recent police strategies to recruit members of visible minorities. Another side issue involves the question of whether women and visible minorities are able to function effectively once they are employed in crimi-nal justice agencies. With respect to women working in criminal justice agencies there is some evidence to suggest that women are not made to feel welcome and that the system has not developed administrative policies which allow women to pursue careers successfully in criminal justice agen-cies. In this respect, Crawford and Stark-Adamec's article "Women in Canadian Urban Policing: Why Are They Leaving?" and Szockyj's article "Working in a Man's World: Women Correctional Officers in an Institution for Men" discuss some of the factors which negatively affect women's employment in criminal justice agencies.

Young Offenders and the Youth Justice System

A recent wave of violent crime by juvenile offenders has focused public attention onto the perceived inadequacies of the Young Offenders Act

(YOA) as an effective tool for controlling youth crime. The one point of agreement among all participants in the debate is that the YOA, which covers all offenders between 12 and 18 years of age, has serious flaws. Most of the participants, and particularly the police, blame the lenient sentences provided in the Act (e.g. first degree murder carries a maximum sentence of five years) for apparently random and increasingly rampant juvenile crime. Academics, social workers and the legal profession generally take a slightly different view. Although most also identify the YOA as the major source of conflict, most place the real blame on the inflexibility of the YOA, which enforces an adversarial and legalistic process on situations which are not suited to such a formal approach. In "Good People, Dirty System: The YOA and Organizational Failure," Hackler argues that, although there are many dedicated, competent people working in the youth justice system, their efforts are hampered by organizational constraints and legal rules which inhibit effective cooperation between the youth justice professionals, and also preclude meaningful contact with the offenders. Hackler contrasts our own legalistic approach with the child-welfare negotiated approach used in France and Austria. He argues that the European inquisitorial emphasis on negotiating an outcome which is in the best interests of the young person is much more effective.

This argument is reinforced by Leschied and Jaffe in "Dispositions as Indicators of Conflicting Social Purposes under the JDA and YOA." They argue that although the unfettered paternalism reflected in the former Juvenile Delinquents Act (JDA) frequently resulted in injustices, the YOA has gone too far in the opposite direction by completely removing any ability to deal flexibly with the "lifestyle" problems which precipitate much juvenile crime. Leschied and Jaffe argue that we treat young offenders like adult criminals and appear to have lost all hope that they can be rehabilitated. They conclude by noting that the use of custodial sentences has actually increased under the YOA, while access to rehabilitative services has declined. In the final analysis, this may well represent the true reason for the upsurge in juvenile crime, and Leschied and Jaffe call for a new generation of "child savers" who will inject some balance back into the youth justice system. This call is echoed by Nicholas Bala in "The Young Offenders Act: A Legal Framework." Bala outlines the major provisions of the YOA and, while he conducts a more balanced review of its strengths and weaknesses, he ultimately concludes that we must continue our search for a youth justice system which will "fairly balance the needs and rights of young persons while adequately protecting society."

Aboriginal Justice

There is little doubt that Aboriginal justice represents one of the most controversial and complex issues involved in the contemporary debate over criminal justice reform. There are several distinct issues involved in the debate, and although they are far too complex to be discussed in this introduction, most centre on the persistent problem of the Aboriginal over-representation in the criminal justice system, and particularly in correctional institutions. The major focus of the over-representation debate is placed on the police and court decision-making processes. In this respect, many different explanations are discussed, often in the absence of reliable empirical data to help decide the issue. The possible solutions are equally complex and elusive, although most Aboriginal leaders and many academics, judges and mainstream politicians appear to favour some form of autonomous justice system for Aboriginal people.

Robert Depew, in "Policing Native Communities: Some Issues in Organizational Theory," reviews some of the reasons why traditional policing approaches are largely inapplicable to Aboriginal communities. He argues that the need for cultural sensitivity to Aboriginal values precludes the imposition of a mainstream crime control policing model, and that the utilization of a community-based model is essential if relations between the police and Aboriginal people are to be improved. Carol LaPrairie, on the other hand, focuses on the role of court decision-making, and particularly the sentencing process, as causes of the over-representation of Aboriginal people in correctional institutions. In "The Role of Sentencing in the Over-representation of Aboriginal People in Correctional Institutions," LaPrairie argues that, although we lack sufficient data to establish the exact causes of Aboriginal over-representation, there is limited data to suggest that the lack of other appropriate sentencing options has resulted in the disproportionate sentencing of Aboriginal people to correctional institutions. She concludes with a call for sentencing reform, and recommends that community-based resources be developed in Aboriginal communities so that incarceration is not the only option for judges who wish to maintain control over Aboriginal offenders.

These issues are subjected to a much broader analysis by Catherine Crow. In "Patterns of Discrimination: Aboriginal Justice in Canada," Crow reviews many of the purported causes of the problem, including systematic or structural racism and cultural conflict. She goes on to discuss some of the possible solutions, focusing on community-based policing and autonomous court systems as the most promising alternatives. She ultimately concludes

that both the reasons for Aboriginal over-representation in the criminal justice system and the effectiveness of the proposed solutions are far from conclusive, and that a "go slow" approach constitutes the best strategy for the
present. In coming to this conclusion, she notes that there are wide disparities in the abilities of Aboriginal communities to assume responsibility for
their own justice systems, and that even greater problems could result if
sweeping changes are imposed on all Aboriginal communities.

The above issues represent the most far-reaching of the issues currently
being debated in the public, legal and political arenas. The remaining articles in this reader deal with important but more narrowly focused and less
controversial issues. One important issue which is not currently considered
particularly controversial involves the degree to which the operation of the
criminal justice system is compromised by the use of an adversarial model of
justice delivery. In this respect, Cohen and Doob's article on plea bargaining
discusses some of the negative aspects of this practice, which usually occurs
without the trial judge's knowledge or approval. Although Cohen and Doob
do not directly link plea bargaining to the adversarial system, it can be
argued that it simply could not occur in non-adversarial systems where
judges play more active roles in all aspects of the criminal justice process.
There is also some evidence to suggest that the nature of the adversarial
process is indirectly linked to the frustration and burnout experienced by
police officers. A further issue which is related to the adversarial model is
the "right to counsel" debate. Because the adversarial model places a heavy
emphasis on the presence and abilities of defence counsel, Canadian courts
place a much greater emphasis on a defendant's right to retain counsel during all phases of the court process, as well as during the police investigation.
Hutchison and Marko's article discusses an important case in which the
Supreme Court of Canada outlined exactly how far police must go to ensure
that defendants are aware of their right to counsel. Thus, the ruling in *R*. v.
Bridges will undoubtedly further restrict police activities, and also result in
increased legal aid costs.

Another series of more narrowly focused issues centre around the
police role. In this respect, Stearns and Moore's article on burnout among
RCMP officers deals with the stresses inherent in police work, whereas
Buckley discusses the possible effects that higher education might exert on
police work as an occupation. A recent development which involves both of
these issues is the introduction of community-based policing in major
Canadian police forces. Leighton, in "Visions of Community Policing:
Rhetoric and Reality in Canada," outlines the various principles of commu-
nity-based policing and discusses the extent to which it is a reality in

Canada, and to what extent it is an attempt to embrace a trend from the "...academic criminal justice and policing enterprise from the US." In any case, many people argue that the widespread adoption of the community-based policing model would help alleviate some of the stresses currently inherent in police work. At the same time, it would also necessitate more highly educated police forces. Leighton argues, however, that there is a need for greater research into the effectiveness of community policing tactics, and calls for the development of a "theory of community policing" to facilitate future evaluations of community policing programs.

This reader concludes with two articles which attempt to explore the future of criminal justice. There is little doubt that the ever-increasing costs of administering justice preclude the continual construction of new prisons, staffed by ever-increasing numbers of correctional officers and prison guards. In "From Big House to Big Brother: Confinement in the Future," Ian Gomme discusses the dilemma of attempting to adequately protect society in times of drastic budgetary restraint. Gomme reviews the impact of technology on criminal justice over the years and discusses how electronic monitoring can be used to reduce the costs associated with high prison populations, while also protecting society from antisocial elements. Under Gomme's proposal, the use of electronic monitoring would be restricted to offenders who were not eligible for such community corrections programs as probation, but did not warrant being sentenced to secure custody.

Although Gomme focuses primarily on control, his proposals are not inconsistent with some of the recent theorizing about rehabilitation and the philosophical underpinnings of the administration of justice. In "A Restorative Lens," Howard Zehr argues that western justice systems are heavily predicated towards the assignment of blame and the enactment of retribution. Zehr suggests that we would be more successful at rehabilitating offenders if we adopted a "restorative" model which promotes healing, forgiveness and, where appropriate, reparation between the parties. This approach accords the victim a more central role in the justice process. It is also consistent with the concept of electronic monitoring proposed by Gomme. After all, when offenders are incarcerated in correctional institutions, it does little good for the victim, and frequently necessitates that the state support the offender's family as well. On the other hand, if offenders are allowed to remain in society, suitably restrained by electronic monitoring, they can support their own families, and also make reparations to their victims. This, in the final analysis, might better serve the elusive notion of "justice" than having the offender suffer the pains of imprisonment in the name of retribution and deterrence.

Endnotes

1   See *Maclean's* editorial "The Need to Crack Down" (*Maclean's*, April 18, 1994, p. 4). This editorial discussed a se\ries of murders in Ontario, and while it correctly pointed out that the murders were unrelated and did not "herald the outbreak of a new crime wave," it still called for tougher measures "to honor the memory" of the victims.

2   C.T. Griffiths and S.N. Verdun-Jones, *Canadian Criminal Justice* (Toronto: Harcourt Brace & Company, 1994).

3   R.S. Ratner and J.L. McMullan, *Criminal Justice Politics in Canada* (Vancouver: UBC Press, 1987).

4   A more detailed discussion of this type of logic is provided by R.W. Thacker, "The Functions of Minority Group Disrepute" in B.D. MacLean, ed., *The Political Economy of Crime: Readings for a Critical Criminology* (Scarborough: Prentice-Hall, Canada, 1986), pp. 272-294.

5   For example, the advantages of including minority groups within criminal justice agencies would include, at the very least, language skills and a greater understanding of the cultural norms of certain groups.

6   An example of this argument can be found in a recent study done on the Winnipeg Police Service which indicated that, although women comprise over seven per cent of Winnipeg police personnel, they make up less than one half of one per cent of management positions (Sergeant and above). This is despite the fact that women have been in the Winnipeg Police for over 20 years, well past the 15 years it normally takes to reach management rank (*Winnipeg Free Press*, April 23, 1994, p A1).

7   This point was noted in several media articles, which then went on to call for drastic crackdowns on crime.

8   J.C. Yerbury and C.T. Griffiths, "Minorities, Crime and the Law" in M.A. Jackson and C.T. Griffiths, eds., *Canadian Criminology: Perspectives on Crime and Criminology* (Toronto: HBJ Holt, 1991), pp. 315-346.

9   For example, the over-representation of Aboriginal people in correctional institutions is largely due to their failure to pay fines and not necessarily because they receive more severe sentences. However, this issue will be addressed later in this introduction.

10   For example, drug enforcement is primarily a federal responsibility. However, provincial and municipal police forces also maintain large drug squads, which frequently work in isolation from the RCMP, who are the main federal force responsible for drug control.

11   It is important to bear in mind that the American teenager had committed the relatively minor offence of vandalism, in which he spray-painted cars with a water soluble paint which could easily be washed off with soap and water.

A Social Systems Approach to Criminal Justice Research: An Overview

Craig Boydell and Ingrid Connidis

The Criminal Justice System in Context

The criminal justice system cannot be fully understood in isolation from the society within which it functions, because it is only a part of a broader social control network. Along with many other societal organizations and institutions, it serves to maintain a level of order that permits society to survive as an ongoing unit. Perhaps the key element in such societal survival is predictability. Knowing with some degree of certainty what is expected of us and what we can expect from others is essential for ongoing social interaction. In one way or another all major social institutions contribute to the articulation of goals, norms and values, and apply or threaten to apply sanctions to those who do not conform.

For example, the entire educational system can be viewed as an attempt to establish expectations (norms) and to see that those expectations, which concern such matters as work standards and classroom decorum, are fulfilled. Expectations are specified, persons failing to meet the expectations can be punished and considerable energy is often invested in correcting the behaviour of those who deviate from the norms. Similarly, the medical system establishes and assumes shared notions concerning sickness and health as well as shared expectations concerning the interactions of medical doctors, nurses and patients. Parents teach children a vast array of social expectations, some of which apply within the home and some of which concern matters well outside its boundaries. Regardless of the means chosen, punishment with the aim of correcting behaviour is an ongoing part of the parenting process. In like fashion, religious leaders specify spiritual expectations and their application to earthly settings. Implicit in most religious teachings is a set of sanctions for the noncommitted as well as a set of the correctives that may be applied to those temporarily living outside the faith.

Thus, all major social institutions are intricately involved in the complex and dynamic process of social control. Moreover, although each institution may appear to carve out a certain realm within which it operates, there is, nonetheless, considerable overlap.

The learning of legal norms, for example, generally takes place within the family and in school. Infractions committed by children, such as shoplifting, are frequently punished by parents and store owners rather than through formal criminal justice proceedings. These sanctions, or the threat of them, provide an essential component of the learning process and for most persons are all that is necessary to ensure conformity to legal norms in adult life. In dealing with younger offenders criminal justice system personnel often consult parents, teachers or the clergy to determine whether problem individuals can be dealt with through the home, school or religious group. Such consultations often result in no further official processing of young offenders. From these examples, it can be seen that the justice system shares with other institutions and organizations the task of ensuring conformity to legal norms and applying sanctions when infractions occur.

A Social Systems Approach to the Study of Criminal Justice

Recognition of the ongoing interactions of the criminal justice system with other organizations and institutions in society leads us to favour a social systems approach.[1] A comprehensive treatment of the systems perspective and its application to the analysis of criminal justice operations is well beyond the scope of this text.[2] We shall, however, describe the basic assumptions of the approach and demonstrate their importance in gaining an understanding of the criminal justice system. There are four major assumptions of a social systems approach that recommend it as a heuristic device in analysing criminal justice operations.

1. Social Systems are Open

All social systems are assumed to be open. This means that they are continually interacting with their environment, both at the level of society as a whole and at the level of particular organizations or social systems. Thus, to understand the operation of any social system it is necessary to understand and appreciate the relationship of that system to the environment.

We have discussed the broad nature of social control, highlighting that social control is carried out in all spheres of social life. While the criminal justice system is the official enforcer of legal norms and sanctions regarding crimes against persons and property, as well as myriad other types of offences, other institutions also have input in these areas. This point is extremely important because it cautions us against placing so much importance on the social control functions of the administration of criminal justice that we fail to take into account the relationship of the system to other institutions and the roles that they play in the social control process.

2. Social Systems are Interdependent

The substantial overlap between the various institutions in society is the basis for the *interdependence* of open social systems. The criminal justice system exists in a political, social and economic setting that influences its operation by both initiating and constraining decision making as well as by providing the mandate for criminal justice operations. Because the criminal justice system constantly interacts with other social systems, it must continually react to these systems as part of its general environment. Even at this most general level there is a need to understand the exchange between the criminal justice system and its environment, because this exchange has an impact on policy and decision making both for the system as a whole and for each of the system's constituent parts.

Simply stated, the substantive law stipulates those acts that are prohibited, and the procedural law sets forth the means through which the substantive law is to be enforced.[3] Because making law is not a criminal justice system function, the law is most accurately viewed as an environmental influence on the criminal justice system. Viewed in this light, it is clear that the criminal justice system cannot be isolated from its environment. At the same time, judicial decisions may set precedents, and thus criminal justice system decisions have repercussions for the law. Given that the criminal justice system receives its mandate from the law, the relationship between them forms an integral part of interdependent system-environment relations (Frank and Faust, 1975: 275; Connidis, 1982). At the same time, it is the particular nature of this legal mandate that distinguishes the criminal justice system from other mechanisms of social control, making it a distinct social system.

In addition to applying this kind of legitimized influence on the criminal justice system, other systems in the general environment sometimes try to manipulate it for nonlegitimized purposes. This is most forcefully illustrated in analyses that show how the manipulation of the criminal justice system functions to satisfy political ends (Turk, 1976, 1977; Blaine and Kettler, 1971). For example, the criminal justice system can be shown to be a political tool used against unpopular challengers of the status quo (Beckman, 1977: 285). Some analysts argue that, because of the political patronage entailed in some local governments, political manipulation of the criminal justice system is inescapable (Moore, 1976: 71). Some recent examples of attempts to use the system for nonlegitimized political objectives are RCMP activities in Canada (Henshel, 1977, 1978; Mann and Lee, 1979) and the Watergate scandal in the United States. Over the past few years it has become evident that the RCMP have engaged in activities intended to destroy "subversive" political movements in order to meet the political ends of those in power. Although those in power have attempted to discredit charges of their involvement in RCMP activities, it appears that politicians were in fact aware of RCMP wrongdoings and may indeed have played a role in directing them.

Although the view that the criminal justice system is subject to political misuse tends to spotlight only one side of the system-environment relationship, political manipulation is in fact precipitated by the potential effects of criminal justice actions on its environment. In this regard, Reich (1973: 385) argues that a crisis in the criminal justice system is a reflection on politicians because it suggests that they are unable to handle their jobs. As a result, politicians are highly motivated to intervene in order to avoid such crises. Thus, the relationship between the criminal justice system and its political environment is one of interaction and reciprocity (Connidis, 1982).

The interdependent nature of social systems applies at all levels. The social systems approach assumes that interdependence characterizes not only the relationship between the criminal justice system and its environment but also the relationships among parts (or subsystems) of the criminal justice system. Although recent trends in criminal justice research suggest that this broader approach is increasing in popularity, by and large the bulk of research tends to focus on activities of a specific stage — for example, the police or courts — without reference to the rest of the system. In this regard, the merit of a systems approach is that it forces us to consider the operations and decision making occurring at any point in the criminal justice system in the context of its interdependent relationship with other parts of the system. As well, a social systems perspective provides a framework within which findings regarding different parts of the criminal justice system can be incorporated and related to one another.

For example, the police depend on the public to report offences and on the courts to bring charges to court. Similarly, prosecutors rely on the police to provide cases and relevant information about them in order to proceed to trial. At the same time defence lawyers need the police to provide clients. These interdependent relationships mean that the effects of one subsystem's activity on the rest of the system can be substantial, since the decisions of one agency directly affect the work of others (Cole, 1970: 51; Cassidy and Turner, 1977: 5). Changes within a specific agency are therefore not confined to it but rather have implications for other parts of the system (Outerbridge, 1973: 3, 35; Munro, 1974: 12).

3. Social Systems Have Formal and Informal Goals

All social systems and parts thereof work toward *goals*. A conceptual distinction can be made between two broad types of goals: formal and informal. *Formal goals* are the professed and/or ideal goals of a social system. *Informal goals* are the operative goals that emerge within social systems in response to the requirements of daily work. In some cases informal and formal goals overlap, so that the accomplishment of informal goals leads to the realization of formal ones. In other cases the attainment of informal goals may involve the subversion of formal goals, thus creating conflict between professed and operative goals. The social systems approach advocated here encourages us to examine the operative, or informal, goals of daily functioning, as well as the formal goals, which do not necessarily dictate daily work patterns in the criminal justice system. Furthermore, this approach assumes that the parts of any social system assign priority to their own goals rather than to the professed formal goals of the total system. The resulting variation in priorities has the potential further to heighten conflict between formal and informal goals.

For example, within the court system the formal goal of adversarial justice, intended to place the crown and defence in open competition, is displaced by the informal goal of processing heavy case loads. The latter is facilitated by co-operation between prosecution and defence rather than by the open court battle of a purely adversarial stance (Feeley, 1973; Blumberg, 1967a, 1967b; Cole, 1970; Skolnick, 1967; Newman, 1966; Mohr, 1976; Grosman, 1969; Neubauer, 1974). Co-operation does not replace adversarial justice as a formal goal but rather is a means to attaining informal goals. Plea bargaining, while jeopardizing the formal goal of adversarial justice, permits the accomplishment of other goals: efficiency and high rates of conviction for prosecutors and judges, and lighter sentences for the clients of defence attorneys (Mohr, 1976; Neubauer, 1974).

Social Systems Have Conflicting Goals

The goals of one social system (or subsystem) may be in conflict with those of another, resulting in either a power play between two or more organizations or a compromise that permits both parties to partially realize their objectives. Which of these two outcomes will result depends on the competitors' relative power and ability to operate autonomously. Where one organization clearly has more power than the other, the first outcome is more likely. Where power differentials are minimal and compromise will be of roughly equal advantage to both parties, the latter outcome is more likely. Once again, the tendency to assign priority to the goals of the immediate organizational unit may further heighten conflict between agencies. This interplay among organizations is evidence of the dynamic nature of organizational relations, which often escapes conventional analyses of the justice system but is readily apparent when considered from a social systems perspective.

Finally, because of the interdependence of social systems, the activities of some subsystems will have an impact on others. On the one hand, this interdependence means that no part of the criminal justice system has the power to operate autonomously. On the other hand, however, all organizations will strive to maintain as much autonomy as possible. This desire for autonomy in an interdependent setting provides the basis for an ongoing tension between conflict and compromise. This facet of system operations is by no means unique to the criminal justice system.

The Administration of Criminal Justice as a System

At a fundamental level the substantive and procedural criminal law provides the basis for defining the administration of criminal justice as a system because the law established the system's mandate and agencies as well as general guidelines for its operations (Myren, 1976; Sallmann, 1978). These guidelines specify the structure of the criminal justice system and the order of the activities that take place within it (ie., arrest before charge, charge before prosecution, and so on). On this basis the criminal justice system is composed of: the police; the courts, including magistrate and appeal courts, prosecutors, defence attorneys and the judiciary; and corrections, including probation, jail, prison and other correctional alternatives.

Some authors include the public as part of the criminal justice system because of the public's offence-reporting function (Reiss, 1971). However, in our view to do so becomes problematic because members of the public play other direct roles in the criminal justice system, such as those of witnesses, jurors and accused persons. To treat these and the various other types of public involvement as a single subsystem becomes rather unwieldy. Therefore, we instead treat the many and varied aspects of involvement as a crucial element in the criminal justice system's environment (Connidis, 1982).

As well, we have chosen to emphasize police and court activities in this book and to pay limited attention to correctional alternatives.[4] This decision is dictated in part by the approach we encourage here. That is, decisions made at the correctional level have fewer repercussions within the system than do decisions made at the police and court levels. This is primarily because corrections is the final receptacle of decisions made at earlier points in the system — decisions that generally cannot be reversed by the corrections subsystem. We emphasize, however, that the decision to focus on the police and the courts is somewhat arbitrary and that the impact of correctional philosophies and alternatives, and the pressures from correctional authorities on earlier decision points, must still be considered. For example, the kinds of sentences handed down by judges may relate to their perception of the kinds and quality of alternatives available to them at the correctional stage. These perceptions may be shaped in part by information directed towards judges from correctional administrators about such matters as the success rates of new programs, security in certain prisons and possible ramifications of overcrowded conditions.

It is possible to specify the activities carried out by each of the parts of the criminal justice system in order to distinguish it further from other social systems. Indeed, the administration of criminal justice can be considered a system of interlocking decisions (Henshel and Silverman, 1975; Sallmann, 1978; Cole, 1970; Brautigam, 1974; Cowan, 1963). The decisions that are exclusively within the bounds of the criminal justice system include arrest, charge, prosecution (bringing charges to court), adjudication (determination of guilt or innocence) and sentencing (Feeley, 1973). Although these decisions may not be smoothly integrated, they are interlocking and sequential. Note that we do not define the criminal justice system by its ideal goals (such as law enforcement, protection of the community and deterrence) but rather by its activities.

The Selection Process: From Criminal Law to Conviction

At each of the decision points in the criminal justice system, personnel are in a position to decide whether or not to process a case. These decisions thus form potential attrition points. More broadly, there are three major realms where selection operates. These are the formulation of substantive and procedural law, the discovery and reporting of criminal events by the public, and the discovery and processing of criminal events by the criminal justice system. Before discussing case attrition within the criminal justice system itself, we will consider the selective definition and processing of offences that occur before the formal processing of offences and offenders.

Formulation of Criminal Law

As previously noted, the substantive and procedural law provides the mandate and boundaries for criminal justice processing. It is therefore the criminal law that initially defines acts (and thus violators) as potentially criminal. The formulation of criminal law determines which events are and which are not within the jurisdiction of the criminal justice system. This is not to say that events not included in the criminal law are not subject to social or even legal control,[5] only that they are not defined within the territory of criminal justice operations. Even with the most liberal interpretation of our wide-ranging criminal code, the actions delineated within it represent a minute proportion of all actions. Consequently, criminal norms are a small subset of all norms. For example, we have many norms specifying how to conduct ourselves in the presence of others, such as those related to physical contact, but violation of only some of these norms is defined as criminal. Although this form of case loss is not properly called case attrition, it is clear that the criminal law does exclude many acts that at different times and in different places could be and are defined as criminal.

Thus, there is a significant degree of selectivity involved in determining which acts will be included in criminal law. Considerable discussion surrounds the debate as to whether criminal law represents a consensus view or instead evolves out of conflict in which the most powerful are victorious. Without entering the debate here we conclude that the criminal law arises from both conflict and consensus. The notion that certain acts, such as homicide, robbery and assault causing bodily harm, are crimes tends to originate from and be supported by a popular consensus. That is, the vast majority of Canadians agree that these acts should be defined as criminal.

However, both the inclusion and exclusion of many other acts in the criminal code may well serve the interests of some groups and individuals at the expense of others. Small's analysis of drug laws (1978) documents a case in which those in power succeeded in defining the drug use of selected others as criminal. In some cases those favouring the definition of a particular act as criminal may not directly gain by it but may have the power to make their preferences become law. In the ongoing debate regarding the legal status of abortion, the issue is fought on the basis of principle rather than personal self-interest. Those both for and against may gain no direct personal advantage from having abortion either legalized or criminalized. Which side wins is a function of which has the greater power as a lobby group. The dynamic processes involved in law formulation thus can provide a basis for selectivity and bias in what is and is not defined as criminal.

This selectivity is compounded by the criminal procedures that define the boundaries, powers and duties of criminal justice agencies. It is clear that the shape these procedures assume will be a significant determinant of what specific kinds of criminal events and persons are discovered, reported and processed through the system. This effect of procedures is a facet of criminal justice to which both lay persons and practitioners are sensitive, although they may not always realize its extent. Nonetheless, the kinds of limits placed on police powers or rules of evidence will certainly have a major impact on both the numbers and the types of offences that will ultimately lead to conviction. This is not an argument for more or less police power or tighter or looser restrictions on the admissibility of evidence, but merely an assertion of the impact procedures themselves have on selective processing of criminal events. Current procedures, the availability and allocation of resources, and the nature of personnel recruitment and training tend to support a criminal justice system that is better able to focus on and process traditional street crimes (such as assault and theft) and criminals than to handle highly organized forms of crime. Discovery and punishment of the latter require more time, training and resources than are available. Corporate and organized crime, with their new technology and high level of organization and power, provide a challenge that the criminal justice system is not currently equipped to meet. The result, in terms of case attrition, is that certain types of offences, even though defined as criminal, are far less likely than others to be formally processed.

In summary, the substantive and procedural criminal law specifies criminal norms by detailing which acts will be defined as criminal, as well as the mechanisms for applying these definition and punishing violators. Hence the criminal law itself, by formally distinguishing between behaviours against which sanctions can and cannot officially be applied, and by establishing a specific set of procedures for applying sanctions, necessarily sets in motion a process that is selective. The absence of any mechanism that permits total surveillance and enforcement necessitates the evolution of a system of identifying, reporting and officially processing crime that relies heavily on chance, individual decisions, subjective evaluations and informal processes.

Discovery and Selective Reporting by the Public

Generally it is only when citizens decide to take action that the criminal law becomes a living reality. The transition from crime in theory to the processing of actual cases and persons can occur only if decision making in the criminal justice system is set in motion through the discovery and reporting of law violations. Because the police are highly reliant on the public to report offences, the decisions of citizens regarding whether or not to report usually constitute the starting point for criminal justice system operations.[6]

The reasons for case attrition can be characterized as *passive* or *active*. When offences are committed but are not known to have occurred, cases are lost prior to criminal justice system operations due to *passive* weeding out. With respect to the police, when the public fail to report an offence, or the police to discover one, or when the police are unable to find a suspect for a known offence, the case attrition that results is also passive. *Active* weeding out occurs when members of the public or criminal justice system personnel are confronted with a crime or information about a crime and decide not to take further action. For the public the situation involves knowing a crime has been committed but deciding not to report it to the police. For the police it could mean failing to respond to a citizen report, deciding not to arrest a suspect, deciding not to lay a charge or withdrawing a charge. At later stages in the criminal justice system virtually all case attrition can be characterized as active, because personnel in the courts cannot fail to acknowledge cases brough t before them.

People become aware of criminal events by being victimized themselves, by seeing a crime in progress, through exposure to the communications media or through social interaction. Although there may be the zealous among us, most citizens do not usually actively seek out crime in their spare time. In an attempt to ascertain the total amount of crime actually committed, some researchers have conducted victimization and self-report studies.[7] *Victimization studies* are surveys in which people are asked whether or not they have been the victims of specific offences. *Self-report studies* approach the issue from the other side by asking people whether or not they have committed a variety of offences. The latter have been conducted most frequently with juvenile populations. Both victimization and self-report studies indicate that there is much more crime committed than is reported by the public to the police and discovered by the police. Clearly, then, a considerable degree of case attrition results from selective reporting by the public.

Victimization and self-report surveys also indicate that the official statistics collected by Statistics Canada and provided by the police and courts cannot be accepted as measures of the total volume of crime. In addition, fluctuations in the rate of crime as recorded in official statistics do not necessarily indicate real changes in the total amount of crime but may instead result from changes in the rate of offence reporting by the public, discovery of crimes by the police, and processing of offences throughout the criminal justice system. Finally, as we have noted and shall continue to emphasize, case attrition is the result of selective decision making. Consequently, official statistics do not represent the actual proportions of different types of offences in relation to all crime committed.[8]

The extent to which crimes are weeded out both passively and actively at the public stage is related to the nature of the offence. Offences that do not involve direct confrontation are most likely to be undetected and therefore least likely to be reported. In addition to the traditional offences that fit this category, such as theft, the entire spectrum of corporate and white-collar crime falls under this heading. Members of the public are often directly and indirectly victims of illegal activities involving contamination of air, water and food, embezzlement and price-fixing, without being aware of their victimization. Even when they are aware of being victims, they may fail to report because they have no idea who is responsible or whether the practice of which they are victims is illegal. In addition, certain types of common street crime, such as pickpocketing and shoplifting, when done well, may not be perceived by the victims as crimes. Finally, so-called victimless crimes (drug use, prostitution, gambling and so on) have infinitesimally small report rates for the obvious reason that in most cases the only persons who are clearly aware of the crime have a vested interest in not reporting it. The failure to report such offences is an example of passive weeding out.

Case attrition based on active decision making can also be traced to the nature of the offence. People tend to operate on the basis of self-interest when deciding whether or not to report offences to the police (Boydell and Connidis, 1974). Some offences provide a clear incentive to report because there is a direct benefit in doing so. Car theft is a case in point because, in order to collect insurance, policy holders are required to report the theft to the police. In addition, the police provide an extremely efficient service for the recovery of stolen vehicles. More generally, if the public believe that reporting crime will have results, such as apprehension and conviction of the offender or the return of stolen property, the likelihood of reporting is higher.

As much as we might like to believe that people report crime on principle, the decision typically rests on an assessment of the costs and benefits of doing so. In many cases, citizens choose not to report because the costs of becoming involved, such as the time spent with the police and serving as witnesses, are not worth the perceived benefits. This assessment is subject to considerable individual variation reflecting the different motivations to report held by members of the public. For example, the crime of rape has a very low report rate owing to such factors as fear of reprisal, the further public humiliation of the victim and the demonstrated failure of the criminal justice system to convert known offenders into convicted offenders (Weiss and Borges, 1973; Kasinsky, 1975).

In summary, people not only fail to detect a great deal of crime but also exercise a broad range of discretion in the reporting of criminal offences about which they have knowledge. The passive and active case attrition that results means that by the time we move into an analysis of the decision making process within the criminal justice system itself a great deal has happened to diminish considerably the volume of criminal activity as well as the kinds of activity with which it will be called upon to deal.

Discovery and Processing in the Criminal Justice System

There are several points in the administration of criminal justice where case attrition takes place. These points coincide with the decision that must be made by personnel in the criminal justice system. As noted, by the time criminal events come to police attention there has already been a substantial amount of case attrition. This attrition, however, by no means cuts the volume to the point where the police can then bring all cases to conclusion. A constant and active type of decision making employed at this stage, therefore, is selection of those cases that can be dealt with effectively, given the constraints of existing resources, subsystem policy, public pressure and the likelihood of success in processing the case through the courts. Obviously, the criteria employed in this situation will vary from department to department, over time and, given the amount of autonomy in certain areas of police work, according to the judgement of individual police officers. In the last case decision may be based on police officers' personal reactions to a case and on the characteristics of the particular offender and victim. Such personal considerations may affect both the kinds of discoveries attempted and the kinds of cases processed.

Once offences are discovered, either through public reporting or proactive police work, the police must find a suspect. When they fail to do so, passive case attrition takes place. When they succeed, the decision of whether or not to arrest must be made. From this point onward case attrition is almost always the result of active decision making in a situation of choice.

There are a significant number of cases in which processing terminates prior to the point of charging an offender because there are no witnesses or insufficient evidence. For many such cases, although continued investigation might be productive, the nature of the case will not justify the investment of additional time and resources. Therefore, although the decision to suspend activity in such cases is discretionary, it is more or less impelled by the situation. If the police were to invest as much effort in solving each petty theft as they do in solving each homicide, the proportion of charges for reported thefts would rise significantly. However, the cost would undoubtedly outweigh the benefit, and police personnel would outnumber private citizens. Operational priorities must develop at all stages of the justice system if it is not to grind to a screeching halt.

Following a decision to arrest, police must lay charges or release the suspect. Once charges are laid by the police it is up to the crown prosecutor to decide whether or not to bring charges to court. As we shall discuss in Part II, decisions made by the police and courts are in part influenced by the expectations and anticipated reactions of other criminal justice personnel. However, at this point it is worth noting that the police and prosecutor consider charges from somewhat different vantage points, with the police emphasizing the facts of a case while the prosecutor focuses on whether guilt can be proved in the courts. For this reason, among others, a fair amount of case attrition takes place between the police and court subsystems.

If charges are brought to court it is the role of the judge or jury to adjudicate and find the defendant innocent or guilty if a plea of guilty has not been entered. Once again case attrition occurs wherein acquittals, dismissals and withdrawals are weeded out of the system while convictions remain a part of it. As cases are processed through these decision points, case attrition continues, so that there are convictions for only a very small proportion of all crimes committed.

Official statistics available over the years indicate that roughly twenty-five per cent of the offences known to the police lead to the laying of formal charges. Of these, about half, or about 12.5 per cent of those originally known, will be prosecuted in the courts. Approximately ninety per cent of charges brought to court, or slightly more than ten per cent of those originally known to police, will result in a conviction.[9] However, just as is true at the discovery and report stage prior to the criminal justice system's involvement, there is considerable variation in the amount of attrition and where it takes place, according to the type of crime.

Variations in case attrition for different crimes are often related to the kind of behaviour involved in the crime itself. For example, homicides not only are likely to be known to the police but also are far more likely to lead to an arrest (eighty per cent), a prosecution (fifty per cent), and a conviction (thirty-five per cent) than a crime generally. Homicide is generally more easily detected because often it is less planned, because considerable resources will be invested in its detection, prosecution and defence and because there is considerable public pressure on police to make arrests. The contrasting pattern for breaking and entering reflects in part the less serious nature of the crime and the difficulty in providing proof — particularly the kinds of evidence that will stand up in court. In contrast to homicide only twenty per cent of breaking and entering offences known to police will lead to an arrest, sixteen per cent to prosecution, and fifteen per cent to conviction. When we add to this the observation that only sixty per cent of those offences known are reported to police in the first place, we end up with an even lower conviction rate of about seven per cent. Another striking contrast is that once an arrest is made for breaking and entering the chances of conviction are proportionally much greater than for homicide; that is, a person arrested for homicide is about half as likely to be convicted as a person arrested for breaking and entering. This last contrast suggests that, although proof of breaking and entering is more difficult to obtain, once obtained it tends to stick. Another reason for this difference may be that a lower proportion of offenders accused of homicide plead guilty, and thus guilt has to be proved at trial.

One must also be attuned to variations in reporting and processing within crimes. For example, those types of homicides that are most calculated, that are committed against displaced persons (such as transients or runaways) or that seem to involve no personal connection between victim and offender will be least likely to be known at all (except to the offender) and, when known, will present far more difficulties in the gathering of the kind of information that would lead to arrests, charges and convictions.

Unplanned domestic homicides, often involving alcohol, bear sharp contrast. Similarly, break-ins committed during the day by the young, inexperienced, intoxicated or boastful against persons with watchful neighbours, security systems, possession inventories or large dogs are much more likely to be processed through the justice system than are more professionally undertaken crimes.

Although such examples may point to the more extreme variations, for all crimes there are specific factors connected to the crime itself, its participants and its victims that will increase or decrease the likelihood of its becoming known, reported, connected to the offender and successfully prosecuted. Clearly, those individuals who go through the entire system to the point of incarceration are unique in ways that extend well beyond their temporary residence.

This has been a cursory review of case attrition and its causes. As a result of the kinds of factors we have outlined, those cases processed through the justice system are far from a representative sample of all crimes committed or reported to the police. The cases become gradually more and more distinctive, as do the victims and offenders attached to them. We turn now to a consideration of how decisions in the criminal justice system are influenced by the interdependence of its agencies.

The Interdependent Nature of Criminal Justice Decision Making

In the preceding section we have outlined the many decision points throughout the criminal justice system at which case attrition can and does occur. In this section we will examine the interdependent nature of criminal justice decision making. Our focus here is on how decisions made by personnel within the criminal justice system are affected by and in turn influence the decisions of other criminal justice personnel. Thus, we are looking at subsystem interactions and confine ourselves to the internal workings of the criminal justice system. In this context we shall also discuss the nature of the work in relation to the goals in each of the subsystems.

Unlike many organizations, the overall criminal justice system does not form a hierarchy of authority. As a result, there is no central authority with the power to manage or enforce rules for the entire system.[10] Instead, each agency of the system derives authority from three levels of government — the municipal, provincial, and federal (O'Leary and Newman, 1970; Cassidy, 1974). In Canada, responsibility for the agencies of criminal justice at the federal level alone is dispersed among departments: Justice, the Solicitor General, Indian and Northern Affairs, Manpower and Immigration,

National Health and Welfare, Public Works, Statistics Canada, Economic Council of Canada and the Privy Council (Kirkpatrick and McGrath, 1976).

This creates a situation in which each part of the criminal justice system places emphasis on its own informal goals. This is the case because, in the absence of a central control, there are no mechanisms for ensuring compliance and subordination to system-wide goals and hence no mechanisms for supervising the operations of each criminal justice agency (Reiss, 1971; Feeley, 1973; Ewing, 1976). At the same time, however, the absence of a hierarchy means that there are no formal provisions for the subordination of one criminal justice subsystem to another. As a consequence, although each part of the system enjoys independence from a central authority, an agency's independence is limited by its inability to exercise control over other parts of the system. Thus, although a certain degree of independence is created by the absence of central control, the inability of personnel at any stage of the system to impel other parts of the system to accept their decisions limits this independence (Roebuck and Barker, 1974).

Hence the stage is set for each agency in the criminal justice system to engage in exchange and bargaining relationships with other parts of the system (Reich, 1973; Cole, 1970). In such a setting, compromise is essential, and conflict is a distinct possibility. These exchange relationships both enhance the accomplishment of informal goals by each agency and create the potential for conflict by limiting each agency's independence.

In order for there to be reciprocal effects on decision making some form of information exchange or feedback must take place. After all, it is only through familiarity with what is happening and expected at other stages that decisions made in any one agency can be influenced. Information exchange among parts of the criminal justice system can involve *direct* or *indirect feedback*. *Direct feedback* is provided by interaction between personnel of different agencies. It is important to note that such feedback takes place between individuals from different parts of the criminal justice system and usually fails to serve as a policy statement from one agency to another. Examples of direct feedback include the following: judicial statements to police officers in the courtroom regarding the inadmissibility of evidence in a specific case (Goldstein, 1968; LaFave and Remington, 1965); a prosecutor's explanation to a police officer of the reasons for failing to bring a case to court; and memos from the prosecutor requesting that the police obtain more evidence before a case is sent to trial (Neubauer, 1974).

Because there is no established system-wide line of command through which communications among agencies are regularly channeled, direct feedback is inhibited. Consequently, criminal justice system personnel are highly reliant on indirect forms of feedback. *Indirect feedback* involves addressing another agency's activities in order to determine which are important for decision making generally and what specific kinds of decisions they suggest. The act of assessment often requires subjective interpretation — and thus opens up the possibility of misinterpretation of the activities observed (Connidis, 1982). An example of indirect feedback is past judicial practices regarding adjudication and sentence, used by both the prosecution and the police as guides to decision making about future arrests and charges.

In summary, then, the interdependent nature of criminal justice system operations stems in part from the necessity, created by the absence of a central command, of entering into exchange relationships. Furthermore, accomplishment of agency-wide goals is enhanced through such exchanges. Information necessary for making decisions involving exchange is based on direct and indirect feedback. Thus, to speak of exchange relationships is not to assume that each decision involves the direct interaction of personnel from different agencies. Instead, agencies take other parts of the criminal justice system into account by using the history of decision making as a guide for current decisions.

The Police

We have already discussed the important role played by the public in initiating police action through offence reporting. At this point we shall focus on the relationship between police and court activities.

Despite extensive discretion allowed police officers (Cumming, Cumming and Edell, 1962; Goldstein, 1963; LaFave, 1964), the police agency's decision making is limited and shaped by the courts in many instances. The position of the police as the first stage in the criminal justice process creates a paradoxical position for patrol officers, who, while controlling whether or not the criminal justice system can process a decision at all, are also subject to the most extensive review when their decisions are considered by all the following stages of the system (Reiss, 1971; Cole, 1970; Coffey, Elder-Fouso and Hartinger, 1974). Because the police are not given a guarantee that the court will comply with their decisions, they attempt to ensure that their decisions will meet the criteria of evaluation employed by the courts, particularly the prosecution and judiciary.[11] If they are successful in meeting these criteria, there will be a greater likelihood that cases will flow from the police to the court stage, and a higher percentage of convictions. This does not necessarily mean that police agree with court decisions but rather that they have shaped their own to match them in order to have cases processed.

There is a tendency to assume that, because conviction and sentence are not police functions, the police are not concerned about adjudication at the court stage (Goldstein, 1968: 18-19). However, findings regarding police views on plea bargaining, conviction and sentence generally point to the importance to the police of conviction and sentence for those cases sent to the prosecutor and courts. That police favour guilty pleas because they demonstrate police effectiveness, create a favourable public image and ensure a high conviction rate (Blumberg, 1967a: 64) attests to the significance the police attach to court outcomes. Findings that the police object to some effects of plea bargaining such as reduction of charge, dismissal of multiple counts and reduction of sentence (Neubauer, 1974; Arcuri, 1977; Bottomley, 1973) further support the contention that the police are very much interested in court decisions and will in fact attempt to influence them (Grosman, 1969). To the police, conviction and the sentence frequently represent confirmation of their competence and the true conclusion of a case (Reiss, 1971; Westley, 1970). Because in many cases arrest alone is not considered satisfactory, the police must depend on the courts to apply further desired sanctions (Neubauer, 1974; Bittner, 1970). Thus, in many cases the police consider court processing of their charges crucial. As a result, the police attempt to satisfy the definition of a successful case held by the prosecutor and judge.

The police look to the history of adjudication and sentence when deciding whether or not to process cases. Rarely do police charge suspects without believing them guilty of some crime, and they typically believe that the offender should be convicted. A history of acquittals may therefore direct the police to reduce the number and kinds of suspects they charge.

The role of court actions in making such factors as the quality of evidence important criteria in police decisions to arrest is exemplified by the case of assault (Black, 1971). Because the refusal of an assault victim to co-operate with the prosecution by serving as a complainant greatly restricts what judges can do, such cases are met with considerable displeasure at the court stage. As a result, police officers may choose to make an arrest only when there is a good chance the victims will agree to co-operate (Goldstein, 1968). In jurisdictions where most assault victims will not carry out a formal complaint, police will arrest only when they actually witness assaults and can thus serve as complainants (Pepinsky, 1976). Thus, the evidence required by the judge in order to convict influences police decisions to arrest for assault, as well as for other types of crime. Similarly, the sentencing histories of the judiciary may be used by the police as criteria in determining whether or not to spend time arresting individuals (Bottomley, 1973). Lenient sentencing for certain types of cases may be interpreted as negative feedback, directing police not to invest much energy in investigating, arresting and charging for cases of that type.

There are times when the police may consider alternatives totally within their control to be satisfactory measures for dealing with specific types of cases or offenders. In this event, court outcomes may be viewed as somewhat irrelevant. Prostitution is an offence for which the police, although aware that the prosecutor is unlikely to process charges, make arrests because arrest alone deters the most blatant forms of streetwalking (Reich, 1973) and may relieve community pressure to act. Similarly, in the case of gambling operations, searches and arrests are often deemed sufficient (LaFave and Remington, 1965). In both these situations, by failing to present charges to the prosecutor the police determine what types of cases the courts will deal with. However, there remains a chicken-or-egg dilemma because police decisions not to charge rest in part on the history of the courts not to bring charges of prostitution and gambling to the stage of trial or conviction. Nonetheless, although the police are dependent on the courts to further process offences, police decisions to lay charges or not directly determine the case load and types of cases dealt with at the court stage.

The Courts

The independent relationship between the police and prosecutor has been described by some as one of antagonistic co-operation (Reiss and Bordua, 1967). Despite the institutional independence of the police and courts there is continual interaction between the prosecutor and the police officer assigned to a particular case (Cole, 1970; Grosman, 1969). While the police must rely on the presecutor to move cases through the courts, the prosecutor is dependent on the police to provide charges and evidence (Cole, 1970; Neubauer, 1974; Blumberg, 1967a). This mutual dependence is the fundamental reason for co-operative relationships between the police and prosecutors.

The important role the police play in securing convictions by providing evidence through good investigations and by serving as witnesses in court (Cole, 1970) is incentive for prosecutors to establish rapport with the police. It also provides a basis for police influence on court activities wherein the police control the information and evidence they pass on to the prosecutor in order to stymie cases they do not want processed at the court stage. Given that prosecutors tend to accept cases on the belief that the evidence can secure convictions (Grosman, 1969; Skolnick, 1975), providing poor evidence may well ensure that a case will not be brought to trial by the prosecutor. The police are also in a position to shape the kinds of charges that may be brought to court in a given case. This may be done in order to ensure convictions that might otherwise have been problematic. Co-operation between the police and the prosecutor is enhanced by a similarity in view regarding both goals and methods. Prosecutors and police share the view that conviction of offenders brought to trial is the most desirable outcome. As well, prosecutors and police often believe that legally required court procedure obstructs the efficient processing of offenders (Arcuri, 1977). These shared opinions lead the police to view prosecutors as being on their side (Neubauer, 1974).

However, the extent of co-operation between the police and the prosecutor is reduced by the latter's ongoing interaction with defence lawyers and the judiciary. This interaction fosters a similarity in view between the prosecution and the defence regarding what criteria must be met in order to bring cases to trial and ensure acceptable sentences (Cole, 1970; Skolnick and Woodworth, 1967; LaFave and Remington, 1965; Neubauer, 1974). This apparent collusion between prosecution and defence can create a sense of betrayal on the part of the police. Thus, the defence exerts influence over police decisions through its relationship with the prosecution.

Although the police have a significant impact on prosecutorial decision making, the prosecutor usually makes the final decision about whether to charge. Because prosecutors can either send cases back to the police for further investigation or reduce charges, they can provide a check on police practices, enhancing police compliance with prosecutorial priorities (Cole, 1970; Newman, 1966).

The judiciary, too, considers other parts of the criminal justice system when making decisions. Charge decisions by prosecutors and judges are influenced not only by general goals of justice but also by more practical considerations, such as the number of people who can be handled in court and in correctional facilities (McIntyre, 1968). In cases brought to trial, judges also take the police into account and will sometimes dismiss cases with the intent of changing police practices (Goldstein, 1968; Bittner, 1970). Occasionally, the decision of guilt or innocence is employed as a means of controlling poor police performance (Newman, 1966). In the United States, judicial assessment of police methods used to obtain evidence places the judiciary in a supervisory role with respect to police operations (Goldstein, 1968). This type of control does not hold in Canada, where illegally obtained evidence is admissible at trial (Wilson, 1970). Such judicial practice as dismissal of cases seems to have the desired effect of altering police practices. When a judge has a history of dismissing cases, police may refuse to take cases before him or her (Cole, 1970; Goldstein, 1968), undermining the prosecutor's control over charge decisions.

Sentencing by trial judges is influenced by their knowledge that harsh sentences may lead defence lawyers to appeal. Since such appeals typically result in sentence reduction by the appeals courts (Neubauer, 1974), moderation in sentencing in the first place may result. However, there is considerable variation among judges in sentencing practices and other decision making — variation that further complicates decision making by the police and prosecution. This is particularly problematic in larger centres where one of many different judges could be hearing a given case. In the face of such variability, the predictability of case outcomes is minimized.

Conclusion

This overview of the systems approach has by no means been exhaustive. The examples provided here should, however, prepare students for the readings that follow by encouraging them to come to terms with the criminal justice system as a dynamic social system. The written law may, to many, be dry and tedious. However, the complex social processes that it sets in motion can offer a challenge and a fascination limited only by the energy, insight and imagination of those practitioners, researchers and laypersons who seek truly to understand it.

Endnotes

1   For some general information about systems analysis in the social sciences, see Parsons, 1967; Berrien, 1968; Attinger, 1970; Easton, 1968; Catanese and Steiss, 1970; Katz and Kahn, 1969; Hagen, 1961; Kuhn, 1974; Sutherland, 1973; Emshoff, 1971; von Bertalanffy, 1968; Gouldner, 1967.

2   For those wishing to pursue systems analysis at this level and to examine its specific application to the criminal justice system, see Connidis, 1982.

3   For a more detailed discussion of this distinction, see Clarke, Barnhorst and Barhorst in Part II of this book.

4   Similarly, Reiss, 1971, does not include corrections in his analysis.

5   For a good discussion of the pervasive influence of law, see Feeley, 1976.

6   Studies done in urban centres suggest that upward of ninety per cent of crimes known to police come to their attention via citizen reports (see, for example, Reiss, 1971). This figure will vary by type of crime and law-enforcement setting. For

example, a study of property offences in a small-town setting indicates that 100 per cent of the property offences in the year of the study came to police attention through public reports. In contrast, the bulk of police knowledge about crimes such as illegal gambling, prostitution and drug use results from their own investigatory activity.

7   For a review of Canadian victimization surveys and a discussion of their general use and interpretation, see Evans and Leger, 1979. For an example of this use of self-reporting in Canada, see Hagan, Gillis and Chan, 1978.

8   For discussions of the limitations of official statistics in Canada, see Connidis, 1979; Giffen, 1976; Silverman and Teevan, 1980; Bell-Rowbotham and Boydell, 1974.

9   Such estimates are made cautiously because of the difficulty in obtaining reliable official statistics, especially when moving from one stage of the justice system to another. For an assessment of these difficulties with respect to the kinds of issues raised here, see Connidis, 1979. The estimates constructed here are based on a tempered fusion of official crime statistics with research on victimization (Bell-Rowbotham and Boydell, 1974; Giffen, 1976; Solicitor General, 1979; Connidis, 1979; Evans and Leger, 1979).

10   See Blumstein and Larson, 1969; Ewing, 1976; Reiss, 1971; Freed, 1969; Blumstein, Cassidy and Hopkinson, 1974. For a more detailed discussion of the nonhierarchical structure of the criminal justice system and its implications, see Connidis, 1982.

11   This applies only when the police want a case to lead to conviction. In some cases, other outcomes may be judged more desirable (see Connidis, 1982).

References

Arcuri, Alan F. 1977. "Criminal Justice: A Police Perspective." *Criminal Justice Review* 2(1): 15-21.

Attinger, E.O. 1970. "Potentials and Pitfalls in the Analysis of Social Systems" in Attinger, E.O. (ed.), *Global Systems Dynamics*. Toronto: Wiley-Interscience.

Beckman, Erik. 1977. "Criminal Justice and Politics in America: From the Sedition Act to Watergate and Beyond." *Journal of Police Science and Administration* 5(3): 285-289.

Bell-Rowbotham, B. and C. Boydell. 1974. "Crime in Canada: A Distributional Analysis" in Boydell, C., G. Grindstaff and P. Whitehead (eds.), *Deviant Behaviour and Societal Reaction*. Toronto: Holt, Rinehart and Winston.

Berrien, F.K. 1968. *General Social Systems*. New Brunswick, NJ: Rutgers University Press.

Bittner, E. 1970. *The Functions of the Police in Modern Society*. Rockville, MD: National Institute of Mental Health.

Black, D. 1971. "The Social Organization of Arrest." *Stanford Law Review* 23: 1087-1111.

Blaine, R.H. and D. Kettler. 1971. "Law as a Political Weapon." *Politics and Society* 1(4): 479-526.

Blumberg, Abraham S. 1967a. *Criminal Justice*. Chicago: Quadrangle Books.

Blumberg, Abraham S. 1967b. "Law as a Confidence Game: Organizational Cooptation of a Profession." *Law and Society Review* 1: 15-39.

Blumstein, Alfred R., Gordon Cassidy and George R. Hopkinson. 1974. "Systems Analysis and the Canadian Criminal Justice System." Statistics Division Report 8/74. Ottawa: Ministry of the Solicitor General.

Blumstein, A. and R. Larson. 1969. "Models of a Total Criminal Justice System." *Operations Research* 17: 199-232.

Bottomley, A. Keith. 1973. *Decisions in the Penal Process*. London: Martin Robertson.

Boydell, Craig L. and Ingrid A. Connidis. 1974. "The Administration of Criminal Justice: Continuity Versus Conflict." *Canadian Journal of Criminology and Corrections* 16(1): 14-34.

Brautigam, Richard K. 1974. "Criminal Justice Decision-making: An Exploratory Empirical Study." *Harvard Journal of Penology and Crime Prevention* 14(1): 53-77.

Canadian Civil Liberties Education Trust. 1974. "Due Process Safeguards and Canadian Criminal Justice" in Boydell, C., P. Whitehead and C. Grindstaff (eds.), *The Administration of Criminal Justice in Canada*. Toronto: Holt, Rinehart and Winston.

Cassidy, R. Gordon. 1974. "A Systems Approach to Planning and Evaluation in Criminal Justice Systems." Statistics Division Report 13/74. Ottawa: Ministry of the Solicitor General.

Cassidy, R. Gordon and Ronald E. Turner. 1977. "Criminal Justice System Behaviour." Unpublished manuscript. Ottawa: Ministry of the Solicitor General.

Catanese, A.J. and A.W. Steiss. 1970. *Systematic Planning: Theory and Application*. Toronto: D.C. Heath.

Clark, Kenneth L., Richard Barnhorst and Sherrie Barnhorst. 1977. *Criminal Law and the Canadian Criminal Code*. Toronto: McGraw-Hill Ryerson.

Coffey, Alan, Edward Elder-Fouso and Walter Hartinger. 1974. *An Introduction to the Criminal Justice System and Process*. Englewood-Cliffs, NJ: Prentice-Hall.

Cole, George F. 1970. "The Decision to Prosecute." *Law and Society Review* 4(3): 331-343.

Cole, George F. 1975. *The American System of Criminal Justice*. North Scituatte, Mass.: Duxbury Press.

Connidis, Ingrid A. 1979. "Problems in the Use of Official Statistics for Criminal Justice System Research." *Canadian Journal of Criminology* 21(4): 397-415.

Connidis, Ingrid A. 1982. *Rethinking Criminal Justice Research: A Systems Perspective*. Toronto: Holt, Rinehart and Winston.

Cowan, Thomas A. 1963. "Decision Theory in Law, Science and Technology." *Rutgers Law Review* 17(2): 499-530.

Cumming, E., I. Cumming and L. Edell. 1962. "Policeman as Philosopher, Guide and Friend." *Social Problems* 12(3): 276-286.

Easton, D. 1968. "A Systems Analysis of Political Life" in Buckley, W. (ed.), *Modern Systems Theory for the Behavioral Scientist*. Chicago: Aldine.

Emshoff, James R. 1971. *Analysis of Behavioral Systems*. New York: Macmillan.

Evans, John L. and Gerald J. Leger. 1979. "Canadian Victimization Surveys: A Discussion Paper." *Canadian Journal of Criminology* 21(2): 166-183.

Ewing, Blair G. 1976. "Criminal Justice Planning: An Assessment." *Criminal Justice Review* 1(1): 121-139.

Feeley, Malcolm M. 1973. "Two Models of the Criminal Justice System: An Organizational Perspective." *Law and Society Review* 7(3): 407-425.

Feeley, Malcolm M. 1976. "The Concept of Laws in Social Science: A Critique and Notes on an Expanded View." *Law and Society Review* 10(4): 497-523.

Frank, Daniel J. 1969. "The Nonsystem of Criminal Justice" in Campbell, James S., Joseph R. Sahid and David P. Stang (eds.), *Law and Order Reconsidered: A Staff Report to the National Commission on the Causes and Prevention of Violence.* Washington, D.C.: U.S. Government Printing Office.

Frank, James E. and Frederic L. Faust. 1975. "A Conceptual Framework for Criminal Justice Planning." *Criminology* 13(2): 271-196.

Freed, Daniel J. 1969. "The Nonsystem of Criminal Justice" in Campgell, James S., Joseph R. Sahid and David P. Stang (eds.), *Law and Order Reconsidered: A Staff Report to the National Commission on the Causes and Prevention of Violence.* Washington, D.C.: U.S. Government Printing Office.

Giffen, P.J. 1976. "Official Rates of Crime and Delinquency" in McGrath, W.T. (ed.), *Crime and Its Treatment in Canada.* Toronto: Macmillan of Canada.

Goldstein, Herman. 1963. "Police Discretion: The ideal Versus the Real." *Public Administration Review* 23(3): 140-148.

Goldstein, Herman. 1968. "Trial Judges and the Police: Their Relations in the Administration of Criminal Justice." *Crime and Delinquency* 14: 14-24.

Gouldner, Alvin J. 1967. "Reciprocity and Autonomy in Functional Theory" in Demerath, N.J. III and Richard A. Peterson (eds.), *System, Change and Conflict.* New York: The Free Press.

Grosman, B.A. 1969. *The Prosecutor: An Enquiry into the Exercise of Discretion.* Toronto: University of Toronto Press.

Hagan, John, Ronald Gillis and Janet Chan. 1978. "Explaining Official Delinquency: A Spatial Study of Class, Conflict and Control." *The Sociological Quarterly* 19: 386-398.

Hagen, E.E. 1961. "Analytical models in the Study of Social Systems." *American Journal of Sociology* 67(2): 144-151.

Hann, Robert J. 1973. *Decision Making in the Canadian Criminal Court System: A Systems Analysis.* Toronto: Centre of Criminology.

Henshel, R.L. and R.A. Silverman. 1975. "Introduction" in Henshel, R.L. and R.A Silverman (eds.), *Perception in Criminology.* Toronto: Methuen.

Henshel, Richard L. 1977. "The Control of Police Power." *Canadian Forum* 57(November): 11-13.

Henshel, Richard L. 1978. "Forgetting About Police Crime." *Canadian Forum* 57(March): 10-11.

Henshel, Richard L. 1979. "Will Police Disruptive Tactics Leave Only the Facade of Democracy?" *Canadian Journal of Sociology* 4(2): 167-171.

Kasinsky, Renee Goldsmith. 1975. "Rape: A Normal Act?" *Canadian Forum* 55(September): 18-22.

Katz, D. and R. Kahn. 1969. "Common Characteristics of Open Systems" in Emery, F.E. (ed.), *Systems Thinking: Selected Readings.* London: Penguin.

Kirkpatrick, A.M. and W.T. McGrath. 1976. *Crime and You.* Toronto: Macmillan of Canada.

Kuhn, Alfred. 1974. *The Logic of Social Systems.* San Francisco: Jossey-Bass Publications.

LaFave, W.R. 1964. *Arrest: The Decision to Take a Suspect into Custody.* Boston: Little, Brown.

LaFave, W.R. and Frank J. Remington. 1965. "Controlling the Police: The Judge's Role in Making and Reviewing Law Enforcement Decisions." *Michigan Law Review* 63: 987-1012.

Mann, Edward and John Alan Lee. 1979. *The RCMP vs. the People.* Toronto: General Publishing.

McIntyre, Donald M. 1968. "A Study of Judicial Dominance of the Charging Decision." *Journal of Criminal Law, Criminology and Police Science* 59: 463-490.

Mohr, Lawrence B. 1976. "Organizations, Decisions and Courts." *Law and Society Review* 10(4): 621-642.

Moore, M.D. 1976. "A Normative Model for Law Enforcement in the Criminal Justice System." *Journal of Police Science and Administration* 4(1): 71-81.

Munro, Jim L. 1974. *Administrative Behavior and the Police Organization.* Cincinnati: W.H. Anderson.

Myren, Richard A. 1976. "Study of Federated Criminal Justice Systems: Research Needs." *Criminal Justice Review* 1(1): 1-10.

Neubauer, David W. 1974. *Criminal Justice in Middle America.* Morristown, NJ: General Learning Press.

Newman, D.J. 1966. *Conviction: The Determination of Guilt or Innocence Without Trial.* Boston: Little, Brown.

O'Leary, Vincent and Donald J. Newman. 1970. "Conflict Resolution in Criminal Justice." *Journal of Research in Crime and Delinquency* 7(1): 99-110.

Outerbridge, W. 1973. "In Search of New Perspectives." Paper presented at the Canadian Congress of Criminology and Corrections, June 24.

Parsons, T. 1967. "The Social System: A General Theory of Action" in Grinker, R.R. (ed.), *Toward a Unified Theory of Human Behavior.* 2nd ed. New York: Basic Books.

Pepinsky, Harold E. 1976. "Police Patrolman's Offence-reporting Behaviour." *Journal of Research in Crime and Delinquency* 13(1): 33-47.

Reich, Robert B. 1973. "Operations Research and Criminal Justice." *Journal of Public Law* 22: 357-387.

Reiss, A.J. Jr. and D.J. Bordua. 1967. "Environment and Organization: A Perspective on the Police" in Bordua, D.J. (ed.), *The Police: Six Sociological Essays.* New York: Wiley.

Reiss, Albert J., Jr. 1971. *The Police and the Public.* New Haven: Yale University Press.

Roebuck, Julian B. and Thomas Barker. 1974. "A Typology of Police Corruption." *Social Problems* 21(3); 423-437.

Sallmann, Peter A. 1978. "Criminal Justice: A Systems Approach." *Australian and New Zealand Journal of Criminology* 11: 195-208.

Silverman, Robert A. and James J. Teevan Jr. (eds.). 1980. *Crime in Canadian Society.* Toronto: Butterworth.

Skolnick, J. 1967. "Social Control in the Adversary System." *Journal of Conflict Resolution* 2: 52-70.

Skolnick, J.H. 1975. *Justice Without Trial: Law Enforcement in Democratic Society.* New

York: Wiley.

Skolnick, J.H. and J.R. Woodworth. 1967. "Bureaucracy, Information and Social Control: A Study of Morals Detail" in Bordua, D.J. (ed.), *The Police: Six Sociological Essays.* New York: Wiley. Pp. 99-136.

Small, S. 1978. "Canadian Narcotics Legislation, 1880-1923" in Greenaway, William and S.L. Brickey (eds.), *Law and Social Control in Canada.* Scarborough, Ont.: Prentice-Hall.

Solicitor General Canada. 1979. *Selected Trends in Canadian Criminal Justice.* Ottawa: Communications Division, Ministry of the Solicitor General of Canada.

Sutherland, John W. 1973. *A General Systems Philosophy for the Social and Behavioural Sciences.* New York: Braziller.

Turk, Austin T. 1976. "Law as a Weapon in Social Conflict." *Social Problems* 23(3): 276-291.

Turk, Austin T. 1977. "Class, Conflict and Criminalization." *Sociological Focus* 10(3): 209-220.

von Bertalanffy, L. 1968. *General Systems Theory.* New York: Braziller.

Weiss, Kurt and Sandra Borges. 1973. "Victimology and Rape: The Case of the Legitimate Victim." *Issues in Criminology* 8(2): 71-115.

Westley, William A. 1970. *Violence and the Police: A Sociological Study of Law, Custom and Morality.* Cambridge, Mass: M.I.T. Press.

Wilson, John Owen. 1970. "The Canadian Courts." *Judicature* 53(6): 254-257.

Visions of Community Policing:
Rhetoric and Reality in Canada[1]

Barry N. Leighton

Introduction

Community policing, sometimes referred to as community-oriented policing, community-based policing, or problem-oriented policing, is currently presented by academic observers of policing as characterizing "modern," "progressive" or "contemporary" policing (Skolnick and Bayley, 1986, 1988a,b; Kelling, 1987; Murphy, 1988a; Greene and Mastrofski, 1988; Trojanowicz and Bucqueroux, 1990; Sparrow, Moore and Kennedy, 1990). While many of these commentators have also actively influenced the direction of community policing, it has been the prevailing wind of change among North American police leaders for the past few decades and a key ingredient of the public and professional discourse on policing reform. Canadian police professionals have also adopted as their conventional wisdom the view that community policing represents the most progressive approach to contemporary policing (Normandeau and Leighton, 1990a,b). Indeed, the majority of police leaders consulted during a series of federal government consultations during 1990 laid claim to their own police force as the most progressive in Canada, if not amongst police forces in the western world, on the grounds that they had adopted or had always been pursuing a community policing approach (Leighton, 1990). Obviously, they cannot all be the leading police agency. Further, community policing appears to be in the eye of the beholder, especially when the beholder is a police executive, mayor or other stakeholder in a local effort to establish community policing or to motivate change in policing.

Despite this conventional wisdom, it is not clear why community-based policing has recently become so popular in North America and elsewhere as the generic, all-purpose police solution to crime and disorder problems, especially given the weak empirical support for its effectiveness. In many ways it is like oat bran: there is general agreement that it has some beneficial effect and it has many devotees, but scientists are not quite sure how or why it works. Indeed, police executives claiming success for their own community-based policing project without a rigorous evaluation is like prematurely announcing a cure for colon cancer. Like oat bran, community policing may have more to do with bulky rhetoric and process; that is, an indirect effect rather than the direct effect of its substance on the desired outcome.

The question posed by Greene and Mastrofski (1988) as to whether community policing in Canada is "rhetoric or reality" is obscured by unrestrained support for the approach. This immense support flies in the face of a lack of agreement over what it means in theory and practice and presents the problematic for this discussion. Accordingly, this paper attempts to present a clear and meaningful definition or description of community policing. It then sketches out some of the community policing initiatives taken by selected police forces across Canada. A number of unresolved issues are raised which may challenge the viability of community policing or, if responded to, may assist in improving its changes for greater effectiveness. Finally, an explanation for the popularity of this approach is sought in a brief review of its apparent origins and an attempt is made to place this policing paradigm within a broader theoretical context.

Definition

What is community policing? As has been observed, the concept has a wide range of meanings (Manning, 1984), resulting in little agreement over even its general nature. Indeed, it could be said that, like the concept of "community," the concept of "community policing" is in the eye of the beholder. However, while it is generally considered to be the "new" approach to policing that has recently begun to sweep through North America, Europe and common law countries such as Australia and New Zealand, community policing might be more correctly referred to as a re-emergence, renewal or revitalization of a former philosophical, organizational and operational approach to urban policing developed last century in Metropolitan London by Peel and his associates. The current version of this approach may be summarized by a central principle followed by a family of subsidiary value statements on the preferred police role, authority, managerial style, organizational arrangements and an operational approach in terms of strategies and tactics.

The central principle underlying this style of urban policing is a full *partnership between the community and their police* in identifying and ameliorating local crime and disorder problems. It claims that crime and disorder problems are the *joint property* of the community as "client" as well as of the police as the local agency delivering public security services. Accordingly, the police and the community are *co-producers of order and civility* (Wilson and Kelling, 1982; Murphy and Muir, 1984) and "co-reproducers of order" (Ericson, 1982). They achieve this remarkable symbiotic state through an interactive, cooperative and reciprocal relationship (Short, 1983) which, in practical terms, means that community members, as clients of the police, participate in shaping police policy and decision making. Underlying this partnership principle is the core assumption that the level of crime, disorder and fearfulness in a community is inversely related to the level of public participation in policing. That is, participation breathes life into the partnership principle.

This relationship of partnership and participation contrasts with the "professional, bureaucratic or traditional" model of policing in which crime is the exclusive property of the police under this "professional policing" or "crime control" model, the police form a "thin blue line" against crime and, in practice, unfortunately also form a thin blue line against the community. In operational terms, the professional model can be characterized in a number of different ways but has been described succinctly by Kelling and Moore (1988) as a technology-driven, rapid response strategy coupled with random motorized patrol. It is as if police forces under the "professional model" operated like a hospital organized as a large emergency ward. Most of the staff would be sitting around waiting for those relatively rare, life-threatening events when the public would call in to ask for a rapid response by ambulance. Ambulances would cruise the accident "hot spots" to be more readily available but also to deter high-risk behaviour such as unsafe driving or driving under the influence of alcohol. Patients would arrive only by ambulance, the regular wards would be largely forgotten and regular health care would be neglected. Certainly, no one would indulge in preventive health care. Community policing can also be portrayed through a medical model. But, rather than being like an emergency ward, community policing is seen as being more like preventive medicine, with an emergency response used for only a small proportion of health care cases. This approach involves promoting and maintaining good health — exercise, a balanced diet, a lot of fibre and less red meat — in the same way as building safer communities that have less crime and disorder problems relies upon the elements of community policing and preventive policing or crime prevention.

This juxtaposition of "community policing" and "professional policing" (see Table 1) is largely a heuristic device, or perhaps a pedagogical technique, that sharpens the contrast at the expense of rigour in the representation of past and present policing practices (as does the "three eras of policing" referred to later). The professional model, which currently serves as a useful straw man for proponents of community policing, nonetheless played an important part in the development of modern policing and meets one of the minimal conditions of public expectations for safety in the form of rapid, reliable response for those relatively rare life-threatening incidents.

While there are a variety of components to various visions of community policing, most of them proceed from the partnership principle which has far-reaching implications for the organization and operations of police forces. For example, the police-community partnership is often seen as providing new resources from the community that combine to form the symbol of a "broad blue line" against crime and disorder in the community or, as Skolnick and Bayley (1986) characterize it, a "new blue line" that has a more general role than merely crime control. Their view of community policing identifies four elements, in terms of police-community reciprocity, a real decentralization of command, reorientation of patrol and civilianization. Others' visions follow the seminal work of Goldstein (1979, 1987, 1990) by identifying it with problem-oriented policing which largely limits community policing to the problem-solving ingredient. Some of the components of the broad blue line are principles or value statements while others represent the routine distinction between strategies (e.g., problem-solving) and tactics (e.g., foot patrol, mini-stations, consultative committees).

There are perhaps sixteen subsidiary ingredients of "community policing" which summarize the conventional wisdom among many police leaders and academics. The following summary is an elaboration on one of the author's contributions to an "official vision" of community policing (Leighton, 1989; Solicitor General, 1990; Normandeau and Leighton, 1990a,b; Leighton, 1990).

(1)   *The central objective or mission of the police* in Canadian society is to ensure peace, order, and civility, to provide related services to the community, and to facilitate a sense of security among the public. In helping to maintain peace, order and security in local communities, police officers exercise their side of the partnership with the community by being routinely — but not exclusively — responsible for the reduction and prevention of crime and the promotion of public order and individual safety.

In the words of Sir Robert Peel's first two police commissioners, Sir Charles Rowan and Sir Richard Mayne, the new police follow the principle "...that the police are the public and that the public are the police..." (Reith, 1975). Accordingly, the police official's role is fundamentally that of a peace officer. By contrast, the objective of the traditional or professional policing approach is more narrow: it is to enforce the criminal law, solve crime, and apprehend criminals. The police role is to serve as law enforcement officers responsible only for crime control; that is, anything else is mere "social work" and not "real policing."

(2)   The police legal authority and their mandate to police local communities is derived from democratic institutions and is delegated by elected representatives to police executives. Where "the community" voices, through one means or another, their public approval of the nature and scope of the policing arrangements, then they are reaffirming their approval of the police mandate as well as their direct consent to be policed. Conferring of consent contributes in no small way to the success of community policing and goes beyond both the legal authority to police as a minimal requirement and a police-community partnership as an operating principle. By contrast, legal authority under the professional model is formal, passing through a chain of clearly circumscribed responsibility to the chief and down in hierarchical, para-military fashion through the chain of command. This authority structure is exclusive and shuts the door on community participation of any kind, at any level.

(3)   Community police agencies are service-oriented organizations. Because police officers serve and protect the public and provide related services to the public for crime and disorder problems, the preferred title of their organizations is now a "police service." This service orientation is consistent with the interpretation of urban policing as another municipal service, along with health, education, etc., which are delivered as legal and social justice entitlements to local taxpayers. It is also a reflection of the growing tendency to view the public as clients of the police who consume their services, in much the same way as they consume other goods and services in the private sector. Hence, private sector standards are being introduced into policing, including performance values such as the "search for excellence" (Peters and Wasserman, 1982; Kanter, 1983) and the search for quality in those services, for "continuous quality assurance" and for continuous improvement (Sensenbrenner, 1991). As a result, the corporate culture and subculture is transformed. The corporate culture becomes that of a service agency to the public, borrowing values from the private sector such as partnerships,

search for excellence, continuous quality assurance, etc. The subculture becomes that of a white-collar profession that is responsible, responsive to community needs, and driven by a code of professional ethics. By contrast, policing under the former model primarily serves the limited outcome of police work focused largely on crime control. This emphasis is symbolically represented by the use of "police force" as the preferred term for their organizations.

(4)   A community consultation process is employed as a key strategy to help the police accomplish the important objective of identifying policing priorities for addressing crime and disorder problems in the community. This process may be done on an annual basis, usually with the assistance of a police governing authority (e.g., police board or commission) and establishes the relatively short-term priorities for the year, as well as providing community feedback on police performance over the past year. This process also assists community representatives to set their agenda for safety and security in their area and to better understand the problems associated with public policing. A variety of consultation mechanisms which facilitate a police community dialogue are currently being explored by Canadian police forces, such as advisory or consultative committees and meeting with local interest groups. This approach differs from the former "professional" model which usually pursued "police-community relations" through a specialized unit rather than at all levels of police service through a variety of means.

(5)   Taking a proactive approach to crime and disorder problems is a key strategy with the community policing approach, although it may also stand alone as part of "problem oriented policing" (Goldstein, 1979, 1990; Fek and Spelman, 1987). Rather than passively waiting for the calls or randomly patrolling for a presumed deterrent effect, the police anticipate future calls by identifying local crime and disorder problems. A first step is a scanning and forecasting process that identifies problems based on demographic and other "social data," including information from other agencies. It also includes input from the local community. The scanning process is accomplished in part by "crime analysis" involving the analysis of patterns among similar crimes and calls for service. "Hot spots" of similar crimes are identified by time, place and type of offence. These hot spots are brought to the attention of street constables at the neighbourhood level, and to police managers and the police commission for community- or city-wide problems. Input from the local community is received in terms of local crime and disorder priorities. A strategic plan may be developed that priorizes the competing crime

and disorder problems at the community level and may be debated in public discussions. This problem-identification strategy contrasts with the "professional model" approach as a knee-jerk, undifferentiated rapid-response to the majority of calls for service which are treated separately, despite any commonalties and prior history. Once responded to, each incident is treated as an event that is closed when the case has been solved.

(6) The main police response strategy to address local crime and disorder problems is a problem-solving strategy, which is developed with a focus on their underlying causes (Goldstein, 1979, 1990; Murphy, 1991). The most appropriate proactive and reactive policing tactics are selected to address particular crime and disorder problems in each neighbourhood, reflecting the reality that crime and disorder problems are not unitary phenomena, nor are the solutions, and nor are neighbourhoods and communities. This "community-specific" approach parallels "client-specific planning" in designing individual treatment within the "something works" paradigm in corrections. Accordingly, flexibility in the use of tactics from the full range is a central principle in this approach and no single tactic can be identified with community policing. Indeed, any means of increasing the level and quality of contact between citizens and the police can be used that will facilitate greater public participation. Tactics might include zone parking, neighbourhood foot patrol, officers dedicated to particular beats, mini-stations or store-front offices, differentially responding to calls for service, volunteers, greater civilianization, flexible shifts, integrated teams (of foot patrol, motorized patrol and investigative functions) and community advisory or liaison committees. Once the problem has been solved or significantly reduced, then an evaluation or assessment is conducted to determine the effectiveness of the tactics for the particular problem and type of neighbourhood. By contrast the professional policing model focuses on discrete incidents which are treated as unrelated to other similar incidents, such as those previously occurring at the same place or time or with the same offender or victim.

(7) A careful balance is maintained between proactive (e.g., prevention, problem solving) and reactive (e.g., emergency response) tactics. Community policing recognizes the reality of a continued requirement for those tactics commonly identified with the professional model, including in particular a rapid-response capability which remains a fundamental requirement for policing when occasional life-threatening incidents arise. It is also necessary to continue maintaining a few specialist units, including homicide investigation teams which might also have responsibili-

ty for family violence where most homicides occur. However, the principle of minimal specialization is observed and the number of specialized units is severely limited, with the functions of "grin-and wave" or community relations squads transferred to generalist constables. Whereas the professional approach preferred the use of rapid-response and random patrol tactics over other tactics, community policing does not reject any tactics that are appropriate to the problem and the neighbourhood.

(8)   Police address the underlying causes of problems using a broader set of longer-term responses, particularly crime prevention activities. These include opportunity reduction tactics such as "target hardening," principally, "crime prevention through environmental design" (CPTED) techniques. As well, "crime prevention through social development" (CPTSD) is recognized as the long-term solution in which prevention strategies focus on the reduction of the motivation of potential offenders or recidivists to engage in criminality by removing the root causes of these motivations. Under this framework, prevention tactics address poverty, unemployment, poor education and work skills, inadequate housing, poor health and other underlying causes of crime. On the other hand, the professional model treated long-term prevention as not within the realm of policing and continued merely to plug the leaking dike on a leak by leak basis.

(9)   Inter-agency co-operation is a key strategy involving a branching out to other service delivery agencies to form strategic partnerships and a more co-operative and productive division of labour. This allows both types of prevention activities (CPTED, CPTSD) to be more efficiently and effectively undertaken. Inter-agency co-operation recognizes the limits of policing beyond what they do extremely well, which is providing a round-the-clock, first rapid-response to crime and related crises. It also recognized the complementarity of police and those other agencies which are better able to provide a longer-term response for victims and to undertake crime prevention by removing the underlying causes of crime. This co-operative response places the police within a service network of agencies addressing urban safety and, more generally, the "healthy cities" approach. On the other hand, the former policing model often over-extended police organizations for many functions better provided by other agencies and presented an "iron agency curtain" by failing to link up with or co-operate with these other agencies. Where police did co-operate with other agencies, then police professionals usually insisted on taking the lead role.

(10)   Information management is emphasized, relying on people-con-

tacts within the community as a major but not exclusive source of information and intelligence. Much of the success of policing depends on how well its personnel operate as information managers who engage in "interactive policing" by routinely exchanging information on a reciprocal basis with community members through close formal contacts and numerous informal networks. While much of the police work is often seen as not being "real" police work because it involves providing services and information unrelated to crime, community police do so on the grounds that not only is policing a service to the public, but it allows the public to become more familiar with their police service and the police to become more knowledgeable about their community. Closer ties with community members are a good investment because they can become sources of valuable information or police "intelligence" when crime problems later arise. By contrast, while some specialized units emphasize human sources of intelligence, the professional model generally exhibits an overreliance on technology, such as cars, radios and computers. Indeed, the professional model tactics appear to be technology-driven rather than technology being used as a means to enhance the efficiency and effectiveness of preferred tactics. Contacts with the community are not only inhibited by a reliance on technology, but distance police from the community. In many police forces contact with the public was once prohibited unless they were explicitly for crime-related business involving victims, witnesses and offenders. Intelligence sources were therefore largely internal to police agencies.

(11)   The composition of community police services is shifting towards a better reflection of the demographic and social composition of the communities they serve, particularly through the recruitment of women, visible and ethnic minorities and Aboriginal police officers. Positions that are not directly related to crime control are increasingly being civilianized. Community volunteers are also being used in mini-stations and other community policing tactics although it is interesting to note that, in the logical extension of the Peelite vision of community policing, it is the police who are the true volunteers, being paid full-time to assist the community to control crime and disorder. These trends facilitate an improved understanding of community views by police professionals.

(12)   More relevant criteria for success of police service effectiveness or performance are now being established. These criteria are now reaching a more appropriate balance between those stressing community policing processes and those stressing its impact. Some of these new indicators of effectiveness include: (1) identifying

local crime and disorder problems through a police-community consultation process; (2) solving local crime and disorder problems through a police-community consultation process; (3) higher reporting rates for both traditional crime categories and for non-traditional crime and disorder problems; (4) reducing the number of repeat calls for service from repeat addresses; (5) improving the satisfaction with police services by public users of those services, particularly victims of crime; (6) increasing the job satisfaction of police officers; (7) increasing the reporting of information on local crime and disorder problems by community residents and increasing the knowledge of the community and its problems by local beat officers; and (8) decreasing the fear of personal victimization. The reduction of the unfounded fear of crime and of being victimized is a legitimate objective within the new approach, including fear reduction tactics directed towards the elderly, children and other vulnerable groups in society. Typically, those with the lowest statistical risk have the greatest fear of being victimized, particularly elderly. The police now have a responsibility to ensure that this fear has constructive rather than debilitating effects so that those who are vulnerable or view themselves a vulnerable may take reasonable crime prevention measures and then enjoy a safe environment. The professional model, by contrast, sees fear reduction as being outside established police responsibilities and accepts as legitimate the established criteria of (1) response time, (2) charges cleared, (3) others which stress the efficiency rather than the effectiveness of policing, and (4) popularity polls on how much community members like their local police force.

(13)   There is a transformed organizational structure in two ways, resulting in greater responsibility and autonomy for front-line street constables to apply community policing strategies and tactics in neighbourhoods. First, the hierarchical, para-military organizational model that exists in many large police services is changed into a flatter profile in which the front line of policing, where police services are provided, is the most important part of the organization. A great deal of responsibility is shifted down a rank, making some levels redundant. In designing more efficient police service delivery organization, there is therefore a "de-layering" of the authority structure. Second, there is a geographical decentralization of many functions including management and resource deployment so that those with responsibility are closer to the consumers of their services. Similarly there is a "temporal decentralization," with service delivery being based on neighbourhoods rather than on shifts. Resources are justified mainly on how well they serve the front-line police officers responsible for neighbourhood policing, problem solving and

rapid response to the rare life-threatening calls or for incidents in progress. Decentralization may result in the dispersal of headquarters specialists, if not the complete break-up of many headquarters' specialized units, with their duties assumed by generalist constables. In larger police services, there may still be a need for a few headquarters specialists (e.g., one victims specialist, one crime prevention specialist, etc.), but only in a support role for the front-line officers. In this way, headquarters staff in larger police services might be reduced by perhaps half its former numbers, thus releasing further resources to front-line policing. This police organization with minimal specialization is in sharp contrast to the complex, specialized, centralized, hierarchical police agency of the past.

(14)   Most police officers are permitted to become career generalists (i.e., the generalist constable model) rather than specialists and are responsible for a broader range of activities than permitted under the "professional" model, including solving neighbourhood crime and disorder problems. In many respects, the generalist constable is as much a specialty as is a physician serving as a general practitioner who has specialized in family medicine. The balance between generalist duties and emergency response duties has not been settled, however, nor has an appropriate proportion of officers pursuing generalist duties and other specialties duties been established. While many officers may still be rotated through specialties as part of career advancement, those who prefer to continue as street constables pursuing community policing may do so and be recognized within the reward structure, with this generalist constable role as a possible life-long career option. Rather than being the "dirty work" of police where street officers apply as soon as possible to transfer to non-street duties or specialized units, this is now an honourable status. Accordingly, community policing street constables are treated as highly trained, relatively well-paid white-collar professionals who have the respect of their colleagues and the local community. By contrast, they were treated generally as "blue-collar workers" under the "professional" model, at least until they reached the respectability of commissioned officer rank.

(15)   As a result of organizational transformation and the re-emergence of the generalist constable model, the loyalties of officers working under a community-policing regime, or the "blue" model (Guth, 1987), are primarily towards the Charter, the *Criminal Code*, the common law and the community. While this "blue model" raises the historically suspect and romantic concept of the autonomous English "village bobby" maintaining the King's Peace in hamlets across the land, it is a more

appropriate reflection of legal status of Canadian police officers as peace officers. A significant outcome is the fostering of a "new police professionalism" that is supported by a code of ethics and many of the other attributes of professions, with one obvious exception being the lack of a self-governing status. By contrast, the loyalties of police officers under the para-military or "brown" model is to the chain of command, working within a narrow range of responsibilities and limited autonomy. These loyalties have created an organizational culture of strict control over its members and a resilient sub-culture characterized by authoritarianism and conservatism.

(16)   Given the priorities supported earlier by the community, there is a degree of accountability to the community in terms of a review of progress on those priorities, possibly conducted through public consultations. To avoid entanglement with established accountability structures, police misconduct is discussed publicly in the form of explanatory accountability. Hence, informal accountability complements legal accountability which is exercised through formal external oversight or review bodies whose authority is delegated from elected officials. This combination of legal and public accountability provides a great measure of protection from misconduct for both the public and the police. Unlike the earlier "professional model," under which police officers in close contact with the local community were regarded with suspicion and as potentially corruptible, the protection of legal and public scrutiny frees the police from the public's fear of police corruption, allowing them to become close to the communities they serve and to direct the most appropriate community policing strategies and tactics towards specific crime and disorder problems in each neighbourhood.

Community Policing in Canada

How well do community policing projects in Canada fulfil the above description of community policing? In other words, how well is it implemented or operationalized to fulfil these sixteen elements and objectives? The performance of Canadian police services under a community policing framework is difficult to assess because there are few evaluations of community policing, most police forces have implemented only a few of the tactics, there is little consensus on the criteria for community policing and the methodology for evaluation has not been agreed upon. Moreover, unlike the U.S. where a rather forthright article by Greene and Taylor (1988) critically reviewed eight major evaluations, Canadian reviewers have yet to provide similar constructive criticism of the few evaluation studies that have been undertaken so far. Yet it is toward these U.S. studies that Canadian

Table 1. Approaches to Policing

ISSUE	TRADITIONAL APPROACH	COMMUNITY-BASED APPROACH
Objective Mission:	To enforce the criminal law, solve crime and apprehend criminals	To ensure peace, order and civility, provide services to the community and facilitate a sense of security
Police Role:	Law enforcement officers	Peace officers
Outcome Orientation:	Police work	Client/consumer, service delivery
Authority/Mandate: source	Delegated from elected representatives; exclusive	Delegated from elected representatives and community; multiplex
Accountability:	Exclusive; formal/legal; often co-opted	Multiple; formal/legal and informal with community; usually independent
Priority Setting:	By police chief	By police governing authorities with community through consultations, etc.
Responsibility For Crime/ Order Problems	Exclusive property of police	Shared/partnership with community as client
Main Strategy:	Incident solving (of discrete incidents seen as unrelated to other similar incidents)	Problem solving (of patterns among similar incidents and their underlying causes) and therefore of future similar incidents, i.e., crime prevention
Criteria For Success: effectiveness	Lower crime rates; higher clearance rates	Absence of crime, disorder and incivility; reduction in repeat calls for service from repeat addresses, offenders and victims; reduced fear; greater community satisfaction
Efficiency:	More rapid response time	Problem identification and solution, in partnership with the local community
Tactics, Police Response: style	Reactive-uniform/standard tactics	Proactive-flexible tactics that are tailored to community needs and the nature of crime or disorder problems
Response To Calls:	Undifferentiated; rapid response to all calls	Differential response; target "hot spots" victims, places, offences, offenders, recidivists

ISSUE	TRADITIONAL APPROACH	COMMUNITY-BASED APPROACH
Predominant Tactic	Random, motorized, preventive patrol	Tailored to community and problem type; e.g., dedicated neighbourhood foot and/or car patrol, directed patrol, zones, mini-stations, flexible shifts, integrated teams, civilization, volunteers, community liaison committees, etc.
Relationship To Community	Distant, few contacts (usually limited to victims, witnesses and offenders)	Close, many contacts (facilitated by the above tactics)
Use Of Technology (cars, radios, computers)	Overreliance, technology driven	Balanced; flexible, not technology-driven (i.e., as a means to a tactic)
Relationship To Other Community Services	Lead role	Partnership; recognizes limits to police mandate and expertise; inter-agency links (e.g., housing, employment, education, victim support, agencies)
Organization And Control: management style	Paramilitary	Participatory/democratic
Authority/Command Structure	Centralized; hierarchical	Decentralized; flatter, more "horizontal"
Scope Of Officer Responsibility	Narrow, little discretion	Broad, delegated; wide discretion and autonomy
Control	Invisible to public; informal internal discipline and formal/bureaucratic control (rules and regulations)	Visible to public; formal internal discipline and external/public complaints mechanisms
Loyalty	To superior via chain of command (i.e., the "Brown" model)	To Charter, Criminal Code, common law, and the community (i.e., the "Blue" model)
Functional Units	Specialized	Integrated (incl. investigation)
Role Definition	Specialized, with many specialists role/units	Generalist constable, with minimal complementary specialist roles/units
Human Resources	Generic police officer rotated through specialist positions	Open to lateral entry, civilianization, part-time staff, career specialization, etc.
Corporate Culture: professional culture	Blue collar (below officer rank); policing as a career	White collar (all ranks); policing as a vocation
Sub-culture	Police as separate from the community; self-image as being superior to clients	Police as members of the community; self-image as partners with the community in crime and disorder control

researchers and police professionals turn when assessing their own projects and designing their evaluations. Like Rosenbaum's (1986b) rejection of all but one evaluation study of crime prevention projects, Greene and Taylor (1988) conclude that "nothing works" because nothing has been scientifically proven to work in community policing on the grounds that none of the studies they reviewed met basic criteria for sound, rigorous evaluations. Other commentators have similarly high standards which seldom seem to be met (Sherman, 1986; Weatheritt, 1983).

To date there are only three published reports of evaluations of community-based policing programs in Canada. The first evaluation, conducted by Lambert (1988), describes the history and development of Metro Toronto Police Force's mini-stations and found them well received by local residents (see also Murphy and de Verteuil, 1986; Murphy, 1988b). The second study is an evaluation of the City of Victoria Community Police Stations (Walker, 1987; Walker, 1989) in which a community survey showed that the majority of respondents were aware that a neighbourhood community station existed and a significant proportion of them had also contacted the local station. Perhaps one of the most rigorous evaluations of a community policing program conducted anywhere (Hornick, Burrows, Tjosvold and Phillips, 1990; Hornick, Burrows, Phillips and Leighton, 1991; Koller, 1990) is of the City of Edmonton Police Service Neighbourhood Foot Patrol Project. This was a pilot project involving twenty-one constables working mainly on foot out of mini-stations strategically located in selected neighbourhoods. The study reported that the project: (a) significantly reduced the number of repeat calls for service in the beat neighbourhoods with foot patrol; (b) improved user satisfaction with police services; (c) improved constables' job satisfaction; and (d) increased constables' knowledge of the neighbourhoods and their problems. As well, Edmonton's police plan to evaluate a planned service-wide implementation as a further step towards becoming (in the words of the chief) the "Mayo Clinic of community policing in Canada."

While there do not appear to be any other evaluations currently underway, there is still a significant number of descriptive and analytic studies of community policing, mainly in municipal police services. As well, there is a surprisingly large number of police forces whose community policing initiatives have yet to be studied or even described, despite the fact that they may be characterized as "police forces of excellence in community policing" (Leighton, 1991). A few of these initiatives deserve to be highlighted.

Over the past three years, the Halifax Police Department has significantly reorganized its traditional structure and operations to become more community oriented, including implementation of zone-based team policing, decentralization of criminal investigation, crime analysis and direct patrol, the expansion of crime prevention and the expansion of foot patrol in core urban areas and the establishment of a "village constable" program (Clairmont, 1990). Fredericton police have also introduced an innovative inter-agency storefront office (the Devon Storefront) in a low income housing project (Dixon, 1990). In late 1986, Le service de police de la communauté urbaine de Montréal (Montreal Urban Community Police) implemented the first stage of a zone community police service designed to prevent crime by getting closer to the residents of communities with high crime rates (Cartier, Grenon and Rizkalla, 1987). Halton Regional Police Force, near Toronto, is another police force of excellence which has introduced community policing innovations, including zone and beat policing, mini-stations, and "Village constables" (Loree, 1988). In Winnipeg, four experimental beat patrols were introduced during 1988 in the city core as its first component of community policing, with at least one beat constable working out of a mini-station (Linden, 1989). Community-based policing has been a stated objective of the Metropolitan Toronto Police Department since the early 1980s (Lambert, 1988) and one notable achievement is the annual airing for public discussion of policing priorities by the Toronto Police Commission. While zone policing was implemented in Calgary and in Ottawa police services and a mini-station was established in Vancouver during the 1970s, these initiatives appear not to have been consolidated until recent years. For example, the Ottawa Police Force has just established the first few of at least five mini-stations, re-organizing around zones and beats once again, and establishing community consultation communities, possibly along focus-group lines.

Turning to provincial policing, Ontario has adopted community policing principles in the preamble to the *Ontario Police Services Act* of 1990 and the Ontario Ministry of the Solicitor General as well as the Ontario Provincial Police are actively promoting community-based policing, particularly in small towns. An Action Plan has been implemented (Ontario Provincial Police, 1990) and monitoring of progress has produced feedback, revealing an impressive range of activities (Ontario Provincial Police, 1991). At the same time, in a 1989 annual Directional Statement, the Commissioner of the Royal Canadian Mounted Police (RCMP) directed that all detachments above a certain size should establish community advisory or consultative committees. As well, a community policing implementation committee is now working with a strategic planning framework to review and enhance the implementation of community policing operational practices (RCMP, 1990). As a police service predominantly serving rural and small town constituencies, the typical RCMP response is that it has always done community policing, is currently doing community policing and plans to continue to do community policing in the future in a systematic way across Canada.

It is interesting to note the role the Canadian federal government department responsible for policing has played in promoting community policing as the vision of appropriate policing. This vision is found in policy papers (Murphy and Muir, 1984; Linden, Barker and Frisbie, 1984), conferences (Loree and Murphy, 1987), and research funding (Hornick *et al.*, 1990). The Solicitor General of Canada, together with its Ontario provincial government counterpart, has also produced a series of reports on community policing that have been designed to serve the information, training, planning and management needs of Canadian police departments implementing community policing (Mitzak and Leighton, 1991). The Canadian Police College, an RCMP service to Canadian police forces, has an ongoing series of dedicated seminars and regional training sessions on community policing and includes this in the content of more general executive-level courses. Finally, the federal department recently distributed a public discussion paper (Normandeau and Leighton, 1990a,b) that was intended to shape the rhetoric of community policing and, in doing so, increase the likelihood that a community policing approach will be implemented in police agencies across the country. This paper argues that community policing is the most appropriate police response to current and future trends in Canadian society and it is noteworthy that it is the first time a Solicitor General of Canada has endorsed a particular approach to policing.

This sketchy, selective review of community policing in Canada shows that the approach is fast becoming part of the operational framework in most progressive police services and that there is a growing number of police departments planning for, experimenting with or implementing community policing programs. There are also some very promising experiments and innovations: some police services have implemented at least part of the core strategies, such as some form of foot patrol, have attempted to decentralize some police activities by establishing storefront offices and zone policing and have facilitated regular contact with the community through advisory committees or other mechanisms. As a result, while some still seek legitimacy for local initiatives by touring the key U.S. community policing sites and soliciting the views of a favoured U.S. academic, there is no longer any need for police professionals to look towards examples of community policing outside Canada for lessons and insights. Nonetheless, some issues and concerns remain. While police executives have got the rhetoric of community policing, there is still a need to bridge the gap between the philosophy and strategies of community policing and the tactics of community policing. As well, while community policing has been widely accepted by Canadian police executives, there is a lack of consensus over its definition as well as considerable variation in both the application of its principles and on its implementation. As a result, few programs resemble each other in more than some core tactics. At the same time, some police executives responsible for these programs claim unqualified success and a national stage to proselytize their approach, despite the lack of a rigorous evaluation. As is the case elsewhere, one of the main issues facing Canadian police executives at this time is how to implement community policing in a systematic way and on a department-wide basis. Further, police leaders need to discover how to obtain feedback on their efforts, i.e., by monitoring followed by a comprehensive impact evaluation. So that others can learn from the more promising of these experiments, there is also an urgent need for these initiatives to be well documented. Despite these drawbacks, one prominent U.S. academic recently found that not only is there no crime or policing crisis, but community policing is alive and well in Canada (Bayley, 1991).

Issues in Community Policing

While the many drawbacks to community policing and many outstanding issues have been addressed elsewhere (Manning, 1984; Waddington, 1984; Greene and Taylor, 1986; Bayley, 1988; Murphy, 1988a; Reichers and Roberg, 1990; Goldstein, 1990; Skolnick and Bayley, 1986, 1988a,b), they are summarized here as issues that need to be addressed over the next decade by those police services seeking to implement a community policing approach. This first group relate to more operational policing or issues surrounding the implementation of community policing while the second half refer to more fundamental and theoretical issues.

(1)   From an operational policing point of view, there is the need to distinguish between the tactics of community policing and the overall strategies of problem solving and a police-community partnership. Both foot patrol and mini-stations are just two tactics which may or may not be appropriate for some neighbourhoods and for some crime problems. Foot patrol is usually inappropriate in low crime areas with less dense populations while mini-stations must do more than serve traditional public relations and crime prevention objectives. The main strategies of community policing are problem solving and community participation in priority setting.

(2)   Placing an emphasis on a particular tactic runs the risk of community policing being regarded as an "add-on" program that is just another specialized and therefore marginalized unit rather than being seen as a department-wide program with implications for most policing operations. Police mini-stations, in particular, are often used merely as public relations outposts, as a stationary "grin-and wave" squad, especially when they do not handle even the low priority centralized calls for service. Police-

community consultative or advisory committees can also become a marginalized tactic, especially when used to divert public attention from the real issues of policing priorities. Nonetheless, it may be necessary to test or demonstrate a program on a partial basis before adopting a program throughout a police service. Whatever approach is used, the introduction of innovation by police executives needs to be supported as a risk-taking exercise that may run the chance of failure.

(3)   A definition of "community" must be developed that identifies a practical way in which a local community or neighbourhood can be recognized and related to by the police to make possible useful dialogue on local crime and disorder. This presents the question of how "community" can be operationalized in terms of who represents that community and through what means or structure (Murphy, 1988a). Attempts at developing a working definition of "community" have generally failed largely because community is in the eye of the beholder (Leighton, 1988). Previous attempts at operationalizing "community" have struggled with democratic representation in neighbourhoods. However, Stenning (1981) found that police committees are generally inadequate ways of representing local communities. Once of the reasons for this failure is that communities are not usually homogeneous social units characterized by a consensus of values, norms and agreements on crime problems (Waddington, 1984; Reichers and Roberg, 1990). More recent suggestions have given up democratic representation at the local level as being too problematic, preferring instead to use existing local interest groups and leaders (Goldstein, 1990).

     As well, it is clear that there is a revisionist history about the nature of communities in the past which romanticizes them (Manning, 1984; Leighton, 1988) as well as romanticizing Peel's London Bobbies (Cain, 1973; Miller, 1977). The so-called "three eras of policing" (Kelling and Moore, 1988) are reminiscent of the three eras of community which have been characterized as the "community lost, community saved and community transformed" models (Wellman, 1979; Wellman and Leighton, 1979; Leighton, 1988). However, there are obvious ways in which communities have changed which explains why the romantic version of Peel's policing cannot be reconstructed in North American cities. These reasons include urbanization, post-industrialization, technological change, transformations in communications and transportation and legal changes, to name but a few of the most obvious societal changes (Mastrofski, 1990).

(4)   The issue of what community policing means in a rural and

small-town context has yet to be explored and examined to
show how policing in this context differs fundamentally from
urban policing (Murphy, 1985, 1988a). This examination
should include: (1) the differences in policing between large
municipal forces and both small-town and rural forces; (2) problems facing small police services with limited resources which
are implementing community policing; (3) the criteria for successful implementation of this approach; and (4) the methods
for evaluating small forces. It has been argued that community
policing is merely an urban application of small town policing
principles.

(5) Because it is not yet clear what impact community policing actually has on crime, it has yet to be proven to "work." While it
may be successful in addressing disorder problems and in reducing fear of crime, it has yet to be demonstrated scientifically that
it actually reduces crime itself. Part of this problem is that community policing generates new clients and "new" types of crime
that the public would not otherwise bother reporting to the
police. It is also not clear what impact, if any, community participation (as a key component of community policing) actually
has on community policing. This question raises further issues
regarding whose criteria are accepted as the appropriate measure of effective policing in a community. Accordingly, "success" depends upon who "owns" crime and disorder issues,
whether it is the exclusive property of the police, of police governing bodies, or shared by police and the community. As well,
the assessment should be scientifically evaluated by an independent agency. But the failure of the old "professional" policing
model is partly demonstrated by the failure sufficiently to address
"non-traditional" crimes, such as sexual assault, spousal assault,
child sexual abuse and so on (Braiden, 1986). It was only when
these categories of crime were secured as legitimate targets for
formal police activities that the success or failure of different
policing models could be more realistically assessed.
Consequently new measures of police service effectiveness or
performance must be developed that stress its impact rather
than the processes and structures for accomplishing community
policing. These criteria must contrast with those of the "professional" model which included such measures as the police
response time and the proportion of charges cleared. On the
other had, some of the "new" measures are not without fault.
For example, community "satisfaction" with the police has been
shown to be practically useless as an indicator of police effectiveness, although it is not yet clear what it does demonstrate
(Clairmont and Murphy, 1990). Indeed, popularity polls are
becoming far too popular with police chiefs as a way of manag-

ing public opinion rather than crime.

Perhaps one of the most difficult tests of this "new" approach to policing is its ability to ameliorate problems associated with disadvantages with vulnerable groups in Canadian society, including police relationships with aboriginal peoples in an urban environment, new Canadians, ethnic and visible minorities, women, the elderly and children and youth at risk. Equally difficult a question is whether community policing would have helped at Oka in the summer of 1990. The answer is likely to be that it might have beforehand and it might be relevant over the next ten years, contingent on the resolution of land claims and self government issues. This answer is a reminder that the reality of policing a complex, diverse, largely urban society characterized by structured inequality occasionally presents police agencies with situations when they are likely to resort to the techniques of "hard policing," such as those associated with riot control, homicide, etc. Accordingly, the strengths and limitations of community policing must be recognized, including the fact that it cannot be a panacea that will solve all crime and disorder problems.

(6)   New criteria must be developed for evaluating police officers working in a police service operating on community policing principles. When the criteria for police service performance change, then the formal position descriptions, performance criteria and rewards (e.g., promotion) must also be changed to reflect these changes. Unless the reward structure is changed in accordance with the new criteria and principles, then community policing strategies and tactics will not be implemented in other than a cosmetic manner.

(7)   Greater community involvement with policing might be interpreted by police executives as providing additional or supplementary resources through volunteers, neighbourhood watch and other forms of community surveillance. But by providing a legitimate link with other service delivery agencies, community policing may result in an attempt by police agencies to exploit other agencies to fill the gap created by a fiscal crisis. However, it may be equally found that other agencies might look to the police to fill their own underfunded needs. On the other hand, co-operation with human service and social service agencies provides additional resources to policing through the pooling of their respective scarce resources. As well, local crime and order problems become joint responsibilities, with the consequent sharing of both successes and of failures or limitations. It is not yet clear whether police co-operation with human service and social service agencies actually results in a bigger bang for the

collective buck in delivering urban services to targeted groups and victims. Nor is it clear whether police executives are equipped to enter into inter-agency co-operation with highly competitive voluntary sector partners.

(8)   As a traditionally reactive agency primed for the key function of providing rapid response to the relatively rare emergency incident, the capacity of policing to shift to a more balanced, proactive stance has yet to be demonstrated. Nor is it clear whether private sector or some other service delivery agencies are an appropriate model for police agencies when, with the exception of health care, they lack this key emergency function. Consequently, it may be inappropriate to import the standards of service, quality, efficiency and effectiveness from private industry into human service delivery professions.

(9)   By advocating a police-community partnership, community policing seeks to empower the community to bring it onto a more equal footing with the police in terms of joint "ownership" of local crime and disorder problems and as "co-producers" of peace, order and security at the local level (Murphy and Muir, 1984; Wilson and Kelling, 1982, 1989). On the one hand, there is the possibility that the community will acquire greater control over local crime and disorder matters (Kinsey, Lea and Young, 1986). More plausible is the prospect, as Bayley (1988) warns, of transforming the community into an interest group on behalf of the police. After all, it is the community side of the "partnership" that is least likely to have the expertise and resources to take advantage of any empowering opportunities. This is particularly relevant when public advocacy is encouraged by establishing police-community consultative committees. As well, public participation through this and similar mechanisms may be a diversionary device used by police leaders to diffuse potential criticism from the community. Indeed, involvement in these committees often appears to degenerate into fundraising and organizing for already established crime prevention programs. As a result, the police rather than the community are likely to be further empowered by a community policing regime (Savage, 1984).

(10)   One aspect of problem solving can get out of control. The logical extension of the "hot spot" approach also covers "hot persons," being victims or groups sharing individual characteristics (*cf* their residences) of statistically at-risk victims, as well as "hot places" and "hot offenders" or potential offenders, with the latter consisting of recidivists or offenders at statistically high risk of re-offending and of potential offenders fitting a profile of

offenders (e.g., drug interdiction activities). However, an "aggressive order maintenance" or "intensive policing" approach which targets people, times and places can also get out of hand, leading not only to focusing mindlessly on the "signs of crime" as a surface symptom, while ignoring its root causes, but also to harassment and bias in the delivery of police services.

(11)   As with most crime prevention programs in practice, community policing exhibits a class bias by finding fertile ground in neighbourhoods and communities where it is needed least in comparison with lower socio-economic areas (Rosenbaum, 1986, 1988). That is, if it could be shown that community policing "works," then there is likely to be a bias in its impact. Consequently, further research is necessary on the exact nature of class bias, and community policing must be tested in neighbourhoods and communities where it is really needed rather than just in those neighbourhoods in which its success can be guaranteed because of lack of need or because of the availability of resources.

(12)   Community policing is a useful rhetorical tool for police chiefs to solicit additional funds. During the 1960s and 1970s, when crime rates were increasing rapidly, chiefs could argue for more officers and resources on the grounds of a crime wave. With overall crime rates settling down, chiefs have had to shift their argument from "quantity policing" to a "quality policing" argument. That is, in order to deliver high quality policing services, as represented by community policing, then they require additional officers and resources.

(13)   Police services are being asked to perform schizophrenic responsibilities, as both "green berets" and "peace corps." On the one hand, they are asked to serve as an armed force permanently at red alert status to provide a rapid response to the relatively rare life-threatening incidents. At the same time they are now being asked to serve as a "peace corps" by becoming a "partner" with the community to address crime and disorder problems, ranging from mediating domestic disputes to solving the underlying causes of crime. But how can police forces designed for an emergency response with a para-military organization be transformed into more "democratic" ones exhibiting the characteristics of participatory management? Indeed, it sometimes appears that the public present the police with contradictory demands by "wanting it all," despite the inherently conflicting nature of their requirements, including the bottom line of a rapid response, seeing the police "on the job" even

when most preventive patrol activities largely serve as public relations, as well as reduced crime rates. Unfortunately, when the full brunt of the fiscal crisis is felt (hastened at the local level by down-loading of police and other human service delivery costs from federal and provincial governments to the municipal level), then the emergency response function may emerge again as the predominant tactic of policing. Perhaps the only positive side to this outcome is that there may be greater local control over an emasculated police service.

(14)   The local focus of community policing generates "sand-box policing" in terms of a bias towards defining problems as local ones, ignoring the regional, national and international nature of many problems, such as drugs, organized crime, corporate and white collar crime and environmental crime. In many ways, community policing trivializes some of these major crime problems by interpreting or stressing them as local problems with local solutions. Instead, attention is focused on local issues which tend to be disorder problems rather than crime problems. Hence, decentralized community policing runs the risk of becoming localized or "going native" by being directed by local values, norms, culture and concerns in contrast to those articulated in the Charter, the Criminal Code, and the common law. The former are community, collective or corporate rights while the latter are primarily individual rights. While it may be justifiable in certain circumstances to allow collective rights to override individual ones, when these collective rights are local ones, then they run the risk of great variations in the meaning and practice of justice between communities (Waddington, 1984; Bayley, 1988; Murphy, 1988a; Klockars, 1986; Sykes, 1986). In the extreme, localization of policing can run amok by expanding police practice beyond the legal boundaries as well as supporting vigilantism by community members (leading to the next point).

(15)   It is not yet clear whether community policing results in tighter or looser "handcuffs" on the community. On the one hand, it may further weaken any control the police now have on crime at the local level. On the other hand, community policing may further penetrate the community to introduce even more intrusive techniques of formal social control. It seems that community policing does widen the net of control beyond crime control by legitimizing an expanded role of the police in terms of the types of behaviour that are addressed, particularly order maintenance problems such as street nuisance behaviour and other "non-crimes" that do not traditionally or technically fall within the legal realm of policing (Manning, 1984; Klockars, 1985;

Walker, 1984; Wilson and Kelling, 1982). As Bayley (1988) points out, the distinction between public and private becomes increasingly blurred. In rare instance, the police might take community involvement as providing a mandate for additional powers which would otherwise be inconsistent with routine policing practices.

(16) A corollary issue arises over how far in a free and democratic society the police should go in performing their role (Klockars, 1985). This is a particularly acute question when there is an ever-increasing demand for expanded police services. The police are in danger of becoming far too politically involved with the community affairs (Goldstein, 1987) and of surrendering their professional neutrality (Sykes, 1986). The question should be addressed as to whether the police should engage in community development activities, as "community catalysts," to create local initiatives and, indeed, to fabricate community where it is weak, not readily apparent to outsiders, or is lacking.

(17) In light of the more prominent role played by the community, a further issue surrounds whether there is a greater or lesser accountability at the local level. Local partnership in policing may be understood as providing local communities with a direct oversight role over their police at the expense of established accountability mechanisms.

(18) Increased police officer autonomy may lead to systematic under-performance. While community police services are being increasingly characterized by a growing formalization of internal regulations and disciplinary procedures and by a "new professionalism" typical of self-governing, white-collar professions, it is too soon to assess whether this trend reduces the likelihood of police taking advantage of the greater professional freedom afforded them. As well, the growing tendency for police services to adopt a code of ethics or professional conduct is likely to have only a long-term impact on the police professional culture and sub-culture.

(19) Police leaders can use community policing as a strategy to avoid criticism for not reducing crime by claiming that, given one new criterion for success in the reduction of the public's fear of crime, this approach can at least reduce the fear of crime. This is akin to looking for a lost coin under the street lamp because that is where the light is shining. As well, the question arises as to how far the police can go in reducing the fear of crime by persuading particular segments of the community, such as the elderly, that their fear is largely unfounded when the statistical risk of them being victimized is considered. Although unlikely, it

is not clear whether the police, as a government agency, incur civil liability for "guaranteeing" public safety.

Origins of Community Policing

Why is community policing so popular and whose interest does it serve? One explanation may lie not so much in its appeal but in the growing recognition that the established policing paradigm has become recognized as exhausted in light of its clearly demonstrated inefficiency and ineffectiveness. Hence, the answer might lie in its origin through the history of policing.

While some commentators see the history of community policing in the U.S. as the direct result of crises occurring during the 1960s which led to national-level attempts to provide solutions during the 1970s (Gennann, 1969; Walker, 1983; Reichers and Roberg, 1990). The current rhetoric of community policing is often associated with the packaging of American police history into three eras (Kelling and Moore, 1988). But despite criticism that these three eras of policing and the linear progression of U.S. policing through these eras is somewhat revisionist (Walker, 1984; Hartman, 1988), it is nonetheless a useful and compelling heuristic device, complete with ideal types pushed to their extreme to present an overly simplified typification and therefore simplistic historical account of the development of policing. Further, this scheme provides an intriguing parallel to Cohen's (1985) "master patterns" in social control which apply more appropriately to correctional control, with limited application to the course of policing history.

As the party line of community policing would have its genealogy, the origins of public urban community policing lie in both American and British policing, with Sir Robert Peel's Metropolitan London police established over 150 years ago providing the first paradigm. But, beginning about the 1930s onwards, the "professional policing" paradigm became established within North American urban police forces, assisted by the efforts of police leaders such as W.O. Wilson and Volmer. This development was largely in reaction to the close ties that police established with their local communities, which were understood to have facilitated the widespread, systemic corruption of police agencies by local political party organizations. In order to minimize corruption in American police forces, they intentionally distanced themselves from the community they served. Tactics were developed to ensure this distancing occurred, assisted by technological developments such as the telephone, then the patrol car and two-way radio, followed by onboard computers. While these new technologies permitted tighter control over individual police officer behaviour, two further policing strategies were even more powerful influences in distancing the police from the local community. These strategies were the invention of random motorized patrol as a presumed deterrent to potential criminals and the invention of rapid response as the uniform response to all calls to the police from the public. Under this "professional" policing model, the two main criteria for police force performance then became: (1) the proportion of charges laid of offences reported to the police; and (2) the response time to calls for service made to the police by the public. However, U.S. evaluations of these two strategies have shown that they are marginally effective in preventing or containing crime and hardly worth the loss of positive police-community relations (Young and Cameron, 1989; Ellickson, Petersilia, Caggiano and Polin, 1983).

While there appear to have been other failures of the "professional model" in the U.S.; a failure of funding as a result of the fiscal crisis, a failure of public confidence, and a failure of legitimacy (Klockars, 1988), they do not seem applicable to the Canadian experience. Nonetheless, as a result of a number of profound failures in the existing paradigm, the U.S. experiment in professional policing eventually revealed its own contradictions and limitations, bringing about a crisis within the paradigm. But rather than compelling it toward a new paradigm, the crisis returned policing to an earlier one. This "new" paradigm turned out to be a romanticized one from the past, in the form of a re-emergence of, and renaissance in, community policing.

How well do this revisionist history and the conveniently packaged paradigms fit the history of policing in Canada? Unfortunately, there has been little rigorous scholarship on the historical development of Canadian policing, from the colonial period to the present. Nothing compares, for example, with the history of New Zealand colonial policing by Hill (1986, 1989). Indeed, the Hollywood version of RCMP visions of order (Walden, 1982) and the popular myth of order preceding settlement and cultural values regarding a "deference to authority" (Friedenberg, 1980) are an enduring element of Canadian popular culture. But what little is known about the history and development of Canadian policing suggests a number of tentative conclusions.

First, Canadian police are held in high regard and there does not appear to be a crisis in public support for the police. Second, Canadian police are relatively well financed and are currently not experiencing a deep fiscal crisis. Third, the reasons for exerting tighter control over police officers in the U.S., as prescribed by the "professional model," were not as applicable to their Canadian counterparts. In the present century at least, there has been a marked absence of routine political influence over Canadian police forces. By comparison with the U.S., there has been a lack of widespread corruption and systemic individual misconduct within Canadian police forces. Of course, there have been exceptions; the use of the police to break up the Winnipeg Strike, the involvement of the RCMP in national security abuses, individual corruption within forces of some of the major municipalities and in many small municipalities which ended largely over a decade ago. In recent decades, other cases involving individual officers and made known to the public have been relatively isolated, although recent commissions of inquiry suggest otherwise, especially with respect to systemic bias in the delivery of police services to Aboriginal people and discrimination against visible minorities. Nonetheless, it might be concluded that the means for exerting tighter control over routine street policing were, in the Canadian context, largely misplaced.

If there were no discernible crisis within public policing in Canada, the question arises as to why there has been a return to community policing in this country. As Murphy (1988a) presents the issue, the lack of internal and external pressures for reform of Canadian policing is a curious phenomenon which demands an explanation and he interprets this situation as being due to the lack of a national police research institutional framework that can critically examine current practices, new developments and innovations in policing. As a result, Canadian police are more vulnerable to trends from the U.S. Much more should be made of the ideological imperative of the academic criminal justice and policing enterprise from the U.S. While there are outstanding individual academics in Canada who contribute to a body of relatively critical research on the police, there is no "critical mass" of academics who are routinely involved in an American-style criminal justice approach with police operational activities. In some respects, police researchers get only one kick at the cat because if they earn the displeasure of the police executive of the police force they studied, they will not only have muddied the local waters for their own colleagues but they are unlikely to have access to other police forces. Accordingly, there is an urgent need to marshall a healthy critique of community policing as the dominant vision of progressive policing and, because this critique must be an independent one that can only be provided by neutral academics, there is also a requirement for independent funding. This requirement is critical because most research on Canadian police services is funded by federal and provincial governments or their agencies which largely set the agenda of police research generally (Brickey, 1989).

Conclusions: Toward a Theory of Community Policing?

Is there now or can there ever be a community policing theory? The "signs of crime" or "broken windows" thesis of Wilson and Kelling (1982, 1989) is usually identified as the theory underlying community policing (Greene and Taylor, 1988; Reichers and Roberg, 1990: Skogan, 1990). This thesis focuses on the cognitive conclusions of potential offenders based on their perceptions of the physical deterioration of neighbourhoods and has the flavour of environmental determinism. It follows W.I. Thomas's sociological dictum on the self-fulfilling prophecy by arguing that if a neighbourhood is defined as being in decay and disorder then it will inevitably become characterized by disorder and crime. However, reviewers such as Greene and Taylor (1988) have found this thesis unsatisfactory on a number of theoretical and empirical grounds. One explanation may be that the "broken windows" notion applies most appropriately to order maintenance and that attempts to expand it to cover crime control generally are simply beyond its capacity. If so, then it could serve only as one part of a broader theory of community policing. Indeed, it hardly addresses the underlying causes of crime, whether as offender motivations or as the foundations of these motivations in structured inequalities, and therefore falls far short of an adequate explanation of crime or of a theory of community policing. Nonetheless, Skogan (1990) presents comprehensive, compelling evidence of a clear link between disorder and crime in American cities. It would appear, therefore, that until a competing theory of community policing is developed, the "broken windows" view is by default the current theory of community policing.

In the face of this conclusion, it is still suggested here that a comprehensive theory of community policing has yet to emerge and that community policing, as it is currently constructed, is a theoretically undeveloped set of policing principles and practices which at best is a "theory sketch" (Dumont and Wilson, 1967). At its core is the principle or "strategy" of a police-community partnership and the hypothesis that the effectiveness of community policing is directly related to the degree of involvement by the community it serves. While these do not constitute a theory, at least they provide the elements of a theory about policing, including at least two fundamental aspects of the approach, much of which were addressed earlier in one form or another. First, a theory about community policing should raise questions over the role of community in policing and social control generally (Duffee, 1990). Second, a theory about community policing should raise questions over the role of policing in the social control of the community.

Concerning the first aspect, the role of formal community participation in public urban policing has had a chequered career, from community relations programs through to crime prevention activities. Beyond participation in these fairly circumscribed programs, how far can community members go in participating in major decisions that govern policing? Does it make sense to argue that police and community can become equal partners in policing, as "co-producers" of order? Or does it make sense, as Kinsey, Lea and Young (1986) suggest, to argue that the community — in the guise of the local state — can possess exclusive authority over local police and can control police policies and priorities? Further, is the conferring of local "consent" on policing (Morgan, 1989) — even if a "community consensus" is possible — merely a masking of vested interests, raising the same issues associated with all claims of consensus? "Legitimate" consensual agreements might only be possible at such a micro-neighourhood level as to be quite impractical for policing arrangements. And, as mentioned earlier, exclusive local authority and "consensus" might remove the neutrality of the police and relegate policing to an arm of local politics and vested interest. Further, it might reduce local policing to local concerns or "sand-box policing." And how "local" does the local state have to become before it loses its legitimacy on the grounds of being undemocratic or out of touch with the common law, the *Criminal Code* and the *Charter*? The question remains, then, about the independence or relative autonomy of the police with respect to the local, regional and national state and about whose interests are served at each of these levels. If the relative autonomy of the police has any meaning, then it is about a type of control over policing resources that is independent of the local community the police serve. One the other hand, it is precisely the local autonomy of police forces that led to the "professional model" of policing and the distancing of police from local concerns and priorities. These and other questions demonstrate the need to locate a theory about community policing, and policing generally, within a broader theory of the state (Ratner and McMullan, 1987).

Regarding the role of the police in social control of the local community, questions arise as to whether it makes sense to restrict policing to crime control so that, as Brogden (1982, 1989) suggests, the penetration of the community by the police will be arrested. After all, as Chapman (1970) warns, the encroachment of policing on the traditional responsibilities of other agencies, such as those covered by order maintenance, the underlying causes of crime, inter-agency cooperation and other community policing objectives, could lead down the slippery slope toward the police state (Gordon, 1984). On the other hand, should the community abandon state sponsored policing, as Taylor (1981) suggests, going it alone as the sole source of order maintenance and crime control? In any event, it is clear that the role of police under a police-community partnership as proposed by the vision of community policing demands critical examination.

In conclusion, this paper has attempted to summarize the rhetoric and reality of the dominant vision of community policing in Canada. It finds that the future of community policing in Canada is probably well assured and will easily survive these and other criticisms. While it may be viewed by some as merely going back to the basics of traditional Peelite policing, the implementation of community policing strategies and tactics will nonetheless have a profound and far-reaching impact on Canadian police services that pursue the approach. By raising some critical issues and identifying a theoretical space that needs to be occupied, the need for a theory about community policing has been demonstrated. There is a need for further research on the working of community policing tactics, such as consultative committees, in order to examine such issues as whether the "broad blue line" of community policing co-opts the community or whether the community co-opts policing. However, an even more urgent need is to set the agenda for a critical discourse on the role and impact of community policing in Canadian society.

Endnotes

1   The views presented in this article are those of the author.

References

Bayley, David H. 1991. "Managing the Future: Perspective Issues in Canadian Policing." User Report No. 1991-02. Ottawa: Ministry of the Solicitor General of Canada.

Bayley, David H. 1988. "Community Policing: A Report from the Devil's Advocate" in Greene, J.J. and S.D. Mastrofski (eds.), *Community Policing: Rhetoric or Reality.* New York: Praeger.

Braiden, Chris. 1986. "Bank Robberies and Stolen Bikes: Thoughts of a Street Cop." User Report No. 1986-04. Ottawa: Ministry of the Solicitor General of Canada.

Brickey, Stephen. 1989. "Criminology as Social Control Science: State Influences on Criminological Research in Canada." *Journal of Human Justice* 1(1): 43-62.

Brogden, Michael. 1982. *The Police: Autonomy and Consent.* London: Academic Press.

Brogden, Michael. 1989. "Social Accountability and Police Power — Squeezing the Discretionary Space." Paper presented at the Society for Reform of the Criminal Law Conference on Police Powers. Sydney, Australia, March.

Cain, Maureen. 1973. *Society and the Policeman's Role.* London: Routledge.

Cartier, Bernard, Sylvie Grenon et Samir Rizkalla. 1987. *Prévention communautaire du crime: Les citoyens visités et les policiers non-intervenant s'expriment sur le programme.* Montréal: Société de Crimimologie du Québec.

Chapman, B. 1970. *Police State.* London: Pall Mall.

Clairmont, Donald. 1990. *To the Forefront: Community-Based Zone Policing in Halifax.* Ottawa: Canadian Police College, RCMP.

Clairmont, Donald and Chris Murphy. 1990. "Rural Victims Survey." Draft paper for Ministry of the Solicitor General of Canada.

Cohen, Stanley. 1985. *Vision of Social Control.* Cambridge: Polity Press.

Dixon, Carol. 1990. "The Resident Perspective: An Evaluation of the Fredericton (Devon) Storefront.." Report written in partial fulfillment of M.A., Carleton University, School of Social Work.

Duffee, David E. 1990. *Explaining Criminal Justice: Community Theory and Criminal Justice Reform.* Prospect Heights, IL: Waveland Press.

Dumont, Richard G. and William J. Wilson. 1967. "Aspects of Concept Formation, Explication and Theory Construction in Sociology." *American Sociological Review*

32: 985-995.

Eck, John E. and William Spelman. 1987a. "Who Ya Gonna Call? The Police as Problem Busters." *Crime and Delinquency* 33(1): 31-52.

Ellickson, Phyllis, Joan Petersilia, Michael Caggiano and Sandra Polin. 1983. *Implementing New Ideas in Criminal Justice.* Washington, D.C.: U.S. Department of Justice, National Institute of Justice.

Ericson, Richard V. 1982. *Reproducing Order: A Study of Police Patrol Work.* Toronto: University of Toronto Press.

Friedenberg, Edgar Z. 1980. *Deference to Authority: The Case of Canada.* White Plains, New York: M.E. Sharpe.

Greene, J.R. and R.B. Taylor. 1988. "Community-based Policing and Foot Patrol: Issues of Theory and Evaluation" in Greene, J.R. and S.D. Mastrofski (eds.), *Community Policing: Rhetoric or Reality.* New York: Praeger.

Gennann, A.C. 1969. "Community Policing: An Assessment." *Journal of Criminal Law, Criminology and Police Science* 60(1): 89-96.

Goldstein, Herman. 1979. "Improving Policing: A Problem-oriented Approach." *Crime and Delinquency* 25: 236-258.

Goldstein, Herman. 1987. "Towards Community-Oriented Policing: Potential, Basic Requirements and Threshold Question." *Crime and Delinquency* 33(1): 6-30.

Goldstein, H. 1990. *Problem Oriented Policing.* New York: McGraw-Hill.

Gordon, P. 1984. "Community Policing: Toward the Local Police State" in Scraton, P. (ed.), *Law, Order and the Authoritarian State.* (Reprinted 1987). Milton Keynes: Open University Press.

Greene, Jack R. and Stephen D. Mastrofski. 1988. "Community-based Policing and Foot Patrol: Issues of Theory and Evaluation" in Greene, J.R. and S.D. Mastrofski (eds.), *Community Policing: Rhetoric or Reality.* New York: Praeger.

Guth, DeLloyd J. 1987. "The Common Law Powers of Police: The Anglo-Canadian Tradition." Paper presented at the Canadian Law in History Conference (8-10 June). Ottawa: Carleton University.

Hartman, Francis X. (ed.). 1988. "Debating the Evolution of American Policing." *Perspectives on Policing, No. 5.* Washington, D.C.: U.S. Department of Justice, National Institute of Justice and Harvard University, John F. Kennedy School of Government.

Hill, Richard S. 1986. *The History of Policing in New Zealand.* Vol. 1: Policing the Colonial Frontier. Wellington: Government Printer.

Hill Richard S. 1989. *The History of Policing in New Zealand.* Vol. 2: The Colonial Frontier Tamed. Wellington: GP Books.

Hornick, Joseph P., Barbara A. Burrows, Ida Tjosvold and Donna M. Phillips. 1990. "An Evaluation of the Neighbourhood Foot Patrol Program of the Edmonton Police Service." User Report No. 1990-09. Ottawa: Ministry of the Solicitor General of Canada.

Hornick, Joseph P., Barbara A. Burrows, Donna M. Phillips and Barry Leighton. 1991. "An Impact Evaluation of the Edmonton Neighbourhood Foot Patrol Program." *Canadian Journal of Program Evaluation* 6(1): 47-70.

Kanter, Rosabeth Moss. 1983. *The Change Masters.* New York: Simon and Schuster.

Kelling, George L. 1987. "Acquiring a Taste for Order: The Community and Police." *Crime and Delinquency* 33(1): 90-102.

Kelling, George L. and Mark H. Moore. 1988. "From Political to Reform to Community: The Evolving Strategy of Police" in Greene, J.R. and S.D. Mastrofski (eds.), *Community Policing: Rhetoric or Reality*. New York: Praeger.

Kinsey, Richard, John Lea and Jock Young. 1986. *Losing the Fight Against Crime*. New York: Basil Blackwell.

Klockars, Carl B. 1985. *The Idea of the Police*. Beverly Hills, CA: Sage.

Klockars, Carl B. 1986. "Street Justice: Some Micro-Moral Reservations: Comments on Sykes." *Justice Quarterly* 3(4): 513-516.

Klockars, Carl B. 1988. "The Rhetoric of Community Policing" in Greene, J.R. and S.D. Mastrofski (eds.), *Community Policing: Rhetoric or Reality*. New York: Praeger.

Koller, Katherine. 1990. *Working the Beat: The Edmonton Neighbourhood Foot Patrol*. Edmonton: Edmonton Police Service.

Lambert, Leah R. 1988. "Police Mini-stations in Toronto: An Experience in Compromise." *Royal Canadian Mounted Police Gazette* 50(6): 1-5.

Leighton, Barry. 1988. "The Concept of Community in Criminology: Toward a Social Network Approach." *Journal of Research in Crime and Delinquency* 25(4): 351-374.

Leighton, Barry. 1989. "Community Policing." Brief presented at the European and North American Conference of Mayors on "Safer Cities." Montréal, October.

Leighton, Barry. 1990. "The Future of Policing in Canada." Paper presented at the Annual Meeting of the American Society of Criminology. Baltimore, November.

Leighton, Barry. 1991. *Community Policing in Canada: A Review*. Ottawa: Ministry of the Solicitor General of Canada.

Leighton, Barry and Joseph Hornick. 1990. "Evaluating Community-based Policing: Lessons from the Edmonton Project." Paper presented at the Canadian Evaluation Society annual meeting. Toronto, May.

Linden, Rick. 1989. "A Report on the Winnipeg City Police Community Officer Program." Winnipeg: University of Manitoba, Criminology Research Centre.

Linden, Rick. 1984. *Working Together to Prevent Crime: A Practitioner's Handbook*. Ottawa: Ministry of the Solicitor General of Canada.

Linden, R., I. Barker and D. Frisbie. 1984. *Working Together to Prevent Crime: A Practitioner's Handbook*. Ottawa: Ministry of the Solicitor General of Canada.

Loree, David J. 1988. "Innovation and Change in a Regional Police Force." *Canadian Police College Journal* 12(4): 205-239.

Loree, Donald J. and Chris Murphy (eds.). 1987. *Community Policing in the 1990s: Recent Advances in Police Programs*. Ottawa: Ministry of the Solicitor General of Canada and Ministry of Supply and Services Canada.

Manning, Peter K. 1984. "Community Policing." *American Journal of Police* 3(2): 205-227.

Mastrofski, Stephen D. 1990. "The Prospects of Change in Police Patrol: A Decade in Review." *American Journal of Police* 9(3): 1-79.

Miller, W.R. 1977. *Cops and Bobbies: Police Authority in New York and London, 1830-1870*. Chicago: University of Chicago Press.

Mitzak, Marsha and Barry Leighton (eds.). 1991. *Community Policing: Shaping the Future*.

Ottawa and Toronto: Ministry of the Solicitor General of Canada and Solicitor General, Ontario.

Morgan, Rod. 1989. "Policing by Consent: Legitimating the Doctrine" in Morgan, R. and D.J. Smith (eds.), *Coming to Terms with Policing: Shaping the Future*. Ottawa and Toronto: Ministry of the Solicitor General of Canada and Solicitor General Ontario.

Murphy, Chris and Graham Muir. 1984. *Community-based Policing: A Review of the Critical Issues*. Ottawa: Ministry of the Solicitor General of Canada.

Murphy, Chris. 1985. "The Social and Formal Organization of Small Town Policing: A Comparative Analysis of RCMP and Municipal Policing." Unpublished doctoral dissertation. Toronto: University of Toronto.

Murphy, Chris. 1988a. "The Development Impact and Implications of Community Policing in Canada" in Greene, Jack R. and Stephen D. Mastrofski (eds.), *Community Policing: Rhetoric and Reality*. New York: Praeger.

Murphy, Chris. 1988b. "Community Problems, Problem Communities, and Community Policing in Toronto." *Journal of Research in Crime and Delinquency* 25(4): 392-410.

Murphy, Chris. 1991. *Problem-oriented Policing*. Ottawa: Ministry of the Solicitor General of Canada, Federal-Ontario Community Policing Report Series.

Murphy, Chris and Jacques de Verteuil. 1986. *Community-Based Policing: A Review of the Critical Issues*. Ottawa: Ministry of the Solicitor General of Canada.

Normandeau, André and Barry Leighton. 1990a. "The Future of Policing in Canada." Discussion paper. Ottawa: Ministry of the Solicitor General of Canada.

Normandeau, André and Barry Leighton. 1990b. "The Future of Policing in Canada." Background paper. Ottawa; Ministry of the Solicitor General of Canada.

Ontario Provincial Police. 1990. "Community Policing Strategy Implementation: 12 Month Action Plan." Toronto: Field Support Division.

Ontario Provincial Police. 1991. "Field Superintendents Workshop: Community Policing and Crime Prevention." Toronto: Field Support Division.

Peters, Thomas J. and Robert Wasserman. 1982. *In Search of Excellence*. New York: Harper and Row.

Ratner, Robert S. and John L. McMullans (eds.). 1987. *State Control: Criminal Justice Politics in Canada*. Vancouver: University of British Columbia Press.

Reith, Charles. 1975. *The Blind Eye of History: A Study of the Origins of the Present Police Era*. Montclair, NJ: Patterson-Smith.

Reichers, Lisa M. and Roy R. Roberg. 1990. "Community Policing: A Critical Review of Underlying Assumptions. *Journal of Police Science and Administration 17(2): 105-114*.

Reichers, Lisa M. and Roy R. Roberg. 1990. "Community Policing: A Critical Review of Underlying Assumptions." *Journal of Police Science and Administration* 17(2): 105-114.

Rosenbaum, Dennis P. (ed.). 1986. *Community Crime Prevention: Does it Work?* Beverly Hills: Sage.

Rosenbaum, Dennis P. (ed.). 1988. "Community Crime Prevention: A Review and Synthesis of the Literature." *Justice Quarterly* 5(3): 323-395.

RCMP. 1990. "Strategic Plan." Ottawa: Royal Canadian Mounted Police, Corporate Services

Branch.

Savage, Steve. 1984. "Political Control or Community Liaison?" *Political Quarterly* (Jan.-Mar.).

Sensenbrenner, Joseph. 1991. "Quality Comes to City Hall." *Harvard Business Review* (March-April): 64-75.

Sherman, Lawrence. 1986. "Policing Communities-What Works?" in Reiss, Albert Jr., and Michael Tonry (eds.), *Communities and Crime: Crime and Justice.* Vol. 8. Chicago: University of Chicago Press.

Short, C. 1983. "Community Policing - Beyond Slogans" in Bennet, T. (ed.), *The Future of Policing.* Cambridge: University of Cambridge.

Skogan, Wesley G. 1990. *Disorder and Decline: Crime and the Spiral of Decay in American Neighbourhoods.* Toronto: Collier Macmillan Canada.

Skolnick, Jerome H. and David H. Bayley. 1986. *The New Blue Line: Police Innovation in Six American Cities.* New York: Free Press.

Skolnick, Jerome H. and David H. Bayley. 1988a. "Theme and Variation in Community Policing" in Tonry, Michael and Norval Morris (eds.), *Crime and Justice: A Review of Research.* Chicago: University of Chicago Press.

Skolnick, Jerome H. and David H. Bayley. 1988b. *Community Policing: Issues and Practices Around the World.* Washington, D.C.: U.S., Department of Justice, National Institute of Justice.

Solicitor General of Canada. 1990. "The Future of Policing in Canada." Discussion paper. Ottawa: Ministry of the Solicitor General of Canada. Prepared by André Normandeau and Barry Leighton.

Sparrow, Malcolm K., Mark H. Moore and David M. Kennedy. 1990. *Beyond 911: A New Era for Policing.* New York: Basic Books.

Stenning, Philip C. 1981. "The Role of Police Boards and Commissions as Institutions of Municipal Government in Organizational Police Deviance" in Shearing, C. (ed.), *Organizational Police Deviance, Its Structure and Control.* Scarborough, Ontario: Butterworths.

Sykes, Gary W. 1986. "Street Justice: A Moral Defense of Order Maintenance Theory." *Justice Quarterly* 3(4): 497-512.

Taylor, Ian. 1981. *Law and Order: Arguments for Socialism.* London: Macmillan.

Trojanowicz, Robert and Bonnie Bucqueroux. 1990. *Community Policing: A Contemporary Perspective.* Cincinnati: Anderson.

Waddington, P.A.J. 1984. "Community Policing: A Skeptical Appraisal" in Norton, Philip (ed.), *Law and Order and British Politics.* Aldershot, England: Gower.

Walden, Keith. 1982. *Visions of Order: The Canadian Mounties in Symbol and Myth.* Toronto: Butterworths.

Walker, Christopher R. 1987. "The Community Police Station: Developing a Model." *Canadian Police College Journal* 11(4): 273-318.

Walker, Christopher R. and S. Gail Walker. 1989. *The Victoria Community Police Station: An Exercise in Innovation.* Ottawa: Canadian Police College.

Walker, Samuel. 1983. *The Police in America.* New York: McGraw Hill.

Walker, Samuel. 1984. "Broken Windows and Fractured History: The Use and Misuse of History in Recent Police Patrol Analysis." *Justice Quarterly* 1(1): 75-90.

Weatheritt, Mollie. 1983. "Community Policing: Does it Work and How do We Know?" in Bennet, T. (ed.), *The Future of Policing*. Cambridge: University of Cambridge, Institute of Criminology.

Wellman, Barry. 1979. "The Community Question: The Intimate Ties of East Yorkers." *American Journal of Sociology* 84(5): 1201-1231.

Wellman, Barry and Barry Leighton. 1979. "Networks, Neighborhoods and Communities." *Urban Affairs Quarterly* 14(3): 363-390.

Wilson, James Q. and George Kelling. 1982. "Broken Windows." *Atlantic Monthly* (March): 29-38.

Wilson, James Q. and George Kelling. 1989. "Making Neighbourhoods Safe." *Atlantic Monthly* (Feb.): 46-52.

Young, Warren and Neil Cameron (eds.). 1989. *Effectiveness and Change in Policing*. Studies Series No. 3. Wellington: New Zealand: Victoria University of Wellington, Institute of Criminology.

Women in Canadian Urban Policing:
Why Are They Leaving?

Belinda Crawford Seagram and Cannie Stark-Adamec

It was the intent of this study to explore the factors related to attrition among women in Canadian urban police forces. Policing is an occupation that traditionally embodies a stereotypical "male" image. Qualities commonly considered necessary for the job are rarely attributed to the feminine sex role.

Is it possible for women in this male-dominated occupation to fulfill the traditional expectations of being a good girlfriend, wife or mother, while simultaneously satisfying their own career goals? Qualities necessary for survival on the street may not be compatible with those expected at home. Women entering law enforcement soon learn that there are multiple, often conflicting expectations for their behaviour.[1] The stresses associated with such conflicts may be so great that they result in dissatisfaction, disillusionment or even a loss of commitment to policing, and may lead to the loss of valuable officers.

Several Canadian police departments have identified higher rates of attrition among female members as compared to male members. By examining the factors related to attrition among both female and male police officers, it is possible to determine whether the reasons for leaving are sex-specific. In order to identify the issues particularly salient to female officers, it is necessary to view the work they do, not only within the policing network, but also within the context of societal expectations.

Women, Work and Policing

The past two decades have seen a tremendous change in the numbers of women entering the labour force. Between 1966 and 1982, the female labor force grew by 119 per cent, while the male labor force increased only by 35.1 per cent.[2] In total, women now comprise forty-one per cent of the Canadian labour force.[3]

A number of factors are taken into consideration when once chooses an occupation. Apart from his or her personal beliefs about the appropriateness of a specific job, an individual must consider ability or opportunity to acquire requisite skills, labor market conditions, one's life circumstances and the attitudes of the "significant others" in one's life.[4] Actual job preference is merely one of many considerations that come into play in job selection.

Many women today hold full-time paying jobs, while continuing to shoulder the bulk of duties in the home. Nieva and Gutek proposed in 1981 that employment fields dominated by women tend to allow women to accommodate their work demands to their family demands, thus allowing them to concentrate their efforts on their roles as wives and mothers. Possibly, the nature of this employment enables women to shape their work responsibilities to fit what has traditionally been perceived as a primary female concern — the domestic sphere.

Despite the fact that women are taking on more work outside the home, they are not automatically being relieved of their domestic obligations. As more women are employed outside the home, demands for equal treatment in the job market and shared responsibility for work in the home may intensify.[5] The advent of dual-career families — whether they have come into being for reasons of self-enhancement, economic necessity or both — limits what employers can reasonably expect of their workers. In short, the family, which was once seen as the ally of the firm, is changing and, in many cases, has become its enemy.[6] Increased involvement of women in the paid labour market, coupled with rising normative expectations of men's involvement with their families, are forcing companies to consider potential impacts on families in making personnel policy decisions.[7]

The area of policing is particularly relevant to these findings in that it is an occupation in which the organization expects high commitment on the part of the individual. Police officers are required to uphold a certain image while coping with job stresses and rotating shifts; none of the factors is necessarily compatible with those of family life. With hiring trends pointing towards increased numbers of women joining the ranks, and with a growing trend for officers to marry within the force (according to personal communication with study participants), we cannot afford to ignore the issue of family-career conflict.

Policing and Job-Related Stress

For the purpose of this study, job stress is seen as probable when demands from the work environment are perceived to be in excess of an individual's abilities to meet them, under conditions where the costs of meeting such demands greatly outnumber the rewards. Margolis and Kroes define job stress as a condition in the work environment that interacts with worker characteristics to disrupt psychological or physiological homeostasis.[8] Typical organizational outcomes include absenteeism, turnover and either increased or decreased quality and/or quantity of job performance.[9] The strains produced by job stressors may be manifested in a number of ways; depression, low self-esteem, feelings of anxiety, low energy levels, sexual disinterest and physical complaints. Loo has theorized that police stressors can be grouped into four broad categories: organizational procedures and characteristics, police work itself, the criminal justice system and its characteristics and the public.[10]

Among those organizational procedures and characteristics that might prove stressful are lack of participation in the decision making structure, poor relationships with supervisors and/or subordinates, inadequate support from management, lack of recognition and transfers without prior consultation — all of which might lead an individual to feel insignificant and unrecognized.

The second category identified by Loo pertains to police work itself. Such stressors may include shiftwork, work overload, negative impacts on family life and periods of inactivity or boredom.

Many officers also feel frustrated in their dealings with the criminal justice system. Problems in scheduling appearances, cross-examinations in court and feelings that the courts are too lenient toward criminals and slow to put justice into motion may all contribute to the stress felt by police officers.

Finally, lack of support from the public, assaults on police and sometimes-biased media reporting add to the feelings of frustration an officer may be experiencing.

One would expect that such stressors would be experienced by both male and female officers; however, women on the force may experience additional stressors particular to female officers. As an occupation, policing is stereotypically "male." Qualities commonly considered necessary for the job are often not those attributed to the feminine sex role.

Because those qualities do not always complement those of wife, mother or lover, the stresses created by the resulting conflicts may be so great that they result in dissatisfaction, disillusionment or even a loss of commitment to policing.

One of the mitigating factors that serves as a buffer against many of these stressors is the type of social support received by the officer. A person may be more or less insulated against the effect of stressors depending upon whether he or she possesses effective social supports.[11] It is important that this support come both from within the organization[12] and from without.[13] Officers who can form meaningful relationships with fellow officers, family and friends will avoid many of the straining aspects of law enforcement work.[14]

Attrition Among Female Officers

It is clear that many aspects of police work are inherently stressful. Should such stressors remain unresolved over an extended period of time, individual police officers may well experience a loss of commitment to policing, and some may eventually decide to leave the force. It remains to be determined which factors are the most salient in contributing to attrition among such officers, as little research has been done in the area of attrition of women in police work. There have been conflicting reports on female/male differences in rates of attrition in military and paramilitary organizations.[15]

In Canada, the Royal Canadian Mounted Police (RCMP) has reported higher rates of attrition among female officers: sixteen per cent of the females employed after September 1975 had left the force by August 1978, compared with 8.7 per cent of the males.[16]

It appears that there are reasons, pertinent to both sexes, that might lead individuals to leave the force. It is clear that when perception of and treatment by others conflict with one's self-perception, serious stress can result. The long-term psychological pain that ensues — depression, cynicism, loss of commitment to policing and even suicide — can be quite significant; hence, the importance of further study in this underdeveloped research area.

The Study

Those studies that have been conducted regarding attrition among Canadian police officers are either outdated or focus on American samples. The study described below was designed to investigate sex-specific factors leading to attrition among men and women in Canadian urban police forces, since identification of these factors enables the development of intervention strategies and administrative reform. By improving the quality of life for police officers, administrators may be able to reduce the loss of valuable trained staff.

Four major Canadian police departments were involved in the study. Four groups of sworn officers from each participating police force were selected to receive questionnaires designed to provide data pertinent to the study questions. In order to identify sex-specific factors contributing to attrition, females who had left the force were compared with their male counterparts; thus, the groups were composed of female officers, female ex-officers, male officers and male ex-officers.

Of the four groups, the smallest population was in the group of female ex-officers. The total population of women who had left each force since January 1, 1982, was identified as the primary study group. For purposes of comparison, equal-sized samples of male and female current officers, as well as male ex-officers, were included in the study. The comparison groups were matched with the primary study group on the variables of age and number of years on the force and, if applicable, the month and year that they left the force.

The following questionnaires were included in the survey:

1. *General Information Questionnaire.* Basic demographic data were obtained from each respondent. A number of specific issues were presented, and participants were asked to indicate how salient each of these items was to them personally. Ex-officers were asked their reasons for leaving, and all participants were questioned on which policies/practices they would like to see implemented in policing.

Figure 1. Satisfaction With Job

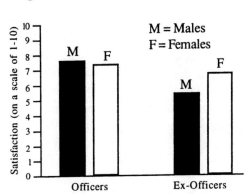

2. The *Police Stress Survey.*[17] On this sixty-item questionnaire, officers were asked to indicate (on a scale of one to a hundred) the amount of stress they feel is associated with specific events. Respondents were instructed to use both knowledge gained vicariously and their own personal experience in judging the amount of time and energy necessary to cope with the events.

3. *Coping Strategies Scale.*[18] This nineteen-item scale was administered to determine the extent to which officers use "appropriate" and "inappropriate" methods to cope with job stress.

4. *Symptom Checklist.* The symptom checklist was comprised of a list of somatic and stress-related complaints. Respondents were asked to identify symptoms experienced in their last year on the force, indicating the degree to which they were bothered by these symptoms.

Results

In total, there were 118 participants in the study: fifty women (thirty-two current officers and eighteen ex-officers) and sixty-eight men (forty-six current officers and twenty-two ex-officers). The participants proved to be well matched on the variables of age, education and number of years on the force, with no significant differences between the groups on these variables. The age of the participants ranged from twenty-three to sixty-one, with a mean age of 33.57.

In general, the sample was fairly well educated, with twenty-one per cent of the participants holding a university or college degree, sixty-five per cent having had at least a year of college or university and thirty-five per cent having completed high school. Individuals in this sample had worked an average of 9.53 years, with experience ranging from one to twenty-six years of police work.

With respect to marital status, it was found that sixty-three per cent of the men were married, ten per cent were single and twenty-six per cent were divorced, with fifty-six per cent having remarried. Half of the women in the sample were married, thirty-four per cent were single and sixteen per cent had divorced, with fifty per cent of those having remarried.

Sixty-five percent of the men in the sample had children (fifty-four per cent of current officers and eighty-six per cent of ex-officers), while only forty-four per cent of the women reported having children (thirty-one per cent of current officers and sixty-seven per cent of ex-officers).

Data on the rates of attrition were available for three of the participating forces. During the years 1982-1986, Force A averaged a 3.8 per cent yearly loss of its female officers (due to voluntary resignation) versus a 1.32 per cent loss of male officers. Similarly, Force B lost an average of 3.4 per cent of its female officers during the years 1982-1987, compared with one per cent of its male officers. Force C, on the other hand, had much higher levels of attrition over the same six-year period, averaging a loss of 7.59 per cent of its female officers and 3.24 per cent of its male officers. Despite these differences, however, women from all forces resigned at a rate approximately three times greater than that of men.

Attitudes of Current Officers vs. Ex-Officers

A number of attitude variables were analyzed using the Analysis of Variance (ANOVA) technique. As illustrated in figure 1, current officers reported feeling significantly more satisfied than ex-officers, with the difference being most apparent in the attitude of male participants.

Ex-officers reported greater levels of distress than current officers over the issue of family-career conflict, and tended to feel less satisfied with the effect that their job was having on their private life (see figures 2 and 3).

Women on the force reported doing a greater share of the domestic chores in their respective homes than did men. As illustrated in figure 4, seventy-seven per cent of the women studied reported doing greater than fifty per cent of the chores at home, with fifty-two per cent reporting that they did at least eighty per cent of the work.

Among those officers with young children, female officers reported significantly higher levels of support from their spouses/closest friends than did female ex-officers, and male ex-officers reported more support than did male officers currently on the force.

Both men and women in the study agreed on the degree to which it is important for officers to demonstrate traditional "masculine" characteristics while on the job; however, women reported feeling significantly less comfortable doing so.

Stress Associated with the Job

As expected, the majority of stressors were given comparable ratings by both men and women, current officers and ex-officers. Nevertheless, a few significant differences emerged between groups. Women reported more stress associated with assignment of an incompatible partner, delivery of a death notification and assignment of new or unfamiliar duties; men reported more stress associated with political pressures from outside the department, attempts to move "up" in the organization and excessive paperwork.

Asked whether they had encountered any particularly stressful work-related experiences in their last year on the force, participants cited a number of circumstances as having been acutely stressful. These included problems with supervisors, finding oneself in dangerous situations, disagreeable aspects of the job (such as searching for dead bodies or giving evidence in court for the first time), the death of a fellow officer, inadequacies of the court system, shift work and its negative impact on family life, competition for promotion and uncertainties associated with the decision making process.

Of note is the fact that eighteen per cent of the female participants cited sex-specific problems as having been particularly stressful. Items in this category include sexual harassment, sexual discrimination, pregnancy and having children while on the force. An example of such discrimination was provided by one the respondents:

> I was off the road and out of uniform at four months' pregnant. I was doing station duty. My supervisor told me that it was best if I do the [specified job]. At this time, I was six months' pregnant and just beginning to wear maternity clothes. It was a job I hoped for until he stated: "It's best you stay away from the front desk. It isn't appropriate that the public sees a pregnant police officer." I was not one to make waves or fight for women's rights. I was afraid of "winning the battle and losing the war." I did nothing.

For purposes of analysis, the Coping Strategies Questionnaire was broken down into seven factors: avoidance of problems, looking to outside resources for help, taking drugs, exercising, seeking support from family and/or church, acting out, talking things over with a friend and having a cigarette.

Multivariate analyses of variance revealed few differences in factor scores across groups. However, there was significant status effect for the exercise factor, with current officers exercising more frequently than former officers had when they were on the force.

Not only did they exercise more than ex-officers, but current officers were also more likely to find pleasant diversions (such as seeing a movie or playing sports) in order to cope with stress. Again, it is noted that ex-officers were asked to answer in terms of their habits while they were on the force.

The Symptom Checklist was broken down into five categories: internalization of feelings (for example, depression, tension, anxiety, fatigue, insomnia, irritability); emotional changes (hostility, cynicism, emotional coldness, interpersonal difficulties); and three separate factors pertaining to physical complaints (headaches, backaches and loss of interest in sex; ulcers, hives and upset stomach; and hemorrhoids). Sex differences were obtained on two of the factors. Women in the study reported having more somatic complaints than men (headaches, backaches and loss of interest in sex) as a result of stress; on the other hand, men reported experiencing more emotional changes towards others than did the women studied.

Reasons for Leaving the Force

When participants were asked their reasons for leaving the force, a number of interesting sex differences emerged. For those women who had left policing, many cited family-related concerns as the primary reason for leaving, as opposed to dissatisfaction with the job. The reasons women gave for leaving their jobs included wanting to raise their families and/or spend more time with them (fifty-six per cent); moving to another city (seventeen per cent); relocation to a now police force (eleven per cent); burnout/negative views on life (six per cent); feelings of inadequacy as a police officer (six per cent) and dissatisfaction with shift work (six per cent).

In contrast, men were more likely to express disillusionment with certain aspects of the job. When asked their reasons for leaving, issues cited included wanting to change vocation/return to school (forty-one per cent); disillusionment with the bureaucracy /judicial system (thirty-two per cent); burnout/negative views on life (twenty-three per cent); dissatisfaction with shift work (eighteen per cent); wanting to raise/spend more time with family (nine per cent); and danger inherent in the job (five per cent).

Discussions and Conclusions

According to Nieva and Gutek, effecting change in sex-role assignments and definitions necessitates basic redefinitions in male responsibilities and rewards in the family arena, just as women expand their responsibilities and rewards in the world of paid employment.[19] Police administrators must acknowledge and respect the role of family among both female and male officers. By accommodating the shifts of couples, allowing time off for important family gatherings and permitting sick-leave time for male or female officers who need to attend to sick children at home, police departments will begin to accommodate to the increase in responsibility that many men are taking at home.

When asked their primary reasons for leaving the force, women tended to cite family-related concerns, whereas men were more likely to express disillusionment/frustration with certain aspects of the job. Despite the fact that women in the study have broken societal norms and entered a traditionally male-dominated occupation, most of them continue to view themselves as having to shoulder the bulk of the domestic responsibilities. As well as fulfilling the expectations of the police department, these women are attempting to attend to the needs of their respective households. It seems hardly surprising, therefore, that among women with young children, those with unsupportive husbands were more likely to be ex-members than those whose families supported their careers.

The results of the study suggest that it is not only women who are experiencing family/career conflict. Family responsibilities are no longer solely the woman's domain. Social changes are increasing the normative share of responsibility that men are expected to take home. In order to keep in tune with employee needs, organizations must acknowledge such changes. The more police forces adapt to family needs, the more committed will be both the officer and his or her family to the institution.

Implications of the Study

Traditionally, there has been an assumption that the socialization a male typically experiences better prepares him for the task-oriented working world than does the socialization of females, which focuses on sensitivity and emotional expression. The results of this study support the notion that, among police officers, the traditional male model of behaviour is that which is deemed most appropriate for the job. Although the women who participated in the study agreed on the extent to which one should display traditional masculine characteristics at work, they did not necessarily feel comfortable doing so. It would appear, on the basis of the findings, that a great deal of pressure is applied to these women to conform to the stereotypical male model. The underlying belief is that in order to survive in a "man's world," one must adopt traditional masculine values and modes of behaviour.

At this point, the question is whether or not the existing model of behaviour in policing, based upon traditional male values and beliefs, is necessarily the most appropriate. With high levels of job stress and decreasing levels of public support, it is becoming increasingly difficult for officers to maintain high levels of commitment and enthusiasm in their work. The emotionally detached, "professional" manner employed by many officers may seem to be an appropriate method of coping with day-to-day stress. In the long run, however, such a coping mechanism may be quite damaging. Although one could speculate on the various ways in which women could be trained to fit into the "male" world of policing, a more productive approach might be to objectively re-examine the values and beliefs inherent in the traditional male model of policing. Perhaps the question is not "What can we do to make women better fit into policing?" but "What is it that the organization can learn from women?"

Endnotes

1   S. Gross, "Women Becoming Cops: Developmental Issues and Solutions," *Police Chief*, January 1984, pp. 32-35.

2   Canadian Advisory Council on the Status of Women, *Women and Work* (Ottawa: Canadian Advisory Council on the Status of Women, 1985).

3   H.M. Lips and N.L. Colwill, "Psychology Addresses Women and Work: Canadian Research in the 1980s," *Canadian Psychology*, 1988, 29:5748.

4   V.F. Nieva and B.A. Gutek, *Women and Work* (New York: Praeger Publishers, 1981).

5   S.S. Tangri, *Research on Women's Work*, edited by Anne Hoiberg, NATO Conference Series III (New York: Plenum Press, 1982).

6   C.B. Derr, *Work, Family and the Career* (New York: Praeger, 1980).

7   M.W. Segal, "The Military and the Family as Greedy Institutions," *Armed Forces and Society*, 1986, 13(1):9-38.

8   B.L. Margolis and W.H. Kroes, "Occupational Stress and Strain," in *Occupational Stress*, A. McLean, ed., (Springfield, IL: Charles C. Thomas, 1974), pp. 15-20.

9   K.D. Love and T.A. Beehr, "Social Stressors on the Job: Recommendations for a Broadened Perspective," *Group and Organizational Studies*, 1981, 6:190-200.

10 R. Loo, "Occupational Stress in the Law Enforcement Profession," *Canada's Mental Health*, September 1984, pp. 10-13.

11 F.T. Cullen, T. Lemming, B.G. Link and L.F. Wozniak, "The Impact of Social Supports on Police Stress," *Criminology*, 1985, 23(3):503-23.

12 F.A. Graf, "The Relationship Between Social Support and Occupational Stress Among Police Officers," *Journal of Police Science and Administration*, 1986, 14(3):178-186.

13 R. Loo, "Police Stress and Social Supports," Paper presented at the 48th Annual Convention of he Canadian Psychological Association, Vancouver, B.C., 1987; also, P.E. Maynard, N.E. Maynard, H.I. McCubbin and D. Shao, "Family Life and

the Police Profession," *Family Relations*, 1980, 29:495-501.

14   Cullen, *et al.*

15   R. Linden, "Attrition Among Male and Female Members of the RCMP," *Canadian Police College Journal*, 1985, 9(1):86-97; and R. Linden and C. Minch, "Women in Policing: A Review," Ottawa: Ministry of the Solicitor General of Canada, cat. no. 1984-92.

16   Linden, "Women in Policing: A Review". 1984.

17   C.D. Spielberger, L.G. Westbery, K.S. Grier and G. Greenfield, "The Police Stress Survey: Sources of Stress in Law Enforcement," Human Resources Institute, Monograph Series Three, No. 6, University of South Florida, Tampa, 1980.

18   C. Maslach, "Coping Strategies Scale," unpublished, University of California-Berkeley.

19   Nieva and Gutek, *op. cit.*

Attitudes Toward Higher Education Among Mid-Career Police Officers

Leslie Brian Buckley[1]

Much has been written about university education for police officers. Studies examining the overall effects education has on police performance, however, are inconclusive. Furthermore, there is a lack of agreement among researchers and police administrators on the usefulness of a university education for the senior ranks and managerial levels. Despite the disagreement with respect to the benefits of educating police officers, recent recruitment practices of many police forces have increasingly been favouring the better educated. Moreover, some police forces are attempting to upgrade their force by encouraging incumbent police officers to attend university.

Police work in North America was once considered as a career requiring little formal education. Finding a police officer with any post-secondary education was rare. In the past, police forces were mainly concerned with a candidate's physical stature with the belief that size enabled officers to handle troublesome or potentially troublesome situations and deter people from physically challenging the police. A good police officer was generally thought of as physical raw material bolstered by on the job training, experience and common sense. Academic knowledge learned in a university environment was deemed irrelevant to everyday police work.

Some observers feel, however, that all police officers, especially those at the senior ranks, would benefit from having formal post-secondary education beyond high school (Grant, 1984). It is believed that such an education would not only improve the status of policing, but would also provide police officers at all levels with a better understanding of modern society and the role of the police in the community. As well, it would also provide them with the knowledge and abilities needed to manage a large organization.

The decision by police administrators to raise the educational standards for police personnel, however, has not been received favourably by some officers. In addition, the new educated police officers may not have looked favourably upon the views of their non-university-educated counterparts.

The minimum basic requirement for entrance into any police force in Canada is grade 12, although, for some time now, some police forces have incorporated scoring systems which include education as one of the criteria in recruitment. A basic premise for recruiting university graduates into police forces is that past performance is a good predictor of an individual's future performance (Lester, 1979; Owens, 1976). The belief is that the attainment of a university degree is indicative of the ability to succeed in a training program or in learning a new job. One's educational achievement may also indicate one's aptitude or intellectual ability to do the job (Merritt-Haston and Wexley, 1983).

A decision to raise police educational standards may partly be a reaction to technological and social change. The police have responded with numerous strategies to meet these concerns. Some strategies are technical and practical in nature and largely designed to improve operational efficiency, while others address such issues as human resource and organizational development. One such strategy which has been identified is to use higher education to improve the overall quality of policing.

Education and Police Professionalism

Police administrators have long been trying to improve the social status of law enforcement through education so that the police may achieve professional standing (Steinman and Eskridge, 1985; Merritt-Haston and Wexley, 1983). Education, in this sense, has been deemed synonymous with professionalization. The meaning of police professionalization, however, remains unclear. The police want the public to perceive policing as a profession and not merely as an occupation (Sherman, 1978a). Some authors have argued that the professionalization of the police is strictly an attempt by administrators to raise public confidence (Muir, 1982; Regoli, 1976). Individual police officers, however, have displayed much skepticism and cynicism over the reasons given for professionalizing the police (Regoli, 1976). In addition, a number of observers have not supported the reasons given for police professionalization. The attempt to use education to attain professional status is, according to Greene and Cordner (1980), less important than improving the quality of police service.

Considering the emphasis placed on the benefits of university education for policing, little, if any research has examined the implications of such requirements for those who are most directly involved — individual police officers themselves. This study is designed to shed some light on this issue by examining whether police officers of differing educational levels have different attitudes about the appropriate qualifications for promotion, different beliefs about appropriate police roles, and different perceptions about the appropriate requirements needed to engage in police work.

Among the important ramifications of increasing educational standards is the effect such a policy change has on serving police officers. When such changes are implemented in any organization, one must consider not only the desired outcomes of the policy, but also concomitant negative consequences. One such consequence may be violation of expectation, and confusion and resentment among the present and incoming personnel.

Police officers with differing levels of education may have different and conflicting styles, approaches and perceived goals of policing. The attitudes of perceptions police officers have about education may be contingent upon the individual's own level of education. In addition, attitudes toward education may be influenced by other police officers having a different level of education. Not much attention has been given to the issue. The problem to be addressed, therefore, concerns the way in which individual police officers perceive the value of university education to their force, to themselves and to their fellow officers.

Research Findings: Education and Police Attitudes

Although education has been shown to correlate with some police attitudes (Fisher, Golden and Heininger, 1985), research to this date has produced findings which unequivocally clarify the benefits of educating the police. From a sample of 118 police officers in Lincoln, Nebraska, Roberge (1980 and 1978) found that university educated police officers are less dogmatic than their non-university educated colleagues. Similar results were found by Parker, Donnelly, Gerwitz, Marcus and Kawalewski (1976) in a study of police officers sampled in the Eastern United States. Dalley (1975) found that RCMP officers with higher levels of education were less authoritarian, less conservative and held less rigid attitudes. Blankenship and Cramer (1976) found that police officers who have higher levels of education and better training in interpersonal skills tend to prefer informal referral to intermediate agencies instead of formal committal to mental hospitals when handling mentally disordered juvenile behaviour.

The research literature on police education tends to stress the police officer's role as a decision maker and emphasizes that this decision making process is a personal and individual one. Finkenauer (1975) suggests that police officers with higher education tend to be less legalistic and less likely to invoke the criminal process. He also suggests that there is a need to condition the police into being less authoritarian and more empathic towards the people with whom they deal.

Weiner (1976), in a study of the attitudes of police officers, found that level of education was unrelated to police cynicism, although Niederhoffer (1967) suggests that education would reduce police cynicism. Studies by Regoli (1976) and Lotz and Regoli (1977), however, found that although less educated officers were more cynical than better educated officers, the better educated also rank high on cynicism scales due to their supposed identification with the "professional ethos" and their inability to practice it. Similar results were reported by Wycoff and Susmilch (1979) from studies examining the attitudes and educational level of command and rank officers.

Education, Performance and Job Satisfaction

While there is no consensus on the value of education, neither is there consensus on the best type of education for police officers. Cross-occupational studies have shown that the type of university degree has little effect on job performance especially at managerial levels (Ariss and Timmins, 1989). Finnegan (1976) found that although education has an effect on attitudes and performance, the officers' type of education made no difference on these factors. On the other hand, Madell and Washburn (1978) found that those who concentrated on police science and business administration fared better at promotions than those who studied liberal arts.

Some support has been found for the notion that education is positively related to receiving better performance appraisals (Hayeslip, 1989), although the specific performance areas are relatively unknown (Sparling, 1975). In a study of 418 Michigan State Police Troopers, Weirman (1978) found that better educated officers performed better on a test of academic ability and had better peer relationships. Weirman (1978), however, also found that better educated officers were more likely to leave policing. On the other hand, Barry (1978) found that although better educated police officers in Illinois were not receiving any pay incentives or preferred promotional advancements, their education was positively related to their performance and they showed a higher level of job satisfaction. In a study of 500 Chicago patrol officers, Baehr, Furcon and Fromel (1968) reported that senior officers who received higher performance ratings had a significantly higher level of education. Similarly, a police chief reported that nineteen of his officers with some college education received subsequently higher performance ratings than did a similar number of officers without a college education (Saunders, 1970). A study by Finnegan (1976) of the Baltimore Police Department found similar results.

An interesting observation made by Wycoff (1987), following visits to a number of American police forces, was that better educated police managers tended to be more creative in devising new supervisory methods. These managers also encouraged thought and creativity in their patrol officers.

Carter and Sapp (1989) suggest that higher education may help reduce the risk of misconduct or negligence by police officers. In a study of the New York Police Department, Cohen and Chaiken (1973) reported that better educated officers received fewer complaints and fewer disciplinary actions, took fewer sick days and had fewer injuries. In a survey of 940 Dade County Officers, Cascio (1977) obtained similar results. It was also found that more highly educated officers had higher intelligence and motivation scores.

Cross occupational studies of education and job satisfaction have not reported consistent findings (Buzawa, 1984; Mottaz, 1984; Glen and Weaver, 1982; O'Toole, 1977; Freeman, 1976). There is, however, increasing evidence that within policing, better educated officers are less job satisfied. In the United States and Britain, a higher percentage of university educated officers leave policing in comparison to those with less education (Fielding and Fielding, 1987; Burbeck and Furnham, 1985; Weirman, 1978). One reason given for the high turnover rate has been the frustration of working in a rigid setting (Griffin et al., 1978). Similar findings regarding job satisfaction have not been shown in Canada.

Contrary to the findings found on job satisfaction in the United States and Britain, Berkley (1969) and Weiner (1974) believe that a university education may be positively related to job satisfaction in that it may enable police officers to see their work from a different and broader perspective. University educated police officers may perceive their job differently and believe that they are having some impact on society whereas non-university educated officers may be more oriented towards law enforcement and believe that given their resources, the police have a limited effect on reducing crime. Police officers with a university education, on the other hand, may be more likely to recognize that although they are having limited influence on curbing crime, they are at least making some people's lives better. They may have a better understanding of the crime situation and may realize their own and their force's limitations. More importantly, they may have an understanding of the police role beyond law enforcement to the maintenance of social order as well as the enforcement of the law. Less educated officers may place less importance on the order maintenance role.

Two primary criticisms have been made of university education for policing. The first, as suggested by Salten (1979), is that university education makes no difference even if it is obtained before entering policing. A second and more serious allegation is that university educated officers may actually perform worse than their non-university educated counterparts. Wilson (1975: 113) suggests that "while college may make a man civil... it also gives him (or reinforces for him) his sense of duty." Because of this, the better educated officer may become excessively aggressive and more likely to arrest, when a gentler approach may be more appropriate. It has also been suggested that better educated officers may not be able to identify with the problem of the lower and working class person with whom they must deal (Sherman, 1978b).

Some senior officers in the United States have expressed the fear that "the new breed (often with a Bachelor's or Master's degree) [sic] is more apt to ask questions and less inclined to accept departmental edicts blindly than did his predecessors of fifteen or more years. This attitude sometimes leads to unrest in departments" (Gerstein, Bowen and Torrance, 1980: 94). The belief is that educated officers are more apt to cause problems within the organization and that they have a tendency to question authority. Therefore, educated officers may be perceived as being difficult to deal with.

Critics of higher education for police officers, especially those who entered policing before the education movement, resent the emphasis placed on education for several reasons (Miller and Fry, 1976). They view the new educational requirements as an unfair change in the rules in the middle of the game. College attendance may be viewed as an infringement on family and recreational activities and the courses themselves may be perceived as irrelevant. These concerns may contribute to the resistance some have displayed towards education for police work.

Despite the inconclusive results concerning policing and education, more candidates entering the police force have a university education and more currently serving officers are improving their level of education. These police officers may believe that education will better enable them to do their present job and improve their abilities and prospects for promotion. They may further believe that those having less education do not perform as well as those who have higher levels of education. Alternatively, officers with less formal education may believe that experience and common sense are more important factors in understanding work than formal education. In fact, these officers may disagree with the policing style of the university educated police officer.

This Study

The purpose of this investigation, therefore, was to address four issues: the extent to which education related to the endorsement by police officers of a wider police role than mere crime control, the extent to which police officers believe higher education is related to performance, the extent to which police officers feel that higher education would be a criterion for promotion, and the extent to which education relates to job satisfaction.

A random sample of 250 police officers was selected from two Canadian midsized regional police forces (125 from each force) and asked to participate in this study. Both forces (referred to as Force A and Force B) provide municipal and rural policing, and both endorse formal education beyond the minimum requirement (grade 12) and encourage members to continue their education. When college or university courses are taken, both forces will pay for course fees upon successful completion of the course.

The respondents were police constables with five to fifteen years of service. Those with less than five years of service were omitted on the basis of McGinnis' (1985) findings on career studies which showed constables under five years of service were generally content and not as anxious about career issues as more senior members. McGinnis suggests that it is at around five years of service that police officers start to have serious concerns regarding promotion or specialized police work. It is this group of police officers that this study wished to target.

The participants voluntarily completed a "Career Attitude Survey" which examined attitudes toward university education for police officers. The respondents were assured that their anonymity would be preserved. Of the 250 questionnaires sent out, 156 (sixty-two per cent) were returned. Eighty-four of the respondents came from Force A, while seventy-two came from Force B.

The questionnaire was designed and pretested twice until problem-free. Part A focused on general background and demographic information, reference groups and the reasons why the respondent elected to take university courses. Part B focused on the respondents' police career and attitudes toward education. There were five sections. The first section examined attitudes toward education as a requirement for recruitment and promotion, and beliefs about education and job performance. Questions dealt with work experience, seniority, job satisfaction and attitudes toward the police role. Section Two examined the extent to which respondents agreed with eight assertions made in support of the Continuing Education Programme of the Canadian Police College on the benefits that a university education has for police officers. Section Three focused on the extent to which respondents believed that university education, work experience, common sense, personality and attitude and training contributed to the performance of a variety of police functions. Section Four sought to determine the respondents' preferred promotion system. Respondents were asked to allocate the number of points they believed appropriate for several factors often used in promotion systems. Among these were performance appraisals, examinations, oral interview boards, education, seniority and an essay or research paper. Section Five dealt with the respondents' level of job satisfaction, career satisfaction and promotion aspirations.

Results

In order to investigate differences between levels of education, the sample population was divided into three groups: "No University" (high school education only); "Some University" (Less than three completed years of university); and "University Degree" (three or more years of university completed).

Extensive data, tables and statistical significance testing results are available from the author, while summaries are provided in the paragraphs below on differences found among these three groups. Percentages, means, etc. are rounded, to simplify presentation — statistical testing determined whether there were significant differences between the two forces with respect to age of the respondents, sex, length of service and education. The only force difference was on educational level.

Forty per cent of the respondents were between thirty-one and thirty-five years of age, with thirty-one per cent being between the ages of twenty-six and thirty years, seventeen per cent between thirty-six and forty years, eleven per cent between forty-one and forty-five years, and two per cent between twenty-one and twenty-five years of age. Approximately forty-six per cent of the respondents had between six and ten years of service, while forty-two per cent had between eleven and fifteen years of service; seven per cent and between sixteen and twenty years, twenty-one per cent had five years of service, and three per cent had over twenty years of service.

The vast majority of the respondents (ninety-five per cent) were male.

Force A had more respondents with partial university and completed degrees (fifty-eight per cent) than Force B (twenty-five per cent). Both forces had similar proportions of officers with at least some community college education (twenty-four per cent for Force A; twenty-six per cent for Force B). More officers in Force B had high school education only (forty-nine per cent) than Force A (eighteen per cent). Approximately nineteen per cent of the respondents from Force A indicated that they were presently enrolled in a university course compared to eleven per cent of the respondents in Force B.

The move to improve the educational level of police officers is fairly recent. Many police forces are actively recruiting those with higher education than before. This will result in older police officers with less formal education. This raises the issue of the relationship between education, length of service and age. The sample in this study, however, was deliberately truncated so that the length of service was limited to between five and fifteen years. This may have resulted in the loss of some officers having no or little university education at the high end (over fifteen years of service) and a number of newly recruited university educated officers at the low end. In order to determine if level of education was associated with age or length of service, correlations were calculated among education, length of service and age. There were no significant correlations between education and length of service or education and age. Therefore, since neither age nor length of service are related to educational level, they can be ruled out as alternative explanations when attitudinal differences are found among respondents of different educational levels.

The three levels of education groups were compared on the respondents' desired weights for components in a promotion system. These components included performance appraisals, written examinations, an oral interview board, level of education, seniority and a research paper, for a total of 100 points. There were significant differences on two components. The some university group indicated that less emphasis should be given to performance appraisals (thirty-one points) than the no university group (thirty-eight points). The university degree group did not significantly differ from the no or some university groups, but it is noteworthy that the university degree group's allocation of points (thirty-four) to the performance appraisal was similar to the some university group. In addition, the university degree group indicated that more points should be allocated to education (fifteen) than the no university group (eleven). On a combined total of 100 points, the three groups on average gave performance appraisals the greatest weight (thirty-five points) followed by examinations (nineteen points), a selection board interview (fourteen points), seniority (fourteen points) education (twelve points) and a research paper (three points) and other (three points).

A comparison was made of the three education groups on attitudes toward education issues, length of service, and loyalty. Five significant questionnaire measures showed differences. These are as follows:

(1)   Compared to the university degree group, the other two groups more strongly believe that the university educated perceive themselves as superior.

(2)   The no university group more strongly believes that the education issue is "political" than the university degree group.

(3)   The university degree group more strongly agrees that university education has overall value for police forces.

(4)   The university degree and some university groups more strongly believe that officers should be encouraged to obtain a university education in order to help professionalize policing than the no university group.

(5)   The no university group believe more strongly than the university degree group that the non-university educated are committed to police professionalism.

Another comparison was made of the three education groups on attitudes toward education and job experience. There are significant differences by educational level on almost all of the measures. Overall, the university degree group believed that a university education enhanced performance. The no and some university groups more strongly endorse "instincts" over education, and less strongly endorse education as providing "perspective." They also provide stronger endorsement of the current minimum education standard (grade 12) than the university degree group. Across the three groups, the respondents generally indicated that work experience, "street education" and recruit training are not sufficient for becoming effective police offices.

An additional comparison was completed of the three education groups on attitudes toward the Canadian Police College positions on Continuing Education. All three groups showed lack of support for these assertions, however the university degree and some university groups provided statistically significant stronger support than the no university group that a university education; (1) helps police officers to develop a better awareness of what goes on around them; (2) enhances one's ability to function in a complex society; (3) increases one's understanding of human behaviour;

(4) better enables one to tolerate differences and ambiguities; (5) gives one a better understanding of the causes of crime; and (6) better prepares one to evaluate situations and arrive at a balanced judgement. Further, compared to the other two groups, the university degree group more positively rated university graduates as leaders.

In a comparison of the three groups on the extent to which they believe that "experience" facilitates the performance of a number of different police functions, no significant differences were found. Similar results were found when the three groups were compared on the extent to which they believe "common sense" facilitates the performance of these same functions. There is, however, an interesting pattern. All respondents indicated that common sense is strongly related to the handling of interpersonal functions such as interpersonal disputes, hostage negotiation, rowdiness and disorder and interviewing witnesses and victims. Common sense was seen as less related to the technical functions such as identification or computer crime.

Significant differences were found among the three groups on most of the police functions in a comparison of the extent to which education is related to these functions. Overall, the university degree group gave higher endorsement for university education in the performance of the various functions than the some or no university groups. The respondents across all education groups indicated that a university education was strongly related to conducting computer crime investigations or preparing budgets. A further comparison of the three education groups on the extent to which personality and attitude are related to the various police functions indicated a similar pattern to that of the common sense variable. Personality and attitude were perceived as strongly related to the handling of the interpersonal functions of police work, and less related to the technical functions.

The differences among the three education groups on the extent to which training is related to the various functions reflected, overall, few significant differences among the three groups. As with experience, all education groups believe that training is important for all aspects of police work. Interestingly, however, the respondents indicated that training was not as important for handling interpersonal disputes as was experience, personality and attitude and common sense. Overall, the respondents endorsed training as being related to some of the technical specialist (i.e., drug investigations) functions.

A final comparison of the three education groups on attitudes toward the police role showed no significant differences among the three groups on any measures dealing with the order maintenance roles. The measure dealing with crime control did approach significance, however, and there is some indication that the university degree group less strongly endorses crime control as the sole role of the police. The university degree group, however, rated helping victims or citizens as being less rewarding than did the other two groups. Across all education groups, the respondents generally indicated that much of their time is taken up with order maintenance duties, that it is an appropriate role of the police to perform this function, and that the order maintenance function, as well as serving and assisting the public, is a source of job satisfaction.

Across the education groups, the respondents were generally satisfied with their jobs as police officers and indicated that their work is not discouraging. The respondents did not indicate that they questioned why they chose or remain in police work. No significant differences existed among the groups on this dimension.

A potential source of variance in police research is the effect of the specific police organization on the respondents' answers to the dependent measures. That is, apart from the respondents' level of education, there may exist at the organizational level, cultural influences that affect responses. Therefore, it is important to examine possible force effects on the variables being measured. In this study, however, such an analysis would be confounded because there is a significantly higher proportion of university educated respondents in Force A than in Force B. This difference itself may reflect a difference of organizational cultures. Analyses partialing out education from the two forces would not be effective since there are so few university degree respondents in Force B. Therefore, the education effect would mask any differences between the two forces. Differences between the forces could well be effects of education.

Discussion

This study has focused on the attitudes of police officers toward university education for policing. Many police administrators have argued that university education would help policing achieve higher status and a more professional image. Recently, police researchers and administrators have suggested that a university education gives police officers a broad and more informed outlook and that higher education elevates one's understanding of society and human behaviour, thereby enhancing performance. The literature to date, however, does not provide conclusive evidence of a positive relationship between higher education and performance. Further, there has been little research examining the relationship between higher education and police officer attitudes and beliefs. In this study, the majority of the differences were between those respondents who have a complete university degree and those who have either no university education at all or some university courses but not a complete degree.   Therefore, the remaining discussion will refer to university graduates and non-graduates.

The data provided strong support for the suggestion that university graduates would weigh education more heavily in their ideal promotion scheme, while non-graduates did not believe that university education should be considered strongly for promotion.   Further, compared to the university graduates, the non-graduates placed more emphasis on the performance measure for determining promotion eligibility.

Compared to non-graduates, university graduates consider university education to be more of an asset in the performance of police functions. The university graduates did not, however, give as strong an endorsement to education as expected.   Instead, the mean scores indicated that they collectively exhibited either less disagreement compared to the non-graduates or expressed the more neutral response of neither agree nor disagree. University graduates did indicate that education was related to the performance of specific police functions more than non-graduates, but the university graduates did not rate education as highly as the attributes of common sense, training, experience and personality and attitude.   The belief, therefore, may be that university education only supplements the other attributes.

The low emphasis placed on university education by the graduates may be the result of job experience, and socializing or associating with a group of coworkers who place little value on university education.   The graduates may have adopted a peer or reference group who perceive little value to university education for police work.   Since most police officers have other police officers as their reference group and, as the data show, there are few graduate police officers in most forces, this explanation fits reference group theory.   University graduates may, therefore, identify with non-graduate officers and incorporate into their belief systems the idea that education is of little value.   Further, the graduates in their day-to-day work may not see the need for a university education and come to believe that it is indeed irrelevant.   They may be failing to recognize, however, that some of the qualities that they have acquired through the university experience are actually affecting how they do police work.   They may not realize that, as suggested by some police researchers (McGrath, 1978; Sherman, 1978b; Weiner, 1974; Berkley, 1969), they have a better understanding of certain situations or are handling these situation differently and perhaps more appropriately.   These officers may not recognize that certain personal qualities or abilities may be associated with a university education.

The data also show that the non-graduates perceive graduates different-ly than graduates perceive themselves. Non-graduates believe that gradu-ates perceive themselves as superior to non-graduates. Further, non-gradu-ates believe that graduates perform no better than themselves. In addition, the non-graduates believe more strongly that the root of the education issue is based upon "politics" and that its purpose may be to satisfy the needs of politicians and academics rather than those of policing itself. On the other hand, university graduates believe that university education for police offi-cers has overall value for police forces and that it may help make policing more professional.

Contrary to expectations, the data show that the non-graduates per-ceived the order maintenance roles to be just as important as the graduates. It is still possible that the university educated are more oriented towards the order maintenance role, but the results suggest that all police officers recog-nize that this is an important and appropriate function of everyday police work. This issue was not explored in depth, and other studies with other measures may produce different results.

It was believed that university graduates might display a higher level of job satisfaction than non-graduates. If they perceived their job and policing from a broader and different perspective, this might result in greater job sat-isfaction. It was believed that educated officers would be less discouraged by the limitations encountered on the job and appreciate such intrinsic rewards as the ability to help others. Contrary to expectations, there were no significant differences among respondents at the three levels of educa-tion on measures and job satisfaction. This finding may be due to the way in which police officers adapt to their job (Buckley, 1989). Becker (1961) and Hughes (1958) believe that individuals adapt and re-adapt themselves to their job as a function of the length of time they have been performing their job and the events that occur at any one time. That is, individuals may enter policing with an idealistic approach to police work. After some time, however, they may come to realize that such views are unrealistic. Therefore, they may adapt by changing attitudes, values and beliefs in order to bring job expectations in line with reality. By adopting a new set of job expectations they may increase their job satisfaction.

Implications

This study has provided evidence that education is related to attitudes toward university education for policing. The predominant pattern is that those who do not have any university education perceive it as having little value for a variety of police functions, whereas university graduates have more positive views of the benefits of education.

Despite the clamour for recruiting university educated police officers and the fact that some forces are actively recruiting university graduates, the data show that few graduates are entering these police forces five or more years ago (this study did not include those with less than five years of service). If police forces desire to increase their number of university educated police officers, police work must become more desirable or appealing to them. This may include pay or promotion incentives, or perhaps showing university graduates that police forces are no longer the authoritarian type of organization the public once envisioned.

The attitudes of non-graduate officers toward university education may stem from some genuine and realistic concerns they have with their career or with genuine beliefs. Some officers, especially those who are more senior and less educated, may not appreciate that university education appears to be forced upon them to enhance their image, especially if these officers believe that education is irrelevant to policing. Lesser educated officers may perceive university education as a threat to their careers, in terms of promotion or preferred postings, especially if they are finding or fear that the new, younger, educated officers will receive advancement over them. On the other hand, some university educated officers may believe that their education is not helping them to advance in their careers as expected and may feel frustrated with the system. In both cases, morale and career satisfaction may be adversely affected.

Despite their attitudes toward higher education, police officers can be made aware that education has general value and, therefore, overall value for police work. This will not be achieved if police administrators advocate education as the panacea for correcting problems encountered in police work and, in turn, pressure their members into obtaining higher education. Instead, education must be presented as only one of a number of possible options for improving the quality of policing. That is, it should be viewed as a factor complementing a number of other factors having the potential of raising the calibre both of individual police officers and, therefore, of police organizations. Not only will higher education raise the overall calibre of the police, but better educated police forces, seen as more representative of society in general, may also increase public confidence and respect for the institution. Improving public confidence is, in itself, reason enough to increase the educational level of police officers.

Education is knowledge and it is difficult to argue that greater knowledge is detrimental to police work. Given the complexities of our different and ever changing society, the vast technical advancements made in recent years, and the multitude of different situations police officers encounter, police officers can only benefit from a broad knowledge from which to make decisions.

References

Ariss, Sonny S. and Sherman A. Timmins. Spring 1989. "Employee Education and Job Performance: Does Education Matter?" *Public Personnel Management* 18 (1): 1-9.

Baehr, M.E., J.E. Furcon and E.C. Froemel. 1968. *Psychological Assessment of Patrolman Qualifications in Relation to Field Performance.* Washington, D.C.: U.S. Government Printing Office.

Barry, Donald M. 1978. "A Survey of Student and Agency Views on Higher Education in Criminal Justice." *Journal of Police Science and Administration* 6(3): 345-354.

Becker, Howard S. 1961. *Boys in White: Student Culture in Medical School.* Toronto: The University of Toronto Press.

Berkley, George E. 1969. *The Democratic Policeman.* Toronto: Beacon Press.

Blankenship, R.L. and J.A. Cramer. December 1976. "The Effects of Education and Training on Police Perceptions of Mentally Disordered Juvenile Behaviours." *Journal of Police Science and Administration* 4: 426:425.

Buckley, Leslie Brian. 1989. "The Influence of Level of Education and Career Orientation on Police Attitudes Toward Higher Education." M.A. Thesis. University of Ottawa.

Burbeck, Elizabeth and Adrian Furnham. 1985. "Police Officer Selection: A Critical Review of the Literature." *Journal of Police Science and Administration* 13(1): 58-69.

Buzawa, Eva S. February 1984. "Determining Patrol Officer Job Satisfaction." *Criminology* 22(1): 61-81.

Carter, David L. and Allen D. Sapp. 1989. "The Effect of Higher Education on Police Liability: Implications for Police Personnel Policy." *American Journal of Police* 8(1): 153-166.

Cascio, W.F. March 1977. "Formal Education and Police Officer Performance." *Journal of Police Science and Administration* 5: 89-96.

Cohen, B. and J.H. Chaiken. 1973. *Police Background Characteristics and Performance.* Lexington, MA: Lexington.

Dalley, A.F. December 1975. "University vs. Non-university Graduated Policemen: A Study of Police Attitudes." *Journal of Police Science and Administration* 3: 458-468.

Fielding, N.G. and J.L. Fielding. 1987. "A Study of Resignation During British Police Training." *Journal of Police Science and Administration* 15(1): 24-36.

Finkenauer, James O. 1975. "Higher Education and Police Discretion." *Journal of Police Science and Administration* 3: 450-457.

Finnegan, J. August 1976. "A Study of the Relationship Between College Education and Police Performance in Baltimore, Maryland." *Police Chief* 60-62.

Fisher, Robert J., Kathryn M. Golden and Bruce L. Heininger. 1985. "Issues in Higher

Education for Law Enforcement Officers: An Illinois Study." *Journal of Criminal Justice* 13(4): 329-338.

Freeman, R. 1976. *The Over-Educated American*. New York: Academic Press.

Gerstein, Bowen and Torrance. 1980. *Policing in Ontario for the Eighties: Perceptions and Reflections*. Ontario: Solicitor General of Ontario.

Glen, N. and C. Weaver. 1982. "Enjoyment of Work by Full-Time Workers in the United States, 1955 and 1980." *Public Opinion Quarterly* 46: 459-468.

Grant, Alan. 1984. *The Police — A Policy Paper*. Ministry of Supply and Services, Canada.

Greene, Jack R. and Gary W. Cordner. Fall 1980. "Education and Police Administration: A Preliminary Analysis of Impact." *Police Studies* 3(3): 12-23.

Griffin, Gerald R., Robert L.M. Dunbar and Michael E. McGill. 1978. "Factors Associated with Job Satisfaction Among Police Personnel." *Journal of Police Science and Administration* 6(1): 77-85.

Hayeslip, Jr., David W. 1989. "Higher Education and Police Performance Revisited: The Evidence Examined Through Meta-Analysis." *American Journal of Police* 8(2): 49-62.

Hughes, Everett Cherington. 1958. *Men and Their Work*. Glencoe, IL: The Free Press.

Lawler III, Edward E. Spring 1985. "Management Style and Organizational Effectiveness." *Personnel Psychology* 38(1): 1-26.

Lester, D. 1979. "Predictors of Graduation From a Police Training Academy." *Psychological Reports* 44: 362.

Lotz, R. and R. Regoli. 1977. "Police Cynicism and Professionalism." *Human Relations* 30(2): 175-181.

Madell, J.D. and P.V. Washburn. August 1978. "Which College Major is Best for the Street Cop?" *Police Chief* 40-42.

McGinnis, James H. 1985. "Career Development in Municipal Policing." *Canadian Police College Journal* 9(2).

McGrath, N. 1978. "Going Beyond Handcuffs 101." *Chronicle of Higher Education* 18: 3.

Merritt-Haston, Ronni and Kenneth N. Wexley. 1983. "Educational Requirements: Legality and Validity." *Personnel Psychology* 36(4): 743-753.

Miller, Jon and Lincoln Fry. 1976. "Re-examining Assumptions About Education and Professionalism in Law Enforcement." *Journal of Police Science and Administration* 4: 187-196.

Mottaz, Clifford. 1984. "Education and User Satisfaction." *Human Relations* 37(11): 985-1004.

Muir, Richard Graham. April 1982. "Considerations in Educating the Police." M.A. Thesis. Simon Fraser University.

Niederhoffer, Arthur. 1967. *Behind the Shield: The Police in Urban Society*. New York: Doubleday.

O'Toole, J. 1977. *Learning and the American Future*. San Francisco: Jossey-Bass.

Owens, W. 1976. "Background Data" in Dunnette, M.D. (ed.), *Handbook of Industrial and Organizational Psychology*. Chicago: Rand McNally College Publishing Co.

Parker, L.C., M. Donnelly, D. Gerwitz, J. Marcus and V. Kawalewski. July 1976. "Higher Education: Its Impact on Police Attitudes." *Police Chief* 33-35.

Regoli, R.M. September 1976. "The Effects of College Education on the Maintenance of Police Cynicism." *Journal of Police Science and Administration* 4: 340-345.

Roberge, Roy R. 1978. "An Analysis of the Relationship Among Higher Education, Belief Systems and Job Performance of Patrol Officers." *Journal of Police Science and Administration* 6(3): 336-344.

Roberge, Roy R. 1980. "Higher Education, Belief Systems and Police Performance: A Reply to Zelig's Critique." *Journal of Police Science and Administration* 8(3): 335-340.

Salten, David G. 1979. "A Harsh Criticism of American Policing and Police Education." *Police Chief* 22-26.

Saunders, Charles B. 1970. *Police Officers: The Relationship of College Education to Job Performance.* Washington, D.C.: The Brooking Institute.

Saunders, Charles B. 1970. *Upgrading the American Police.* Washington, D.C.: The Brookings Institute.

Sherman, L.W. 1978a. *The Quality of Police Education: A Critical Review with Recommendations for Improving Programs in Higher Education.* San Francisco: Jossey-Bass.

Sherman, L.W. 1978b. "College Education for Police: The Reform that Failed?" *Police Studies* 1(4): 32-38.

Sparling, Cynthia L. 1975. "The Use of Education Standards as Selection Criteria in Police Agencies: A Review." *Journal of Police Science and Administration* 3: 332-335.

Steinman, Michael and Chris W. Eskridge. February 1985. "The Rhetoric of Police Professionalism." *Police Chief* 26-29.

Weiner, N.L. 1976. "The Educated Policeman." *Journal of Police Science and Administration.* 4: 450-458.

Weiner, Normal L. 1974. "The Effects of Education on Police Attitudes." *Journal of Criminal Justice.* 2(4): 317-323.

Weirman, C.M. August 1978. "Variances of Ability Measurement Scores Obtained by College and Non-College Educated Troopers." *Police Chief* 45: 34-36.

Wilson, J.Q. 1975. *Thinking About Crime.* New York: Basic Books.

Wycoff, Mary Ann. June 1987. "New 'Yes Person' Managers." *Police Manager: Newsletter of the Police Management Association* 2(3): 18.

Wycoff, Mary Ann and Charles E. Susmilch. 1979. "The Relevance of College Education for Policing: Continuing the Dialogue" in Peterson, D.M. (ed.), *Police Work: Strategies and Outcomes in Law Enforcement.* Beverly Hills, CA: Sage.

The Recruitment and Selection of Visible Minorities in Canadian Police Organizations, 1985-1987

Harish C. Jain

Introduction

Federal Initiatives

Since 1971 Canada has had a national multicultural policy,[1] intended to be both a social and cultural policy for all Canadians. However, the focus of program delivery until the late 1970s was largely on cultural retention.[2] The social policy aspects, such as removal of barriers to the full participation of all Canadians, especially participation by increasing numbers of immigrants from third world countries, and native-born non-white Canadians, were largely ignored.[3] By 1981 increasing levels of racism and discrimination against non-whites led to initiatives designed to promote institutional change and to increase public understanding and acceptance of the multicultural reality of Canada. The federal government established a race relations unit in the Multiculturalism Directorate of the Department of the Secretary of State and the directorate's funding was increased considerably. As Bowie has indicated, this ushered in a new era of multiculturalism as an advocate ministry.[4]

At the present time, multiculturalsim has become mere than a federal government policy. It was enshrined in the 1982 Constitutions Act as part of the Canadian Charter of Rights and Freedoms.[5] The federal government also brought in the Employment Equity Act and the federal Contractors Program in 1986. The act requires federally regulated employers with 100 or more employees to provide improved access to employment opportunity for four target groups: women, visible minorities, the disabled and Aboriginal peoples.[6] The federal Contractors Program affects employers with 100 or more employees who bid on federal contracts for goods and services worth $200,000 or more.[7] In addition, the federal government, through the Treasury Board, has undertaken affirmative action (or employment equity) measures for the public Service of Canada. Numerical goals have been established for all four target groups.

In December 1987 the federal government introduced the Canadian Multiculturalism Act. This legislation would set up a ministry, a program and an advisory council to the minister. It would provide for the tabling of an annual report by the minister to the Parliament, a review of the act and an annual report by the Parliamentary Standing Committee on Multiculturalism and a co-ordinating responsibility to the minister for the implementation of multicultural policy on the part of all government institutions.[8]

Provincial Initiatives

Multiculturalism is not restricted to the federal or other levels of the government. A 1985 poll conducted by Environics found that eighty-one per cent of the people polled perceived Canada as a multicultural society.[9] All provinces have human rights codes which prohibit discrimination in employment, housing and services on the basis of race, colour, origin and religion, etc. All jurisdictions are covered by the Canadian Charter of Rights and Freedoms. Six provinces have formal multicultural policies: Saskatchewan has had a Multiculturalism Act since 1974 and four other provinces have legislation that relates to multiculturalism to varying degrees. Five provinces have cabinet committees relating to multiculturalism and one has a senior interdepartmental committee. However, as the parliamentary standing committee on multiculturalism has noted. no province has a minister or department designated solely for multiculturalism.[10]

Like the federal government, several provinces have taken initiatives to provide for equality of opportunities for racial minorities. For instance, Ontario has a race relations directorate within the Ministry of Citizenship and has included visible minorities (non-whites) in its employment equity program for the civil service. Ontario's new minister of citizenship, in his role as chairman of the Cabinet Committee on Race Relations, has been assigned the duty of co-ordinating government-wide race relations and multiculturalism initiatives, such as the provincial task force on access of visible minorities and others to Ontario professions and trades, in order to determine whether qualifications obtained abroad are being adequately recognized by professional and trade associations in Ontario.[11]

Visible minorities have also been included in employment equity programs for civil service in Manitoba and Nova Scotia, as well as in public and private sector programs in Quebec.[12]

Municipal Initiatives

At the municipal level, numerous cities have formed race relations or multiculturalism advisory committees to the mayor or city councils.[13] At its annual meeting in 1986, the Federation of Canadian Municipalities (FCM) adopted a policy entitled "Improving Race Relations in Canadian Municipalities."[14] The FCM commissioned a survey of municipal activities in multiculturalism and race relations, sponsored a national symposium in 1986, and established a national action committee on race relations in 1987. Through these activities, the FCM hopes to make municipal leaders and community leaders aware of the need to develop policies and programs in race relations at the local level. Some municipalities, such as the City of Toronto and Vancouver, have been proactive in promoting race relations for some time. At the Toronto City Hall, for instance, the visible minority proportion of the work force has moved "from a minuscule proportion in the early 1980s to ten per cent today," according to Kilbourn.[15] Kilbourn goes on to point out that in March 1988 city hall departments "will set hiring goals for visible minorities that range as high as twenty-one per cent in some cases."

Initiatives by Police Organizations

It is within the above described policy contexts, at the three levels of government, that police organizations' initiatives affecting recruitment and selection of visible minorities can best be analysed.[16] The first major initiative was launched by the federal multiculturalism Directorate in October 1984 in the form of a national symposium on policing in multicultural/multiracial urban communities in Vancouver. The symposium was attended by police chiefs, visible minority representatives and government officials. Following the symposium, a National Police Multiculturalism Liaison Standing Committee consisting of visible minority community leaders and selected police chiefs was established under the auspices of the Canadian Association of Chiefs of Police (CACP), funded by the government. The committee's role was to work with the CACP membership to implement major recommendations from the symposium aimed at increasing the number of visible minorities in police forces, improving cross-cultural training for police, and promoting liaison between ethnic and visible minority communities and the police.[17] The committee was established in 1986.

Following the symposium, CACP commissioned a survey of recruitment and selection of visible minorities in selected Canadian police organizations in 1985. The study was funded by Multiculturalism Canada. At the same time, several police organizations had started proactive programs to recruit visible minorities. These included the Metropolitan Toronto and the Montreal Urban Community police organizations. The Royal Canadian Mounted Police had for quite some time mounted special programs to recruit females and aboriginals, and had developed and implemented cross-cultural education courses beginning in 1976. In 1987 the RCMP announced a new national recruiting team to attract visible minorities and others to the RCMP.[18] In January 1988 Commissioner Inkster announced several initiatives, including a survey of all members of the RCMP, an examination of systemic barriers to the entry of visible and other minorities to the force, and enhancement of the cross-cultural training for all members of the RCMP, with special consideration for those involved in recruiting, interviewing, instructing and supervising new members.[19] In addition, the Commissioner recently announced that the number of visible minority police officers will increase from the estimated one per cent at present to five per cent in fifteen years.[20]

The Importance of Visible Minority Recruitment and Selection

Police are frequently the only front-line public officials with whom many citizens are likely to interact.[21] This is especially so in the case of non-whites, including recent third world immigrants. All too often they perceive police as insensitive and vested with far-reaching and oppressive powers. Police, on the other hand, proclaim their commitment to non-discriminatory law enforcement, contending that their efforts are unappreciated and their motives misunderstood. Irrespective of where the truth lies, it is important to realize that police attitudes and behaviour are crucial to better community relations. Therefore, in an increasingly multicultural and multiracial society, police have a very special role, which requires that they have a workforce which reflects the ethno-cultural make-up of the communities they serve in all its diversity. Therefore, in the interests of employment equity and social justice, society must ensure the participation of various racial and ethnic groups who until now, because of history and systemic job barriers, have had little place in police organizations across Canada. This is not necessarily incompatible with the recruitment of high-quality individuals into police organizations.[22]

The 1987 Study

This study is an update of the 1985 survey of visible minority recruitment and selection policies in fourteen police organizations across Canada.[23] The study has three principal aims: to examine the impact of police staffing policies on the recruitment of visible minorities; to make recommendations with a view to increasing the representation of visible minorities in Canadian police organizations; and to assist the Canadian Association of Chiefs of Police in their efforts to improve race relations within their member police organizations.

Visible minorities comprise close to two million people or approximately seven per cent of the country's population. They represent more than 4.5 per cent of the Canadian labour force according to the 1981 census. Visible minorities consist of nine non-white groups: Chinese, Black, Indo-Pakistani, West Asian or Arab, Filipino, Japanese, Southeast Asian, Korean and Oceanic.[24]

The police organizations in the 1987 study co-operated willingly in completing a comprehensive questionnaire, and several selected police representatives allowed themselves to be interviewed for the project.[25] The participating police organizations were: the RCMP, Vancouver Police Department, Edmonton Police Department, Calgary Police Department, Regina Police Service, City of Winnipeg Police, Metropolitan Toronto Police, Ottawa Police Force, Ontario Provincial Police (OPP), Montreal Urban Community (MUC), Quebec Police Force (QPF), St. Hubert Police, Moncton Police Force and the Halifax Police Department.

Representation of Visible Minorities in Canadian Police Organizations

The representation of visible minority police officers ranged from zero to 3.4 per cent of all the police officers in ten of the fourteen police organizations covered by the study (see Table 1). Four police organizations did not keep records of the distribution of police officers by visible minority police status. Nine of the remaining ten organizations had some visible minority police officers. Three of the police organizations had between approximately two to 3.4 per cent visible minority police officers. These were Metropolitan Toronto (3.4 per cent), Vancouver (2.3 per cent) and Halifax (1.9 percent).

Table 1. Availability of Visible Minorities in the Labour Market, Aged Fifteen Years and over and Visible Minority Representation in Police Forces in 1985 and 1987.

Police Force	Visible Minorities				Area	%
	1985		**1987**			
	% **Men**	% **Women**	% **Men**	% **Women**		
RCMP	N/S	N/S	N/S	N/S	Canada	4.3
Vancouver	1.2	.2	2.1	.2	Vancouver	12.6
Edmonton	N/S	N/S	.7	-	Edmonton	6.9
Calgary	.7	.1	.4	.2	Calgary	7.3
Regina	.3	0	.6		Regina	2.9
Winnipeg	.2	0	N/S	N/S	Winnipeg	5.2
Toronto	2.7		3	.04	Toronto	12.1
(men and women)						
Ottawa	.3	0	.3	N/S	Ottawa/Hull	4.6
OPP	0	0	N/S	N/S	Ontario	5.7
Montreal	.1	0	.3		Montreal	4.7
QPF	N/A	N/A	N/A	N/A	Quebec	2.3
Moncton	0	0	.07		New Brunswick	0.6
Halifax	1.9		1.9		Halifax	3.1
St. Hubert	0	0	0	0	St. Hubert	N/A

Source: *Availability of Visible Minorities in the Canadian Labour Market.* (Ottawa: Public Service Commission of Canada, December, 1986).
N/S=not supplied
N/A=not available

Several organizations had increased the number of visible minority officers from 1985 to 1987. Montreal (MUC) had increased from five to fifteen; Toronto from 143 to 157; Vancouver from sixteen to twenty-four and Regina from one to two. Halifax and the Ottawa police organizations maintained their 1985 strengths of five and two respectively. Overall, some improvement in the recruitment of visible minority police officers was evident.

Five of the eight police organizations had visible minority police officers above the rank of constable. Metropolitan Toronto had the following ratios of visible minorities to non-visible minority offices as of October 1986: constable, 134 to 3,849; sergeants, seventeen to 899; staff sergeants, five to 278; inspectors, one to thirty-seven. The remaining ranks were all non-visible minorities. As of February, 1987, MUC had thirteen to 3,197 constables, and two to 569 sergeant detectives. Vancouver had twenty-two to 707 constables, one to fifty-three corporals, and one to twenty-eight staff sergeants. Edmonton had seven to 785 constables and one to 240 sergeants in early 1987. Calgary promoted one black officer, in April 1987, above the rank of constable.

Almost all the visible minority police officers were males. Female visible minority police officers were employed by four police organizations at the constable rank. As of February, 1987, Metropolitan Toronto had six female visible minority officers, Calgary and Vancouver had two, and Edmonton one.[26]

As Table 1 indicates, most police organizations have some distance to travel before they approach the representation of visible minorities in the labour markets of their respective jurisdictions.[27]

Recruitment

Recruitment is designed to locate, identify and attract individuals who have the basic skills, personal characteristics and motivation to become successful employees. Effective recruitment programs ensure a pool of potential employees in order to meet an organization's requirements. In recent years, societal pressures and human rights legislation have affected the recruitment process. As a result, employers have had to go out and actively seek job applicants from groups of people, such as racial minorities, who might not otherwise apply for employment because they have been denied such employment in the past. For instance, organizations cannot fill their recruiting needs solely through walk-in candidates or word-of-mouth referrals by friends or relatives on their payroll.

As Table 2 indicates, there was little change in the recruitment sources used by the organizations from 1985 to 1987. While thirteen of the fourteen police organizations recruited through high schools in 1985, this had dropped to eleven organizations in 1987. The remaining sources of recruitment are used by exactly the same number of police organizations in both 1985 and 1987. Eleven recruited through walk-ins and personal contact with police organizations and ten and nine respectively through newspapers and employee referrals in both 1985 and 1987. High schools, walk-ins and employee referrals are traditional channels of recruitment that tend to perpetuate the existing make-up of police organizations which is exclusively or predominantly white.[28] The employee referral and walk-in applicants approach relies on employees or police officers' contacts with family and friends. Naturally, employees are going to tell members of their own race of job openings. Since visible minorities are not well represented on most police organizations in Canada, the word-of-mouth approach tends to exclude them.

Visible minorities may not apply to police organizations because of artificial barriers, prejudice and the "chill factor," a phrase used to describe the lack of visible minorities as police officers.

Table 2. Recruitment Practices of Selected Canadian Police Organizations, 1985 and 1987.

	1985		1987	
Recruitment Sources	**No.**	**%**	**No.**	**%**
High schools	13	93	11	79
Walk-ins and personal contact with police organizations	11	79	11	79
Newspapers, recruitment brochures, etc.	10	71	10	71
Employee referrals	9	64	9	64

Walk-ins was cited most frequently (by ten or seventy-two per cent organizations) as being successful in generating candidates in 1985.

The other side of the story is that visible minorities may not apply to police organizations because of inadequate understanding of the police role. The police may be perceived as a repressive force of the state and the white status quo. There may, therefore, be a lack of natural enthusiasm and desire on the part of some visible minorities to enter the profession of policing.

Chief Cohoon of the Moncton police organization has noted that the Atlantic region and his police organizations, in particular, do not follow the employee referral procedure described above. Chief Cohoon states that most police organizations in New Brunswick, Nova Scotia and Prince Edward Island recruit "primarily directly from the APA [Atlantic Police Academy], and APA cadets usually make application to police organizations of their choice just prior to their cadet graduation."[29]

Whatever the reasons for lack of applications from visible minority applicants in most police organizations, the walk-ins and employee referral approach should be made supplementary to a more open process of recruitment to attract visible minority candidates, such as an outreach program. There is evidence that several police organizations have been using such an approach, and at least two of these forces, Montreal and Toronto, have met with some success. For instance, in Metro Toronto, from January to April 1987, 13.5 per cent (144 of 1,066) of all applicants for cadet and constable positions were visible minorities. Inspector Young of the Metropolitan Toronto organization attributes the success in hiring visible minorities to focused recruiting. Such a policy can work in communities such as Toronto which have a high mix of visible minorities, can use visible minority role models such as Chinese police officers in the Chinese community, and which have visible minority community leaders and both visible minority and non-visible minority church leaders.

Table 3. Strategies Used by Police Organizations to Recruit Visible Minority Police Officers in 1985 and 1987.

	1985		1987	
	No.	%	No.	%
Visible minority group presentation	6	43	7	50
Police officers with visible minority contacts	6	43	7	50
Visible minority role models	3	21	6	43
Trained recruiters	4	29	6	43
High school presentations with visible minority role models	4	29	4	29
Asking high school teachers etc. to identify visible minority candidates	1	7	3	21

As shown in Table 3, more police organizations were using outreach recruiting sources to attract visible minority applicants in 1987 than in

1985. For instance, six organizations were using both visible minority role models and trained recruiters in 1987 compared to three using the former and four using the latter in 1985. The technique of visible minority group presentations and police officers with visible minority contacts was being utilized by seven police organizations in 1987 relative to six in 1985. The data on success of these sources in attracting and hiring visible minority applicant are unavailable. These data would be most helpful in directing police efforts in the right direction, as indicated by the experience of the Montreal and Metropolitan police organizations.

Selection

Human rights statutes in all jurisdictions across Canada prohibit discrimination on the basis of race, religion, colour, national or ethnic origin, marital status and age. Age groups protected vary among jurisdictions, with the most common being between the ages of eighteen to sixty-five and forty-five to sixty-five. Other prohibited grounds are also included, depending on the jurisdiction. These statutes put the burden on the employer to prove that, in case of a valid complaint, hiring standards such as height, weight, cut-off scores on tests, age, etc., are reliable and valid or job-related. Human rights tribunals and courts have ruled that any requirement that has a disproportionate effect on minority group applicants is illegal, unless it is related to job success or business necessity.

The selection process among the fourteen police organizations in this survey in both 1985 and 1987 consisted of basic minimum mandatory requirements and a multiple-hurdles approach. As Table 4 indicates, the most common minimum standards related to age, educational level, citizenship status, physical and medical fitness, a valid driver's licence, visual acuity, and/or vision and height and weight standards (in most police organizations).

Once the minimum standards were satisfied, a multiple-hurdles procedure was followed. As indicated in Table 5, this consisted of completed application forms, interviews, physical fitness and medical examinations, character reference checks, background investigation, fingerprint check and performance during recruit's training and probationary period. Several organizations used police officer selection tests, English/French language tests (spelling, grammar, essays), personality and polygraph tests. Only two organizations used the assessment centre method.

As is evident from Table 5, almost all the police organizations used the same selection standards in 1987 as in 1985. The only important changes were in the use of polygraph tests and the officer selection test. The officer selection test was dropped by three organizations, while the polygraph test was not used by two additional organizations.

Dress Code

At the time of the last study in 1985, only the Edmonton police organization allowed for the wearing of a turban. Two additional police organizations have since changed their policy and were allowing the followers of the Sikh faith to wear turbans as a part of the police officer's uniform. These were the Metropolitan Toronto and the Ottawa Police organizations. Nine organizations allowed the wearing of a beard; four of these organizations allowed beards only under special circumstances, such as the officer being a member of the Sikh religion or on special assignment. Several police organizations are legally prohibited from changing the dress code.

Table 4. Minimum Mandatory Qualifications for a Constable's Job in Fourteen Selected Canadian Police Organizations, 1985 and 1987.

	1985		1987	
	No.	%	No.	%
Age	14 (18-21 years, to less than 30 or 35 years, in some organizations).	100	13	93
Education	14 (grade 12 or equivalent in most cases).	100	14	100
Citizenship status	12	86	14	100
Physical and medical fitness	14	100	14	100
A valid driver's licence	14	100	14	100
Visual acuity/vision	10	71	14	100
Height and weight*	8	57	12	86

*Most police organizations require weight commensurate to height. Only three police organizations specified male and female standards as well as age limits in both 1985 and 1987.

Table 5. Selection Methods Used by Fourteen Selected Canadian Police Organizations, 1985 and 1987.

	1985		1987	
	No.	%	No.	%
Applicant forms	14	100	14	100
Interviews	14	100	14	100
Psychological tests:				
A. intelligence and aptitude tests	9	64	8	57
B. personality tests	9	64	10	71
Reference checks	14	100	14	100
Background investigation	14	100	14	100
Fingerprint check	14	100	13	93
Officer selection test	11	79	8	57
English/French tests	9	64	9	64
Polygraph tests	6	43	4	29

The Job Interview

The interview is the most widely used of all selection techniques. Several studies have reported that interviews were the most important aspects of the selection process, and that ninety per cent of all organizations surveyed had more confidence in interviews than any other sources of selection information.[30] The popularity of interviews stems from their flexibility and adaptability to managerial, professional and other types of employees. They can disclose information that other techniques cannot, such as the candidates' ability to express themselves verbally, their social assurance and adeptness, their manner of self-presentation and enthusiasm. Thus, interviews provide useful information on several observable interpersonal dimensions of behaviour. Interviews also allow the organization to expose job candidates to accurate information about the job, which might help create realistic job expectations for the candidates. Interviews are also perhaps the only way that a personal contact can be made prior to the selection decision and can be used for accomplishing objectives unrelated to the selection decision, such as selling the candidate on the job and for public relations purposes.[31]

Interviews have serious shortcomings, however. Several reviews of the literature have revealed that the interview has relatively low reliability (that is, different interviewers come to quite disparate conclusions) and low validity (that is, interview ratings and job performance scores are not closely related). A recent positive development, however, is that structured interviews improve predictive validity relative to unstructured interviews.[32]

Several studies have found that job applicants are more likely to be hired if they look straight ahead rather than down. People who look the interviewer straight in the eye are rated as being confident, responsible and having more initiative. As well, applicants who demonstrate a greater amount of eye contact, head moving, smiling and other non-verbal behaviours are rated higher than applicants who do not.[33]

Each of the factors in non-verbal communication[34] such as facial expression, body gesture, eye contact, gesture and such things as hesitations in speech and the tone and volume of our voice, is culturally determined. Therefore, these findings have severe implications for visible minority men and women, especially recent immigrants from third world countries.

Performance in selection interviews was considered to be extremely important for job applicants by several police organizations. In the present study, two police organizations assigned 100 per cent weight to interviews in the overall selection decision; two organizations allotted eighty or up to eighty per cent; four organizations allocated sixty per cent; an additional three assigned forty per cent. Thus, eleven of the fourteen organizations considered selection interviews to be extremely important in the overall selection decision and assigned anywhere from forty to 100 per cent weight.

Twelve organizations conducted more than one job interview; seven organizations interviewed each candidate twice while four did three interviews and one conducted three to four interviews. Ten organizations had structured interviews, but only seven of these ten organizations scored the interviews. Only two organizations had visible minority job interviewers, and interview scores were not broken down by minority status by any of the police organizations. No validity data were kept to relate scores on job interviews to subsequent job performance by any of the organizations.

As suggested earlier, while interviews provide useful information on some behavioural dimensions, and the structured interviews have good predictive validity, they have relatively low reliability and validity and do not contribute significantly to the interviewer's decision to hire or to reject. Interviews are subjective and therefore susceptible to the covert prejudices of individual interviewers.

In our view, performance in interviews should not be considered to be the "make or break point" for applicants. Interviews should be used by police organizations as one of several selection techniques, but the number of points allocated to them should be reduced considerably and interviewers should not be allowed to make hiring or rejection decisions.[35] Every effort should be made to collect data on reliability and validity of the interviews. For instance, since most of the organizations conducted several interviews, they should collect data on inter-rater reliability. In order to reduce the possible discriminatory effects of oral interviews upon visible minorities and others, police organizations should carefully structure the interviews. The questions should be based on formal job analytic information, and every attempt should be made to maximize the reliability of the structured interview by scoring them. Structured interviews have more face validity and might be more acceptable to courts and human rights policy-makers. Interviewers should be trained and their hiring recommendations should be monitored to determine whether individual interviewers are rejecting a disproportionate number of minorities.

Age, Height and Weight Standards

Preference for various ages, height and weight standards or award of differing numbers of points for various ages or weight and height standards as selection criteria can be discriminatory when they result in the exclusion of a disproportionate number of visible minorities and other groups of applicants. A study was conducted in the United States by the Police Foundation and the International Association of Chiefs of Police in co-operation with the Urban Institute, to determine if there was a correlation between the height and performance of police officers in several police organizations. Findings indicated that height differences generally had no statistically significant effect on police performance.[36]

In the case of Ann Colfer against Ottawa Police Commission, a board of inquiry decided that the commission's minimum height and weight requirements had an adverse effect upon the number of females hired relative to males. Therefore the height and weight requirements were declared illegal since these were not related to successful job performance. Ottawa's was not the only case: numerous other boards of inquiry and courts have rendered similar decisions.[37] For instance, the RCMP modified its height and weight requirements after an Oriental complained to the Canadian Human Rights Commission.

In both 1985 and 1987 the age requirements ranged from a minimum of eighteen to thirty-five in thirteen of the fourteen police organizations. In 1985, eight police organizations had height and weight standards. In 1987, three police organizations specified height and weight standards (5'8" and 150 lbs. for men, and 5'4" and 120 lbs. for women). Another police organization had a system of point allocation. No points were awarded to candidates who were older than thirty-five years of age and under 5'8". Several police organizations had a standard of weight commensurate with height.

One large police organization, the Quebec Police Force, has replaced height and weight standards with a physical aptitude test since the last study. Several other organizations were considering the possible elimination of height and weight standards. In some cases, the provincial legislation prescribed the minimum height and/or weight standards. At least two police organizations had initiated physical fitness testing.

In our view, age and weight need not be used as a proxy measure of fitness. These standards should be replaced with a physical fitness test and medical examination. This is because the burden of showing job-relatedness of an employment selection device such as height, weight and age cannot be carried by the assertion of an obvious but unmeasured relationship between a selection standard and job performance. It is essential that the selection devices be validated by professionally accepted methods. The fact that several police organizations are able to select police officers successfully without specific height requirements makes it difficult for other organizations that retain specific height requirements to justify their use as necessity.[38]

Preference for various ages or differing numbers of points for various ages and heights and weights without these being bona fide occupational qualifications may be contrary to both the human rights statutes and the equality clause in the Canadian Charter of Rights and Freedoms.

Conclusions and Recommendations

Several general conclusions can be drawn from this study. First, there has been some improvement in the recruitment of visible minority police officers in at least five police organizations since the 1985 study. As the availability figures indicate, however, police organizations have some distance to travel before they approach the representation of visible minorities in their respective communities. This would require constant vigilance on the part of visible minority communities and a continuous dialogue between the police organizations and visible minority organizations so that the chilling effect could be reduced or eliminated. Moreover, police organizations would have to use proactive recruitment methods. In this respect, the community outreach method used by the Montreal and Metropolitan Toronto police organizations may be worth emulating.

Secondly, policy-making at the federal, provincial and police commission levels would have to examine the police legislation in their respective jurisdictions[39] with a view to amending the provisions of these laws in order to bring them into compliance with the Canadian Charter of Rights and Freedoms and the human rights statutes. This is especially true with respect to provisions pertaining to dress code, age and height and weight standards. These standards can and do have an adverse impact on members of visible minority groups and do not appear to be job-related.

Thirdly, police organizations need to review their selection policies in order to make them job-related and to avoid disproportionate impact on visible minorities. This is especially true in the case of job interviews, psychological tests and the like. Job interviews should be structured, scored and related to subsequent job performance; points allocated to interviews should be considerably reduced.[40] Psychological tests can also have adverse impact on minorities. In *ATF* v. *CN* (1984)[41] a Canadian human rights tribunal struck down use of the Bennett Mechanical Comprehension Test for selection into several entry-level positions because the test had a discriminatory impact on women. Issues of employment test reliability, validity, bias and fairness are of great concern to human rights commissions and the courts. As Cronshaw points out, work is required to assess the suitability of selection tests developed in other countries for Canadian use on minorities such as single group/differential validity of employment tests for groups protected by human rights legislation.[42] The use of the Minnesota Multiphasic Personality Inventory Test, for example, by several police organizations requires close scrutiny.

Finally, the RCMP, the OPP, the Winnipeg police organization and the QPF should be required to collect data on visible minority police officers. For instance, the RCMP operates Canada-wide, and its influence is pervasive.[43] It must collect data on visible minority officers and adopt policies to increase the representation of visible minority officers in order to perform its role effectively.

Mechanisms Needed within Police Organizations to Insure Equitable Employment

First, police organizations, especially large ones as in Toronto, Vancouver and Montreal and including the RCMP, the OPP and the QPF need to monitor their recruitment and selection procedures to ensure that no systemic discrimination exists at any step of the recruitment and selection process. For instance, each police organization can examine the track record of each recruitment source being used to attract and to retain minority and non-minority candidates. Similarly, data can be collected on the rejection and success rate of each of the selection procedures being used in order to determine whether a disproportionate number of minority candidates relative to non-minority candidates are being rejected. Secondly, police organizations can use independent experts to review their recruitment and selection programs to ensure that no adverse impact exists in order to recruit visible and other minorities. In order to obtain funding to conduct such reviews, police organizations can approach federal, provincial and municipal governments, as the Metropolitan Toronto police organization has done. Thirdly, those police organizations that do not have data available on the visible minortuiy composition of their officers can obtain funding from the Canada Employment Immigration Commission to conduct a self-identification survey of their civilian and sworn officers, as the Hamilton-Wentworth Regional Police has done. Fourthly, police organizations need to be proactive in recruitment and selection of minority candidates and not rely exclusively on visible minorities to knock at their doors.

Steps Needed by Police Organizations to Ensure Job-Relatedness of Their Selection Policies

Police organizations either need to hire or obtain outside expertise in order to ensure that their selection instruments are reliable. Industrial psychologists, in particular, have expertise in this area and both the American Psychological Association and the Canadian Psychological Association have issues guidelines for employee testing. It is important that police organizations use only those selection methods that are both reliable and job-related or valid. This is important in order to withstand legal scrutiny in case of a charge of discrimination by minorities. Even more important is the fact that reliable and valid selection instruments or procedures can save money to an organization, are legally defensible, and are normally approved by both minority and non-minority candidates since they are job-related.

Mechanisms to monitor police organizations progress towards employment equity

The community at large has an interest in ensuring that police organizations reflect the multi-racial nature of the society. To this end, it is important to monitor the progress that police organizations make towards employment equity. One mechanism is to lobby provincial governments to appoint visible minorities to police commissions at the local community level and the provincial level. A second strategy might be to urge police organizations, through chiefs of police, to report regularly to local race relations committees or police-minority advisory committees on the progress of police organizations are making towards employment equity. This is already in Winnipeg, Vancouver, Toronto and Hamilton. Another strategy is to lobby the federal and provincial governments to put pressure on the CACP and its provincial counterparts to ensure that it encourages its member police organizations to continue employment equity initiatives by holding federal and provincial symposiums such as the 1984 national symposium and the Ontario symposium in the fall of 1988; and by providing "success" models to other police organizations that have either not started or are hesitating, to undertake employment equity programs.

Endnotes

1   The policy, endorsed by all the political parties, accepted the linguistic duality of Canadian Society. See *The Place of Multiculturalism in Canada's Long-term Economic Development.* A Brief by the Minister of State of Multiculturalism submitted to the Macdonald Commission (Ottawa: Multiculturalism Directorate, 15 November, 1983).

2   The policy was widely criticized by the media and minorities for its "song and dance" approach. Breton, in his recent study for the Macdonald Commission, has noted the policy's deficiencies as degrading the value of cultural diversity and its contribution to Canadian society. See Raymond Breton, *"Multiculturalism and Canadian Nation Building,"* in *The Politics of Gender, Ethnicity and Language in Canada,* edited by Alan Cairns and Cynthia Williams (Toronto: University of Toronto Press, 1986, for the Royal Commission on the Economic Union and Development Prospects for Canada).

3   In 1967 the federal government made changes to the Immigration Act which removed discriminatory barriers (that is, racially based restrictions) and dramatically increased the arrival of Asian and Caribbean immigrants, beginning in the late 1970s. See Rosalie Abella, *Equality in Employment: A Royal Commission Report* (Ottawa: Minister of Supply and Services, October, 1984) and the Daudlin Report, *Equality Now!* Report of the Parliamentary Committee on Visible Minorities, Ottawa, House of Commons, March, 1984.

4   Douglas Bowie, "Notes for an address," Multiculturalism Canada, Ottawa, 16 November, 1985.

5   Section 15(1) of the Charter states that "every individual is equal before and under the law and has the right to the equal protection and equal benefit of the law without discrimination based on race, colour, relgion, sex, age or mental or physical disability." Section 27 states that the Charter will be interpreted in a manner consistent with the preservation and enhancement of the multicultural heritage of Canadians. In addition to the Charter, the Candian Human Rights Act provides legal safeguards against discrimination based on race, origin or religion, and other grounds. However, unlike the Charter, the act applies only to employers under federal juris-

diction, covering ten per cent of the labour force in Canada. Human rights codes exist in all other jurisdictions and provide similar protection against discrimination based on race, origin, colour or religion.

6   The law requries that employers prepare annual reports for submission to the Canada Employment and Immigration Commission (CEIC), beginning June 1988. These reports must include information on geographic location, industrial sector and employment status. In addition to the annual report, employers are also required to develop an employment equity (affirmative action) plan and retain it for at least three years.

7   The program requires that the contractors sign a Certificate of Commitment to design and carry out an employment equity program which meets eleven specified criteria. Failure to implement employment equity does not result in the cancellation of the contract but excludes the contractor from future government business.

8   The proposed act has been criticized for ignoring two major recommendations of the parliamentary standing committee on multiculturalism, contained in its June 1987 report *Multiculturalism: Building the Canadian Mosaic*. These were the establishment of a full department of multiculturalism to oversee multicultural issues and programs and a commissioner of multiculturalism with powers like those of the Commissioner of Official Languages, in order to monitor progress under the act. See "Multicultural Bill Raked in Commons," *Hamilton Spectator*, 19 March 1988, p. B5.

9   Bowie, "Notes for an address."

10 See *Multiculturalism: Building the Canadian Mosaic* (Ottawa: Report of the Standin Committee on Multiculturalism, June, 1987). Ontario, however, may be the exception to this rule. As of fall 1987, Ontario has a Minister of Citizenship and another Minister for Culture and Communications. The Minister of Citizenship is also the minister responsible for race relations and the Ontario Human Rights Commission. In addition, the minister chairs the cabinet committee on race relations.

11 Gerry Phillips, "Notes for Remarks" by the Minister of Citizenship to the reception celebrating multicultural heritage, 16 February, 1988, Toronto.

12 Harish C. Jain. "Affirmative Action/Employment Equity and Racial Minorities in Canada: Issues and Policies," background paper for the Conference on Canada 2000: Race Relations and Public Policy, Ottawa, Carleton University, 30 October to 1 November, 1987.

13 Judith Mastai, "A Report to the Federation of Canadian Municipalities on Municipal Initiatives for Improving Race Relations in Canada." Ottawa: National Symposium on Multiculturalism and Race Relations, 14-15 February, 1986.

14 *Multiculturalism: Building the Canadian Mosaic.*

15 William Kilbourn, "The Changing of the Guard," *Toronto,* 1988, March, p. 69.

16 In Canada, there are three main types of police organizations: the federal police (the RCMP), the provincial police and the municipal police organizations. The municipal and the provincial police organizations enforce municipal by-laws and provincial laws respectively. The RCMP enforces federal laws in all ten provinces and the two territories. Ontario and Quebec are the only two provinces that have provincial police organizations. In all other provinces, the RCMP acts as the provincial police under federal-provincial contracts, and also as the police of some urban areas under federal-provincial and Federal-provincial-municipal contracts. See J.J. Juliani, C.K.

Talbot and C.H.S. Jayewardene, Urban Centurions: A Development Perspective of Municipal Policing in Canada (Ottawa: Crimcare Inc., 1984).

17   Jack Murta, in Report of Proceedings of the Symposium on Policing in Multicultural Multiracial Urban Communities (Ottawa: Multiculturalism Canada, 1984). The 1984 symposium also recommend that provincial symposia should be held bringing together police chiefs, racial and ethnic minority representatives and government officials. One such symposium took place in Vancouver in January 1988. The Ontario Symposium, funded by the Ministry of the Solicitor General, took place in October 1988.

18   Commissioner's 1987 Directional Statement (Ottawa: RCMP, 1987).

19   Norman Inkster, "Multiculturalism and Policing," speech to the B.C. Conference on Policing, Vancouver, January, 1988.

20   "Mountie recruiters on trail of more visible minorities," Globe and Mail, 29 March, 1988, p. A-10. The five per cent over fifteen years estimates were supplied to the author by a spokesperson for the RCMP.

21   It is estimated that 80 percent of calls for police service are for non-crime related activities. Police officers deal with the effects of familly upheaval, racial discord, youth unemployment and general states of isolation and alienation. Police, therefore, are both service and enforcement organizations. See Daniel Hill, "The Future of Policing in Multicultural and Multiracial Urban Communities in Canada," in Report of Proceedings of the Symposium on Policing in Multicultural/Multiracial Urban Communities (Ottawa: Multiculturalism Canada, 1984).

22   Reva Gerstein, et al., Report of the Task Force on the Racial and Ethnic Implications of Police Hiring, Training, Promotion and Career Development. Policing in Ontario for the Eighties: Perceptions and Reflections (Toronto: Solicitor General of Ontario, July, 1980).

23   Harish C. Jain, "Recruitment and Selection of Visible Minorities in Selected Canadian Police Organizations," in Mark Thompson, (ed.), Is There a New Canadian Industrial Relations? (Winnipeg: Canadian Industrial Relations Association Proceedings, 1986), pp. 174-89.

24   Availability of Visible Minorities in the Canadian Labour Market (Ottawa: Public Service Commission of Canada, December, 12986). The seven per cent estimate includes Native persons; see Equality Now!

25   The study was sponsored by the CACP and partially funded by the federal multiculturalism sector in the Department of the Secretary of State.

26   The latest information supplied by the CACP, subsequent to the survey; indicates that Edmonton had 1,082 police officers as of 1 December 1987. Of these, seventeen were visible minorities (eight being Native Indian and Métis). Calgary had twelve visible minority police officers in late 1987. The Metropolitan Toronto police organization had surpassed the goals set for 1987. In 1987, thirty-five visible minorities were hired. The RCMP has announced its intention, as noted earlier, to have the organization reflect the Canadian mosaic and has appointed a national recruiting team that will itself reflect this mosaic.

27   It should be noted, however, that there has been a dramatic influx of visible minorities in Canada beginning in the late 1970s. At the same time, some police organizations were caught by a hiring freeze during the early 1980s. Hence, the lack of hiring in general and of visible minorities in particular.

28   Harish C. Jain, *Anti-discriminatory Staffing Policies: Implications of Human Rights Legislation for Employers and Trade Unions* (Ottawa: Department of the Secretary of State, January, 1985).

29   Personal telephone conversation with Chief Cohoon, 8 May, 1987.

30   Steven Cronshaw, Carol Corriveau and Harish Jain, "A 16-Year Update on Managerial Recruitment and Selection in the Canadian Manufacturing Industry." See also, James W. Thacker and R. Julian Catteneo, "The Canadian Personnel Function: Status and Practices" in Thomas Stone (ed.), *Personnel and Human Resources*. Proceedings of the annual conference of the Administrative Sciences Association of Canada (Toronto, June, 1987), pp. 56-66; and William F. Glueck, *Personnel: A Diagnostic Approach* (Plano, Texas: Business Publications, Inc., 1982).

31   Jain, *Anti-discriminatory Staffing Policies.*

32   W.H. Wiesner and Steve Cronshaw, "A meta-analytic investigation of the impact of interview format and degree of structure on the validity of the employment interview," *Journal of Occupational Psychology* 61 (1988).

33   J.G. Amalfitano and N.C. Kalt, "Effects of eye contact on the evaluation of job applicants," *Journal of Employment Counselling* 14 (1977); and D.M. Young and E.G. Beier, "The Role of Application Non-Verbal Communication in the Employment Interview," *ibid.*

34   It has been estimated that more than sixty-five to seventy per cent of the meaning conveyed in a message during interviews is non-verbal. In fact, one of the reasons that non-verbal clues are so powerful is that in most cases interviewers are not aware of the cues as possible agents of impression formation. See J.D. Hatfield and R.D. Gatewood, "Nonverbal cues in the selection interview," *Personnel Administrator* (January, 1978).

35   Some police organizations have argued that their interviewers did not make hiring decisions but were authorized to reject candidates. In the case of one police department, at the last interview, recommendations were made to a review board of senior officers who could accept or reject the recommendation.

36   Cynthia Sulton and Roi D. Townsey, *A Progress Report on Women in Policing* (Washington, D.C.: Police Foundation, 1981).

37   Harish C. Jain, *Anti-discriminatory Staffing Policies.*

38   Cynthia Sulton and Roi D. Townsey, *op. cit.*

39   In several cases, including Quebec and Ontario, the provincial legislation (Police Act) sets the minimum standards. However, the municipal police organizations can and do set higher standards, as in the case of educational qualifications, etc.

40   Interviews should be used as one of the selection techniques. A final hiring decision should not be made on the basis of one or even several interviews but by combining all the information received from the other selection tools in addition to the interviews.

41   *Action Tracail Des Femmes* v. *Canadian National and Canadian Human Rights Commission*, 24 August 1984 (translation from French).

42   Steven Cronshaw, "The status of employment testing in Canada: A review and evaluation of theory and professional practice," *Canadian Psychology* 27 (1986), pp. 183-93.

43   A survey in 1980 revealed that more than sixty per cent of police officers in the public police services were employed by municipalities, 28,725 out of 47,499. In addition, more than twenty-five per cent of police officers employed by the RCMP were engaged in municipal policing, 2,609 out of 10,283; and 401 municipal police organizations were autonomous while 195 were RCMP-contracted. Thus, the RCMP provided almost half (48.6 per cent) of the municipal policing in Canada. There were no RCMP-contracted municipal organizations in Ontario and Quebec. The OPP with its 4,052 members polices those areas of Ontario which are not covered by municipal police organizations. There were 128 police organizations in Ontario, including the OPP in 1980. See Gerstein, *et al.*, *Report of the Task Force*.

The Physical and Psychological Correlates of Job Burnout in the Royal Canadian Mounted Police

Gerry M. Stearns and Robert J. Moore

Introduction

Stress has been a popular topic in the police literature since the 1970s and 1980s (Grier, 1982; Jackson and Maslach, 1982; Kankewitt, 1986; Lester, 1982; Lester and Gallagher, 1980; Loo, 1984, Loo, 1985; Stratton, 1984). A number of publications have focused on the sources of police stress (Ellison and Genz, 1978; Perrier and Toner, 1984; Stratton, 1984) while others have considered its possible consequences, such as job burnout (Jackson and Maslach, 1982), cynical and negative attitudes toward the public (Niederhoffer, 1967; Violanti and Marshall, 1983), conservative and authoritarian belief systems sometimes referred to as the "John Wayne Syndrome" (Chandler and Jones, 1979), frustrations with the criminal justice system (Ellison and Genz, 1978), and derogatory attitudes toward the human service professions (Adlam, 1982). There is also evidence in the literature to support the notion that police officers suffer moderate to high levels of job burnout (Colegrove, 1983; Jackson and Maslach, 1982; Stearns and Moore, 1990). Few studies, however, have integrated the correlates of job burnout in to a multivariate study of job burnout, particularly in Canadian police. In order to conduct such a study, a review of the literature was initially undertaken to identify some of the possible correlates of job burnout.

Demographic Characteristics

Maslach (1982) suggested that age, length of tenure in a helping profession, marital status and the sex of the respondent would be related to burnout scores; Colegrove (1983) studied such correlates and found that amount of police experience and age were significant predictors of scores on the Maslach Burnout Inventory (MBI) scale for *Emotional Exhaustion* in a sample of American policewomen. Contrary to Maslach's statement, Colegrove did not find significant relationships between burnout and marital status, presence or absence of children and level of education attained. Further research is needed to clarify the relationships between such demographic variables and burnout.

Attitudes

The presence of cynical (i.e., toward government, the criminal justice system, the public, social services) and authoritarian attitudes has been a fairly well established finding in the police literature (Adlam, 1982; Niederhoffer, 1967; Rafky, Lawley and Ingram, 1976; Regoli, 1976; Tifft, 1974). A number of theoretical perspectives on attitude development might apply to the origins of such attitudes in police. For example, more than four decades ago, sociologists began to use the concept of conformity to explain attitude formation, suggesting that people adapt their attitudes to be consistent with a particular reference group (Shibutani, 1955). More recently, it became popular to explain attitude development in terms of organizational culture and socialization (Niederhoffer, 1967; Regoli, 1976). In an alternative conceptualization, cynical and authoritarian attitudes are considered to be a form of coping with the demands of working in the helping professions (Maslach, 1979, 1982; Jackson and Maslach, 1982; Violanti and Marshall, 1983). The concept of job burnout, as initially used by Freudenberger in the 1970s (1974, 1975) and later extended by Maslach and Jackson (1981) refers to the development of cynicism or depersonalization as one dimension of job burnout.

Specifically referring to police, some authors have considered cynicism to be either serving a functional purpose, such as insulating the police from society (Niederhoffer, 1967; Tifft, 1974), or acting as an ineffective coping mechanism (Violanti and Marshall, 1983). Although cynicism is suspected of being related to the stressful nature of police work, empirical evidence of this relationship is necessary to determine if it is indeed another component of police officers' reactions to stress, i.e., an additional dimension of the burnout syndrome in police officers.

Other authors have implicated the "John Wayne Syndrome" in police, referring to authoritarian attitudes which include conservatism as one component (Genz and Lester, 1976; Varsos, 1970). Vastola (1978) and Violanti and Marshall (1983) considered the adoption of these attitudes to be yet another ineffective attempt at coping with the stresses of police work while Chandler and Jones (1979) described such attitudes as an "escape mechanism" for the police. Research focusing on the relationship between conservative and authoritarian attitudes, the role of police officers and job burnout is needed.

Personality Constructs

The literature addressing police personality has reported findings that might stimulate research into the investigation of job burnout. For example, Maslach (1982) found that those individuals who appear to be weak and unassertive, reserved and conventional and unable to express or control their emotions (e.g., hostility, fear, impatience, empathy) are more prone to burnout.

A measure indicating the individual's level of psychological adjustment (e.g., the MMPI *Ego Strength* scale) is another dimension that would be useful in job burnout research. According to Duckworth (1979), the *Ego-Strength* scale is one of the MMPI's best indicator of psychological health and a person's ability to "bounce" back from crises. It might be expected that, as a person suffers increased levels of burnout, he/she would experience lower levels of *Ego Strength.* Empirical validation of this hypothesis would provide useful information about job burnout and its effect on the psychological health of police.

Research on police personality has consistently found elevations on the MMPI *K* Scale (Klopsch, 1983; Nowicki, 1966). Originally, the *K* Scale was developed to serve as an indicator of defensiveness where high scores represent an attempt to present oneself in a positive light. Alternatively, in groups of individuals form higher socio-economic levels, high scores might suggest that their lives are running smoothly, i.e., in these cases the *K* Scale can be interpreted as an indicator of positive well-being. It is not entirely clear how the significantly elevated scores for the police should be interpreted; however, studying its correlates might clarify this point.

Health-related Concerns

In addition to the above variables being possible correlates of job burnout, a number of researchers have explored the existence of a relationship between job burnout and health-related concerns (e.g., headaches, hives, backaches); some have specifically investigated this relationship in police officers and have found stress to be related to high incidence of illness (Bergen and Bartol, 1983; Kreitner, Sova, Wood, Friedman and Reif, 1985; Vulcano, Barnes and Breen, 1984; Wood, Kreitner, Friedman, Edwards and Sova, 1982). Alcohol abuse, another health concern often associated with stress in general (Peyser, 1982), has been considered to be a problem for the police (Kankewitt, 1986; Stratton, 1984; Violanti, Marshall and Howe, 1985) and has been related to the stressful nature of police work (Violanti *et al.*, 1985).

Rationale

From the review of the literature, there appears to be considerable support for the notion that attitudes, personality and health concerns are all related to job burnout. Few empirical studies, however, have employed a multivariate approach in investigating the nature of the relationships among these variables. The present study investigated the correlates of job burnout in male and female Canadian police officers through a multivariate approach in an attempt to determine more fully the nature of the burnout syndrome.

Method

Measures

Job Burnout

To obtain a measure of job burnout, an adaptation of the Maslach Burnout Inventory (MBI) was employed. The MBI provides scores on a total of six sub-scales and has been used extensively in research on job burnout (Colegrove, 1983; Golembiewski and Munzenrider, 1981; Jackson and Maslach, 1982; Maslach, 1979). Although thoroughly researched norms have not been published, acceptable validity and reliability data have been offered (Maslach and Jackson, 1981).

The twenty-two-item MBI scale has been found to measure three dimensions of burnout. Each item (e.g., "I feel emotionally drained from my work") is answered twice, once for how often the feeling occurs (frequency) and once for how strongly (intensity). This format allows for each of the three burnout dimensions to be evaluated on frequency and intensity resulting in six sub-scales. *Emotional Exhaustion* Frequency and Intensity, *Depersonalization* Frequency and Intensity and *Personal Accomplishment* Frequency and Intensity. In addition past research (Golembiewski and Munzenrider, 1981) has indicated the utility of combining all the burnout items into a total burnout score.

Attitudes

Previously employed items measuring opinions about the law (e.g., "How much effort should be put into law enforcement?") and priorities for government spending (e.g., "How much effort should be put into health and medical care?"), cynicism (e.g., "Generally, those elected to Parliament soon lose touch with the people"), authoritarianism (e.g., "A few strong leaders would make this country better than all the laws and talk") and conservatism (e.g., "Unemployment is high these days because it is too easy to get welfare assistance") were adapted from Moore's (1985) research on Canadians' perceptions and evaluations of the law in the 1980s. Additional questions from this study assessing attitudes regarding interpersonal trust (e.g., "Most people would try to be fair"), happiness and life satisfaction were also included.

Personality Measures

The MMPI is the most frequently used instrument in the study of police personality (Murphy, 1972). The *Ego Strength, Psychology and Control* and *K* Scales of the MMPI were used in the present research because previous research supported their validity (Barron, 1956; Cuadra, 1956; Gottesman, 1959) and because research on police personality using these scales has yielded interesting and significant findings relevant to job burnout (Klopsch, 1983; Nowicki, 1966). In addition, the *Dominance* Scale of Jackson's Personality Research Form (PRF) was employed as an indicator of assertiveness and leadership.

Health-related Concerns

Traditional items requesting information about health concerns (e.g., physical fitness, smoking, alcohol consumption and psychosomatic complaints) were also included.

Procedure

Permission to conduct the study was obtained from the Officer in Charge, RCMP Training Academy and the Commanding Officer of "F" Division (Saskatchewan). In all instances, there was a high level of interest and support.

Questionnaires were sent to a sample of 225 regular members of the RCMP who were actively involved in police work in Saskatchewan at the time of the study. Names were taken from a complete list of RCMP regular members in Saskatchewan that was arranged in ascending order of regimental number (the higher the regimental number, the longer the individual has been employed by the RCMP as a regular police officer). To obtain an adequate and representative sample of constables, every fifth individual from this list was sent a questionnaire. Because the resulting sample of 125 male and female constables only identified six female members, permission was granted to obtain a list of all fifty-three female RCMP members in Saskatchewan. Each of the police officers on this list was sent a questionnaire.

Selection of the sample of non-commissioned officers (NCOs; i.e., corporals, sergeants, staff/sergeants and sergeant majors) followed a similar procedure to that used for constables with the exception that every eighth individual from a list of RCMP NCOs in Saskatchewan was chosen. This yielded a sample of forty-three NCOs to whom the questionnaires were mailed.

To obtain a sample of members of the RCMP who had little or no operational police duties, an announcement was made to five troops of recruits at the RCMP's Recruit Training Academy in Regina, Saskatchewan, informing the recruits of the general nature of the research and inviting them to take part. In order to obtain data from recruits at different stages of training, troops completed the questionnaire on four separate dates. Both male and female recruits were included.

Finally, approximately thirty additional questionnaires were distributed to sworn police officers of the RCMP who were serving as instructors at the RCMP Training Academy in Regina.

Statistical Analyses

All statistical analyses were performed using SPSSx (SPSS Inc., 1986). Descriptive statistics provided sample means and measures of variance while principal components analyses (varimax rotation) were used to combine various variables into conceptually simplified and statistically validated factors. Stepwise-multiple regression analyses were then employed to determine which set of variables best accounted for the variance in the mea- sure s of job burnout (i.e., Total Burnout score. *Emotional Exhaustion, Depersonalization, Personal Accomplishment*).

Results

The results of the study will be presented as follows: (1) description of the sample in terms of various demographic variables. (2) principal compo- nents analysis of items concerning health-related problems, priorities for government spending, and socio-political views, and (3) multiple regression analyses identifying the strongest correlates of the four measures of job burnout: Total Burnout score, *Emotional Exhaustion Frequency, Depersonalization Frequency, and Personal Accomplishment Frequency.*

Sample Characteristics

A total of 138 (61.3 per cent) of the 225 questionnaires sent to the experienced police officers in Saskatchewan were completed and returned to the researchers while seventy per cent (21/30) of the RCMP Training Academy instructors participated.   Because the overall rate of sixty-six per cent was considered to be acceptable, non-responders were not followed- up. All of the 131 recruits who attended the sessions that were specifically organized for data collection completed the questionnaire.

Demographic items

Although women were underrepresented in the experienced police group (n = 27, 19.5 per cent) and were totally absent in the RCMP instruc- tors' group, they constituted the majority of the RCMP recruits (n - 80. 61.6 per cent).

Experienced male police officers (X = 33.0 years, SD - 6.9) were older than their female counterparts (X = 27.1 years, SD = 3.2) while male and female RCMP recruits were approximately the same age (X_M = 23.9 years, SD = 3.7; X_F = 24.3 years, SD = 3.5). Experienced male officers had an average of 11.9 years of service (SD = 7.1); females an average of 5.0

years (*SD* = 2.8). Instructors averaged 20.0 years (*SD* = 5.0) of service with the RCMP

Eighty-one per cent (*n* = 112) of the experienced police officers were constables; thirteen were corporals, nineteen (6.5 per cent) were sergeants, and five (3.6 per cent) were at the staff/sergeant rank or above. All instructors were NCOs: twelve corporals, five sergeants and four members ranking at the staff/sergeant level or higher.

Evaluation of the Sample

The sample of experienced police officers responding to the survey adequately represented the RCMP population in Saskatchewan. The smaller number of female officers may be accounted for by the recruiting practices of the RCMP which did not include hiring women until 1974. This policy would also explain why all the females held the rank of constable and reported less police experience than the males sampled. The larger number of female recruits sampled can also be considered to be representative of current RCMP recruiting policy. The sample of instructors represented a broad cross-section of the population of available instructors at the time the data were collected.

Scale Development

To facilitate data reduction, the items tapping health concerns, priorities for government spending and socio-political attitudes were submitted to a principal components analysis using a minimum eigenvalue of 1.0 as a cutoff point. The resulting factors were rotated using the varimax (orthogonal) method; interpretation was based on variables that achieved loadings greater than 0.3 (Tabachnick and Fidell, 1983). The regression technique (SPSS Inc., 1986) was employed to compute factor scores for each resulting factor.

Health-related Items

The first factor analysis considered thirteen health concerns (e.g., how often the respondent experiences nervousness, insomnia, irritability). Three factors emerged and accounted for forty-six per cent of the total variance. The first factor included items relating to psychological distress and was comprised of the following items: nervousness, worry, depression, irritability and loss of energy. The items surveying frequency of experiences with hemorrhoids, loss of interest in sex, insomnia and ulcers all loaded on the second factor labeled psychosomatic concerns. Miscellaneous health complaints comprised the third factor and included the items backaches and hives (Table 1).

Table 1. Factor Loading for Health-Related Items.

Variables	Factor loadings		
	I	II	III
Factor 1 (Psychological distress):			
Nervousness	.69	-.05	.33
Worry	.63	.15	.23
Depression	.58	.33	-.09
Irritability	.46	.46	-.01
Loss of energy	.45	.22	.12
Upset stomach	.28	.24	.25
Factor II (Psychosomatic concerns):			
Hemorrhoids	.05	.54	.06
Loss of interest in sex	.26	.37	.07
Insomnia	.31	.37	.13
Ulcers	.06	.30	.00
Headaches	.23	.27	.23
Factor III (Miscellaneous health concerns):			
Backaches	.20	.37	.54
Hives	.04	-.04	.34

Priorities for Government Spending

Four factors which accounted for fifty per cent of the total variance were extracted from the variables surveying respondents' attitudes toward priorities for government spending. They can be interpreted as being related to (1) national economy (e.g., dealing with unemployment, helping the poor, controlling inflation); (2) women's issues (e.g., eliminating discrimination against women); (3) social issues (e.g., prison reform, crime prevention, health and medical care, supporting the business community); and (4) the criminal justice system (e.g., law enforcement, law reform) (Table 2).

Table 2. Factor Loading for Items Surveying Priorities for Government Spending.

Variables	Factor loadings			
	I	II	III	IV
Factor 1 (National economy):				
Dealing with unemployment	.71	.15	.12	.06
Helping the poor	.42	.28	.24	.09
Controlling inflation	.38	.02	.17	.03
Factor II (Women's issues):				
Eliminating discrimination against women	.10	.81	.26	.09
Eliminating pornography	.28	.36	-.02	.20
Factor III (Social issues):				
Prison reform	.17	.02	.48	.01
Crime prevention	.14	.23	.42	.18
Health and medical care	.27	.17	.32	.16
Supporting the business community	.14	.15	.17	.06
Factor IV (Criminal justice system):				
Law enforcement	.13	.10	.08	.72
Reform of our laws	.00	.14	.33	.33

Socio-political Attitudes

Table 3 summarizes the outcome of the factor analysis of the socio-political items which accounted for fifty-eight per cent of the total variance. Cynicism toward the public is characterized by the first factor which was comprised of "most people would try to be fair" (negative loading), "most people are just looking out for themselves," and "you can't be too careful in dealing with people." Factor Two can be labeled as cynicism toward the government. Interpretation of this factor was based on four items: "I don't think that the government cares much what people like me think;" "Those elected to Parliament soon lose touch with the people;" "People like me don't have any say about what the government does;" and "People with high incomes should pay a greater share of the total taxes than they do now." A sense of well-being ("I am satisfied with my life as a whole" and "I am happy") typified the next factor. Two items comprised the fourth factor: "There is too much of a difference between rich and poor in this country" and "The government should provide jobs for Canadians who want to work but cannot find a job" which seemed to reflect liberal political views. Conservatism (e.g., "During a strike, management should be prohibited by law from hiring workers to take the place of strikers" [negative loading] and "Unemployment is high these days because it is too easy to get welfare assistance") characterized the fifth factor. The last factor comprised one item suggestive of alienation ("Sometimes politics and government seem so complicated that a person like me can't really understand what's going on").

Correlates of Job Burnout

Pearson product-moment correlation coefficients between the four burnout scales and the demographic, personality and attitude measures were first computed to examine the intercorrelations amongst the variables (Table 4).

Step-wise multiple regression analyses were then carried out to determine which set of variables was most strongly related to the four measures of burnout. Total MBI, *Emotional Exhaustion, Depersonalization, Personal Accomplishment* served as the criterion variable while a set of demographic items (i.e., age, sex, marital status, presence of children, years of police service, level of education), attitude factors (e.g., cynicism toward the public, cynicism toward the government), priorities for government spending (e.g., national economy, women's issues), personality scales (e.g., *Ego-strength, Dominance*) and the various health concerns were employed as potential predictor variables in four step-wise multiple regression analyses.

Table 3. Factor Loadings of Socio-Political Attitudes.

Variables	Factor loadings					
	I	II	III	IV	V	VI
Factor I (Cynicism toward the public):						
Most people would try to be fair	-.73	-.07	.00	-.10	-.05	-.11
Most people are just looking out for themselves	.68	.15	.00	-.15	.05	-.01
You can't be too careful	.60	.02	-.10	.23	.05	-.11
Factor II (Cynicism toward the government):						
I don't think that the government cares much what people like me think	.14	.79	-.11	.13	.14	.14
Those elected to Parliament soon lose touch with the people	.14	.58	.05	.10	.14	.00
People like me don't have any say about what the government does	.13	.40	-.26	.30	.24	.13
People with high incomes should pay a greater share of the total taxes than they do now	-.11	.33	.06	.26	-.01	-.13
Factor III (Well-being):						
I am satisfied with my life as a whole	-.01	-.02	.76	-.03	.01	.05
I am happy	-.09	.03	.65	.16	-.05	-.03
I am not in control of my life, what happens is out of my hands	-.02	.06	-.17	-.04	.12	.14
Factor IV (Liberal political views):						
There is too much of a difference between rich and poor in this country	.02	.13	.12	.45	.01	-.06
The government should provide jobs for Canadians who want to work but cannot find a job	.06	.10	.01	.38	-.03	-.02
Factor V (Conservative political views):						
During a strike, management should be prohibited by law from hiring workers to take the place of strikers	.16	-.06	.02	.20	-.47	-.06
Unemployment is high these days because it is too easy to get welfare assistance	.26	.08	-.10	.23	.47	-.02
Union leaders and workers who fail to obey back-to-work legislation should be fined or jailed	.03	.05	.03	-.04	.35	-.02
A few strong leaders would make this country better than all the laws and talk	.12	.10	-.13	.17	.33	.03
Factor VI (Alienation):						
Sometimes politics and government seem so complicated that a person like me can't really understand what's going on	-.01	.03	.01	.21	-.02	.70

Table 4. Correlations Between Predictor and Criterion Variables.

Predictor	Criterion			
	Total MBI	EEF[1]	DPF[2]	PAF[3]
Demographic items				
Age	.02	.04	-.07	-.04
Sex	.00	.09	.00	.04
Marital Status	.06	-.08	.09	-.05
Children	-.04	.07	.00	.03
Years of police service	.06	.04	-.03	-.08
Education	-.07	.04	-.02	.15**
Attitudes				
Cynicism toward the public	.22**	.23**	.30***	-.20
Cynicism toward the government	.14*	.06	.11	.14*
Well-being	-.41***	-.48***	-.38***	.15
Liberal attitudes	-.03	.02	-.06	-.04
Conservative attitudes	.19*	.09	.26**	-.10
Alienation	.03	.07	.08	-.06
Priorities for government spending				
National economy	-.01	.04	-.13	-.08
Women's issues	-.12	.03	-.05	.17*
Social issues	-.18*	-.06	-.13*	.17*
Criminal justice system	.23**	.18*	.25***	-.10
Personality scales				
Ego-strength	-.29***	-.32***	-.21***	.18***
Control	.38***	.31***	.33***	-.15***
Dominance	-.17**	-.11*	-.05	.19***
K Scale	-.36***	-.33***	-.35***	.16**
Health Concerns				
Psychological distress	.29***	.43***	.27***	-.04
Psychosomatic complaints	.24**	.25**	.17*	-.02
Somatic disorders	.26***	.27***	.15*	-.17*
Physical fitness	.07	.06	.00	-.09
Frequency of exercise	-.15**	.09	-.11*	.27***
Smoking	-.03	.02	-.03	.04
Drinking	.03	.04	-.07	-.18
Time for hobbies	-.33***	-.36***	-.19**	.12*

* $p \le .05$ 1 *Emotional Exhaustion Frequency*
** $p \le .01$ 2 *Depersonalization Frequency*
*** $p \le .001$ 3 *Personal Accomplishment Frequency*

Table 5. Multiple Regression Analysis Identifying the Strongest Correlates of MBI.

Total MBI

Step	Variable	Mult R	Adj. R^2	R^2 Change	Beta Weight
1	Well-being	.41	.16	.17	-.41
2	Control	.49	.23	.07	.28
3	Criminal justice system	.55	.28	.05	.23
4	Dominance	.58	.32	.04	-.21
5	Time for hobbies	.61	.35	.04	-.20
6	Social issues	.64	.39	.04	-.20
7	Miscellaneous health concerns	.66	.40	.02	.16
8	Conservative	.67	.42	.02	.13

Emotional exhaustion frequency

Step	Variable	Mult R	Adj. R^2	R^2 Change	Beta Weight
1	Well-being	.48	.22	.23	-.48
2	Psychological distress	.59	.34	.13	.36
3	Criminal justice system	.62	.37	.03	.18
4	Frequency of exercise	.64	.39	.02	.14
5	Time for hobbies	.65	.40	.02	-.14

Depersonalization frequency

Step	Variable	Mult R	Adj. R^2	R^2 Change	Beta Weight
1	Well-being	.38	.14	.14	-.38
2	Criminal justice system	.47	.21	.07	.27
3	K Scale	.52	.26	.06	-.25
4	National economy	.55	.28	.03	-.18
5	Psychological distress	.58	.31	.03	.18

Personal accomplishment frequency

Step	Variable	Mult R	Adj. R^2	R^2 Change	Beta Weight
1	Frequency of exercise	.27	.07	.07	.27
2	Dominance	.34	.10	.04	.20
3	Social issues	.39	.14	.04	.20
4	Miscellaneous health concerns	.43	.16	.03	-.17

The first multiple regression analysis, using total MBI score as the criterion variable, and the various attitude, personality and health related factors and variables as potential predictors, produced a solution that accounted for a total of forty-two per cent of the variance and included the factors or varia total of forty-two per cent of the variance and included the factors or variables measuring *Well-being, Control, Criminal Justice System, Dominance, Time for Hobbies, Social Issues, Miscellaneous Health Concerns* and *Conservatism.*

As in the other analyses, *Well-being* accounted for a large proportion of the variance in the multiple regression analysis for *Depersonalization Frequency. Criminal Justice System, K* Scale, *National Economy* and *Psychological Distress* accounted for the remainder of the thirty-one per cent of the total variance.

Only sixteen per cent of the total variance in *Personal Accomplishment Frequency* was explained in the regression equation. The primary correlates included *Frequency of Exercise, Dominance, Social Issues* and *Miscellaneous Health Concerns* (Table 5).

Discussion

The present study examined a number of variables that previous research had suggested were significant correlates of job burnout in police officers. In addition to determining individual correlations between those variables and burnout, the set of variables that were the most efficient correlates of burnout was identified through multiple regression analyses.

The factor labeled *Well-being* proved to be the strongest correlate of three of the four measures of job burnout (i.e., *Emotional Exhaustion Frequency*, Depersonalization Frequency, and Total BMI score). This finding is considered to have one of the most important results of the study: job burnout amongst police officers is highly correlated with officers' happiness and life satisfaction in general, suggesting that when police officers are suffering from burnout, they perceive their entire lives more negatively. Perhaps this could be interpreted as meaning that a lack of well-being — i.e., not being satisfied or happy — is an additional dimension of the general construct of job burnout. This notion is further reinforced by the statistically significant negative zero-order correlations between the various burnout dimensions and the MMPI *Ego Strength* scale, one of the MMPI's best indicators of psychological health and well-being.

Heath-related issues also proved to be significantly related to burnout suggesting that, as levels of job burnout increase, so do complaints about psychological distress and other health concerns. On the other hand, as individuals increased their frequency of exercise, their levels of depersonalization and job burnout in general decreased, while their levels of personal accomplishment increased. The direction of the relationship between exercise and job burnout in general decreased, while their levels of personal accomplishment increased. The direction of the relationship between exercise and job burnout is unknown; for example, exercise could serve to prevent job burnout or, more likely, it seems that reduced level of exercise is another symptom of the burnout construct. Furthermore, the more frequently the police officers felt that work interfered with sports or hobbies, the higher their burnout officers felt that work interfered with sports or hobbies, the higher their burnout scores on all scales. Although correlational research is not appropriate for determining causality, these data provide additional support for the notion that exercise and involvement in sports or hobbies may serve as buffers against the negative consequences of police work.

Higher scores on conservatism/authoritarianism were also consistent with higher levels of burnout, confirming the Vastola (1978) and Violanti and Marshall (1983(notion that the "John Wayne Syndrome" is related to police stress and seems to be yet another component of burnout for police officers.

Although neither cynicism toward the government nor the public entered into the multiple regression equations for the various scales of burnout, the letter was significantly correlated with three of the four burnout scales (i.e., Total Burnout score, *Emotional Exhaustion Frequency*, and *Depersonalization Frequency*), indicating that, with higher levels of burnout, police are more likely to believe that one cannot be too careful in dealing with people, that most people are just looking out for themselves, and that most people would try to take advantage of others. It would appear that, in this sample of the RCMP officers, the more cynical and negative their attitudes toward the people they deal with in their work were (i.e., increased MBI *Depersonalization* Scores), the more likely they were to be negative and cynical about people in general. Perhaps these negative and cynical attitudes toward the public are additional dimensions of the burnout syndrome for police officers, providing further support for the notion that burnout is a more global construct than originally thought — i.e., it goes beyond emotional exhaustion, depersonalization and lack of personal accomplishment.

Despite significant correlations with the various burnout scales, the personality variables were rarely identified in the stepwise multiple regression analyses that accounted for significant proportions of the variance in the MBI scales. This might suggest that, although personality has weak to moderate correlations with burnout (i.e., $.05 < r < .38$) accounting for up to fourteen per cent of the variance, the particular set of personality constructs tapped in this study were not the most efficient correlates of job burnout for police officers.

Theoretical implications

This research has added to the body of knowledge on job burnout in police in demonstrating that, in addition to attitudes of cynicism and conservatism, health-related factors (e.g., psychological distress, psychosomatic and miscellaneous health concerns) and general well-being are important correlates of job burnout. It is especially noteworthy that as levels of burnout increased, police officers indicated less satisfaction with life and tended to report less happiness. Such findings are valuable because they identify some additional consequences of burnout and how the stress of police work extends beyond the work environment into the entire lives of police officers.

It can also be concluded that the environment in which a police officer works may be an important antecedent to burnout (i.e., the finding that work interferes with time to pursue sports or hobbies). This underscores the need for theorists, researchers and police administrators to consider the effects of the environment in which our Canadian police officers work instead of suggesting that officers who suffer the negative consequences of police work must be weak, ineffective or psychologically maladjusted individuals.

Practical implications

A number of practical recommendations regarding the prevention of burnout follow from the present study. Having sufficient time to pursue sports or hobbies and exercising frequently were found to be important correlates of job burnout. Police departments might prevent some of the negative effects of burnout by providing opportunities for, and encouraging their officers to pursue, outside activities. For example, since shift work often interferes with such activities, the organization might consider implementing policies permitting more flexible shift schedules. Initiating fitness programs might be another preventive measure that could be undertaken by police administrators.

Conclusions

The current research has provided information regarding the correlates of job burnout in members of the RCMP in Saskatchewan, Canada. While many questions are left unanswered, this research has contributed further evidence that the negative consequences of police stress extend beyond work and that a lack of well-being, cynical attitudes and the "John Wayne Syndrome" are likely additional dimensions of the job burnout construct in police officers. Further evidence of the existence of a relationship between physical and psychological health and burnout has been provided.

Appendix A. Correlations Between Predictor Variables.

	1	2	3	4	5	6	7	8	9	10	11	12	13	14	15	16	17	18	19	20	21	22
1 Ego strength	1.00																					
2 Control	-.20***	1.00																				
3 Dominance	0.19***	0.08	1.00																			
4 K scale	0.47***	-0.47***	0.12	1.00																		
5 Psych. distress	-0.42***	0.24***	-0.16	-0.34***	1.00																	
6 Psychosomatic	-0.38***	0.15*	0.00	-0.14*	0.26	1.00																
7 Miscellaneous	-0.17*	0.02	-0.22**	-0.12	0.27***	0.14*	1.00															
8 Nat'n econ.	-0.07	-0.02	-0.13	0.03	0.19***	0.05	0.26***	1.00														
9 Women's issues	-0.04	-0.08	-0.20**	0.09	-0.01	0.15*	0.22**	0.30***	1.00													
10 Social issues	-0.14*	-0.01	-0.20**	0.02	0.09	-0.01	0.15*	0.22**	0.30***	1.00												
11 Crim. just.	-0.03	0.05	0.08	-0.08	0.08	-0.01	0.07	0.15*	0.19***	0.14*	1.00											
12 Cynic. pub.	-0.07	0.20**	0.18*	-0.30***	0.15*	-0.09	-0.01	0.02	-0.10	0.19***	0.14*	1.00										
13 Cynic. gov't.	-0.18**	0.02	-0.05	-0.24**	-0.05	0.13*	-0.09	-0.08	0.01	0.01	-0.03	0.22**	1.00									
14 Well being	0.17	-0.28***	0.01	0.24***	-0.16*	-0.20**	-0.14*	-0.04	-0.10	-0.05	0.11	-0.04	-0.09	1.00								
15 Liberal views	0.00	0.02	-0.05	-0.08	0.00	-0.01	0.04	0.22**	0.19***	0.27***	0.04	-0.09	0.04	0.19***	1.00							
16 Conservative	-0.07	0.06	0.15*	-0.18*	0.16*	0.09	-0.09	-0.14*	0.04	0.19***	0.19***	0.13*	0.04	0.16*	0.07	1.00						
17 Alienation	-0.19**	0.07	-0.09	-0.16*	0.15*	0.16*	-0.06	0.07	-0.23**	0.02	0.09	0.13*	0.02	0.16*	-0.15*	0.11	1.00					
18 Physically fit	-0.09	0.10	-0.13*	-0.03	-0.03	0.13	0.04	-0.09	0.02	0.12	0.03	-0.02	0.16*	0.15*	-0.01	0.14*	0.04	1.00				
19 Freq. of exer.	0.09	-0.10*	-0.06	0.10*	-0.02	-0.16*	0.25***	0.20**	-0.01	0.09	-0.12	-0.03	0.05	0.19***	-0.16*	0.19**	-0.02	-0.27***	1.00			
20 Smoking	0.04	-0.16***	-0.19***	0.09	-0.01	-0.05	-0.10	0.07	0.08	0.11	0.04	-0.08	-0.03	-0.09	0.11	-0.13	-0.23**	-0.09	-0.05	1.00		
21 Drugs	-0.08	-0.12*	-0.04	-0.01	-0.05	0.01	-.01	0.01	0.18*	0.18*	0.01	0.04	-0.03	0.02	0.07	-0.02	-0.16*	0.02	-0.01	-0.02	1.00	
22 Hobbies	0.21***	-0.14*	0.04	0.19*	-0.38*	-0.29***	-0.21***	-0.14*	0.03	0.03	-0.02	-0.06	-0.17*	0.10	0.24**	-0.03	-0.03	0.12	-0.08	0.02	-0.06	1.00

* p ≤ .05
** p ≤ .0?
*** p ≤ .00?

Endnote

Requests for reprints should be sent to Dr. Robert J. Moore, Campion College, University of Regina, Regina, Sask. S4S 0A2.

References

Adlam, D.R. 1982. "The Police Personality: Psychological Consequences of Being a Police Officer." *Journal of Police Service and Administration* 10: 344-349.

Barron, F. 1956. "An Ego-Strength Scale Which Predicts Response to Psychotherapy," in Welsh G.S. and W.G. Dahlstrom (eds.), *Basic Readings on the MMPI in Psychology and Medicine.* Minneapolis: University of Minnesota Press.

Bergen, G.T and C.R. Bartol. 1983. "Stress in Rural Law Enforcement." *Perceptual and Motor Skills* 56: 957-958.

Chandler, E.V. and C.S. Jones. 1979. "Cynicism—An Inevitability of Police Work?" *Journal of Police Science and Administration* 7: 65-68.

Colegrove, S.B. 1983. "Personality and Demographic Characteristics as Predictors of Burnout in Female Police Officers." Unpublished Doctoral dissertation, The California School of Professional Psychology, Berkeley, 1983. *Dissertation Abstracts International* 41(4-B: 1232-1233.

Cuadra, C.A. 1956. "A Scale for Control in Psychological Adjustment (Cn)," in Welsh G.S. and W.G. Dahlstrom (eds.), *Basic Readings on the MMPI in Psychology and Medicine.* Minneapolis: University of Minnesota Press.

Duckworth, J.C. 1979. MMPI *Interpretation Manual for Counselors and Clinicians.* 2nd ed. Muncie, Indiana: Accelerated Development Inc.

Ellison, K.W. and J.L Genz, 1978. "Burned-out Samaritan." *FBI Law Enforcement Bulletin* 47: 2-7.

Freudenberger, H.J. 1974. "Staff Burnout." *Journal of Social Issues* 30: 159-165.

Freudenberger, H.J. 1975. "The Staff Burnout Syndrome in Alternative Institutions." *Psychotherapy: Theory, Research and Practice* 12: 73-82.

Genz, J.L. and D. Lester. 1976. "Authoritarianism in Policemen as a Function of Experience." *Journal of Police Science and Administration* 4: 9.

Golembiewski, R.T. and R. Munzenrider. 1981. "Efficacy of Three Versions of One Burnout Measure: MBI as Total Score, Sub-scale Scores, or Phases?" *Journal of Health and Human Resources Administration* 4: 229-246.

Gottesman, I.I. 1959. "More Construct Validation of the Ego-Strength Scale." *Journal of Consulting Psychology* 23: 342-346.

Grier, K.S. 1982. "A Study of Job Stress in Police Officers and School Teachers'" Doctoral dissertation University of South Dakota, 1982. *Dissertation Abstracts International* 13: (1-B): 271.

Jackson, S.E. and C. Maslach. 1982. "After-effects of Job Related Stress: Families as Victims." *Journal of Occupational Behaviour* 3: 63-77.

Kankewitt, B. 1986. *The Shattered Badge* Toronto: Methuen.

Klopsch, J.W. 1983. "Police Personality Change as Measured by the MMPI: A Five-Year Longitudinal Study." Doctoral dissertation, Fuller Theological Seminary, 1983. *Dissertation Abstracts International* 44(6B): 2001.

Kreitner, R., M.A. Sova, S.D. Wood, M.E. Friedman and W.E. Reif. 1985. "A Search for the U-Shaped Relationship Between Occupational Stressors and the Risk of Coronary Heart Disease." *Journal of Police Science and Administration* 13: 122-131.

Lester, D. 1982. "Perceived Stress in Police Officers and Belief in Locus of Control." *The Journal of General Psychology* 107: 157-158.

Lester, D. and J. Gallagher. 1980. "Stress in Police Officers and Department Store Managers." *Psychological Reports* 46: 882.

Loo, R. 1984. "Occupational Stress in the Law Enforcement Profession." *Canada's Mental Health* 32: 10-13.

Loo, R. 1985. "Policy Development for Psychological Services in the Royal Canadian Mounted Police." *Journal of Police Science and Administration* 13: 132-137.

Maslach, C. 1979. "Burned-out Cops and their Families." *Psychology Today* May: 58-62.

Maslach, C. 1982. *Burnout — The Cost of Caring*. Englewood Cliffs, NJ: Prentice Hall.

Maslach, C. and S.E. Jackson. 1981. *Maslach Burnout Inventory Research Edition*. Palo Alto: Consulting Psychologists Press Inc.

Moore, R.J. 1985. "Reflections of Canadians on the Law and the Legal System: Legal Research Institute Survey of Respondents in Montreal, Toronto and Winnipeg," in Gibson D. and J.K. Baldwin (eds.), *Law in a Cynical Society? Opinion and Law in the 1980s*. Calgary: Carswell Legal Publications, Western Division.

Murphy, J.J. 1972. "Current Practices in the Use of Psychological Testing by Police Agencies." *Journal of Criminal Law, Criminology and Police Science* 63: 570-576.

Niederhoffer, A. 1967. *Behind the Shield*. NY: Doubleday.

Nowicki, S. 1966. "A Study of Personality Characteristics of Successful Policemen." *Police* 10(3): 39-41.

Perrier, D.C. and R. Toner. 1984. "Police Stress: The Hidden Foe." *Canadian Police College Journal* 8: 15-26.

Peyser, H. 1982. "Stress and Alcohol" in Goldberger L. and S. Breznitz (eds.), *Handbook of Stress. Theoretical and Clinical Aspects*. New York: Collier Macmillan Publishers.

Rafky, D.M., T. Lawley and R. Ingram. 1976. "Are Police Recruits Cynical?" *Journal of Police Science and Administration* 4: 352-360.

Regoli, R.M. 1976. "The Effect of College Education on Maintenance of Police Cynicism." *Journal of Police Science and Administration* 4: 344.

Shibutani, T. 1955. "Reference Groups as Perspectives." *American Journal of Sociology* 60: 562-569.

SPSS Inc. 1986. *User's Guide*. 2nd ed.. Chicago: SPSS Inc.

Stearns, G.M. and R.J. Moore. 1990. "Job Burnout in Royal Canadian Mounted Police Officers: Preliminary Findings of a Saskatchewan Sample." *Journal of Police Science and Administration* 17: 183-193.

Stratton, J.G. 1984. *Police Passages*. Manhattan Beach California: Glennon Pub. Co.

Tabachnick, B.G. and L.S. Fiddell. 1983. *Using Multivariate Statistics*. New York: Harper and Row Pub. Inc.

Tifft, I.L. 1974. "The 'Cop Personality' Reconsidered." *Journal of Police Science and Administration* 2: 266-278.

Varsos, M.M. 1970. "A Report on the Diverse Psychological Characteristics of Law Enforcement Personnel." *Law and Order,* Nov.

Vastola, A. 1978. "The Police Personality: An Alternative Explanatory Model." *The Police Chief*, April: 50-52.

Violanti, J.M. and J.R. Marshall. 1983. "The Police Stress Process." *Journal of Police Science and Administration* 11: 389-394.

Violanti, J.M., J.R. Marshall and B. Howe, 1985. "Stress, Coping and Alcohol Use: The Police Connection." *Journal of Police Science and Administration* 13: 106-110.

Vulcano, B.A., G.B. Barnes and I.J. Breen. 1984. "The Prevalence of Psychosomatic Disorders Among a Sample of Police Officers." *Social Psychiatry* 19: 181-186.

Wood, S.D., F.G.M. Kreitner, M.E. Friedman, M. Edwards and M.A. Sova. 1982. "Cost-Effective Wellness Screening: A Case Study of 4,524 Law Enforcement Officers." *Journal of Police Science and Administration* 10: 273-278.

The Police, the Crowns and the Courts:
Who's Running the Show?

Glenn Wheeler

They hang around the hallways, smoking cigarettes and talking, waiting for 10 o'clock, like people standing around a theatre lobby.

This, however, is serious, even though the charges that have brought most of the people to Toronto's Old City Hall courtrooms are not. The diet of crime at the provincial court level is heavy on theft, drunkenness and assault. But a bad break on trial day still has serious consequences for the accused — it can mean the difference between discharge and fine, freedom and jail, unblemished character and criminal record.

On the other hand, to the Crown attorneys who prosecute the cases, they're part of a caseload to be dealt with as best they can, because, the Crowns says, their job has become less of a search for justice than a battle against the clock.

Crowns and defence lawyers agree that can be bad news for the accused, not at all a ticket to an easy time of it in court, because too often it leaves the police officers, who collected the evidence with the aim of getting a conviction, also running the show in court. In such circumstances, the Crown — who's supposed to be a check on the power of the police, and a protector of rights as well as prosecutor — is relegated to an extension of the police apparatus.

That situation was an underlying issue in the Ontario Crown attorneys' recent pay dispute, which threatened to turn into a work-to-rule campaign. The Ministry of the Attorney General staved that off by offering more money and better working conditions. But observers agree that even though the province's 314 Crowns have accepted the deal, it will do little to right the fundamental wrongs of an under-financed court system.

The office of Crown attorney has a long history in English criminal law. Central to the office, says University of Toronto law professor John

Edwards, is a concern with the wider public interest — not merely in getting convictions.

"It would be very wrong to think that the responsibility of the Crown attorney is merely to put criminals behind bars," says Edwards, an authority on such matters.

However, under increasingly frugal financing of the court system, critics argue that the protections embodied in the office of Crown attorney have become more rhetorical than real.

While the courts, like prisons and other corrections services, get twelve per cent of money spent in criminal justice, the police get seventy per cent. "Since the 1970s, the gap between police and other types of costs has become even more evident," according to *Selected Trends in Canadian Criminal Justice*, an annual publication of the federal Solicitor General's department.

That means that while there are plenty of police to lay charges, it's hard for the rest of the criminal justice system to deal with them. Bonnie Wein, a veteran Crown, says the physical facilities are bad (crumbling courthouses and interview rooms whose walls don't go up to the ceilings), and the Crown attorneys are overextended and underpaid.

"Having a salaried system saves the public a lot of money," she says, since overtime is a regular part of the job. But Wein says the accused gets shortchanged as well. She allows that in some cases, poor Crown preparation results in people beating charges that, by rights, they should be convicted of. But she also says the accused can end up languishing in jail, just waiting for their case to make it into the clogged court system.

More often, she said in a later interview, scheduling delays result in charges being dismissed without the court ever hearing the merits. And judges often react more leniently in bail hearings because of the long waiting lists for trial.

Once minor cases do make it into court, they're mostly in the hands of the police, according to some lawyers. In Toronto, for example, the Crown does not keep a file on a case unless it is a major one and the Crown is assigned immediately. A routine file "stays in the custody of the police," says lawyer Paul Trollope. "It doesn't come into the Crown's hands, except on the days that the case is up in court for trial or if the Crown wants to request the file specifically."

Usually, however, there's no such request, especially at the provincial court level, where ninety per cent of criminal charges are heard — mostly the less serious ones. The Crown first sees the file on the morning of trial, along with the dozen or more others to be prosecuted that day.

Michael Martin, Ontario's director of Crown attorneys, says this scant attention to individual cases isn't necessarily a bad thing. "Perfect justice is something one strives for at all times as a Crown attorney," he says. "But it doesn't necessarily involve agonizing attention over a protracted period of time. If someone is charged with shoplifting and there are only one or two witnesses, an experienced Crown could glance at the file for a couple of minutes and appreciate the issues."

Wein, however, doesn't accept this reasoning whole cloth. She says Crowns worry that seemingly routine cases can slip through that involve serious points of law. And she says Crowns sorely miss their lack of time to prepare members of the public before they appear as witnesses.

A former head Crown at the district court in Toronto also has his doubts. Robert McGee says the working conditions mean a Crown often has to make concessions to expediency.

"In a perfect world, he would want to interview the witnesses himself, but in fact he can't do it," says McGee. "He has to rely on what the police tell him the witnesses are going to say. Sometimes that may be faulty. Sometimes what a witness says under oath in a witness box is completely different from what he told a policeman six months before."

McGee says the Crown is also required to follow a lot of suggestions from the police about the case, especially if it's a fairly new Crown dealing with a veteran police officer — a common situation these days as experienced Crowns desert the public service to use their acquired knowledge in more lucrative defence work.

The Crown "really doesn't have time to sit down and think about his role as a quasi-judicial official," says McGee. "When you get a young Crown in there with fifteen trials, it's pretty hard for him to give much thought to each one. Maybe he has fifteen trials crammed into a courtroom with fifty or sixty witnesses clamouring to see him. It's hard for him to give an intelligent appraisal of each case.

"When I was a Crown, I relied a great deal on what the police advised me — what they thought and how they saw the case. The Crown isn't bound by that. It's not something that he should feel compelled to follow in every case. But it certainly has an effect. It means a lot, especially if you're young and have a lot of work on the list."

It's not only on trial day that the police exert influence on prosecutions. They also play a role in the behind-the-scenes bargaining that's part and parcel of criminal cases.

"I don't know another profession where there are so many hitches that [lawyers] could employ," says civil liberties lawyer Charles Roach. "If you worked strictly to rule, you wouldn't get anything done."

Although the two sides can hash out anything from admissibility of evidence to adjourning the trial, the bargaining often involves the accused pleading guilty in return for a lesser charge or an agreed-upon sentence.

Although it's a common activity, plea-bargaining is a controversial one, and law reform commissions, some defence lawyers and others have called for its abolition. There have been suggestions that it encourages the police to lay more serious charges than warranted by the evidence, or charges for which they have little evidence at all, in order to give them leverage in plea bargaining — thereby extracting a guilty plea without a time-consuming trial in which their case will be challenged and possibly fail.

But, says Roach, defence lawyers are willing participants. "If you don't [plea] bargain [the outcome] for the accused could be worse," he says. "So sometimes they will plead guilty to things they are not guilty of, in order to escape being found guilty of something much worse — which they may not be guilty of either. One thing people can't stand is uncertainty."

Plea-bargaining is especially repugnant, say its critics, because it not only encourages the police to be especially harsh when laying charges, but because they are integral participants in the dealing.

"The Crown attorney is so busy, his list is so long, and he's got so many things to do that he says, 'Why don't you go speak to Sergeant So-and So'," says Roach.

Noted criminal lawyer Brian Greenspan is one who disputes this. He says plea bargaining is an essential part of the judicial process, and that even if the courts had optimum financing and ran at under-capacity rather than the reverse, "we would still have negotiated resolutions of criminal proceedings." He added that in cases in which overworked Crowns have little time to prepare for prosecution, the advantage often falls to the accused, who get improved odds of acquittal.

Greenspan, as vice president of the 600-member Criminal Lawyers Association, disagrees that police are taking over prosecutions. "The Crowns consult the police, as so they should. But the police aren't running the cases. We don't hear that from our members."

The issue of plea bargaining recently caused public argument between two prominent barristers in Toronto. First, Clayton Ruby wrote to a newspaper that "friendly" defence lawyers were able to obtain lighter sentences from the Crown for their clients. In a published reply Earl Levy accused him of suggesting, without proof, that a shady conspiracy existed between judges, Crown and the defence bar. "Shame on you, Clayton Ruby, for attempting to perpetuate the myths and misconceptions of plea negotiations," Levy concluded.

Such intimate dealings are something that police officers aren't trained for, says lawyer Rebecca Shamai, and something that they shouldn't be involved in.

"The police are there to get crime off the streets. The prosecutor has a very different role. When you get the police stepping too far into the prosecutor's shoes, you interfere with the right of the accused to be tried impartially."

It was the similar reasoning by the Supreme Court of Newfoundland that led to a ruling that having police officers act as prosecutors even in minor traffic offences is unconstitutional because it denies the accused the right to a fair trial. The ruling was overturned by the Newfoundland Court of Appeal, but the case will likely find its way to the Supreme Court of Canada.

Michael Martin says he's not worried that Ontario police are too involved in prosecutions. "Sometimes the police officer might speak to a Crown and convey to the Crown the attitude of defence counsel. But the actual decision is made by the Crown. It's like a reporter telling the publisher of a rival newspaper, 'Hey, our publisher wants to sell. Do you want to buy it?'"

Counters Roach: "Over the years, Crown attorneys have lost their power to really say, 'Look, this case shouldn't proceed.' Right now, it looks like the police are calling all the shots."

Research by University of Toronto criminologist Richard Ericson tends to support Roach's perception. During fieldwork with detectives in Peel Region, to the west of Toronto, Ericson found that they sent files to the Crown with a scrawl across the front indicating the sentence they expected. Ericson also found the police officers were not averse to expressing their displeasure to unco-operative Crowns.

"The police are able to fundamentally affect the outcome of a case both in terms of what the accused is convicted on and in terms of sentencing — deciding first of all what they're going to charge a person with, what's a reasonable outcome and then getting other parties to agree. They're having a fundamental effect on the case from beginning to end."

Greater police role in prosecutions means less chance to keep an eye on their work, the criminologist says. "It means that [prosecutions] are not as subject to checks and balances as formal legal procedures would have it. In only a tiny fraction of cases does the accused actually have a trial. In the vast majority, the 'trial' is the plea bargaining session and the accused is not allowed to attend. So he is excluded from his own trial."

Is There a Place for the Victim in the Prosecution Process?

Patricia Clarke

Victims of crime once were the central actors in bringing offenders to justice. Today they are neglected outsiders in a system which could not function without them, yet is not accountable to them, provides no role for them and does not necessarily serve them, for ours is "an adversary system in which the victim is not one of the adversaries" (Federal-Provincial Task Force, 1983: 5).

Victims are organizing, in one of the significant developments in the justice system, to complain of their expulsion and to demand more participation. Sometimes they bypass the system entirely, either by systems of private justice or in extreme cases by becoming their own prosecutor, judge and executioner.

A number of jurisdictions have tried a number of ways over the past twenty years to answer the demands of victims, and in Canada a Federal-Provincial Task Force on Justice for Victims has made recommendations some of which have been embodied in legislation. The question is no longer, the Task Force says, "whether the victim should participate in the (criminal justice) process or not. The question is rather the extent of that participation" (1983: 7).

This paper will look at the current status of the victim in the prosecution process, the reasons for that status in the historic development of the process, and some reasons for the growth of the victims' rights movement. It will review proposals to change the victim's status but will argue that, as far as genuine participation is concerned, the proposed changes will be more cosmetic than real. That is because of the nature of the process, the nature of bureaucratic systems to resist change, and the aims and purposes of the criminal justice system. The exclusion of victims is not an accident or oversight which can be remedied by minor tinkering with a process whose purpose is to provide justice for victims. It is a necessary and inevitable fact of a process with a totally different purpose. If victims dare to find remedies for their victimization, they must find them outside the prosecution process.

Evolution of the Prosecution Process

Before there was a formal legal system, all wrongs were private wrongs. Victims and their families exacted the penalties. To temper and regulate such private justice, in Anglo-Saxon law there gradually grew a system of restitution with fixed payments for various wrongs. At the same time there grew the notion that while some incidents were private disputes, which in the developments of law became torts to be dealt with in civil courts, other acts threatened the fabric of society and destroyed "the King's peace." For such acts the offender made payment not only to the victim but also to the lords or the King. Holdsworth (1909: 38) claims this was "the germ of the idea that wrong is not simply the affair of the injured individual — an idea which is the condition precedent to the growth of a criminal law."

Gradually as this idea developed, the victim lost control of the conflict and it became the property of the state. The focus shifted from a dispute between the offender and the victim, in which the offender was bound to make reparation to the person he had injured, to the relationship between the offender and society, in which the offender had injured society and must be punished by society. Common law developed to prevent victims from receiving reparations until they had done all they could to bring the offender to justice and prohibited victims from aggreeing not to prosecute in order to get back their property. Individuals could not condone a crime against the state (Hudson and Galway, 1975: 24).

The key to a criminal proceeding thus became, in essence, the exclusion of the victim as one of the parties. Full participation by the victim, Christie says (1977: 3), presupposes elements of civil law.

Just as the state came to replace the victim as the injured party, so it gradually replaced the victim as the prosecuting party. Until the late eighteenth century, trials normally were conducted by the victim-prosecutor and the defendant (Beattie, 1986: 13). By the nineteenth century Blackstone was able to state categorically that the sovereign "is therefore the proper person to prosecute for all public offences and breaches of the peace, being the person injured in the eye of the law" (Hagan, 1983: 268).

In the evolution of the prosecution process, then, two important things have happened, according to Christie (1977: 3) one, that both parties are being represented; and second, that the one represented by the state, the victim, "is so thoroughly represented that for the most part he has been pushed completely out of the arena." The victim is a double loser: his property may have been stolen by the offender, but "his conflict has been stolen by the state" (Christie, 1982: 93). When the private conflicts become state property, they are made to serve "the ideological interests of state-subject authority relations and the organizational interests of the individual citizens" (Ericson and Baranek, 1982: 4).

Role of the Victim in the Prosecution Process

This transfer of the dispute between two persons into a dispute between one of them and the Crown means, according to Shearing and Stenning (1983: 9), that victim neglect is not a "minor deficiency" in the justice system but arises from a "fundamental feature." The state owns the conflict and the roles left to victims are: (1) to supply the system with raw material; (2) to give the evidence the system requires; and (3) to serve as a "ceremonial" or "symbolic presence" (Hagan, 1983: 7) which legitimizes the mobilization of the law against the accused.

The fundamental policy objectives of the criminal justice system are based on a classical concept of society as a contract between a neutral arbitrating state and rational individuals. The state provides society and its members with a reasonable degree of security, and ensures just treatment for the accused (Griffiths *et al.*, 1980: 6). Punishments must be established if the sovereign is to "defend the public liberty, entrusted to his care, from the usurpation of individuals" (Vold, 1979: 24), and they must be fixed, known and in relation to the crime. These policy objectives ignore the victim as such, other than as a member of society. The second objective implies, far from participation by the victim, a moderation and rationality in the punishment the accused might otherwise receive from those who believe themselves wronged. The resulting court process may be seen as a sort of morality play where certain values are publicly affirmed, certain conduct publicly denounced, and certain persons identified, blamed and rejected as "criminals." "The process uses accused persons to help define the relationship between the individual and the state" (Ericson and Baranek, 1982: 215). Victims and their needs simply are not part of the script.

As the process has evolved, the chief power left to victims is the power not to surrender their conflict to the state — not to report the victimization. More than half of victims appear to exercise this right (Federal-Provincial

Task Force, 1983: 14). Once the state takes over, they lose virtually all other power. They have no right to testify, although they may do so if they are called by the Crown and if theirs is the uncommon case which goes to trial. Approximately up to seventy per cent of cases are settled by a guilty plea.[1] They have no right to express their views on bail or sentencing, though a judge or prosecutor is free to ask for them. They have no right to receive restitution, although they may in certain circumstances have a right to apply for it.[2]

In the prosecution, the Crown represents the interests of the community, which may or may not coincide with the interests of the victims. The Crown must consider, for example, priorities on police time and court time for investigating and prosecuting, availability of evidence, chances of a conviction, public attitudes toward the offence, desirability of plea negotiations, the protection of the community and the rehabilitation of the offender. The victim has no way to challenge the Crown decisions.

Not only does the Crown have to consider wider concerns than those of the victim, but it can be argued that to seem to represent the victim, or to press the victim's claim, might prejudice the Crown's function as an impartial presenter of all the evidence. Indeed, for the Crown to give any assistance or status to the alleged victim, which would not be given to any witness, might compromise the rights of the accused. Even to equate the complainant with a victim could prejudge facts to be proved, for instance in a sexual assault case where consent is an issue.

The Victim Movement

Having been detached over the centuries from the prosecution process, some victims have organized to attempt to get back in. In the last few years such groups have mushroomed across North America. In Canada twenty - eight groups claim 150 chapters in every province and 250,000 to 400,000 members (*Toronto Star*, Nov. 11, 1984: 1). Their numbers comprise an effective lobby, but are only a fraction of those eligible. Individual victims in Canada number at least 1.6 million a year.[3] Organizational victims may be even more numerous: in a study by Hagan (1983: 35) they made up to two-thirds of a random sample.

A number of factors appear to be involved in the birth and growth of victim groups. First is "a widespread and apparently increasing fear of crime" of which Taylor (1983: 93) says "countless research studies" have provided evidence. The fear, partly justified and partly promoted by the media, is expressed in purchases of burglar alarms and double-locks, in self-defence classes, in private security patrols and programs such as Neighbourhood Watch and in victim groups.

Second is the law and order movement, which argues that the criminal justice system is "soft on criminals," thereby turning them loose to create more victims. It supports more "rights" for victims to balance what it claims are too many rights for "criminals."

Third is the woman's movement, which began with advocacy and assistance for rape victims and in some jurisdictions achieved changes in statutes and rules of evidence which provided more rights for victim-witnesses.

Fourth is the self-help movement, growing out of the protest movements of the 1960s, which leads people who don't trust big government or bureaucracy to form their own groups to represent themselves.

Fifth is the general humanitarian impulse to help people in trouble (and earn political points) which in other fields has led to worker compensation programs or the motorists' unsatisfied judgement fund.

Victim advocacy groups differ in their concerns and their goals. Some complain most about neglect, carelessness and insensitivity from police and the courts. They can't find out what is happening in their case, they can't understand what goes on in court and they are not notified when their case is coming up or when it is settled. These groups want more information, more support services, more "sensitivity."

Others complain that victims cannot get restitution for their losses, or even get back their stolen property promptly. According to a 1976 survey in Alameda County, California (Karmen, 1984: 148), thirty per cent of victims never got back the stolen property used as evidence, forty-two per cent never learned the outcome of their case and sixty-one per cent of those eligible for the state's crime compensation fund were not informed of its existence. These victims want more effective compensation schemes and help in applying to them.

Still others such as Mothers Against Drunk Driving want stiffer laws for active role in the prosecution process. They ask to be acknowledged as a party to the proceedings, to be given access to the Crown case, to be supplied with reasons for every decision, even given a veto on plea negotiations and sentence submissions. Donald Sullivan, spokesman for a Canadian conference of victims' groups, says they want laws to give victims "a place in the courtroom" and rights in court "equal to those of the offender" (*Toronto Star*, Feb. 11, 1985: 2).

Source of Rights for Victims

A right has three key features (Federal-Provincial Task Force, 1983: 130). It is a legal recognition of interest, in this case the victim's interest in this court proceeding. A right for one party implies a responsibility or duty on another party. And it must be legally enforceable, so that one can secure either the right or damages.

At present the justice system is a balance (equal or not) of rights between prosecution and accused. If victims are to have more rights in the prosecution process, are they to come at the expense of the rights of police or the Crown or court officials? These have the greatest interest in encouraging the co-operation of victims, for as much as eighty-seven per cent of police workload — and consequently much of the court workload — comes from incidents reported by citizens (Griffiths *et al.*, 1980: 33). Clearly it is in the bureaucratic interests of the system to encourage a steady and increasing clientele. The more incidents that are reported, the higher the crime rate; and high crime rates are an effective argument for bigger budgets. Yet as we have seen, more than half of victimizations are not reported, and many victims "appear to feel that the system would only fail them or ignore them if they involved it" (Federal-Provinvial Task Force, 1983: 3).

Victims are essential not only to bringing in the cases but, as witnesses, to prosecuting them successfully. Treating victims in a "sensitive manner" will encourage their "constructive assistance," says a paper prepared for the federal department of justice (Weiler and Desgagne, 1984: 27). Or as Weigend (1983: 93) puts it, "Happy victims make better witnesses" — a claim he says is unsubstantiated by any evidence except the "feelings" of the staff of victim-witness assistance programs.

Sensitivity however does not confer power. It is not a right enforceable by law (Federal-Provincial Task Force, 1983: 131). It does not conflict with any of the prerogatives of the prosecution. None of the proposals of the Task Force on Justice for Victims involves any mandatory transfer of power from police or court to victims. They contain phrases such as "to be considered" or "where appropriate." Indeed, the Task Force says the key words in its proposals for victims are "concern, consideration and communication" and that these words sum up how the system can respond to the concerns of victims "without compromising its basic aims" (1983: 152).

But the "basic aims," as we have seen, have no necessary connection with justice for victims. There is no transfer of power to victims in proposals which allow them to participate in their cases only at the discretion of judge or Crown. There is no transfer of power either in the guidelines for fair treatment of victims set out by the Victim Committee of the American Bar Association and quoted with approval by the Task Force (1983: 152). They deal mainly with ways to improve communication between victims and decision-makers in the criminal justice system. Similarly, a case management program in British Columbia "improved convenience" for victims with no change in the "aims and purposes of the system (Federal-Provincial Task Force, 1983: 96).

If rights for victims are not to come from the prosecution, then they must come from the accused. If the victim of sexual assault, for instance, wins the right not to have evidence of sexual reputation considered, the accused loses the right to present that evidence. The transfer of rights is particularly evident in the California Victims' Bill of Rights of 1982 (Karmen, 1984: 232-3), which limits the accused's opportunities for bail, restricts plea bargaining, restricts insanity defences, broadens standards for admissibility of evidence and permits victims to press for greater penalties in sentencing, to appeal sentences they view as lenient and to argue against parole.

That is further than Canadians appear willing to go. The rhetoric is that the rights of the accused are inviolate, and the Task Force cautions that in focusing on the plight of the victim "we must not lose sight of the need to safeguard the accused" (1983: 5). Perhaps it would be more realistic to say, with Ericson and Baranek (1982: 223), that both accused and victim are dependents in the prosecution process and that neither has more "rights" than is expedient to allow and not "upset the operation of criminal control in the interests of the state."

Proposals for Change

It appears then that victims have almost no enforceable rights in the prosecution process. It also appears that they are excluded from any real rights in the process by its very nature as a conflict between the state and the accused. Within those limits, several ways have been suggested to recognize and recompense the victim.

One is financial reparation. Three of the seventy-nine recommendations of the Task Force dealt with this. A second is a "victim impact" statement, to be requested before sentencing, the subject of another Task Force recommendation. A third is a "victim's advocate" who attempts to influence the prosecution process. Two such experiments have been tried in the United States (McDonald, 1976: 153). In one a lawyer was employed as a "victim advocate" to attempt to influence the process through out-of-court negotiations. In the other, a volunteer group of victim advocates attended court hearings en masse for a time, until they tired of it, and claimed fewer charges were dismissed or remanded when they were present. The second program raises questions about fairness to the accused. As Griffiths says (1980: 32), "The prototype of community involvement...is the lynch mob." The first raises questions about who pays the advocate. If the victims pay, they may feel twice victimized. If the state pays, that may compromise its stance that the community, not the victim, is the injured party. In any case, such advocates have no standing in court since the victim is not one of the adversaries.

Restitution and Compensation

The Task Force proposals on reparation would: (1) amend section 653 of the Criminal Code to require judges to consider restitution "in all appropriate cases" and to provide an opportunity for victims to make representations about their ascertainable losses; (2) empower the court to impose a jail term for wilful default on a restitution order; and (3) amend section 388 to raise its present limit on restitution for property damage from $50 to $500. Restitution as part of a probation order under section 663 would continue unchanged.

"Whenever possible," the Task Force explains, "victims should be restored to the position they enjoyed prior to the victimization" (Task Force, 1983: 35). The Law Reform Commission of Canada in its paper on Restitution and Compensation describes restitution as a "natural and just response" to the victim's plight which should be a "central consideration" in sentencing (Law Reform Commission of Canada, 1974: 6, 8).

Yet such remedies for the victim already exist. Several sections of the Criminal Code make it possible for the court to order restitution.[4] These remedies appear to be seldom used. While Canadian data are lacking (Burns, 1980: 29), the Task Force thinks judges are "reluctant" to use them (Federal-Provincial Task Force, 1983: 54). It does not explain why judges would be less reluctant to use its new proposals.

Outside the criminal process, victims may apply to provincial crime injury compensation boards in all provinces except Prince Edward Island, or collect for property losses from private insurance, or file a civil suit both for property loss and for suffering and get judgement not only against the offender but, where negligence can be proved, against third parties.[5]

Restitution provisions in other jurisdictions appear to be an ineffective remedy for victims. In Britain, after passage of new restitution legislation in

1972, of those sent to custody and also given restitution orders only twelve per cent paid the whole sum (Burns, 1980: 15). In practice, said the British Advisory Council on the Penal System, a victim's prospects for restitution through a criminal court order "are remote" (Burns, 1980: 15). After a study of United States restitution schemes, Burns found them of relatively little use to victims and concluded that their popularity reflected a conception of them as "potentially useful tools for rehabilitating the offender rather than as devices for restoring the victim" (Burns, 1980: 12).

The compensation schemes outside the criminal process are not well used either. They are usually limited to victims of violent crime but are available regardless of whether an offender has been identified or convicted. In Ontario, one in fifty-five eligible victims actually seeks compensation (*Globe and Mail*, April 10, 1984: 2). A study of the New York and New Jersey schemes showed that fewer than one per cent of all victims of violent crime even applied to the boards, and only thirty-five per cent of those who applied were compensated (Elias, 1983: 219).

As for the possibility of civil suit, Allen Linden reported that 1.5 per cent of victims surveyed collected anything by suit, although 74.2 per cent of those studied suffered some economic loss (Linden, 1968: 29).

Whether or not restitution is a "natural response," there appear to be a number of reasons why judges are reluctant to use the existing provisions and legislators are reluctant to impose more effective ones — reasons involving the nature of the criminal process, the objectives of sentencing, constitutional division of powers and sometimes no doubt a combination of ignorance and inertia. Judge Cartwright of York County, in *Regina v. Kalloo* (quoted in Moskoff, 1983: 11), commented:

> those few Crown counsel who are even aware
> of the existence of this section (653) which
> allows the victim of an indictable offence to
> apply for an order to satisfy loss or damage to
> property caused in the commission of a crime
> are equally indifferent to its application.

He went on to suggest that if the Attorney General were paid by commission on completed restitution orders, "blood would be flowing from stones" all over Ontario (Moskoff, 1983: 11).

The difficulty of getting blood from stones, however, is one reason restitution orders are seldom made, and civil suit is often useless as well. In making restitution a condition of probation under section 663(2)(e), a judge is bound to consider an offender's ability to pay. (He is not so bound under section 653). Observation of the courts indicates that many offenders, particularly against property, have neither jobs nor assets.

A further reason for caution is the Supreme Court of Canada ruling in *R. v. Zelensky* (1978; 2 C.R. (3d) 107 (S.C.C.)) that proceedings for restitution under section 653 must not take on any character of a civil suit, and therefore the criminal court must not determine issues regarding the amount to be awarded. Restitution can be imposed, then, only when the amount is not in dispute, which Moskoff comments makes the section a "toothless tiger" (Moskoff, 1983: 11). Burns comments that judges hesitate to order restitution under section 663 as well, first because they fear using criminal law to enforce civil obligations, and second because they see it as suitable only for simple cases in which there is no dispute either over the amount involved or over the offender's ability to pay (Burns, 1980: 25).

In addition, a restitution order once made is hard to enforce. Those made under section 653 must be enforced by the victim as a civil judgement, if the offender has assets and can be located. Those made under section 664(2)(e) are intended to be monitored by probation officers. If the probation officers notice that payments have not been made, and if they decide to charge the offender with failure to comply with probation, and if the offender can be located, they must prove the offender "wilfully" defaulted. If they succeed, the maximum penalty is a $500 fine and/or six months in jail. Note that the victim is not the complainant in the enforcement procedure.

The most serious problem with restitution involves the nature of the criminal process. Civil wrongs have grown in law to be those for which injured persons seek their own monetary compensation. Criminal wrongs have become a public relationship between offenders and the state with a public response applied through penal sanctions. The historical tie between the two remains in the Criminal Code provisions for restitution (section 653 and section 663) which the Law Reform Commission describes as carryovers "grudgingly grafted onto penal law to save the victim the expense of a civil suit" (Law Reform Commission of Canada, 1974: 9). They enable the victim to circumvent civil procedure by obtaining a criminal judgement, enforceable as if it were civil, by a more expeditious and less expensive process. An example of the civil nature of section 653 is that it comes into operation "on application" of the victim, not on the initiative of the court.

The British North America Act gives jurisdiction over criminal law and procedure to the federal parliament (section 91(27)) but authority over property and civil rights to the provinces. This division, says Burns, means "an almost insurmountable obstacle to the establishment of efficient restitution systems in Canada" (1980: 29).

Further, criminal courts are constituted to determine a person's criminal responsibility, not his/her civil liability. The two have different standards of proof and different rules of evidence. For example, examination for discovery is a civil procedure not available in the criminal court. An accused person would not have the same safeguards around challenging a victim's claim for damages in criminal court than would be available in civil court. For the criminal court to try to make such a determination raises the danger of infringing on the powers reserved to the civil court. Widespread use of restitution orders might encourage use of the criminal courts as a collection agency, and lead to threatening prosecution to collect a debt.

A further set of problems arises because the focus in sentencing is not on what is pleasing to the victim but on what is good for the offender and for society. Though the Law Reform Commission saw restitution as a "rational sanction" and the Zelensky decision accepted its "valid character" as part of the sentencing process, restitution cannot be argued in the criminal court on the basis that it would return the victim to wholeness or compensate for suffering. The only constitutional way to make the civil liability to the victim a valid part of the criminal sentence is to actively locate it within criminal laws. The purpose which has been alleged is that it will provide the offender of the fruits of crime, deter those who might hope to profit illegally and facilitate the rehabilitation of the accused.

> The Law Reform Commission argues that restitution "involves acceptance of the offender as a responsible person with the capacity to undertake constructive and socially approved acts.... To the extent that restitution works toward self-correction and prevents or at least discourages the offender's commitment to a life of crime, the community enjoys a measure of protection.... The offender, too, benefits.... He is treated as a responsible human being" (1974: 7-8).

These desirable effects, Burns comments, are "entirely speculative" (1980: 8). The momentum toward restitution as a sentence seems to him to depend on little more than "an intuitive sense of its rationality" (1980: 7).

The Task Force, although it supports expanded restitution proposals, admits "there is little of this kind of 'hard' evidence which might allow us to decide conclusively whether the benefits of restitution outweigh its costs" (1983: 92). To be fair, there is little hard evidence on whether any other sentencing dispositions work any better (Griffiths et al., 1980: 233-34). The "safest conclusion," says Klein, is that restitution "as a correctional measure simply will not make any difference" (1978: 400).

And finally, there are difficulties in implementing effective and just restitution schemes.

Crown attorneys will have discretion whether to recommend restitution, and judges will have discretion whether to order it. Can justice then be equal for offenders, or victims? The victims cannot "shop" for a judge who is known to make restitution orders.

Would the law fall unevenly on the person who steals $10 million and cannot possibly make restitution, and the person who steals $100 and can? If restitution is a correctional measure, imposed for the good of the offender, should it not then be imposed regardless of whether the victim has been paid for the loss by insurance?

Defence counsel often tell the court, in a bid for a more lenient sentence, that full or partial restitution has been made. If this does in fact result in leniency, does that mean that if a rich man and a poor man both break a window and the rich man can afford to replace it, then he receives a less severe sentence than the poor man for the same offence?

What happens if there are several offenders? If one has no ability to pay, or reneges on payment, do the others pay more to make up the victim's total loss? Suppose there are multiple victims, and as part of plea negotiations some charges are dropped. Which victims are then to receive restitution?

Finally, if victims of crime are entitled to be restored to their original status, why not every victim? Why limit the recompense to those cases of property loss in which an offender can not only be identified, charged, convicted and sentenced to make restitution but can actually pay damages?

Yet with all their flaws, restitution programs (inside the criminal process) and compensation schemes (outside of it) have been legislated in may jurisdictions in the last twenty years. Though often underfunded, unadvertised and underused, obviously they have merits for lawmakers. For one, they enable governments faced with rising crime rates and rising public concern over crime to say, "Look what we're doing for the victims." Roger Meiners points out that large numbers of compensation programs were established at least in part as a palliative for increasing crime and relatively inefficient restitution (Meiners, 1978: 9-44). Voters are told that something will be done for them when and if they are victimized and few will find out otherwise. Elias claims compensation has:

> justified strengthened police forces, provided
> political advantages to its supporters, facilitated
> social control of the population and yet sub-
> stantially failed in providing most victims with
> assistance (1983: 213).

A second purpose is to keep the victim from demanding a real role in the prosecution process. As Hagan says, such programs open the possibility of bringing the victim back into the system without actually doing it, symbolically conveying a sense of concern while doing little to alter the actual origin of the concern (1983: 160).

Victim Impact Statements

The other proposal of the Task Force, aside from restitution, to bring the victim back into the prosecution process was to amend the Criminal Code to "permit" the introduction of a victim impact statement "to be considered" at the time of sentencing (Task Force, 1983: 157). Such a statement would presumably enable victims to tell the judge of their suffering and of any monetary loss as a result of the crime. Presumably they would then feel that somebody was paying attention to what happened to them.

At present nothing, except pressure of time, prevents a judge from asking to hear from a victim, or when ordering a pre-sentence report from asking that the victim be consulted. The intent of the Task Force proposal is to require the judge to request such a statement.[6]

That proposal raises serious questions. To the degree that the statement dealt with monetary loss, it could be considered in assessing restitution as part of a sentence, subject to concerns already discussed about the purposes of sentencing and conflict with civil courts, particularly if the amount of the loss were in dispute. Questions arise whether the determination of loss would have to be based on receipts of appraisals, which might be difficult for some victims to produce; whether the statement would have to be sworn; whether it would be subject to contest by the accused; and if contested, whether the whole question would not then have to be referred to a civil court for adjudication.

To the degree that the statement dealt with pain or suffering, its usefulness would be questionable as long as the focus in sentencing is on the protection of society and the rehabilitation of the accused. A shut-in widow whose television set is stolen may suffer more from its loss than the wealthy bachelor who is seldom home, but that should weigh less with the judge than the characteristics of the offence, the previous record of the offender and the perceived need to deter such behaviour in the community. If the purpose of the sentence is to rehabilitate the offender, then its nature should be determined by presumed experts. If its purpose is deterrence, then it should be certain and predictable, not subject to modification by the victim. If the purpose is retribution, then the punishment must fit the crime rather than the victim (Karmen, 1984: 155).

Then there is the problem of how the statement will be submitted, Ninety-eight per cent of cases are concluded in the provincial courts (Griffiths *et al.*, 1980: 146-147) and about seventy per cent of these without a trial. Dockets are crowded, hearings are rushed and pre-sentence reports are rare. If the victim is not present when the accused pleads guilty, how often will judges be willing to delay sentence to hear from the victim?

Perhaps too, it is only an assumption that many victims really want this input, or any input, into their cases. A Philadelphia judge, Lois Porer, who routinely offers victims a chance to speak on sentence, says they seldom do (Karmen, 1984: 230-231). Since victim impact statements were legislated in Connecticut in 1981, only three per cent of victims appear at sentence hearings. When as an experiment victims were invited to take part in plea-bargaining sessions on their cases in Dade County, Florida, only a third attended. Those who were present generally spoke only in answer to questions, approved what the professionals suggested and were "passive and docile" (Heinz and Kerstatter, 1980: 172).

Resistance to Change

Having looked at the "rights" of the victim in the prosecution process and at proposals to give victims a larger role, it remains to ask: would these proposals, or any proposals, make any real difference in the conduct of the courts?

As we have seen, restitution is seldom ordered. Compensation schemes are seldom used. The majority of victims do not accept the limited opportunities to participate which are offered to them. It is not clear whether the last is because they don't care, or because they don't think it will make any difference, or because as the Dade County study suggests the system is not diligent in notifying them of opportunities (Heinz and Kerstatter, 1980: 173).

One of the reasons advanced for helping victims is to encourage them to co-operate with the system in reporting more victimizations. In the United States, the percentage of incidents of violence which were reported to police went from forty-six per cent in 1973 to forty-seven per cent in 1981, and of household burglaries from forty-seven per cent in 1973 to fifty-one per cent in 1981, despite the launching of numerous victim-assistance programs during that period (Karmen, 1984: 168).

After reviewing a decade of action and advocacy on behalf of victims in the United States, Weigend concluded it has generated "much rhetoric, more knowledge...but little change" (1983: 91).

Criminal justice systems are like any bureaucracy. They operate in their own interests. They are subject to what Karmen calls "goal displacement" (1984: 169), which means that they substitute, for the official goals of doing justice and serving the public, the unofficial goals of getting through the workload expeditiously, covering up mistakes and making themselves look as essential as possible so funding won't be cut. As King points out:

> Imagine for example the approach of the victim of a serious crime. He wishes to see the offender punished and deterred from further offences. Now compare that approach with that of a court administrator, whose major concern is the efficient running of the system, clearing the workload for the day and avoiding any unnecessary delays.... The one looks to the magistrate to revenge his loss...and to compensate him, the victim, while the other looks at his watch and wonders how long the case is going to last and whether the morning list will be completed by one o'clock" (1981: 13-14).

A place for victims in the prosecution process is limited to one that does not interfere with the smooth working of the system or the privileges and convenience of its principles.

Most reforms, as we have seen, seem to be intended to inform or assist or conciliate the victim, and these are worthy goals, but they involve no real rights or participation. Where the victim has been granted a role in the process, it appears to be subject to foot-dragging (the Dade County experiment), discretion (to be "considered" or to be applied "where appropriate") or co-opting.

The fate of reforms in the role of the victim is not surprising. Ericson and Baranek state:

> It is a common feature of bureaucratic organi-
> zations that rules intended to influence the
> action of agents are routinely absorbed by the
> agents to conform with their existing practices
> (1982: 224).

Exciting reforms are "translated into mechanisms of convenience by control agents and relegated to their pragmatically appropriate place" (1982: 231).

Conclusion

If the public criminal justice process is impervious to change which would allow the victim any real participation, what then?

Organizational victims already bypass the public prosecution and set up their own system to deal with incidents which are classified not as "crime" (which by definition involves the public interest) but as "loss" (Shearing and Stenning, 1983: 7). In these victim-oriented systems, run by and for victims, the priority is on restitution or compensation for the loss and prevention of future losses.

Then there are proposals, for example Christie's (1977, 1982), for similar decriminalization of offences against individuals. Christie argues that we "create crime by creating systems that ask for the work" (1982: 74). He proposes to remove conflicts from the professionals and return them to the accused and the victims, and to set up quasi-civil procedures to assess compensation and penalties. Pointing out that "several less-industrialized countries" apply civil law where Europe applies criminal law (1982: 92), he asks, "Could we imagine social systems where the parties by and large relied on civil solutions?" (1982: 96).

Ericson and Baranek, discussing such proposals, are skeptical. Decriminalization may simply imply some other form of social control. Diversion programs may lead to more cumbersome procedures and increase the number of persons subject to control (1982: 228). They add, "All reform alternatives include an added role for some group of professionals" (1982: 233).

It is also important to note that there is the vigilante, who tries his own case and administers his own justice, celebrated in the movies *Death Wish* and *Deadly Force* ("When the cops won't and the courts can't...he will give you justice!" (Karmen, 1984: 247)) and emulated by Bernhard Goetz of New York.

In Canada, at least, rates of reported crime are not escalating in a way that justifies the vigilante. But one of the arguments for compensating victims of crime rests on the assumption that they do not carry out their own justice. In Taylor's analysis (1983), a crucial function of the capitalist state is to maintain conditions under which production can flourish. One of these conditions is a "justice" system. There must be an overall sense in society of a free contract whereby the state protects the person and the property of its citizens, in exchange for those citizens subjugating themselves to the state. The loss of liberty thereby involved is offset and made legitimate by the overall protection of the freedom of the citizen which is provided by a police force and a legal and penal system (1983: 135). In other words, citizens give up the right to protect themselves and to pursue their own vengeance, and the state contracts to protect them to do so. Therefore, it can be argued that if the state fails in its side of the contract, it should compensate the victim.

Similar arguments for compensating crime victims can be raised on the basis of sociologist Emile Durkheim's theories that crime is normal, even necessary to a healthy society (Vold, 1979: 204-208). Durkheim argued that society makes certain demands on its members, and fulfilling these demands is an important source of social solidarity. But the demands are constructed so that inevitably a certain identifiable group will not be able to fulfill them. This enables the rest to feel a sense of moral superiority which he says is the primary source of the social solidarity.

Durkheim informed us that it is not only inevitable that some will oppose the collective conscience, it is also healthy. Progressive social change comes about because some people dare to differ. Thus crime is the price society pays for the possibility of progress — all the more reason why society should compensate those few who are martyrs to its health.

What would we do if we were really serious about helping victims of crime? We would fund adequately and advertise widely a government-supported compensation fund. It would not be funded, as is often suggested, by a group of convicted offenders, for that would imply that offenders are a distinct group and would hold all in that group, who happened to be caught, liable for the damage inflicted by some. Rather it might be funded like medical insurance (one might contribute to OHIP and to VICE — Victims Insurance (against) Criminal Enterprises), recognizing first that there are more offenders than ever that are caught, second that their definition of which acts are crimes and therefore which persons are offenders is made by society and changes from time to time and third that society has an obligation to those who suffer from one of its inevitable features. We would allow compensation both for material loss and for pain and suffering, and whether or not an offender has been identified. Yes, there would be cheating, just as people cheat now on claims for private insurance. But if private insurers live with that risk, surely a public scheme can.

Endnotes

1   Justice statistics do not distinguish between guilty pleas and guilty verdicts in keeping records of those convicted. This figure is based on Griffiths *et al.* (1980: 147) and on Ericson and Baranek (1982: 156) and studies reported in Note 2, p. 248.

2   Section 653 of the Criminal Code provides that where the accused is charged with an indictable offence, the victim may apply at the time of sentencing for an order that the accused pay an amount as satisfaction for loss or damage to property caused as a result of the commission of the crime. If the accused does not pay forthwith, the victim may file the order as a civil judgement with the superior court of the province and execute upon it as if it were a civil judgement. The court may also take the amount awarded out of monies found in the possession of the accused at the time of arrest, as long as there is no dispute over the right of ownership or possession of that money.

3   This figure is based on the Canadian Urban Victimization Study, reported by the Federal-Provincial Task Force on Justice for Victims of Crime (1983: 14), which estimated that in seven major Canadian centres in 1981 there were more than 700,000 individual victims of personal crimes and almost 900,000 victims of household crimes.

4   The major references in the Criminal Code to compensation and restitution are as follows:

Section 388(2). A summary conviction court can order the accused to pay up to $50 for willful destruction or damage to property, in addition to any other punishment which may be imposed, and failure to pay can result in an additional prison sentence of up to two months.

Sections 653, 654 and 655 cover restitution as a sentence for an indictable offence.

For Section 653 see Note 2 above.

Section 654 confers the same rights as 653 on innocent purchasers of stolen property.

Section 655 empowers the court to order that any property obtained by an indictable offence of theft be restored to the victim, so long as the property is before the court at the time of trial and there is no dispute as to ownership.

Section 616 suspends a restitution order made under any of these sections until the appeal process has been exhausted, and the court of appeal may vary or annul any such order.

Section 663(2)(e) allows a probation order to require the offender to make restitution or reparation to any person aggrieved or injured by the commission of the offence for the actual loss or damage sustained by that person as a result of the offence.

5   The *Globe and Mail* (1985b: A10) reports an Ontario Supreme Court decision awarding a rape victim damages jointly from the offender and the owner of her apartment building who was found negligent.

6   Statement made by Task Force Chairman Donald Sinclair in a personal conversation Feb. 11, 1985.

References

Beattie, J. 1986. "Administering Justice Without Police: Criminal Trial Procedure in Eighteenth-Century England" in Donelan, R. (ed.), *The Maintenance of Order in Society: A Symposium*. Ottawa: Canadian Police College.

Burns, P. 1980. *Criminal Injuries Compensation*. Vancouver: Butterworths.

Christie, N. 1977. "Conflicts as Propert." *British Journal of Criminology* 1.

Christie, N. 1982. *Limits to Pain*. Oxford: Martin Robertson.

Elias, R. 1983. "Symbolic Politics of Victim Compensation." *Victimology* 18.

Ericson, R.V. and P.M. Baranek. 1982. *The Ordering of Justice: A Study of Accused Persons as Dependents in the Criminal Process*. Toronto: Butterworths.

Federal-Provincial Task Force. 1983. *Justice for Victims of Crime*. Ottawa: Ministry of Supply and Services.

Globe and Mail. 1984. "Justice Secretary Proposes Fund Finances by Convicted Offenders." Toronto, April 10.

Griffiths, C.T. *et al*. 1980. *Criminal Justice in Canada*. Toronto: Butterworths.

Hagan, J. 1983. *Victims Before the Law: The Organizational Domination of Criminal Law*. Toronto: Butterworths.

Heinz, A.M. and W.A. Kerstatter. 1980. "Victim Participation in Plea Bargaining: A Field Experiment" in McDonald, W.F. and J. A. Cramer (eds.), *Plea Bargaining*. Lexington, MA: D.C. Heath.

Holdsworth, J. 1909. *A History of English Law*. Vol. II, Part II, Section II. London: Methuen.

Hudson, J. and B. Galway. 1975. *Considering the Victim: Readings in Restitution and Victim Compensation*. Springfield, IL: Charles Thomas.

Karmen, A. 1984. *Crime Victims: An Introduction to Victimology*. Monterey: Brooks/Cole.

King, M. 1981. *The Framework of Criminal Justice*. London: Croom Helm.

Klein, J. 1978. "Revitalizing Restitution: Flogging a Horse that May Have Been Killed for a Just Cause." *Criminal Law Quarterly* 20.

Law Reform Commission of Canada. 1974. Working Paper 5: "Restitution and Compensation." Ottawa: Information Canada.

Linden, A.M. 1968. "Report of Osgoode Hall Study on Compensation for Victims of Crime." Toronto: Osgoode Hall Law School.

McDonald, W.F. 1976. *Criminal Justice and the Victim*. Beverly Hills: Sage.

Meiners, F. 1978. *Victims Compensation: Economic, Legal, and Political Aspects*. Toronto: D.C. Heath.

Moskoff, F. 1983. "Compensation and Restitution as Part of the Criminal Process." *Advocates Society Journal* 10.

R. v. Zelensky et al. 1978. 2 C.R. (3rd) 107 (S.C.C.).

Shearing, C.D. and P.C. Stenning. 1983. *Private Security and Public Justice: The Challenge of the 80s.* Montreal: Institute for Research on Public Policy.

Taylor, I. 1983. *Crime, Capitalism, and Community.* Toronto: Butterworths.

Toronto Star. 1985. "Crime Victims — Conference Approves Organization of National Lobby Groups." Feb. 11.

Toronto Star. 1984. "Victims of Violence: Too Many to Ignore." Nov. 11.

Vold, G.B. 1979. *Theoretical Criminology.* New York: Oxford.

Weigend, T. 1983. "Problems of Victim-Witness Assistance Programs." *Victimology* 3.

Weiler, D. and J.D. Desgagne. 1984. *Victims and Witnesses of Crime in Canada.* Ottawa: Ministry of Supply and Services Canada.

Sentencing as a Gendered Process:
Results of a Consultation

Renate M. Mohr

Introduction

There is one striking feature of sentencing reform in Canada and other jurisdictions that has recently surfaced in the literature (Daly, 1989; Morris, 1988). Historically, sentencing reforms, like all other law reform efforts, have been gender-neutral in form and substance (Boyle, 1985; Gavigan, 1983). Feminist literature critically examines the significance of gender-neutral research as it reveals itself in androcentricity, overgeneralization and gender insensitivity (Eichler, 1988). Symptomatic of gender-neutrality in sentencing reform efforts is research that consists of constructing our thinking around men rather than women and men, research that involves the gathering of information with regard to one sex and treating it as if it applied to both sexes and, finally, research that ignores sex as "a socially significant variable in cases in which it is, in fact, significant" (Eichler, 1988). This paper seeks to reveal ways in which gender-blindness in law reform efforts inevitably results in formal, rather than substantive, justice. As a recent consultation with a women's organization illustrated, understanding sentencing as a gendered process is the beginning, not the end, of a new process of reform (Canadian Association of Elizabeth Fry Societies CAEFS, 1988: 32).

> There is much work to be done. Little has been written about the status of women in conflict with the law. Few people have been educated to understand how attitudes regarding gender, race and class influence decision-making on a daily basis. Sentencing data is inadequate at best, and little exists on women as a distinct group.

Gender-blind Reform Efforts

Gender-neutral research is necessarily blind to the reality that "[r]egardless of individual judge's commitment to the abstract values of fairness and impartiality, unconscious gender-based myths, biases and stereotypes can and often do influence judicial decision making, fact-finding, and the conduct of a court room environment" (Wikler, 1987). The role of gender in shaping decision making is key in understanding the sentencing process, since, as Freda Steel (1987) writes of family law, "...the subject is essentially a fact-based arena of decision-making, where legal principles are merely guidelines to extraordinary amounts of flexibility granted to the judiciary." Blindness to the impact of gender biases, sex roles and stereotypes on decision making, law making, and law reform has been reinforced rather than challenged by law school training (Wikler, 1987). It is not surprising, therefore, to learn that sentencing reform has long been guided by gender-blindness.

Interestingly, although gender bias has been overlooked, there has long been a recognition in the literature on sentencing that unconscious biases and personal characteristics of judges shape their individual approaches to sentencing. Over 200 years ago, Beccaria (1764: 10) expressed concern over the subjective nature of sentencing decisions and how, due to the judges unbridled discretion, "...the spirit of the law would be the product of a judge's good or bad logic, of his good or bad digestion; it would depend on the influence of his passions, on the weakness of the accused, on the judge's connection with him and on all those minute factors that alter the appearance of an object in the fluctuating mind of man." Then, as now, although there was a concern with personal biases, the gender of the sentencer and the person subject to the sentence was left unquestioned.

In the last two decades, the relationship of social class and race to the exercise of judicial discretion has been studied in mainstream Canadian literature on sentencing (Hogarth, 1971). Hogarth's study on the background characteristics of magistrates revealed that a number of extra-legal factors were central to their sentencing behaviour. These factors included political affiliation, social class, background, age, religion and ethnic background. Gender is once again conspicuous in its absence. Although this study remains an important contribution to sentencing literature, its gender-blindness is revealed in the gender-neutral title of the text. Hogarth studied the sentencing behaviour of an almost (if not totally) exclusively male judiciary yet the book was given the title, *Sentencing as a Human Process*. To use the word human to describe what is almost exclusively a male process serves further to obscure the significance of the gender of those who sentence.

In their first major report on sentencing reform in Canada, the Law Reform Commission of Canada (LRCC) (1977) stated that their work was based on "the assumption that perceptions, attitudes, practices and expectations are the primary forces in shaping our approach to crime." Again, although the LRCC raised social class and race as personal attributes that affect attitudes and perceptions, their work too remained gender-neutral. That concern that the individual attitudes and perceptions of judges were largely responsible for unwarranted disparity in sentences was to be a guiding theme in the following law reform efforts (Canadian Sentencing Commission, 1987). The Canadian Sentencing Commission was created in 1984 with the broad mandate requiring it to address this issue of unwarranted disparity which was, according to the terms of reference, "inconsistent with the principle of equality before the law." Unlike previous reform efforts which continued to propose that multiple rationales should guide the sentencing of judges (Department of Justice, Canada, 1984), the Commission proposed the imposition of a single rationale to structure the decision-making process and ensure a "uniformity of approach" to sentencing. The Commission recommended that the paramount principle governing the determination of sentence should be that the sentence be proportionate to the gravity of the offence and degree of responsibility of the offender. The just deserts solution proposed by the Commission was the first serious attempt to ensure that individual judges sitting in courts of different levels across the country would no longer sentence according to their personal rationales but would share a uniform approach.

In the next part of this paper, the limitations of the just deserts rationale will be explored as they were revealed in a recent consultation that raised the significance of gender, in form and substance. The consultation revealed, as feminist literature asserts, that legislative change must be accompanied by change at the personal level if it is ever to achieve goals of substantive equality. Just deserts may be the rationale that will ultimately lead to a more just process of sentencing, but so long as it remains gender-neutral (as well as colour-blind and class-less), it will remain on the level of the abstract. As feminists have long agreed, and as the consultation reveals, treating unequals equally will not result in equality. Rather than neutralize gender, race and class, a sentencing rationale must ensure that, as in the development of equality rights under the Charter of Rights and Freedoms, unequals are treated "in proportion to the inequality existing between them" (Bayefsky, 1987).

Results of the Consultation

To assert that sentencing is a gendered process is to suggest that the gender of both the sentencer and the subject of the sentence is a crucial element in understanding and defining the roots of unwarranted disparity. In January 1988, the Department of Justice provided funding to a national women's organization to respond to the report of the Canadian Sentencing Commission (1987). The Canadian Association of Elizabeth Fry Societies (CAEFS) represents nineteen community-based agencies across the country that work with and on behalf of women involved in the justice system. As an organization structured to work with women, CAEFS was uniquely situated to raise issues of gender so long ignored in the sentencing reform process. As the title of one of the first books on Canadian women in conflict with the law suggests, to date, the criminal justice system has considered women "too few to count" (Adelberg and Currie, 1987). As the results of a consultation that drew from the experiences of women and men working with women reveals, when women are counted, both the form and substance of the approach to sentencing reform changes.

As set out in the consultation (CAEFS, 1988: 8), the purpose of the consultation was not simply to gather responses to the Sentencing Commission's lengthy report, but rather to build on concerns and issues raised by the participants who had a wealth of first-hand knowledge of the impact of current sentencing practices and laws on women.

> Although the Commission's report has many worthy proposals, we do not set out in this consultation to deal with the proposals in the order and framework established by the Commission. Again, the reason for this is simple. If we are to take context seriously, then we must first uncover the experiences of women in conflict with the law. It is those experiences that will provide us with a framework for reform proposals, if they are truly to address the daily sources of inequities experiences by women.

This has been described as a feminist methodology because it takes "the experiences of women as the initial starting point for the formulation of legal critiques and political agendas" (Boyle, 1985; Greshner, 1987; Lahey, 1985). Although neither the methodology nor the results of the consultation can be described fully, some of the results of the interviews will be highlighted below.

Eighteen of the nineteen member societies located in communities from Sydney, Nova Scotia to Prince George, British Columbia, participated in this consultation. Two telephone interviews were conducted with each of the participants (a staff member or society board member). In order to facilitate preparation for the first interview, each participant received a list of open-ended questions to consider. The questions sought to uncover the views and perceptions of participants as to the problems that — in their particular community — were the greatest source of unwarranted disparity and inequity in sentencing (CAEFS, 1988: Appendix B).

As a result of the first telephone interviews, a clear picture of issues and problems of greatest concern to women in conflict with the law emerged. In spite of the regional differences, the differences in size of the community, etc., there was a general consensus on all of the major issues raised by participants coast to coast.

The second telephone interviews were to draw on the context or picture that emerged as a result of the first interviews. In the second set of interviews, participants were asked to respond to reform proposals that would address the concerns they raised. If the Sentencing Commission proposed a recommendation that was relevant to a particular concern raised, it was presented to the participant as a suggested reform. Again, just as the context painted by participants came through with remarkable clarity, so did their suggestions for the directions of sentencing reform. Social services, education and communication were the primary concerns repeated in the conversations. Many participants stressed that before legislators, judges, lawyers and other actors in the criminal justice process can be educated as to the "realities of women and crime," they must first understand something about the inequalities women suffer in Canadian society generally. The report sets the context for understanding the status of women in Canada through citing Statistics Canada figures that show women's wages in 1985 remained at 64.9 per cent of their male counterparts.

> Unfortunately, the majority of the poverty stricken are women, the phenomen becoming known as the feminization of poverty. Families headed by women are 4.5 times more likely to be poor than families headed by men. A full 44% of female-headed households are poor. In 1981, women as single-parent headed almost one in every ten Canadian families.

In addition, the consultation document listed other "realities" of women's lives raised by participants, including violence, in pornography or in fact, and other "historical barriers which go far beyond issues of choice in reproduction." The consequences of sentencing reform efforts that overlook the "realities of women's lives" were far-reaching in the eyes of the participants:

> Commonly-held social values and attitudes to women are not in touch with the real life experiences of women, nor are the social institutions established to provide services to them. Despite billions of dollars of federal and provincial programming, women have still had to establish their own separate institutions such as interval houses for battered women and their dependents, health care collectives, child care centers, and multi-service facilities for aboriginal women, immigrant women, and other identifiable social groups in need of support. While some of this may be anticipatory planning by women's groups, much of it stems from the "reality gap" — the difference between services provided to women by traditional institutions and the real life requirements of women.

One question that emerged from a discussion of the significance of gender to sentencing practices and laws was a question that would never have been raised in the course of a traditional consultation. The question asked by one participant was the following: given the realities, why do law makers ask "why" women come into conflict with the law instead of questioning how it is that so few women come into conflict with the law? The very fact that this question is never asked should give great hope to critical scholars — for if it is taken seriously, it suggests that there may be answers in this "different voice" to which we have just begun to listen.

The problem facing women in conflict with the law that was most often raised by participants was the lack of social services available to women. Interestingly, the lack of social services was raised in response to the question about what it is that causes the most unwarranted disparity.

> The answers to this question were very revealing as to the context which would ultimately unfold. The answers did not focus on issues like unreasonably high maximum penalties or on the need for presumptive guidelines for judges. Instead, the answers read as follows:

> Poverty, Race, Socialization, Power imbal-
> ances, Class bias, Violence, Access to legal
> representation, Attitudes, Lack of knowledge
> about the context of women's lives.

These answers have never emerged in the course of traditional consultations on state reform efforts. The reason, once again, is that once in
print the structure of the reform efforts themselves is so powerful that their
very foundation is rarely questioned. Meaningful reform requires that the
form itself be challenged. It requires an understanding of women in conflict
with the law that very few people have. The reason for this is that very few
women and men have an understanding of the social significance of gender
in Canada today. Significantly, education and communication were the two
major areas raised by participants as areas of priority to be addressed in any
re-thinking of sentencing. Stereotypes and other biases that are shared by
many Canadians were also cited as causes of unwarranted disparity.

The proposed solution to this problem was not that "a uniformity
approach" to sentencing be imposed on judges, but that "...the agendas of
continuing education seminars for lawyers and judges give priority to issues
of gender, race and class." The report stressed that "[u]ntil judges are
taught about the violence and poverty that exists in homes across the country, we cannot expect them to understand the 'impact' of their decisions on
the lives of the women they sentence daily." The call for education was
overwhelming. All those who work in the criminal justice process were singled out as in need of attention, given the decision-making power that goes
along with their roles. A broad recommendation was made urging "...the
Department of Justice to meet with provincial departments of education
and to call upon them to provide education, at all levels of schooling, on the
operation and limitations of the criminal law and criminal justice system."

The issue of communication was invariably raised whenever sentencing
was discussed as a "process." Participants agreed that there was no sense
of process, either as experienced by the women they worked with or by
themselves as court workers. Currently, the report acknowledges, few decision-makers get feedback "as to either the impact or the effectiveness of
their decisions." The importance of good communication between the volunteer court workers and the judge was stressed by many participants and
those communities that reported a good relationship between the volunteer
court-worker and the judge had the greatest success in using community-
based sanctions. An interesting observation was made by one of the participants regarding how simple it would be to improve communication
between the community and the actors in the "process." In her particular

community, a committee had been set up to discuss renovations of the new court house. The committee includes judges, lawyers, court workers, police officers and a variety of community representatives. If it is possible to get these people talking to one another about the renovation of a building, she suggested, it should be possible to get them together to discuss the work they do every day. Once again, this is a small but significant example of the creative recommendations that spring from a form of consultation that listens to and values experience.

Conclusion

The essential connection between gender and the criminal law was perhaps best summarized in the conclusion of the CAEFS report:

> The criminal law has never been "our" criminal law, if "our" is to reflect the lives of women and men. It has been drafted, enforced and reformed primarily by men, for men. Although beyond the purview of this consultation, the substantive criminal law is in need of reform efforts that take issues of gender, race and class seriously (1988: 20).

Although this is but a brief description of a women-centred consultation, it is evident that the issues central to the reform of sentencing laws and practices, as seen by women and as felt by women, are different from those that have been raised in previous reform efforts. The popular "just deserts" sentencing rationale proposed by the Sentencing Commission as a solution to unwarranted disparity was felt by participants to leave too many questions unresolved and too many attitudes unchecked.

> If we are ever to achieve the goal of proportionality — that the "punishment fit the crime," we need contextual information about not only the crime but also the punishment. Judges must be aware of the pains of imprisonment that cannot be measured in time alone (CAEFS, 1988: 21).

Although it was conceded that the "just deserts" rationale may be the best solution to unwarranted disparity in a society where there is true equality, until we attain that goal, we must continue to search for an approach that requires judges and law reformers to uncover, rather than cover up, gender, race and class differences.

References

Adelberg, E. and Claudia Currie. 1987. *Too Few to Count*. Vancouver: Press Gang Publishers.

Bayefsky, Anne F. 1987. "Defining Equality Rights Under the Charter," in Martin, Sheilah and Kathleen Mahoney (eds.), *Equality and Judicial Neutrality*. Toronto: Carswell.

Beccaria, Caesar. 1764. *On Crimes and Punishments*. New York: Bobbs-Merrill.

Boyle, Christine. 1985. "Criminal Law and Procedure: Who Needs Tenure?" *Osgoode Hall Law Journal* 23: 427.

Canadian Association of Elizabeth Fry Societies (CAEFS). 1988. "Sentencing in Context: Revealing the Realities of Women in Conflict with the Law." Ottawa: Unpublished Consultation document.

Canadian Sentencing Commission. 1987. *Sentencing Reform: A Canadian Approach*. Ottawa: Ministry of Supply and Services.

Daly, Kathleen. 1989. "Rethinking Judicial Paternalism: Gender, Work-Family Relations, and Sentencing." *Gender and Society* 3: 9.

Department of Justice, Canada. 1984. *Sentencing*. Ottawa: Government of Canada.

Eichler, Magrit. 1988. *Nonsexist Research Methods: A Practical Guide*. Boston: Allen and Unwin.

Gavigan, Shelley. 1983. "Women's Crime and Feminist Critiques: A Review of the Literature." *Canadian Criminology Forum*. 6: 75.

Greshner, Donna. 1987. "Judicial Approaches to Equality and Critical Legal Studies," in Martin, Sheilah and Kathleen Mahoney (eds.), *Equality and Judicial Neutrality*. Toronto: Carswell.

Hogarth, John. 1971. *Sentencing as a Human Process*. Toronto: University of Toronto Press.

Lahey, Kathleen. 1985. "Until Women Themselves Have Told All That they Have to Tell." *Osgoode Hall Law Journal* 23: 519.

Law Reform Commission of Canada. 1977. *Guidelines: Dispositions and Sentences in the Criminal Process*. Ottawa: Minister of Supply and Services.

Morris, Allison. 1988. "Sex and Sentencing." *The Criminal Law Review*: 163.

Steel, Freda M. 1987. "Alimoney and Maintenance Orders," in Martin, Sheilah and Kathleen Mahoney (eds.), *Equality and Judicial Neutrality*. Toronto: Carswell.

Wikler, Norma J. 1987. "Identifying and Correcting Gender Bias," in Martin, Sheilah and Kathleen Mahoney (eds.), *Equality and Judicial Neutrality*. Toronto: Carswell.

R. v. Brydges:
Let Them Eat Cake or, The Poor Person's Right to Counsel

Scott C. Hutchison and John G. Marko

> The Constitution requires I inform you that you have the right to remain silent; anything you say can and will be used against you in court; you have the right to talk to a lawyer now and have him present now or at any time during questioning, and if you cannot afford a lawyer one will be appointed for you without cost.
> Standard Warning given by Minneapolis Police Department.

The Facts: "I Just Think that I Should Talk to Someone."

In December 1985, Edmonton City Police finally caught up to Bill Brydges.

Brydges, wanted in relation to a 1979 murder, was arrested in Strathclair, Manitoba. He was taken to the RCMP detachment in Brandon, where Edmonton City Police Detective Ron Harris interviewed him. During the course of the interview Harris took care to tell Brydges of his right to counsel. Harris reminded Brydges of his warnings given to him on his arrest in Strathclair and continued the interview in the following terms:

Ron: Ah I informed you there that ah, it was our duty to inform you that you had the right to instruct counsel. And I asked you if you understood what that meant. And you said yes.

Bill: Yeah.

Ron: Okay. Ah...You didn't want to phone a lawyer out there. Ah you can phone one from here if you want. If you know one.

Bill: I don't know of any.

Ron: Did you want to try and get hold of one here.

Bill:	Well. Do they have any free Legal Aid or anything like that up here?
Ron:	I imagine they have a Legal Aid system in Manitoba. I'm...
Bill:	(Unintelligible)
Ron:	...not familiar with it but.
Bill:	Won't be able to afford anyone, heh? That's the main thing.
Ron:	Okay. You feel ah there's a reason for you maybe wanting to talk to one right now?
Bill:	Not right now no.
Ron:	Okay. Ahh. I'm just gonna read from this blue card again.
Bill:	Okay.
Ron:	Umm. Do you wish to say anything to me. Ah you're not obliged to say anything unless you wish to do so. Okay. But whatever you do say could be given in evidence. Do you understand that?
Bill:	Um hum.[1]

The interview continued with questioning in relation to the murder and inculpatory remarks by Brydges, but turned back to the issue of counsel when he asked "I just think that I should talk to someone. Maybe from Legal Aid or something then I.... Is that gonna be possible for me to get hold of someone?" Detective Harris replies:

Ron:	I can try and arrange it, sure.
Bill:	I'd like to try to talk to someone first.
Ron:	Okay.
Bill:	And that way, I might feel, feel a little bit easier about talking.
Ron:	About what happened?
Bill:	About everything, yeah.
Ron:	Okay, I don't know if I can get hold of a Legal Aid lawyer.
Bill:	I can't afford anyone else.
Ron:	But, well, what, I don't think they're gonna charge you for advise [sic]. (Pause) Do you want me to try to get one?
Bill:	Yeah, if you can get a Legal Aid, first.
Ron:	Do they have Legal Aid in Manitoba?
Bill:	I don't know, I don't know.
Ron:	Okay, I'll check. (Noise of chair moving)[2]

After that Detective Harris arranged a lawyer for Brydges. After speaking to this Manitoba lawyer Bridges made no further comments to the police.

In Court

Brydges did not speak to a lawyer again before his return, in police custody, to Alberta. There he was tried on the charge of murder and acquitted. The trial Judge excluded from evidence the statements made during the interview after Brydges indicated that he wanted a lawyer but did not think he could afford one.[3] The Court of Appeal split, two of the judges finding that the statement should have been allowed in, while the third agreed with the trial Judge.[4]

In the Supreme Court of Canada

All along the issue had been whether *after Brydges began asking about funded counsel* the police had a duty to tell him about the availability of legal aid. That is, until the case was heard in the Supreme Court, the issue was not related to the initial information provided to the detainee, but rather the duty on the officer conducting the interrogation to respond with information when the detainee indicates some desire to contact counsel or to have more information about the availability of legal aid.

On this point the Supreme Court is unanimous. All the Judges agreed with the comments of Mr. Justice Lamer (now Chief Justice) when he said:

> Once the appellant in effect requested the assistance of counsel it was incumbent on the police officer to facilitate contact with counsel by giving the appellant a reasonable opportunity to exercise his right to counsel. On the specific facts of this case, the court is faced with the following question: when an accused expresses a concern that his inability to afford a lawyer is an impediment to the exercise of the right to counsel, is there a duty on the police to inform him of the existence of duty counsel and the ability to apply for Legal Aid? In my view there is. I say this because imposing this duty on the police in these circumstances is consistent with the purpose underlying the right to retain and instruct counsel. A detainee is advised of the right to retain and instruct counsel without delay because it is upon arrest or detention that an accused is in *immediate need of legal advice*. As I stated in *Manninen, supra* at p. 392, one of the main functions of counsel at this early stage of detention is to confirm the existence of the right to remain silent and to advise the detainee about how to exercise that right. It is

> not always the case that immediately upon
> detention an accused will be concerned about
> retaining the lawyer that will eventually repre-
> sent him at a trial, if there is one. Rather, one
> of the important reasons for retaining legal
> advice without delay upon being detained is
> linked to the protection of the right against
> self-incrimination. This is precisely the reason
> that there is a duty on the police to cease ques-
> tioning the detainee until he has had a reason-
> able opportunity to retain and instruct
> counsel.[5]

This reasoning took comfort from the judgement of Mr. Justice Watt in *R. v. Parks*,[6] where a similar rule had been applied.

Thus far it is difficult to criticize Lamer J.'s judgement. The issues dealt with were squarely before the Court, placed there by the parties and fairly developed in written and oral submissions.

Moreover, the reasons are consistent with the underlying purpose of section 10(b) of the Charter of Rights and Freedoms as developed by the Court in *Therens*[7] and other cases.[8] An accused who indicates a desire to have counsel is entitled to have the police take reasonable steps to facilitate that desire. If the accused, by word or conduct, suggests that he believes in some barrier to counsel which does not exist then the officer has a duty to make it clear that such a barrier does not exist. The police cannot cultivate or take advantage of unreal impediments to counsel which exist in the mind of the detainee.

Too Tempting to Resist: "[I]t is Not Wise for this Court to Make Pronouncements."

The real problem with Mr. Justice Lamer's judgement is that it does not stop with this common sense and fair disposition of the case before the Court. His Lordship goes on to a broad consideration of the relationship between section 10(b) of the Charter[9] and the nature of funded counsel in this country. None of this was raised by the parties and no submissions were made on this issue. Lamer J. admits that his reasons on the issues already discussed were sufficient to dispose of the appeal. He felt "com-pelled," however, to go on and consider the "broader question" of whether the informational component of section 10(b) should *always* include refer-ence to the existence and availability of funded counsel.

This is a particularly difficult area and it is disturbing to see the Court entering into exploration of it without the benefit of any assistance from counsel. What is ironic is that Lamer J. was himself quick to criticize other members of the Court when they entered into a similar excursion in *Thomson Newspapers Ltd. v. Canada (Director of Investigations and Research)*.[10] There the effect of a challenge on a provision of the Combines Investigation Act[11] had significant impact on other provisions of the Canada Evidence Act.[12] Lamer J. expressed distress that some other members of the Court had entered into the case without recognizing or allowing a proper consideration by way of presentations to the Court on that issue. He writes:

> It would be most undesirable that we do this as a result of a challenge of the wrong section of the *Combines Investigations Act* and without a genuine challenge of s. 5(1) of the *Canada Evidence Act*, affording the constitutional validity of that section a full hearing. Second, this improper s. 52 challenge circumvents a challenge of s. 5(1) which, quite undoubtedly, would have attracted different interventions from the Attorneys-General.[13]

It would have been equally desirable to have the Court consider the issue of the section 10(b) of the Charter warning with some input from other provinces and it is likely that if they had been given proper notice many provinces would have had views to put before the court. As a result of Lamer J.'s determination to dispose of this issue, however, the Court has crossed a major threshold in the development of the right to counsel without any representations from those governments or bodies which are responsible for providing these services. As one author has noted:

> Lamer J.'s judicial digression in *Brydges* itself raises questions of basic fairness to interested parties. He noted himself the absence of input on the legal aid point from the police, the bar or the government. Nevertheless, he moved on to decide an issue with sweeping consequences for these parties. Surely these parties should have had the opportunity to seek to intervene.[14]

It is ironic that in attempting to make the criminal process fairer to accused, the Court has breached one of the most basic rules of fairness itself. While Lamer J.'s conduct is "most undesirable" the deed is done and it is now necessary to look at the major changes his Lordship has wrought in the law.

The Right to Funded Counsel

The issue which Lamer J. raises is "whether it should be part of the information component of the constitutional guarantee under s. 10(b) that accused persons should be told as a matter of routine *in all cases* of arrest or detention of the existence and availability of duty counsel and Legal Aid plans."[15]

Lamer J.[16] concludes that it should. His Lordship writes:

> In fact, it is most often the indigent and the disadvantaged in our society that are not as aware of the schemes that the state has set up on their behalf. In this respect I quote from the landmark decision of the United States' Supreme Court in *Miranda* v. *Arizona,* 384 U.S. 426 (1965), at p. 473:
>
> "The warning of a right to counsel would be hollow if not couched in terms that would convey to the indigent — the person most often subjected to interrogation — the knowledge that he too has a right to have counsel present. As with the warning of the right to remain silent and of the general right to counsel, only by effective and express explanation to the indigent of this right can there be assurance that he was truly in a position to exercise it."
>
> In my view then, these policy concerns in respect of making police officers' duties under the Charter clear and of ensuring that all detainees are made aware of the existence of duty counsel and Legal Aid, complement each other and support the view that information about the existence and availability of duty counsel and Legal Aid plans should be part of the standard s. 10(b) caution upon arrest or detention.[17]

After discussing his impressions of the existing funded counsel systems in Canada (about which more will be said later), Lamer J. concludes:

> All of this is to reinforce the view that the right to retain and instruct counsel, in modern Canadian society, has come to mean more than the right to retain a lawyer privately. It now also means the right to have access to

counsel free of charge where the accused meets certain financial criteria set up by the provincial Legal Aid plan, and the right to have access to immediate, although temporary, advice from duty counsel irrespective of financial status. These considerations, therefore, lead me to the conclusion that as part of the information component of s. 10(b) of the Charter, a detainee should be informed of the existence and availability of the applicable systems of duty counsel and Legal Aid in the jurisdiction, in order to give the detainee a full understanding of the right to retain and instruct counsel.[18]

Counterbalance: The Heightened Obligation on the Accused

In counterbalance to this new duty on the police to ensure that the detainee is aware of funded counsel, Lamer J. has presented the possibility of a new, or at least heightened, duty on detainees to seek out counsel. There may be a concomitant increase in the requirement that an accused or detainee show "reasonable diligence" in the exercise of his right to counsel. That is, an accused who tries and fails to contact a specific lawyer may be obliged to take advantage of the generic, though competent, duty counsel provided by the state. A refusal by an accused to accept this arrangement may be said to constitute unreasonable conduct amounting to a waiver or abandonment of the right to counsel.

Lamer J. declines to go further with this point than to suggest as follows:

> It may appear to some, as it does to me, that the additional duty imposed on the police combined with the increasing presence of duty counsel services, irrespective of a means test, may well have an effect on the consideration of what constitutes "reasonable diligence" of a detainee in pursuing the right to counsel. The purposive approach which leads us to the conclusion that a detainee has the right to be informed of the availability of Legal Aid and of duty counsel also raises questions as to how long the police must wait for counsel of the detainee's choice to become available. Indeed, if the purpose of s. 10(b) is to assist initially

persons upon their being detained as regard their rights and as regard their exercise thereof, we might well have to put time limits, not on access to counsel, but on access to counsel of one's choice. It may be that it is unreasonable not to seek the advice of available counsel when the only one available is either duty counsel or a Legal Aid lawyer. We must not, as a court, lose sight of the realities of crime investigation and the functioning of modern police forces of varying sizes, with shifts, labour agreements and limitations put on overtime for financial considerations of course, but also, if not more important because police officers have a right to a personal and family life. Waiting for eight to ten hours for counsel of the detainee's choice to become available may not be justified in a purposive approach when duty counsel has been available all along. But this issue and these considerations were not before the court, and were not addressed in this court nor in the courts below. The court has not had the benefit of the views of the police, government or the bars as to what would constitute "reasonable diligence" in the exercise of the right to counsel in the light of the additional burden, and of the specific availability of duty counsel. As such, it is not wise for this court to make pronouncements on that issue. It is sufficient to note that, as a corollary to the obligation imposed on the police to inform detainees of the existence and availability of duty counsel services and Legal Aid plans, there may have to be an adjustment to the meaning of "reasonable diligence".[19]

Even Lamer J. realized that his case marked the imposition on police of a significant new burden. Ill-defined and unexpected, this new duty requires the police to make the accused aware of the "existence and availability of the applicable systems of duty counsel and Legal Aid." His Lordship gives no real guidance to law enforcement officers or Crown counsel as to what the police should be saying to detainees. Instead of advice or a "bright line" for police, Lamer J. allows a thirty-day grace period in which this right might be ignored while the impact of the judgement is worked out. With the release of the judgement on February 1, 1990, law enforcement officials had until March 3, 1990 to work up their new standard operating procedures.

What to Say Now?

In Alberta, where the case arose, the following wording has been adopted:

> You have the right to retain and instruct coun-
> sel without delay. You may call any lawyer you
> want or you may get immediate advice from a
> lawyer from Legal Aid without charge.
>
> Do you understand?
> Do you want to call a lawyer now?

In Ontario the following wording has been adopted:

> You have the right to retain and instruct coun-
> sel without delay.
> You have the right to telephone any lawyer
> you wish.
>
> You also have the right to free advice from a
> Legal Aid lawyer.
> If you are charged with an offence you may
> apply to the Ontario Legal Aid Plan for legal
> assistance.
>
> Do you understand?
> Do you wish to call a lawyer now?

The scramble to formulate wording has left the country with a number of different wordings for the *Brydges* warning. Every province, the RCMP, the Judge Advocate General's office and the territories have all had to respond without any chance at proper co-ordination to this drastic change in the law.

In conjunction with this new informational right, services have been put into place to provide quick access to basic legal advice. In Ontario, a province-wide telephone service has been established since the decision in *Brydges*.[20] An accused is now told of the right to counsel in the language set out above and given an opportunity to call any lawyer he wishes. If that lawyer is not available, the province-wide "dial-a-duty counsel" is put into service. Alberta has responded with a similar scheme.[21]

This is all fine for a province like Ontario where a highly developed system of legal aid and a growing duty counsel service makes compliance with the Supreme Court's edict manageable. Other provinces, including, ironically, Alberta, where *Brydges* originated, have no such scheme in place or in development. The stresses of putting such a system in place on the 30-day shock treatment prescribed by the Supreme Court are obvious.

The whole *Brydges* experience is unsatisfactory. What the Court has in effect done is to write into the Constitution a significant new right without offering any real assistance to law enforcement officers called upon to respect that right. The weaknesses in the judgment demonstrate the problems which arise when judges try to legislate without regard to the cases before them. It is ironic and disappointing that a judgment which stresses the importance of basic fairness in the criminal justice system should itself be the product of such a flawed process.

Endnotes

1   [1990] 1 S.C.R. 190, [1990] 2 W.W.R. 220, 71 Alta. L.R. (2nd) 145, C.C.C. (3d) 330 at 334-335.

2   Ibid. at 335 (C.C.C.).

3   See the passages from the Judge's ruling reproduced in Lamer J.'s (now C.J.C.) judgement in the Supreme Court, ibid. at 336.

4   Ibid. at 330 (Alta. L.R.).

5   Ibid. at 342-343 (C.C.C.).

6   (1988), 33 C.R.R. 1 (Ont. H.C.).

7   *R. v. Therens*, [1985] 1 S.C.R. 613, [1985] 4 W.W.R. 286, 32 M.V.R. 153, 45 C.R. (3d) 97, 38 Alta. L.R. (2d) 99, 18 C.C.C. (3d) 481.

8   *R. v. Manninen*, [1987] 1 S.C.R. 1233, 61 O.R. (2d) 736 (note), 34 C.C.C. (3d) 385.

9   Canadian Charter of Rights and Freedoms, Part I of the Constitution Act, 1982, being Schedule B of the Canada Act 1982 (U.K.), 1982, c. 11.

10 [1990] 1 S.C.R. 425, 72 O.R. (2d) 415, 76 C.R. (3d) 129, 54 C.C.C. (3d) 417.

11 R.S.C. 1970, c. C-23 [now Competition Act, R.S.C. 1985, c. C-34].

12 R.S.C. 1970, c. E-10 [now R.S.C. 1985, c. C-5).

13 Above, note 10 at 430 (C.C.C.).

14 P.B. Michalyshyn, "Brydges: Should the Police be Advising of the Right to Counsel?" (1990) 74 C.R. (3d) 151 at 154-155.

15 Above, note 1 at 347 (C.C.C.).

16 And the three judges who concur with his opinion on this issue.

17 Above, note 1 at 347 (C.C.C.).

18   Ibid. at 349.

19   Ibid. at 350.

20   John Zado, Duty Counsel for the York County Law Association, responsible for Metropolitan Toronto and the surrounding area, reports that such a service was in the works before *Brydges*. The judgemnet simply made imperative a program which was in the planning stages.

21   Above, note 14 at 155.

Public Attitudes to Plea Bargaining

Stanley A. Cohen and Anthony N. Doob

In a 1975 working paper on *Control of the Process*[1] the Law Reform Commission of Canada strongly condemned the practice popularly known as plea bargaining. The Commission was not convinced by the then-prevalent arguments that plea bargaining was an administrative necessity. Referring to the scarcity and inconclusiveness of available evidence the Commission declared that:

> Even if the necessity of the practice were conclusively demonstrated, we would legitimize it as a part of the procedural law only with that reluctance that inevitably accompanies any sacrifice of principle to expediency. Plea bargaining may save time and money. We doubt that the saving is worth the cost.[2]

The inclusion of these statements in a working paper (as opposed to a Report to Parliament) indicates that they were the Commission's tentative, not its final, views on the subject. Much has occurred in the intervening years to merit a reconsideration of those views. Perhaps the two most significant developments have been the increased availability of legal aid to persons accused of serious crime and the advent of the Canadian Charter of Rights and Freedoms.[3] These two phenomena have resulted in an enhanced capacity in the system to provide legal representation to accused persons and this in turn has alleviated some of the potential dangers posed by the plea bargaining process. Coincident with these events has been the development and formalization in some locations of the pre-trial conference, a process explicitly designed to promote the early resolution of disputes in criminal matters.[4] In essence what has transpired, and continues to unfold, is a subtle but significant change in the working relationships of prosecutors and defence counsel. Given this evolving reality, the challenge for the Commission was to assess and propose workable reforms for a system known to possess serious flaws. Such was the genesis of the Commission's recent working paper to Parliament on "Plea Discussions and Agreements."[5]

The need for reform in this area of the law is pervasive. it extends, as the very title of the paper indicates, even to the basic vocabulary that is employed. "Plea Bargaining" is a term which, over time, had taken on pejorative connotations and thus had lost much of its utility. The paper concludes that new terms such as "plea discussions" and "plea agreements" were necessary to replace the old ones.

When the Commission first considered the issue of plea bargaining in 1975 it concluded that an appropriate definition of the phenomenon was "any agreement by the accused to plead guilty in return for the promise of some benefit."[6] It had become clear in the literature and the jurisprudence on the subject that the range of activity to be encompassed by any definition was of deceptive breadth. Amongst other things plea negotiations could involve:

(a)   a reduction in the charge;

(b)   a withdrawal of charges;

(c)   a promise not to proceed on other charges;

(d)   a recommendation or promise as to the type of sentence to be expected (fine, probation, imprisonment, etc.)

(e)   a recommendation as to the severity of sentence;

(f)   a Crown election to proceed by summary rather than indictable procedure where the offence involves a Crown option;

(g)   a promise not to seek a sentence of preventive detention;

(h)   a promise not to seek an enhanced penalty where the Code allows for one in the event of a prior conviction for the same offence;

(i)   a promise not to charge other persons;

(j)   a promise concerning the nature of any submissions to be made to the sentencing judge (e.g., not to mention aggravating facts or circumstances when they are in dispute);

(k)   a promise not to compel a jury trial through resort to a preferred indictment or by means of the power given under section 568 of the Code;

(l)   a recommendation or promise as to the place of incarceration or arrangements concerning release (e.g., day parole);

(m)   an arrangement for the sentencing to take place before a particular judge;

(n)   a promise not to appeal the sentence imposed.

In its 1989 reconsideration of the subject, the Law Reform Commission concluded that while it was valid to define plea bargaining as it had in 1975 the compass had been set rather too wide. The considerations affecting plea arrangements that resulted in a guilty plea were of a different nature than those applicable when the accused person was prepared to offer such benefits as evidence or information. In its view, the treatment of immunities and informers should be a matter of separate study and consideration. This decision did not have any direct bearing on the question of definition although it did affect the scope of the ultimate recommendations. What was unfortunate and of relevance was the emphasis in the 1975 definition on the exchange of "benefits." If the prevailing system of plea discussion and agreement were to be regularized and if there were to be any prospect of plea bargaining's shedding its unsavoury image it was important to discard the vocabulary of bartered justice. A new definition was required. Thus, the 1989 paper concludes that "plea discussion" and "plea agreement" should become the operative terms.

The term "plea agreement" was defined to mean "any agreement by the accused to plead guilty in return for the prosecutor's agreeing to take or refrain from taking a particular course of action." "Plea discussion" was defined as "a discussion directed toward the conclusion of a plea agreement."

The Law Reform Commission's 1989 Working Paper

The 1989 paper contends that the practice of "plea bargaining" is not inherently shameful and ought not, even on a theoretical level, to be characterized as a failure of principle. Plea discussions and agreements, where properly conducted, are necessary mechanisms in a system which aspires to do justice by matching the offender's alleged misconduct with the offence that is ultimately charged and by imposing sanctions appropriate to the misconduct involved.

The Commission's rejection of the abolition option necessitated its addressing, in concrete terms, the very problems which had previously been marshalled as arguments in support of abolition. Primary among these arguments were the low visibility of the phenomenon and the consequent absence of accountability. The *sub rosa* nature of plea bargaining, coupled with a reluctance in the legal and judicial communities to accept its legality, has resulted in a relative absence of standards and an unwarranted degree of looseness in practice. Openness and accountability thus were felt to be among the necessary conditions of effective reform.

Accountability entails a need to consider to what degree, if any, judicial involvement in the practice should be tolerated or encouraged. Accountability is also a primary guarantor of equality in the operation and enforcement of the law. Openness, by the same token, is seen as a guarantor of the voluntariness of any arrangements that are ultimately agreed upon. The accuracy and the appropriateness of such arrangements can only be scrutinized if the processes themselves are opened up to the public gaze.

Ultimately, the paper supports the development of an open and accountable process within which acceptable plea agreements may be reached. Under the proposed scheme improper blandishments offered during the course of discussions are prohibited and where discovered, as a result of increased scrutiny, are capable of effective repudiation. Judicial involvement, although highly circumscribed, is permitted. Under the proposals a judge before whom the parties are to appear is allowed to inquire whether plea discussions have taken place and, where they have not, the judge may indicate the possible benefits of such discussions and inquire whether the parties wish to engage in discussions. While plea discussions can initially occur in a relatively sequestered environment, the scheme mandates the full disclosure of the nature of and the reasons for any agreement by the parties in open court. This openness requirement may be dispensed with where compelling reasons, such as the likelihood of serious harm to the accused or to another person, require otherwise. The judge would, of course, retain ultimate authority to impose a sentence independent of any agreement entered into between the Crown and defence counsel under this scheme.

The notion of bringing the plea negotiations process out from behind closed doors is hardly novel, or even untried. Commentators have urged the adoption of more open plea discussion processes for Canada over a period of many years.[7] More recently the Canadian Sentencing Commission, in its report *Sentencing Reform: A Canadian Approach*, advocated the creation of mechanisms requiring the disclosure in open court of the facts and considerations which formed the basis of any plea agreement.[8]

The American Federal Rules of Criminal Procedure provide detailed rules for the regulation of plea bargaining practices.[9] The federal rules were the culmination of a lengthy process wherein the American Law Institute[10] and the National Conference of Commissioners on Uniform State Law,[11] supported by a great deal of academic and professional commentary,[12] urged the promulgation of standards that recognized the legitimacy of negotiated pleas in the context of a highly structured process involving judicial supervision.[13]

The Commission's proposals had been subjected to extensive discussion and consultation. In addition to the regular internal consultations on work in progress, working drafts are scrutinized in periodic advisory sessions convened with five major groups. The first of these groups is a panel of senior judges from different courts and jurisdictions across Canada. A second advisory group is a delegation of defence lawyers nominated by the Canadian Bar Association, while a third consists of representatives of the federal and provincial departments of the Attorney-General who present a prosecution perspective on the reform proposals. Another group that the Commission meets with is made up of police representatives nominated by the Canadian Association of Chiefs of Police and the final panel contains legal scholars working in the field of criminal procedure who are selected by the Canadian Association of Law Teachers. On occasion the Commission also organizes special workshops with other groups, institutions or professionals who are familiar with its work. Several of these special workshops were convened on the subject of plea discussion during the past year. Joint sessions involving specialist representatives from the bench and the prosecuting and defence bar from across the country were convened and discussions on the reform of plea bargaining practices were held in Winnipeg, Vancouver, Toronto and Montreal.

By contrast, the Commission's study of the area led it to conclude that certain attributes of plea bargaining as presently practiced in various regions of the country are of doubtful or questionable legality. What, for example, is the legal status of a plea bargain arrived at with the active participation of a judicial officer who, in the course of a closeted discussion with counsel, not only indicates the nature of the range of sentence but, indeed, stipulates the actual sentence that he or she believes to be acceptable? What form can judicial intervention lawfully take and what are the limits of judicial intervention? These questions are incapable of precise answers inasmuch as there is neither a statutory framework upon which to base a conclusion nor are there relevant established precedents of high authority addressing the issues.

The Commission also had been told that certain judges refuse to participate in the plea bargaining process because of their view of the ethics, if not the legality, of the process. This preoccupation with the ethics or appropriateness of the practice, in the Commission's view, arises primarily because the law on the subject cannot be confidently stated, given its uncodified status. The present mélange of common law, local practice and canons of professional ethics is replete with contradictions and gaps in coverage. The resulting uncertainty is in turn productive of controversy concerning what are essentially matters of policy.

This is an unhealthy state of affairs. The policy questions ought to be squarely confronted. If the practice is one that should continue then it should find clear expression in legislation. The legal and the ethical standards of application in this area of the practice of law should coincide. Judges, of all people, should not have to speculate whether a well-known and much-resorted-to part of the legal process is legally deficient or ethically dubious.

The Issue of Public Attitudes

The commissioner's paper proceeded on the premise, often asserted in the literature, that plea bargaining is a practice held in low esteem by the general public. For some, this fact alone provides a significant reason for reform. Somewhat to the Commission's surprise, many of its consultants questioned the validity of the low-public-esteem assertion. Questions were repeatedly raised concerning who the "public" was and as to the accuracy of the observation that the public believed the present system to be defective. The conclusion that this state of affairs was damaging to the reputation of the administration of justice was also questioned. Rather, most consultants contended that the present system worked well and was remarkably free of problems. While not questioning the beliefs of these actual users of the system, the Commission was aware, from its travels across the country, that the system, however one may assess its operation, certainly works differently in different parts of the country. Consultants thus expressed a largely unanimous positive reaction to an essentially multifarious reality.

The Commission found itself unable to counter satisfactorily the consultants' belief that public confidence in the system was not being undermined by plea bargaining practices. Reproducing the empirically unsubstantiated assertions of the literature was an obviously insufficient response. While convinced of the theoretical soundness of its approach to the reform of this area of the law, the Commission recognized that the concerns raised deserved an authoritative answer, if that was possible.

Even in the absence of empirical data, the case for reform is strong. Despite the low visibility of the phenomenon, the case law has unearthed a variety of abusive practices that the courts have struggled to remedy over the years. Over-charging in order to induce pleas to lesser offences,[14] the suppression by counsel of material facts in representations made to the court,[15] the inducing of guilty pleas from innocent individuals,[16] the solicitation of guilty pleas by means of apparently attractive inducements when it was known to the prosecutor that a case for conviction could not be established with the available evidence[17] and the repudiation of regularly struck bargains on appeal[18] are just some of the dubious stratagems that have surfaced in the jurisprudence. Practical reforms could be justified on this basis alone. Nevertheless, the views of the public are important, not because legislators should respond to the passing whims and fancies of a transitory majority of the general population, but because it is important for the law to enjoy the respect of those who are served by it. Secondly, the profession, by which we mean all professionals who serve the criminal justice system (judges, lawyers and police officers) should not be tainted by participation in what is regarded as an unseemly process, albeit one that is imperfectly understood by the public. Moreover, if the profession is truly of the view that the general public has confidence in the system it presently operates then that assumption should be verified.

Assessing Public Attitudes: Method

Because of this importance of public views of the criminal justice system generally, and of the plea bargaining process in particular, the Law Reform Commission of Canada decided to assess directly the views of the Canadian public on the issue of plea bargaining through the use of a survey. In this way, systematic views could be obtained in contrast with the potentially unrepresentative views of those who might spontaneously express their views on the subject. It is easy to speculate that the public is, or is not, upset with the process. It is more sensible to attempt to find out what the public actually feels.

For most people, the mass media are the major source of information about the operation of the courts. The media typically present information about specific cases. Members of the public, in turn, normally form opinions about specific practices as a result of being exposed to a number of such stories. We decided, therefore, to try to assess the public's view of various aspects of plea bargaining by asking members of the public to respond to scenarios involving plea bargaining. Although the scenarios involved what is commonly termed "plea bargaining," this was done without using that term so as to avoid attaching any connotation those words have to the process being described. By getting responses to different forms of plea bargaining from equivalent groups of respondents, we could determine whether particular kinds of practices with respect to plea bargaining would be likely to have different impacts on how the public would view the criminal system.

In an attempt to determine both the over-all public view of plea bargaining and to understand what aspects of plea bargaining upset the public, an experiment, embedded in a public opinion survey, was conducted. The survey, sponsored by the Law Reform Commission of Canada, was administered by Gallup, Canada, in late February, 1988. The Gallup organization defines its sampling procedure as being "designed to produce an approximation of the adult civilian population, 18 years or older, living in Canada except for those persons in institutions such as prisons or hospitals, or those residing in far Northern regions."

We asked respondents two types of questions. First, we asked them for their responses to one of five different scenarios depicting a criminal case which ended in a guilty plea to one charge and the withdrawal of another charge. Seven questions were asked assessing their reactions to the scenario they read. Approximately 200 people were given each of five different scenarios. Second, respondents were asked for their over-all views of plea bargaining and of sentences. A total of 1,049 Canadians were interviewed for the study.

The five scenarios differed in the description of how the case was resolved. Comparisons across scenarios allow us to see how different forms of resolution of the case affect public perceptions of the process. The content of the five scenarios can be summarized as follows:

A   *No bargain*: a case was described in which a person was charged with robbery and using a firearm during the offence. The accused was described as having pleaded guilty to the robbery. The second charge was dropped by the Crown. The reader was told that counsel had not discussed the case prior to the court appearance and that similar sentence submissions were made. The sentence handed down was described as falling between the two submissions.

B   *Standard bargain*: this scenario differs from A in the following ways. The reader was told that crown and defence had met in the Crown's office prior to the court hearing and an agreement had been made on a joint submission on a sentence for the robbery and a dropping of the other charge. The sentence handed down was what counsel had recommended.

C   *Bargain — explanation given*: the difference between this and B is that, in addition, counsel were described as having given, in open court, an explanation on how they had arrived at the decision to drop the weapons charge and to make the joint submission.

D   *Bargain — judge present*: this is essentially the same as B except that the plea bargaining was described as having taken place in the judge's office with the judge present.

E   *Bargain — judge involved*: this is the same as D except that the judge was described as having rejected (in his chambers) a preliminary suggestion from counsel on the outcome of the case and subsequently accepting a second suggestion.

Public Attitudes Toward Plea Bargaining: Results

Plea Bargaining, Generally

The most simple way of determining the public's view of plea bargaining is to look at the responses to a direct question about it (asked *after* the questions related to the scenarios). The findings are simple and straightforward: most Canadians disapprove of plea bargaining (defined, in this question, as "the practice whereby an accused person agrees to plead guilty in return for the promise of some benefit such as agreement that certain charges be dropped and/or certain recommendations be made to the judge on what the sentence should be") (see Appendix, Table 1).

Because the figures are rounded off to the nearest percentage, totals may not equal exactly 100 per cent.

On this question, 68 per cent of adult Canadians, or 79 per cent of those who had at least some opinion about the practice, disapprove of plea bargaining. The scenario that the respondents had read a few minutes before had no effect on their responses.

There is little important demographic variation in this view.

Disapproval of plea bargaining was expressed by at least 60 per cent of the following demographic breakdowns: each of the five regions of Canada, three age groupings, both sexes, three levels of educational achievement, four income groupings, mother tongue and size of community. Students were the only occupational grouping whose over-all level of disapproval dropped below 60 per cent (to 58 per cent). In general, demographic variation in the responses to all of the questions we asked did not appear to be important and, therefore, will be ignored in this article.

When faced with questions concerning the scenarios, respondents could, of course, indicate that they did not feel confident enough to give a response. This would not be a surprising outcome, given that only a small amount of information on which to base a response was given. As it turned out, the refusal to state an opinion was related to the scenario that was read. The presence of a plea bargain of any sort (i.e., conditions B, C, D, or E) appeared to make respondents *more* confident in giving answers of any kind to the evaluative questions that were asked of them. On seven of the nine questions, respondents were significantly more likely to indicate that they did not know or could not respond in the "No bargain" condition than any of the other "plea bargaining" conditions.

It would appear that the presence of a plea bargain is definite information to the respondent on the appropriateness of the procedure. When a person simply pleads guilty, a larger portion of the public indicates that they simply do not have enough information to evaluate what went on. When the guilty plea is as a result of a plea bargain, however, it is easier to elicit a view.

Are Views of Sentence Severity and Plea Bargaining Linked?

It appears that views of plea bargaining and views of sentencing are linked in the public's mind. In each of the five (experimentally created) groups, those who disapproved of plea bargaining tended to be more likely to think that sentences were too lenient (see Appendix, Table 2).

In this survey sixty-nine per cent of the general population (seventy-six per cent of those who had any opinion on the matter) thought that sentences generally were too lenient. Clearly this view is related to views about plea bargaining. Of those who indicated approval of plea bargaining, "only" fifty-five per cent thought that sentences were not severe enough.

From these data alone, it is not clear that the existence of plea bargaining — or perceptions of it — is really a cause of the public's concern about the severity of sentences. These data do suggest, at a minimum, that the two views are linked: those who find plea bargaining to be an unacceptable practice are more likely to think that sentences are not severe enough.

There are, however, other indications that "plea bargaining" is seen by members of the public as a mechanism by which people receive lower levels of punishment than they deserve. The question dealing with the respondents' opinion on the severity of sentences (generally) came immediately after the seven questions that related to the scenario. Although it was prefaced with the statement "Now we would like to ask you two general question," it seems that the scenario it followed influenced the responses. Specifically, those who had just read a scenario involving *any* kind of plea bargaining (standard bargain, bargaining — explanation given, bargain — judge present, or bargain — judge involved) were significantly more likely to think that sentences were not severe enough than those who had read the "no bargain" scenario. Put differently, of those who expressed an opinion about sentencing, thirty-two per cent of those who had not been exposed immediately beforehand to plea bargaining thought that sentences were too severe or about right. This fell to twenty-three per cent among those for whom plea bargaining had been made salient (see Appendix, Table 3).

Impact of Plea Bargaining on the Perception of the Sentence in the Particular Case Being Described

We have shown thus far that views of sentences and opinions about plea bargaining are linked. Making plea bargaining salient to people immediately before asking them what they thought about sentencing had an impact on their views of the appropriateness of the sentences coming from the courts.

One of the questions asked of respondents who had just read one of the five scenarios was whether they would assume, on the basis of the information provided in the scenario, that the sentence given the offender was likely to be appropriate. It should be noted that no sentence was specified; differences among experimental conditions, then, would reflect differences in the public's perceptions of how likely it was that the *process* described in the question would lead to an appropriate outcome (see Appendix, Table 4).

There are two findings that stand out in this table. The first is the contrast of "No bargain" with "Standard bargain." Belief that the sentence will be appropriate drops dramatically when the public hears that the Crown and defence have bargained.

The second is the effect of giving an explanation for the bargain in open court (condition C). It is quite clear that a good portion of the detrimental effects of the normal plea bargain is erased by having a full explanation given in court.

Having the judge present, but not as an active participant (condition D) appears to lead the public to anticipate a more acceptable outcome than the standard bargain; however, having the judge actively involved in the plea bargaining process leads the public to expect a less acceptable outcome.

Expectation that All of the Relevant Information Was Brought to the Attention of the Judge Before Sentencing

Part of the difference in the expected appropriateness of the sentence may be due to the large differences in the expectation of whether all of the relevant evidence would be brought to the attention of the judge before he made his sentencing decision (see Appendix, Table 5).

Clearly, one effect of having a case resolved by a standard plea bargain (condition B) is that the public will be slightly (but not significantly) more likely to believe that the judge did not have access to all relevant information about the case.

More dramatic is the finding that where an explanation is given in court of how the "bargain" had been arrived at (condition C), or the judge had direct knowledge of how the bargain had been arrived at (conditions D and E), the public was more likely to believe that the relevant information was available to the judge than in the standard-bargain condition (condition B). Indeed, where the public perceived that the judge had information about how the decision to plead guilty had been arrived at (conditions C, D and E), the respondents were more likely than in the "No bargain" condition (condition A) to believe that all relevant information was brought before the judge.

Belief that the Judge Took All Relevant Factors Into Account In Sentencing the Offender

The previous question suggests that people believe that in a standard plea bargaining situation (or to some extent, even in a case where there is a plea of guilty without plea discussions) the judge does not have access to all appropriate information. Not surprisingly, then, people in the standard plea bargaining situation (condition B) are less likely (than in the other conditions) to believe that the judge took into account all relevant information than in the other conditions (see Appendix, Table 6).

On this question, the condition that stands out is condition B — the standard plea bargaining situation. Respondents in this condition were considerably less likely to think that the judge took into account all relevant factors in deciding on the sentence.

Perception of the Performance of Counsel

Other evidence supporting the view that plea bargaining is seen as a way for the accused to get a "bargain" disposition comes from two questions in which respondents were asked to evaluate the performance of the Crown and defence.

In one question, they were asked whether they thought that defence counsel had done a good job in representing the offender's interests. As shown below, it appears that the performance of defence counsel is seen in more favourable terms if bargaining of any sort took place (see Appendix, Table 7).

Over-all, it is clear that defence counsel are seen by most people as doing a good job of representing the offender's interests. The one condition that stands out as being different from the rest is condition A (no bargaining). Respondents are somewhat less sure in this condition than in the other four conditions (where some form of bargaining takes place) that the defence has done a good job.

It is likely that the public believes that "doing a good job in representing the accused's interests" involves getting a lenient sentence. However, disclosing the nature of the "bargain" to the court (conditions C, D and E) did not interfere with the public's generally positive evaluation of the defence counsel's performance on behalf of the accused. As long as the lawyer entered into some form of plea bargaining, counsel is evaluated in more positive terms than in the non-bargained guilty plea (condition A).

In the second question — where people evaluated the Crown — the evaluations were not as favourable. Fewer than forty per cent of the respondents with an opinion thought that the Crown did a proper job of presenting all appropriate information in any condition (see Appendix, Table 8).

The one condition that stands out among the rest is the "standard bargain" (condition B). Clearly in this condition, respondents assumed that the

Crown would not do a good job of bringing the appropriate information to the court.

Did the Judge Act in Proper and Fair Manner in Handling the Case?

There was a lot of variation in how the judge was perceived. Of those who expressed an opinion, more saw the judge behaving properly in the "no bargain" condition than in any other. Indeed, only in this condition did a majority of those who expressed a view see the judge as behaving in a proper and fair manner in handling the case (see Apendix, Table 9).

Clearly, one of the conditions under which the judge is likely to be viewed in unfavourable terms is where there is a "standard bargain" with no disclosure of any sort. It is possible that the judge is being criticized, implicitly, for presiding over a hearing where he/she is perceived not to be taking into account all relevant information (as noted above). Respondents in this condition are also critical of the Crown for not bringing the information before the court. Thus the Crown is being criticized for not bringing the information before the court and the judge is being criticized for allowing the hearing to proceed on the basis of this presumed inadequate information.

It is worth noting, however, that where an explanation is given for the plea agreement (condition C), the judge is rated significantly more favourably than he is in the "standard bargain" condition.

Finally, there is an indication that the public does not approve of the judge getting heavily involved in the plea bargaining process. The rates of the actions of the judge are slightly (but not significantly) lower in the condition where he is actively involved (condition E) than when he is present, but inactive (condition D).

Over-all, it is clear that most people in *all* experimental conditions want the judge more involved in the case. It is possible that one factor common to all scenarios — the dropping of the second charge against the accused — is responsible for this. Even in condition E — where the judge is actively involved in the plea discussions — fifty-six per cent of those expressing an opinion believe that the judge should have been more involved in the case (see Appendix, Table 10).

The condition that clearly stands out on this question is condition E (bargain — judge involved). Only in this one instance did a sizable portion of the respondents believe that the judge was too involved.

Summary of Findings

On the basis of the survey data, we are confident in making the following summary statements about the findings:

Over-all View of Plea Bargaining

(1) Plea bargaining has a bad public image. Most of those polled disapproved of the practice (Table 1).

(2) Believing that plea bargaining is an unacceptable practice and believing that sentences are too lenient are attitudes that are related (Table 2).

(3) Plea bargaining is seen by members of the public as a mechanism by which people receive lower levels of punishment than they deserve (Table 3).

Plea Bargaining and Opinions About the Resulting Sentence

(4) When explanations are given in open court on the reasons for a negotiated outcome of a case, or the judge is present at the negotiations, the public has greater confidence that all appropriate information will be transmitted to the judge than in the standard plea bargaining situation (Table 5).

(5) In comparison to the situation where no bargaining took place, or where bargaining took place in the presence of the judge or where the judge was made aware of the reasons for the bargain, the judge in the standard bargaining situation was seen as being less likely to have taken into account all relevant information when deciding on the appropriate sentence (Table 6).

(6) Similarly, judges' decisions made after a standard plea bargaining session are seen in less favourable light than are decisions made in the absence of plea bargaining or where there is knowledge, on the part of the judge, of why the agreement was arrived at (Table 4).

(7)   Defence counsel is seen as doing a better job when plea bar-
        gaining takes place than when there is no plea bargaining
        (Table 7).

(8)   The Crown Attorney, however, is seen as doing a less ade-
        quate job when plea bargaining takes place, although this is
        ameliorated by disclosure to the court of the nature of the bar-
        gain or by the presence of the judge at the plea bargaining ses-
        sion (Table 8).

(9)   Judges are least likely to be seen as acting in a fair and proper
        manner when they sentence on the basis of a plea bargain
        where there was neither open disclosure nor the presence of
        the judge during the negotiations. The perception of the judge
        improves (toward the situation where there was no bargaining)
        as the judge's involvement increases, unless the judge partici-
        pates actively in plea bargaining (Table 9).

(10)   The only situation where a sizable portion of respondents
        thought that the judge was too involved in the process leading
        to a plea was when the judge was an active participant in the
        plea discussions (Table 10).

Conclusion

It is clear from these results that the legitimacy of court processes and
outcomes as perceived by the Canadian public are affected by the nature of
the plea discussions that take place between Crown and defence counsel.
Certain procedures — in particular plea bargaining taking place behind
closed doors in the absence of the judge and without disclosure to the judge
— appear to reduce public confidence in the criminal process. Plea bargaining appears to have an effect not only on the view of the public about a
particular sentence that resulted from the process but also sentences generally coming out of the court. Most Canadians disapprove of the process of
plea bargaining. It may lower the public's confidence in the ability of the
sentencing judge to deal with the case in a fair and appropriate manner.
However, much of this detrimental impression is removed if the full explanation of the process is given in open court. Enhancing the awareness of
the judge of the facts of the process or actually having the judge present at

key stages of the process appears to foster greater public confidence and render the outcome more acceptable than would be the case if the judge is not so involved.

However, there are limits to what the public will accept as proper judicial activity. Where the judge takes too active a role in the process, this can impact negatively on the acceptability of the outcome. At the other end of the spectrum, where the judge is not regarded as being sufficiently involved in the plea bargaining process, the public's confidence that all appropriate information is before the court diminishes.

Where explanations are given in open court or in the presence of the judge, the public perceives the process to be more appropriate and perceives the likelihood of the prosecutors' being taken advantage of as being lower. Defence counsel is seen in an equally positive light whether or not disclosure of the plea bargaining process takes place.

The results of this study would suggest that, as with other areas of the criminal justice system such as sentencing,[19] the public responds to rather specific aspects of the operation of the criminal justice system and is clearly able to distinguish among different procedures for making decisions.

Appendix

Table 1.
View of Plea Bargaining.

	Overall	Excluding no opinion and DK/NS*
Strongly approve of the practice	2%	2%
In general, approve of the practice	16%	19%
No opinion about the practice	9%	–
In general, disapprove of the practice	39%	45%
Strongly disapprove of the practice	29%	34%
Do not know or not stated	4%	
Total	100%	100%

*   Do not know/Not Stated

Table 2.[20] View of Sentencing.

	Too severe/ about right	Not severe enough	Total
Opinion of Plea Bargaining:			
Approve of it:	45%	55%	100%
Disapprove of it:	17%	83%	100%

Note: Chi square = 60.4, df = 1, p<.001

Table 3. Opinion of Sentence (Generally) Handed Down by the Courts.

	Too severe/ about right	Not severe enough	Total
Scenario:			
No bargain (A)	68%	32%	100%
Some form of bargaining (B, C, D, E)	77%	23%	100%

Note: Chi square = 7.17, df = 1, p<.01

Table 4. Did the Respondent Assume that the Sentence was Likely to be Appropriate?

	Yes	Probably not	Definitely not	Total
Condition:				
No bargain (A)	35%	35%	30%	100%
Standard bargain (B)	21%	37%	42%	100%
Bargain — explanation given (C)	27%	40%	34%	100%
Bargain — judge present (D)	28%	39%	33%	100%
Bargain — judge involved (E)	23%	34%	43%	100%

Note: Chi square (over-all) = 16.29, df = 8, p<.05
Chi square (A vs. B) = 11.21, df = 2, p<.01
Chi square (A vs. E) = 7.79, df = 2, p<.05
Chi square (A vs. C) = 3.24, df = 2, not significant
Chi square (C vs. E) = 3.36, df = 2, not significant

Table 5. Was All Appropriate Information Brought to the Attention of the Judge Before Sentencing?

	Yes	Probably not	Definitely not	Total
Condition:				
No bargain (A)	31%	42%	27%	100%
Standard bargain (B)	27%	37%	37%	100%
Bargain — explanation given (C)	36%	43%	21%	100%
Bargain — judge present (D)	46%	39%	16%	100%
Bargain — judge involved (E)	40%	38%	22%	100%

Note: Chi square (over-all) = 35.43, df = 8, p<.001
Chi square (A vs. C, D and E pooled) = 7.72, df = 2, p<.05
Chi square (A vs. B) = 4.34, df = 2, not significant
Chi square (B vs. C, D and E pooled) = 27.79, df = p<.001

Table 6. Did Judge Take Into Account All Relevant Information?

	Yes	Probably not	Definitely not	Total
Condition:				
No bargain (A)	45%	26%	28%	100%
Standard bargain (B)	24%	34%	42%	100%
Bargain — explanation given (C)	39%	42%	18%	100%
Bargain — judge present (D)	42%	35%	22%	100%
Bargain — judge involved (E)	40%	38%	22%	100%

Note: Chi square (over-all) = 50.04, df = 8, p<.001

Table 7. Did Defence Do A Good Job?

Condition:	Definitely yes	Probably yes	No	Total
No bargain (A)	24%	51%	25%	100%
Standard bargain (B)	40%	36%	24%	100%
Bargain — explanation given (C)	43%	39%	18%	100%
Bargain — judge present (D)	42%	43%	15%	100%
Bargain — judge involved (E)	35%	42%	23%	100%

Note: Chi square (over-all) = 24.29, df = 8, p<.001
Chi square (A vs. B, C, D and E pooled) = 16.19, df = 2, p<.001

Table 8. Did the Crown Prosecutor Do a Proper Job of Presenting All Appropriate Information?

Condition:	Yes	Probably not	Definitely not	Total
No bargain (A)	34%	37%	29%	100%
Standard bargain (B)	28%	31%	40%	100%
Bargain — explanation given (C)	36%	39%	25%	100%
Bargain — judge present (D)	37%	33%	29%	100%
Bargain — judge involved (E)	38%	36%	26%	100%

Note: Chi square (over-all) = 15.89, df = 8, p<.05

Table 9. Did Judge Act in Proper and Fair Manner?

Condition:	Yes	Probably not	Definitely not	Total
No bargain (A)	52%	25%	23%	100%
Standard bargain (B)	31%	34%	35%	100%
Bargain — explanation given (C)	44%	29%	27%	100%
Bargain — judge present (D)	42%	29%	29%	100%
Bargain — judge involved (E)	33%	32%	35%	100%

Note: Chi square (over-all) = 24.227, df = 8, p<.01
Chi square (B vs. C) = 8.51, df = 2, p<.02
Chi square (D vs. E) = 2.237, df = 1, not significant

Table 10. Opinion of Judge's Level of Involvement in the Case.

Condition:	Too involved	Appropriate	Should be more involved	Total
No bargain (A)	2%	30%	69%	100%
Standard bargain (B)	4%	23%	73%	100%
Bargain — explanation given (C)	5%	23%	72%	100%
Bargain — judge present (D)	7%	26%	67%	100%
Bargain — judge involved (E)	21%	23%	56%	100%

Note: Chi square (over-all) = 63.480, df = 8, p‹.01
Chi square (D vs. E) = 15.48, df = 2, p‹.01

Endnotes

1   "Criminal Procedure: Control of the Process," Working Paper No. 15 (1975).

2   Ibid., at p. 48.

3   Note especially section 10(b) guranteeing the right of an arrested or detained person to retain and instruct counsel without delay and to be informed of that right.

4   The aim of the pre-trial conference is to ensure that the parties are adequately infomed about the nature of the case and the areas of disagreement that separate them.

5   Law Reform Commission of Canada, "Plea Discussions and Agreements," Working Paper No. 60 (1989).

6   "Control of the Process," *supra*, footnote 1, at 45.

7   See, e.g., G. Ferguson and D. Roberts,"Plea Bargaining: Directions for Canada Reform" (1974), 52 Can. Bar Rev. 497; S.A. Cohen, *Due Process of Law: The Canadian System of Criminal Justice* (Toronto, Carswell Co. Ltd., 1977): and S. Verdun-Jones and D. Cousineau, "Cleansing the Augean Stables: A Critical Analysis of Recent Trends in the Plea Bargaining Debate in Canada" (1979), 17 Osgoode Hall L.J. 227 at p. 230 *et seq.*; and P. Russell, *The Judiciary in Canada: The Third Branch of Government* (Toronto, McGraw-Hill Ryerson Inc., 1987), p. 212.

8   (1987), at pp. 414-27.

9   Rule 11.

10   See *A Model Code of Pre-Arraigment Procedure*, American Law Institute (1975), Article 350.

11   *Uniform Rules of Criminal Procedure: Model Penal Code* (1974), Rules 441-4.

12   The American debate is well summarized by S. Verdun-Jones and D. Cousineau, *supra*, footnote 7, at p. 232, note 25.

13   Opponents of structured plea bargaining in the U.S. have been vocal. The National Advisory Commission on Criminal Justice Standards and Goals urged the complete abolition of plea bargaining in 1973 in its Report, *Courts.* More recently, A. Alschuler condemned American developments and urged Canadians to resist the lure of structured plea bargaining: see A. Alschuler, "Background note on Plea Bargaining for Seminar on Reform of the Law of Sentencing," Conference on Reform of the Criminal Law, July 28, 1987, London, England.

14   See M. Manning "Abuse of Power by Crown Attorneys" in Law Society of Upper Canada, Special Lectures, *Abuse of Power* (1979), at p. 571.

15   *See, The Dewar Review: A Report Prepared by the Honourable A.S. Dewar at the Request of the Attorney General of Manitoba,* October, 1988, at pp. 52-3.

16   Counsel should "emphasize that the accused must not plead guilty unless he committed the acts constituting the offence charged:" *R.* v. *Turner,* [1970] 2 All E.R. 281 at p. 285 (C.A.); and should make clear the necessity for the accused's having had the requisite mental state: *R.* v. *Turner,* ibid., and G.A. Martin "The Role and Responsibility of the Defence Advocate" (1969-70), 12 C.L.Q. 376 at p. 387.

17   Some commentators have expressed the fear that suppression of the fact that a vital witness will not be available at trial may not be viewed as a violation of professional conduct standards: A. Hooper, "Discovery in Crime Cases" (1972), 50 Can. Bar. Rev. 445 at p. 471; and White,"A Proposal for the Reform of the Plea Bargaining Process" (1971), 119 U.Pa. L. Rev. 439 at p. 459.

18   See, e.g., *A.-G. Can.* v. *Roy* (1972), 18 C.R.N.S. 89 (Que. Q.B.); *R.* v. *Agozzino,* [1970] 1 C.C.C. 380 6 C.R.N.S. 147, [1970] 1 O.R. 480 (C.A.); *R.* v. *Brown* (1972), 8C.C.C (2d) 227 (Ont. C.A.); *R.* v. *Fleury* (1971), 23 C.R.N.S. 164 (Que. C.A.); *R.* v. *Mouffe* (1971), 16 C.R.N.S.257 (Que. C.A.).

19   See A.N. Doob and J.V. Roberts "Public Punitiveness and Public Knowledge of the Facts: Some Canadian Surveys," in Walker, N. and M. Hough, *Public Attitudes to Sentencing* (Aldershot, England: Gower, 1988).

20   This and all subsequent tables in this paper should be read as follows. Each row of numbers represents a group of people. In this table, the first row of numbers represents those whose "Opinion of plea bargaining" is that they "Approve of it." Of this group, then, forty-five per cent think that sentences are "too severe or about right" and fifty-five percent think that sentences are "not severe enough." The total "100 per cent" is included simply to show in which direction the percentages are meant to add. In this and all subsequent tables, only data from those who gave an answer are presented. For all questions at least ninety per cent (pooled across conditions) responded to each question.

The second row shows that views of sentence of those respondents who "disapprove" of plea bargaining. Clearly, their responses are different. The statistic "Chi square" is a way of evaluating this difference. Chi square is a statistical test used, in the context of the data in this paper, as a way of evaluating the size of the differences across scenarios in the way in which people responded to questions. The "degrees of freedom" (df) of a table is a function of the size of the table and is used to evaluate the Chi square statistic. Since small amounts of variation can occur simply "by change," the Chi square statistic is a way of estimating how likely it is that the observed difference could have occurred by chance. Thus in this case, the statement that "p<.001" indicates that the changes (probability or "p") are less than one in one thousand ("<.001") that the observed differences could have occurred by chance. Effectively, then, the difference is a "real" one (i.e., it is unlikely to have occurred by chance), indicating that with a high level of certainty, those who disapprove of plea bargaining are more likely (than those who approve of it) to feel that sentences are not severe enough.

In this and subsequent tables, response categories have been combined (e.g, "strongly approve..." and "In general, approve..." are combined into "Approve..."). Generally, categories have been combined where one or more of the original alternatives was chosen by few respondents.

Risky Business:
The Classification of Dangerous People in the Canadian Carceral Enterprise[*]

Robert Menzies, Dorothy E. Chunn
and Christopher D. Webster

If there is an overall political issue around the prison, it is not therefore whether it is corrective or not; whether the judges, the psychiatrists or the sociologists are to exercise more power in it than the administrators or the supervisors; it is not even whether we should have prison or something other than prison. At present, the problem lies rather in the steep rise in the use of these mechanisms of normalization and the wide-ranging powers which, through the proliferation of new disciplines, they bring with them.

> Michel Foucault, *Discipline and Punish* (1977: 306)

Introduction

The idea for this chapter emerged out of our individual and collective writing, on a number of convergent topics in the areas of critical social control and feminist theory (Chunn and Gavigan, 1991; Chunn and Gavigan, 1988; Lowman, Menzies and Palys, 1987; Menzies, 1989; Webster, 1990), homicide and violence (Grant, Boyle and Chunn, forthcoming; Menzies, Webster and Sepejak, 1987), the clinical prediction of dangerousness (Webster and Menzies, 1987; Webster, Ben-Aron and Hucker, 1985), and the forensic evaluation of women and other medico-legal subjects in pre-trial assessment clinics (Chunn and Menzies, 1990; Menzies, 1989; Menzies, Chunn and Webster, 1992; Webster, Menzies and Jackson, 1982).

Permeating these related subjects are various recurrent themes reflecting structures of control and cultural concerns: about the securing of social order in private and public realms of contemporary society; about the apprehension of various forms of risk to that order; about the development of policies and practices for the regulation of threatening people, thoughts and things; and about the circulation of knowledge and emergence of experts in the identification of the endangered and the dangerous, the protection of the former, and the surveillance, containment and control of the latter. The idea of dangerousness — whether applied to the crimes and victimization of women, the social construction of homicide, the relationship between violence and mental disorder or the psychiatric prediction of criminal and violent conduct — is a central feature of contemporary correctional and therapeutic systems. In its various manifestations the construct throws open many important windows for comprehending the complex processes through which the carceral apparatus is constituted, and through which, conversely, it can potentially be deconstructed and rearranged.

In what follows we examine the expert attribution of dangerousness in the Canadian penal apparatus. In the context of current developments in the critical revisionist literature on penality and social control (Chunn and Gavigan, 1988; Cohen, 1985; Cohen and Scull, 1983; Garland, 1985, 1990; Garland and Young, 1983; Lowman, Menzies and Palys, 1987; Melossi, 1990), we look at the classification of danger and risk as a central property of contemporary carceral discourses and practices in this country. We review some recent trends in the administration of danger by legal and mental health institutions and professionals. We review contemporary movements toward the bifurcation of systems designed to treat and control psychiatric populations, and we address current trends in the Americanization of the Canadian mental architecture.

Following the observations of Foucault (1977, 1978), Garland (1985, 1990) and Castel (1991), we argue that the mutual attractions of parallel and frequently overlapping control systems, along with the increasingly scientized, technocratic and managerial character of the penal business itself (Chan, 1990; Cohen, 1988; Ericson and Shearing, 1986; Lowman and MacLean, 1992; Young, 1988), have been instrumental in both proliferating and fundamentally transforming the dangerousness construct. Finally, by enlisting some of our own work on the outcomes of forensic evaluation activities in a medico-legal assessment agency in Toronto (Chunn and

Menzies, 1990; Menzies, 1989; Menzies, Chunn and Webster, 1992; Webster and Menzies, 1987; Webster, Menzies and Jackson, 1982), we consider the implications of dangerousness decisions for the careers of penal and psychiatric subjects and for the deployment of judicial and therapeutic organizations in which they are immersed.

The Dangerousness Discipline in Perspective

Like a variety of allied and inter-related constructs — endangerment, disorder, dependency, delinquency, depravity, deficiency and so forth — dangerousness is deeply engrained in the correctional culture and in the knowledge systems embraced by its practitioners (Castel, 1991; Foucault, 1977, 1978; Menzies, 1986, 1989; Petrunik, 1983; Pfohl, 1978, 1979; Rennie, 1978). From the late eighteenth century to the present (Monahan, 1981; Shah, 1978; Webster, Ben-Aron and Hucker, 1985), ideas about punishment and treatment have been recurrently fuelled both by the imagery of dangerousness circulating through public and private realms and by official claims to scientific expertise in its diagnosis, prediction, prevention and treatment (cf. Britzer and Crowner, 1988; Brody, 1990; Hamilton and Freeman, 1982; Hall, 1987; Hinton, 1983; Toch and Adams, 1989).

The notion that risky people — and classes of people — can be precisely calibrated and contained has a powerful discursive and pragmatic appeal. It offers assurances that public protection is to be found not just in the law's retroactive response to criminal behaviour, but more so in the capacity of science to extend the reach of law beyond human behaviour and into the future tense. A purely reactive penal system, constrained by its reliance on formal categories of legality, individual responsibility, evidence and guilt, is a relatively blunt, if potentially brutal, instrument of punishment. It measures up violent behaviour and other social wrongs, and it responds in kind.

In comparison, the infusion of scientific and technical knowledge in the service of criminal law opens and re-focuses the carceral lens on the multitude of threats posed by defective human subjects across a broad and potentially indefinite band of time and space. For the purposes of penal intervention, dangerous people are dangerous because they present personalities, patterns and possibilities that transcend their own behaviour and seemingly elude the normal safeguards conferred by law.[1] So to neutralize the apparent threat, specialist systems are constructed at the frontiers of criminal law and in parallel institutions such as mental health, and psychiatrists and other professionals are designated as authoritative experts in the detection and defusion of social danger. And according to Foucault's well-known passage from *Discipline and Punish*, this dispersal of normalizing power is by no means exclusively confined to the attribution of dangerousness alone:

> Throughout the penal procedure and the implementation of the sentence there swarms a whole series of subsidiary authorities. Small-scale legal systems and parallel judges have multiplied around the principal judgment: psychiatric or psychological experts, magistrates concerned with the implementation of sentences, educationalists, members of the prison services, all fragment the legal power to punish.... The whole machinery that has been developing for years around the implementation of sentences, and their adjustment to individuals, creates a proliferation of the authorities of judicial decision-making and extends its powers of decision well beyond the sentence (Foucault, 1977: 21).

None of the above should be read as an essentialization of the construct (see Cameron, 1990; Diamond and Quinby, 1988; Eisenstein, 1988; Harding, 1987; Nicholson, 1990; Palmer, 1990), nor as a suggestion that understandings of dangerousness are in any way autonomous from historical process or from the structural-cultural context of state and civil control institutions. To the contrary, we conceive dangerousness as a highly elastic, even "protean" idea (Rennie, 1978), which indexically reflects and conditions historically specific moments in the life cycles of carceral programs and practices. From its overtly class-conscious usage in nineteenth-century social commentary (Brace, 1872; Mayhew, 1861), dangerousness has undergone a number of discursive shifts through its absorption, respectively, into the words and deeds of criminal anthropologists (Rennie, 1978), turn-of-century social reformers (Bacchi, 1983; McLaren, 1990; Rothman, 1980; Valverde, 1991), second-wave psychiatrists (Castel, Castel and Lovell, 1982), sexual and chemical prohibitionists (Boyd 1991; Coward, 1985; Dorn, 1987; Mort, 1987; Weeks, 1989) and, more recently and most intriguingly, of deinstitutionalists, social critics and civil libertarians (Floud and Young, 1981; Stone, 1984; Warren, 1982).

What unites these various incarnations of the construct is their common adherence to pervasive belief systems about the causes, consequences and cures of social (dis)order. Whereas the symbolic assailants may be consistently changing faces and forms, and while new cohorts of social defence specialists may be in constant succession or rotation, still the constructed dangerosities of any given society open up important windows toward an understanding of its main problems and preoccupations. The people, practices and ideas which are defined as most dangerous at any conjunction of time and space, however real or ideological in substance, are sharp representations of the social order's main vulnerabilities and contradictions. Taking the shape of witches or foreigners or homosexuals or heretics or communists or unmarried women or drug dealers or paedophiles, they hold up a mirror to the most profound apprehensions of those who invest in established formations and practices, and hence they paradoxically reveal the power relations and hegemonies that perpetuate the status quo and hold these structures in place.

In practice, of course, these collective iconographies of danger are often woefully misconstrued and misapplied. The personalization of dangerousness in the twentieth century, like the individualization of carceral practices more generally (Foucault, 1977; Garland, 1985; Rose, 1990; Smart, 1989), has functioned to drain the dangerousness construct of its social and political content.

Images of peril become inscribed on solitary human subjects, typically pathological or psychopathic, and social defence becomes a matter of simply segregating the dangerous and potentially dangerous from the endangered through authoritative exercises in scientific sorting. The diagnosis and prevention of inter-personal violence and other individual harms become the main task of penal systems, which are increasingly cut off from the collective and normalized hazards inherent in modern life, whether these take the form of nuclear arsenals, genocidal wars, ecological atrocities, state terrorism, institutionalized poverty, racism, sexism or violations of human rights. Such dangers are typically seen to fall outside the realm of penality, and hence are left to other, more "politicized" institutions. The criminal law and its supporting systems are instead concerned with the depredations of sick and sinful beings. And while the legal power to punish and correct is immense (Garland, 1990; Garland and Young 1983; Pepinsky and Quinney, 1991; Smart, 1989), the weaponry is trained downward and inward, away from the structures and ideas that spawn the most terrifying kinds of collective endangerment. Constrained by such a myopic conception of risk, the state's carceral apparatus is simply not equipped to protect its citizens from the most systemic and supreme perils.

More than this, through the twentieth-century interventions of psychiatry and other mental sciences, danger has become increasingly pathologized and equated with a wide range of personal defects and disorders. Amid a sustained exercise in Foucauldian normalization (Diamond and Quinby, 1988; Garland, 1985; Rose, 1990), the routine, mundane features of violence and other social harms have been progressively submerged in political and public culture, and supplanted by the sense that dangerous people are somehow different and unique — walled off from the rest of us by some discoverable material, mental or moral barrier. From Garofalo's theories of dangerosity (1914) to contemporary sociobiologies of homicide and violence (Daly and Wilson, 1988; Wilson and Herrnstein, 1985; see Caputi, 1987; Hanmer and Maynard, 1987), experts have time and again been commissioned to chart the correlates of dangerous conduct; to draw distinctions between the innocuous and the threatening; to mine for cues and clues in the bodies and minds of risky subjects; and to construct actuarial scales and clinical methods for the scientific forecasting of dangerous events (Deitz, 1985; Dix, 1980; Hall, 1987; Mulvey, Blumstein and Cohen, 1986; Schmidt and Witte, 1990; von Hirsch, 1987).

These efforts continue, despite recurrent demonstrations of the construct's ontological orneriness — its stubborn resistance to the overtures of technicians or clinicians who propose to classify dangerous people and predict their transgressions (Menzies, 1986, 1989; Monahan, 1981; Steadman and Cocozza, 1974; Thornberry and Jacoby, 1979; Webster, Dickens and Addario, 1985; Webster and Menzies, 1987).

According to critics, the scientific normalization of dangerousness is a hapless pursuit, condemned by the ideological character of the concept itself, and by the political contexts in which it is typically invoked (Castel, 1991; Petrunik, 1983; Pfohl, 1978, 1979). And a small library of research is now available to document the meagre correspondences between violent behaviour and such personal categories and conditions as psychiatric status, criminal history and social class (Bieber, Pasewark, Bosten and Steadman, 1988; Menzies, Webster and Sepejak, 1987; Mesnikoff and Lauterbach, 1975; but see Harris, Rice and Cormier, 1991). Even those factors that do demonstrate a differential effect—for example age, gender, and prior violence—are notoriously deficient in predictive power (American Psychiatric Association, 1974; Monahan, 1981). The intuitive judgments of practising psychiatrists and other experts, in turn, show little promise (Coleman, 1984; Dix, 1980; Menzies, Webster and Sepejak, 1985a; Webster and Menzies, 1987). Statistical and psychometric instruments, while less strikingly inaccurate, are nonetheless of little practical value in the clinical or penal classification of perilous persons (Menzies, Webster and Sepejak,

1985b; Monahan, 1981; von Hirsch, 1987).

Yet the enterprise endures. Indeed, perhaps the most remarkable aspect of the danger sciences is their resilience in the face of such a prolonged legacy of unremittingly bad reviews. Over the past decade, in fact, the power to apply dangerous labels to legal and medical subjects, and to confine and correct them on the grounds of these imputations, has escalated. Moreover, some of the most vocal critics of these practices fifteen or twenty years ago (Ennis and Litwack, 1974; Monahan and Cummings, 1975; Steadman, 1973; Morris and Hawkins, 1970) have revised their positions and are now endorsing the qualified use of the dangerousness construct, or some variant, in carceral and psychiatric decision-making (Litwack, 1985; Monahan, 1988; Steadman, Robbins and Monahan, 1991; Morris and Miller, 1985).

None of this should come as much of a shock to anyone versed in the behaviour of scientific paradigms, and in their power to propel "normal" theory and practice through countless minefields of empirical anomalies (Harding, 1987; Kuhn, 1970; Lakatos and Musgrave, 1968; Ritzer, 1975; Spruill, 1983). Nor should we be surprised that the dangerousness concept survives and thrives in medico-legal settings, given its embeddedness in the very fabric of forensic discourse (Menzies, 1986; Castel, 1991), and given its many contributions to the projects of penal systems and the ventures of their agents (Garland 1985; Garland and Young, 1983). Indeed, in the Canadian carceral complex as elsewhere, we are witnessing yet another in a long series of dangerousness revivals (see Bottoms, 1977), and the new versions of this vintage construct are taking a variety of legal, institutional and discursive forms.

Dangerous Trends in the Canadian Carceral Complex

The renaissance of dangerousness in Canadian correctional and therapeutic systems has been gathering momentum since the middle 1970s. The authors of provincial mental health laws across the country, caught in the convulsions of the "deinstitutionalization" movement (Dear and Wolch, 1987; Johnson, 1990; Lerman, 1982; Scull, 1984, 1989; 1990; Torrey, 1988), and inspired by the rights rhetoric emanating from the Charter of Rights and Freedoms and from developments in the United States (Gordon and Verdun-Jones, 1988; Robertson, 1987; Savage and McKague, 1987; Stone, 1984; Wexler, 1981), have turned to dangerousness as a focal criterion for the involuntary confinement of psychiatric subjects.

The remarkable depopulation of inclusionary mental institutions over the past quarter-century has been largely premised on and justified by expert assertions that ex-patients present no threat to the "communities" into which they are being unloaded (Ashford, 1989; Brahams and Weller, 1986; Steadman, Cocozza and Melick, 1978). Conversely only those persons evaluated to be both mentally ill and dangerous (to others, or to themselves through risk of suicide or grave disablement) are legally liable to be mentally confined against their will (Robertson, 1987; Savage and McKague, 1987; Schiffer, 1978, 1982).

The results have been predictable. The grim realities of the "community mental health movement" — the fiscal minimalism of right-wing legislators, the naive deconstructionist mentality of their liberal counterparts, the condemning of an entire generation of emotionally damaged and poor people to lives of urban decay, homelessness, petty crime and endless cycles of psycho-legal discipline — are obscured by a danger discourse that indelibly colours psychiatric practice and legal process, and purports to inform these policies with just measures of both scientific precision and legalistic propriety. In practice, the predication of involuntary mental hospitalization on diagnoses of dangerousness has led to the bifurcation of mentally disordered populations. The non-dangerous are cast into the transcarceral complex (Lowman, Menzies and Palys, 1987; Webster and Menzies, 1987), and into a desultory drift through the inner-city landscape, and between the assortment of state and private agencies left to contend with the chaos. The dangerous, often so defined on the grounds of their violent histories and carceral records, come to typify chronic hospital populations and in the process to escalate the general criminalization of psychiatric settings.

Dangerousness has also been an organizing theme in recent amendments to the Criminal Code of Canada. After an initial latency period following its passage in 1977, Part XXIV of the Code (formerly Part XXI), providing for the indefinite incarceration of convicted offenders judged to be dangerous in a quasi-criminal sentencing tribunal involving expert testimony, has been invoked over recent years with increasing regularity (Jakimiec, Porporino, Addario and Webster, 1986).[2] Dangerous offender legislation was originally proposed by the 1969 federal Ouimet Committee (see Petrunik, 1983; Price, 1970; Webster, Dickens and Addario, 1985), and was conceived in the tradition of various statutes in other jurisdictions which permit extraordinary sentences for individuals posing a perpetual risk to the public (Floud and Young, 1981; Morris and Miller, 1985; von Hirsch, 1987). Following the conviction of criminal offenders for specified violent or sexual offences, the Attorney-General has the discretion to order a dangerous offender hearing, which is conducted under civil standards of evidence and proof, and which enlists expert testimony about the subject's alleged dangerousness in determining whether to invoke an indeterminate prison sentence. Ultimate parole or release is at the discretion of the National Parole Board which reviews cases after three years, and every year thereafter. To date, of the more than 100 Canadians declared to be dangerous offenders since 1977, only one has been discharged from prison.

Dangerous offender legislation has been widely denounced by sociolegal scholars and civil libertarians who dispute its constitutionality, its efficacy in protecting the public from violent offenders, and its reliance on dubious expert judgments about the dangerousness of criminal defendants (Grant, 1985; Klein, 1976; Price, 1970; Menzies, 1986). Indeed, the Canadian Sentencing Commission (1987: 213) has recommended that it be revoked. But in response to numerous legal challenges under the Charter of Rights and Freedoms, the courts have consistently upheld its provisions (Gordon and Verdun-Jones, 1988; Webster, Dickens and Addario, 1985).

The 1986 dangerous offender trial of Robert Noyes, a British Columbia teacher convicted of nineteen counts of indecent and sexual assault involving school children, was a watershed case. Noyes' offences involved no violent coercion or penetration; the previous average sentence for such sex crimes was a three year prison term; and witnesses testified at the hearing that Noyes was a "classic" paedophile who presented little risk to re-offend while under appropriate supervision and medication. Nonetheless the court rejected defence arguments that an indefinite sentence was in violation of Charter sections 7, 9 and 12,[3] and declared Noyes a dangerous offender. Six years later he remains in prison, and the appeal is still before the courts (Koutetes, forthcoming; see Caputi, 1987).

During the 1980s the dangerousness construct also converged increasingly with decisions to release federal prisoners into the community. Prompted by a few highly publicized instances of violent crime perpetrated by ex-inmates on parole or mandatory supervision[4] during the early part of the decade (Birnie, 1990; Taylor, 1981; Voumvakis and Ericson, 1984), Parliament passed amendments in 1986 to the Parole Act and the Penitentiary Act[5] which authorized the "gating" of persons otherwise eligible for Mandatory Supervision after two-thirds of their sentence, on the grounds that they are likely to commit a violent crime during their term of supervision (MacLean, 1986; Mandel, 1986; Ratner, 1987).

Parole boards, which have since their inception been involved in the evaluation of criminal recidivism, and been institutionally endowed with exceptional discretionary powers, are now also firmly entrenched in the business of predicting dangerousness. But there is little evidence that they are any more successful in these endeavours than their clinician colleagues, or that the many actuarial and semi-structured instruments designed to facilitate release decisions (see Farrington and Tarling, 1985; Gottfredson and Gottfredson, 1986; Nuffield, 1982; von Hirsch, 1987) are capable of separating dangerous from non-dangerous parole or MS applicants with any degree of validity or regularity. The 1986 amendments were a textbook Canadian occurrence of "political prediction" (Thornberry and Jacoby, 1979), designed to impress the public and press with a display of raw carceral power in the middle of the most repressive decade in Canadian penal history (Mandel, 1991). As an operation in correctional management or social defence, it has had no demonstrable impact.

The 1991 Supreme Court of Canada decision in *Regina* v. *Swain*[6] has opened one further aperture for admission of the dangerousness construct. This case promises to have the greatest bearing on the disposition of criminally insane Canadians since Daniel McNaughtan himself was acquitted of murder in 1843 and shipped off to Bedlam at the "pleasure" of the sovereign.[7]

In *Swain*, the Court found section 614(2) of the Criminal Code, ordering the mandatory indeterminate hospitalization of persons judged not guilty by reason of insanity (NGRI) under Warrants of the Lieutenant-Governor,[8] to violate both the Charter of Rights guarantee of life, liberty and security of the person under section 7, and the protection against arbitrary detention contained in section 9. The holding on its surface appeared effectively to dismantle the Canadian system for confining NGRI subjects at the discretion of provincial Advisory Review Boards and Cabinets (Schiffer 1982; Hucker, Webster and Ben-Aron, 1981; Whitley, 1984). Moreover, it was to hasten parliamentary amendments to the Criminal Code[9] designed to place upper limits on the length of detention to which persons found "not criminally responsible on account of mental disorder"[10] are subject. The civil libertarian dimensions of the case seemed self-evident. Yet, despite initial enthusiasm from some legal quarters, particularly on the apparent abolition of indeterminacy as a sentencing principle for mentally disordered offenders, the recently enacted legislation (Bill C-43, section 4) passed by Parliament in February 1992, soon proved to hold out some potentially dangerous prospects.

The amendments restrict the court's initial hospital order to ninety days maximum. In addition, insanity acquittees will now receive absolute or conditional discharges. The provincial review boards[11] are empowered to render initial dispositional decisions in the absence of a court decision, and to administer all cases which have not received an absolute discharge. The initial order for custody or discharge is to be governed by "the need to protect the public from dangerous persons, the mental condition of the accused, the reintegration of the accused into society and the other needs of the accused" (Verdun-Jones, 1991: 20). Ceilings are imposed on the duration of psychiatric detention, namely life for murder and high treason, ten years (or the maximum Criminal Code penalty, whichever is less) for a variety of indictable offences, and two years or the maximum (again, whichever is shorter) for all other crimes. As Verdun-Jones (1991) observes, it is unlikely, given the length of these proposed ceilings, that the period of confinement for most insanity acquittees will be measurably reduced. Further, there are provisions for the court to extend the internment to life where the defendant has been acquitted of a "serious personal injury offence" and found upon application to be a "dangerous mentally disordered accused" (Verdun-Jones, 1991: 21).[12]

Once more we find dangerousness being inserted into law as a symbolic palliative, affirming the alleged capacity of judicial and forensic specialists to classify people on the basis of mental status and violent propensities, and in the apparent interests of public safety. The amendments reproduce on a different institutional terrain several of the tendencies reviewed earlier in this chapter. Dangerousness is summoned as a signifier which infuses these legal manoeuvres with discursive meaning, paradoxically allowing the perpetuation, and even escalation, of carceral power to be accomplished using the language of law reform, individual rights and scientific method.

In effect, the legislation is yet another instance in the continuing trend toward a mutual merging of criminal and therapeutic systems (Lowman, Menzies and Palys, 1987; Menzies, 1989, 1991). It is also consistent with the hastening transformation of legal psychiatrists and other forensic practitioners from therapists into experts in mental classification (Castel, 1991; Foucault, 1977; Garland, 1985; Garland and Young, 1983; Rose, 1990). In future, the Canadian criminal defendant pleading an insanity defence will be exposed to a protracted series of diagnoses of her or his psychiatric condition and danger to others, beginning with pre-trial examinations by defence and Crown witnesses, and continuing into the judicial judgment to order custody or discharge; the determination of "dangerous mentally disordered accused" status for violent offenders; the ninety-day initial confinement, which becomes in essence a protracted post-dispositional psychiatric assessment under review board authority; and finally, for custodialized subjects, the annual evaluations by the board to decide about eligibility for release (again based on ascriptions of mental status, dangerousness to the community, the prospects of successful "reintegration into society," along with unspecified "other" considerations).

This also imports yet another kind of dichotomy into the social control of psycholegal subjects. For mentally disordered persons acquitted of homicide and other personal injury offences, on the one hand, lengthy terms of security hospitalization will remain the status quo. Their purported danger to the public will become a more explicit rationale to justify what amounts to their indeterminate mental detention by another name. On the other hand, for those deemed non-dangerous (in practice, mentally disordered non-violent offenders) there will be a proliferation of insanity pleas, given the new two-year maximum for minor crimes and even the possibility for absolute or conditional discharge at trial. These people will become the criminal equivalent of non-dangerous informal psychiatric patients, who move rapidly and repeatedly through and between systems. They will become an increasingly prevalent feature of criminal trials, expert assessments and forensic institutions. Many will circulate into the civil hospital system, or will be deinstitutionalized or trans-institutionalized into alternative agencies (or more likely the streets), upon their release.

And in the process, psychiatric and psychological classification work, concentrating on the criminal responsibility and public risk of mentally disordered subjects, will escalate in frequency and significance. There will be yet another influx of professional gatekeepers, alternatively aligned with judicial authorities, defence attorneys and review boards, into these critical junctures between court, criminal and civil hospitals, prison and community. Much of this process has already unfolded in various U.S. states (Sales and Hafemeister, 1984), where reforms to the insanity defence have resulted in elevated numbers of insanity acquittees, confined for shorter periods if assessed to be non-dangerous, who are subjected to more classification and less treatment while under criminal control, and who flow with accelerating volume and speed between penal, psychiatric and other institutional settings (Cohen, 1985; Lowman, Menzies and Palys, 1987; Menzies, 1989; Ryan, 1987). Simultaneously, provisions for the designation of "mentally disordered dangerous offenders" (Bill C-43, section 4) will undoubtedly multiply populations of persons deemed to be criminally dangerous. Here above the forty-ninth parallel, with *Swain* and the proposed legislation we are experiencing the Americanization of our own criminal insanity apparatus.

What bridges these various scenarios is the disarming facility through which danger discourse gets injected into the routine operations of carceral control. It is no coincidence that the construct has achieved such prominence on so many parallel fronts over the past few years. The law-and-order culture of the 1980s was in many respects an ideal environment for a new wave of anti-crime projects, of "great and desperate cures" (Valenstein, 1986), and of political promises to secure a brave new world of public safety and security (Box, 1987; Ericson and Baranek, 1982; Hall, Critchley, Jefferson, Clarke and Roberts, 1978; Spitzer, 1987; Taylor, 1983). Experts in the diagnosis and containment of dangerousness simply rode the wave. And the impetus continues into the 1990s. More and more people are becoming self-professed authorities on violence. Predictive tests and instruments abound. The danger business has become an extraordinarily profitable enterprise, with numerous branch plants, a nearly insatiable clientele, and a seemingly endless supply of raw material. So the search for the magic bullet marches relentlessly onward.

The Construction and Deconstruction of Dangerousness at MET-FORS

In the research conducted over the past fifteen years at a pre-trial assessment agency called the Metropolitan Toronto Forensic Service (MET-FORS), one major focus has been on predictions about the dangerousness of criminal defendants that are formulated by psychiatrists and other clinical practitioners during the course of brief and protracted forensic remands. METFORS originally opened in 1977, and over the intervening years its personnel have conducted assessments of such attributes as fitness to stand trial, general mental status, treatability and dangerousness to self and others in the service of criminal courts throughout the greater Toronto area (Chunn and Menzies, 1990; Menzies, 1989; Menzies, Chunn and Webster, 1992; Menzies and Webster, 1988; Webster and Menzies, 1987; Webster, Menzies and Jackson, 1982).

METFORS occupies a central position in Toronto's forensic infrastructure. It is funded by the provincial Ministry of the Attorney-General; administered by a board under the auspices of the A-G along with the Ministries of Health and Community and Social Services; located on the grounds of the Queen Street Mental Health Centre on the west side of the city; and affiliated with the Clarke Institute of Psychiatry and the University of Toronto. Nearly 10,000 subjects have been evaluated at the agency since its inception. It was originally intended as a prototype for the development of other such agencies across the country, and its research unit has attracted a wealth of public and private funding on a variety of socio-legal and clinical subjects (Webster, Menzies and Jackson, 1982).

From the outset, dangerousness was a key interest. When METFORS opened its doors and the work began in earnest during the late 1970s and early 1980s, the concept had already attained a high profile in the literature of the time, and was clearly a focal concern in forensic practice across judicial and correctional contexts (Hinton, 1983; Monahan, 1981; Walker, 1978; Webster, Ben-Aron and Hucker, 1985). For the purpose of establishing a research agenda and amassing data, the initial mandate seemed obvious, namely, an appraisal of the clinical forecasting of violent and other dangerous conduct. Only a few methodologically sound evaluations of dangerousness predictions had yet been performed (Monahan, 1981; Pfohl, 1978; Steadman and Cocozza, 1974; Thornberry and Jacoby, 1979), and this void needed to be filled.

Consequently one of us (CDW), then in charge of research, set out to assess the accuracy of clinical predictions of dangerousness at METFORS. A research team was assembled, funds secured, clinicians recruited and protocols developed to facilitate an intensive series of investigations into the correspondences between clinical judgments about the dangerousness of METFORS forensic subjects, and the institutional and community violence and criminality of these people during the years subsequent to their psychiatric evaluation. With the participation of the clinical teams (including psychiatrists, psychologists, social workers, nurses and correctional officers) detailed research instruments were constructed, a dangerousness rating scale was produced, files were tracked down and compiled on more than 800 accused persons remanded during seventeen months of the clinic's operation, and Ontario correctional and hospital records were secured on the subsequent activities of these people for a period of twenty-four months after their initial assessments.

As the results came in during the early and mid-1980s, it soon become apparent that the relationships between the danger predictions and outcomes were at best tenuous, and at worst non-existent or even inverted. We could establish positive associations (signifying a measure of predictive accuracy) for some of the clinicians some of the time, and we could entice at least a fragment of forecasting validity out of semi-structured instruments applied by trained coders (Menzies, Webster and Sepejak, 1985b), but there was little doubt that we were consistently falling far short of the .40 "sound barrier" for prediction correlations that was a prominent threshold image in the prevailing research literature on dangerousness (Hall, 1987; Monahan, 1981; Menzies, Webster and Sepejak, 1985a).

Some of these findings were published in 1984 and 1985 (Menzies, Webster and Sepejak, 1985a,b; Webster, Sepejak, Menzies, Slomen, Jensen and Butler, 1984), complete with myriad caveats about the methodological limitations associated with work of this kind, and about the relative invalidity of the prediction scale that we had invented (called the Dangerous Behaviour Rating Scale or DBRS). Therefore the authors of these papers were dumbfounded to find themselves soon being inundated with requests for the instrument coming from clinicians and agencies across North America and Europe (including the US Secret Service), all of whom were evidently desperate for whatever "scientific" tools they could enlist in aid of their predictive practices, to the point of ignoring what we had guile-lessly believed were the irrefutable indications of our near-total failure.

These developments were highly interesting for a number of reasons. Researchers and clinicians were apparently reading our work through a variety of different ideological screens.[13] At the same time, we found our-selves surrounded too by a swarm of similar interpretive alternatives, which inevitably forced us back onto the very political, discursive and epistemologi-cal terrain that was carved out in earlier sections of this chapter. Put crude-ly, why the failure to establish any compelling evidence for the clinical or technical ability to predict dangerousness in this particular clinic? Was this a purely methodological problem or empirical limitation? Was the difficulty situation-specific? Were the inadequacies our own? Had we failed to meet the minimal standards for a critical test of predictive validity? What about the specificity of the prediction indicators, or the cavernous black holes in the outcome data set,[14] or the absence of information on subjects outside the province of Ontario, or the restrictions imposed by a mere two-year outcome term? Was our study, in short, methodologically unsound? Had we "under-tested" (Webster, 1990) our clinical and actuarial subjects? Was there insufficient science in our evaluation?

These queries led to one line of theorization. On another front, a very different set of considerations emerged that propelled our thinking more toward a challenging of dangerousness itself as a discursive construct, and as an institutionalized idea that is as deeply and dialectically embedded in the understandings of researchers as it is in the practices of the clinicians being studied. Perhaps, in other words, we had been asking the wrong questions altogether. Maybe "the-clinical-and-scientific-ability-to-predict-dan-gerousness" is an entirely inappropriate frame for structuring research of this kind. What if the entire problem is not a matter of predictive acumen at all, or even of establishing the standards and conditions for improving per-formance? What if the researchers are as ideologically and institutionally confined as their clinical subjects, and that only through a fundamental and paradigmatic reworking of the entire issue — through a devolving of dan-gerousness and of the accepted meanings which have been built up around it over decades of "scientific" activity — will they stand any prospect of liberating the idea of dangerousness and engaging it for progressive ends?

Clearly, such a self-consciously deconstructionist approach lends itself to a very different mode of inquiry. The evaluation of dangerousness becomes an exploration of scientific authority itself, and of the material and cultural conditions that authorize the attribution of danger to some people and problems to the exclusion of others. New subjects emerge: for example; (1) the constitution and impact of the dangerousness construct itself in relation to hierarchies of dominance and subordination, in realms of social life beyond the walls of mental and carceral institutions; (2) how ideas about danger and related categories flow through organizational structures to condition the beliefs and judgments of professional experts, and in turn to shape the carceral careers of their subjects; and (3) how ideologies and institutions, law and science, people and practices are recursively bound together in the implementation of dangerousness depictions along with such related constructs as endangerment, dependency, delinquency, deficiency, disorder and so on (see above).

These two competing strands — the empiricist and the deconstructionist — have been woven together, with no small degree of intermittent friction, in subsequent research on the subject of dangerousness at METFORS. Over the past five years a new project has been undertaken in an effort simultaneously to refine the conceptual and empirical bases of the earlier work, and to situate it within this more overtly critical framework. The return to METFORS for what can loosely be called a "replication" represented an attempt to push up against the methodological boundaries of this kind of longitudinal study, on the presumption that a more ambitious approach might reveal something about the nature of the limitations themselves (along with the forces that influence forensic practices and outcomes), and could possibly get more completely at the structures and discourses that make dangerousness such a pivotal phenomenon in psychiatry and law.

The current project, then, represents an enhancement of the work both internally and externally: internally, to elaborate the data base, supplement background, prediction and outcome variables and extend the follow-up to a full six years covering the entire breadth of the country; and externally, to design the research not only as an evaluation of predictive validity, but in addition this time as a survey of the organizational currents and legal-scientific understandings to which both experts and subjects are exposed in the forensic construction of carceral and therapeutic careers.

Accordingly, beginning in 1986 two cohorts of defendants were selected from the original METFORS dangerousness studies (see Menzies, 1989;

Menzies, Webster and Sepejak, 1985a,b), and the project has been designed to elicit as much information as possible about these people from their official judicial, correctional and hospital records. The exercise for one of these groups — 162 subjects who were originally assessed at METFORS between March and June 1979 — has now been completed. Detailed files were collected on these defendants' legal and clinical histories, their criminal and psychiatric condition at the time of assessment and their socio-demographic attributes and social circumstances. Information was assembled on the original clinical decisions about a variety of medico-legal issues from all members of clinical teams, which included the completion of the Dangerous Behaviour Rating Scale (see above), and added were myriad measures of dangerousness furnished at the time of original assessment by three trained coders. This was followed by an attempt to collect the most comprehensive pool of data possible on the institutional experiences and conduct of these people for the six years subsequent to their initial METFORS remand, which included federal and provincial correctional records from across the country,[15] hospital records from fifteen different institutions, National Parole Board files, Canadian Police Information Centre (CPIC) printouts and Ontario Death Registry records. For each case the final data set totalled 5040 variables, comprising detailed information on background, assessment and outcomes (the latter specifying each correctional and psychiatric contact during the seventy-two months, along with year-by-year synopses of experiences and activities in correctional and mental institutions and in the community).

Armed with this comprehensive collection of materials we have been hoping to shed some light on the issues raised in earlier sections of this chapter, and perhaps to address questions that were left largely unanswered in our earlier work. How, for example, is the perceived and lived dangerousness of forensic subjects related to the expectations and decisions of authorities and to institutional parameters? To what degree do refinement of the measures, and extension of the knowledge base, contribute to predictive accuracy when it comes to dangerous behaviour? Who predicts well and badly, and under what circumstances? How do the experts fare in relation to laypersons, and what do systematization and science contribute to these comparisons? Is dangerousness person-, situation- or institution-specific? Is it chronologically structured — does it amplify or decay with the passage of time? In general does dangerousness emerge from these data as a stable construct that retains its reality across time, space and perception? Or are we dealing with a construct so mired in the complexities of cultural and institutional life that it necessarily resists the ontological overtures of clinical, criminological and other "scientific" classifiers?

Given limitations of time and space, we can barely scratch the surface of these phenomena and problems in what follows. Elsewhere (Menzies, Webster, McMain and Staley, forthcoming a,b) we present a far more detailed review of the research findings and their implications for the dangerousness construct and its place in carceral practice. Here we offer just a brief synopsis in the context of this chapter's main themes. Among the most striking observations:

(1)   The subjects of METFORS assessments, like the subjects of most medico-legal institutions, had already experienced extensive levels of correctional control and treatment prior to their initial forensic remand. Nearly three-quarters (seventy-three per cent) had been charged with a previous criminal offence, and more than two out of every five (43.5 per cent) had been incarcerated. One-third were unemployed, thirty-four per cent had attempted suicide at some time in their lives, and sixty-four per cent and thirty-three per cent were moderate or heavy users respectively of alcohol or other non-prescription drugs. For a large segment of the cohort this forensic stopover at MET-FORS was just one in a series of carceral interventions in their continuing experiences of marginality and trans-institutionalization.

(2)   As in the earlier prediction assessment work involving two-year outcomes, there was little demonstration of either clinical or psychometric capacity to forecast the future dangerous conduct of METFORS subjects. The strongest positive correlations among the grouped clinical disciplines (for presiding psychiatrists) were about +.20, indicating that less than five per cent of future dangerousness (measured in three different ways: by total number of recorded official incidents, number of violent incidents and number of criminal charges) was being accounted for by the predictions. Some individual practitioners, on the other hand, fared better than others, with one nurse, one correctional officer and two psychiatrists achieving correlations above +.30 (explaining about ten per cent of the six-year outcome conduct). For most groups and individuals, the correlations peaked at about two to three years, and there was a subsequent deterioration in predictive capacity with the further elapse of time.

(3)   Efforts to construct complex predictive instruments generally met a similar fate. The Dangerous Behaviour Rating Scale, item- and factor-analysed and honed down to thirteen items[16] to maximize efficiency, contributed negligibly at best to the predictive power of clinical and other raters of dangerousness. In the hands of psychiatrists in particular, the psychometric instruments were virtually useless (see Menzies, Webster, McMain and Staley, forthcoming a,b).

(4)   Predictions of dangerousness based solely on the background attributes of subjects were clearly more successful than generic clinical judgments, raising important questions about the relevance of expert input into the decision making process. For example, multiple classification analyses involving just three variables (age, prior violence and prior number of psychiatric hospitalizations) elicited a multiple correlation of .48 with total violent incidents during the subsequent six years. Although these operations still embraced less than one-quarter of the officially recorded dangerousness exhibited by METFORS subjects, the simple scrutiny of prior records generated far better results than either the professional projections of clinical practitioners or the technical instruments of social researchers.

(5)   During the six years of intensive follow-up through carceral institutions, psychiatric settings and the community, it became apparent that the measure of dangerousness, and its very construction, varied dramatically across time and space. One dimension of this volatility was the extraordinary range of registered deviance and danger according to institutional context. For every subject-year spent in the community during the outcome period, for example, there were 2.82 official incidents and 0.34 acts of violence. In prison the respective figures were 2.70 and 0.50. This contrasts starkly with the records of mental hospitals, where 19.30 incidents and 3.38 acts of violence were reported for every patient-year.[17] It is highly doubtful that psychiatric inpatients are substantially more dangerous or prone to violence than prisoners or persons at liberty to any remote approximation of these statistics (cf. Mesnikoff and Lauterbach, 1975; Steadman, Cocozza and Melick, 1978). Instead, the diverse patterns of surveillance and containment, and the differential sensitivity of various organizations to acts of non-compliance and violence, necessarily become central

features in the understanding and measurement of dangerousness. Such powerful institutional forces consistently have been ignored in writing on the subject of social danger. Yet without a comprehension of structure and discourse, and of the complex practices that infuse the production and distribution of dangerous knowledge, the predictive enterprise is unlikely to progress.

(6)   One final preliminary observation from this new research pertains to the cycles of carceral and psychiatric contact to which the 159 defendants were subject. In general through the years after their forensic "diversion" these people remained highly institutionalized. Over the course of the follow-up over ninety per cent experienced pre-trial jail; about the same got parole, probation or bail; seven out of ten were sentenced to at least one term of imprisonment; fifty-seven per cent were psychiatric inpatients; and twenty-seven per cent were outpatients. Altogether they averaged 4.47 psychiatric contacts and 3.92 carceral contacts each. At the same time there was evidence of a decay in the intensity of control and supervision over time. For example, only forty-five of 159 people experienced any period of full liberty in the community during the first year after their assessment, whereas the number gradually rose to 128 by year six. Still — and this may be the single most graphic finding of the entire project — the sheer volume of criminal and mental censures was quite spectacular. Even in the final year one-quarter of the sample spent time in prison, another one-fourth was on probation, parole or bail, fifteen per cent in pre-trial lock-up, and fourteen per cent in psychiatric hospital. The story of dangerousness is very much the story of penal and therapeutic institutions, and how it is that they converge to shape the dangerous careers of psycho-legal subjects.

Conclusion: From Dangerousness to Risk

In arguably the most important paper to be written on the subject of dangerousness since the English translations of Foucault's work (1977, 1978) first appeared, Robert Castel recently (1991) published his observations on the currently evolving transformation, in the theories and activities of academics and practitioners alike, from dangerousness into risk (see Floud and Young, 1981; Monahan, 1988; Steadman, Robbins and Monahan, 1991). Castel argues that the positive idea of a dangerous subject in psychiatry has always been an uncertain and fallible instrument of power. In focussing on the individual attributes of dangerous people, the experts can too easily be proven wrong, with potentially dire consequences for both clinical authority and public security. Moreover, the inclination "to treat dangerousness as an internal quality of the subject" (Castel, 1991: 284) is itself a cumbersome and inefficient control device, limited in scope and confined to the sporadic detection and prevention of isolated forms of danger: "One cannot confine masses of people just out of simple suspicion of their dangerousness, if only for the reason that the economic cost would be colossal and out of all proportion to the risks prevented" (1991: 284).

In response to these contradictions, in concert with massive innovations in the constitution of postmodern knowledge systems (with new forms of instrumentation, data inscription and governmentality [Foucault, 1977; Garland, 1985; Rose, 1990]), the attribution of social liability is becoming increasingly objectified, depersonalized, actuarialized, applied to whole populations instead of isolated individuals, and transferred from the clinical scrutiny of experts into the hands of administrators and managers (see Cohen, 1988; Young, 1988). In the process, the designators of risk become insulated from the negative consequences of erroneous ascriptions, because their judgments are no longer applied to single subjects, but rather to entire categories of people and populations whose status is "based on the collation of a range of abstract factors deemed liable to produce risk in general...which render more or less probable the occurrence of undesirable modes of behaviour" (1991: 281, 287).

In other words, to be risky (or to be at risk), ceases to be an attribute emerging from within and discoverable only by those with the appropriate scientific or technical "gaze" (Foucault, 1978). It is simply a set of probabilities, a position in statistical relation to a cluster of variables, to be applied from without by anyone with the requisite data. It is not a "prediction" at all, but merely an allocation, a correlation of indices and classes: "To be suspected, it is no longer necessary to manifest symptoms of dangerousness or abnormality, it is enough to display whatever characteristics the specialists responsible for the definition of preventive policy have constituted as risk factors" (Castel, 1991: 288). And the range of risky categories, once detached from the bodies and minds of dangerous individuals, can become virtually infinite: "[n]ot just those dangers that lie hidden away inside the subject, consequences of his or her weakness of will, irrational desires or unpredictable liberty, but also the exogenous dangers, the exterior hazards and temptations from which the subject has not learnt to defend himself or herself, alcohol, tobacco, bad eating habits, road accidents, various kinds of negligence and pollution, meteorological hazards, etc." (Castel, 1991: 289).

These are expansive powers, which are manifesting themselves not only in the legislative and systemic trends we reviewed earlier in this chapter, but throughout the carceral complex and beyond. Paradoxically, the very failings of the dangerousness construct have become a catalyst (yet again) for its re-emergence in new form, as an organizing concept for the bureaucratic mapping and managing of damaged and damaging cohorts in accordance with their socio-demographic configurations, their actuarial risk gradients and test profiles, their cross-referencing on composite data banks and computer libraries, their approximation to the attributes of typical risk classes and categories. Throughout the remainder of this decade, we can expect these developments to continue and expand, with profound implications for social understandings and programs on the subject of social danger, and for the practices of experts invested with the authority to define the dangerous and prevent them from inflicting harm. And efforts to curb these powers, to hold authorities accountable and define the limits of carceral interventions, will need increasingly to contend with these profound transformations in the detection and detention of "dangerous" people.

Now whether any of these reflections have any lingering value beyond their basic heuristics is another question altogether. The tenuous lines of communication between correctional research and practice, and more generally between knowledge and policy in the carceral realm, present some daunting obstructions to the formation of any kind of progressive or humane approach to the phenomenon of social danger. Old mythologies die hard, and it is not at all certain that social, legal and clinical researchers — working as they usually do outside of the public eye and political arena — can effectively neutralize or even contend with the relentless deluge of imagery about malignant monsters and pathological beings that is being endlessly reproduced in the media and public culture (Caputi, 1987; Jones, 1980). Nor is it easy to deconstruct the hegemonic promises of a danger-free and secure society to be somehow achieved through tougher laws, more professional police, more painful punishment, more effective treatment, bigger prisons, better science, more rigorous classifications and precise predictions.

But the effort to deconstruct is at least a beginning (Code, 1991; Mitchell and Oakley, 1976; Smart, 1989; Spelman, 1988). And perhaps through the vehicle of research we can inch toward new discourses and practices that offer a more realistic appraisal of dangerousness, shaped by the understanding that what is to be feared most is not the random and rare assaults of predatory psychopaths and unwell beings, but the systematic

ideological and structural conditions that create these people and throw
them into our midst, just as they foster the celebration of war and weaponry, the economic partitioning of the planet into north and south, the industrial poisoning of the biosphere, the co-existence everywhere of outrageous
affluence and poverty, the subordination of women and minorities in private
and public, in the workplace and homeplace, and the kind of criminogenic
criminal justice system that makes this society, for virtually everyone, a very
dangerous place to live.

Endnotes

* Thanks are expressed to Debbie Slomen, Diana Sepejak, Shelley McMain and
Shauna Staley, who co-ordinated data collection during various stages of the project
described in this chapter. Acknowledged as well is the assistance of the many
research assistants, and representatives of mental health, police, justice and correc-
tional agencies (too numerous to list here by name), who collaborated in the compi-
lation of the information described below. Funding was supplied by the Social
Sciences and Humanities Research Council of Canada, the Canadian Psychiatric
Research Foundation, the Solicitor General Canada, the LaMarsh Research
Program on Violence and Conflict Resolution, the Ontario Department of Health,
Simon Fraser University, the University of Toronto Centre of Criminology and the
Clarke Institute of Psychiatry.

1   Even the pursuit of peace during time of war can be defined as dangerous activity.
See Wiltsher's (1985) history of women peace campaigners during World War I.

2   Section 753 of the Code reads in part:

> Where, upon an application made under this Part following the conviction of a
> person for an offence but before the offender is sentenced therefor, it is estab-
> lished to the satisfaction of the court (a) that the offence for which the offender
> has been convicted is a serious personal injury offence [defined in
> s.752(a)]...and the offender constitutes a threat to the life, safety or physical or
> mental well-being of other persons on the basis of evidence establishing (i) a
> pattern of repetitive behaviour by the offender, of which the offence for which
> he has been convicted forms a part, showing a failure to restrain his behaviour
> and a likelihood of his causing death or injury to other persons, or inflicting
> severe psychological damage on other persons, through failure in the future to
> restrain his behaviour, (ii) a pattern of persistent aggressive behaviour by the
> offender, of which the offence for which he has been convicted forms a part,
> showing a substantial degree of indifference on the part of the offender respect-
> ing the reasonably foreseeable consequences to other persons of his behaviour,
> or (iii) any behaviour by the offender, associated with the offence for which he
> has been convicted, that is of such a brutal nature as to compel the conclusion
> that his behaviour in the future is unlikely to be inhibited by normal standards of
> behavioural constraint, or (b) that the offence for which the offender has been
> convicted is a serious personal injury offence [defined in s.752(b)]...and the
> offender, by his conduct in any sexual matter including that involved in the com-
> mission of the offence for which he has been convicted, has shown a failure to
> control his sexual impulses and a likelihood of his causing injury, pain or other
> evil to other persons through failure in the future to control his sexual impulses,
> the court may find the offender to be a dangerous offender and may thereupon
> impose a sentence of detention in a penitentiary for an indeterminate period, in

lieu of any other sentence that might be imposed for the offence for which the offender has been convicted.

3.   Section 7 of the Charter reads: "Everyone has the right to life, liberty and security of the person and the right not to be deprived thereof except in accordance with the principles of fundamental justice." Section 9 stipulates that: "Everyone has the right not to be arbitrarily detained or imprisoned." Section 12 provides that: "Everyone has the right not to be subjected to any cruel and unusual punishment or treatment."

4.   Introduced through revisions to the National Parole Act in 1969, mandatory supervision provides for the supervised release of inmates not qualifying for regular parole after two-thirds of their sentence has been served (cf. Ratner, 1987: 294).

5.   Bill C-67, R.S.C. 1986.

6.   *Regina v. Swain* (1991), 63 C.C.C. (3d) 481.

7.   *MacNaughtan's Case.* (1843), 8 E.R. 718. See Moran (1981) and West and Walk (1977).

8.   Criminal Code of Canada, section 614(2).

9.   The Court originally gave Parliament six months to enact replacement legislation. The "grandparenting" period was later extended to nine months (expiring in February 1992).

10. This is the new wording, which will supplant the present legal category of "not guilty by reason of insanity."

11. Under the new legislation, each province must have a review board comprising no fewer than five people, one of whom must be a registered psychiatrist. The board chair must be a senior or retired judge or someone so qualified. The provisions resemble those pertaining to restriction orders (Peay, 1989) in England and Wales (Verdun-Jones, 1991: 20).

12. The criteria for release review, under the auspices of the Advisory Review Boards, will approximate those currently applying to parole boards in the case of dangerous offenders (see Verdun-Jones, 1991: 21). Not insignificantly, the Dangerous Offender provisions, formerly contained in Part XXIV of the Criminal Code, have been moved into these new sections.

13. For a more recent illustration of the same phenomenon, see Arboleda-Florez, 1991; Rogers and Bagby, 1990; Menzies, 1991.

14. In this initial two-year outcome study, the correctional data search was restricted to Canadian Police Information Centre (CPIC) and Ontario correctional files, along with six provincial mental hospitals other than METFORS.

15. Access to National Parole Board files permitted the documentation of incarcerations, transfers and releases for persons confined in the federal system, along with incarceration misconducts incurred during terms of imprisonment. Similar information was obtained at the provincial level, from all provinces with the exception of Manitoba and Nova Scotia, for all persons who registered a criminal offence in the specified province in CPIC records.

16. These are passive aggressive, hostility, anger, rage, guilt, capacity for empathy, capacity for change, self-perception as dangerous, control over actions, tolerance, environment support, ability to manipulate and provide accurate information.

17. Altogether the 159 METFORS subjects spent 8931 months in the community, during which they registered 2102 incidents and 252 acts of violence. The corresponding statistics for prison and hospital were, respectively, 1784 months, 401 incidents

and seventy-four violent occurrences (prison) and 462 months, 743 incidents and 130 violent acts (hospital).

References

American Psychiatric Association. 1974. *Clinical Aspects of the Violent Individual.* Washington, DC: APA.

Arboleda-Florez, J. 1991. Book review. "Survival of the Sanest: Order and Disorder in a Pre-trial Psychiatric Clinic." *Canadian Journal of Criminology* 33: 215-220.

Ashford, J.B. 1989. "Offence comparisons between mentally disordered and non-mentally disordered inmates." *Canadian Journal of Criminology* 31: 35-48.

Bacchi, C.L. 1983. *Liberation Deferred? The Ideas of the English-Canadian Suffragists, 1877-1918.* Toronto: University of Toronto Press.

Bieber, S.L., R.A. Pasewark, K. Bosten and H.J. Steadman. 1988. "Predicting criminal recidivisn of insanity acquittees." *International Journal of Law and Psychiatry* 11: 105-112.

Birnie, L.H. 1990. *A Rock and a Hard Place: Inside Canada's Parole Board.* Toronto: Macmillan.

Bottoms, A.E. 1977. "Reflections on the renaissance of dangerousness." *The Howard Journal of Penology and Crime Prevention* 16: 70-96.

Box, S. 1987. *Recession, Crime and Punishment.* London: Macmillan.

Boyd, N. 1991. *High Society.* Toronto: Key Porter.

Brace, C.L. 1872. *The Dangerous Classes of New York and Twenty Years' Work Among Them.* New York: Wynkoop and Hallenbeck.

Brahams, D. and M. Weller. 1986. "Crime and homelessness among the mentally ill." *Medico-Legal Journal* 54: 42-53.

Britzer, D.A. and M. Crowner (eds.). 1988. *Current Approaches to the Prediction of Violence.* Washington, DC: American Psychiatric Press.

Brody, B.A. 1990. "Prediction of dangerousness in different contexts." *Ethical Practice in Psychiatry and the Law* 7: 185-196.

Cameron, D. (ed.). 1990. *The Feminist Critique of Language: A Reader.* London: Routledge.

Canadian Sentencing Commission. 1987. *Sentencing Reform: A Canadian Approach.* Ottawa: Supply and Services Canada.

Caputi, J. 1987. *The Age of Sex Crime.* Bowling Green, OH: Bowling Green State University Popular Press.

Castel, R. 1991. "From dangerousness to risk" in Burchell, G., C. Gordon and P. Miller (eds.), *The Foucault Effect: Studies in Governmentality.* Chicago: University of Chicago Press.

Castel, R., J. Castel and A. Lovell. 1982. *The Psychiatric Society.* New York: Columbia University Press.

Chan, J. 1990. "Decarceration: A case for theory building through empirical research." *Law in Context* 8: 32-77.

Chunn, D.E. and S.A.M. Gavigan. 1988. "Social control: Analytic tool or analytic quagmire?" *Contemporary Crises* 12: 107-124.

Chunn, D.E. and S.A.M. Gavigan. 1991. "Women and crime in Canada" in Jackson, M.A. and C.T. Griffiths (eds.), *Canadian Criminology: Perspectives on Crime and Criminality*. Toronto: Harcourt, Brace and Jovanovich.

Chunn, D.E. and R.J. Menzies. 1990. "Gender, madness and crime: The reproduction of patriarchal and class relations in a pre-trial psychiatric clinic." *Journal of Human Justice* 2: 33-54.

Code, L. 1991. *What Can She Know? Feminist Theory and the Construction of Knowledge*. Ithaca, NY: Cornell University Press.

Cohen, S. 1985. *Visions of Social Control: Crime, Punishment and Classification*. Cambridge, UK: Polity.

Cohen, S. 1988. *Against Criminology*. New Brunswick, NJ: Transaction.

Cohen, S. and A. Scull. 1983. *Social Control and the State: Historical and Comparative Essays*. Oxford, UK: Martin Robertson.

Coleman, L. 1984. *The Reign of Error: Psychiatry, Authority and Law*. Boston: Beacon.

Coward, R. 1985. *Female Desires: How They Are Sought, Bought and Packaged*. New York: Grove Press.

Daly, M. and M. Wilson. 1988. *Homicide*. New York: A. de Gruyter.

Dear, M. and J. Wolch. 1987. *Landscapes of Despair — From Deinstitutionalization to Homelessness*. Princeton, NJ: Princeton University Press.

Diamond, I. and L. Quinby (eds.). 1988. *Feminism and Foucault: Reflections on Resistance*. Boston, MS: Northeastern University Press.

Dietz, P.E. 1985. "Hypothetical criteria for the prediction of individual criminality" in Webster, C.D., M.H. Ben-Aron and S.J. Hucker (eds.), *Dangerousness: Probability and Prediction, Psychiatry and Public Policy*. New York: Cambridge.

Dix, G.E. 1980. "Clinical evaluation of the 'dangerousness' of 'normal' criminal defendants." *Virginia Law Review* 66: 523-581.

Dorn, N. 1987. *A Land Fit for Heroin? Drug Policies, Prevention and Practice*. London: Macmillan.

Eisenstein, Z. 1988. *The Female Body and the Law*. Berkeley: University of California Press.

Ennis, B.J. and T.R. Litwack. 1974. "Psychiatry and the presumption of expertise: Flipping coins in the courtroom." *California Law Review* 62: 693-752.

Ericson, R.V. and P.M. Baranek. 1982. *The Ordering of Justice: A Study of Accused Persons as Dependants in the Criminal Process*. Toronto: University of Toronto Press.

Ericson, R.V. and C.D. Shearing. 1986. "The scientification of police work" in Bohme G. and N. Stehr (eds.), *The Knowledge Society: The Growing Impact of Scientific Knowledge on Social Relations*. Dordrecht, GER: Reidel.

Farrington, D.P. and R. Tarling (eds.). 1985. *Prediction in Criminology*. Albany: State University of New York Press.

Floud, J. and W. Young. 1981. *Dangerousness and Criminal Justice*. London: Heinemann.

Foucault, M. 1977. *Discipline and Punish: The Birth of the Prison*. New York: Pantheon.

Foucault, M . 1978. "About the concept of the 'dangerous individual' in 19th-century legal psychiatry." *International Journal of Law and Psychiatry* 1: 1-18.

Garland, D. 1985. *Punishment and Welfare: A History of Penal Strategies*. Aldershot, UK: Gower.

Garland, D. 1990. *Punishment and Modern Society: A Study in Social Theory*. Chicago: University of Chicago Press.

Garland, D. and P. Young. 1983. *The Power to Punish: Contemporary Penality and Social Analysis*. London: Heinemann.

Garofalo, R. 1914. *Criminology*. Trans. R.W. Millar. New York: Patterson Smith, 1964.

Gordon, R.M. and S.N. Verdun-Jones. 1988. "The trials of mental health law: Recent trends and developments in Canadian mental health jurisprudence." *Dalhousie Law Review* 11: 833-863.

Gottfredson, S.D. and D.M. Gottfredson. 1986. "Accuracy of prediction models" in Blumstein, A., J. Cohen, J.A. Roth and C.A. Visher (eds.), *Criminal Career and Career Criminal*. Vol. 2. Washington, DC: National Academy Press.

Grant, I. 1985. "Dangerous offenders," *Dalhousie Law Journal*. 9: 347-382.

Grant, I., C. Boyle and D.E. Chunn. Forthcoming. *The Law of Homicide*. 2nd ed. Toronto: Carswell.

Hall, H.V. 1987. *Violence Prediction: Guidelines for the Forensic Practitioner*. Springfield, IL: Charles C. Thomas.

Hall, S., C. Critchley, A. Jefferson, S. Clarke and B. Roberts. 1978. *Policing the Crisis: Mugging, the State, Law and Order*. London: Macmillan.

Hamilton, J.F. and H. Freeman (eds.). 1982. *Dangerousness: Psychiatric Assessment and Management*. London: Gaskell.

Hanmer, J. and M. Maynard (ed.). 1987. *Women, Violence and Social Control*. Atlantic Highlands, NJ: Humanities Press International.

Harding, S. (ed.). 1987. *Feminism and Methodology*. Bloomington: Indiana University Press.

Harris, G.T., M.E. Rice and C.A. Cormier. 1991. "Psychopathy and Violent Recidivism." *Law and Human Behaviour* 15: 625-637.

Hinton, J.W. (ed.). 1983. *Dangerousness: Problems of Assessment and Prediction*. London: Allen and Unwin.

Hucker, S.J., C.D. Webster and M.H. Ben-Aron (eds.). 1981. *Mental Disorder and Criminal Responsibility*. Toronto: Butterworths.

Jakimiec, J., F. Porporino, S. Addario and C.D. Webster. 1986. "Dangerous offenders in Canada, 1977-1985." *International Journal of Law and Psychiatry* 9: 479-489.

Johnson, A.B. 1990. *Out of Bedlam: The Truth About Deinstitutionalization*. New York: Basic.

Jones, A. 1980. *Women Who Kill*. New York: Fawcett Crest.

Klein, J.F. 1976. "The dangerousness of dangerous offender legislation: Forensic folklore revisited." *Canadian Journal of Criminology and Corrections* 18: 109-123.

Koutetes, B. Forthcoming. "I, Robert Olav Noyes." Unpublished M.A. Thesis. Simon Fraser University School of Criminology.

Kuhn, T.S. 1970. *The Structure of Scientific Revolutions*. 2nd ed. Chicago: University of Chicago Press.

Lakatos, I. and A. Musgrave (eds.). 1968. *Problems in the Philosophy of Science*. Amsterdam: North-Holland.

Lerman, P. 1982. *Deinstitutionalization and the Welfare State*. New Brunswick, NJ: Rutgers University Press.

Litwack, T.R. 1985. "The prediction of violence." *The Clinical Psychologist* (Fall): 87-91.

Lowman, J. and B.D. MacLean (eds.). 1992. *Realist Criminology: Crime Control and Policing in the 1990s*. Toronto: University of Toronto Press.

Lowman, J., R.J. Menzies and T.S. Palys (eds.). 1987. *Transcarceration: Essays in the Sociology of Social Control*. Aldershot, UK: Gower.

MacLean, B.D. 1986. *The Political Economy of Crime: Readings For a Critical Criminology*. Scarborough, ON: Prentice-Hall.

McLaren, A. 1990. *Our Own Master Race: The Eugenic Crusade in Canada*. Toronto: McClelland and Stewart.

McMain, S., C.D. Webster and R.J. Menzies. 1989. "The post-assessment careers of mentally disordered offenders." *International Journal of Law and Psychiatry* 12: 189-201.

Mandel, M. 1986. "The legalization of prison discipline in Canada." *Crime and Social Justice* 26: 79-94.

Mandel, M. 1991. "The great repression: Criminal punishment in the nineteen-eighties" in Samuelson, L. and B. Schissel (eds.), *Criminal Justice: Sentencing Issues and Reform*. Halifax, NS: Garamond.

Mayhew, H. 1861. *London Labour and the London Poor*. London: Griffin.

Melossi, M. 1990. *The State of Social Control: A Sociological Study of Concepts of State and Social Control in the Making of Democracy*. New York: St. Martin's Press.

Menzies, R.J. 1986. "Psychiatry, dangerousness and legal control" in Boyd, Neil (ed.), *The Social Dimensions of Law*. Scarborough, ON: Prentice-Hall.

Menzies, R.J. 1989. *Survival of the Sanest: Order and Disorder in a Pre-Trial Psychiatric Clinic*. Toronto: University of Toronto Press.

Menzies, R.J. 1991. "Counterpoint: Response to book review." Survival of the Sanest: Order and Disorder in a Pre-trial Psychiatric Clinic (by Richard Rogers and Michael Bagby). *Health Law in Canada* 11: 79-83.

Menzies, R.J. 1992. "The empire strikes back: Response to book review." Survival of the Sanest: Order and Disorder in a Pre-trial Psychiatric Clinic. *Canadian Journal of Criminology* 34.

Menzies, R.J., D.E. Chunn and C.D. Webster. 1992. "Female follies: The forensic psychiatric assessment of women defendants." *International Journal of Law and Psychiatry* 15: 179-193.

Menzies, R.J. and C.D. Webster. 1988. "Fixing forensic patients: Psychiatric recommendations for treatment in pre-trial settings." *Behavioural Sciences and the Law* 6: 453-478.

Menzies, R.J., C.D. Webster, S. McMain and S. Staley, Forthcoming. *Dangerous liaisons: Part 1. The formulation of dangerousness decisions*.

Menzies, R.J., C.D. Webster, S. McMain and S. Staley. Forthcoming. *Dangerous liaisons: Part 2. The outcome behaviour of dangerous people*.

Menzies, R.J., C.D. Webster and D.S. Sepejak. 1985a. "Hitting the forensic sound barrier: Predictions of dangerousness in a pre-trial psychiatric clinic" in Webster, C.D., M.H. Ben-Aron and S.J. Hucker (eds.), *Dangerousness: Probability and Prediction, Psychiatry and Public Policy*. New York: Cambridge University Press.

Menzies, R.J., C.D. Webster and D.S. Sepejak. 1985b. "The dimensions of dangerousness: Evaluating the accuracy of psychometric predictions of violence among forensic patients." *Law and Human Behaviour* 9: 35-56.

Menzies, R.J., C.D. Webster and D.S. Sepejak. 1987. "'At the mercy of the mad': Examining the relationship between violence and mental disorder" in Rieber, R.W. (ed.), *Advances in Forensic Psychology and Psychiatry*. Vol. 2. Norwood NJ: Ablex.

Mesnikoff, A.M. and C.G. Lauterbach. 1975. "The association of violent dangerous behaviour with psychiatric disorders: A review of the research literature." *Journal of Psychiatry and Law* 3: 1-31.

Mitchell, J. and Ann Oakley (eds.). 1976. *The Rights and Wrongs of Women*. Harmondsworth, UK: Penguin.

Monahan, J. 1981. *Predicting Violent Behaviour: An Assessment of Clinical Techniques*. Beverly Hills, CA: Sage.

Monahan, J. 1988. "Risk assessment of violence among the mentally disordered: Generating useful knowledge." *International Journal of Law and Psychiatry* 11: 249-257.

Monahan, J. and L. Cummings. 1975. "Social policy implication of the inability to predict violence." *Journal of Social Issues* 31: 153-164.

Moran, R. 1981. *Knowing Right From Wrong: The Insanity Defence of Daniel McNaughtan*. New York: The Free Press.

Morris, N. and G. Hawkins. 1970. *The Honest Politician's Guide to Crime Control*. Chicago: University of Chicago Press.

Morris, N. and M. Miller. 1985. "Predictions of dangerousness" in Tonry, M. and N. Morris (eds.), *Crime and Justice: An Annual Review of Research*. Vol. 6. Chicago: University of Chicago Press.

Mort, F. 1987. *Dangerous Sexualities*. London: Routledge.

Mulvey, E.P., A. Blumstein and J. Cohen. 1986. "Reframing the research question of mental patient criminality." *International Journal of Law and Psychiatry* 9: 57-65.

Nicholson, L.J. 1990. *Feminism/Postmodernism*. London: Routledge.

Nuffield, J. 1982. *Parole Decision Making in Canada: Research Toward Decision Guidelines*. Ottawa: Supply and Services Canada.

Palmer, B.D. 1990. *Descent into Discourse: The Reification of Language and the Writing of Social History*. Philadelphia, PA: Temple University Press.

Peay, J. 1989. *Tribunals on Trial: A Study of Decision-Making Under the Mental Health Act 1983*. Oxford, UK: Oxford University Press.

Pepinsky, H.E. and R. Quinney (eds.). 1991. *Criminology as Peacemaking*. Bloomington, IN: Indiana University Press.

Petrunik, M. 1983. "The politics of dangerousness." *International Journal of Law and Psychiatry* 5: 225-246.

Pfohl, S.J. 1978. *Predicting Dangerousness: The Social Construction of Psychiatric Reality*. Lexington, MA: Heath Lexington.

Pfohl, S.J. 1979. "Deciding on dangerousness: Predictions of violence as social control." *Crime and Social Justice* 5: 28-40.

Price, R.R. 1970. "Psychiatry, criminal-law reform and the 'mythophilic' impulse: On Canadian proposals for the control of the dangerous offender." *Ottawa Law Review* 4: 1-61.

Ratner, R.S. 1987. "Mandatory supervision and the penal economy" in Lowman, J., R.J. Menzies and T.S. Palys (eds.), *Transcarceration: Essays in the Sociology of Social Control*. Aldershot, UK: Gower.

Rennie, Y.F. 1978. *The Search for Criminal Man: A Conceptual History of the Dangerous Offender*. Lexington, MA: Heath Lexington.

Ritzer, G. 1975. *Sociology: A Multiple Paradigm Science*. Boston: Allyn and Bacon.

Robertson, G.B. 1987. *Mental Disability and the Law in Canada*. Toronto: Carswell.

Rogers, R. and R.M. Bagby. 1990. Book review. "Survival of the Sanest: Order and Disorder in a Pre-trial Psychiatric Clinic." *Health Law in Canada* 11: 251-244.

Rose, N. 1990. *Governing the Soul: The Shaping of the Private Self*. London: Routledge.

Rothman, D.J. 1980. *Conscience and Convenience: The Asylum and its Alternatives in Progressive America*. Boston: Little, Brown.

Ryan, L. 1987. *Harry and the Bus*. University of Toronto Centre of Criminology. Unpublished.

Sales, B. and T. Hafemeister. 1984. "Empiricism and Legal Policy on the Insanity Defence." in Tepplin, L.A. (ed.), *Mental Health and Criminal Justice*. Newbury Park, California: Sage.

Savage, H. and C. McKague. 1987. *Health Law in Canada*. Toronto: Butterworths.

Schiffer, M.E. 1978. *Mental Disorder and the Criminal Trial Process*. Toronto: Butterworths.

Schiffer, M.E. 1982. *Psychiatry Behind Bars*. Toronto: Butterworths.

Schmidt, P. and A. Dryden Witte. 1990. "Some thoughts on how and when to predict in criminal justice settings" in *New Directions in the Study of Justice, Law, and Social Control*. School of Justice Studies, Arizona State University. New York: Plenum.

Scull, A. 1984. *Decarceration. Community Treatment and the Deviant — A Radical View*. 2nd ed. New Brunswick, NJ: Rutgers University Press.

Scull, A. 1989. *Social Order/Mental Disorder: Anglo-American Psychiatry in Historical Perspective*. Berkeley: University of California Press.

Scull, A. 1990. "Deinstitutionalization—cycles of despair." *Journal of Mind and Behaviour* 11: 301-312.

Shah, S.A. 1978. "Dangerousness: A paradigm for exploring some issues in law and psychology." *American Psychologist* 33: 224-238.

Smart, C. 1989. *Feminism and the Power of Law*. London: Routledge.

Spelman, E.V. 1988. *Inessential Woman: Problems of Exclusion in Feminist Thought*. Boston: Beacon Press.

Spitzer, S. 1987. "Security and control in capitalist societies: The fetishism of security and the secret thereof" in Lowman, J., R.J. Menzies and T.S. Palys (eds.), *Transcarceration: Essays in the Sociology of Social Control*. Aldershot, UK: Gower.

Spruill, C.R. 1983. *Power Paradigms in the Social Sciences*. Lanham, MD: University Press of America.

Steadman, H.J. 1973. "Some evidence on the inadequacy of the concept and determination of dangerousness in law and psychiatry." *Journal of Psychiatry and Law* 1: 409-426.

Steadman, H.J. and J.J. Cocozza. 1974. *Careers of the Criminally Insane*. Lexington, MA: Heath Lexington.

Steadman, H.J., J.J. Cocozza and M.E. Melick. 1978. "Explaining the increased arrest rate among mental patients: The changing clientele of state hospitals." *American Journal of Psychiatry* 135: 816-820.

Steadman, H.J., P.C. Robbins and J. Monahan. 1991. "Predicting community violence among the mentally ill." 50th Annual Conference of the American Society of Criminology. San Francisco, CA.

Stone, A.A. 1984. *Law, Psychiatry and Morality: Essays and Analysis*. Washington, DC: American Psychiatric Press.

Taylor, I. 1981. *Law and Order: Arguments For Socialism*. London: Macmillan.

Taylor, I. 1983. *Crime, Capitalism and Community: Three Essays in Socialist Criminology*. Toronto: Butterworths.

Thornberry, T.P. and J.E. Jacoby. 1979. *The Criminally Insane: A Community Follow-up of Mentally Ill Offenders*. Chicago: University of Chicago Press.

Toch, H. and K. Adams. 1989. *The Disturbed Violent Offender*. New Haven, CT: Yale University Press.

Torrey, E.F. 1988. *Nowhere to Go: The Tragic Odyssey of the Homeless Mentally Ill*. New York: Harper and Row.

Valenstein, E.S. 1986. *Great and Desperate Cures: The Rise and Decline of Psychosurgery and Other Radical Treatments For Mental Illness*. New York: Basic.

Valverde, M. 1991. *The Age of Light, Soap, and Water: Moral Reform in English Canada, 1885-1925*. Toronto: McClelland and Stewart.

Verdun-Jones, S.N. 1991. "The insanity defence in Canada: The Supreme Court of Canada strikes down the system providing for the indefinite incarceration of those acquitted by reason of insanity and the Canadian government proposes an alternative system." *International Bulletin of Law and Mental Health* 3: 19-21.

von Hirsch, A. 1987. *Past or Future Crimes: Deservedness and Dangerousness in the Sentencing of Criminals*. New Brunswick, NJ: Rutgers University Press.

Voumvakis, S.E. and R.V. Ericson. 1984. *News Accounts of Attacks on Women: A Comparison of Three Toronto Newspapers*. Toronto: University of Toronto Centre of Criminology.

Walker, N. 1978. "Dangerous people." *International Journal of Law and Psychiatry* 1: 37-51.

Warren, C.A.B. 1982. *The Court of Last Resort: Mental Illness and the Law*. Chicago: University of Chicago Press.

Webster, C.D. 1990. "Prediction of dangerousness polemic." *Canadian Journal of Criminology* 32: 191-196.

Webster, C.D., M.H. Ben-Aron and S.J. Hucker (eds.). 1985. *Dangerousness: Probability and Prediction, Psychiatry and Public Policy*. New York: Cambridge University Press.

Webster, C.D., B. Dickens and S. Addario. 1985. *Constructing Dangerousness: Scientific, Legal and Policy Implications*. Toronto: University of Toronto Centre of Criminology.

Webster, C.D. and R.J. Menzies. 1987. "The clinical prediction of dangerousness." in

Weisstub, D.N. (ed.), *Law and Mental Health: International Perspectives*. Vol. 3. New York: Pergamon.

Webster, C.D., R.J. Menzies and M.A. Jackson. 1982. *Clinical Assessment Before Trial: Legal Issues and Mental Disorder*. Toronto: Butterworths.

Webster, C.D., D.S. Sepejak, R.J. Menzies, D.J. Slomen, F.A.S. Jensen and B.T. Butler. 1984. "The reliability and validity of dangerous behaviour predictions." *Bulletin of the American Academy of Psychiatry and the Law* 12: 41-50.

Weeks, J. 1989. *Sex, Politics and Society: The Regulation of Sexuality Since 1800*. 2nd ed. London: Longman.

West, D.J. and A. Walk. 1977. *Daniel McNaughtan: His Trial and its Aftermath*. London: Gaskell.

Wexler, D.B. 1981. *Mental Health Law: Major Issues*. New York: Plenum.

Whitley, S. 1984. "The lieutenant-governor's advisory boards of review for the supervision of the mentally disordered offender in Canada: A call for change." *International Journal of Law and Psychiatry* 7: 385-394.

Wilson, J.Q. and R.J. Herrnstein. 1985. *Crime and Human Nature*. New York: Simon and Schuster.

Wiltsher, A. 1985. *Most Dangerous Women: Feminist Peace Campaigners of the Great War*. London: Pandora.

Young, J. 1988. "Realist criminology in Britain: The emergence of a competing paradigm." *British Journal of Criminology* 28: 159-183.

THE GREAT REPRESSION:
CRiMiNAL PUNisHMENT iN THE NiNETEEN-EiGHTiES[1]

MicHAEL MANdEL[2]

Introduction

Even before the stock market plummeted in October of 1987, parallels were being drawn between our era and the years just before the Great Crash of 1929. According to the experts, in each era an extraordinarily narrow concentration of wealth was aided and abetted by governments that were strikingly similar in their non-doctrinaire support for big business, combining handsome subsidies on the one hand with a laissez-faire approach to regulation and taxes on the other. Each era was seized by a takeover/merger mania financed by spiralling debt and fragile credit devices such as "margin buying" (in the 1920s) and "junk bonds" (in the 1980s). The stock market was widely believed, in each era, to be completely out of touch with the strength of the economy, and based instead on pure specula-tion (Davis 1987; Thomas 1987; Galbraith 1987), the whole thing resem-bling a mass game of chicken. Both periods saw quantum leaps in Canada's integration into the American economic orbit: the twenties was the decade in which U.S. capital bought out Canadian manufacturing and extraction industries, and the eighties was the decade of the Free Trade Agreement. Each decade started with a severe recession and the second half of each saw a boom which created unheard-of wealth, but also unheard-of inequali-ty; spectacular profits were made amid falling wages and farm incomes. Even the moral crusade of the late eighties, the "War on Drugs," seemed like a replay of Prohibition, complete with its hypocrisy, international adventurism, official and unofficial violence and, naturally, the fortunes being made from it (Thompson 1985: 63-69, 77-96, 138-157, 193-195; Granatstein *et al.* 1986: 197-203).

Conventional wisdom holds that a crash of 1929 dimensions would be very different this time around, what with social "safety nets" and the "general cushioning effect" of Keynesian fiscal policies (Galbraith 1987: 64). But there is reason to believe that the results of the next crash will be much *worse* than they were after 1929 because, on at least one very important index, the appropriate comparison for our times is not with the period just before the Great Depression but with its very depths. This is the index of *repression*. In criminal punishment terms, the Great Depression was more repressive than any period before, and as repressive as any period since, *except our era*.

As far as criminal punishment is concerned, the 1980s was the most repressive decade in Canada's history. During that decade, the *per capita* prison population reached and sustained an all-time post-confederation high. This occurred at a time when the official philosophy of corrections emphasized "community" above all else. The emphasis on community was due to the fact that in *relative* terms — but only in relative terms — imprisonment is a declining form of punishment. Since the 1960s, imprisonment has been greatly outstripped by the growth of penal measures that operate outside of the traditional prison setting. The most prominent of these is the probation order, a device of infinite variety: from the occasional meeting with a probation officer, through unpaid work ("community service") to conditions identical to imprisonment ("Probation hostels"). On any given day, there are now three times as many people serving sentences of probation as there are in prison. Of course, this should not be allowed to obscure the fact that our imprisonment rate is higher than it has ever been. And this is *in addition to* a probation population never before seen in Canada's history.

Canada's Most Repressive Decade

The prison population

In determining the relative repressiveness of various periods in Canadian history, we are at the disadvantage of lacking consistent, comprehensive data. Comparable adult imprisonment figures covering all of Canada are only available since 1955. However, the method of reporting has changed significantly in two major respects. In the first place, since 1979 a distinction has been made between those "on register" and those "actually in" a given prison. This reflects the growth in the 1970s and

1980s of lawful absences from prison, especially "day parole." Since these mechanisms are part of the new "community" form of punishment, it would be misleading to include them in a comparison of *prison* populations in the past, especially since there were no comparable forms of lawful absences during the periods of high prison populations prior to the current one (e.g., 1961-1965 and 1931-1935). Consequently, I have tried to stick to the "actual in" counts, though sometimes these have had to be estimated. The second major change affecting comparability of data is the Young Offenders Act (YOA), which came into force in April 1985. The effect of this was to transfer a large number of offenders from adult court and adult punishment to youth court and youth punishment because it raised the age of majority for criminal law purposes from between sixteen and eighteen, depending on the province, to a uniform national age of eighteen. This, *and this alone*, is responsible for the apparent fall-off in the adult prison population after 1985. However, to adopt the new definitions for comparison purposes would also be misleading, because sixteen- and seventeen-year olds are still being imprisoned; in fact they are being imprisoned in greater numbers than they were before the YOA. The only real difference is that they are being imprisoned under different legislative mandates. To merely accept the reclassification as determinative would make long-term historical comparisons impossible. I have tried, therefore, to adjust the figures to counteract this "Young Offenders Act effect."

Ontario keeps separate figures for sixteen- and seventeen-year olds sentenced under the YOA and I have used these to project a national effect (based on Ontario's share of the relevant measures). I have then simply added these projected national figures to the conventionally reported adult imprisonment figures.[3] It turns out that, even apart from the YOA, the 1980s were the most prison-prone decade in Canada's history, but not to take account of the YOA effect would be to unnecessarily minimize the trends of the decade. Furthermore, excluding these numbers gives the completely misleading impression that the prison population started to fall drastically in the late 1980s.

Appendix I shows that in each of the years 1983 through to 1988 the per capita prison population exceeded the previous record high (for the period covered by the table) of 1963 by between 2.7 per cent and 9.5 per cent. The average prison population per 100,000 Canadian population for the five-year period 1984-1988 exceeded the five-year period 1961-1965 (the previous five-year high) by 111.3 to 103.6 (a difference of 7.4 per cent). The decade average for 1980-1988 exceeded the 1960s average by 105.6 to 99.7.[4] The average prison rate for the 1970s was only 89.3 per

100,000, with a high of 96.4 in 1977. Since 1955, therefore, the current period is clearly the most repressive in terms of the proportion of the Canadian population in prison on any given day.

To reach back farther, we have to use proxy figures. The "total institutional population" (Appendix II) has the advantage of going back to 1916; but it has the considerable disadvantage of not distinguishing between adult and juvenile detention. This table shows that the high imprisonment period of 1961-1965 was also higher, on average (123.2 per 100,000), than any other period since 1916, including 1930-1934 (117.3), though the rate for its highest year in total institutional terms (1964: 125.9) was slightly lower than the rate for 1932 (126.1), the depths of the Depression. To estimate the adult rate for the Depression so that it can be compared with the 1980s requires deflating the Depression figures to remove the element of juvenile imprisonment. This results in an average adult imprisonment rate for 1934 of between 98.6 and 105.3 per 100,000 (depending on the assumptions one makes),[5] putting the Depression's worst years well below the levels reached in the 1980s. The most repressive year of the Depression era, 1932 (0.2 percentage points above the most repressive year of the early 1960s), would, on this calculation, be assigned an adult imprisonment rate of between 105.7 and 113.2[6] per 100,000 Canadian population, still below the 1987 level of 114. If the entire decade of the 1930s is considered, the relative severity of our era becomes even more obvious. The average total (including juvenile) imprisonment rate for the 1960s was 118.7 per 100,000; it was 99.7 for adult institutions. For the 1930s as a whole, the average total institutional population was 113.1 per 100,000, from which can be estimated an adult population of between 95 and 101.5 adult prisoners per 100,000 population, compared to the 1980s adult institution average of 105.6.[7]

The only figures we have going back all the way to 1867 are for the *penitentiary* population (Appendix III; Figure 1). In Canada, "penitentiary" has a specialized meaning: prisons administered by the federal government. Consequently, these figures leave out of account those prisoners serving sentences in provincially administered institutions, a varying percentage of the prison population which has always constituted more than half of the total prisoners. The penitentiary population has varied as a percentage of the total prison population from a low of 26.7 per cent in 1937 to a high of 43.5 per cent in 1974. On the other hand, while "penitentiary" is a purely jurisdictional term and does not designate any particular type of prison, Canadian criminal law has always reserved "penitentiaries" (i.e., federally-administered prisons) for prisoners serving sentences of two years or more, i.e., the longest sentences. So the penitentiary population can serve as an index of penal severity: at any given time, what proportion of the Canadian population are serving prison sentences of two years or more? Here, too, the current era takes the prize. The average penitentiary population for 1984-1988 was 42.9 per 100,000, while for 1931-1935 it was only 38.2.

So, in terms of imprisonment, the 1980s were the most repressive years in Canada's history, including the years of the Great Depression.[8] Of course, imprisonment is not the only form of state repression and certain other forms were more typical of the Great Depression than of our own era. One such form was the death penalty (Appendix IV). There were eighty-three executions for murder in the years 1931-1935, almost twice as many as during the five-year period either preceding or following, and over one-third more than any other period in Canada's history (the next blood thirstiest period was 1946-1950, with sixty-two executions). The Depression was more violent in terms of the death penalty than any era before or since. There have been no judicial executions in Canada since 1962. In purely quantitative terms, these numbers are very insignificant: adding them to the prison population does not change the rounded per 100,000 population rate at all. But state-sanctioned killing cannot just be ignored. On the other hand, our era has no right to be complacent about its lack of capital punishment. Deaths "by legal intervention" (that is, killings by police or prison guards), judicially sanctioned, were far from unknown in the 1980s. In the years 1980-1986 (the latest for which figures are available), such deaths numbered sixty-three, or nine per year (Statistics Canada 1980-86). Furthermore, deaths of prisoners averaged seventy-seven a year for the last ten years for which information is available (1979-1988); of these, thirty-three per year were suicides—about 6.5 times the Canadian rate (Statistics Canada 1987-1988: Table 31; 1980-86). There are no readily available figures with which to compare our era and the 1930s in this respect.[9]

In quantitative terms, far more significant than deaths were the great number of deportations that took place during the Depression (Appendix V). The deportations for the years 1930-1933 were almost triple the per capita rate for any four years in the 1980s. Adding deportations to imprisonment changes the picture considerably, making the 1980s at most only slightly more repressive than the 1930s (122.7 to 121.3), and perhaps even less repressive (122.7 to 127.8), depending on the formula used. Whatever the formula, adding deportations to imprisonment means that the period 1930-1934 was substantially worse than 1984-1988 (146.4/153.1

to 124.7); it also means that the high rate of repression for 1932 far out-weighed the rate for the fiscal period 1982-1983 (178.7/186 to 130.4).

Table 1. Penitentiary Population Per 100,000 Total Population.

Decade	Decade Average	Decade High
1980-88	40	44.2 (1986)
1970-79	38	41.3 (1973)
1960-69	37	38.7 (1964)
1950-59	34	36.0 (1959)
1940-49	29	33.1 (1940)
1930-39	35	43.1 (1933)
1920-29	26	29.6 (1922)
1910-19	24	26.6 (1910)
1900-09	24	26.9 (1900)
1890-99	26	27.9 (1898)
1880-89	26	28.5 (1880)
1870-79	22	28.7 (1879)
1867-69	25	28.1 (1867)

It is important to determine whether the number of persons deported should be added to the number of persons imprisoned. Should deportation be regarded as on the same level of repression as imprisonment? There is no question that a large number of Depression deportations were meant to supplement the criminal law system. In the first place, there are many documented cases of the use of deportation to rid the country of political radicals, some of whom had been convicted of crimes and had already served terms of imprisonment (Roberts, 1988: 48-52). Secondly deportation was used "as an alternative to relief," an explicit means of "'shovelling out' the unemployed" (1988: 162,169). On the other hand, there are a number of documented cases of people who *wanted* to be deported, especially to the British Isles (where most of the deportees wound up) because of the desperate situation in Canada (1988: 185). Things could be substantially better at home and deportation meant a free, if uncomfortable, passage. While the government's claim of ninety per cent voluntary deportees was certainly exaggerated (1988: 181-82), it is hard to know where the truth lies. More importantly, there is a great difference between imprisonment and deportation to one's home country (assuming one is not claiming to be a refugee). For one thing, the state's concern with the deportee ends at the border; the deportee, as such, is under no sentence of any sort in the home country. For another thing, the element of enforced isolation is lacking; in the 1930s, whole families were deported along with the breadwinner (Roberts, 1988).

Of course, the point is not to minimize deportation, or even the desperate conditions of working people neither deported nor imprisoned. What we are trying to grasp, and what distinguishes certain periods in our history, especially our own, is the level of *state* repression, the repression of the public sphere as opposed to the private sphere. In this regard, deportation seems much more like probation than imprisonment. Imprisonment localizes punishment and surveillance in an isolated institution. Probation and related measures, such as parole, extend punishment and surveillance beyond the walls of the prison into the community, where, at various levels of restraint, the offender is kept under surveillance and required to carry out certain duties, more or less onerous depending on the circumstances of the case. Some probation can certainly be more repressive than deportation. Deportation, where involuntary, follows the offender to the border and then says goodbye; probation and related measures follow the offender into the community and keep an eye on him or her for years.

Whether or not the correct analogy for deportation is probation, it is clear that probation must be taken into account in any quantification of repression. If that is so, then the Depression, deportations and all, is not a match for the current era in terms of repression.

The Probation Population

In comparison to the prison population, the probation population has grown not only steadily but spectacularly. This is almost entirely a post-World War II development. There was some probation before the War, but it was on a tiny scale. Ontario appointed the first two adult probation officers in 1922, but progress was slow and there were only eight of them altogether in Ontario between 1930 and World War II (McFarlane, 1966: 31-32). These were the only adult probation officers in the entire country (Department of Justice, Canada, 1956: 13-14; Sheridan and Konrad, 1976: 254). Only fourteen officers in all had been appointed in Ontario by 1951 (McFarlane, 1966: 62). Then, suddenly, between 1952 and 1956, the complement grew from 15 to 94 (1966: 67). By 1965 there were 167 (1966: 96-97). Subsequent developments in admissions can be seen from Appendix VI. While jail admissions outnumbered probation admissions by 9:1 in 1965, this ratio had dropped to under 7:1 by 1972, to under 3:1 by

1976, down to just over 2:1 in 1979, where it has hovered since. At the same time, the rate of probation admissions grew from about ninety-eight per 100,000 population in 1965 to 367 per in its peak year of 1982. Another indication of the rate of growth is that between 1951 and 1979 Ontario's adult probation officer complement went from fifteen to 429 (including supervisors) (Hatt, 1985: 300).

Other provinces shared this experience. Alberta was the second province with adult probation services in 1940 and British Columbia followed in 1946 (Sheridan and Konrad, 1976: 254). The number of probation officers in British Columbia just about doubled every five years from 1950 through 1975, from six officers to 266, an increase in rate from about .5 per 100,000 British Columbia population to eleven per 100,000 (Sheridan and Konrad, 1976: 254-255). The adult probation system in British Columbia employed 350 officers in 1979-1980 (13.5 per 100,000 population) (Hatt, 1985: 300). National probation figures do not exist for earlier than 1978-1979, and since that time they have remained fairly stable, with probation accounting for roughly one in every four admissions to the correctional system (Appendix VIII) (Ontario's roughly one in three is high on the national scale).

But *admission* rates are nothing compared to *average daily population* rates (Figure 2). Somewhere between 1965 and 1972, the number of adults on probation in Ontario, which had been insignificant, indeed verging on non-existent prior to 1950, surpassed the number of adults in prison. By 1975 the figure, which had more than doubled in relation to Ontario's total population, was also more than twice as high as the prison population. By 1979 it was more than three times as high, and by 1983 Ontario's adult probation population was more than four times its adult prison population (Appendix VII).[10] Once again the national dimensions are similar, if slightly more modest, with the adult probation population at approximately three times the prison population (Appendix IX).

We can now return to our comparison with the Great Depression. During the 1980s (1980-1988), the average daily adult population under judicially ordered control and supervision, including prison, probation, parole and mandatory supervision, was 429.8 per 100,000 (422.4 for 1979-1988), with a high of 462 in 1987. If deportations are added to this, the total "repression rate" can be calculated at 446.8 per 100,000 for 1980-1988 with a high of 471.6 in 1986-1987. This is 3.5 *times* our best estimate for the 1930s, a rate of between 121.3 and 127.8. The particularly repressive years of 1984-1988 had an average rate of 465.8 per 100,000, more than three *times* the most repressive Depression years of

1930-1934, with an estimated rate of between 146.4 and 153.1. The peak year of 1987, with a rate of 471.6, was more than 2.5 *times* the Depression high rate of between 178.7 and 186 in 1932.

It is true that there was some minor Depression probation activity which probably should be added to the figures we have already calculated, if only for the sake of completeness. They do not change the picture at all, however. There were only eight probation officers operating in Ontario during the Depression compared to 429 in 1979. Ontario accounted for all of the Depression probation for adults, but only about fifty-two per cent of probation in the 1980s (Statistics Canada, 1987-1988: 125). There was also a form of parole in the pre-War period, but it was entirely lacking in enforceable conditions, or the parole officers to enforce them. This means that probation/parole levels during the Depression could be no more than about one per cent of what they are now, even assuming constant caseloads, which seems very unlikely, as caseloads appear to have more than doubled between 1965 and 1979 alone.[11] But even assuming constant caseloads, this would mean a maximum of about 900 cases in total during the Depression, or about nine per 100,000; adding this to the figures for the 1930s does not change things at all. The 1980s remain more than three times as repressive as the 1930s, the late 1980s 2.9 times as repressive as the early 1930s (the worst years of the Depression), and 1987 2.4 times as repressive as 1932, which, until the 1980s had been Canada's worst year for repression.[12] In other words, the 1980s were easily the most repressive years in Canada's history.[13]

Understanding Decarceration

Official ideologists have described the community corrections movement in the most glowing terms imaginable:

> Diversion is a promise!
> It is a promise that the poor, the uneducated,
> the disadvantaged and the abandoned who
> come in conflict with the law will receive the
> support and compassion of their communities
> (Canada, 1978: 10).

Even among left-wing criminologists it is possible to find the rising rate of repression and the proliferation of community corrections treated as "contradictory" or as "a momentous liberal compromise" (Taylor, 1985: 331). It is obvious that community corrections is neither promise nor compromise. The level of imprisonment has not only not abated, but has actually increased with community corrections, which have added to the arsenal of the state techniques of repression that are sometimes as intrusive as the traditional forms — indeed indistinguishable from them in some cases — and often more insidious. One thinks, for example, of the electronic bracelet to keep the probationer or parolee under constant Orwellian surveillance; or of the "probation hostel," minimum security prisons where persons under sentence of probation mix with persons under sentence of imprisonment (*R. v. Degan,* 1985). The community corrections phenomenon has expanded the power of the state's repressive apparatus, and has been predictably employed to increase enormously the proportion of the population under criminal sentence and surveillance, with no observable impact on the level of crime. It is hard to imagine a more important object of criminal law reform than the reversal of this trend. In Foucault's words:

> If there is an overall political issue around the prison, it is not therefore whether it is corrective or not; whether the judges, the psychiatrists or the sociologists are to exercise more power in it than the administrators or the supervisors; it is not even whether we should have prison or something other than prison. At present, the problem lies rather in the steep rise in the use of these mechanisms of normalization and the wide-ranging powers which, through the proliferation of new disciplines, they bring with them (1977: 306).

In order to stop something, though, you usually have to know why it is happening in the first place. Do we know what is causing all of this repression? Do we know anything about what causes variations in the repression rate?

What strikes even the casual student of the history of punishment in the twentieth century is how closely changes in the repressive rate seem to parallel changes in economic conditions or what is often called the "business cycle." The Great Depression of the 1930s, and the recessions of the late 1950s and the early 1980s have all been accompanied by a steep rise in the rate of repression. The recovery periods of the late 1930s and the mid-1960s were both periods of falling repression. During the sustained period of rising repression that Canada has experienced since the Second World War, there has been an "upward drift" of unemployment rates; in other words "the unemployment floor has been at a successively higher level"

(Ostry and Zaidi, 1979: 146).

Greenberg (1977) has shown a striking correlation between oscillations in the annual unemployment rate for ages sixteen and over and annual admissions to Canadian penitentiaries during the years 1945-1959, a correlation of ninety-two per cent with only a slight time lag of imprisonment behind unemployment. U.S. data are reported to be remarkably similar. In fact, the relationship between unemployment and repression is fairly well-established in the criminological literature (Crow *et al.*, 1989). What is not so well-established is the mechanism at work. Most conventional explanations of the connection between repression and unemployment are via an assumed relationship between *crime* and unemployment. The conventional explanation is that economic recession causes crime, and this rather predictably brings forth more repression. For example, Ehrlich argues that high unemployment and an otherwise contracting economy create greater material incentives for property crime and diminish disincentives such as the loss of earning capacity one might experience from a sentence of imprisonment (1973: 529-30, 538-39, 555). Tepperman has provided a more subtle analysis of the Great Depression in Canada along similar lines: severe conditions resulted in crimes of protest, crimes of "day-to-day survival" and crimes of just plain "craziness" (1977: 176-79).

The problem with the conventional explanation is the persistently weak relationship shown between the crime rate and the unemployment rate. In Greenberg's (1977) study, the rate of penitentiary admissions had nothing to do with the criminal conviction rate and little to do with the crime rate itself. The relation between the homicide rate and the unemployment rate, though substantial (.22), was too weak to support the changes in penitentiary admissions. Greenberg concluded that:

> It thus appears that in both Canada and the United States, changes in commitments to prison can be explained almost entirely by changes in the unemployment rate. Changes in the number of cases entering t'he criminal justice system and potentially available for imprisonment seem to be unimportant, as does the crime rate (1977: 650).

Like American rates, Canadian rates of reported crime since 1960 bear no apparent relation to the oscillations of the prison population over the same period. Crime rates have risen more or less steadily, while repression rates have fluctuated with the business cycle. The same was true during the Great Depression: conviction rates had been rising steadily from the beginning of the century and merely continued to rise through the Depression, albeit at an accelerated rate in some categories (Tepperman, 1977: 181, 216).

Such observations have led to more complicated hypotheses. Some studies have emphasized the sentencing system. For example, one study found that when controls for average prison sentences were imposed, the amount of variation in U.S. federal prison population explained by the unemployment rate dropped from seventy per cent to fifty-four per cent. Thus, a little more than one-fifth of the connection between prison population and unemployment was explained by sentencing, with nothing explained by the conviction rate (Yeager, 1979). Greenberg, too, concluded that the answer lay in the sentencing system. Though he doubted that judges consciously "orient their sentencing policies to the requirements of the labour market and that they agree on how this can best be done" (1977: 650), he was willing to "speculate" along two lines: either that "judges are less willing to grant probation to offenders when they are unemployed, or that unemployment affects levels of community tolerance toward offenders, to which judges respond in sentencing" (Greenberg, 1977:650).

Both hypotheses have their adherents. A recent study of English courts emphasized the way "unemployment restricts options" in sentencing (Crow et al., 1989: 27). Controlling for offence and record, the authors found that an offender's employment status made a significant contribution to the severity of the sentence: an unemployed offender was less likely to be fined and was more likely to get probation, a community service order or prison. The effect varied from community to community. It was most pronounced in traditionally low unemployment areas, in punitive courts and in areas where unemployment was increasing from low to high (Crow et al., 1989: 47). Even where unemployment was high, it made a difference in a negative way: judges felt it important to keep an employed person out of jail so as not to jeopardize employment status (1989: 61-62).

In Canada, employment status is both an empirically observable and legally accepted factor in determining a sentence, despite the lack of any plausible philosophical justification (Mandel, 1984). On the other hand, employment status is not considered by judges as an end in itself, but rather as a part of the assessment of the offender's "character." "Fault," even in matters of unemployment, is an important part of this. It seems far too legalistic — especially since sentencing is the most "unlegal" aspect of criminal law — to let the courts off the hook by assuming that they would *inadvertently* ignore the general economic climate in assessing the offender's character.

The hardening of official, including judicial, attitudes seems a more likely explanation of increased repression. Tepperman makes a strong case for an increase in "official punitiveness," as well as in real crime during the Depression, with sentencing severity and conviction rates rising to unheard-of heights in the early thirties and then falling back again (1977: 62-65). The most striking evidence is the execution rate. As Appendix IV shows, the years 1931-1935 had the most executions for any five-year period before or since, but they had fewer homicides and murder charges than the prior five-year period. What they had was an eighty-nine per cent higher conviction-to-charge rate for murder charges, and a fifty per cent higher likelihood of a death sentence being carried out. In other words, despite the lower homicide rate, a person charged with murder was almost twice as likely to be executed during 1931-1935 than during 1926-1930.

The Depression was a period not only of severe deprivation but of extremely high working class militancy. The Communist Party achieved its greatest popularity and influence, the Co-operative Commonwealth Federation was founded, and the real fear of revolution led to severely repressive actions on the part of the government. This included the outlawing of the Communist Party, the imprisonment of its leaders and violent confrontations between workers and police, such as during the "On-to-Ottawa Trek" (Thompson and Seager, 1985: 222-35):

With mounting discontent with the way Canada was being run during the Depression, the government, police and courts may have organized more tightly to punish and control the discontent throughout the country (Tepperman, 1977: 176).

Tepperman's general hypothesis is that "the worse socioeconomic conditions become, the more punitive judges and juries become" (1977: 63). Stephen Box has advanced a version of this to explain a similar rise of repression in the 1980s in the United Kingdom, where prison sentence admissions rose from 117 per 100,000 population in 1956 to 187 in 1983, and the average prison population went from sixty-four to eighty-seven per 100,000 during the same period (1987: 12). Box demonstrates that increases in the official crime rate, while reflecting real increases in crime (as shown by victimization studies) greatly exaggerate them.[14] One United Kingdom study showed that about eighty-five per cent of the increase in burglary between 1972 and 1983 was attributable to increased reporting (Box, 1987: 18-21). Box argues that some of this is due to increased willingness to report crime on behalf of victims and better record keeping by police, but that it also reflects greater official punitiveness and fear of rebellion:

> As unemployment rises, so the surplus labour
> force becomes a body viewed more suspicious-
> ly by the governing elite, not because it actually
> does become disruptive and rebellious, but
> because it might (1987: 62).

Nevertheless, even those advancing a "punitiveness" hypothesis have attributed at least *some* of the increase in repression to real increases in crime. Recent studies have suggested that it may be stronger than we have thought and that the problem with the studies so far is that they have not been sufficiently sensitive to different *types* of crime. When crime rates are "disaggregated" into different types, a much closer relationship between repression and crime can be observed. A sophisticated cross-national study has found that prison rates correlate with serious crimes (homicide, robbery, aggravated assault, fraud) but not with minor ones (theft, burglary) (Moitra, 1987: 71, 86). This difference is something we should expect from the changing roles of prison and probation mentioned above. Furthermore, disaggregated unemployment data have shown a closer relationship between unemployment and crime: certain age groups are more vulnerable than others to being affected by unemployment, and their situation is better grasped by certain measures of unemployment (e.g., participation rates) rather than others (Crow *et al.*, 1989: 6-10). Once again, there is clearly an exaggeration effect: for example, unemployed people are searched more often by police (1989: 10-11).

There is much scepticism among eminent criminologists about the reality of the increase in crime. Chan and Ericson have shown that most of the post-war increase in minor crime can be accounted for by increases in per capita policing alone (Chan and Ericson, 1981: 51-53). Furthermore, the steady rise in official U.S. crime rates has not been matched by victimization surveys which show the crime rate stable through the 1970s and actually falling through the 1980s (Hagan, 1986: 59; Siegel, 1989: 62-63; Chambliss, 1988: 32-35). On the other hand, victimization surveys exclude the homicide rate, which has also increased substantially. This increase is extremely unlikely to be artificial because of the difficulty in manufacturing homicides that have not really occurred and the high likelihood that those that occur will come to official attention. There is very little doubt, even among statistic sceptics, about the reality of the homicide increase (Chambliss, 1988: 40-41; Hagan, 1986: 175). Indeed, the homicide rate during the late 1920s and the early years of the Depression, though a historical high water mark until the mid 1960s, was far below the averages Canada has experienced for the last two decades. Homicide averaged 1.1

per 100,000 between 1936 and 1966, while for the 1930s, the average was 1.4 per 100,000. The worst five years for homicide in the Depression era (1928 to 1932) averaged 1.7 per 100,000; since the 1970s, the homicide rate has averaged 2.6 per 100,000 population, and the murder rate (only the most serious homicides) 2.4. The worst year for homicide during the Depression was 1930, with a rate of 2.1 per 100,000; since 1972, the *murder* rate in Canada has *never fallen below* 2.1, and the homicide rate, never below 2.3 (Reed, 1983: 21-27). Indeed, it has been argued that homicide rates *underestimate* the increase in the rate of lethal violence:

> Faster ambulances, better communications, transportation, and emergency room service meant better treatment for seriously injured persons, so that many who previously would have been homicide statistics were surviving (Hagan, 1986: 177).

It is worth noting that the *attempted* murder rate increased more than four times as rapidly as the murder rate between 1962 and 1987 (Dominion Bureau of Statistics, 1962a, 1965, 1968; Statistics Canada, 1971b, 1975a, 1980, 1983a, 1984, 1985a, 1986, 1987b).

If murder has genuinely increased, there is good reason to believe that violence in general has as well, even if some part of the official increase is a reporting phenomenon. On the other hand, it is also clear that violent offenders make up a small part of the clientele of the total population under sentence, and can in no way account for either the increase in prison populations or for the explosion in probation. Thus it is clear from the sheer numbers that many of those in community corrections would never have gone to prison. Furthermore, with what we know about the increasing punitiveness and intrusiveness of community corrections, it is also clear that those who would not have gone to prison would not have been subject to anything like the supervisory regime they now experience. This also lends support, indirectly, to the notion that much of the conduct now attracting probation would not even have reached the level of official notice before. It is hard to see the incentive for the police bothering to take notice of things about which nothing or virtually nothing is going to be done.

None of the alternatives — increased crime, increased repression or both — is very appetizing, of course. Either we are more repressed because we are more victimized or we are merely more victimized by being more repressed. But on the best evidence, we seem to be left with this: downturns in the business cycle cause real crime to rise, and this is met by increased repression, but in a way that exaggerates, sometimes to a great extent, the real increase in crime. How is it though, that we are now more punitive than during the Depression? If unemployment is responsible, then the Depression should have been far more repressive than our own era. The Depression was a "total and massive disruption of the economy" with unemployment rates reaching more than nineteen per cent, almost twice the worst post-Depression rate of 11.8 per cent in 1983.

It is possible to dispute the comparability of unemployment figures. Modern statistics clearly underestimate unemployment by excluding "discouraged workers," those who have given up actively looking for work because there are no jobs (Chen and Regan, 1985: 20-21). Also, unemployment rates do not take into account the growing substitution of part-time for full-time jobs. Between 1975 and 1985 part-time workers as a percentage for all workers increased from 10.6 per cent to 15.2 per cent (Rinehart, 1987: 165-66; van Cleef, 1985). On the other hand, it is clear that there was nothing in the 1980s to match the severity or abruptness of the economic downturn of the early 1930s, when unemployment, however measured, increased threefold between 1929 and 1930 and sixfold between 1929 and 1933, and when average per capita income was cut in half between 1928 and 1933 (Thompson and Seager, 1985: 350-51). Furthermore:

> The unemployed of that period were mainly adult males — the sole family earner — and there was no "safety net" of unemployment insurance or other income-support measures which today greatly reduce the disastrous economic effects of unemployment on the working population (Ostry and Zaidi, 1979: 145).

In other words, the reasons for the greater repressiveness of our era must be sought outside of the short-term economic fluctuations, which have been the object of most studies of crime and unemployment. The reasons must have something to do with long-term differences between our era and the Depression.

Several theorists have postulated a kind of self-perpetuating expansion of the repressive capacity of the state, which is supposed to have an inbuilt tendency to spread from the enclosed institutions and to penetrate society ever more deeply. The foremost proponent of this thesis was Foucault. Foucault argued that the disciplinary technique, which first flourished in factories, schools, hospitals and prisons from very early on exhibited a "swarming" tendency, a "tendency to become 'deinstitutionalized,' to emerge from the closed fortresses in which they once functioned and to circulate in a 'free' state" (1977: 211). At the beginning of the penitentiary system in the late eighteenth century one already sees the use of disciplinary mechanisms, not in the form of enclosed institutions, but "as centres of observation disseminated throughout society." Foucault gave the example of the Paris charity associations that sent out their missionaries on regular family visits for the purpose of reforming proletarian life (1977: 212):

> On the whole, therefore, one can speak of the formation of a disciplinary society in this movement that stretches from the enclosed disciplines, a sort of social "quarantine," to an indefinitely generalizable mechanism of "panopticism" (1977: 216).

For Foucault the prison held a special place in the disciplinary design. It was the mechanism which fashioned the "delinquent" (the dangerous individual — whose dangerousness does not reside solely in the offence — needing supervision) from the "offender" (the mere violator of laws needing no supervision). Delinquency, "with the generalized policing that it authorizes, constitutes a means of perpetual surveillance of the population: an apparatus that makes it possible to supervise, through the delinquents themselves, the whole social field." Foucault argued that this surveillance was at first "able to function only in conjunction with the prison" because of the powers of surveillance it authorized over the prisoner and ex-prisoner population (1977: 281). But soon there began to develop a "carceral archipelago," a series of institutions "beyond the frontiers of criminal law" (Foucault, 1977: 298). The frontiers of criminal law

> tended to disappear and to constitute a great carceral continuum that diffused penitentiary techniques into the most innocent disciplines, transmitting disciplinary norms into the very heart of the penal system and placing over the slightest illegality, the smallest irregularity, deviation or anomaly, the threat of delinquency. A subtle, graduated carceral net, with compact institutions, but also separate and diffuse methods, assumed responsibility for the arbitrary, widespread, badly integrated confinement of the classical age (1977: 297).

The formation of this "archipelago" had for Foucault some important implications. One of these was the tendency to dissolve the distinction between crime and abnormality. Instead:

> A certain significant generality moved between the least irregularity and the greatest crime; it was no longer the offence, the attack on the common interest, it was the departure from the norm, the anomaly; it was this that haunted the school, the court, the asylum or the prison.... You will end up in the convict-ship, the slightest indiscipline seems to say; and the harshest of prisons says to the prisoners condemned to life: I shall note the slightest irregularity in your conduct (Foucault, 1977: 299).

Extending the carceral system beyond legal imprisonment succeeded "in making the power to punish natural and legitimate, in lowering at least the threshold of tolerance to penalty" (1977: 301). It did this by giving legal legitimacy to all of the disciplines through their connection with the law (1977: 302) and by freeing legal punishment from the appearance of excess and violence:

> Between the latest institution of "rehabilitation," where one is taken to avoid prison, and the prison where one is sent after a definable offence, the difference is (and must be) scarcely perceptible. There is a strict economy that has the effect of rendering as discreet as possible the singular power to punish, the carceral "naturalizes" the legal power to punish, as it "legalizes" the technical power to discipline. By operating at every level of the social body and by mingling ceaselessly the art of rectifying and the right to punish, the universality of the carceral lowers the level from which it becomes natural and acceptable to be punished. (1977: 302-03)

The spread of disciplinary power involved its fragmentation and dispersal to ubiquitous practitioners:

> The judges of normality are present everywhere. We are in the society of the teacher-judge, the educator-judge, the "social worker"-judge; it is on them that the universal reign of the normative is based.... The carceral

network...has been the greatest support, in
modern society, of the normalizing power
(1977: 304).

Foucault's vision of the localized penitentiary mechanism inexorably dissolving into the invisibly carceral city is obviously a profoundly disturbing
one. An ever larger section of the population comes under the sway of an
increasingly superior means of exercising power, superior because it is
more subtle, more finely tuned, less visible and, therefore, more acceptable.
The central locus of Bentham's "Panopticon" turns out to have limited its
ability to "see without being seen." Most disturbing of all is the implication
that the growth of this power is inevitable and completely detached from
the history of political struggle that (even on Foucault's account) gives rise to
it. It represents an inevitable technological impulse which, once set in
motion, we are powerless to stop. Though Foucault did counsel opposition,
nothing in his work provides any theoretical foundation for it actually to
occur. Indeed, in his view, if discipline had not already eliminated politics
altogether, it eventually would.

There are a number of reasons, however, to doubt this bleak view. If
there are really no political forces driving these mechanisms, how is it that
the decarceration boom had to await the aftermath of the cataclysmic
events of the mid-twentieth century? Why does repression rise and fall with
the business cycle? How is it that these community measures are compatible with a great expansion in the traditional overt, "compact" repression of
the penitentiary? Why has the growth of the carceral city not seen the
decline of the penitentiary? Has Foucault unduly neglected the purely
repressive features of imprisonment, of the penitentiary as an institution for
punishment, in his concern with the disciplinary "addition"? Repression
implies resistance, or at least a lack of discipline. How can an increasingly
"disciplinary society" also be an increasingly chaotic one where resort must
increasingly be had to undisguised repression?

A useful contribution to a resolution of these contradictions has been
made by Santos who argues that there is a "structural combination"
between the community therapy of decarceration and the retributive renaissance in punishment (1980: 386). Both, he argues, are ways of replicating
the social status quo while appealing to symbols of autonomy. Santos relies
on the notion of "chaosmic power" to describe the repressive aspects of
decarceration and other forms of informal or community justice. By leaving
people to their own devices, these reforms *replicate* and therefore reinforce
social power. They "integrate the sanctioning power in the ongoing social

relationships connecting cosmic power to the chaosmic power which up until now had been outside its reach" (Santos, 1980: 391). Where retribution legitimizes the status quo through the fiction of free will, community therapy does so by prescribing the status quo (the "community") as therapy. In other words, it is the "community" not the "therapy" that is the key to the concept.

In using the community, the state "*is expanding through a process which on the surface appears to be a process of retraction*" (emphasis in original):

> In other words, the state is expanding in the form of civil society and that is why the dichotomy of state/civil society is theoretically not useful anymore if ever it was. And because the state expands in the form of civil society, social control may be exercised in the form of social participation, violence in the form of consensus, class domination in the form of community action. In other words, the state power expands in a kind of indirect rule.
> (Foucault, 1980: 391)

The community corrections movement fits this description very well. Whereas the prison was meant to be the egalitarian penalty (Foucault, 1977: 232), probation represents the fruition of the penitentiary technique's replication of the inegalitarianism of the private sector. Probation is an infinitely *flexible* instrument for the distribution of offenders. It can use the entire community, with its diversity, to situate the offender in the proper designated role. The desired power relations can be enforced (or not enforced as in the case of privileged offenders) *in situ*, where and when they are supposed to take place, not, as with prison, after some period of preparation. One not only teaches the delinquent habits of industry, one actually puts the delinquent to work.

Apart from the enormous growth in the *dimensions* of the penal system which can be credited to the advent of community measures —"net widening," etc. — this added flexibility itself represents a net increase in power. Indeed, flexibility is what unites the developments in probation with the expansion and elaboration of the prison itself. Increases in the use of both probation and imprisonment have been accompanied by further changes in the nature of both imprisonment and probation. Both have become more fungible, in the sense that each measure contains such great variety in levels of intrusiveness that imprisonment can be very much like probation and probation very much like imprisonment. Flexibility means that the differences within the notions of prison and community become as important as the differences between them. The specific designation of the sanction is increasingly irrelevant. Even the conviction itself is of decreasing importance as the conviction melts into the discharge which melts into the diversion program with no admission of guilt. All of these form a great continuum along which offences and offenders can be subtly distributed, according to their prescribed role in the structure of social power relations.

Thus, while in the case of *R. v. Malboeuf* (1982), in which the defendant was a young Native in need of "stabilization," probation meant the equivalent of a minimum security prison for his breaking and entering, for businessman A. (*R. v. A.,* 1974), it meant a $1000 payment as "restitution" to the employee he tried to rape; and while for thousands of Ontario offenders probation meant menial tasks such as snow-shovelling, for Keith Richards, caught in Toronto with 22 grams of heroin, it meant two free concerts for the blind at the earliest convenience of the Rolling Stones (*R. v. Richards,* 1979).

Accepting that we have a new, insidious form of power to contend with, we are still left trying to explain why this should be happening now. One attempted explanation comes from the frequently heard official defence of community corrections in terms of economics, i.e., that they constitute a great money savings over imprisonment. The embrace of community measures coincided with the "fiscal crisis" of deficit financing that hit Western governments in the 1970s, so many commentators have sought to explain community corrections this way. Santos himself favours a fiscal crisis explanation, supplemented by the ideological appeal of notions of "community" in an era in which real community is disappearing. Legitimacy in a time of economic contraction is more a matter of symbols than of "goods and services," thus the appeal to "transcendental values" (Santos, 1980: 391) such as "community" and "responsibility" (Law Reform Commission of Canada, 1976a, 1976b; Canada, 1977: Chapter 4). Santos believes that "state sponsored community organization will be the specific form of disorganization [of the oppressed classes] in late capitalism" (Santos, 1980: 390). Like Foucault, Santos foresees:

> A dislocation of power from formal institutions to informal networks. Social networks will then become the dominant unit of power production and reproduction, a source of power which is diffuse and interstitial and which as a consequence is as familiar as it is remote (1980: 392).

The fiscal crisis explanation has also been adopted by Scull (1977, 1984) who treats "decarceration" as a form of carceral "privatization."

Privatization has both fiscal and correctional aspects. It is the ideal-term designation of the 1980s movement by right-wing provincial and federal governments, following the example of the United Kingdom, to raise billions of dollars by selling off large chunks of the public sector, often at bargain-basement prices (Corcoran, 1990); at the same time, the private sector itself has been turned over to the free play of market forces, through such deregulation initiatives as the Canada-U.S. Free Trade Agreement. The movement has many counterparts in the correctional system. One of these is the delivery of correctional services by private enterprise.

In the United States privatization of prison services, indeed of entire prisons in some states, has been a way governments have attempted to solve the problem of the costs of building new prisons to cope with overcrowding (Wilson, 1989: 175ff.; *Globe and Mail*, 24 July 1986: A11, 25 July 1986: A8). In Canada, privatization has so far been restricted to community corrections, but that has meant that most of the expansion of such services has come in non-governmental form, through agencies of both the "not-for-profit" and, increasingly, the "for-profit" form (Griffiths and Verdun-Jones, 1989: 592-93). In Ontario, all community residential centres and agencies are privately run on contract with the government, as are two-thirds of the community service order programs (Ontario, 1985: 46). In the mid-eighties, the federal government also began to contract agencies run privately for profit to provide parole supervision and half-way houses (*Globe and Mail*, 9 December 1986: A19).

When public services are privatized by right-wing governments under a free market ideology, they generally operate more in accordance with market principles, which means a deterioration in those services delivered primarily to poor people. Even when the government is the main consumer in privatized service, the quality is reduced, because the government is seeking to reduce costs (often in wages to skilled, unionized employees), and because the private service exists to make profit. But the prison is not just another social service; besides meeting the needs of its clientele, it must also control and discipline them. Thus, we should not be surprised to learn that in the context of prison, privatization can mean something quite different from what it means in the context of other social services; in fact, prison privatization means quite the opposite of neglect. When a major privatization initiative in parole supervision was announced in 1986, the government reassured the public by promising that the reporting requirements for parolees had been *doubled* (*Globe and Mail*, 20 September 1986: A11).

So privatization in corrections does not entail a loosening of the grip on offenders; on the contrary, it gives the government "more bang for its buck" and thus becomes a form of expansion and intensification of penal discipline.

Privatization takes other forms. The rather sudden concern by the penal system for "the victim" can be seen in this light. Victims and their grievances are obviously not new; what is, is the attention paid to them by the penal system. Practically, this has meant making restitution an important part of punishment, usually as part of a probation order. In Ontario, restitution orders are included in fifteen per cent of all probation orders, amounting to $5 million worth for adult offenders and another half million dollars for young offenders in 1987 alone (Ontario, 1987: 12, 16). Restitution orders seem to function both as an alternative to prison for respectable offenders with the ability to pay (Jackson, 1982: 23-24) and as a means of toughening up an otherwise non-incarcerative sentence, in either case placating actual and potential victims. Both the community service order and the restitution order appeared with the denunciatory rationale of punishment (Law Reform Commission of Canada, 1974a, 1974b, 1975, 1976a), and were conceived as *punitive*, not therapeutic, devices. A greater role in sentencing is also being given to the victim through "victim-impact" statements (Criminal Code, section 735 (1.1) in force January 1, 1989) and mediation alternatives (Baskin, 1988). As with community service orders and other community measures, it appears that the offenders sentenced to restitution are drawn primarily from offenders who would not have gone to prison in the first place. The authors of one study of a popular Ontario restitution/mediation program concluded:

> On the whole VORP [Victim/Offender Reconciliation Program] has contributed little to sparing offenders imprisonment. Instead of avoiding problems created by the use of the prison system, another sentencing option has been implemented which pulls a different set of offenders deeper into the system of social control and inevitably increases cost (Dittenhoffer and Ericson, 1983: 346).

The net result of the restitution initiative is to leave the punishment increasingly to a negotiation between victim and offender. No less than in the case of economic privatization, the private sphere is not an equal one; negotiation is inevitably influenced by the bargaining strength of the parties. The availability and onerousness of a restitution order depends on the financial status of the offender (*R. v. Hudson*, 1981; *R. v. Sugg*, 1986; *R. v. Collard*, 1987; *R. v. Wilcox*, 1988). The more the offender can pay, the more likely the offender will be able to buy off a more intrusive sentence. Furthermore, the more the offender can pay, the more likely it is that the victim can be persuaded to ask the court to make a restitution order instead of ordering a prison sentence (*R. v. A.*, 1974; *R. v. Davies*, 1988). If the offender cannot pay, then the offender works, either for the victim, or more often, under a community service order. The latest development combines restitution and community service through fines. Increasingly, offenders without money are given the choice of working off their fines instead of serving the time in prison (Ontario, 1986: 13; *R. v. Hebb*, 1989; *Globe and Mail*, 10 February 1989: A11). These fines in turn are being earmarked for victim-assistance programs, as in the 1989 "victim-fine surcharge" amendment to the Criminal Code or the 1985 "fine-option" amendment (Criminal Code, sections 718.1; 727.9). Of course, people who can afford their fines (which are still not set according to ability to pay) just pay them. This seems rather appropriate for our economic system: those without property must work while those with property need not bother.

We have been examining the "fiscal crisis" explanation of community measures. The problem with *purely* fiscal explanations of this phenomenon, however, is that it has not resulted in a diminution of traditional repressive measures; it is part of the expansion, not the contraction, of the state's repressive capacity. In other words, though community measures clearly cost less than prisons, when both are expanding, the explanation cannot be restricted to governments trying to save money (Chan and Ericson, 1981).

In their important work on the origins of the penitentiary system, Melossi and Pavarini (1981) have also offered a plausible interpretation of the developments we have been examining. Their main point is to show how changing productive relations can account for the rise of the penitentiary as the specific form of social control in competitive capitalism; but they also argue that the radical changes which have since taken place in productive relations in the twentieth century can similarly account for the nature of modern social control. They point to the concentration, centralization and changing organic composition of capital, the rise of unions, state involvement in the economy and the disintegrating effect this has all had on the once firm lines between public and private spheres. In late capitalism the marketplace becomes more and more the object of organization by business, union and state:

> The sphere of circulation and consumption
> were subjected to the direct rule of capital:
> decisions on prices, the organization of the
> market and at the same time of a consensus,
> all became part of one and the same thing. Not
> only were the traditional instruments of social
> control strengthened — those areas of "the
> sphere of production" outside the factory from
> capitalism's inception — but also new instru-
> ments were created. The new strategy was
> towards dispersion, towards the extension and
> pervasion of control. Individuals are no longer
> locked up; they are got at where they are nor-
> mally locked up: outside the factory, in society
> as a whole. Propaganda, the mass media, a
> new and more efficient network of police and
> social assistance, these are the bearers of a
> new kind of social control (Melossi and
> Pavarini, 1981: 6).

More control of the marketplace is necessitated by ever more severe
market dislocations, such as that of the Great Depression itself; inefficiency
and unemployment abound and capital can no longer afford to follow its
own logic. Rising unemployment even diminishes the need to prepare people for the factory; more and more what they have to be prepared for is
idleness in the community. Community measures become part of this
attempt to organize the community coercively when it can no longer be
relied upon to regulate itself efficiently. This was, in fact, the express rationale of those who advocated an increased role for probation in the 1940s
in Canada. Blaming rising prison populations on the breakdown of "proper
home training during the past quarter century," the call went out for better
funding, co-ordination and "legal authority" for the state's efforts to "step in
and apply the necessary remedy where parents are failing in their duties"
(Ontario, 1943: 6):

> Parents who have failed are rather likely to fail
> again unless they are sufficiently strengthened
> and helped by probation officers and others
> who are capable. Very often that support and
> help are non-existent. In much of this province
> there are no regular probation officers, and
> where there are their time and energies are
> spread over too many cases (Ontario, 1945:
> 6-7).

Not for one moment was probation to be confused with leniency in punishment; it was *more* and not less intervention that was being called for:

> Probation without proper supervision is dangerous. Too frequently it is worse.... Akin to the abuse of probation is the practice of suspending sentences without a proper follow-through. Generally there is no follow-through. Delinquents and criminals are well aware of that fact. The chance that they will be brought back and sentenced for breach of recognizance or the offence on which sentence is suspended is so small that they boldly ignore it and pursue their way (Ontario, 1945: 6-7).

Thus the ideology underpinning the rapid expansion of the Ontario probation system in the early 1950s was an explicitly *disciplinary* one. The increase in prison population was blamed on a lack of proper supervision *in situ*, which could only be solved by state intervention in the form of probation supervision. Probation was advocated as a kind of penal Keynesianism, a state intervention into a malfunctioning private sphere. It is thus no coincidence that the great post-war increases in the proportion of economic activity taking place through the state and the increase in public sector employment coincide with the dramatic increase in community measures. But, rather than one causing the other, they turn out both to be products of the same underlying contradiction, the increasing inability of an economy structured upon private profit to (a) reproduce itself without violence and (b) meet our basic economic needs. Instead of the full development and use of the energy and talent of the entire population, improved standards of living and decreasing inequality, we have precisely the opposite: ever higher levels of unemployment (Ostry and Zaidi, 1979), a stagnating economy (Statistics Canada, 1988: 21-22, 28) and increasing inequality (Ross and Shillington, 1989: 34; CALURA, 1988: 28-29, 56; Davis, 1987: 36; *Globe and Mail*, 30 December 1989: E11).

This leads to a much different assessment than the one offered by Foucault (1977), who saw "decarceration" as a purely technological movement detached from politics and bound to fix humanity in a seamless web of inescapable discipline. Instead of an invincible movement, decarceration becomes merely a strategy for holding on to an increasingly unstable social situation, a strategy which seems, furthermore, to be fraught with its own contradictions, such as escalating costs and the debasement of the coinage of punishment through overuse (Matthews, 1979). The community measures phenomenon can be seen as the late capitalist breakdown in the separation between public and private spheres as applied to the penitentiary system: an attempt to expand state discipline ever more deeply into the community as capitalism becomes ever less capable of "standing on its own two feet" and traditional penal measures and levels of punishment become ever less capable of holding things together.

Endnotes

1   From L. Samuelson and B. Schissel (eds.), *Criminal Justice: Sentencing Issues and Reform*. (Halifax, N.S.: Garamond Press, 1991).

2   The author wishes to thank William Evans and Elain Bright for their help compiling tables and graphs, Caroll Barrett and Maggie Stockton for their stenographic work, and Harry Glasbeek, as always, for his friendly advice. For reasons of space, several sections of this paper had to be omitted, which may account for (some of) the disjointedness.

3   As adult and juvenile regimes become more alike, the justification for considering adult repression separately, as the present study does, diminishes; however, for most of Canada's history adults and children have been subjected to very different legal punishment regimes.

4   If we leave out the low year of 1969 to make the comparison more symmetrical, the difference is slightly less: 105.6 to 100.4.

5   If we assume that the relationship between adult imprisonment and juvenile imprisonment was more or less constant between 1930-34 and 1961-1965, an adult rate for 1930-1934 can be estimated by applying the known adult-total ratio of 1961-1965 to the figures for 1930-1934. This would give an adult rate of $(103.6/123.2 \times 117.3 = 98.6)$.

But was the relationship constant? There seems no statistical way of knowing this for sure. The relative use of training school as a disposition for those found delinquent was similar for the periods 1930-1934 (3464/38815 or 8.9 per cent) and 1961-65 (9771/87096 or 11.2 per cent), but not identical (Reed, 1983: Z238-291). On the other hand, the per capita use of training school as a disposition was 6.6 per 100,000 in 1930-1934, while it was 10.3 in 1961-1965. Per capita use of a disposition is a far cry from institution population per capita, but these figures still suggest that a higher proportion of the later than of the earlier total institutional population involved training schools, which means that the assumption of constant ratios underestimates the severity of the repression of adults in the 1930s.

To attempt to correct for this, we can apply the 1930-1934/1961-1965 disposition ratio of 6.6/10.3 to the proportion of the population during the 1961-1965 period that we know constituted juvenile detention: 123.2 - 103.6 = 19.6, or 15.9 per cent of the total institutional population for 1961-1965. At most, training school seems to have been used 6.6/10.3 less in 1930-1934 than in 1961-1965, so the juvenile component of the 1930-1934 population can be reckoned at 6.6/10.3 x 15.9 per cent = 10.2 per cent. Therefore, to estimate the 1930-1934 adult population, the period's total population should be deflated by only 10.2 per cent = .898 x 117.3 = 105.3 per 100,000 population. This is well below the average for the worst five-year period of the 1980s which was 111.3 per 100,000.

6   On the assumption of a constant ratio between adult and juvenile imprisonment: 126.1/125.9 x 105.5 = 105.7; on the more generous deflator outlined in the prior footnote: 126.1 x .898 = 113.2.

7   On the assumption of a constant ratio between adult and juvenile imprisonment: 99.7/118.7 x 113/1 = 95.0; deflated by the formula of endnote 5 (which works out to .897 in this case): .897 x 113.1 = 101.5.

8   Imprisonment figures just released show a rise in the per capita adult prison population for the fiscal year 1988-1989; it had fallen slightly in 1987-1988. The rise, not adjusted for the effect of the Young Offenders Act, was 1.9 per cent for all institutions and 3.2 per cent for penitentiaries (Statistics Canada, 1988-89).

9   A 1990 medical report claimed that prisoner deaths were at an all-time historical high (*Globe and Mail*, 3 May 1990: A8).

10   The reason for the difference between admission and daily population ratios is the fact that probation terms are generally so much longer than prison terms, meaning that fewer admissions result in high average daily populations. The median prison sentence for provincial admissions (more than ninety per cent of all admissions) in 1984-1985 was thirty-two days, whereas the median probation term was twelve months (Statistics Canada, 1984-1985: 165,173).

11   McFarlane reports 244 probation officers in Ontario in 1965 with an adult probation population of 5225 (McFarlane, 1966: 90), while the 429 Ontario probation officers reported by Hatt for 1979 had to take care of at least 26,362 adult probationers (Hatt, 1985: 300; Appendix VII).

12   It is possible that the early 1960s surpassed the Depression, or at least equalled it, but lacking better figures on probation it is difficult to be sure.

13   Probation figures just released show a rise in the per capita adult probation population for the fiscal year 1988-1989; it had fallen slightly for the two prior years. The rise, not adjusted for the effect of the Young Offenders Act, was 1.1 per cent. However, a simultaneous fall in the parole population kept the total non-custodial supervised population at a constant per capita level (Statistics Canada, 1988-1989).

14   There are parallel Canadian data on crime rates and social class area. It appears that the higher reported crime rates of lower social class areas are accounted for partly, but only partly, by higher rates of victimization. Another important contributing factor is the level of policing which, in effect, exaggerates the higher level of crime (Hagan, Gillis and Chan, 1978).

References

Bala, N. 1988. "The Young Offenders Act: A Legal Framework" in Hudson, Joe, Joseph P. Hornick and Barbara A. Burrows (eds.), *Justice and the Young Offender in Canada*. Toronto: Wall and Thompson.

Baskin, D. 1988. "Community Mediation and the Public/Private Problem." *Social Justice* 15: 98.

Beattie, J.M. 1986. *Crime and the Criminal Courts in England 1660-1800*. Princeton University Press.

Blumstein, A. 1988. "Prison Populations: A System Out of Control?" in Tonry, Michael and

Norval Morris (eds.), *Crime and Justice: A Review of Research*, Volume 10.

Bochel, D. 1976. *Probation and After-care, Its Development in England and Wales.* Edinburgh: Scottish Academic Press.

Box, S. 1987. *Recession, Crime and Punishment.* Totowa, New Jersey: Barnes and Noble Books.

Braithwaite, J. 1979. *Crime, Inequality and Public Policy.* London: Routledge and Kegan Paul.

CALURA. 1988. *Annual Report of the Minister of Supply and Services Canada under the Corporations and Labour Unions Returns Act.* Part I — Corporations 1986.

Canada. 1938. *Report of the Royal Commission to Investigate the Penal System of Canada.* Ottawa: King's Printer.

Canada. 1956. *Report of a Committee Appointed to Inquire Into the Principles and Procedures Followed in the Remission Service of the Department of Justice of Canada.* Ottawa: Queen's Printer.

Canada. 1969. *Report of the Canadian Committee on Corrections. Toward Unity: Criminal Justice and Corrections.* Ottawa: Queen's Printer.

Canada. 1977. *Third Report of the Sub-Committee on the Penal System in Canada, House of Commons Standing Committee on Justice and Legal Affairs.* Ottawa: Queen's Printer.

Canada. 1978. *Diversion: A Canadian Concept and Practice. A Report of the First National Conference on Diversion* October 23-26, 1977, Quebec City. Ottawa: Solicitor General of Canada. 1979/80 to 1987/88.

Canada. 1982. *The Criminal Law in Canadian Society.* Ottawa: Government of Canada.

Canada. 1983. *Sentencing Practices and Trends in Canada: A Summary of Statistical Information.* Ottawa: Department of Justice Canada.

Canada. 1984. *Sentencing.* Ottawa: Government of Canada.

Canada. 1987. *Sentencing Reform: A Canadian Approach. Report of The Canadian Sentencing Commission.* Ottawa: Minister of Supply and Services Canada.

Canada. 1988. *Taking Responsibility. Report of the Standing Committee on Justice and Solicitor General on its Review of Sentencing, Conditional Release and Related Aspects of Corrections.* Ottawa: Minister of Supply and Services Canada.

Canadian Bar Association. 1988. "Imprisonment and Release." *Justice Report* 5, 4: 9.

Caputo, T. and D.C. Bracken. 1988. "Custodial Dispositions and The Young Offenders Act" in Hudson, Joe, Joseph P. Hornick and Barbara A. Burrows (eds.), *Justice and the Young Offender in Canada.* Toronto: Wall and Thompson.

Chambliss, William J. 1988. *Exploring Criminology.* New York: Macmillan Publishing Company.

Chan, Janet B.L. and R.V. Ericson. 1981. *Decarceration and the Economy of Penal Reform.* Toronto: University of Toronto Centre of Criminology.

Chen, Mervin Y.T. and T.G. Regan. 1985. *Work in the Changing Canadian Society.* Toronto: Butterworths.

Clement, W. 1975. *The Canadian Corporate Elite: An Analysis of Economic Power.* Toronto: McClelland and Stewart.

Collier, P. and R. Tarling. 1987. "International Comparisons of Prison Populations." Home

Office Research and Planning Unit Research Bulletin 23: 51.

Conklin, J.E. 1989. *Criminology*. 3rd edition. New York: Macmillan Publishing Company.

Corcoran, T. 1990. "The Big Sell-Off." *Globe and Mail Report on Business Magazine*, January 1990: 25.

Correctional Service of Canada. 1983. *Directory of Community-Based Residential Centres in Canada 1983-84*. Ottawa: Minister of Supply and Services Canada.

Crow, I., P. Richardson, C. Riddington and F. Simon. 1989. *Unemployment, Crime, and Offenders*. London: Routledge.

Culhane, C. 1985. *Still Barred from Prison: Social Injustice in Canada*. Montreal: Black Rose Books.

Davis, L.J. 1987. "The Next Panic: Fear and Trembling on Wall Street." *Harper's Magazine* 274: 35, (May).

Dittenhoffer, T. and R.V. Ericson. 1983. "The Victim/Offender Reconciliation Program: A message to correctional reformers." *University of Toronto Law Journal* 33: 315.

Dominion Bureau of Statistics. 1940. *The Canada Year Book 1940*. Ottawa: King's Printer.

Dominion Bureau of Statistics. 1957-59 to 1970. *Crime Statistics, 1962, 1965, 1968*. Ottawa: Queen's Printer.

Dominion Bureau of Statistics. 1962a. *Correctional Services 1957-59; 1960-61; 1962; 1963; to 1964; 1965-65; 1965-66; 1966-67; 1967-68; 1968-69; 1969-70, 1969-70; 1970*. Ottawa: Queen's Printer.

Ehrlich, I. 1973. "Participation in Illegitimate Activities: A Theoretical and Empirical Investigation." *Journal of Political Economy* 51: 521.

Ekstedt, J.W. and C.T. Griffiths. 1984. *Corrections in Canada: Policy and Practice*. Toronto: Butterworths.

Employment and Immigration Canada, *Annual Reports* 1979/80-1987/88.

Foucault, M. 1977. *Discipline and Punish: The Birth of the Prison*. Trans. Alan Sheridan. New York: Pantheon.

Galbraith, J.K. 1987. "The 1929 Parallel." *The Atlantic Monthly* 62: 259 (Jan).

Glasbeek, H.J. 1988. "The Corporate Social Responsibility Movement — The Latest in Maginot Lines to Save Capitalism." *Dalhousie Law Journal* 11: 363.

Granatstein, J.L. I.M. Abella, D.J. Bercuson, R.C. Brown and B.J. Neatby. 1986. *Twentieth Century Canada*. 2nd edition. Toronto: McGraw-Hill Ryerson Limited.

Greenberg, David F. 1977. "The Dynamics of Oscillatory Punishment Processes." *The Journal of Criminal Law and Criminology* 68: 643-51.

Griffiths, C.T. and S. Verdun-Jones. 1989. *Canadian Criminal Justice*. Toronto: Butterworths.

Hagan, F.E. 1986. *Introduction to Criminology: Theories, Methods, and Criminal Behaviour*. Chicago: Nelson-Hall.

Hagan, J., A.R. Gillis and J. Chan. 1978. "Explaining Official Delinquency: A Spatial Study of Class, Conflict and Control." *The Sociological Quarterly* 19: 386.

Hatt, K. 1985. "Probation and Community Corrections in a Neo-Correctional Era." *Canadian Journal of Criminology* 27: 299.

Hay, D. 1975. "Property, Authority and the Criminal Law" in Hay, D. *et al.* (eds.), *Albion's*

Fatal Tree: Crime and Society in Eighteenth-Century England. London: Allen Lane.

Hornick, J.P., B.A. Burrows, J. Hudson and H. Sapers. 1988. "Summary and Future Directions" in Hudson, Joe, Joseph P. Hornick and Barbara A. Burrows (eds.), *Justice and the Young Offender in Canada.* Toronto: Wall and Thompson.

Hunter, Alfred A. 1981. *Class Tells: On Social Inequality in Canada.* Toronto: Butterworths.

Jackson, M.A. 1982. *Judicial Attitudes Towards Sentencing Options.* Toronto: Ontario Ministry of Correctional Services.

Jaffe P. 1985. "Young Offenders System Tougher than Adult Court." *Ontario Lawyers' Weekly* 7: 4.

Kulig, P. 1990. "Lawyers Knock Report Suggesting Counsel to Blame for Increase in YOA Custody Rate." *Law Times,* April 9-15: 8.

Landerville, P., M. Hamelin and S. Gagnier. 1988. "Opinions of Quebec Inmates Regarding Questions Raised by the Mandate of the Canadian Sentencing Commission." Ottawa: Department of Justice Canada. Research Reports of the Canadian Sentencing Commission.

Law Reform Commission of Canada. 1974a. "Working Paper No. 3: the principles of sentencing and dispositions." Ottawa: Information Canada.

Law Reform Commission of Canada. 1974b. Working Papers 5 and 6: "restitution and compensation;" "fines." Ottawa: Information Canada.

Law Reform Commission of Canada. 1975. "Working Paper 7: Diversion." Ottawa: Information Canada.

Law Reform Commission of Canada. 1976a. *Community Participation in Sentencing.* Ottawa: Information Canada.

Law Reform Commission of Canada. 1976b. *Report: Our Criminal Law.* Ottawa: Information Canada.

Leacy, F.H., ed. 1983. *Historical Statistics of Canada.* 2nd ed. Ottawa: Minister of Supply and Services Canada.

Leschied, A.W. and P.G. Jaffe. 1988. "Implementing the Young Offenders Act in Ontario: Critical Issues and Challenges for the Future" in Judson, Joe, Joseph P. Hornick and Barbara A. Burrows (eds.), *Justice and the Young Offender in Canada.* Toronto: Wall and Thompson.

Lynch, J.P. 1988. "A Comparison of Prison Use in England, Canada, West Germany and the United States: A Limited Test of the Punitive Hypothesis." *The Journal of Criminal Law and Criminology* 79: 180.

Madden P.G. and C.A. Carey. 1982. *Bail Verification and Supervision in Ontario.* Toronto: Ontario Ministry of Correctional Services.

Madden P.G. and S. Hermann. 1983. *The Utilization of Community Resource Centres.* Toronto: Ontario Ministry of Correctional Services.

Mandel, M. 1975. "Rethinking Parole." *Osgoode Hall Law Journal* 13: 501.

Mandel, M. 1983. "McDonald and the R.C.M.P." in CBC *"Ideas:" "Law and Social Order."* Toronto: CBC Transcripts. Part I: 1.

Mandel, M. 1984. "Democracy, Class and Canadian Sentencing Law" *Crime and Social Justice* 21-23: 163, also in Brickey, Stephen and Elizabeth Comack (eds.), *The*

Social Basis of Law in Canada: Critical Readings in the Sociology of Law.
Toronto: Garamond Press, 1986.

Mandel, M. 1985. "Democracy, Class and the National Parole Board." *Criminal Law Quarterly* 27: 159.

Mandel, M. 1986. "The Legalization of Prison Discipline in Canada." *Crime and Social Justice* 26: 79.

Mandel, M. 1987. "'Relative Autonomy' and the Criminal Justice Apparatus" in Ratner, R.S. and John L. McMullan (eds.), *State Control: Criminal Justice Politics in Canada.* Vancouver: University of British Columbia Press.

Mandel, M. 1989. *The Charter of Rights and the Legalization of Politics in Canada.* Toronto: Wall and Thompson.

Marx, K. 1853. "Capital Punishment" in Cain, Maureen and Alan Hunt (eds.), *Marx and Engels on Law.* London: Academic Press.

Mason, B. 1988. "Implementing the Young Offenders Act: An Alberta Perspective" in Hudson, Joe, Joseph P. Hornick and Barbara A. Burrows (eds.), *Justice and the Young Offender in Canada.* Toronto: Wall and Thompson.

Matthews, R. 1979. "'Decarceration' and the fiscal crisis" in Fine, Bob *et al.* (eds.), *Capitalism and the Rule of Law: From Deviancy Theory to Marxism.* London: Hutchinson & Co.

McFarlane, G.G. 1966. *The Development of Probation Services in Ontario.* Toronto: Queen's Printer.

Melossi, D. and M. Pavarini. 1981. *The Prison and the Factory: Origins of the Penitentiary System.* Trans. G. Cousin. London: The Macmillan Press Ltd.

Moitra, S.D. 1987. *Crimes and Punishments: A Comparative Study of Temporal Variations.* Freiburg i. Br.: Max Planck Institute for Foreign and International Penal Law.

Nettler, G. 1982. *Killing One Another.* Cincinnati: Anderson Publishing Company.

Niosi, J. 1985. "Continental Nationalism: The Strategy of the Canadian Bourgeoisie" in Brym, Robert J. (ed.), *The Structure of the Canadian Capitalist Class.* Toronto: Garamond Press.

Ontario. 1891. *Report of the Commissioners Appointed to Inquire into the Prison and Reformatory System of Ontario.* Toronto: Legislative Assembly of Ontario.

Ontario. 1941-45. *Annual Reports 1941, 1942, 1943, 1945.* Department of Reform Institutions of Ontario.

Ontario. 1968-70. *Annual Report of the Minister 1968, 1969, 1970.* Department of Correctional Services of Ontario.

Ontario. 1981-88. *Annual Reports of the Minister 1981-1988.* Ministry of Correctional Services.

Ontario. 1987. *Corrections in Ontario: Everyone's Business.* Toronto: Ontario Ministry of Correctional Services.

Osberg, L. 1981. *Economic Inequality in Canada.* Toronto: Butterworths.

Ostry, S. and M.A. Zaidi. 1979. *Labour Economics in Canada.* 3rd edition. Toronto: Macmillan of Canada.

Pate, K.J. and D.E. Peachey. 1988. "Face-to-Face: Victim-Offender Mediation Under the Young Offenders Act" in Hudson, Joe, Joseph P. Hornick and Barbara A. Burrows (eds.), *Justice and the Young Offender in Canada*. Toronto: Wall and Thompson.

Pease, K. 1980. "Community Service Orders" in *International Conference on Alternatives to Imprisonment Report* Solicitor General of Canada (Workshop 6: 41). Ottawa: Minister of Supply and Services Canada.

Polonski, M.L. 1981. *The Community Service Order Program in Ontario*. 4. Summary. Toronto: Ontario Ministry of Correctional Services.

Powell, C.M. 1976. *Arrest and Bail in Canada*. 2nd ed. Toronto: Butterworths.

Reed, P. 1983. "Section Z: Justice" in Leacy, F.H. (ed.), *Historical Statistics of Canada*, 2nd ed. Ottawa: Minister of Supply and Services Canada.

Rinehart, J.W. 1987. *The Tyranny of Work: Alienation and the Labour Process*. 2nd ed. Toronto: Harcourt Brace Jovanovich.

Roberts, B.A. 1988. *Whence They Came: Deportation from Canada 1900-1935*. Ottawa: University of Ottawa Press.

Roberts, J. 1988. "Early Release From Prison: What Do the Canadian Public Really Think?" *Canadian Journal of Criminology* 30: 231.

Ross, D.P. 1980. *The Canadian Fact Book on Income Distribution*. Ottawa: The Canadian Council on Social Development.

Ross, D.P. and E.R. Shillington. 1989. *The Canadian Fact Book on Poverty — 1989*. Ottawa: The Canadian Council on Social Development.

Rusche, G. and O. Kirchheimer. 1938. *Punishment and Social Structure*. New York: Russell and Russell.

Santos, B. 1980. "Law and Community: The Changing Nature of the State Power in Late Capitalis." *International Journal of the Sociology of Law* 8: 379-397.

Schwendinger, J. and H. Schwendinger. 1981. "Rape, Sexual Inequality and Levels of Violence." *Crime and Social Justice* Winter: 3.

Scull, A.T. 1977. *Decarceration: community treatment and the deviant: a radical view*. Englewood Cliffs, N.J.: Prentice-Hall.

Scull, A.T. 1984. *Decarceration: community treatment and the deviant: a radical view*. 2nd ed. New Brunswick, N.J.: Rutgers University Press.

Sheridan A.K.B., and J. Konrad. 1976. "Probation" in McGrath, W.T. (ed.), *Crime and Its Treatment in Canada*. 2nd edition. Toronto: Macmillan.

Siegel, L.J. 1989. *Criminology*. 3rd edition. St. Paul, Minnesota: West Publishing Company.

Solicitor General of Canada. 1979. *National Inventory of Diversion Projects*. Ottawa: Solicitor General of Canada.

Solicitor General of Canada. 1980. *International Conference on Alternatives to Imprisonment Report*. Ottawa: Minister of Supply and Services Canada.

Solicitor General of Canada. 1981-85. *Annual Reports 1981-82, 1982-83, 1983-84, 1984-85*. Ottawa: Minister of Supply and Services Canada.

Solicitor General of Canada. 1983. "Victims of Crime." Canadian Urban Victimization Survey, Bulletin No. 1.

Solicitor General of Canada. 1984. *Long Term Imprisonment in Canada*. "Working Paper No. 1: An Overview of the Long Term Prisoner Population and Suggested Directions for Further Research." Ottawa: Ministry of the Solicitor General of Canada.

Solicitor General of Canada. 1985. *Ministry Facts*. Ottawa: Minister of Supply and Services Canada.

Solicitor General of Canada. 1987. "Patterns in Violent Crime." Canadian Urban Victimization Survey, Bulletin No. 8.

Solicitor General of Canada. 1988. "Patterns in Property Crime." Canadian Urban Victimization Survey, Bulletin No. 9.

Statistics Canada (listed by title date, no publication date).

Statistics Canada. 1971a. *Correctional Institutions Statistics 1971; 1972; 1973; 1974; 1976; 1977; 1978; 1979*. Ottawa: Information Canada (1974-75); no publisher (1976, 1979); Minister of Supply and Services Canada (1979-81).

Statistics Canada. 1971b. *Crime Statistics*. Ottawa: Information Canada (1973).

Statistics Canada. 1971c. *Traffic Enforcement Statistics*. Ottawa: Information Canada (1973).

Statistics Canada. 1973b. *Statistics of Criminal and Other Offences* 1973. Ottawa: no publisher (1978)

Statistics Canada. 1975a and 1980. *Crime and Traffic Enforcement Statistics*. Ottawa: Information Canada (1977); Minister of Supply and Services Canada (1982).

Statistics Canada. 1975b. *Penitentiary Statistics 1975*. Ottawa: no publisher (1978).

Statistics Canada. 1980-86. *Vital Statistics, Part IV: Causes of Death*. Ottawa, Minister of Supply and Services Canada.

Statistics Canada. 1980-88. *Adult Correctional Services in Canada 1980-81; 1981-82; 1982-83; 1983-84; 1984-85; 1985-86; 1986-87; 1987-88*. Canadian Centre for Justice Statistics. Ottawa: Minister of Supply and Services Canada (1982, 1983, 1984, 1986, 1986, 1987, 1988).

Statistics Canada. 1983a, 1984 and 1985a. *Canadian Crime Statistics 1983-1987*. Ottawa: Minister of Supply and Services Canada (1985, 1986).

Statistics Canada. 1983b. *Homicide Statistics 1983*. Ottawa: Minister of Supply and Services Canada (1984).

Statistics Canada. 1985b. *Historical Labour Force Statistics — Actual Data, Seasonal Factors, Seasonally Adjusted Data, 1985*. Household Surveys Division. Ottawa: Minister of Supply and Services Canada (1986), 205, 228.

Statistics Canada. 1986. *A Description of Bail: Verification and Bail Supervision Programs in Western Canada*.

Statistics Canada. 1986a. *Criminal Injuries Compensation 1986*. Canadian Centre for Justice Statistics. Ottawa: Minister of Supply and Services Canada.

Statistics Canada. 1986b. *Juristat Service Bulletin*. Vol. 6, No. 1.

Statistics Canada. 1986c. *Policing in Canada 1986*. Ottawa: Minister of Supply and Services Canada.

Statistics Canada. 1986d. *A One-Day Snapshot Profile of all Persons in Provincial Adult Correctional Institutions*. Ottawa: Canadian Centre for Justice Statistics. May, 1986.

Statistics Canada. 1987. *Income after tax, distributions by size in Canada 1987*. Household Surveys Division. Ottawa: Minister of Supply and Services Canada, 1989.

Statistics Canada. 1987a. *Homicide in Canada 1987: A Statistical Perspective*. Ottawa:

Minister of Supply and Services Canada.

Statistics Canada. 1988. *Income Distributions by Size in Canada 1988*. Household Surveys Division. Ottawa: Minister of Supply and Services Canada.

Statistics Canada. 1989a. *Income Distributions by Size in Canada 1988*. Household Surveys Division. Ottawa: Minister of Supply and Services Canada.

Statistics Canada. 1989b. *Labour Force Annual Averages 1981-1988*. Household Surveys Division. Ottawa: Minister of Supply and Services Canada.

Taylor, I. 1985. "Criminology, the Unemployment Crisis, and the Liberal Tradition in Canada. The Need for Socialist Analysis and Policy" in Fleming, Thomas (ed.), *The New Criminologies in Canada: State, Crime and Control*. Toronto: Oxford University Press.

Tepperman, L. 1977. *Crime Control: The Urge Toward Authority*. Toronto: McGraw-Hill Ryerson.

Thomas, M. 1987. "Why This Is 1929 All Over Again" *The Nation* 244: 641 (May 16).

Thompson, J.H. with A. Seager. 1985. *Canada 1922-1939: Decades of Discord*. Toronto: McClelland and Stewart.

Tonry, M.H. 1987. *Sentencing Reform Impacts*. Washington: U.S. Department of Justice, National Institute of Justice.

Urquhart, M.C. and K.A.H. Buckley (eds.). 1965. *Historical Statistics of Canada*. Cambridge: University Press.

van Cleef, D. 1985. "Persons Working Long Hours" in Statistics Canada, *The Labour Force*, May.

West, W.G. 1984. *Young Offenders and the Canadian State: A Canadian Perspective on Delinquency*. Toronto: Butterworths.

Wilson, D.G. 1989. "The Impact of Federal Sentencing Guidelines on Community Corrections and Privatization" in Champion, Dean J. (ed.), *The U.S. Sentencing Guidelines: Implications for Criminal Justice*. New York: Praeger.

Yeager, M. 1979. "Research Note: Unemployment and Imprisonment." *The Journal of Criminal Law and Criminology* 70, 586-88.

Zay, N. 1965. "Section Y: Justice" in Urquhart, M.C. and K.A.H. Buckley (eds.), *Historical Statistics of Canada*. Cambridge: University Press.

Statutes

An Act for the More Speedy Trial and Punishment of Juvenile Offenders 20 Victoria, c. 29 (1857).

An Act to Permit the Conditional Release of First Offenders in Certain Cases, S.C. 1889, c. 44.

The Bail Reform Act 1972, R.S.C. 1970 (2nd Supp.), c. 2.

The Criminal Code, R.S.C. 1970, c. C-34.

The Criminal Records Act, R.S.C. 1970, C. 12 (1st Supp.).

The Juvenile Delinquents Act, R.S.C. 1970, Chap. J-3 (originally, 7-8 Edward VII, c. 40,

1908).

The Narcotic Control Act, R.S.C. 1970, c. N-1.

The Opium and Narcotic Drug Act, S.C. 1929, c. 49.

The Parole Act, R.S.C. 1970, c. P-2.

The Young Offenders Act, R.S.C. 1985, c. Y-1.

Cases

R. v. *A.* (1974), 26 C.C.C. (2d) 474 (Ontario High Court of Justice).

R. v. *Collard* (1987), 39 C.C.C. (3d) 471 (Manitoba Court of Appeal).

R. v. *Davies* (1988), 26 O.A.C. 382 (Ontario Court of Appeal).

R. v. *Degan* (1985), 20 C.C.C. (3d) 293 (Saskatchewan Court of Appeal).

R. v. *Drew* (1978), 45 C.C.C. (2d) 212 (British Columbia Court of Appeal).

R. v. *Hebb* (1989), 47 C.C.C. (3d) 193 (Nova Scotia Supreme Court).

R. v. *Hudson* (1981), 65 C.C.C. (2d) 171 (Ontario Court of Appeal).

R. v. *Jones* (1975), 25 C.C.C. (2d) 256 (Ontario County Court).

R. v. *Kergan* (1985), 21 C.C.C. (3d) 549 (Alberta Court of Appeal).

R. v. *Malboeuf* (1982), 68 C.C.C. (2d) 544 (Saskatchewan Court of Appeal).

R. v. *Richards* (1979), 11 C.R. (3d) 193 (Ontario Court of Appeal).

R. v. *Sidley* (*Le Roy* versus *Sr. Charles Sidley*) (1675), 82 E.R. 1036.

R. v. *Sugg* (1986), 28 C.C.C. (3d) 569 (Nova Scotia Supreme Court, Appeal Division).

R. v. *Wilcox* (1988), 43 C.C.C. (3d) 432 (Northwest Territories Supreme Court).

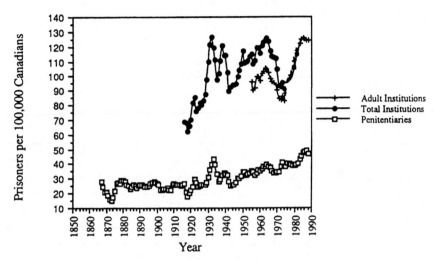

Figure 1
Per Capita Prison Population
1867-1988 (Canada)

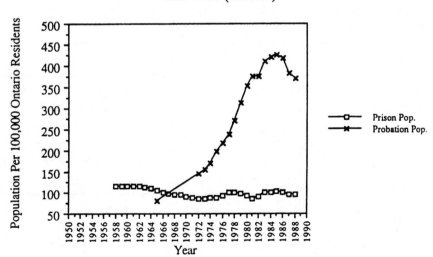

Figure 2
Per Capita Prison Population
1867-1988 (Canada)

The Canadian Criminal Justice System

Appendix I.

	Adult Institution Population 1955-1988					
	Daily Adult Institution Population Population On Register (Actual Count)		Rate per 100,000 Canadian		Actual Count Adjusted for YOA Effect*	
1988	31,750(e)	(26,634)	123.9	(103.9)	(28,873e)	(112.7)
1987	31,378(e)	(26,893)	124.0	(106.2)	(28,864e)	(114.0)
1986	31,647(e)	(27,392)	124.8	(108.0)	(28,277e)	(111.5)
1985	31,540(e)	(27,634)	125.5	(110.0)		
1984	30,992(e)	(26,980)	124.5	(108.4)		
1983	30,044(e)	(26,924)	122.0	(109.3)		
1982	27,484(e)	(24,064)	112.9	(98.9)		
1981	25,678(e)	(22,502)	106.8	(93.6)		
1980	24,539(e)	(21,936)	103.3	(92.4)		
1979a	25,201(e)	(21,956e)	107.2	(93.4)		
1979b	22,076		92.9			
1978	22,034		93.7			
1977	22,337		96.4			
1976	21,821		94.9			
1975	20,009		88.2			
1974	18,484		82.7			
1973	18,913		85.8			
1972	18,259		83.7			
1971	18,165		84.2			
1970	19,218		90.2			
1969	19,655		93.6			
1968	19,712		95.2			
1967	19,506		95.7			
1966	19,695		98.4			
1965	20,141		102.5			
1964	20,210		104.8			
1963	19,974		105.5			
1962	19,222		103.4			
1961	18,559		101.8			
1960	17,240		96.5			
1959	17,461		99.9			
1958	16,962		99.3			
1957	15,171		91.3			
1956	14,503		90.2			
1955	15,053		95.9			

Sources: Statistics Canada, 1979, 1982-1983, 1983-1984, 1984-1985, 1985-1986, 1986-1987, 1987-1988; Reed, 1983: Z292-304; Chan and Ericson, 1981: 77.

"On register"

> includes prisoners temporarily out of the institution, whereas "actual custody" does not. The on-register figures are estimates based on figures for the federal government and all provinces excluding B.C. for the whole period, NWT for the whole period except 1982, Ontario for 1979a-1985 and the Yukon for 1988. It includes day paroles (sixty-nine per cent of those on register but not in custody in the federal system for 1987-88: Statistics Canada, 1987-1988: 91), unlawfully at large (twelve per cent), in hospital (five per cent), at court (seven per cent), out on bail (two per cent), temporary absence (one per cent) and unspecified (four per cent). Figures in the table prior to 1979 are from a different series of publications which purport to be based on the same principle, viz., "on register" whether or not in actual custody, but notice the similarity between "actual count" of 1979a (new series) and "on register" of 1979b (old series). On the other hand, the same does not hold for penitentiary statistics where there is a divergence between the on-register population of the old series and the actual count of the new (see Appendix III).

(e)   both sets of figures for 1979a-1988 are average daily or less frequent count for the fiscal year ending March 31st of the year named. In 1972-1979b the prison population is as of December 31st of the year named. For 1971 it is December 31st for federal and Quebec institutions and March 31st for all other provincial institutions. For 1955-1970 it is March 31st. The Canadian population bases for the rates are as of June 1st of year named 1955-1979b and as June 1st of the year before the year named 1979a-1988.

The "YOA effect"

> is the effect on the prison population of changing (as of April 1, 1985) the age of adulthood so far as the penal system is concerned: sixteen- and seventeen-year-olds, who were classified as adults before that date, now became young offenders. An adjustment has been made to correct for the fact that sixteen- and seventeen-year-olds are still being imprisoned, but under a different label. The adjustment is not a projection; it is based on the number of sixteen- and seventeen-year-olds actually imprisoned during the years mentioned. The difference is that they are now imprisoned under the authority of the Young Offenders Act. On the other hand the figures are only estimates based on data pertaining to the Ontario system only. These figures have undergone complicated calculations in order to derive a national figure. One perhaps controversial move is to treat "open custody" as part of the institutional population. There are good legal and practical grounds for doing this, though the differences are not great. If open custody had been treated as non-institutional, the figures for 1986-88 would have been: 1988: 28,009 (109.3); 1987: 28,168 (111.3); 1986: 28,277 (110.9).

Appendix II.

	Total Institutional Population 1916-1974				
	Daily Population of All Penal Institutions Including Training Schools	Rate per 100,000 Canadian Population		Daily Population of all Penal Institutions Including Training Schools	Rate per 100,000 Canadian Population
1974	20,407	91.2	1944	11,212	93.9
1973	20,966	95.1	1943	10,862	92.1
1972	20,136	92.4	1942	10,451	89.7
1971	20,124	93.3	1941	11,763	102.2
1970	22,329	104.8	1940	12,951	113.8
1969	23,448	111.7	1939	12,874	114.3
1968	23,368	112.9	1938	13,348	120.5
1967	23,111	113.4	1937	12,208	110.5
1966	23,455	117.2	1936	11,154	101.9
1965	24,179	123.1	1935	10,550	97.3
1964	24,288	125.9	1934	11,899	110.8
1963	23,512	124.2	1933	12,657	119.0
1962	22,747	122.4	1932	13,255	126.1
1961	21,960	120.4	1931	12,549	120.9
1960	20,628	115.4	1930	11,223	109.9
1959	20,790	118.9	1929	9,796	97.7
1958	20,382	119.3	1928	8,561	87.0
1957	18,301	110.2	1927	7,964	82.6
1956	17,352	107.9	1926	7,593	80.3
1955	18,048	115.0	1925	7,543	81.2
1954	17,369	113.6	1924	7,126	77.9
1953	16,383	110.4	1923	6,849	76.0
1952	15,846	109.6	1922	7,601	85.2
1951	15,295	109.2	1921	7,191	81.8
1950	16,012	116.8	1920	6,004	70.2
1949	14,573	108.4	1919	5,442	65.5
1948	13,454	104.0	1918	5,026	61.7
1947	12,481	99.4	1917	5,468	67.8
1946	11,651	94.8	1916	5,459	68.2
1945	11,334	93.9			

Sources: Reed, 1983: Z198-208, Z292-304, A1-14.

Figures are for the last day of the fiscal year: for 1916-1948 this is September 30th, excepting Ontario (March 31st), Nova Scotia (November 30th) and Quebec (December 31st); for 1949-1970 it is March 31st except for Quebec (December 31st); for 1971 it is March 31st excepting training schools, federal penitentiaries and Quebec (all December 31st); for 1972-1974 it is December 31st with no exceptions.

Appendix III.

Penitentiary Population 1867-1988				
	Daily Penitentiary Population on Register (Actual Count)		Rate per 100,000 Canadian Population	
1988	11,969	(10,557)	46.7	(41.2)
1987	12,318	(11,106)	48.7	(43.9)
1986	12,281	(11,214)	48.4	(44.2)
1985	11,872	(10,857)	47.2	(43.2)
1984	11,359	(10,438)	45.6	(41.9)
1983	10,638	(9,775)	43.2	(39.7)
1982	9,765	(8,938)	40.1	(36.7)
1981	9,452	(8,651)	39.3	(36.0)
1980	9,305	(9,465)	39.2	(35.6)
1979a	9,219	(8,370)	39.2	(35.6)
1979b	9,290		39.1	
1978	9,309		39.6	
1977	9,335		40.1	
1976	9,285		40.4	
1975	8,700		38.3	
1974	8,499		38.0	
1973	9,111		41.3	
1972	8,253		37.9	
1971	7,483		34.7	
1970	7,337		34.5	
1969	7,117		33.9	
1968	7,026		33.9	
1967	7,167		35.1	
1966	7,438		37.2	
1965	7,514		38.2	
1964	7,651		39.7	
1963	7,219		38.1	
1962	7,156		38.5	
1961	6,738		36.9	
1960	6,344		35.5	
1959	6,295		36.0	
1958	5,770		33.8	
1957	5,432		32.7	
1956	5,508		34.3	
1955	5,507		35.1	
1954	5,120		33.5	
1953	4,934		33.2	

Appendix III (cont'd.).

	Penitentiary Population 1867-1988	
	Daily Penitentiary Population on Register (Actual Count)	Rate per 100,000 Canadian Population
1952	4,686	32.4
1951	4,817	34.4
1950	4,740	34.6
1949	4,260	31.7
1948	3,851	30.0
1947	3,752	29.9
1946	3,362	27.4
1945	3,129	25.9
1944	3,078	25.8
1943	2,969	25.2
1942	3,232	27.7
1941	3,688	32.1
1940	3,772	33.1
1939	3,803	33.8
1938	3,580	32.1
1937	3,264	29.6
1936	3,098	28.3
1935	3,586	33.1
1934	4,220	39.3
1933	4,587	43.1
1932	4,164	39.6
1931	3,714	35.8
1930	3,187	31.2
1929	2,769	27.6
1928	2,560	26.0
1927	2,480	25.7
1926	2,474	26.2
1925	2,345	25.2
1924	2,225	24.3
1923	2,486	27.6
1922	2,640	29.6
1921	2,150	24.5
1920	1,931	22.6
1919	1,689	20.3
1918	1,468	18.0
1917	1,694	21.0
1916	2,118	26.5

Appendix III (cont'd.).

	Penitentiary Population 1867-1988	
	Daily Penitentiary Population on Register (Actual Count)	Rate per 100,000 Canadian Population
1915	2,064	25.9
1914	2,003	25.4
1913	1,970	25.8
1912	1,895	25.6
1911	1,865	25.9
1910	1,859	26.6
1909	1,765	26.0
1908	1,476	22.3
1907	1,423	22.2
1906	1,439	23.6
1905	1,367	22.8
1904	1,328	22.8
1903	1,250	22.1
1902	1,214	22.1
1901	1,382	25.7
1900	1,424	26.9
1899	1,445	27.6
1898	1,446	27.9
1897	1,383	27.0
1896	1,361	26.8
1895	1,277	25.4
1894	1,223	24.6
1893	1,194	24.2
1892	1,228	25.1
1891	1,249	25.8
1890	1,251	26.2
1889	1,195	25.3
1888	1,094	23.4
1887	1,159	25.1
1886	1,200	26.2
1885	1,112	24.5
1884	1,039	23.2
1883	1,113	25.1
1882	1,127	25.8
1881	1,218	28.2
1880	1,213	28.5
1879	1,200	28.7

Appendix III (cont'd.).

Penitentiary Population 1867-1988		
	Daily Penitentiary Population on Register (Actual Count)	Rate per 100,000 Canadian Population
1878	1,110	26.9
1877	1,108	27.3
1876	1,069	26.7
1875	848	21.4
1874	679	17.4
1873	567	14.8
1872	605	16.1
1871	692	18.8
1870	756	20.9
1869	745	20.9
1868	861	24.5
1867	972	28.1

Sources: Statistics Canada, 1979, 1982-83, 1983-84, 1984-85, 1985-86, 1986-87, 1987-88; Reed, 1983: Z173-174, A1-14, Z-292-304. The 1980-88 figures are average daily counts for the fiscal year ending March 31st of the year named; they are in all respects like the figures in Appendix I; the 1979a figures are estimates derived from a census figure reduced by the proportion of average population to census given in the 1982-83 report for the year 1980 for which we have both figures (Actual Count: 8465/8627 x 8530 = 8370; On Register: 9305/9519 x 9431 = 9219); the 1960-1979b figures are a single census taken on December 31st; the 1906-1959 figures are as of March 31st; 1877-1905 figures are as of June 30th; 1867-1876 figures are as of December 31st. Canadian population bases for the rates are as of April 1st from 1867-1901 and as of June 1st from 1902-1987.

Appendix IV.

Execution Statistics				
	Number of Executions	Per Death Sentences	Per Murder Charges	Per Homicides
1879-80	11	.579 (19)	.180 (61)	———
1881-85	30	.508 (59)	.216 (139)	———
1886-90	23	.535 (43)	.198 (116)	———
1891-95	14	.412 (34)	.135 (104)	———
1896-1900	26	.591 (44)	.234 (111)	———
1901-05	29	.580 (50)	.206 (141)	———
1906-10	42	.656 (64)	.204 (206)	———
1911-15	51	.405 (126)	.166 (308)	———
1916-20	47	.420 (112)	.162 (290)	———
1921-25	49	.538 (91)	.166 (295)	———
1926-30	46	.523 (88)	.190 (242)	.058 (796)
1931-35	83	.783 (106)	.359 (231)	.108 (772)
1936-40	42	.477 (88)	.205 (205)	.062 (674)
1941-45	34	.523 (65)	.198 (172)	.054 (626)
1946-50	62	.544 (114)	.232 (267)	.085 (731)
1951-55	41	.554 (74)	.198 (207)	.056 (735)
1956-60	10	.159 (63)	.053 (190)	.019 (945)
Average (excluding 1956-58)		.539	.203	.071

Sources: Zay, 1965: 649 (Y61-67); Reed, 1983: Z21.

Appendx V.

Deportation and Imprisonment 1929/1939-1980/1988				
	Deportation		Prison	Total of Deportation and Prison
Year	Number	Rate per 100,000 Population	Average Daily Population per 100,000	
(Adult Institutions)				
1929	1,964	19.6	97.7	
1930	3,963	38.8	109.9	
1931	6,583	63.4	120.9	
1932	7,647	72.8	126.1	
1933	5,138	48.3	119.0	
1934	1,701	15.8	110.8	
1935	675	6.2	97.3	
1936	605	5.5	101.9	
1937	421	3.8	110.5	
1938	439	3.9	120.5	
1939	413	3.7	114.3	
(Adult Institutions)				
1979-80	5,107	21.5	92.4	
1980-81	5,376	22.4	93.6	
1981-82	5,191	21.3	98.9	
1982-83	5,197	21.1	109.3	
1983-84	5,099	20.6	108.4	
1984-85	3,950	15.8	110.0	
1985-86	2,467	9.8	111.5	
1986-87	2,446	9.6	114.0	
1987-88	2,809	11.0	112.7	
Average	1930-39	26.2	95.1*	121.3*
		26.2	101.6**	127.8**
	1930-34	47.8	98.6*	146.4*
		47.8	105.3**	153.1**
	1932	72.8	105.9*	178.7
		72.8	113.2**	186.0**
Average	1980-88	17	105.6	122.7
	1984-88	13.4	111.3	124.7
	1983			130.4

The figures with asterisks have been adjusted to make them comparable with figures for adult institutions only as per footnote 5 in the text

* denotes deflator of 99.7/118.7

** denotes deflator of .898

Sources: Roberts, 1988: 38; Dominion Bureau of Statistics, 1940: 160; Employment and Immigration Canada, Annual Reports 1979/80-1987/88.

Appendix VI.

	Prison	Probation	(Rate)	Ratio	Prison	Probation	(Rate)	Ratio
				Adult Prison and Probation Admissions in Ontario 1964-1988				
1987-88	66,170	24,168	(261)	2.7:1	72,093	30,266	(326)	2.4:1
1986-87	64,311	23,237	(255)	2.8:1	69,719	29,296	(322)	2.4:1
1985-86	64,466	24,555	(271)	2.6:1	68,166	28,999	(320)	2.4:1
1984-85	67,785	30,053	(336)	2.3:1				
1983-84	68,138	28,997	(329)	2.3:1				
1982-83	71,090	29,500	(338)	2.4:1				
1981-82	65,576	31,665	(376)	2.1:1				
1980-81	65,776	31,107	(361)	2.1:1				
1979-80	60,701	29,775	(350)	2.0:1				
1978-79	61,834	27,822	(329)	2.2:1				
1977-78	59,072	21,413	(256)	2.8:1				
1976-77	59,362	18,851	(228)	3.1:1				
1975-76	54,791	19,323	(235)	2.8:1				
1974-75	54,721	17,386	(215)	3.1:1				
1973-74	56,072	13,691	(172)	4.1:1				
1972-73	56,754	11,225	(143)	5.1:1				
1971-72	65,664	10,270	(133)	6.4:1				
1970-71	76,284							
1969-70	66,595							
1968-69	62,097							
1967-68	61,120							
1966-67	61,343							
1965-66	58,230	6,547	(97)	8.9:1				
1964-65	58,431							

Sources: Ontario, 1967, 1968, 1969, 1970, 1981, 1982, 1983, 1984, 1985; Statistics Canada, 1976, 1977, 1978, 1979, 1982-1983 through 1987-1988; McFarlane, 1966: 89 (for 1965); Reed, 1983: Z175-197.

All admissions save probation admissions for 1965-1966 are for the fiscal year ending March 31st. Probation admissions for 1965-66 are for the calendar year 1965. The Canadian population bases for the rates are as of June 1st of the fiscal year comprehended by the admissions.

The YOA effect is calculated as in Appendix I, with "open custody" treated as imprisonment. Had it not been so treated, the differences would again be small, with the ratios for 1986-1988 each being 2.3:1 instead of 2.4:1.

Appendix VII.

	Prison (Rate)	Probation (Rate)	Ratio	Adjusted for YOA		
1987-88	8,701 (94)	34,493 (371)	1:4.0	9809 (106)	40853 (e) (441)	1:4.2
1986-87	8,610 (95)	34,868 (383)	1:4.0	9575 (105)	41,187 (453)	1:4.3
1985-86	8,927 (99)	37,771 (417)	1:4.2	9372 (103)	39,915 (441)	1:4.3
1984-85	9,090 (102)	37,974 (425)	1:4.2			
83-84	8,741 (99)	36,902 (419)	1:4.2			
82-83	8,739 (100)	35,666 (409)	1:4.1			
81-82	7,864 (91)	2,406 (376)	1:4.1			
80-81	7,334 (86)	32,011 (374)	1:4.4			
79-80	7,779 (92)	29,941 (352)	1:3.8			
78-79	8,236 (98)	26,362 (312)	1:3.2			
77-78	8,437 (101)	22,631 (271)	1:2.7			
76-77	8,254 (100)	19,672 (238)	1:2.4			
75-76	7,538 (92)	17,838 (218)	1:2.4			
74-75	7,010 (87)	15,832 (197)	1:2.3			
73-74	6,899 (87)	13,561 (171)	1:2.0			
72-73	6,567 (84)	12,044 (154)	1:1.8			
71-72	6,464 (84)	11,237 (146)	1:1.7			
70-71	6,669 (88)					
69-70	6,746 (91)					
68-69	6,811 (94)					
67-68	6,812 (96)					
66-67	6,749 (97)					
65-66	6,748 (99)					
64-65	6,934 (105)	5,225 (79)	1:3.1			
63-64	7,157 (110)					
62-63	7,205 (113)					
61-62	7,232 (116)					
60-61	7,072 (116)					
59-60	6,791 (114)					
58-59	6,712 (115)					
57-58	6,475 (115)					

Average Daily Adult Prison and Probation Population—Ontario 1957-1988

The prison data are a combination of the population of Ontario correctional institutions and federal penitentiaries located in Ontario. For 1978/9-1987/8 they consist of average daily counts for the fiscal year ending March 31st; for 1957-1958 to 1969-1970 they are the average of the counts for March 31 of each year; for 1970-1971 to 1977-1978 they are the average of the counts for March 31st of each year for the provincial prisons only, while for the federal penitentiaries they are the count for December 31st of the first year mentioned. The probation data are the average daily counts for 1978-1979 to 1984-1985; for 1970-1971 to 1977-1978 they are the average of the counts for March 31 of each year; for 1964-65 they are the population under supervision for January 1, 1965; Rates are per 100,000 Ontario population as of June 1st comprehended by the fiscal year.

The YOA effect is calculated as in Appendix I, with open custody assigned to prison and not to probation. If it were assigned to probation, the ratios for 1986, 1987 and 1988 would be 1:4.3, 4.5 and 4.4 respectively.

Sources: Dominion Bureau of Statistics, 1957-1959, 1960-1961, 1962, 1963, 1964, 1964-1965, 1965-1966, 1966-1967, 1967-1968, 1968-1969, 1969-1970, 1970; Statistics Canada, 1971a, 1972, 1973a, 1974, 1975, 1976, 1977, 1978, 1982-1983 through 1987-1988; Ontario, 1985; McFarlane, 1966: 89.

Appendix VIII.

Yearly Admissions to Custodial and Supervised Population—Canada 1978-1988					
	Provincial Custody	Probation	Total	Rate Per 100,000 Canadian	Custody as % of Total
1987-88	196,552 (e)	53,521	250,073	976	78.6
	(208,607)(e)	(64,408)	(273,015)	(1,065)	(76.4)
1986-87	190,108	52,749	242,857	960	78.3
	(200,973)	(63,954)	(264,927)	(1,047)	(75.9)
1985-86	190,286	54,838	245,124	967	77.6
	(197,729)	(63,034)	(260,763)	(1,028)	(75.8)
1984-85	193,602	62,986	257,714	1,026	75.2
1983-84	199,852	63,567	263,419	1,058	75.9
1982-83	201,690	65,550	267,240	1,085	75.5
1981-82	183,450	66,245	249,695	1,026	73.5
1980-81	170,874	62,875	233,749	972	73.1
1979-80	160,078	58,631	18,709	921	73.2
1978-79	158,428	56,342	214,770	913	73.8

Admissions are "from liberty" not including transfers.

Figures in brackets are adjusted for YOA, assuming as in Appendix I that open custody should be assigned to prison and not to probation. If it were assigned to probation, the percentage custody for 1986, 1987 and 1988 would be 75.7 per cent, 75.3 per cent and 75.7 per cent respectively.

Sources: Statistics Canada, 1982-83 through 1987-88; Ontario, 1985.

Appendix IX.

Average Daily Custodial and Supervised Population — Canada 1978-1988					
	Average Daily Probation	Parole and Mandatory	Total Non-Custodial	Custodial and Non-Custodial	Total Custodial
1987-88	66,405	11,526	77,931	26,634	104,565
	(76,291)		(87,817)	(28,873)	(116,690)
1986-87	67,133	10,887	78,020	26,893	104,913
	(77,078)		(87,965)	(28,864)	(116,829)
1985-86	72,249	9,994	82,243	27,392	109,635
	(75,646)		(85,640)	(28,277)	(113,917)
1984-85	74,707	10,191	84,898	27,634	112,532
1983-84	74,386	10,042	84,428	26,980	111,408
1982-83	71,880	9,032	80,912	26,924	107,836
1981-82	65,123	9,182	74,305	24,064	98,369
1980-81	62,656	8,131	70,787	22,502	93,289
1979-80	59,248	8,037	67,285	21,936	89,221
1978-79	53,937	7,801	61,738	21,956	83,694
Rates Per 100,000 Canadian Population					
	Custodial	Non-Custodial	Total	Non-Custodial as % of Total	
1987-88	104 (112.7)	304 (343)	408 (455)	74.5 (75.3)	
1986-87	106 (114.0)	308 (348)	415 (462)	74.4 (75.3)	
1985-86	108 (111.5)	324 (338)	432 (449)	75.0 (75.2)	
1984-85	110	338	448	75.4	
1983-84	108	339	448	75.8	
1982-83	109	328	438	75.0	
1981-82	99	305	404	75.5	
1980-81	94	294	388	75.9	
1979-80	92	283	376	75.4	
1978-79	93	263	356	73.8	

Figures in brackets are adjusted for YOA effect, assuming as in Appendix I that open custody should be assigned to prison and not to probation. If it were assigned to probation, the percentage non-custodial for 1986, 1987 and 1988 would be 75.3 per cent, 75.9 per cent and 76.0 per cent respectively.

Sources: Statistics Canada, 1982-1983 through 1987-1988; Ontario, 1985.

Note: The 1987-1988 Statistics Canada report excludes lock-up data for the first time. In the interests of comparability they have been included in the table nevertheless. This required an estimate to be made for 1987-1988, based on the Statistics Canada report for 1986-1987 where lock-ups for 1986-1987 are included and the report for 1987-1988 where lock-ups for 1986-1987 are not included. It was assumed that the proportion of lock-ups to ordinary imprisonment was the same for both years. Therefore the 1987-1988 figure of 190,141 without lock-ups was multiplied by 190,108/183,907 to get the total of 196,552. The same reasoning applies to daily population figures, but the numbers in this case are tiny due to the short duration of lock-up imprisonment, so no attempt has been made to include them in the tables on population.

Appendix X

Reported Crime per 100,000 Population 1962-1987

Year	Murder	Attempted Murder (Wounding)	Manslaughter	Sexual Assault	Aggravated Assault	Other Assault	Robbery	Break and Enter	Theft	NCA/FDA	Total Driving*	Impaired Driving
1987	2.3	3.6	.19	87	10.5	650	88	1,421	3,712	241	1,584	570
1986	2.1	3.5	.17	81	11.4	603	92	1,440	3,656	222	1,599	585
1985	2.6	3.4	.19	73	11.0	558	90	1,416	3,593	227	1,630	609
1984	2.5	3.7	.17	59	12.5	529	93	1,429	3,622	220	1,648	632
1983	2.5	3.6	.21	48	14.6	507	98	1,462	3,700	221	1,662	671
1982	2.5	3.6	.17	57	10.5	502	111	1,505	3,676	263	1,769	681
1981	2.5	3.7	.18	55	11.1	486	101	1,509	3,797	309	1,889	721
1980	2.1	3.3	.40	53	10.0	477	102	1,454	3,569	309	1,894	704
1979	2.5	3.2	.16	52	9.7	466	88	1,248	3,274	273	1,843	692
1978	2.5	3.2	.24	49	9.2	440	84	1,184	3,021	258	1,723	663
1977	2.7	2.9	.33	47	8.9	438	84	1,163	2,944	283	1,655	666
1976	2.7	3.0	.21	46	8.7	448	67	1,167	3,004	274	1,657	645
1975	2.8	2.8	.28	48	9.4	440	94	1,146	2,998	245	1,622	649
1974	2.4	2.3	.24	50	9.3	424	76	1,043	2,782	262	1,579	651
1973	2.2	2.2	.30	54	8.3	407	60	698	2,693	239	1,410	565
1972	2.2	1.9	.18	50	7.8	391	54	676	2,449	132	1,217	499
1971	2.0	1.6	.22	52	8.6	385	52	674	2,468	111	1,082	449
1970	2.0	1.2	.16	52	7.7	363	55	834	2,308	88	979	379
1969	1.6	1.0	.21	51	7.8	343	48	770	2,026	50	856	239
1968	1.5	.9	.29	51	6.2	322	40	700	1,854	26	785	218
1967	1.4	.7	.27	48	5.1	290	35	586	1,662	14	714	202
1966	1.1	.7	.14	44	4.9	267	29	510	1,529	7	680	198
1965	1.2	.6	.17	38	4.2	227	28	491	1,405	4	N/A	191
1964	1.1	.6	.18	39	4.3	210	29	504	1,429	3	N/A	180
1963	1.1	.6	.18	37	6.7	173	31	498	1,359	5	N/A	172
1962	1.2	.4	.26	36	6.8	150	27	442	1,263	5	N/A	176
Factor by which 1987 figure exceeds 1962 figure:	1.9	9	(?)	2.7 (est)	1.5	4.3	3.3	3.2	2.9	48.2	2.3 (66.87)	3.2 (est)

* Total Driving includes the offences of criminal negligence causing death, criminal negligence causing bodily harm, criminal negligence in the operation of a motor vehicle, driving while impaired or with more than the allowed alcohol/blood ratio (Criminal Code), failure to remain at the scene of an accident, dangerous driving, and driving while disqualified (Criminal Code and provincial statute).

** Driving while impaired or with more than the allowed alcohol/blood ratio and refusal to provide a breath sample.

*** Commencing 1986, changes were made to the Criminal Code, which affect the comparability of driving offence statistics. Offences were expanded to include boats and aircraft as well as motor vehicles. In 1986 and 1987 such offences constituted less than one per cent of the total, but the way statistics are reported makes it impossible to determine the precise numbers. The figures in the table attempt to exclude offences committed with boats and aircraft. Including them would change the figures to 1589 and 572 for 1987, and 1604 and 587 for 1986. Also, as of 1986 the offences of impaired operation of a motor vehicle etc. causing bodily harm or causing death were added. Theoretically these should be included in the impaired offences because they would have constituted such offences before the change. But most certainly some of these offences, perhaps all of them, would have been prosecuted under other charges (criminal negligence causing death or bodily harm) before, and to include them now would suggest more of an increase or less of a decrease in the impaired category than has actually occurred. I have therefore excluded them. If they were included, the figures for 1987 would be 579 (with boats and aircraft) or 577 (without) and for 1986 594 (with) and 591 (without).

Calculations for 1986: Total driving: 406,635 (1604); without boats: 405,333 (1599); impaired driving: 150,571 (594); without harm: 148,794 (587); impaired driving without boats: 149,932 (591); impaired driving without boats and without harm: 148,316 (585).

Calculations for 1987: Total driving: 407,087 (1589); without boats: 405,836 (1584); impaired driving: 148,320 (579); without harm: 146,586 (572); impaired driving without boats: 147,741 (577); impaired driving without boats and without harm: 146,107 (570).

**** In 1983 several changes in the Criminal Code came into effect which affect comparability. For the category of "Sexual Assault:" the offences of "rape" and "indecent assault" were replaced by three categories of "sexual assault" in 1983; while the figures under "sexual assault" for 1962-1982 include not only rape and indecent assault but also various forms of sexual intercourse with minors and seduction, as well as the offences of "gross indecency" and "buggery and bestiality," the figures for 1983 and afterwards are restricted to pure sexual assault. For the category "Aggravated Assault (Wounding):" Wounding was redefined in 1983 and partially replaced by "aggravated assault." The figures under "Aggravated Assault (Wounding) for 1962-1982 include all offences under the former section 228 of the Criminal Code, including discharging a firearm; but the 1983 offence of aggravated assault is somewhat narrower. However, separate statistics are now kept on discharging firearms and I have included these in the category for 1983 and following to maintain rough comparability. "Other Assault:" this category excludes wounding before 1983 and aggravated assault after 1982; it includes unlawfully causing bodily harm in all years.

***** In 1969, the offence of driving while intoxicated was repealed and the offences of driving with a higher than permitted alcohol to blood ratio and of refusing to provide a breath sample were created. This appears to have led to an immediate increase in the reported offence rate.

Sources: Dominion Bureau of Statistics, 1962a, 1962b, 1965a, 1965b, 1968a, 1968b and
Statistics Canada, 1971a, 1971c, 1975a, 1980, 1984, 1987a, *Juristat Service
Bulletin*, Volume 7, No. 4 (September, 1987); for driving offences in 1986 and
1987: unpublished statistics kindly provided to me by the Canadian Centre for
Justice Statistics of Statistics Canada.

Corrections and Community (In)Action

K.R.E. McCormick and L.A. Visano

"Propaganda begins when dialogue ends."
Jacques Ellul

Introduction

The concept of community pervades all levels of the criminal justice system. Throughout the last few decades we have witnessed a proliferation of programs, strategies and policies ostensibly designed to encourage a greater degree of "community" participation (Boostrom and Henderson, 1983; Visano, 1983). This passionate rediscovery of viable alternatives in the community has been sought to supplement traditional and more formal methods of control. To elaborate, such ideological manipulations of this concept in community policing, criminal trials, sentencing and corrections has attained a heightened significance within the criminological "chatter" of control (Foucault, 1977: 304) This shift towards community crime prevention, compensation, restitution, victimization and the simple return of the bad or the mad (Scull, 1977: 41) to the community echo a lingering pastoral nostalgia.

The corrections industry has been busy in promoting a community argument in ensuring greater degrees of co-operation and input. As Commissioner of Corrections Ingstrup celebrates:

> Accepting that the community is the only environment in which the offender can fully demonstrate the ability to function as a law-abiding citizen, gradual release to the community, and quality community supervision and support are essential to achieve our Mission of protecting society by facilitating the timely reintegration of offenders (1987: 7).

Moreover, as Ingstrup elucidates:

> We will also strive to enhance public under-
> standing and acceptance of our role through
> active, responsive and honest communication
> with the public (1987: 9).

Likewise, provincial counterparts continue to highlight in their annual reports their respective governments' commitment to community service orders. Typically, community alternatives are singled out in terms of their effectiveness, that is, in responding to such criteria as the protection of society and the rehabilitation of offenders. Ontario's 1984 *Annual Report of the Ministry of Correctional Services*, which virtually remains unchanged currently, cites the following goals:

> "To encourage and develop community-based
> work programs" and "To facilitate the partici-
> pation of both individual citizens and the com-
> munity at large in the criminal justice system."
> (Ontario, Annual Report: Ontario Ministry of
> Correctional Services, 1984: 5)

What emerges from the plethora of government documents is the theme that the community plays an incredibly vital role in the overall corrections process, a critical element in forging new relationships with offenders and state agencies. The general public concurs, as indicated by Doob and Roberts (1988) who report that seventy per cent of Canadians indicate that they would rather put money into the development of community sanctions than in building more prisons. Admittedly, the government sanctions directly and symbolically the processes of community participation. The notion of community in these contexts, however, remains poorly operationalized within a normatively illusory framework that masks any connotations of politics and struggle.

The purposes of this paper are to evaluate critically the concept of community in corrections, provide a case study of a much celebrated exercise in federal corrections — the Citizens' Advisory Committee — and to focus attention on the need to transform community inaction into communities-in-action.

Within the correctional marketplace of rhetoric, jargon and clichés, the concept of community has become a negotiable commodity the value of which is conveniently determined by the state. The community concept provides more than ideological legitimacy. Rather, as currently manipulated by sophisticated cadres of state bureaucrats committed to public relations campaigns, the community concept is designed to discipline "outside" participation, pre-empt criticism and discourage much needed critical dialogue. How then does the public participate in corrections? Much is known about the efforts of the state in infiltrating, penetrating and getting connected to local initiatives. Yet relatively little information exists documenting the extent to which the community actually participates in its own right in government activities. That is, a paradox is apparent regarding non-governmental community initiatives. What happens when, for example, representatives of community-based organizations, who are all carefully appointed according to bureaucratic criteria, demand an agenda that departs from state-filtered priorities?

Citizens' Advisory Committee: Maintaining An Inactive Community

According to Correctional Service of Canada (1984), the Citizens' Advisory Committee (C.A.C.) benefits from a rich heritage of citizen participation. C.A.C.s have not only helped wardens become more aware of community concerns but have also encouraged citizens in a free society to make valuable educational, cultural and employment opportunities to offenders (Correctional Service of Canada, 1981). C.A.C.s open the operation of federal corrections to the public and are influential in bringing the offender and the community together in work projects which benefit both (Correctional Service of Canada, 1981). In 1965 there were at least three formal committees — Saskatchewan Penitentiary, Matsqui in British Columbia and Beaver Creek Correctional Camp in Ontario. Throughout the 1970s as federal corrections expanded centralized control, the C.A.C. evolved to become a more objective check on corrections within a "watchdog" orientation (Thorne and Detlefsen, 1986: 6). In 1977 the Solicitor General accepted the recommendations of the MacGuigan Parliamentary Sub-committee which fully supported the value of C.A.C.s. Recommendation 25 of the MacGuigan Report clearly stated that the Penitentiary Service should be open and accountable to the public. Recommendation 49 further declares that: C.A.C.s should be established in all penal institutions; members should be recruited from a cross-section of society representing a wide variety of interests as well as ethno-cultural diversity; and C.A.C.s should advise directors of local attitudes towards the institution and programs; C.A.C.s should inform and educate the public — to name but a few recommendations (MacGuigan, 1977). Correctional Service of Canada (C.S.C.) requires these committees in every correctional institution and district parole office (Commissioner's Directive 600-4-08.1). C.A.C.s have the following roles:

(1)   to promote communication between inmates, C.S.C. staff and the public;

(2)   to participate in the overall development of the institution or district parole office;

(3)   to improve the local population's knowledge and understanding of these activities;

(4)   to provide conditions that will encourage public participation in correctional activities;

(5)   to participate in developing community resources designed to support correctional programs (Correctional Service of Canada, 1984).

Responsibilities include advising the responsible local administrator or regional deputy commissioner on the overall development of the institution or district parole office and its programs, assisting in developing community resources, educating the local community and providing continuing advice to the local administrator or regional deputy commissioner regarding the sensitivities, problems, needs and pulse of the community (Correctional Service of Canada, 1984). Commissioner LeBlanc's Directive (#023; January 1, 1987) details the policy objective:

> To contribute to the functioning of the Service and humane treatment of offenders by involving citizens in the overall development of Service installations and by strengthening the ties between the field units and the local communities through the establishment of Citizen Advisory Committees.

This directive stipulates that members are appointed by the local Director with the consent of the Deputy Commissioner of the Region. C.A.C.s would consist of no less than five members, appointed for no less than two years. Disagreements about the role and responsibilities of the C.A.C. which cannot be resolved locally may be referred to the Deputy Commissioner of the Region, or if necessary to the Commissioner (Correctional Service of Canada, 1984). *Taking Responsibility*, the Report of the Standing Committee on Justice and Solicitor General recommends that the C.S.C. allocate more resources to the C.A.C. "so that community participation in their activities may be more widespread" (Daubney, 1988: 205).

In light of the above context of governmental support for the C.A.C., the following examination of the treatment of one of the largest C.A.C.s in Canada — the Central Ontario Citizens Advisory Committee — is

extremely illustrative of institutional manipulations, the politics of corrections and the culture of contradictions that characterize corrections in
Canada.

The Central Ontario C.A.C. which operated in Metropolitan Toronto
was unilaterally disbanded on 7 October 1988 (*Globe and Mail*, 19
October 1988; *The Toronto Star*, 18 October 1988; *The Toronto Sun*,
19 October 1988). The District Director of the C.S.C., the most senior
official in the Toronto area, sent letters to committee members informing
them that as a result of "emotional crises," the current C.A.C. was disbanded and indicated that new members would be appointed. The Toronto area
had been a hotbed of controversy since the C.S.C. began to issue contracts
to private agencies. The matter surfaced in early 1988 with the murder of
Tema Conter. For months the local C.A.C. had been critical of the government's move to privatize halfway houses. Although the monthly meetings
were congenial, the Chair and the Vice-Chair echoed numerous concerns
about the levels of supervision, the "for profit" contracts and the failure of
local officials to keep committee members informed of pressing cases. On
several occasions, for example, the acting chair, like many other committee
members learned much about events not from local C.S.C. officials but
from the media. Despite his contacts as a former parole officer in the
region, the C.S.C. was often not forthcoming. More importantly, his presence on the committee was endorsed by the well-respected Social Planning
Council of Metropolitan Toronto and the Access Action Council of which
he was a representative. As a result of too many thorny questions about privatization asked by the chair, vice-chair, the secretary and several members,
the District Director moved quickly to muzzle any complaints.

Just hours after disbanding this public advisory group, the C.S.C.
reversed its decision and restored the committee. In a news release the
Deputy Commissioner noted that the dismissal was the result of a "misunderstanding" (*Globe and Mail*, 20 October 1988: A21). According to this
senior official:

> The real problem arises when you are into the
> land of policy.... There are ambiguities here
> and there..[they] are not a watchdog or an
> ombudsman. They do not have authority to
> legislate change in the service. Their role is an
> advisory one, nudging here and there, or push-
> ing here and there.

The chair of this C.A.C. commented:

> We should be part of the fabric of the

> correctional service. The role we have played
> in the past is a very important one.... We have
> no vested interests. We are not paid...(*Globe
> and Mail*, 20 October 1988: A21).

In the above example, members of the C.A.C. had been working productively for years. But they mistakenly believed that the C.A.C. was a legitimate mechanism for genuine public input into the operations of the C.S.C.

This illustration demonstrates clearly the consequences of assuming one's responsibility as a community representative. State authorities define the appropriateness of conduct, the parameters of a "partnership" and the levels of accountability. Although the C.A.C. was committed to its advisory mandate, members were often ill-informed of the activities of local parole offices. Material was often screened or edited by the local director.

The C.A.C. is a persuasive ideological device that conceals state coercion by projecting images of community participation and public accountability. When dissent could no longer be trivialized, state agents exaggerated the threat ("emotional crisis") and subsequently sought to remove the trouble. But, to the surprise of many officials, the media — television newscasts, newspapers and interview shows — demonstrated considerable interest in carrying the story of a disbanded governmental advisory committee. The political embarrassment resulted in a series of damage control manoeuvres. Although the Deputy Commissioner reinstated the local C.A.C., none of the key actors on the committee accepted the invitation. The community was treated like a contained colony. Administrators avoided dangerous collisions with community members, defined as meddlesome, by segregation and banishment. The firing of the entire C.A.C. was a vulgar expression of the politics of containment that emerges whenever accommodation fails. Committed to social justice, integrity and a uncompromising rapport with diverse interests in the community, the C.A.C. was "permitted" to function as long as the rhetoric of public consultation was maintained. Once members took their mandate more seriously, authorities were increasingly uncomfortable. By attributing this rebuke to a misunderstanding, the Deputy Commissioner destroyed what little confidence in the C.S.C. existed among the leadership of the C.A.C. The failure to silence criticism, however quiet and in-house, resulted in de-authenticating, de-valuing and negating the C.A.C. altogether. That is, as long as compliance with the ethos of secrecy was secured, as long as the appointed members were well disciplined to reproduce the official ideologies and as long as the C.A.C. served as an instrument for public relations and not advocacy; the concept of community was distorted for self-serving governmental schemes. Essentially, the community was ideologically incarcerated. The ethics of membership and the concomitant oath of office prevented disclosures.

Community participation as a viable and complex script involves more than reading and rehearsing well prepared government roles. Participation occurs within wider interactive contexts and articulates discourses of power and privilege. The appropriation of community resources by the state to legitimate programs, re-socialize volunteers and to discredit discordance subverts any meaningful dialogue. The C.S.C. seeks a banal accommodation to bureaucratic propaganda — image building, rather than the capacity of the community to "advise." Palliatives like re-instating the C.A.C. are shallow gestures and bankrupt slogans that fail to confront structural deficiencies oriented towards the maintenance of dependency relations. An advisory committee truly independent of the discretionary whims of the C.S.C. holds the prospect of restoring community confidence. Within the former's calculus, the community has limited options since the C.A.C. is a creation of the state.

Organizational analyses clearly suggest that bureaucracies are designed to maintain stability while concurrently generating limited outside input. Centralization protects the distribution of power. Controls in decision making and policy formulations are deliberately complex and blurred thereby defying facile access to and understanding of the vagaries of administrative privileges. A characteristic feature of the C.S.C. is to shift from goal-oriented mission statements to procedural priorities. Thus, professionalism, not voluntarism, overwhelms. In unmasking authority structures it is evident that the work in corrections is clouded in secrecy. Decisions, policies and strategies are effectively insulated and immune from general inspection. Secrecy is rationalized, in turn, as organizational imperatives. The norm of secrecy or the cowardice of anonymous committees is a valuable tool in controlling information and avoiding accountability. Secrecy is a screen behind which incompetence is protected. Keeping secret their expertise and motives, organizations treat knowledge as a very powerful commodity which is differentially distributed even within the bureaucracy. Experts are assigned exclusive tasks. Mysteries are perpetuated. Specialization dislocates and subordinates public input. Once the public has succeeded in participating in formal discussions, a further institutional layer surfaces — informal occupational cultures that do not necessarily share the political enthusiasm of community involvement. Within corrections, the rank and file seeks to protect its own control, self-interests and immunities from the encumbrances of management. The occupational culture arguably has reasons to suspect management-driven initiatives such as citizens advisory committees.

Labour is seldom consulted in the wholesale array of impression management schemes that promote the progress and success of administrative plans. The C.A.C. operated much as an appendage of the administration. Alternatives that depart from co-optation are needed despite the resistance from bureaucrats who continue to act with impunity in disregarding the interests of constituencies in favour of their own organizational and political exigencies. As Doob (1990: 420) admonishes: "we often do little to ensure that alternatives work as alternatives rather than as mere supplements to imprisonment." Likewise, Cohen (1985: 44) suggests: "community control has supplemented rather than replaced traditional methods."

An examination of advocacy and community-based empowerment provides a conceptually more comprehensive appreciation of community action in corrections. From a public policy perspective, however, a focus on "communities-in-action" is threatening. This commitment to meaningful action does not suffer from the vagueness and vulnerability of state-sponsored "community" constructions. Changes in legislation, administrative rules and regulations that protect independent community input are long overdue. Moreover, vigilance is needed by community groups to reclaim the influence which more appropriately belongs to them.

The unilateral dismissal of the local C.A.C., because on occasion it echoed sentiments that were inconsistent with the practices or views of the local director or the deputy commissioner, smacks of institutional arrogance. The subsequent reinstatement, especially after the media were notified, qualifies as a transparent politically motivated exercise in damage control.

Clearly, the C.A.C. can provide a valuable contribution to the C.S.C. But, long- and short-term interrelated changes at the organizational, interorganizational, systemic and societal levels are warranted. Immediately, the C.S.C. at the local level must confront numerous barriers that include, for example:

(1)   the denial of a problem, the refusal to recognize the significance of community input;
(2)   a self-arrogated sense of professionalism that fears change and is suspicious of critical inquiry;
(3)   a lack of commitment to change;
(4)   a dysfunctional public accountability;
(5)   a displacement of responsibility.

The following changes could easily be implemented; the C.S.C., for instance, needs to:

(1)   develop an understanding of community interests that moves beyond trite public statements;

(2)   increase the flow of information;

(3)   permit the C.A.C. to distance itself from the C.S.C.;

(4)   field questions from all community groups;

(5)   encourage the proactive consultation of the C.A.C.;

(6)   utilize community resources;

(7)   invite participation in the program planning and development stages;

(8)   select C.A.C. members from a cross-section of the community who will articulate issues of inequality, rampant in the criminal justice system, such as the treatment of the First Nations People, race, gender, class, homophobia, biases against the differentially abled;

(9)   use volunteers effectively.

If the C.S.C. is serious about improving access, it needs to take concrete steps in eradicating barriers. In other words, it is now necessary to move from a posture of reflection to one of action. Individual C.A.C.s need to implement initiatives that confront traditional barriers. During the initial stages of involving community groups the C.A.C. would be well advised to:

(1)   provide information to prospective volunteers from labour, police, business, tenant/ ratepayers associations, advocacy groups, academics, service providers, inmate committees;

(2)   develop a brokerage role that would help volunteers become aware of the responsibilities of senior administrative officials;

(3)   publicize in a culturally sensitive manner the activities of the C.S.C. and the C.A.C.;

(4)   reach out to identify and encourage community- or neighbour-hood-based organizations;

(5)   develop a capacity for inter-organizational collaboration not just with the police alone but a wider representation of perspectives;

(6)   organize resources so that they have the maximum impact on volunteers;

(7)   evaluate the services of the C.A.C. and adjust policies to

accommodate to the community rather than strictly to the C.S.C.;

(8) develop and implement explicit policies to improve community participation with appropriate protections against unilateral dismissals;

(9) emphasize more modern management approaches with an emphasis on human resource development and human relations skills especially;

(10) co-ordinate community events and workshops with other agencies to avoid confusion and enhance resource sharing;

(11) encourage joint ventures with other voluntary organizations;

(12) integrate linkages with service providers in health, education, employment, social assistance, etc.;

(13) assist in joint funding, personnel exchanges, joint planning and support services;

(14) collaborate with service providers and advocacy groups that work with the socially disadvantaged;

(15) monitor the activities of the local C.S.C.;

(16) evaluate the objectives of the Mission Statement;

(17) provide referrals to community agencies.

According to Warren (1977: 251), even when organizations are transformed into something closer to the heart's desire, they may still remain as islands in a very hostile sea. The need for change directed at the societal level is crucial. As Galper (1975: 46) argues in reference to reform:

> They express concern for individual and social welfare, but they do so in a form shaped to limited and distorted values and structures, and thus ultimately undermine the pursuit of human welfare. They are established within a political and economic context. This context, we believe, acts to subvert.

Figure 1 illustrates that access is a central dynamic that influences interplay between the community and the state agencies. Access is not limited only to voluntary participation at the local level of community relations. But more significantly, access refers to the level of involvement in policy formulation, advising senior bureaucrats, setting directions for change in the C.S.C. and C.A.C., ongoing consultations with both community leaders and C.S.C. officials. Access is not just the enjoyment of a few opportunities made available by the government; access refers to the ownership of the agenda that to date has been exclusively controlled by the C.S.C.

Figure 1.

Community
and
State Interface

Community ⟺ Access ⟺ C.S.C./C.A.C.
Service
Delivery

Communities-In-Action: Responding to Barriers

The struggle for change is a challenge, a political process that cannot be left to the "benevolent" gestures of authority agents. By defying the defining authoritative gaze of the C.S.C., alternative formulations are required. In the previous section we detailed the responsibilities of the C.A.C. and the C.S.C.; in the following discussion we highlight the responsibilities of communities.

Briefly, problem solving is a *collective* accomplishment despite the rancorous cacophony of authorities denouncing the involvement of volunteers. Authorities will designate as deviant or subversive the objections of participants. Despite attenuated ties with state officials, public input and pressure ought to continue. Ameliorative action, dispute settlements or the management of grievances may be handled by applying existing practices, rules and policies (Lyman and Scott, 1970). Alternatively, radically more compelling measures are required to secure even a modicum of social justice. The C.S.C., as evident in the case study of the Toronto C.A.C., is institutionally deficient in enhancing community confidence. The norms and values displayed during this episode were inappropriate, confusing and woefully insufficient. Frustration characterized the response of the C.A.C. members. Structural barriers such as the rigid bureaucratic framework, inadequate legislation, systemic bias against any challenge to authority and ineffective accountability prevailed. Mobilization of outside support, therefore, is justified. But, efforts to mobilize a large number of people to bring about change (Clarke *et al.*, 1975: 1; Stone, 1986) are determined by several contingencies.

Mobilization, "the activation of human resources for collective participation" (Clarke *et al.*, 1975: 12) is shaped by the following factors: ideology, an able leadership and channels of communication or networks of cooperative relationships.

Ideology sustains participation by providing a litany of invaluable rationalizations. This set of interrelated values re-socializes volunteers or activists to become receptive to new competing definitions. Additionally, ideology is a reflexive process that is directed at the self and recasts present troubles through past experiences. Ideological challenges invite, as Lofland (1985) suggests, ongoing conversions in social and personal identities. A change in consciousness emerges as long as alternative visions are explored and a distance from official accounts is maintained. Logically, this quasi-resistance is, in effect, an expression of agency, autonomy and accountability. Gradually, the self becomes oriented toward unlearning the conventions of corrections and increasingly familiar with more compelling, albeit more unorthodox, explanations of power and the consequences of non-compliance. By moving beyond convenience and self-serving rationales, community representatives ideologically situate themselves as committed participants.

Ideology does not alone ensure a successful protest. The potential for mobilization is determined by the cohesiveness of the group, strengths of opposing control agents and the resources available. For Tilly (1978), mobilization is the process of creating commitments that generate a willingness to contribute resources. Group cohesiveness, with its attendant collaborative orientations toward advocacy, constitutes a pressure to change the state's approach to community interests. This emphasis on cojoint activities will undoubtedly empower any C.A.C. to demand accessibility. Also, coalition building with the socially disadvantaged, economically deprived, community-based organizations, feminist, anti-racist action groups, labour, Aboriginal associations, open and well established communication networks with the media, opposition party members of the legislatures, civil liberties, etc. is a formidable force. Attempts by the state to promote inter- and intra-group conflicts in an effort to construct "the community" in its own image and likeness will falter.

Figure 2

CONTINUUM
OF
COMMUNITY INVOLVEMENTS:
Volunteers in Corrections

STATE SPONSORED (N.P.B.)	PUBLIC/PRIVATE (C.A.C. J.H.S)	COMMUNITY NEIGHBOURHOOD-BASED (Black Action Defence Committee Inmate Councils)
ADVISORY COMMITTEES	SERVICE PROVIDERS	ADVOCACY/ACTION COUNCILS
ROYAL COMMISSIONS	GOVERNMENT CONTRACTS	INFORMATION REFERRALS
GOVERNMENT APPOINTEES	UNITED WAY	DONATIONS
DIRECTORS		UNDER-RESOURCED POORLY-FUNDED

Conclusions

The "community" is an elusive concept that has been too easily appropriated by the state to engineer support for limited initiatives that fail to grapple with fundamental inequalities in corrections. This term is contextually determined and discursively constructed to satisfy organizational interests. Without reference to the context of power, the community concept has become a pretext for intervention and exclusion. A commitment to local contests, for example, is perceived as counter-hegemonic and subject to coercive measures. This sponge-like term enables the state to celebrate and parade representations that it has effectively screened — to appoint those individuals and organizations who subscribe deferentially to authority/subject relations and enjoy the benefits of such complicity and deception that something is being done "for" the community.

Admittedly, the case study of the C.A.C. suffers from anecdotal oversimplification and remains suspiciously idiosyncratic. Nevertheless, there are generic principles that are readily applicable to other research sites that demand a more rigorous investigation. This brief discussion urges students of penology to juxtapose the rhetoric inviting community input with actual content and structure of community involvement, the imposed limitations that silence the voices of the concerned. Given the proliferation of chatter about increased community participation, students are further asked to problematize the relationship between the state and democratic accountability. Interestingly, one wonders curiously what price is paid by those who dare to question authority not from the outside community but from behind bars.

Community inaction is rewarded by the exaggerated privilege of being permitted to sit on committees struck by state functionaries. Communities-in-action, however, mobilize, advocate and articulate an agenda that provides an ongoing critique of power. Inequalities in corrections are ubiquitous. Victims feel ignored by an alienating system of justice; inmates, parolees and their families suffer deprivation; correctional officers complain about the insensitivities of management, stress and poor working conditions; and the general public remains ignorant and fearful of "alarming" crime rates, statistics that are often advanced to secure support for state practices.

References

Boostrom, R. and J. Henderson. 1983. "Community Action and Crime Prevention: Some Unresolved Issues." *Crime and Social Justice* 19 (Summer): 24-30.

Clarke, H. *et al.* 1975. *Prophecy and Protest.* Toronto: Gage.

Cohen, S. 1985. *Visions of Social Control.* Cambridge: Polity.

Commissioner's Directive "Citizens' Advisory Committee." #023, January 1, 1987.

Correctional Service of Canada. 1981. *Citizens' Advisory Committee: Aid to Corrections.*

Correctional Service of Canada. 1984. *Working Together: Citizens' Advisory Committees and the Correctional Service of Canada.*

Daubney, 1988. "Report of the Standing Committee on Justice and Solicitor General on its review of the sentencing, correctional release and related aspects of corrections" in *Taking Responsibility*. Ottawa.

Doob, A. 1990. "Community Sanctions and Imprisonment: Hoping for a miracle but not bothering even to pray for it." *Canadian Journal of Criminology,* 32, 3: 415-428.

Doob, A. and J. Roberts. 1988. "Public Punitiveness and Public Knowledge of the Facts: Some Canadian Surveys" in Walker, N. and M. Hough (eds.), *Public Attitudes to Sentencing: Surveys From Five Counties*. Aldershot, U.K.: Gower.

Foucault, M. 1977. *Discipline and Power*. N.Y.: Pantheon.

Galper, J. 1975. *The Politics of Social Services*. Englewood Cliffs, N.J.: Prentice-Hall.

Globe and Mail, "Ottawa Fires Watchdog Group Critical of Halfway House Plans." 19 October 19 1988.

Ingstrup, O. 1987. *Mission Statement of the National Parole Board*. National Parole Board, Communications Division.

Lofland, J. 1985. *Protest*. New Brunswick, N.J.: Transaction.

Lyman, S. and M. Scott. 1970. *Revolt of the Students*. Columbus: Charles E. Merrill.

MacGuigan, M. 1977. *Report: The Penitentiary System In Canada*. Ottawa: Supplies and Services.

Ontario, 1984. *Annual Report, Ministry of Correctional Services;* Toronto: Government Services.

Scull, A. 1977. *Decarceration*. Englewood Cliffs, N.J.: Prentice-Hall.

Stone, S. 1986. "The Lesbian Mothers' Defence Fund" Paper presented at the Qualitative Research Conference, Univ. of Waterloo, May 13-16.

Thorne, B. and M. Detlefsen. 1986. "Advisory Citizen Participation in the Correctional Systems of Canada, the United Kingdom and Ireland." Unpublished monograph.

Tilly, C. 1978. *From Mobilization to Revolution*. Reading: Addison-Wesley.

Toronto Sun, "Feds Can Watchdog." 19 October 1988.

Toronto Star, "Critics Dumped By Government." 18 October 1988.

Turner, R. 1978. "The Public Perception of Protest" in Manis, J. and B. Meltzer (eds.), *Symbolic Interaction*. Boston: Allyn and Bacon.

Visano, L. 1983. "Tramps, Tricks and Troubles: Street Transients and Their Controls" in Fleming, T. and L. Visano (eds.), *Deviant Designations*. Toronto: Butterworth.

Warren, R. 1977. *Social Change and Human Purpose*. Chicago: Rand McNally.

Webber, D. 1987. *Community-Based Corrections and Community Consultation — A How to Manual. Solicitor General*: Ontario Region.

Bilateral Legitimation:
The Parole Pendulum*

R.S. Ratner

Introduction

For all its material affluence and its apparent triumph over communist economic orders, capitalist societies are scored by deep inequalities and, consequently, suffer chronic legitimation problems (Habermas, 1975; Wolfe, 1977; Offe, 1984, 1985). When adjustments in the accumulative sphere prove inadequate to manage or dispel recurrent crises, the burden of social control falls on coercive systems — occasionally in the form of foreign military exploits, more often as intensified domestic repression. This was evident in the late 1970s when worrying economic trends precipitated recessionary cutbacks, a weakening of democratic institutions and the emergence of so-called "exceptional states" (Hall *et al.*, 1978; Ratner and McMullan, 1983). The neo-conservative politics unleased by the negative trajectories of that period were no less visible in Canada, where subsequent developments accentuated problems of legitimation (Taylor, 1983, 1987).

Without doubt, the spread of a reactive political climate in this country was fuelled by growing anxiety over crime. In 1981, for example, forty per cent of respondents to a Canadian Urban Victimization Survey said they felt unsafe walking alone in their own neighbourhood at night.[1] A 1984 Decima Quarterly Report poll found a similar level of concern among Canadians. Of those surveyed, forty-four per cent agreed with the statement: "I don't feel safe when I go out alone at night in my neighbourhood" (Johnson, 1988: 24). Substantiating this fear, a 1988 survey by Statistics Canada estimates that nearly five million Canadians were victims of at least one crime, and that over half of the crimes were personal — theft, robbery, assault and sexual assault.[2]

Public anxieties about crime often fixate on the issue of parole, partly because it presents the spectre of unknown offenders legitimately "at large." But controversy over the pros and cons of the parole system often reaches such crescendos as to suggest a symptomatic reading of social crisis,[3] indicative of far more than public attitudes toward the disposition of a relatively small number of offenders. For example, while only 7,000 plus federal prisoners in Canada were on some form of parole in 1991,[4] and although the National Parole Board (NPB) actually grants parole only in about one-third of the cases reviewed, a widely shared public myth persists that the NPB is "soft" on criminals and that the recidivism rate of inmates on parole is astronomical. On the other hand, recent government efforts to allay public fears and encourage a policy of community corrections have been frustrated by a rash of murders committed by prisoners who had been released on parole or on mandatory supervision[5] and who were placed in community correctional facilities despite long histories of sexual violence.[6] No more than a dozen such horrific incidents have occurred over the past several years, but these were sufficient to send up the hue-and-cry of "Scrap parole!" Oddly, government commissions and task forces have arrived at radically different recommendations about the use of prison and parole in combatting crime. The Government Task Force on Program Review (Nielsen, 1986) urged restrained use of incarceration, since imprisoning criminals had become a fiscal "luxury."[7] The Canadian Sentencing Commission (Archambault, 1987), arguing the need to make sentences "real," recommended the abolition of parole,[8] while the Parliamentary Justice Committee (Daubney, 1988) strongly supported parole, community alternatives and improved treatment programs.[9] In the very same week that the Daubney Report was released, the then Solicitor General James Kelleher proceeded to introduce a bill to tighten the Parole Act and lengthen the proportion of sentences that inmates serve in prison. Paradoxically, the Pepino inquiry into one of the sensationalized parolee murders ended with a qualified endorsement of the halfway house concept.[10]

All of the varied proposals raise important questions about the sources of public misinformation and media bias in the reporting of parole violations, the role of privatization in the corrections service, and the general problem of restoring public credibility in the parole system. Their contradictory recommendations, however, can best be grasped through contrasting an understanding of parole geared to a concept of "rehabilitation" with parole as a mechanism of societal "regulation."

Parole as Rehabilitation

The main tenets of Enlightenment philosophy — social contract, rationality, free choice — formed the basis of the Classical School of Criminal Law (Beccaria, 1963; Bentham, 1982) during the late eighteenth and nineteenth centuries. These juristic assumptions were articulated in a tight grid of offences and corresponding punishments that prescribed a whole catalogue of property crimes, thus protecting the foundations of a nascent capitalist economy. A powerful nineteenth-century Tory State in Canada, bent on "peace, order, and good government" (Horowitz, 1968), eagerly incorporated classicist doctrine, so that by the turn of the century, classical modes of thinking dominated the Canadian criminal justice system and disparaged "mollycoddling" reforms.[11]

Parole began in Canada with the passage of the Ticket-of-leave Act in 1899 by the Federal Parliament. Like the British legislation from which it was drafted, the Act was vague regarding its essential purpose. Some members of Parliament believed Tickets-of-leave would assist convicts in becoming law-abiding citizens. Others thought it would solve the problem of overcrowding in the prisons. Some saw the new system simply as a means of granting clemency to young and first offenders. By 1905, the Ticket-of-leave experiment was considered to be a success, and by the end of WWI, it had become an established institution,[12] centred on the principle of rehabilitation. This focus was blurred by the social unrest after WWI, which led to increases in crime and criticisms of leniency in the criminal justice system. But the granting of Tickets-of-leave was again liberalized to counter the escalating prison population during the Depression years, and later to allow prisoners to join the armed forces or to accept employment in war industry. This development coincided with a theoretical shift away from juristic-deductive reasoning to scientific study of the offender (Lombroso, 1912). This new positivist thrust, combined with the practical need to mould a well disciplined work-force, eclipsed the classical philosophy of retribution and deterrence in favour of rehabilitation. Reformist intentions were officially endorsed by the 1938 Archambault Report, which recommended humanitarian changes in correctional institutions and commented approvingly on the "rehabilitative ideal." A subsequent government report on corrections — Fauteux Committee (1956) — went further in urging the abandonment of the retributive philosophy, the provision of treatment facilities for specific categories of offenders, the development of professional specialties to serve prisoners, probation departments and after-care agencies and the establishment of criminology as "the study of crime and its treatment" (1956: 85).

In commenting on the Ticket-of-leave system, the Fauteux Committee was "astonished" that "such antiquated legislation" could provide "such satisfactory results" (1956: 55); nevertheless, it called for creation of a parole authority organizationally independent from the parole service.

The recommendations of the Fauteux Report were implemented in 1959 with the proclamation of the Parole Act and the creation of a National Parole Board. In transferring authority to grant conditional release to the NPB, the concept of rehabilitation was incorporated into law, with parole envisioned as a logical step between confinement and freedom. Accordingly, a National Parole Service was established to prepare cases for Board consideration and to supervise parolees in the community. In 1969, the rehabilitative strategy was extended to cover those inmates released automatically at the two-thirds mark of their prison sentence, owing to earned remission.[13] The Ouimet Committee, appointed partly in response to the civil rights movements in the late 1960s (which called the criminal justice system into question), expressed concern that inmates deemed unfit for parole were being released without any of the controls or benefits of supervision provided to the better risk parolees. On the Committee's recommendation, amendments to the Parole Act of 1969 were passed which required that inmates released as a result of remission be supervised in the community for the remainder of the sentence under a program known as Mandatory Supervision (MS).[14] The provision of counselling services to assist high-risk MS releasees through a transitional period of statutory conditional release seemed to establish the dominance of the "rehabilitative ideal."

Even with its apparent entrenchment, the rehabilitative philosophy has been continually assailed on grounds of "undue lenience," a characterization which many prisoners would regretfully dispute. This incongruity reveals the extent to which parole remains a politically charged issue, obtaining erratic and unprincipled support, at best, from public and governmental sectors. This was evident in the notorious "gating" controversy, where, between September 1982 and May 1983, eleven MS releasees with histories of violence or serious sexual offences, were "gated" (i.e., had their release revoked at the penitentiary gate).[15] The practice was then challenged in the courts as an unreasonable reading of sections of the Parole Act and as violative of section 9 of the Charter of Rights, which prohibits arbitrary detention or imprisonment. In May 1983, the Supreme Court of Canada declared gating to be illegal, and all gated individuals who were still incarcerated were released on MS. This prompted the Solicitor General to introduce amendments to the Parole Act that would, in effect, legalize gating.

Bills C-67 and C-68, passed in June 1986, gave authority to the National Parole Board to "detain," until warrant expiry, prisoners deemed unsuitable for automatic release under MS.[16] While mollifying public criticism of the parole system, this legislation seemed to undermine the logic of conditional release, since mandatory supervision had been recommended by the Ouimet Committee precisely in order to prevent dangerous offenders from being discharged without first undergoing a transitional period of supervision in the community.

This inconsistency is reflected in the public's persistent failure to differentiate parole, with its moderately respectable success rate (approximately sixty-five per cent), from mandatory supervision, with its significantly lower success rate (approximately forty per cent).[17] The reasons for the distorted public perception are not clear, but it is unlikely that media bias can be the sole explanation, since a lack of assiduousness on the part of correctional officials in clarifying these terms for public consumption has invited general confusion.[18] The conflating of parolees with MS and other high-risk offenders creates the impression of a uniformly high recidivist rate, which then negates the argument for rehabilitation. Undifferentiated high recidivism rates in the context of increasing inmate populations[19] and sharply escalating state expenditures in corrections (MacLean, 1986: 125-127; 1989), ultimately sink therapeutic expectations to the level of "nothing works" (Martinson, 1974). Moreover, inherent restraints on acclaiming the successes of parole,[20] the dwarfing of positive outcomes by newer forms of criminalization (e.g., child-abuse, wife-battering) and the failure to link the rehabilitation of offenders to opportunity-structures in the economy,[21] all undermine the "rehabilitative ideal" and contribute to its antithesis, the movement to "abolish parole."

So we are drawn to the paradoxical conclusion that while the rehabilitative approach must count as a modest success, its general impact sustains a pattern of overall failure. Parole has not reduced incarceration rates, or halted the growth of criminal justice expenditures, or mobilized enthusiastic public support. This brings to mind W.T. McGrath's contention that "Parole and mandatory supervision cannot be assessed in isolation from the rest of the criminal justice system. It is the system as a whole that needs review" (1982: 10).

The question is, what is the "system as a whole"?

Parole as Regulation

In a political economy of crime control, the "system as a whole" is nothing less than the entire social formation. This means that any single institutional element, such as parole, cannot be understood in isolation from the socio-economic totality in which it functions,[22] and certainly not apart from the societal mode of production. In capitalist societies, the mode of production is characterized by relations of domination and subordination, wherein exploitation and the appropriation of surplus value do not occur smoothly or without inciting resistance. Periodic crises, reflecting economic disjunctures at the national and global levels, are registered at the political level. In order to maintain order and protect the assets of capital, power over the working and "redundant" classes must be legitimated. Continued compliance in the interests of "productive efficiency" requires that human material must be defined as "worthy" or "unworthy" in terms of "good" and "bad" investments in human capital. Through ideological hegemony ("consent armed with coercion" — Gramsci, 1971), a stable social order is achieved which seeks to ensure that production and exchange remain unimpaired. In advanced capitalist societies, the state becomes the primary mechanism to articulate, co-ordinate and direct this rationalization process (Spitzer, 1979),[23] and the "criminal justice system" becomes an indispensable element of this "modern technology of subjection" (Foucault, 1977).

From this vantage-point,[24] parole is understood as one of the managerial solutions to the problem of surplus labour,[25] especially in recessionary periods of the capitalist economy. Structurally, it operates to harmonize institutional imperatives of the "corrections" sub-system with the ubiquitous state functions of accumulation, coercion, and legitimation.[26]

(1)   Parole serves the accumulative function by helping to regulate the size and growth of penitentiary populations and by stimulating the development of community corrections (including needed facilities, as well as personnel). As in the case of mandatory supervision, parole allows for a level of de-institutionalization that contains prohibitive costs of prison construction while alleviating institutional overcrowding.[27] On the other hand, parole policy can also be shaped to lengthen the control of the state over penitentiary inmates, thereby fostering organizational expansion.[28] Unsurprisingly, budgetary expenditures and personnel for both Corrections Service Canada (CSC) and the National Parole Board have increased regularly since their

formation. By increasing employment in this manner, and thus facilitating the realization of surplus value, economic and political crises are to some degree averted, at least in the short term.

(2)   Parole serves the coercive function by placing individuals officially "at risk" in the community, thus permitting an extension of surveillance in order to monitor "trouble" and widen the involvement of agencies of "criminal justice." In this respect, parolees and MS releasees each represent sectors of the population that must be subjected to unrelenting control, since their relative vulnerability to economic crisis constitutes them as a core of potential dissent.[29] By placing these groupings under permanent scrutiny (through "supervisory" powers that often result in a return to custody), dissidence can be stifled both within and beyond the penitentiary setting.

(3)   Parole serves the legitimative function through claims of protecting the public and "rehabilitating" individual offenders. But, while the rhetoric of "reintegration" is bruited, public safety takes priority and usually short-circuits the reintegration schema. Moreover, legitimation strategies net greater political dividends when invoked on behalf of greater coercive control, such as when public outcries over egregious parole violations are used to justify more repressive policies. In this respect, parolee "failures" serve as psychological scapegoats for the systemic failures of capitalism.

Although there are no Canadian studies which offer historical validation of these correlative functions of the criminal justice system, Mandel, in attempting to account for variations in the repression rate (and for his own assessment of the 1980s as the most repressive decade in Canadian history), makes the following observation (1991: 186): "What strikes even the casual student of the history of punishment in the twentieth century is how closely changes in the repressive rate seem to parallel changes in economic conditions or what is often called the "business cycle."' In tracing the relationship between recessionary periods (1930s, late 1950s, early 1980s) and steep rises in the rate of repression, Mandel, using Greenberg's analysis (1977) of the oscillatory relationship between annual *unemployment* rates and annual admissions to Canadian penitentiaries, finds that connection to be the crucial indicator, rather than the conventionally assumed relationship between *crime* and repression. Studies by Tepperman (1977) and Box

(1987) also point to the significance of the employment/repression ratio, leading Mandel to adopt a qualified version of the extra-punitive hypothesis.[30] While this is short of offering adequate historical substantiation for the political economy analysis that needs to be made in this area, Mandel's interpretation is suggestive of the links between parole decision-making and labour market opportunities. His exploration offers empirical grounds to conceptualize parole and mandatory supervision as homeostatic devices for regulating the flow of surplus labour through the penitentiaries,[31] producing the "quasi-normalization of deviant populations" (Spitzer, 1975), and helping to preserve the stability of bourgeois rule (Mandel, 1985).[32]

If this depiction is correct, the ultimate effect of such palatably repressive "solutions" is to ensure the continuation of high incarceration and recidivism rates,[33] along with a consequent expansion of the carceral system. From the perspective of parole as societal regulation, we are led, therefore, to the ironic observation that the purported "failures" of the correctional system add up to an uninterrupted success. Not liberal-cynicism, but the *sardonicism* of Foucault best grasps the inverted logic of this situation:

> For the observation that prison fails to eliminate crime, one should perhaps substitute the hypothesis that prison has succeeded extremely well in producing delinquency — so successful has been the prison that, after a century and a half of "failures" the prison still exists, producing the same results, and there is the greatest reluctance to dispense with it (1977: 277).

Bilateral Legitimation

Interestingly, both the rehabilitative and regulative notions of parole (and corrections, generally) infuse the recent "mission" statements of the National Parole Board and the Correctional Service:

> The Board, by facilitating the timely integration
> of offenders as law-abiding citizens, contributes
> to the protection of society (National Parole
> Board Mission Statement, 1986: 1).

The Correctional Service of Canada, as part of the criminal justice system, contributes to the protection of society by actively encouraging and assisting offenders to become law-abiding citizens, while exercising reasonable, safe, secure, and humane control (Correctional Service of Canada Mission Statement, 1989: 4).

This merger of control philosophies occurs through sequential implementation of inclusionary strategies (rehabilitation) and exclusionary strategies (regulation), as dictated by economic conditions and political exigencies.[34] Periods of relative affluence ordinarily feature inclusionary (or "re-integration") strategies emphasizing "treatment" and "community corrections" programs.[35] The expansion of community corrections, which entails a re-commodification of "bad" human material, provides an accumulative stimulus and boosts legitimation, since an increased investment in "rehabilitation" is generally perceived as enhancing social equity. Thus, domestic repression is less visible during periods of economic prosperity, operating mainly at the level of "noiseless surveillance."[36] As regards parole, a more lenient policy of conditional release is tactically appropriate.

During periods of economic crisis and downturn, the state confronts a contradictory situation. The reduced availability of funds for state-sponsored treatment and corrections, combined with a growing public resentment towards programs that provide various forms of assistance to "less-deserving" offenders,[37] makes "community corrections" politically untenable and forces the state to re-adopt exclusionary control strategies, especially since the increased economic vulnerability of the poor and working-class sectors of the population *does* result in more crime, which then "justifies" the recourse to coercion. But punishment and imprisonment is costly, requiring an investment of state revenues that must be diverted from more profitable sources of accumulation. The costs of new custodial facilities, increased policing, and more sophisticated technology, can be reduced, to some extent, via privatization,[38] but this presents a further contradiction — the dangers of abuse and non-accountability should the state lose control over the enforcement and administration of "criminal justice." In this quandary, the corrections sector performs a vital legitimative function alongside its intensified coercive activity, through such programs as victim assistance and "target-hardening" and by strident law-and-order campaigns. Such concrete manoeuvres re-invigorate the political status quo and prevent mass public disaffection. In this context, parole risks previously adjudged "assumable" become "undue risks." Parole grant rates go down and revocation rates go up.[39]

If then, corrections performs an ideological "system-maintenance" function in good times and bad, this oscillation nevertheless poses serious problems for practitioners, especially during periods of fiscal austerity when the rehabilitative component must be curtailed. One danger in promoting carceral expansion, whatever the short-term legitimation benefits, is that it may suppress tolerable behaviour and dissent, controverting the declared principles of democratic society, principles to which most people working in corrections avowedly adhere. Moreover, the stimulation of "moral panics" as a means of coping with legitimation crises could result in an over-investment in incarceral expansion, compounding the problem of fiscal instability.[40] The end result of such regulative strategies would be to alienate both managerial technocrats and rank-and-file operatives of the coercive state. Professional "training," organizational expansion, and the authority of "science"[41] offer only limited inducements to collaborate in abandonments of the rehabilitative philosophy. Either covert strategies proliferate to circumvent neo-conservative policy and rhetoric,[42] or resignation prevails, with practitioners sustained only by the belief that the "rehabilitative ideal" will be disinterred when the "new realism" fails.

That government tinkering with conditional release policy does little to dispel these contradictions was illustrated by Solicitor General James Kelleher's 1988 proposals. Responding to constitutional challenges to Bills C-67 and C-68[43] (which attempted to legalize "gating"), and wishing to restore flagging public confidence in the parole system,[44] Kelleher declared that, henceforth, "risk to society" would be the overriding factor in conditional release decisions. Four major changes to parole legislation were proposed:

(1) Earned remission and mandatory supervision would be abolished.[45]

(2) Mandatory supervision would be replaced by a period of supervised statutory release for the last one-third of the sentence or one year before the expiry of the term of imprisonment, whichever was less.

(3) The parole eligibility date would change from one-third of the sentence to one-half of the total sentence.

(4) The day parole eligibility date would change from one-sixth of the sentence to a date which is six months prior to the full parole eligibility date.

Many observers surmised that the net effect of these changes would be longer prison sentences, an outcome which exacerbates the criminogenic effects of imprisonment by extending incarceration beyond the period where the inmate normally would have "earned" a remission release. Rather than contributing to a safer society, the ultimate effect of these measures could be to increase the likelihood of danger. Moreover, the proposed period of "statutory release," which limits the disciplinary incentive of earned remission to a maximum of twelve months, could well increase the difficulty of maintaining order within prison institutions since abolishment of the MS remission period reduces the incentive for "good behaviour."

A further "balancing" proposal to improve the system's ability to differentiate between low-risk and high-risk offenders through more frequent reviews was expected to result in the expeditious release of inmates who posed little or no risk to the community. In practice, however, plans to increase the frequency of parole hearings are often waived or delayed because the system lacks the resources to conduct accelerated reviews and to supervise more releasees in the community.[46]

In sum, the Kelleher proposals, in deferring to public demands for retribution, would have overloaded prisons and furthered the absorption of non-violent offenders into the prison subculture. In their criticism of these proposals as "hastily and speculatively formulated in response to public misconceptions," the Canadian Criminal Justice Association noted that:

> By projecting the impact of these proposals on the penitentiary admissions for 1985-86, one concludes that [the] resources would result in that group of inmates serving 23% more time, which would translate into a total of 1471 additional prison years to be served at a cost of $58,840,000 to the taxpayers for that one group of inmates.[47]

Recognizing the potential impact on prison populations, Kelleher modified his proposals to reduce parole by aiming them primarily at "violent" offenders. Presumably this adjustment would neither undermine the principal criterion of public safety[48] nor overtax institutional capacity. But if tinkering with parole eligibility dates can purchase a temporary measure of legitimation, it cannot relieve the criminal justice system of the weight of contradictions implicit in such an opportunistic posture. Whether through "rehabilitation" or "regulation," correctionalist policy is wedded to system-maintenance, not change or transformation. The intent of either orientation is to legitimate the state and leave fundamentally unchanged the system of institutionalized class interests which the state is beholden to represent, if in an erratic and contradictory fashion. The rhetoric for popular consumption is that parole is an integral feature of the "liberal" state, but that it justifies only a limited investment. Precisely why the costs of effective rehabilitation are insupportable escapes scrutiny.

Whither Parole?

The vicissitudes of parole depend upon the flow of human merchandise through the criminal justice system, which in turn determines whether prison institutions are likely to disappear, contract, or expand. In the class-based society of Canada, prison abolition is unfortunately a quixotic goal, given the need to create and maintain an offender class whose treatment and disposition would deter those in similarly deprived circumstances from electing to misbehave.[49] The rationale for the existence of such a class will only evaporate with the disappearance of subsistence labour and derivative inequalities. Barring some major societal transformation, this prospect is inconceivable. Current de-skilling and divestment trends in the globalization phase of capital are more likely to swell the reserve labour supply.[50]

Even a moderate contraction of the prison population is unlikely, taking into account the legislative curtailments of mandatory supervision and parole, the inflexibly long sentences imposed on capital offenders, and the intensified scrutiny of those who do get discharged.[51] Bureaucratic subversion of new legislative strictures will doubtless occur, but parole and correctional officers will balk at assuming detectable risks when organizational fidelity (as well as political legitimacy) is at stake. Demographically, more people are bound to be proletarianized by the movements of international capital, increasing their susceptibility to crime and to stigmatization within the carceral order. New prison construction may be unaffordable,[52] but the cost of managing a widening pool of offenders will be reduced by technological means, a development now widespread in the U.S. (McCarthy, 1987) and taking root in Canada with the paired use of electronic monitoring and home confinement.[53] In correctional terminology, these developments are euphemistically described as "striving for consistency and balance between *rehabilitation* and *deterrence*,"[54] but either orientation yields similar overall results — continuing high recidivism rates, an expansion of the carceral system and reinforcement of the dominant ideology. Whether it be economic boon or crisis that impacts social order, state policy is adjusted to shift the parole pendulum so as to recoup legitimation and ensure the continued commodification of crime control. But what else should we expect of a "downstream" auxiliary control institution functioning in a dependent role and demonstrating its impotence against the more salient priorities of capitalist society?[55]

We must ask, however, whether the minimalist strategy of bilateral legitimation is necessarily all that the state can hope to achieve within the structural conditions imposed by capital. Does the ideologically fixed arc linking rehabilitation and regulation mean that rehabilitation is necessarily a spurious concept or one that cannot be implemented to real effect? Is genuine reform not possible within the system-imperatives outlined herein? Let us assume, for the moment, that the most profound pessimism is never total, and that possibilities for progressive action do reside even in the present situation. The report of the Parliamentary Justice Committee (Daubney), as well as a like-minded report of the Canadian Bar Association, did, after all, urge the retention of parole and a switch of priorities from imprisonment to community alternatives. And partly owing to such recommendations, the government did reject the advice of the Canadian Sentencing Commission to abolish parole and adopt a system of fixed sentences. While the mandatory supervision program *is* being eroded, and though more stringent rules now govern the release of violent criminals, the need for fiscal constraint and the realization, however grudging, that there can be no "responsibility" without rehabilitation, has, at least, halted a headlong shift to the right. But for rehabilitation to be more than a mere shibboleth, "community corrections" must become a priority of correctional reform, and Citizens' Advisory Committees (CACs), acting as liaisons between the public and prison institutions, must become an important and valued catalyst of change. In fact, there has been a rapid growth in Corrections Service Canada's use of existing community residential facilities,[56] and CSC is on record as favouring an expansion of the role of the CACs.[57] Yet there is little evidence of CSC plans to open new halfway houses under its aegis, despite the fact that a periodic shortage of beds impedes the National Parole Board in carrying out its parole plans for specific inmates.[58] Many federal inmates remain in prison despite reaching eligibility for parole, not only because of information logjams in the federal parole bureaucracy, but because assignments to community projects are often made before such projects even exist.[59] Moreover, increased concern over residential standards and staff safety issues such as security requirements, staff quality and financial liability, have sapped morale amongst halfway house workers and induced private agencies to drop contracts with CSC.[60] A Toronto CAC was abruptly disbanded by the Correctional Service because it became too critical of CSC's hurried efforts to privatize more of its community facilities.[61]

Amidst these contradictions, the "community" side of program services was given a decided boost with the appointment of Ole Ingstrup, a reform-minded veteran of the Danish correctional system, to the office of Corrections Commissioner. A main architect of the parallel Mission Statements of the NPB and CSC, Ingstrup fought public cynicism and reactionary staff attitudes in channelling resources toward more institutional treatment programs and community corrections, partly by using incentives such as higher pay rates or favourable parole evaluations to entice prisoners into programs.[62] While this new momentum is continually jeopardized by bureaucratic intransigence, public disapprobation and various "privatization" fiascos, for now it appears that Ingstrup's reforms have halted the slide back to "warehousing" offenders. Under his leadership, the "challenge of re-integration" restored fading correctionalist motifs of rehabilitation, treatment and community corrections. Since 1987, the pages of *Liaison*, *Let's Talk* and *Justice Report* have been filled with exhortations linking expanded programming to "long-range protection against recidivism."

Seeking a balance between the "tough-minded" reforms that had been proposed by former solicitor general James Kelleher — proposals sidetracked by the 1988 federal election — and the liberal-reformist ideology implicit in the Mission Statements engineered by Ingstrup, the government tabled the Corrections and Conditional Release Act (Bill C-36) on October 8, 1991, an omnibus bill to reform sentencing, prison and parole, replacing the Penitentiaries Act (1868) and the Parole Act (1958). While the proposed Act is purportedly aimed at public safety and protection in order to rebuild trust in the corrections system, it also contains elements that project a rehabilitative scope. Significant changes to conditional release policy are the following:[64]

(1) Eligibility for full parole for violent offenders can be delayed, at a judge's discretion ("judicial determination"), for one-half of the sentence from the current one-third.

(2) Sexual offences against children and serious drug offences are re-categorized as crimes for which offenders can be detained in prison custody until warrant expiry (i.e., these offenders are eligible for "gating").

(3) Day parole eligibility, which currently becomes available at one-sixth of the sentence, is now fixed at six months before the date of full parole eligibility.

(4) More resources will be focused on violent eligible offenders by streamlining the parole review process for less serious, non-violent, first-time offenders ("accelerated review"), who will now ordinarily be released as soon as they become eligible for

         parole at the one-third mark in their sentence.

(5)   Earned remission is abolished and converted to statutory release of inmates at the two-thirds mark in their sentence, unless they are paroled earlier or detained by the parole board past the two-thirds mark. Mandatory supervision is retained from the time of statutory release to sentence expiry, to ensure control and assistance.

6.   The system of granting passes from prison is tightened. No unescorted temporary absence passes will be allowed for those classified as maximum security inmates.

Whether the above proposals merely represent a pastiche of concessions that will have little effect on re-integrating offenders and reducing prison populations depends upon the development of institutional and community programming for both violent and non-violent offenders. The provision of such programs is crucial and would refute the main criticism of the new legislation that it is all "smoke and mirrors."

Some indication that the desired array of programs might not materialize was hinted in earlier statements by Ingstrup that tied the Mission's strategic objectives "to the realities of government restraint."[65] While Ingstrup offered grounds for claiming a relationship between "good programs" and a "positive effect on recidivism,"[66] leading to estimates that the overall effect of the provisions of Bill C-36 would result in no more than 160 added penitentiary inmates in the six years after the bill became law,[67] the Correctional Investigator's assessment of programming options and prospects belies such optimism.[68] There is no reason to believe that current shortages in institutional programming, of personnel to enable timely access of inmates to existing programs, and of occupational employment and training to boost after-release employment prospects, will significantly improve with the passage of Bill C-36.[69] Framers and supporters of the bill hope, of course, that a delicate balancing of priorities (alternating between retribution and rehabilitation) can be sustained, and that enough "legitimation" will be purchased at either end of the liberal-conservative arc so that "justice" and "reform" need not be construed as mutually exclusive objectives.[70] Barring a complete failure to fund programming and to manage public disapproval, a minimalist strategy of bilateral legitimation does seem tenable, although this would not fulfil the more thoroughgoing reformist vision advanced by correctionalists such as Ingstrup. A genuinely reformist vision, however, would prove difficult to establish if not grounded in a new understanding of social order and change, one that transcends the limited discourse of corrections.[71] Unless a wider commitment is won for the redistribution of resources that could extend the possibilities for "law-abiding" behaviour, unless the role of control institutions in societal regulation is plainly acknowledged, and until the communal re-integration of offenders is generously supported, no significant change can occur, and the present option will have the sole virtue of preventing rehabilitation from dissolving into the punitive cauldron of law and order. Is any other option possible? Not so long as we engage in the ideological practices that validate the current order.

Endnotes

* The author wishes to thank the various members of staff at the British Columbia offices of the National Parole Board and Corrections Service Canada for granting the interviews that helped to inform this study.

1 1981 was a peak year for victimization in the United States (Bastian and Deberry Jr., 1991).

2 "Nearly 24 percent of Canadians Victims of Crime," Globe and Mail, 26 April 1989. Violent crimes increased steadily from 648 to 856 per 100,000 between 1980 and 1987 (Canadian Social Trends, Statistics Canada, No. 11, Winter, 1988, p.31).

3 The past U.S. presidential election between Bush and Dukakis may have been won/lost on the symbolic politics of the "furlough" issue.

4 The reality is that Canada has the highest incarceration rate in the Western world: 112.7 per 100,000, surpassed only by the United States. See Basic Facts About Corrections in Canada, 1991 (hereafter referred to as BFACC, 1991), Correctional Service Canada, August, 1988, p. 11. See also Waller and Chan, 1974, for an earlier comparison of international incarceration rates.

Parole is the discretionary conditional release of an inmate prior to the end of the court's sentence. Mandatory supervision is automatic release of the inmate at the two-thirds mark of the court sentence, owing to earned remission.

6 The most troubling incident was the 1985 murder of Celia Ruygrok, a young correctional employee working in an Ottawa halfway house. She was sexually assaulted and murdered by a resident of the facility who was a diagnosed sexual psychopath on parole from a sentence of non-capital murder.

7 See Improved Program Delivery: Justice System, chapter on "Parole," pp. 325-348.

8 See Sentencing Reform: A Canadian Approach, Chapter 10, "The Meaning of a Sentence of Imprisonment," pp. 231-268.

9 See Taking Responsibility, Chapter 12, "The Future of Conditional Release," pp. 185-196.

10 See, "Man who raped...." Globe and Mail, 24 August 1989 and "Commission Praises Stricter Convict-release System," Globe and Mail, 9 June 1990.

11 See, for example, the Reports of the Inspectors of Penitentiaries in the early 1900s,

which defined the object of imprisonment in strictly classicist terms.

12   In 1913, a special section called the Remission Service was created in the Justice Department to advise on matters coming under the Royal Prerogative of Mercy and the Ticket-of-Leave Act. (For a "short history of parole" in Canada, see MacLean and Ratner, 1987.)

13   Remission, or "time off for good behaviour," can comprise as much as one-third of an inmate's sentence.

14   For a detailed review of the history of MS legislation, see Ratner, 1987. See, also, Shewan, 1985, for a comparative evaluation of MS and Parole legislation and policy outcomes.

15   See summary of the then Solicitor General Robert Kaplan's "Rationale for Gating," *Contact*, Vol. 2, No. 1, Summer, 1983, National Joint Committee of the CACPG FCS, pp. 5-6.

16   810 detention orders have been issued since Bill C-67 became law in 1986. (Testimony of current National Parole Board Chairman, Fred Gibson, at the hearings of the Justice and the Solicitor General Standing Committee regarding the provisions of Bill C-36, November 28, 1991).

17   Estimates obtained from data supplied by the NPB Pacific Regional Office, Abbotsford, British Columbia — follow-up of all full parole releases in Canada (15,340) and all mandatory supervision releases (25,660) for the 1975-1985 period.

18   NPB Chairpersons habitually apologise for the failure to communicate adequately with the public, without analysing or publicly stating the reasons for that failure. (See "An Interview with the Chairman," *Liaison*, Vol. 15, No. 2, February 1989, pp. 9-14.)

19   See *Let's Talk*, Vol. 11, No. 11, September 1986, Corrections Service Canada, pp. 1-2.

20   Successful parolees are not inclined to divulge their "criminal" backgrounds just in order to tout the virtues of rehabilitation.

21   "Rehabilitation" traditionally focuses on individual attitudes and behaviour, but opportunities for employment, without which rehabilitation seldom succeeds, are largely determined by structural factors (e.g., the labour market) rather than individual factors.

22   The geo-political boundaries of such totalities are usually equated with "nation-states," although the effects of the internationalization of capital now render such definitions moot.

23   This synopsis of the political economy of crime control draws on the work of Spitzer (1975, 1979).

24   The "political economy" lineage of crime control is not traced in this paper. For a highly condensed review, see Cohen (1985: 107-111).

25   A "reserve army of labour" is an inherent feature of capitalist society, created and reproduced directly by the accumulation of capital itself. The size of this pool in advanced capitalist economies is increasing under the pressures of capital flight to low wage unregulated regions, shifts in world markets and "post-industrial" transformations to either capital-intensive work sites or a low-paying service sector.

26   This discussion of the regulatory effects of parole is adapted from a previous analysis

of the functions of mandatory supervision in the penal economy (Ratner, 1987). The gross impact of correctional policy on the two groups of inmates is roughly similar.

27   Over 13,000 individuals at an annual average cost of approximately $51,000 per inmate are presently incarcerated in Canadian federal correctional institutions. The average monthly number of federal offenders on parole, day parole and mandatory supervision is over 8,000. The average annual cost of supervising an offender on parole or mandatory supervision is approximately $8,000 (BFACC, 1991). The combined number of federal inmates released annually on parole and mandatory supervision amounts to about one-third of the total federal inmate population.

28   Approximately fifty per cent of the combined total of federal parolees and MS releasees are revoked on technical grounds or for new offences. This obviously augments the carceral power of both the NBB and CSC, enabling an expansion of correctional resources.

29   For a description of how technical restrictions imposed on parolees by the Parole Board accomplish this objective, see Ratner, 1986.

30   The "greater punitiveness" hypothesis assumes that higher unemployment leads to greater official punitiveness (e.g., through tougher sentencing) due to rising fears of a restive surplus labour force. Mandel concludes that "...on the best evidence, we seem to be left with this: downturns in the business cycle cause real crime to rise, and this is met by increased repression, but in a way that exaggerates, sometimes to a great extent, the real increase in crime" (1991: 192).

31   Numerous studies document that the great majority of penitentiary inmates come from the poor working class or "lumpenproletariat" underclass (e.g. Gosselin, 1982; Reiman, 1984; Braithwaite, 1979; Nettler, 1984). Although criminality is spread throughout the class structure, anomic pressures are unevenly distributed (Merton, 1938); moreover, the system-ethos requires that the "criminal class" be equated with the economic "underclass." Samuelson (1991) argues that the criminal justice system of post-industrial states has moved from "normalizing deviants for labour" to "managing the marginalized." Of course, mainstream analyses focusing on individual rehabilitation (and its failures) show little cognizance of class analysis. Marxist analytic categories are disdained and conceptions of state class conjunctures are embryonic or dissolve into pluralist fictions of state neutrality.

32   A detailed analysis along the analytic lines suggested here would require an integration of the "economic regulationist" model with the symbolic model of the "blameworthy" group herded into penitentiaries or otherwise punitively controlled.

33   Approximately forty per cent of Canadian federal penitentiary inmates have served one or more previous sentences in federal penitentiaries (BFACC, 1991).

34   For an insightful analysis of "inclusive" and "exclusive" visions of social control, see Cohen, 1986, Chapter 6. The alternation of these complementary strategies is only sketched in this paper and awaits empirical substantiation, a task that correctionalist researchers appear to avoid studiously. Indeed, correctionalists deny that reducing prison populations is one of the purposes of parole. As the NPB Chairman recently asserted, "The National Parole Board is not a mechanism for controlling prison or penitentiary populations.... Parole in Canada explicitly rejects this approach. The Parole Act does not allow it. The National Parole Board's commitment to public protection does not allow it" (Gibson, 1990: 488). That this is sheer rhetoric is connoted by the fact that Canada has one of the highest imprisonment rates in the western world, yet prison over-crowding is not a major problem. Brodeur, too, notes

that "The use of parole to reduce the prison population has been repeatedly disclaimed by the NPB.... It is nonetheless occurring, sometimes on a massive scale" (1990: 507).

35   See *Let's Talk*, Vol. 123, No. 5, June 1988, pp. 9-10; and November/December, 1988, pp. 6-9, Correctional Service Canada.

36   I.e., social control operates most effectively through state ideological apparatuses rather than through state repressive apparatuses. See Althusser, 1971.

37   In more formal terms, a re-activation of the "principle of less eligibility." See Rusche and Kirchheimer, 1939.

38   See *Let's Talk*, Vol. 11, No. 8, June 1, 1986, p. 3.

39   An observation offered by a senior member of the British Columbia National Parole Board, August 11th, 1988.

40   A daily average of approximately 30,000 federal and provincial prisoners are held in 225 correctional institutions in Canada, involving a staff of over 26,000 (BFAAC, 1991). The total annual cost of adult correctional services in Canada is now approximately two billion dollars. Two new penitentiaries have been built, and others are being renovated, mainly in order to avoid new capital construction costs. But even the costs of renovation are astronomical (10 to 30 million dollars per institution). The construction of more custodial facilities seems inevitable, however, since Canada's ten to twenty-five year sentences prior to parole eligibility for capital offences has already resulted in a population of over 1900 "lifers" (BFAAC, 1991). Attempts to cope with overcrowding by "double-bunking" — the practice of containing two inmates in a single cell — have raised constitutional questions and are generally deemed unsatisfactory.

41   Behaviourist treatment modalities and socio-biology, each of which places the onus of blame/change/incorrigibility on the individual offender, are the privileged perspectives of neo-conservative criminology.

42   With uncommon candor, Fred Gibson, the Chairman of the National Parole Board, commented that, "Any abolition of earned remission and mandatory supervision would put pressure on the Board to take further risks and exercise discretion positively, since a progressive parole policy absolutely requires a period of supervision in the community." (Remarks following his lecture "Parole in Canada Today," Douglas College, New Westminster, B.C., September 19, 1988.)

43   In a 1986 court challenge in British Columbia, the Supreme Court of Canada held that the plaintiff, Perry Ross, was deprived of fundamental rights guaranteed by the Canadian Charter of Rights, since his defence counsel had been refused the right of cross-examination regarding "evidence" pertaining to his detention under Bills C-67 and C-68.

44   Suspicion abounded that Kelleher's chief intent was to gain some political mileage through "anti-crime" legislation introduced just prior to a federal election.

45   For further details of the Kelleher plan, see *Let's Talk*, Vol. 13, No. 6, July 1988, pp. 5-8; also, *Liaison*, Vol. 14, No. 7, July-August, 1988, pp. 4-9.

46   This was the experience under the parole eligibility review provision of Bill C-67 where hearings were supposed to be held for all inmates at the one-sixth mark of their confinement. Such hearings were frequently waived, often upon the recommendation of case management officers, and usually because treatment programs within the prison and/or community were simply unavailable.

47   See *Justice Report*, Vol. 5, No. 3, Summer 1988, pp. 1-2, 9-10.

48   *Vancouver Sun*, 4 August 1988.

49   This theoretical requirement for an offender class nullifies the otherwise plausible arguments put forth by abolitionists such as Claire Culhane (1980, 1985) and the prisoners contributing to the inaugural issue of the *Canadian Journal of Prisoners on Prison*, Vol. 1, No. 1, Summer, 1988. The British "left realist" wing of critical criminology also concedes the unlikelihood of eliminating prisons from class society (Matthews, 1989).

50   Even Simon Reisman, Canada's chief negotiator in the Canada-U.S. Free Trade Agreement, has joined the chorus of protests against U.S. implementation of the deal, which has so far resulted in a massive transfer of capital and jobs from Canada to the U.S. and Mexico. ("Top Trade Negotiators Assail U.S.," *Vancouver Sun*, 18 January 1992.)

51   See *Let's Talk*, Vol. 13, No. 8, September 1988, pp. 4-5.

52   "Double-bunking" may soon be viewed as an acceptable solution to the problem of prison overcrowding. A state court of appeal in California recently overturned a blanket ban on the controversial practice, ruling that it was not cruel and unusual punishment in violation of the Eighth Amendment (*Los Angeles Times*, 13 December 1988). Also in support of institutional confinement, a recent U.S. Justice Department study has tried to show that it costs less to build new prisons than to relieve overcrowding in jails by releasing repeat offenders, given the cost of crimes they commit in the community ("New Prisons Make Sense, Study Says," *Vancouver Sun*, 4 July 1988).

53   An electronic monitoring pilot project sponsored by the British Columbia Solicitor General's Department was recently completed and is now being replicated in other Canadian provinces. The B.C. project has won the confidence of correctional administrators and is now being slotted into the provincial corrections system on an enlarged scale. (See the *Report of the Electronic Monitoring Advisory Committee*, submitted to the Corrections Branch of the Ministry of Solicitor General of British Columbia, March 2, 1989.) Utilization of electronic monitoring has also increased rapidly in the U.S. since its first implementation in 1984 (Schmidt, 1989).

54   See *Liaison*, Vol. 14, No. 8, September 1988, pp. 14-18.

55   Assuming that the correctional component of the criminal justice system did have the wherewithal to promote an aggressive reform agenda, clearly one major constraint on its "relative autonomy" would be the danger of reducing its clientele and jeopardizing its own organizational base. Not much relative autonomy is evident when the Chairman of the National Parole Board remarks that, "I think that co-operation and co-ordination are nearly as important to the Board as its independence, and I think we should not lose sight of the fact that we are still part of the Government of Canada. The way we do business should be in tune with government policies" (Nielsen, 1986:19).

56   See *Let's Talk*, Vol. 14, No. 3, May 1989, pp. 12-13.

57   See *Let's Talk*, Vol. 14, No. 2, March 1989, pp. 12-14.

58   Currently, there are beds available in many community residential facilities, primarily because fewer inmates are being granted day parole. The reason for this seems to be that inmates who don't participate in treatment programs within the prisons are not likely to qualify for day parole. Since few programs are available (especially for

sex offenders), day parole is granted in fewer instances.

59   "Paperwork Delaying Parole Hearings," *Globe and Mail,* 23 September 1988.

60   "Halfway Houses ending Contracts because of Corrections' Policies," *Globe and Mail,* 10 December 1988.

61   "Ottawa Fires Watchdog Group Critical of Halfway House Plans," *Globe and Mail,* 19 October 1988.

62   Ingstrup has acknowledged that some discharged inmates, especially some of those released on mandatory supervision, are quite dangerous. In such cases, he favours recourse to "dangerous offender" legislation, which, on application by the Crown, allows a judge to apply an "indeterminate sentence" with release contingent on a parole board determination that the inmate can be safely discharged (*Vancouver Province,* 22 September 1987).

63   "The primary mandate of Canada's criminal justice system is protection of the public" (Campbell and Cadieux, 1990).

64   See *Directions for Reform: A Framework for Sentencing, Corrections, and Conditional Release,* 1990, pp. 21-24.

65   See *Let's Talk*, Vol. 14, No. 5, July 1989, p. 4; and Vol. 14, No. 6, August 1989, p. 7.

66   "Testimony before the Standing Committee of Justice and the Solicitor General on Bill C-36," House of Commons, Issue No. 17, November 27, 1991, p. 10.

67   Ibid., p. 30.

68   "Testimony before the Standing Committee of Justice and the Solicitor General on Bill C-36," House of Commons, Issue No. 19, December 3, 1991, pp. 7, 10, 11, 16.

69   This is especially so when judges continue to believe that the courts are "hog-tied" by reforms (*Vancouver Sun,* 13 December 1991), and when the penitentiary system serves the government as a readily available source of cost-cutting, as was the case, for example, when Ottawa slashed spending ($14 million taken from the prison service) to pay for Canadian forces in the Persian Gulf (*The Province,* 25 November 1990).

70   Criminologists who evaluate correctionalist quandaries by locating the merits of a position at one end of the arc or the other ignore the plausibility of bilateral legitimation. Mohr (1990) for example, is strongly opposed to retribution and punishment as correctional guidelines, while Brodeur (1990) argues for the abolition of parole, granting too much importance to the issue of the "effectiveness" of rehabilitation. The fact that rehabilitation prospects are compromised by the "attrition of parole" is irrelevant to whether it can nevertheless obtain some measure of legitimation. Appearances are crucial, so failure to "act" on the rehabilitation-parole front can contribute to disorder and a consequent legitimation crisis.

71   Even the most sympathetic liberal analyses fail to emphasize the necessity of fundamental social and economic change in order to reduce crime (e.g., Cullen and Gilbert, 1982: 268-291; Reiman, 1984: 143-162). Identifying the starting points of such change is no easy matter, but they are unlikely to originate within the criminal justice system.

References

Althusser, Louis. 1971. "Ideology and Ideological State Apparatuses" in *Lenin and Philosophy and Other Essays*. London: New Left Books.

Andrews, D.A. 1990. "Some Criminological Sources of Anti-rehabilitation Bias in the Report of the Canadian Sentencing Commission." *Canadian Journal of Criminology* Vol. 32, No. 3, 511-524, 525-529.

Archambault, J. 1938. *Report of the Royal Commission to Investigate the Penal System of Canada*. Ottawa: King's Printer.

Archambault, J.R. 1987. *Sentencing Reform: A Canadian Approach. Report of the Canadian Sentencing Commission*, Canada.

Bastian, Lisa D. and Marshall M. Deberry Jr. 1991. "Criminal Victimization 1990." Bureau of Justice Statistics Bulletin, October. U.S. Department of Justice; see also 1992. "National Update." Bureau of Justice Statistics Vol. 1, No. 3, January.

Beccaria, Cesare. 1963. *An Essay on Crimes and Punishments*. Bobbs-Merrill, Indianopolis.

Bentham, Jeremy. 1982. *An Introduction to the Principles of Morals and Legislation*, Edited by J.H. Burns and H.C.A. Hart. London: Methuen.

Box, Steven. 1987. *Recession, Crime, and Punishment*. Totowa, New Jersey: Barnes and Noble Books.

Braithwaite, John. 1979. *Inequality, Crime, and Public Policy*. London: Routledge and Kegan Paul.

Brodeur, Jean-Paul. 1990. "The Attrition of Parole." *Canadian Journal of Criminology* Vol. 32, No. 3, 503-509.

Campbell, A. Kim and Pierre H. Cadieux. 1990. *Directions for Reform: A Framework for Sentencing, Corrections and Conditional Release*. Minister of Supply and Services, Canada.

Cohen, Stanley. 1985. *Visions of Social Control*. Cambridge: Polity Press.

Correctional Service of Canada. 1989. *Mission Statement*. Ottawa: Correctional Service of Canada.

Culhane, Claire. 1980. *Barred From Prison*. Vancouver: Pulp Press.

Culhane, Claire. 1985. *Still Barred From Prison: Social Inequities in Canada*. Montreal: Black Rose Books.

Cullen, Francis and Karen E. Gilbert. 1982. *Reaffirming Rehabilitation*. Cincinnati: Anderson Publishing Co.

Daubney, David. 1988. *Taking Responsibility, Report of the Standing Committee on Justice and Solicitor General on its Review of Sentencing, Conditional Release, and Related Aspects of Correction*. Ottawa: Canadian Government Publishing Centre.

Doob, Anthony N. and Jean-Paul Brodeur. 1989. "Rehabilitating the Debate on Rehabilitation." *Canadian Journal of Criminology* Vol. 31, No. 2, 179-192.

Fauteux, G. 1956. *Report of a Committee Appointed to Inquire into the Principles and Procedures Followed in the Remission Service of the Department of Justice of Canada*. Ottawa: Queen's Printer.

Foucault, Michel. 1977. *Discipline and Punish: The Birth of the Prison*. New York: Pantheon Books.

Gendreau, Paul. 1989. "Programs that do not Work: A Brief Comment on Brodeur and Doob." *Canadian Journal of Criminology* Vol. 31, No. 2, 193-195.

Gibson, Fred E. 1988. "The Future of Parole in Canada" in *The State of Corrections* (Proceedings: ACA Annual Conferences). Etkins, Jeanne-Marie (ed.), The American Correctional Association, pp. 123-130.

. 1990. "The Renewal of Parole." *Canadian Journal of Criminology* Vol. 32, No. 3, 487-491.

Gosselin, Luc. 1982. *Prisons in Canada*. Montreal: Black Rose Books.

Gramsci, Antonio. 1971. *Selections from the Prison Notebooks of Antonio Gramsci*. Hoare, Q. and G. Nowell Smith (eds.). Lawrence and Wishart.

Greenberg, David F. 1977. "The Dynamics of Oscillatory Punishment Processes." *The Journal of Criminal Law and Criminology* Vol. 68, 643-651.

Habermas, Jurgen. 1975. *Legitimation Crisis*. Boston: Beacon Press.

Hall, Stuart *et al.* 1978. *Policing the Crisis: Mugging, the State, and Law and Order*. London: MacMillan Press Ltd.

Horowitz, Gad. 1968. *Canadian Labour in Politics*. Toronto: University of Toronto Press.

House of Commons. 1986. "Setting a New Course." *Liaison*. Vol. 12, No. 11, 16-19.

Johnson, Holly. 1988. "Violent Crime." *Canadian Social Trends, Statistics 1988 Canada*. Summer, 24-29.

Lombroso, Cesare. 1912. *Crime: Its Causes and Remedies*. Boston: Little Brown and Company.

MacLean, Brian. 1986. "State Expenditures on Canadian Criminal Justice" in MacLean, Brian D. (ed.), *The Political Economy of Crime*. Prentice-Hall, 106-133.

MacLean, Brian. 1988/89. "What is to be done about the Correctional Enterprise in Canada?" *Journal of Prisoners on Prisons* Vol. 1, No. 2, Winter 59-74.

MacLean, Brian and R.S. Ratner. 1987. "An Historical Analysis of Bills C-67 and C-68: Implications for the Native Offender." *Native Studies Review* Vol. 3, No. 1, 31-58.

Mandel, Michael. 1985. "Democracy, Class, and the National Parole Board." *The Criminal Law Quarterly* Vol. 27, No. 2, 159-181.

Mandel, Michael. 1991. "The Great Repression: Criminal Punishment in the Nineteen-Eighties," in Samuelson, Les and Bernard Schissel (eds.), *Criminal Justice: Sentencing Issues and Reform*. Toronto: Garamond Press, pp. 177-226.

Martinson, R.M. 1974. "What Works? — Questions and Answers about Prison Reform." *Public Interest* Vol. 55, Spring, 22-54.

Matthews, Roger. 1989. "Alternatives to and in Prison: A Realist Approach" in Carlen, P. and D. Cook (eds.), *Paying for Crime*. Milton Keynes: Open University Press, pp. 128-150.

McCarthy, Belinda. 1987. *Intermediate Punishments: Intensive Supervision, Home Confinement and Electronic Surveillance*. New York: Criminal Justice Press.

McGrath, W.T. 1982. "Parole and Mandatory Supervision." *Bulletin of the Canadian Association for the Prevention of Crime* Vol. XI, No. 6, March, 10.

Merton, Robert. 1938. "Social Structure and Anomie." *American Sociological Review* Vol. 3, 672-682.

Mohr, J.W. 1990. "Sentencing Revisited." *Canadian Journal of Criminology* Vol. 32, No. 3,

531-535.

National Parole Board. 1986. *Mission Statement.* Ottawa: Ministry of Supply and Services, Canada.

Nettler, Gwynn. 1984. *Explaining Crime.* New York: McGraw-Hill.

Nielsen, Erik. 1986. *Improved Program Delivery: Justice System, A Study Team Report to the Task Force on Program Review.* Ottawa: Canadian Government Publishing Centre.

Offe, Claus. 1984. *Disorganized Capitalism.* Cambridge: MIT Press.

Offe, Claus. 1985. *Contradictions of the Welfare State.* Cambridge: MIT Press.

Ouimet, A. 1969. *Report of the Canadian Committee on Corrections.* Ottawa: Queen's Printer.

Ratner, R.S. 1986. "Parole Certificate as Dominant Hegemony" in Currie, Dawn H. and Brian MacLean (eds.), *The Administration of Justice.* Social Research Unit, Department of Sociology, University of Saskatchewan, 205-214.

Ratner, R.S. 1987. "Mandatory Supervision and the Penal Economy" in Lowman, John . Robert Menzies and Ted Palys (eds.), *Transcarceration: Essays in the Sociology of Social Control.* Gower Publishing Co., 291-308, 391-392.

Ratner, R.S. and John L. McMullan. 1983. "Social Control and the Rise of the 'Exceptional State' in Britain, the United States, and Canada." *Crime and Social Justice* No. 19, Summer, 31-43.

Reiman, Jeffrey. 1984. *The Rich get Richer and the Poor Get Prison* 2nd edition. New York: Macmillan.

Rusche, Georg and Otto Kirchheimer. 1939. *Punishment and Social Structure.* New York: Columbia University Press.

Samuelson, Les. 1991. "Social Reproduction and Social Control: A Political Economy of Sentencing Reform in Canada" in Samuelson, Les and Bernard Schissal (eds.), *Criminal Justice: Sentencing Issues and Reform.* Toronto: Garamond Press, pp. 59-80.

Schmidt, Annesley K. 1989. "Electronic Monitoring of Offenders Increases." *National Institute of Justice, NIJ Reports,* January/February, No. 212, pp. 2-5.

Shewan, Ian. 1985. "The Decision to Parole: Balancing the Rehabilitation of the Offender with the Protection of the Public." *Canadian Journal of Criminology* Vol. 27, No. 3, 327-339.

Spitzer, Steven. 1975. "Toward a Marxian Theory of Deviance." *Social Problems* Vol. 22, 638-651.

Spitzer, Steven. 1979. "The Rationalization of Crime Control in Capitalist Society" *Contemporary Crises* No. 3, 187-206.

Standing Committee on Justice and the Solicitor General House of Commons. *Minutes of Proceedings and Evidence.* Chairperson, Bob Horner, Issue No. 16, November 26, 1991, Honourable Doug Lewis, Solicitor General of Canada, pp. 3-35; Issue No. 17, November, 27, 1991, Ole Ingstrup, Commissioner of Corrections, pp. 3-34; Issue No. 18, November 28, 1991, Fred Gibson, National Parole Board Chairman, pp. 3-32; Issue No. 19, December 3, 1991, Ron Stewart, Correctional Investigator, pp. 3-26. Ingstrup, Ole. 1986. Mission Statement of the National Parole Board, Ottawa.

Taylor, Ian. 1983. *Crime, Capitalism and Community: Three Essays in Socialist Criminology.* Butterworths: Toronto.

Taylor, Ian. 1987. "Theorising the Crisis in Canada" in Ratner, R.S. and John L. McMullan (eds.), *State Control: Criminal Justice Politics in Canada.* Vancouver: University of British Columbia Press, pp. 85-125.

Tepperman, Lorne. 1977 *Crime Control: the Urge Toward Authority.* Toronto: McGraw-Hill Ryerson.

Waller, Irvin and Janet Chan. 1974/75. "Prison Use: A Canadian and International Comparison" *The Criminal Law Quarterly* Vol. 17, No. 1, 47-71.

Wolfe, Alan. 1977. *The Limits of Legitimacy: Political Contradictions of Contemporary Capitalism.* New York: Free Press.

Sentenced to Death? HIV Infection and AIDS in Prisons: Current and Future Concerns

Louis A. Pagliaro and Ann M. Pagliaro

AIDS, the acquired immune deficiency syndrome, is a communicable, uniformly fatal viral disease caused by infection with the human immune virus (HIV). HIV is a retrovirus, which has also been referred to as the Human T-Lymphotropic Virus type III (HTLV-III) or Lymphadenopathy-Associated Virus (LAV) and exists in several forms (e.g., HIV-I, HIV-2) (Berkelman and Curran, 1989; Greig, 1987; Orenstein, 1989). Worldwide, the number of reported AIDS cases is currently reported at over six million. Because of generally poor reporting practices in most developing countries, however, this number is probably a significant underestimate.

Since the first case of AIDS was reported in North America in the early 1980s, the number of cases has risen geometrically, as has occurred in other parts of the world, so that currently over 150,000 North Americans have been diagnosed with AIDS and over 3,000 new cases are reported each month. In addition, it is estimated that well over one million people in North America are currently infected with HIV (Centers for Disease Control, 1987) and that virtually all of these, as well as untold numbers of contacts to whom the HIV is spread, will eventually develop AIDS.

From 1981 through 1990, over 100,000 AIDS related deaths were reported to the U.S. Centers for Disease Control with approximately one-third of these deaths reported during 1990 alone (Centers for Disease Control, 1991). During the next two years, it is estimated that approximately 200,000 North Americans will die of AIDS (Centers for Disease Control, 1991). These data are particularly significant in relation to understanding the potential seriousness of the increased prevalence of HIV infection and AIDS among inmates in correctional institutions over this decade, if effective prevention and intervention strategies are not developed and implemented.

HIV Infection and AIDS in Correctional Institutions

Prisons have been noted as being fairly effective barriers to the unscheduled egress of inmates, but they are entirely ineffective in terms of preventing the entrance, exit and spread of HIV infection and AIDS. In fact, cases of AIDS have been reported in prison systems throughout western Europe and North America since the mid 1980s (Brewer, Vlahov, Taylor, Hall, Munoz and Polk, 1988; Coates, 1991; Falkenrodt, Schwartz, North, Schwartz, Weill, Schmitthauesler, Hun, Malgras and Mayer, 1984; Goldsmith, 1987) and reported seroprevalence rates are extremely high. For example, among inmates in several different Spanish prisons, the overall seroprevalence rate has been reported at 66.8 per cent (de Guevara, 1989; Estebanez, Colomo Gomez, Zunzunegui Pastor, Rua Figueroa, Perez, Ortiz, Heras and Babin, 1990); drug addicted inmates in Sardinia (Italy) reportedly have a HIV seropositive rate of fifty-five per cent (Cherchi, Mura, Calia, Gakis, Ginanneschi, Zara, Flumene, and Andreoni, 1987; and an incidence rate of forty per cent HIV seropositive has been reported from a study of delinquent drug abusing girls in Germany (Paschelke, Altvater-Kremer, Meyer, and Kremer, 1987). Prisons are now considered as high risk areas for the spread of HIV infection and AIDS (Pagliaro, 1991a).

A lack of uniform regulations for testing of inmates in prisons (e.g., inmates in U.S. federal facilities may undergo mandatory HIV testing, while inmates in Canadian federal facilities are not subject to mandatory HIV testing) makes it difficult to obtain baseline statistics regarding the percentage of inmates who are currently HIV seropositive in North America. Some data, however, are available for correctional institutions in North America. A study (Vlahov, Munoz, Brewer, Taylor, Canner and Polk, 1990) performed in the State of Maryland indicated that approximately 7.9 per cent of over 5,000 consecutive incoming male inmates were confirmed HIV seropositive. A Canadian study from the Province of Quebec (Hankins, Gendron, Richard, and O'Shaughnessy, 1989) found a similar incidence (i.e., 7.7 per cent) of HIV seropositive results among women inmates at a medium security prison. Other reports range from less than one per cent to ten per cent HIV seropositive rate among inmates (see Table 1). No data were found regarding the reported incidence among inmates in Mexican prisons.

Currently, AIDS is the leading cause of death among inmates in many correctional institutions, including those in New York (Morse, Truman, Hanrahan, Mikl, Broaddus, Maguire, Grabau, Kain-Hyde, Han and Lawrence, 1990) and Maryland (Vlahov, Brewer, Munoz, Hall, Taylor and

Polk, 1989). Because of the high incidence of HIV seropositive status among inmates (in comparison with the general population) and because of the factors that tend to foster the transmission of HIV in prisons, it is expected that AIDS will be the leading cause of inmate death across North America by the end of this decade.

The currently observed rates of the incidence of HIV seropositive status among inmates, alarming as they may seem, are probably only a prelude of what can be expected in North America by the end of this decade. This expectation is based upon two things: 1) an assumption that no significant progress will be made in relation to finding a preventive vaccine or effective treatment for the cure of AIDS during this decade; and 2) the reported HIV seropositive rates among inmates in various European prisons.

Table 1. Reported Incidence of HIV Seropositive Status Among Inmates in Various Correctional Jurisdictions in North America.

Incidence	Jurisdiction	Reference
less than 1 per cent	Iowa	Glass, Hausler, Loeffelholz and Yesalis, 1988
less than 1 per cent	Wisconsin	Hoxie, Vergeront, Frisby, Pfister, Golubjatnikov and Davis, 1990
1.2 per cent	Oregon	Andrus, Fleming, Knox, McAlister, Skeels, Conrad, Horan and Foster, 1989
2.4 per cent	Nevada	Hotsburgh, Jarvis, McArthur, Ignacio and Stock, 1990
4.1 per cent	Philadelphia	van de Beck, 1990
7.7 per cent	Quebec	Hankins, Gendron, Richard and O'Shaughnessy, 1989
7.9 per cent	Maryland	Vlahov, Munoz, Brewer, Taylor, Canner and Polk, 1990
8.0 per cent	Rhode Island	Dixon, DeBuono, Carpenter, Laurie, Zinner and Scott, 1990

The alarmingly high rates of HIV seropositivity in correctional institutions for both men and women is related to several factors, particularly the common behaviours observed among inmates that have been determined to be high risk in relation to HIV infection and AIDS (see Table 2). Inmates generally engage in a greater number of these high risk behaviours and engage in these behaviours (e.g., anal intercourse, needle sharing) more frequently than do members of the general population (Pagliaro, 1991b). In addition, because they engage in many of these behaviours while confined within prisons, in which they interact with a limited population that is itself at high risk for HIV infection and AIDS, their risk becomes compounded.

It should also be noted that even though anal intercourse has been the major mode of HIV transmission worldwide to date, currently in North America (Pagliaro, Pagliaro, Thauberger, Hewitt and Reddon, 1990), and Europe (de Guevara, 1989; Papaevangelou, Roumeliotou, Kotsianopoulou and Trichopoulou, 1990), the greatest percentage of new cases of AIDS are due to sharing of HIV contaminated needles and syringes. Thus, even though homosexual activity among male prison inmates, including situational homosexuality, is a significant, widely-recognized behaviour pattern in prisons, it is not the major risk factor for the spread of AIDS in prisons (Morse, Truman, Mikl, Smith, Broaddus and Maguire, 1989; Vlahov et al., 1989). In fact, higher rates of the incidence of HIV seropositive status are usually found among female, as compared to male, inmates (Dixon, DeBuono, Carpenter, Laurie, Zinner and Scott, 1990; Hotsburgh, Jarvis, McArthur, Ignacio and Stock, 1990).

Table 2. Risk Factors for HIV Infection and AIDS.[1]

Needle Sharing
Anal Intercourse
Tattooing
History of Multiple Sexual Partners
History of Multiple Sexually Transmitted Disease
Poor Physical and/or Mental Health
Risk Taking Personality/Behaviour

1   The HIV infection risk factors are listed in this table in their approximate order of importance.

There are several reasons for these observations. Pagliaro, Pagliaro, Thauberger, Hewitt, and Reddon (in press) reported, for a sample of over one hundred intravenous drug users in the Province of Alberta who were incarcerated at the time of their individual structured interviews, that: 1) the most frequently reported "usual occupation" for adolescent girls and women while on the "outside" was prostitution, which typically involved unprotected sexual contact with multiple clients; and 2) the overwhelming majority of inmates, both men and women, routinely shared previously used needles and syringes.

The issue of HIV transmission and AIDS in prisons is further compounded by inmates. These problems include: lack of adequate, unbiased and scientifically/medically correct information for both inmates and correctional staff regarding the prevention and transmission of HIV infection; prejudices in relation to homosexual and needle use behaviours; vested interest of the different divisions and branches of the administrative structures within correctional systems; inadequate counselling programs for inmates and correctional staff; lack of adequately defined and evaluated administrative and health related protocols and procedures in relation to the prevention and control of HIV infection and AIDS; and general fear of inmates and correctional staff regarding contracting AIDS.

In addition, the prolonged incubation period of HIV infection prior to developing into full-blown AIDS and the increased medical effectiveness in dealing with the infectious complications of AIDS (e.g., pneumonias, fungal infections) have contributed to the increasing co-incidence of HIV seropositive status, or AIDS, and other infectious conditions, particularly hepatitis and tuberculosis, among prison inmates (Benezech, Rager and Beylot, 1987; Braun, Truman, Maguire, Di Ferdinando, Wormser, Broaddus and Morse, 1989; Espinoza, Bouchard, Buffet, Thiers, Pillot and Etienne, 1987; Fackelmann, 1989; Morse, Truman, Braun, Di Ferdinando, Maguire and Broaddus, 1989; Salive, Vlahov and Brewer, 1990). The spread of AIDS-related medical conditions, particularly tuberculosis and hepatitis, both of which are themselves communicable diseases, poses additional concerns and reasons for addressing the issue of HIV infection and AIDS in prisons.

Strategies for Prevention and Control

In an attempt to begin dealing with the increasingly serious issue of HIV infection and AIDS in prisons, several correctional facilities in the United States have begun to implement a number of strategies (Dubler and Sidel,

1989; Olivero and Roberts, 1989), including:

(1)   mandatory HIV testing of inmates;
(2)   segregation (quarantine of HIV positive inmates);
(3)   denial of inmate conjugal visits;
(4)   denial of early paroles for HIV positive inmates; and
(5)   provision for condoms to inmates.

Each of these strategies will be briefly discussed.

Mandatory Testing

Testing for HIV seropositive status is accomplished by an indirect measure that actually tests serum for immune antibodies that develop in response to HIV infection. This test, although very specific, is not completely satisfactory because the human immune system generally requires one to three months, after exposure to HIV, to develop a sufficient quantity of antibodies to be detected by the test (Blumberg, 1990; Sandler, Dodd and Fang, 1988). There is, therefore, a period of time during which people are capable of transmitting the HIV virus to others, even though their HIV test results may be negative (Blumberg, 1990; Hotsburgh *et al.*, 1990). Thus, inmates would need to be tested once and then retested after a three month *totally* risk-free period in order to be able to assert with any significant degree of confidence that they were or were not HIV seropositive. Currently, the Canadian Federal Government deems mandatory testing of inmates incarcerated in Canadian correctional facilities "unwarranted" (Health and Welfare Canada, 1989).

Segregation

Segregation or medical quarantine of HIV seropositive inmates from the general inmate population has been put into effect in several prison systems. However, segregation and quarantine are options that significantly restrict fundamental individual rights and must therefore be undertaken, even in prison (e.g., protective custody, solitary confinement), only after careful consideration is given to the rights of the individual inmate versus potential risks and benefits to others. Even then, the question arises, "Who should be segregated?" (i.e., any inmates testing HIV seropositive, or with AIDS who are "irresponsible" in their behaviour and thus pose a significant risk of transmission of HIV to others). Denial of conjugal visits and consideration of early parole for HIV seropositive inmates are other examples of segregation that have been implemented in some prisons, but which require careful individual consideration. In addition to concerns regarding human rights, segregation or quarantine also raises concerns of feasibility in relation to the physical space, staffing patterns and financial resources involved in such decisions.

Provision of Condoms

As previously noted, a significant amount of homosexual activity occurs among male inmates in correctional institutions (Nacci and Kane, 1983; Wooden and Parker, 1982). Because anal intercourse is commonly recognized as the highest-risk sexual practice in relation to the transmission of HIV infection (Glasel, 1988; Winkelstein, Padian, Rutherford and Jaffe, 1989), most AIDS prevention programs, including several in prisons, have recommended the provision of condoms to inmates in an attempt to decrease the risk of HIV transmission (Greig, 1987). However, a number of problems have been noted in relation to the effectiveness of condom use in relation to the prevention of HIV transmission. These problems include breakage and slippage during sexual intercourse and lack of compliance with use (Fischl, 1988).

Provision of Sterile Injection Equipment

The provision of sterile needles and syringes to injection drug users is based on the philosophy of harm minimization (Hart, Woodward and Carvell, 1989). This strategy, although widely implemented in Europe, has been both advocated and opposed amid much debate in North America (McConnell, 1988; O'Brien, 1989). While several needle/syringe exchange programs have been implemented in high-risk community settings (e.g., inner cities) across the United States and Canada, including San Francisco, New York, Vancouver, Edmonton, Toronto and Montreal with some preliminary promising results (Fournis, 1991), conclusive data regarding the effectiveness of this strategy are not as yet readily available.

The provision of sterile injection equipment to inmates in correctional institutions in an effort to control HIV transmission has not been attempted, not even suggested in the literature. Injection drug use, however, is routinely practiced in prison settings and administrators must not continue to ignore this serious behaviour that is currently considered to be the highest risk behaviour associated with the transmission of HIV infection (Pagliaro, 1991b; Pagliaro *et al.*, 1990). Serious thought must be given to implementing research-based programs aimed at decreasing injection drug use in prisons together with the possible consideration of interim provision of sterile needles and syringes to inmates who inject drugs. The simple denial of the problem of injection drug use within correctional institutions will likely result in increased sharing of HIV contaminated injection equipment among inmates and the resultant increased spread of HIV infection.

Summary

Current and future concerns regarding HIV infection and AIDS in correctional institutions have been posed, and several strategies (e.g., HIV testing, segregation of HIV seropositive inmates, provision of condoms to inmates) that have already been implemented in some correctional facilities, in an effort to address the control of HIV infection and AIDS in prisons, have been briefly described. These strategies, as discussed, are far from being definitive solutions to the problem of HIV infection and AIDS in prisons. In fact, as noted by Harding (1987):

> A survey carried out in 17 countries on behalf of the Council of Europe shows how prison doctors and administrations have reacted to the AIDS epidemic in ways that are not always scientifically and ethically sound.

Attention must be given by correctional administrations to each of the major issues now confronting their institutions in relation to HIV infection and AIDS (see Table 3). At a minimum, it is recommended that the following four needs be addressed and that related strategies and programs be appropriately developed and implemented:

(1)   the need for unbiased and factually correct information concerning HIV infection and AIDS for both inmates and correctional staff;

(2)   the need for scientifically and ethically sound protocols effectively toprevent, or at least minimize, the spread of HIV infection in correctional institutions;

(3)   the need for psychological counselling for both inmates and correctional staff, and their families, to deal with both the fear of becoming HIV seropositive and the issue of coping with AIDS in the event that is diagnosed; and

(4)   the need for scientifically and ethically sound protocols effectively to meet the health care and living/work requirements of inmates and correctional staff who are HIV positive or who have AIDS.

Table 3. Issues related to HIV infection and AIDS in Prisons.

1.   Do a significant number of inmates test seropositive for HIV?
2.   Is HIV being transmitted in prisons from one inmate to another?
3.   Is there significant risk of HIV transmission from an HIV seropositive inmate to correctional staff?
4.   Should HIV screening be mandatory for all inmates?
5.   Should HIV screening be mandatory for all correctional staff?
6.   Should HIV seropositive inmates be segregated from the general population of inmates?
7.   Should HIV seropositive correctional staff be segregated from direct inmate contact (i.e., should job or workplace restrictions be placed on correctional service staff who test HIV seropositive or who have AIDS)?
8.   Who should have access to information about inmate HIV status (e.g., prison health care staff, guards, other inmates living in the same unit or cell)?
9.   Who should have access to information about correctional staff HIV status (e.g., administrators, health care staff, other correctional staff, inmates)?
10. Should condoms be distributed and otherwise made generally available to inmates?
11. Should sterile needles and syringes be distributed and made generally available to inmates?
12. Should HIV seropositive inmates have limited access to selected workplace settings (e.g., kitchen, medical unit)?
13. Should HIV seropositive inmates be denied conjugal visits?
14. Should HIV seronegative inmates be denied conjugal visits to decrease risk of introducing HIV infection into prisons from contact with their partner(s) who themselves may be HIV seropositive or at risk for contracting HIV (e.g., practicing prostitute, injection drug user)?
15. Should HIV seropositive inmates be denied early parole?
16. Should inmates who are dying of AIDS be granted early parole or release?
17. Taking into consideration such concerns as cost, feasibility and effectiveness, what role should universal precautions play in correctional institutions?

HIV infection and AIDS have become an integral and constantly increasing part of prison life (World Health Organization, 1990). Because AIDS is an invariably fatal disease and because the spread of HIV infection and AIDS among prison populations is expected significantly to increase during this present decade, appropriate prevention and control strategies must be implemented at every correctional institution. To ignore this problem would be negligent in that ultimately the result would be a death sentence for numerous inmates and for a relatively small but significant number of correctional staff who will become HIV seropositive as a result of exposure within the correctional system

References

Andrus, J.K., D.W. Fleming, C. Knox, R.O. McAlister, M.R. Skeels, R.E. Conrad, J.M. Horan and L.R. Foster. 1989. "HIV Testing in Prisoners: Is Mandatory Testing Mandatory?" *American Journal of Public Health.* 79:840-842.

Benezech, M., P. Rager, and J. Beylot. 1987. "Sida et hépatite B dans la population carcérale; une réalité épidémiologique incontournable" ["AIDS and Hepatitis B in the Prison Population: An Unavoidable Epidemiologic Reality"]. *Bulletin de l'Académie Nationale de Médecine.* 171(2):215-218.

Berkelman, R.L., and J.W. Curran. 1989. "Epidemiology of HIV Infection and AIDS." *Epidemiologic Reviews.* 11:222-238.

Blumberg, M. 1990. *AIDS: The Impact on the Criminal Justice System.* Columbus, Ohio: Merrill Publishing Company.

Braun, M.M., B. Maguire, G.T. DiFerdinando, G. Wormser, R. Broaddus and D.L. Morse. 1989. "Increasing Incidence of Tuberculosis in a Prison Inmate Population: Association with HIV Infection." *Journal of the American Medical Association.* 261:393-397.

Brewer, T.F., D. Vlahov, D. Hall, A. Munoz and B.F. Polk. 1988. "Transmission of HIV-1 Within a Statewide Prison System." *AIDS.* 2:363-367.

Centers for Disease Control. 1987. "Human Immunodeficiency Virus Infection in the United States." *Morbidity and Mortality Weekly Report.* 36:804.

Centers for Disease Control. 1991. "Mortality Attributable to HIV Infection/AIDS." *Morbidity and Mortality Weekly Report.* 40:41-44.

Cherchi, G.B., M.S. Mura, M.G. Calia, G. Gakis, R. Ginanneschi, G.M. Zara, A. Flumene and G. Andreoni. 1987. "L'inferzione da HIV nella Sardegna nord occidentale." *Bollettino dell Istituto Sieroterapico Milanese.* 66:448-452.

Coates, L. 1991. "Coming to Grips with Substance Abuse in the Federal Prison System." *CCSA Action.* 2:6-9.

de Guevara, J.L. 1989. "HIV-1, HIV-2, HTLV-a in Spanish Inmates." *AIDS* 3:320-321.

Dixon, P., B. DeBuono, C. Carpenter, J. Laurie, S. Zinner and H. Scott. 1990. "A Comprehensive Program of Health Care for HIV-infected Prisoners." *International Conference on AIDS.* 6(1):349 (abstract).

Dubler, N.N. and V.W. Sidel. 1989. "On Research on HIV Infection and AIDS in Correctional Institutions." *The Milbank Quarterly.* 67:171-207.

Espinoza, P., I. Bouchard, C. Buffet, V. Thiers, J. Pillot and J.P. Etienne. 1987. "Forte prévalence de l'infection par le virus de l'hépatite B et le virus HIV chez les toxicomanes français incarcérés." *Gastroentérologie Clinique et Biologique.* 11(4)288-292.

Estebanez, P., C. Colomo Gomez, M.V. Zunzunegui Pastor, M. Rua Figueroa, M. Perez, C. Ortiz, P. Heras and F. Babin. 1990. "Carceles y SIDA. Factores de riesgo de infeccion por el VIII en las carceles de Madrid." *Gaceta Sanitaria.* 4(18):100-105.

Fackelman, K.A. 1989. "Early AZT Use Slows Progression to AIDS." *Science News.* 136:135.

Falkenrodt. A., G. Schwartz, M.L., North, M. Schwartz, D. Weill, R. Schmitthauesler, H. Hun, J. Malgras and S. Mayer. 1984. "Exploration biologiques et recherches de deficits immunitaires chez les donneurs de sang en milieu carcéral." *Revue Française de Transfusion et Immuno-Hématologic.* 27(4):525-529.

Fischl, M.A. 1988. "Prevention of Transmission of AIDS During Sexual Intercourse" in DeVita V.T. Jr., S. Hellman and S.A. Rosenberg (eds.), *AIDS: Etiology, Diagnosis, Treatment, and Prevention.* 2nd ed. Philadelphia, PA: J.B. Lippincott.

Fournis, K. 1991. "Montreal AIDS/IV-use Hot spot." *The Journal.* April 1:1.

Glasel, M. 1988. "High-risk Sexual Practices in the Transmission of AIDS" in DeVita, V.T. Jr., S. Hellman and S.A. Rosenberg (eds.), *AIDS: Etiology, Diagnosis, Treatment, and Prevention* 2nd ed. Philadelphia, PA: J.B. Lippincott.

Glass, G.E., W.D. Hausler, P.L. Loeffelholz, and C.E. Yesalis. 1988. "Seroprevalence of HIV Antibody Among Individuals Entering the Iowa Prison System." *American Journal of Public Health.* 78:447-449.

Goldsmith, H.F. 1987. "Inescapable Problem: AIDS in Prison [News]." *Journal of the American Medical Association.* 258(22):3215.

Greig, J.D., 1987. "AIDS: What Every Responsible Canadian Should Know." Ottawa, Canadian Public Health Association.

Hankins, C., S. Gendron, C. Richard and M. O'Shaughnessy. 1989. "HIV Infection in a Medium Security Prison for Women — Quebec." *Canadian Diseases Weekly Report.* 15:168-170.

Harding, T.W. 1987. "AIDS in Prison." *Lancet.* 2(8570):1260-1263.

Hart, G., N. Woodward and A. Carvell. 1989. "Needle-exchange in Central London: Operating Philosophy and Communication Strategies." *AIDS Care.* 1(2):125-134.

Health and Welfare Canada. 1989. "Human Immunodeficiency Virus Antibody Testing in Canada." *Canada Diseases Weekly Report.* 15:37-43.

Hotsburgh, C.R., J.Q. Jarvis, T. McArthur, T. Ignacio and P. Stock. 1990. "Seroconversion to Human Immunodeficiency Virus in Prison Inmates." *American Journal of Public Health.* 80:209-210.

Hoxie, N.J., J.M. Vergeront, H.R. Frisby, J.R. Pfister, R. Golubjatnikov and J.I. Davis. 1990. "HIV Seroprevalence and the Acceptance of Voluntary HIV Testing Among Newly Incarcerated Male Prison Inmates in Wisconsin." *American Journal of Public Health.* 80:11290-1131.

McConnell, H. 1988. "Scientists Back Needle Exchange." *The Journal.* August 1:1.

Morse, D., B. Truman, M. Braun, G. DiFerdinando, B. Maguire and R. Broaddus. 1989. "Increasing Tuberculosis in Association with AIDS/HIV Among New York State Prison Inmates." *International Conference on AIDS.* 5:82 (abstract).

Morse, D.I., B.I. Truman, J.P. Hanrahan, J. Mikl, R.K. Broaddus, B.H. Maguire, J.C. Grabau, S. Kain-Hyde, Y. Han and C.E. Lawrence. 1990. "AIDS Behind Bars. Epidemiology of New York State Prison Inmate Cases, 1980-1988." *New York State Journal of Medicine.* 90(3):133-138.

Morse, D., B. Truman, J. Mikl, P. Smith, R. Broaddus and B. Maguire. 1989. "The Epidemiology of AIDS Among New York State Prison Inmates." *International Conference on AIDS.* 5:761 (abstract).

Nacci, P.I., and T.R. Kane. 1983. "The Incidence of Sex and Sexual Aggression in Federal Prisons." *Federal Probation.* 47(4):31-36.

O'Brien, M. 1989. "Needle Exchange Programs: Ethical and Policy Issues." *AIDS and Public Policy Journal.* 4(2):75-82.

Olivero, J.M., and J.B. Roberts. 1989. "The Management of AIDS in Correctional Facilities: A View From the Federal Court System." *The Prison Journal.* 69(2):7-17.

Orenstein, M. 1989. *AIDS in Canada: Knowledge, Behaviour, and Attitudes of Adults.* Toronto, University of Toronto Press.

Pagliaro, L.A. 1991a. "The Straight Dope: Focus on Prisons." *Synopsis.* 13:8.

Pagliaro, L.A. 1991b. "The Straight Dope on HIV Infection and AIDS in Prisons." Paper presented at a symposium conducted at the meeting of the Alberta Solicitor General Provincial Corrections Conference, Edmonton, Alberta.

Pagliaro, A.M., L.A Pagliaro, P.C. Thauberger, D.S., Hewitt and J.R. Reddon. 1990. "Knowledge and Behaviours of Intravenous Drug Users in Relation to HIV Infection and AIDS: The PIARG Pilot Study." *Medical Pharmacotherapy: An International Journal.*

Pagliaro, A.M., L.A. Pagliaro, P.C. Thauberger, D.S. Hewitt and J.R. Reddon. 1990. "AIDS and Injection Drug Use: Changing Dimensions of the Epidemic." *Alberta Psychology.* 19(5):5-7.

Papaevangelou, G., A. Roumeliotou, M. Kotsianopoulou and E. Trichopoulou. 1990. "Prevalence of HIV Infection in Imprisoned Injecting Drug Users. An Eight Year Study." *International Conference on AIDS.* 6(2):237 (abstract).

Paschelke, G., G. Altvater-Kremer, W.D. Meyer and H. Kremer. 1987. "HTLV-III Antibody Prevalence Among Young Delinquent Drug Abusers in Long-term Residential Treatment at a North-German Drug Clinic." *Klinische Wochenschrift.* 65(1):22-26.

Salive, M.W., D. Vlahov and T.F. Brewer. 1990. "Coinfection with Tuberculosis and HIV-I in Male Prison Inmates." *Public Health Reports.* 105:307-310.

Sandler, S.G., R.Y. Dodd and C.T. Fang. 1988. "Diagnostic Tests for HIV Infection: Serology" in DeVita, V.T. Jr., S. Hellman, and S.A. Rosenberg (eds.), *AIDS: Etiology, Diagnosis, Treatment, and Prevention.* 2nd ed. Philadelphia, PA: J.B. Lippincott.

van de Beck, M.L. 1990. "Provision of HIV Related Services to Persons Entering the Philadelphia Prison." *International Conference on AIDS.* 6(1):349 (abstract).

Vlahov, D., F. Brewer, A. Munoz, D. Hall, E. Taylor and B.F. Polk. 1989. "Temporal Trends of Human Immunodeficiency Virus Type 1 (HIV-1) Infection Among Inmates Entering a Statewide Prison System, 1985-1987." *Journal of Acquired Immune Deficiency Syndrome.* 2(3):283-290.

Vlahov, D., A. Munoz, F. Brewer, E. Taylor, C. Canner and B.F. Polk. 1990. "Seasonal and Annual Variation of Antibody to HIV-1 Among Male Inmates Entering Maryland Prisons: Update." *AIDS.* 4:345-350.

Winkelstein, Jr. W., N.S. Padian, G. Rutherford and H.W. Jaffe. 1989. "Homosexual Men" in Kaslow, R.A. and D.P. Francis (eds.), *The Epidemiology of AIDS — Expression, Occurrence, and Control of Human Immunodeficiency Virus Type 1 Infection.* New York, NY: Oxford University.

Wooden, W.S., and J. Parker. 1982. *Men Behind Bars: Sexual Exploitation in Prison.* New York, NY: Plenum.

World Health Organization. 1990. *Drug Abusers in Prisons: Managing Their Health Problems.* Copenhagen: World Health Organization.

Working in a Man's World: Women Correctional Officers in an Institution for Men[1]

E. Szockyj

Introduction

During the 1970s and 1980s, the federal and provincial governments introduced women correctional officers into prisons for men. The integration movement was the product of affirmative action and equal employment policies. Prior to this shift in policy, women had been excluded from the entry level correctional officer positions and, since corrections has adopted the tradition of selecting from within its institutional ranks for promotions, women had been, to a large extent, deprived of a major employment avenue.

Although females have shown their competence at handling female and youthful prisoners, a population of adult men presents a myriad of questions. There are some perceived drawbacks to employing women on an equal basis with men; for the most part, these involve issues of inmate rights to privacy[7, 24, 25] and the physical abilities of the female correctional officers.[4, 9, 12, 14, 16] Yet, in Canada, minimal attention has been paid to the receptivity of the institutional organization and co-workers to the presence of women or their effectiveness in the performance of correctional duties.[2]

Method

Between June and October 1985 the experiences and perceptions of the staff and prisoners at a provincial pre-trial centre in western Canada was solicited. The highly sophisticated complex, housing up to 150 prisoners, affords added privacy for the inmates. A random sample consisting of prisoners, male correctional officers and supervisors was selected to complete the questionnaire[3] and interview. Subsequently, the questionnaire was distributed to the remaining population. Since the responses between the randomly chosen participants and the rest of the population were comparable, the items were collapsed for analysis. The entire population of nine actively employed female correctional officers participated in both the interview and questionnaire portion of the study.

Discussion

The major findings of the study, based on the responses of the male and female officers, supervisors and prisoners, reveal an overall picture that is consistent with the results from similar studies in other countries. Various dimensions regarding the employment of females are assessed under the following subheadings: interactive abilities, physical abilities, protective attitudes, acceptance of female officers and privacy concerns.

Interactive Abilities

It was found that the presence of female officers contributed to a more relaxed, calm environment as well as an increase in morale. In the discussions, most of the females felt that the approach women used was more "laid back"; women did not have a "macho" or abrasive attitude.[17] It was stated by many of the females that inmates handled themselves differently in a female's presence and were less prone to violence because they had nothing to prove to a woman. A male officer confirmed this by stating:

> The effect they [female officers] have on the
> prisoners is that they are more subdued. They
> don't become as agitated. It seems they have
> more of a calming effect naturally, rather than
> if it was a male they wouldn't think twice of
> flipping out or whatever. If it's a female they
> seem to hold it back.

A number of the prisoners said they responded to orders by females quicker with less retaliation.[16] For example, one inmate stated:

> They're glad to do it if a female says some-
> thing.... Women can tell an inmate to do
> something and most of the time they don't
> mind. They do things quicker for women.

> The job is easier for them. Men have more
> hassles.

Thus, prisoners gave female correctional officers fewer problems and they appeared to be more responsive to them.

The vast majority had a positive image of the female officer's interactive abilities because, as one inmate said, "they sit down and talk to you like people, with respect, and the males treat you like shit." Another prisoner commented:

> It's more than a job for women. Some males
> put in their hours and then get out. But the
> women are interested in you and what you're
> feeling and how things are going with you.
> They're more feeling. You need to know that
> someone's interested in your welfare.

Some of the women felt that they tend to be more sensitive to the needs of inmates. As one female officer stated, "Little things are important to us like getting a visit or special phone call or family pictures brought in — women see that is important to prisoners. A lot of men let it go." A large number of prisoners noticed this difference in atmosphere as well. Moreover, the attentiveness and thoroughness that the female officers exhibited may pay off in other ways. For instance, a supervisor claims that:

> I've got my best leads on contraband in units
> and breaking up cliques that are in units from
> one or two female staff that work here.

The ability to defuse potentially violent behaviour is a beneficial skill in this setting. All the respondent groups felt that women were equally or more effective in "cooling down" an angry prisoner.[15, 18] In the interviews, the females indicated that women tend to rely on their communication skills to a greater extent than men.[10, 15, 18] As one officer said:

> Men are more aggressive to begin with;
> women are pacifiers. Men will use their fists;
> women will use their tongues. They'll use their
> heads to talk themselves out of a situation.

Although many male correctional officers mentioned in the interviews that the women generally did have better interpersonal skills, a few saw this as creating problems or difficulties for the male staff who take over a unit from a female officer since they do not have the same relationship with the prisoners.

Physical Abilities

There was a tendency for male correctional officers, supervisors and prisoners to rate men as more effective in dealing with situations which may require physical strength. The women correctional officers, though, believed that they were just as effective in handling such situations.[5, 15] The ability of female officers to cool out or calm prisoners and their more positive relationship with prisoners may explain why more of the respondents felt they were just as effective in controlling or separating prisoners. Although females, in the interviews, admitted that men were physically superior to women they did not believe this fact speaks deleteriously for their own performance. It was felt that women were new to corrections and lacked the experience of physically subduing inmates or even physically fighting in general. As a result, men may be better in a one-to-one situation but, it was stated by some female officers and supervisors, brute force was rarely required.[7, 8] All officers, male and female, received the same training; it was the competence and ability of the individual not their sex that was important.

In relation to backup, the following feelings were expressed by the females:

> What kind of back-up is any guy going to be when the ratio is seventeen prisoners against two.

> It doesn't matter who your partner is, because they're not allowed to move by themselves to help you anyway. Either way you're looking at a whole group of people. So I don't think it really matters.

The females were not worried about working with other females and did not believe male officers were justified in any concerns they might put forth. One inmate reflected on the situation as follows:

> Guards don't step into a fight when there's inmates fighting. They don't step into it alone. All they do is push a button. Both can do that equally well.

But most of the prisoners interviewed felt that female correctional officers lacked the physical strength in a fight situation. This was perceived as one of the few disadvantages to their employment.

One male officer commented:

> I think the biggest question that we had when we first opened was would they [female officers] be able to back us up in a situation where it was warranted. I think that was the biggest concern at the time, but since then it's no longer the question or issue because we've had situations where the backup was a women; it was handled quite good. So I can't believe that it's much of a worry anymore.

Nevertheless, in the discussion, the majority of male officers expressed a preference for male backup in a violent situation. A number of officers cited as reasons the feeling that either most females are simply not as physically capable as some of the men, or, those who indicated that the females could handle such occurrences, that an instinctive or protective attitude to females in general prevailed. Less than one-third of the males interviewed stated that they were comfortable with female backup.

Protective Attitudes

It was generally stated by all the women that inmates were more protective of female officers than males in the sense that striking a female was frowned upon by the prisoners. It seemed to be almost an unwritten law that "you do not hit a female" and if an inmate did "his name would be mud." A female officer confided that:

> One inmate had me literally pinned against the wall and I talked my way out of it. A few of the inmates came to me and said "we would not have let him touch you."

Whether this would be true in a riot situation was debated but in a normal setting the women felt they had an advantage.

The prisoners confirmed this assessment in the interviews. Not only did they feel inmates were more likely to help a female correctional officer in trouble but they were also apprehensive about taking physical action against females.[12, 15, 19] The male officers, on the other hand, were divided on this issue. Some thought that inmates would be slightly more inclined to protect female correctional officers whereas others stated that prisoners would treat both male and female staff alike with respect to protecting them in dangerous situations.

Initially, there seemed to be evidence of protective behaviour on the part of the staff,[5, 8, 11,12, 15, 7, 9] especially from the older officers. In the interviews, a few male staff felt that some males were more likely to put themselves in a precarious situation to aid or protect a female. Others said that they simply did a few extra checks if a female was working with them. And still others stated that there was generally no difference in their treatment. As one male reflected:

> If there's a code yellow on a female unit, then the officers' response is no quicker and no more efficient, but is more fervoured.

The women reported that male officers felt there was favouritism because females were stationed in "easier" units or received more attention. The women countered this by saying that some men were also given preferential treatment. One female stated that in emergency situations there did not appear to be a difference in gender, rather:

> As far as the riots and code yellows go, they'll do that [demonstrate protective behaviour] with the guys as well. They'll pick somebody who's...a big strapping guy known for his roughness over a guy who's maybe not like that. So I don't necessarily know if it's just because they're female. They pick and choose who they want anyhow regardless of what sex.

The women wanted to perform the job on the same terms as men. A representative response was:

> I don't want to be treated any differently. I don't want any favouritism. I want to find out if I can do it myself. How else are we going to build our own self-confidence up?

By the initiative of the females, male favourtism appeared to have declined considerably at this facility. Still, some males felt it existed. They argued that the females hired tended to be more outgoing and received more attention from the male officers and supervisors.

Privacy Concerns

All of the females and most of the male correctional officers and prisoners interviewed thought inmates have enough privacy and did not believe it was an issue for the prisoners.[8, 10, 17, 19, 21, 24]   The building was designed to protect inmate privacy: the cells have a solid door rather than bars and the toilet is in an area which is not visible from outside the cell. The women indicated that they respect the privacy of the male inmates; if the door is closed they will knock before entering. The females are restricted from working in the area of the institution where incoming or outgoing prisoners are changing. Moreover, they may not perform skin search on the male prisoners. The only complaint cited by a few of the prisoners was a resentment toward females frisking them.

Acceptance of the Female Correctional Officers

On the whole, the majority of the respondents approved of female correctional officers.[15, 16, 9, 11] Yet female officers still did not feel fully accepted by their male peers. It appeared that this negative sentiment was specifically aimed at a small segment of the male staff that adhered to the "old boy" traditions. The biggest obstacle reported by most of the women was having the male officers accept them and allow them to perform the duties that the job entails.[9, 10, 13, 18]

The female officers are very sensitive about drawing attention to themselves. Many felt that they were "being watched," that their performance was singled out due to the recent entrance of women into the field and the small number employed. The comment, "When a male staff member makes a mistake then it's forgotten, but if a woman makes a mistake then it's talked about for weeks," was typical of the opinions expressed by the female officers.

Many prisoners and male officers interviewed were also aware of this. They mentioned that being recognized and treated as equals by the male staff was one of the biggest problems faced by the female correctional officers.[19] Some of the male officers went on to say that women must also perform at a higher level to prove they were just as capable of performing the job. And, in general, the perceived performance of the female officers was comparable to or better than that of their male counterparts.[6, 11, 15, 16, 19, 23]

Limitations

Only one institution was surveyed extensively. Not only was this a new provincial pre-trial facility but its modern design provided additional privacy and security benefits. Unlike other integration attempts into an existing male officer network, female correctional officers were present when the institution opened. Consequently, responses provided by its inhabitants may not be representative of those from other institutions across Canada. Furthermore, since the research site was a provincial facility it was not subject to an affirmative action program as are the federal prisons.

The results were not cross-checked using institutional records. As a result, the extent to which the perceptions of the respondents correspond to the behaviour in question is unknown. Moreover, because the principal researcher was female, this may have coloured the responses obtained. Nonetheless, answers to the questionnaires distributed to the population of male officers and prisoners were quite similar to those received in the more intimate one-to-one questionnaire/interview approach used initially. The results are also reflective of those reported by others who have researched this area (some of whom were male).

Future Research

Only the perceptions of correctional staff and prisoners were discussed; observational data and record inspection could offer alternative perspectives. For example, a researcher's observation of the interactions amongst staff and with prisoners could flesh out the fine subtleties touched upon in this study. Moreover, an analysis of institutional records could indicate whether there is a difference, based on gender, in the number of charges laid against prisoners, the types of charges laid and the outcome of the charges. Such an approach has yet to be implemented.

It appears that the role of the institution plays an integral part in the shaping of correction officers' attitudes and perceptions. The literature suggests that this is perhaps more important than gender. One study has shown that the security level of the family has an effect on the attitudes of the staff toward female officers.[32] Furthermore, Jurik and Halemba[13] and Zupan[25] expound on the similarities between male and female officers, emphasizing the influence of the job on determining behaviour and attitudes. It is therefore necessary to examine the impact of the setting on the officers.

The contrast between the provincial policy of equal employment opportunity and the federal affirmative action program needs academic attention. The provincial "merit principle" criterion of hiring and promotion requires scrutiny to ensure it does not result in discrimination against females, whereas the females hired under the affirmative action program may face resentment and devaluation of their abilities. A more intensive examination of the impact of the affirmative action program would be informative for policy analysts.

Finally, consideration needs to be given to the proportion of females at the facility. The changes in the institutional environment and the relationships and performance of staff as well as any procedural modifications made when different ratios of females are employed should be examined. It is hoped that these suggestions will plant the seeds for future endeavours.

Endnotes

1   Acknowledgements are given to the staff at the correctional facility surveyed and to C.T. Griffiths and M.A. Jackson from the School of Criminology, Simon Fraser University, British Columbia.

2   Systematic and comprehensive studies in Canada are lacking. The Human Rights Commission[7] completed an interview study soon after female correctional officers were introduced into the federal prison system, and recently Plecas and Maxim[20] have incorporated a sex factor into their longitudinal analysis of Correctional Service of Canada recruits.

3   Used by permission from the creator P.J. Kissel, Research Analyst, Bureau of Prisons, Federal Correctional Institution, Colorado and J. Seidel, Director of Computer Center, University of Colorado School of Nursing, Colorado.

4   Andersen, L. 1978. *A survey of female and male correctional officers' attitudes at the Central Detention Facility*, Washington, D.C. Washington, D.C.: D.C. Dept. of Corrections.

5   Bowersox, M.S. 1981. "Women in corrections: Competence, competition and the social responsibility norm." *Criminal Justice and Behavior*. 8(4), 491-499.

6   Breed, A.F. 1981. "Women in correctional employment." *American Correctional Association Monographs*. 1(1), 37-44.

7   Canadian Human Rights Commission. 1981. *Special employment program to integrate women into the correction officer occupational group (CX-COF and CX-LUF) in male penitentiaries*. Ottawa: Correctional Service Canada.

8   Côté, J.E., L. McCarthy and J. Lavoie. 1977. *A study of the existing sex restrictions in the correctional group CX (COF-LUF-STI)*. Ottawa: Public Service Commission.

9   Fox, J.G. 1982. *Organizational and racial conflict in maximum-security prisons*. Lexington, Massachusetts: Lexington Books.

10   Harm, N.J. 1981. "Female employees in male institutions." *American Correctional Association Monographs*. pp. 269-274.

11   Holeman, H. and B.J. Krepps-Hess. 1983. *Women correctional officers in the California Department of Corrections*. Sacramento, California: California Department of Corrections.

12   Ingram, G.L. 1981. "The role of women in male federal correctional institutions." *American Correctional Association Monographs*. pp. 275-281.

13   Jurik, N.C. and G.J. Halembra. 1984. "Gender, working conditions and the job sat-
        isfaction of women in a non-traditional occupation: Female correctional officers in
        men's prisons." *The Sociological Quarterly*. 25, 551-556.

14   Kinsell, L.W. and R.G. Sheldon. 1981. "A survey of correctional officers at a medi-
        um security prison." *Corrections Today*. pp. 40-51. January/February.

15   Kissel, P.J. and P. Katsampes. 1980. "The impact of women corrections officers on
        the functioning of institutions housing male inmates." *Journal of Offender
        Counseling, Service and Rehabilitation*. 4(3), 213-231.

16   Kissel, P.J. and J. Seidel. 1980. *The management and impact of female correc-
        tions officers at jail facilities housing male inmates*. National Institute of
        Corrections.

17   Nicholson, R. 1984. "Women's function in N.S.W. male prisons" in Hatty, S.E.,
        Women in the prison system. Canberra, A.C.T.: Australian Institute of Criminology

18   Owen, B.A. 1985. "Race and gender relations among prison workers." *Crime and
        Delinquency*. 3(1), 147-159.

19   Peterson, C. 1982. "Doing time with the boys: An analysis of women correctional
        officers in all-male facilities" in Price, B.R. and N.J Sokoloff (eds.), *The criminal jus-
        tice system and women: Women offenders, victims, workers*. New York: Clark
        Boardman Co. Ltd.

20   Plecas, D. and P. Maxim. 1985. *CSC Correctional officer development study: A
        nine-month follow-up survey of 1984 CSC recruits*. Ottawa: Correctional Service
        of Canada.

21   Pollock, J.M. 1986. *Sex and supervision: Guarding male and female inmates*.
        Westport, Connecticut: Greenwood Press.

22   Simpson, S. and M.F. White. 1985. "The female guard in the all-male prison" in
        Moyer, I.L. (ed.), *The changing roles of women in the criminal justice system:
        Offenders, victims and professionals*. Illinois: Waveland Press.

23   Women's Advisory Committee. 1978. *Recommendations resulting from the pilot
        project: Staff exchange programme for correctional officers at Vanier Centre for
        Women and Brampton Adult Training Centre*. Ontario: Ministry of Correctional
        Services.

24   Zimmer, L.E. 1982. "Female guards in men's prisons: Creating a role for them-
        selves." Doctoral dissertation, Cornell University.

25   Zupan, L.L. "Gender-related differences in correctional officers' perceptions and
        attitudes." Unpublished paper, Dept. of Political Science, Washington State
        University, undated.

The Young Offender's Act:
A Legal Framework

Nicholas Bala[1]

Since the beginning of legal history, there have been special rules for dealing with young persons who violate the law. Under English common law, the special *doli incapax* (Latin for incapacity to do wrong) defence developed. A child under the age of seven years was deemed incapable of committing a criminal act. For children between seven and thirteen years, there was a presumption of incapacity, but this could be rebutted if there was evidence to establish that the child had sufficient intelligence and experience to "know the nature and consequences of the conduct and to appreciate that it was wrong" (Criminal Code, 1970, section 13). While the *doli incapax* defence afforded certain protections to children, those children who were convicted faced the same penalties as adult offenders, including hanging and incarceration in such places as the old Kingston Penitentiary.

In the latter part of the nineteenth century, social movements that sought to promote better treatment of children developed in Britain, the United States and Canada. These movements led to such reforms as the establishment of child welfare agencies and the creation of a juvenile justice system, which had a distinct philosophy and provided facilities separate from the adult system. The reformers of this time considered their paramount objective to be saving destitute and wayward children from a life of crime and destitution. Thus they did not draw a clear distinction between neglected and criminal children. W.L. Scott, one of the principal drafters of Canada's early delinquency legislation stated that:

> there should be no hard and fast distinction between neglected and delinquent children, but...all should be dealt with with a view to serving the best interests of the child. (Archambault, 1983: 2)

The efforts of these early reformers culminated with the enactment of the Juvenile Delinquents Act (JDA) in 1908. This federal legislation provided that children were to be dealt with by a court and corrections system separate from the adult system. The JDA clearly had a child welfare, or *parens patriae* philosophy. The Latin term *parens patriae* literally means "father (or parent) of the country," but it has come to mean a philosophy of state intervention based on an assessment of a child's best interests. This philosophy was reflected in section 38 of the JDA (1908):

> ...the care and custody and discipline of a juvenile delinquent shall approximate as nearly as may be that which should be given by his parents, and...as far as practicable every juvenile delinquent shall be treated, not as a criminal, but as a misguided and misdirected child...needing aid, encouragement, help and assistance.

The Juvenile Delinquents Act created a highly discretionary system, which gave enormous power to police, judges and probation officers to do whatever they considered in a child's "best interests." There were no legislative guidelines governing judicial sentencing, and youths who were sent to training school (reformatory) were generally subject to indeterminate committals. Release from reformatory occurred when correctional officials felt that rehabilitation had been accomplished. While the system created by the JDA in 1908 marked an enormous improvement in the treatment of children and adolescents over earlier times, many serious, interrelated problems still existed, and by the 1960s juvenile justice in Canada was subject to criticism from a variety of different sources.

One major criticism of the JDA was that it created a system that tended to ignore the legal rights of children. This was true to such an extent that there were occasions when guilt seemed to be presumed so that "treatment" would not be delayed by "unnecessary formalities." In many parts of Canada, lawyers rarely, if ever, represented youths charged in Juvenile Court, and until relatively recently many of the judges in Juvenile Court lacked legal training. Thus, some critics charged that the juvenile justice system was unfair and unduly harsh with the same youths. Other critics, however, pointed out that certain judges exercised their broad powers to promote their perceptions of the best interests of children in such a way that their dispositions were too lenient and did not adequately protect society.

The substantial discretion that the JDA gave to juvenile judges and probation officers was not the only reason for criticism. The Act also vested very significant control over the system in provincial administrators. As a consequence, there were enormous disparities across Canada in how juveniles were treated (Bala and Corrado, 1985). The maximum age of juvenile jurisdiction varied from province to province, ranging from the sixteenth to the eighteenth birthday, and the minimum age varied from seven to fourteen years; children under the minimum age in each province were dealt with exclusively in the child welfare system. There were also great disparities in respect of diversion from the formal juvenile justice system, access to legal representation and use of community-based sentencing options.

The 1965 release of a report on juvenile delinquency in Canada marked the beginning of a lengthy period of debate and gradual reform (Canada, Department of Justice, 1965). Some provinces, most notably Quebec, took steps to change their juvenile justice system by, for example, ensuring that young persons had access to lawyers and establishing a formal system of juvenile diversion. Other provinces lagged behind. On a federal level, discussion papers and draft legislation were released and commented upon, but no action was taken. The constitutional entrenchment of the Canadian Charter of Rights and Freedoms in 1982 gave a greater sense of urgency to federal reform efforts. Many of the provisions of the JDA appeared to ignore the legal rights guaranteed in the Charter and the provincial disparities invited challenge under section 15 of the Charter, a provision that guaranteed Equality Rights and was scheduled to come into force in April 1985. As a result, in 1982, with the support of all political parties, the Young Offenders Act received Parliamentary approval. Most of the YOA came into force April 2, 1984. Some parts of the legislation gave rise to controversy from the moment of their initial introduction in Parliament. Most notably, a number of provinces were dissatisfied with the establishment of a minimum age jurisdiction of twelve years, and a maximum age jurisdiction running to the eighteenth birthday. The proclamation of the uniform maximum age provision was delayed until April 1, 1985, to allow all provinces sufficient time to adapt. It soon became apparent that there were a number of problems with the YOA and in 1986 some relatively minor amendments were enacted through the passage of Bill C-106. These did not alter the philosophy or basic provisions of the Act, but did facilitate implementation.

Principles of the Young Offenders Act

The YOA constitutes a clear departure from the JDA. There is a uniform national age jurisdiction of twelve through seventeen years, as of the date of the offence, and the YOA is unmistakably criminal law, not child welfare legislation. The discretion of police, judges and correctional staff is clearly circumscribed by the YOA. The only justification for state intervention under the YOA is the violation of criminal legislation, and this must be established by due process of law. Society is entitled to protection from young offenders, and young offenders are to be held accountable for their acts. However, the YOA is not simply a "Kiddies' Criminal Code." It establishes a justice and corrections system separate and distinct from the adult system, and it recognizes that young persons have special needs as compared with adults, require special legal protection and are not to be held as fully accountable as adults for their violations of the criminal law.

In section 3 of the YOA, Parliament offers an express Declaration of Principle for those responsible for the implementation of the Act.

3. *Policy for Canada with respect to young offenders.*

(1)   It is hereby recognized and declared that

(a)   while young persons should not in all instances be held accountable in the same manner or suffer the same consequences for their behaviour as adults, young persons who commit offences should nonetheless bear responsibility for their contraventions;

(b)   society must, although it has the responsibility to take reasonable measures to prevent criminal conduct by young persons, be afforded the necessary protection from illegal behaviour;

(c)   young persons who commit offences require supervision, discipline and control, but, because of their state of dependency and level of development and maturity, they also have special needs and require guidance and assistance;

(d)   where it is not inconsistent with the protection of society, taking no measures or taking measures other than judicial proceedings under this Act should be considered for dealing with young persons who have committed offences;

(e)   young persons have rights and freedoms in their own right, including those stated in the *Canadian Charter of Rights and Freedoms* or in the *Canadian Bill of Rights*, and in particular a right to be heard in the course of, and to participate in, the processes that lead to decisions that affect them, and young persons should have special guarantees of their rights and freedoms;

(f)   in the application of this Act, the rights and freedoms of young persons include a right to the least possible interference with freedom that is consistent with the protection of society, having regard to the needs of young persons and the interests of their families;

(g)   young persons have the right, in every instance where they have rights or freedoms that may be affected by this Act, to be informed as to what those rights and freedoms are; and

(h)   parents have responsibility for the care and supervision of their children, and, for that reason, young persons should be removed from parental supervision either partly or entirely only when measures that provide for continuing parental supervision are inappropriate.

Some commentators have suggested that the principles articulated in section 2 are inconsistent and hence offer no real guidance for the implementation of the YOA. One youth court judge commented that section 3 reflects, if not "...inconsistency, [then] at least ambivalence about [what] approaches should be taken with young offenders..." (Thomson, 1983: 27). It is apparent that there is a level of societal ambivalence in Canada about the appropriate response to young offenders. On the one hand there is a feeling that adolescents who violate the criminal law need help to enable them to grow into productive, law-abiding citizens; this view is frequently reflected in media stories about inadequate facilities for treating young offenders. On the other hand, there is widespread public concern about the need to control youthful criminality and protect society. This view is reflected in media stories and editorials commenting on the inadequacy of the thirty-year maximum disposition that can be applied to young offenders, a particular public concern in regard to those youths who commit very serious, violent offences.

While it is not inaccurate to suggest that the Declaration of Principle reflects a certain societal ambivalence about young offenders, it is also important to appreciate that it represents an honest attempt to achieve an appropriate balance for dealing with a very complex social problem. The YOA does not have a single, simple underlying philosophy; there is not single, simple philosophy that can deal with all situations in which young persons violate the criminal law. When contrasted with the child welfare-oriented philosophy of the JDA, the YOA emphasizes due process, the protection of society, and limited discretion. In comparison to the adult Criminal Code, however, the YOA emphasizes special needs and the limited accountability of young persons. There is a fundamental tension in the YOA between such competing ideals as due process and treatment; in some situations the Act gives precedence to due process, while in others treatment is emphasized at the expense of due process. The underlying philosophical inconsistencies and tensions in the YOA reflect the very complex nature of youthful criminality. There is no single, simple philosophy and no single type of program that will "solve" the "problem." Judges and the other professionals who work with young persons who violate the criminal law require a complex and balanced set of principles like those found in the YOA.

The balance of this chapter will be devoted to a consideration of the substantive provisions of the Young Offenders Act, with a discussion of how they reflect the principles found in section 3 of the Act and how the courts have interpreted these principles in different contexts.

Arrests and Police Questioning

In addition to those rights guaranteed to all under the Charter of Rights, the YOA affords special rights and protections to young persons who are arrested. Some of these provisions are premised on the notion that many young persons lack the maturity and sophistication fully to appreciate their situation, and hence require special legal rights; other provisions are intended to involve parents in the process, both to protect the rights of their children and to recognize their supportive role.

The Charter of Rights provides:

s. 8	Everyone has the right to be secure against unreasonable search or seizure.
s. 9	Everyone has the right not to be arbitrarily detained or imprisoned.
s. 10	Everyone has the right on arrest or detention
(a)	to be informed promptly of the reason therefor;
(b)	to retain and instruct counsel without delay and to be informed of that right; and
(c)	to have the validity of the detention determined...and to be released if it is not lawful.

The rights that are guaranteed to all under the *Charter* may be of special significance to young persons, as they are particularly prone to police supervision and even harassment in certain situations. In *R. v. Ina Christina v.* (1985: 7211) a police officer observed a 15-year-old girl chatting quietly on a street corner in a place known by the officer to have an "...almost magnetic appeal for children who have run from home, some of whom have become the so-called 'street kids' and acts as a focal point for many persons involved in prostitution and drug trafficking." The officer concluded she was either "loitering:" (not a criminal offence) "or possibly a runaway," and purported to arrest her under provincial child welfare legislation. A struggle ensued and the girl was charged with assaulting the police officer. In acquitting the girl of this charge, the judge observed:

On the basis of the evidence presented, there

is more than sufficient to find that Christina V.'s rights were infringed under ss. ...8 and 9 of the Charter and denied under para.10(b) of the Charter. In regard to the latter, although she was advised of her right to retain and instruct counsel without delay, there is no evidence that she was provided with the opportunity and means to do so. In advance of that, she was deprived of her liberty, the security of her person was invaded, her property was unjustly seized and searched and she was arbitrarily detained and imprisoned. These gross violations of her fundamental rights were totally out of proportion with the situation and prescribed nowhere by law. Even if the law had provided for such interference, it would be unreasonable to find that such was demonstrably justified in a free and democratic society....

The phenomenon of the runaway child is, in the first instance, a social problem. Left unaddressed, it too often escalates into a legal issue involving either or both child welfare authorities and law enforcement officers. The magnitude of the problem as it relates to downtown Toronto...requires an urgent response. Undoubtedly, as a result of pressure from concerned parents, politicians and business people in the area, the Metropolitan Toronto Police Department has felt obliged to provide that response. Unfortunately, the standard law enforcement approach to the problem is woefully inadequate as well as improper.

As was exhibited in this case, good faith and a sense of duty on the part of the police falls far short of adequately addressing the situation. The runaway child who has been reported missing but has not committed any criminal offence, may indeed be a child at risk. That is the issue that must be addressed first and it can only be accomplished in a competent and caring fashion by trained child care workers. (R. v. Ina Christina V., 1985: 7212)

In addition to the protections afforded under the Charter of Rights, special provisions found in section 56 of the YOA are intended to ensure that there is no improper questioning of young persons by police and other persons in authority:

s.56(2) *When statements are admissible.* —No oral or written statement given by a young person to a peace officer or other person who is, in law, a person in authority is admissible against the young person unless

(a) the statement was voluntary;

(b) the person to whom the statement was given has, before the statement was made, clearly explained to the young person, in language appropriate to his age and understanding, that

    (i) the young person is under no obligation to give a statement,

    (ii) any statement given by him may be used as evidence in proceedings against him,

    (iii) the young person has the right to consult another person in accordance with paragraph (c), and

    (iv) any statement made by the young person is required to be made in the presence of the person consulted, unless the young person desires otherwise;

(c) the young person has, before the statement was made, been given a reasonable opportunity to consult with counsel or a parent, or in the absence of a parent, an adult relative, or in the absence of a parent and an adult relative, any other appropriate adult chosen by the young person; and

(d) where the young person consults any person pursuant to paragraph (c), the young person has been given a reasonable opportunity to make the statement in the presence of that person.

Section 56 is based on the recognition that young persons may lack the sophistication and maturity to appreciate fully the legal consequences of making a statement, and so require special protection when being questioned by police. It is also premised on the notion that some youths are easily intimidated by adult authority figures, and may make statements that they believe those authority figures expect to hear, even if the statements are false. It is hoped that consultation with a parent or lawyer will preclude the making of such false statements.

Section 56 has been invoked in a number of cases by the courts to exclude statements made by young persons. In *R. v. M.A.M.* (1986) a sixteen-year-old youth with a learning disability was charged with gross indecency. The police officer who arrested the youth purported to inform him of his rights by reading from a form that recited the words used in section 56.

The young person then waived his right to have a lawyer or parent present. In ruling the statements inadmissible, the British Columbia Court of Appeal wrote:

> ...it appears...that the learned trial judge was confronted with the requirements of s.56 and concluded that having the contents of the two forms read to him, the young person did not know what to do in the circumstances and did not know why a lawyer would be necessary....
>
> In my opinion, the course followed by the police officer in the present case did not meet the requirements of s.56 of the *Young Offenders Act*. The forms themselves appear to be clear, but Parliament indicated the requirement that before the statement was made there must be a clear explanation to the young person. I am not persuaded that reading the contents of those two forms met the requirements imposed by Parliament before the statement could be taken from the young person....
>
> Parliament has paid special attention to the needs of young people for protective advice and has called on the police to provide it. There should be a genuine endeavour by the person in authority to describe the function of the lawyer and the benefits to the young person of having a lawyer, or parents, or relatives, or an adult friend present. That endeavour should be designed to lead to an appreciation on the part of the young person of the consequences of the choices that he makes.
>
> Even had this young person been a person without any learning disability, the mere reading over of these two statements and then asking the young person to sign them, without any explanation to him whatsoever, would not, in my opinion, have been compliance with ss.(2)(b) and (c) of s.56 of the *Young Offenders Act*. (R. v. M.A.M., 1986: 571, 573)

An interesting and difficult issue that has arisen in some cases is the extent to which individuals such as school teachers, principals or social workers may be "agents of the state" and hence should be expected to comply with the requirements of the Charter of Rights and section 56 of the YOA. In *R. v. H.* (1985) a thirteen-year-old boy was charged with theft and the prosecutor sought to have the court hear statements made by the youth to his teacher and the school principal. Prior to the statements being made, the teacher promised that if the money was returned, nothing further would happen. Not surprisingly, neither the teacher nor the principal complied with the Charter or section 56 of the YOA. The court ruled the statements inadmissible because of the violation of the YOA and section 10 of the Charter of Rights. *R. v. H.* does not require school personnel to afford young persons the right to counsel in all situations, but it does indicate that if this right is not afforded a youth prior to questioning, statements that are made may later be ruled inadmissible in youth court proceedings.

A somewhat different approach was taken in *R. v. J.M.G* (1986), where a fourteen-year-old boy was charged with possession of a small amount of marijuana that had been discovered by his school principal after a search of the youth. The Ontario Court of Appeal emphasized that the search was carried out in the context of the principal's normal duties of maintaining discipline in the school, and hence did not constitute a violation of the Charter of Rights. The Court recognized that while the relationship between student and principal was not like that of policeman and citizen, "there may come a time when such [significant legal] consequences are inevitable and the principal becomes an agent of the police in detecting crime" (*R. v. J.M.G.*, 1986: 712). In such a situation a school principal or teacher might be expected to comply strictly with the warning requirements of the Charter. *R. v. H.* and *R. v. J.M.G.* illustrate that the courts will closely scrutinize each situation to determine the extent to which a principal or other person would be treated as an agent of the state. It may also be significant that *R. v. J.M.G.* involved the seizure of physical evidence, which was clearly indicative of the fact that the crime in question had been committed, while *R. v. H.* only involved a statement and the YOA has special provisions in regard to statements.

Section 9 of the YOA provides that if a young person is arrested or detained, a parent must be notified "as soon as possible." A parent must also be notified in writing of any youth court hearings. If a parent is not available, notice may be given to an adult relative or other appropriate adult. The Act also allows a youth court to order that a parent attend any proceedings if such attendance is considered "necessary or in the best interest of the young person." While parents are not parties to youth court proceedings, they have a statutory right to address the court prior to disposition, disposition review or possible transfer to adult court.

Paragraph 3(1)(h) of the Declaration of Principle recognizes the role of parents in the lives of their children, and sections 9 and 56 ensure that parents have notice of arrest, detention and youth court proceedings. These provisions are premised on the notion that parents will normally provide emotional support and ensure that a youth's legal rights are protected. It should be emphasized that under section 56(2) it is the youth who has the right to decide whether or not a parent will be present during police questioning. Some youths may be unwilling to have parental involvement, and there may be cases where such involvement is clearly not appropriate. Parents will normally not be considered "persons in authority," and statements made to them by their children will usually be admissible, despite the absence of any form of caution (*R. v. A.B.*, 1986; YOA, 1982, s. 56(6)).

There may, however, be cases in which parental questioning will amount to duress, and a statement in such circumstances could be ruled inadmissible. In *R. v. S.L.* (1984), the judge felt that a father who became actively involved with the police in the questioning of his son about a suspected homicide became a "member of the investigation team." The court ruled the youth's confession inadmissible, saying:

> There is no doubt that most well-thinking parents in a situation involving the death of a youngster would be anxious to co-operate in finding the truth, but when that involves co-operating with the police and obtaining some incriminating evidence against their own child, and without being made aware of all the information that the police had against the child, it is, I feel, not a rightful situation and can constitute an abuse of the very special relationship of authority and influence that a parent has on his child. (*R. v. S.L.*, 1984: 4085)

Youths who are arrested for relatively minor charges are normally released pending a hearing, but those charged with more serious offences, with long records of convctions or who might not appear for trial, may be detained pursuant to the order of a youth court judge or a justice of the peace. The law governing pre-trial detention of young persons is generally the same as that applicable to adults, but section 7 of the YOA specifies that such detention will normally be separate from adults. The YOA allows for detention with adults only if a court is satisfied that this is necessary for the safety of the youth or others, or if the youth is in a remote location and no youth detention facilities are available within a reasonable distance.

While pre-trial detention is normally separate from adults, youths awaiting trial are often kept in the same facilities as young offenders who are serving sentences in custody.

Pre-trial detention has the potential of being extremely disruptive to a young person, as it may result in sudden removal from familiar surroundings and placement in an often intimidating, institutional environment. Such detention will usually interfere with schooling or employment, and with familial and peer relationships. To minimize such disruptions, section 7.1 of the YOA allows a youth court judge or justice of the peace to order that a young person who would normally be detained be placed under the care and control of a "responsible person"; a "responsible person" would normally be a parent or other friendly adult. This will only be done if the "responsible person" undertakes in writing to exercise control over the youth and satisfy such other conditions as may be imposed, for example ensuring that the youth refrain from consuming alcohol pending trial. A "responsible person" who "willfully fails" to comply with the undertaking may be charged with an offence under section 7.2 of the YOA.

The YOA provides in section 13 that if there is a question about a young person's mental capacity to stand trial, or if there is an application for transfer of the case to adult court, the youth court may order a medical, psychological or psychiatric assessment prior to trial. In other situations, there is no jurisdiction for a mandatory pre-trial assessment. Assessments and transfer applications are discussed more fully below.

Alternative Measures

Paragraph 3(1)(d) of the Declaration of Principle recognizes the value of "taking measures other than judicial proceedings" under the YOA. Section 4 of the YOA creates a legislative framework for "alternative measures," that is to say for dealing with young persons outside the formal youth court process.

Alternative measures are a form of diversion from the court process and are typically used for first-time offenders charged with relatively minor offences. An alternative measures program allows a youth to be dealt with in a relatively expeditious, informal fashion and enables a youth to avoid a formal record of conviction. It is felt that some youths may be unnecessarily harmed by being "labelled" as "young offenders" through the formal court process, and that they may benefit from relatively informal treatment. Use of alternative measures is also consistent with the principle of "least possible interference," which is articulated in section 2(1)(f) of the YOA. Further, alternative measures programs may increase the scope for involvement of parents, victims and the community. Such programs may also be less expensive for society to operate than the formal youth court system.

In most provinces, responsibility for alternative measures is given to a community agency with a paid staff or volunteers, though in some provinces, government social workers or juvenile probation staff are responsible (Rabinovitch, 1986). Case referrals must initially be made by the police or Crown Attorney, who must be satisfied that alternative measures would be "appropriate, having regard to the needs of the young person and the interests of society," and that sufficient evidence exists to take the case to court. The program administrator then meets with the young person and proposes some form of alternative measures that might involve, for example, an apology, restitution, some form of volunteer work or a charitable donation. The young person is not obliged to participate, and always has the option of going to youth court for judicially imposed disposition. Youths must "fully and freely consent" to participating and must "accept responsibility" for the offence alleged to have been committed; if the young person denies responsibility, the matter must go to court for a judicial finding of guilt or innocence. The young person must be advised of the right to consultation with a lawyer prior to participation.

If a young person agrees to participate and successfully completes the alternative measures agreed to, the charges must be dropped. Whether or not there is successful completion, no statement made by a youth, in the process of consideration of whether alternative measures should be imposed, may be used in later court proceedings.

While there is some controversy over the efficacy of alternative measures as opposed to court in terms of reducing future offences (Moyer, 1980), until April 1988 every province except Ontario had implemented section 4 of the YOA. It is generally felt that alternative measures represent a socially useful experiment for dealing with first-time offenders in a humane, socially inexpensive fashion. The failure of Ontario to implement section 4 of the YOA has been successfully challenged in the Ontario Court of Appeal, as a violation of the Equality Rights guaranteed by section 15 of the Charter of Rights. In *R. v. Sheldon S.* (1988) it was held that the absence of such programs in Ontario constituted a "denial of equal benefit and protection of the law" on the basis of place of residence, and hence was in violation of section 15 of the Charter. This decision is under appeal to the Supreme Court of Canada and it remains to be seen whether the Charter can be invoked to force a provincial government to provide services and programs in accordance with the YOA. *Sheldon S.* may be a significant precedent for ensuring all youths access to a minimum level of services, regardless of their province of residence.

The Declaration of Principle in section 3(1)(d) mentions "taking no measures" as well as alternative measures. In *R. v. David L.* (1985) a thirteen-year-old boy who had been placed in a group home under child welfare legislation was charged with an assault as a result of an altercation in which the boy punched a staff member. The court dismissed the charge, relying in part on section 3(1)(d) of the YOA, and stated that staff who occupy a "parent-like" role should not look to the courts to deal with relatively minor disciplinary matters.

Youth Court Proceedings

Proceedings under the YOA are conducted in a specially designated "youth court." In a number of provinces, the Family Court, which is responsible for such matters as child protection and adoption, has been designated as the youth court. In other jurisdictions, the Provincial Court, which deals with most adult criminal charges, has been designated as the youth court, although the proceedings must be held at a separate time from those involving adults.

Ontario and Nova Scotia have adopted a two-tier youth court model. As was the practice under the Juvenile Delinquents Act, twelve- to fifteen-year-olds are dealt with in Family Court, while sixteen- and seventeen-year-olds are proceeded with in the adult Provincial Court, albeit with adult court judges who are nominally sitting as youth court judges. Critics have argued that Ontario and Nova Scotia have simply acted in an expedient fashion and have failed to implement the spirit of the YOA by maintaining the court jurisdiction in effect under the JDA (Bala, 1987; Stuart, 1987). However, the courts have held that the two-tier implementation model is permitted under the YOA and does not violate the Charter of Rights (*R. v. R.C.*, 1987).

In section 52, the YOA stipulates that proceedings in youth court are to be similar to those governing "summary conviction offences" in adult court. This means that the proceedings are less complex and more expeditious than those applicable to the more serious adult "indictable offences." More specifically, this means that there are no preliminary inquiries, and all trials are conducted by a judge alone; there are no jury trials in youth court. It is felt that it is particularly important for young persons to have the more expeditious resolution of their cases available through summary procedures. The courts have held that the failure to afford young persons an opportunity for trial by jury does not violate the provisions of the Charter of Rights that guarantee equality and the right to jury trial to persons facing imprisonment of five years or more. In *R. v. Robbie L.* (1986) the Ontario Court of Appeal emphasized that the maximum penalty under the YOA is three years, as opposed to the life sentence an adult may face for certain serious offences. Justice Morden wrote:

> ...the *Young Offenders Act* is intended to provide a comprehensive system for dealing with young persons who are alleged to be in conflict with the law which is separate and distinct from the adult criminal justice system. While the new system is more like the adult system than was that under the *Juvenile Delinquents Act* it nonetheless is a different system. As far as the aftermath of a finding of guilt is concerned, the general thrust of the *Young Offenders Act* is to provide less severe consequences than those relating to an adult offender.... the establishment of the legal regime...for dealing with young persons, which is separate and distinct from the adult criminal justice system, is of sufficient importance to warrant the overriding of the equality right alleged to be infringed in this proceeding.... (*R. v. Robbie L.,* 1986: 219, 225).

While a young person being tried in youth court is denied the opportunity to a preliminary inquiry and a jury, a youth is afforded all of the procedural protections that are given to an adult who faces a summary charge. There is a constitutionally based presumption of innocence (Canadian Charter of Rights and Freedoms, 1982, section 11(d)) with the onus upon the prosecution to prove its case. If a "not guilty" plea is entered, the Crown will call witnesses to establish its case and each witness will be subject to cross-examination. The youth is entitled to call witnesses and to testify, subject to the Crown's right of cross-examination, but there is no obligation upon the accused to adduce any evidence or testify. After all the witnesses are called, there may be submissions (or arguments) and the judge then renders a verdict. If the judge is satisfied, beyond a reasonable doubt, that the offence charged has occurred, a conviction is entered, and the case proceeds to disposition under the YOA. Otherwise, an acquittal is entered and this ends the YOA proceedings, though in appropriate cases the youth might still be dealt with under the provincial child welfare or mental health legislation.

Most cases under the YOA do not in fact result in trials, but rather result in guilty pleas. Frequently the youth recognizes that an offence has occurred and wishes to plead guilty. If a guilty plea is entered, the Crown Attorney will read a summary of the evidence against the youth. Section 19 of the YOA has a special provision requiring a judge in youth court to be satisfied that the facts read by the Crown support the charge. If they do not, the judge must enter a plea of not guilty and conduct a trial. This provision recognizes that a youth may not appreciate the significance of a guilty plea as fully as an adult.

It is not uncommon for a guilty plea in youth court to be the product of "plea bargain." A plea bargain is typically the result of informal discussions between the Crown Attorney and the lawyer representing the youth. There is an agreement to plead guilty to certain charges in exchange for dropping of other charges or a request by the Crown to the court for a particular disposition. Though considered controversial by some, plea bargaining is not regarded as unethical or illegal. It should be noted that if there is a plea bargain, the judge is not bound to impose the disposition requested by the accused.

The YOA affords very important rights in regard to the provision of legal representation. Section 11 requires that as soon as a young person is arrested or appears in youth court, the youth is to be advised of the right to counsel. If the young person is "unable" to obtain counsel, the youth court judge shall "direct" that legal representation be provided. While adults have the right to retain counsel, if they are unable to afford a lawyer, they must rely on legal aid, which has fairly stringent criteria for deciding whether to provide representation. The YOA guarantees that whenever a youth is "unable" to obtain counsel, it will be provided. It has been held that when assessing financial ability to retain counsel, the court should not have regard to parental resources (*R. v. Ronald H.*, 1984; *R. v. M.*, 1985). Since few young persons have significant financial resources, in practice this means that most youths are represented by lawyers who are paid by the state.

While a youth is not obliged to be represented by a lawyer and may choose to appear unrepresented or assisted by some other adult, like a parent, the effect of the YOA has been to ensure that most youths are represented by counsel. This has proven controversial to some observers, who have argued that securing legal representation often results in unnecessary delays and that lawyers often fail to promote the "best interests" of adolescent clients (Leschied and Jaffe, 1987: 428). However, the YOA is clearly criminal law and it is understandable that those subject to potential punishment by the state are entitled to full legal representation; young persons without lawyers are rarely in a position to appreciate the significance of their involvement in the legal system or to protect their rights. It may well be that in some localities administrative difficulties do result in delays in obtaining legal counsel, and that some lawyers involved in the representation of young persons lack the training or sensitivity to provide truly adequate legal services. However, denial of access to counsel does not seem to be an appropriate strategy for dealing with these problems.

The YOA has a number of provisions intended to protect the privacy of young persons involved in the youth court process and to minimize the stigmatization they may face. Section 38 provides that the media cannot publish identifying information about a young person, though there is a special exception if a youth is at large and considered "dangerous to others" by a judge. Section 39 stipulates that while youth court proceedings are generally open to the public, the judge may make an exclusion order if their presence "would be seriously injurious or seriously prejudicial" to the young person. Sections 40 and 46 govern records; access to records of youths involved with the court system is generally restricted. While police may fingerprint and photograph youths charged with indictable offences, the central records of the Royal Canadian Mounted Police must be destroyed five years after the completion of any sentence for an indictable offence, provided the youth commits no further offences in that five-year period. Local police forces and others who have records related to young offenders are not obliged to destroy their records, but their use is severely restricted after the five years have passed. Section 36 of the YOA prohibits employers governed by federal law from asking whether a potential employee has ever been convicted of an offence under the YOA. These provisions recognize the "limited accountability" of young persons and are intended to afford a "second chance" to those who are convicted under the YOA.

Disposition and Disposition Review

Young persons convicted of offences under the YOA receive a "disposition," or "sentence," pursuant to section 20 of the Act. Available dispositions consist of the following:

(1)   an order for restitution or compensation;
(2)   an order for up to 240 hours of community service;
(3)   an absolute discharge;
(4)   a fine up to $1,000;
(5)   an order for up to two years probation;

(6)   an order for treatment for up to three years; or

(7)   an order for custody for up to three years.

For less serious offences, a court may make a disposition immediately after a finding of guilt. However, for more serious offences, the court will normally adjourn to allow preparation of a report to assist the court. Most commonly the youth court will request a "predisposition" report, or social history. A youth court worker will prepare such a report. The worker will interview the youth, the youth's parents, the victim and any other significant individuals, and will summarize the youth's background and provide information about the offence. Frequently the report will include a recommendation about disposition. Although not binding on the court, these recommendations are usually influential. The youth, of course, has the right to challenge the report, and may introduce independent evidence about the disposition. Parents also have the right to make submissions prior to disposition.

In more serious cases, or in cases where there is particular concern about a young person, the court may order a psychiatric, medical or psychological assessment to assist in arriving at an appropriate disposition.

Since the enactment of the YOA, appellate courts in different Canadian provinces have gradually articulated a dispositional philosophy for young offenders. In *R. v. Richard I.* (1985: 523) the Ontario Court of Appeal acknowledged that in comparison to sentencing adults "...the task of arriving at the right disposition may be considerably more difficult and complex given the special needs of young persons and the kind of guidance and assistance they may require." In *R. v. Joseph F.* (1986: 304), Justice Morden of the Ontario Court of Appeal wrote:

> While undoubtedly the protection of society is a central principle of the Act...it is one that has to be reconciled with other considerations, such as the needs of young persons and, in any event, it is not a principle which must inevitably be reflected in a severe disposition. In many cases, unless the degree of seriousness of the offence and the circumstances in which it was committed militate otherwise, it is best given effect to by a disposition which gives emphasis to the factors of individual deterrence and rehabilitation. We do not agree that it puts the matter correctly to say the whole purpose of the Act is to give a degree of paramountcy to the protection of society with the implication

> that this is to overbear the needs and interests of the young person and must result in a severe disposition.

One controversial issue is the extent to which courts making dispositions under the YOA should take into account the principle of general deterrence. In *R. v. G.K.* (1985) the Alberta Court of Appeal declined to impose a custodial disposition on a youth without a prior record who was convicted of armed robbery, emphasizing that a psychiatric report indicated that there was no likelihood of recurrence of delinquent acts. Justice Stevenson wrote:

> We...reject the suggestion that the young offender's sentence should be modeled on the sentence that would be imposed on an adult offender. If a custodial sentence is warranted then it ought not to be lengthier than that which would be imposed on an adult.... In any event, deterrence to others does not, in my view, have any place in the sentencing of young offenders. It is not one of the principles enumerated...in s.3 of the Act which declared the policy for young offenders in Canada. (*R. v. G.K.*, 1985: 560)

However, most other appellate courts have held that general deterrence may play a role in the sentencing of young offenders. The Ontario Court of Appeal specifically rejected the approach of the Alberta Court of Appeal in *R. v. G.K.*:

> The principles under s.3 of the *Young Offenders Act* do not sweep away the principle of general deterrence. The principles under that section enshrine the principle of the protection of society and this subsumes general and specific deterrence. It is perhaps sufficient to say that...the principles of general deterrence must be considered but it has diminished importance in determining the appropriate disposition in the case of a youthful offender. (*R. v. Frank O.*, 1986: 377).

Another controversial issue is the extent to which courts should consider the promotion of the welfare of a youth as a basis for imposing a custodial sentence. In *R.R. v. R.* (1986) the Nova Scotia Court of Appeal upheld a sentence of five months open custody imposed on a fourteen-year-old youth without a prior record who was convicted of the theft of a skateboard. The Court felt the youth "desperately requires strict controls and constant supervision" (*R.R. v. R.*, 1986: 3461–34). The commission of the offence was considered a justification for imposing needed care, even though the sentence was grossly disproportionate to the offence and far in excess of what an adult would have received for the same offence.

A more common approach, however, has been to reject the use of the YOA simply as a route for providing treatment. In *R. v. Michael B.* (1987) the Ontario Court of Appeal overturned an order for five months open custody imposed upon a youth who committed a relatively minor assault and had no prior record. The trial judge had been concerned that the boy was suicidal and neither his family nor the mental health facility he had been staying in wanted to accept him. Justice Brooke concluded that incarceration under the YOA "was not a sentence that was responsive to the offence, but in reality was what seemed at the time a sensible way of dealing with a youth who had a personality problem and needed a place to go" (*R. v. Michael B.*, 1987: 574). The Court of Appeal suggested that involuntary mental commitment was the appropriate route to follow; in fact this had occurred by the time the case came before that Court.

As a result of the YOA's distinctive dispositional philosophy and reflecting the fact that many youths involved in the criminal justice system have not committed serious offences, the vast majority of convicted young offenders receive dispositions that keep them in their communities. Section 20(1)(9) of the YOA allows the imposition of an absolute discharge if the court considers "it to be in the best interests of the young person and not contrary to the public interest." This disposition is usually reserved for minor first offenders and results in no real sanction being imposed, other than the fact of conviction. Restitution, community service and fines allow the court to impose a real penalty on the youth, without unduly restricting freedom. In appropriate cases, victims may be compensated by restitution.

The most frequently imposed disposition under the YOA is probation. The nature of a probation order depends on the circumstances, and various conditions may be imposed. These might include that a youth maintain a curfew, attend school or reside with parents. Probation may also entail regular reporting to a probation officer, and might even be used to require a youth to live in a foster home or with a suitable adult person (*R. v. W.G.*, 1985).

The most serious disposition that can be ordered under section 20 of the YOA is placement in a custodial facility. For most offences the maximum custodial disposition is two years, but for offences for which an adult may receive life imprisonment, the maximum is three years. The YOA requires a judge placing a youth in custody to specify whether the sentence will be served in "open custody" or "secure custody."

Section 24.1 of the *YOA* specifies that an open custody facility means a "community residential centre, group home, child care institution, or forest or wilderness camp, or any other like place or facility" designated as "open" by the provincial government, while "secure custody" means a place "for the secure containment or restraint" of young persons that is designated as secure by the provincial government. The intention of the Act is that judges should have control over the level of restraint imposed on a youth. Provincial governments also retain significant control because they are able to designate the level of facilities. The courts have indicated, however, that they will cautiously review provincial designation. In one case, a Prince Edward Island court ruled that the provincial government could not simply designate as a place of "open custody" one floor of a building that had formerly served as an adult jail and which was then serving as a secure custody facility for young offenders.

> Undoubtedly the physical characteristics are not the only things to be looked at. Other factors which make a place suitable for open custody would include the security that is in place, the number of staff, the qualifications of the staff, bearing in mind that one of their primary functions is to teach young offenders how to better achieve in society. Additionally, a place of open custody will have a program set up for the benefit of the offenders. (*Re L.H.F.*, 1985: 46).

A very disturbing trend immediately following the enactment of the YOA was a significant increase in the use of custodial placements for young persons who violated the criminal law (Leschied and Jaffe, 1987; Wardell, 1987). This trend can in part be attributed to the attitudes of many youth court judges who initially emphasized the protection of society and the youth's responsibility over recognition of special needs and limited accountability. It also seems that in those provinces where the age jurisdiction was raised, older youths who had been appearing in adult court as "first-time offenders" (their juvenile records being ignored), were appearing in youth court with long records of prior offences. Further, it seems that some youth court judges were making extensive use of open custody as a "middle option" for youths who had not committed serious offences but who "needed some help." Prior to the enactment of the YOA, many of these youths had been helped through the child welfare system.

It remains to be seen whether this trend toward increased us of custody will continue. There is some evidence that there may be a decline in the use of custody. In most provinces, the appellate courts have rendered decisions that reduce the length of custodial dispositions for young offenders, and emphasize limited accountability and recognition of special needs. As originally enacted, the YOA placed certain restriction on the use of custody, requiring predisposition report before any custodial disposition was made, and restricting the use of secure custody to cases where a more serious offence occurred or where there was a record of prior offences. In amending the YOA in 1986, Parliament also provided that a youth court should not place a young offender in open or secure custody unless this was considered "necessary for the protection of society...having regard to the seriousness of the offence and...the needs and circumstances of the young person" (section 24(1)). Under the original legislation, this consideration only applied to secure custody. It is to be hoped that these signals from the appellate courts and Parliament may be having the effect of curbing the excessive use of custodial placements by the youth courts.

When a youth is ordered into custody, provincial correctional officials have significant control over the youth's placement. While the youth court specifies a level of custody, correctional officials select the specific facility a youth will reside in and can move the offender from one facility to another in that level. Provincial officials may also permit the temporary release of the youth from custody, either to engage in employment, education or other activities, or to return home for a specified period of time. Correctional officials also have the authority under the YOA to transfer a youth from an open to a secure custody facility for up to fifteen days. A youth may be transferred if there has been an escape or attempted escape, or if in their opinion, this is "necessary for the safety of the young person or others" in the open custody facility. Section 24.5 of the YOA allows correctional officials to apply to a youth court judge to transfer a young offender who has reached eighteen into a provincial adult correctional facility for the remainder of the youth's custodial sentence. Such a transfer shall only be allowed if the youth court, after a hearing, is satisfied that it is "in the best interests of the young person or in the public interest."

The YOA provides that once a disposition has been imposed on a young offender, the youth court retains the authority to conduct a review hearing to ensure that the disposition remains current and appropriate to the needs of the youth. For youths placed in custody, there is a mandatory review hearing by the court after one year, with the possibility of an earlier review, but there is not parole for young offenders. Correctional officials may release a youth from custody into probation or may transfer a youth from secure to open custody, but these decisions are subject to the approval of a youth court judge; normally these processes can be carried out without a hearing, though sometimes one is required. At a review hearing, the youth court cannot increase the level of security that was specified in the original disposition, though if there has been a wilful failure to comply with a disposition, such as a breach of probation or an escape from custody, this would constitute an offence for which a new disposition can be imposed.

One of the most controversial dispositional provisions of the YOA deals with "treatment orders," which allow a youth to be placed in a psychiatric hospital or other "treatment facility" instead of custody. Such orders may only be made on the recommendation of a psychiatric or psychological report ordered under section 13, and only if the youth consents; normally parents must also consent to such an order being made. The requirement that the youth consent has been criticized, as relatively few youths are prepared to admit that they need treatment even if they are highly disturbed, and very few of these orders have been made. Some critics have advocated removal of the requirement for a youth's consent to such a treatment order, although they acknowledge that "the efficacy of compulsory treatment for young offenders is an are laden with considerable debate" (Leschied and Jaffe, 1987: 427). It should be noted that forms of rehabilitative services, therapy and counselling are provided in most custodial facilities. Also, in cases of severely disturbed youths, the insanity provisions of the Criminal Code or provincial mental health legislation may be invoked to require that a youth be involuntarily confined in a mental health facility.

Transfer to the Adult System

The most serious thing that can happen to a young person charged with an offence is transfer to the adult system. Such a transfer can only occur after a youth court hearing, which must be held prior to an adjudication of guilt or innocence. If a youth court judge orders transfer, there will be a trial in adult court. If there is a conviction in an adult court, sentencing will be in accordance with the principles applicable to adults. Although it is theoretically possible for a youth to seek transfer in order, for example, to have the benefit of a jury trial, it is invariably the Crown that seeks transfer in order to subject the young person to the much more severe maximum penalties that can be imposed in adult court. Usually transfer applications are made where the adult maximum of life imprisonment is considered a more appropriate response than the three years under the YOA.

Under section 16 of the YOA an application for transfer can be made in regard to any serious indictable offence alleged to have been committed by a young person of fourteen years or older at the time of the alleged offence. Transfer is only to be ordered if the youth court "is of the opinion that, in the interest of society and having regard to the needs of the person" it is appropriate. In deciding whether to transfer a case, section 16(2) instructs the courts to consider: the seriousness of the alleged offence; the age, character and prior record of the youth; the adequacy of the YOA as opposed to the Criminal Code for dealing with the case; the availability of treatment or correctional resources; and any other relevant factors.

Transfer hearings are adversarial in nature, but are not formal criminal trials. The rules of evidence are greatly relaxed, and the court will receive hearsay (or second-hand) evidence about the youth's background and the circumstances of the alleged offence. The court need not be satisfied beyond a reasonable doubt that an offence occurred, but rather decides what is the appropriate forum for the trial and disposition of the charge in question (*R. v. S.J.H.*, 1986). Witnesses are often called to describe the differences between the likely fate of the youth if placed in custody under the YOA as opposed to incarceration pursuant to the Criminal Code. A predisposition report must be presented at a transfer hearing and there is usually a section 13 psychiatric report prepared as well. Often, a central issue at transfer hearings is the amenability of the youth to rehabilitation within the three-year period prescribed as the maximum YOA disposition.

There has been substantial judicial disagreement about the appropriate interpretation of the YOA's standard for transfer, "the interest of society...having regard to the needs of the young person." The courts have compared this to the standard articulated under section 9 of the Juvenile Delinquents Act: that transfer was to occur only if "the good of the child and the interest of the community demand it."

Justice Monnin of the Manitoba Court of Appeal wrote:

> The test under this Act [the YOA] is different than that under the old *Juvenile Delinquents Act*.... In the new test there is at least a slight emphasis on the interest of society having regard to the needs of the young person. (*R. v. C.J.M.*, 1985: 229).

Another Manitoba decision commented:

> With the advent of the *Young Offenders Act* the transfer provisions ensure a more realistic approach to transfer. The fact that transfer exists in certain cases for those over the age of fourteen, by implication, considers that in some instances those youths will face a period of adult incarceration. While the primary concern has not shifted so that the interests of society would appear to be of primary importance, the needs of the young person are still to be addressed and these needs might well be so addressed with the treatment available in an adult institution. (*R. v. J.T.J.*, 1986: 3409-32)

The Manitoba approach has led to a relatively high transfer rate, not only for such offences as murder and attempted murder, but also for such offences as robbery.

The approach of the Manitoba Courts can be contrasted with the more restrictive approach taken in a number of jurisdictions. In *R. v. Mark Andrew Z.* (1987) the Ontario Court of Appeal refused to transfer a youth who, at the age of fifteen, shot and killed his mother and sister. Justice MacKinnon observed that "a charge of murder does not automatically remove a youth from the youth court" (*R. v. Mark Andrew Z.*, 1987: 158). The judge stressed the amenability of this youth to treatment and wrote:

> In light of s.3 [of the YOA] I do not think that the interests of society or the needs and interests of the young person are to be given greater importance one over the other. They are to be weighed against each other having regard to the matters directed to be considered in subs.16(2). (*R. v. Mark Andrew Z.*, 1987: 162. See also *R. v. N.B..*, and *R. v. E.E.H.*, 1987)

In *Mark Andrew Z.*, the Ontario Court of Appeal did note that in a case such as this, involving first-degree murder, the court was faced with a choice between the three-year maximum disposition under the YOA and the possibility of life imprisonment with no opportunity for parole for at least twenty-five years. While deciding against transfer, Justice MacKinnon stated:

> Put bluntly, three years for murder appears
> totally inadequate to express society's revulsion
> for and repudiation of this most heinous of
> crimes.... This is obviously an area for consid-
> eration and possible amendment by those
> responsible for the Act. (R. v. *Mark Andrew
> Z.*, 1987: 162)

A leading juvenile forensic psychiatrist, Dr. Clive Chamberlain, has supported the view that for homicides, judges acting under the YOA should be
able to impose sentences of longer than three years, noting that for a few
highly disturbed youths it may be necessary to have five to ten years of
treatment in a secure setting. Dr. Chamberlain commented on the problem
with the YOA's three-year maximum disposition, saying that it

> ...puts pressure on the Crown to move these
> kids into the adult court, where a 25-year mur-
> der sentence is available. As a result some of
> them will wind up in the adult prison popula-
> tion, where there is not treatment for them and
> where they just get worse.... Society would be
> better served, I believe, if the three-year maxi-
> mum term of the youth system of which the
> greater part involved counselling—were
> extended in the rare cases where kids kill
> somebody. (Bagley, 1987: 61)

Conclusion

The Juvenile Delinquents Act came into force close to the start of the
twentieth century, and by the 1980s major reforms were inevitable. The
Young Offenders Act created a relatively uniform, national scheme for dealing with adolescents who violate the criminal law. While these youths are
not afforded a child welfare approach, used for children under twelve whose
behaviour may be a threat to others, nor are they subject to the full rigours
of the adult criminal justice system.

The YOA has clearly achieved certain objectives, most notably protecting the legal rights of young persons, and provides recognition of the right
of society to appropriate protection. It seems unlikely for the foreseeable
future that Parliament will engage in a major revision of the YOA or change
its fundamental principles. However, there remain many issues for the
courts, provincial administrators and the federal Parliament to address
before we will have achieved a system of youth justice truly worthy of the

close of the twentieth century. Our search for a youth justice system that fairly balances the needs and rights of young persons while adequately protecting society must be an ongoing one.

Endnote

1   The author wishes to thank Deidre Rice (LL.M. Candidate, Queen's University) for her helpful comments about a draft of this chapter.

References

Archambault, O. 1983. "Young Offenders Act: Philosophy and Principles." *Provincial Judges Journal* 7(2), 1-7.

Bagley, G. 1987. "'Oh, What a Good Boy I Am': Killer Angels Chose When Friends Die." *The Medical Post*, December 8, 1897, 9 and 15.

Bala, N and R. Corrado. 1985. *Juvenile Justice in Canada: A Comparative Study.* Ottawa: Ministry of the Solicitor General of Canada.

Bala, N. 1987. Annotation to *R. v. Robert C., Young Offenders Service,* 7353-3 to 7353-6.

Canada, Department of Justice, Special Committee on Juvenile Delinquency. 1985. *Juvenile Delinquency in Canada.*

Leschied, A. and P. Jaffe. 1987. "Impact of the Young Offenders Act on Court Dispositions: A Comparative Analysis." *Canadian Journal of Criminology* 30, 421-430.

Moyer, S. 1980. *Diversion From the Juvenile Justice System and its Impact on Children: A Review of the Literature.* Ottawa: Ministry of the Solicitor General of Canada.

Rabinovitch, P. 1986. "Diversion Under Section 4: Is There a Future for it in Ontario?" *Young Offenders Service,* 7533-7542.

Stuart, D. 1987. Annotation to *R. v. R.C., Criminal Reports* (3d), 56,185-186.

Thomson, G. 1983. "Commentary on the Young Offenders Act." *Provincial Judges Journal* 7(2), 27-29, 34.

Wardell, W. 1987. "The Young Offenders Act: A Report Card 1984-86." *Journal of Law and Social Policy* 2, 39-72.

Legislation

An Act to Amend the Young Offenders Act, the Criminal Code, the Penitentiary Act and the Prisons and Reformatory Act (Bill C-106), Statutes of Canada 1984-85-86, c. 32.

Canadian Charter of Rights and Freedoms, Part I of the Constitution Act, 1982, being Schedule B of the Canada Act 1982 (U.K.), 1982, c.11.

Criminal Code, Revised Statutes of Canada 1970, c. C-34.

Juvenile Delinquents Act, Revised Statutes of Canada 1970, c. J-3.

Young Offenders Act, Statutes of Canada 1980-81-82-83, c.110.

Cases

R. v. A.B. (1986), 50 Criminal Reports 247 (Ont. C.A.)

R. v. Michael B. (1987), 36 Canadian Criminal Cases (3d) 572 (Ont. C.A.).

R. v. N.B. (1985), 21 Canadian Criminal Cases (3d) 374 (Que. C.A.).

R. v. R.C. (1987), 53 Criminal Reports (3d) 185 (Ont. C.A.).

R. v. Joseph F. (1986), 11 Ontario Appeal Cases 302.

Re L.H.F. (1985), 57 Newfoundland and Prince Edward Island Reports 44 (P.E.I.S.C.).

R. v. J.M.G. (1986), 57 Ontario Reports (2d) 705, Young Offenders Service 86-135 (Ont. C.A.).

R. v. W.G. (1985), 23 Canadian Criminal Cases A(3d) 93 (B.C.C.A.).

R. v. H. (1985), Young Offenders Service 4140 (Alta Prov. Ct-Youth Div.).

R. v. E.E.H. (1987), 35 Canadian Criminal Cases (3d) 67.

R. v. Ronald H. (1984), Young Offenders Service 3319 (Alta Prov. Ct).

R. v. S.J.H. (1986), 76 Nova Scotia Reports (2d) 163 (N.S.S.C.).

R. v. Richard I. (1985), 17 Canadian Criminal Cases (3d) 523.

R. v. J.T.J. (1986), Young Offenders Service 3409-31 (Man. Prov. Ct-Fam. Div.).

R. v. G.K. (1985), 21 Canadian Criminal Cases (3d) 558 (Alta C.A.).

R. v. David L. (1985), Young Offenders Service 3103 (B.C. Prov. Ct).

R. v Robbie L. (1986), 52 Criminal Reports (3d) 209 (Ont. C.A.).

R. v. S.L. (1984), Young Offenders Service 4085 (Ont. Prov. Ct-Fam. Div.).

R. v. M. (1985), Young Offenders Service 3322 (Ont. Prov. Ct-Fam. Div.).

R. v. C.J.M. (1985), 49 Criminal Reports (3d) 226 (Man. C.A.).

R. v. M.A.M. (1986), 32 Canadian Criminal Cases (3d) 567 (B.C. C.A.).

R. v. Frank O. (1986), 27 Canadian Criminal Cases (3d) 376 (Ont. C.A.).

R.R. v. R. (1986), Young Offenders Service 3461-34.

R. v. Sheldon S. (1986), Young Offenders Service 7375 (Ont. Prov. Ct-Fam. Div.); affirmed (1988), as yet unreported decision, summarized in *The Lawyers Weekly*, April 1, 1988, p. 1 (Ont. C.A.).

R. v. Ina Christina V. (1985), Young Offenders Service 7211 (Ont. Prov. Ct-Fam Div.), per Main Prov. J.

R. v. Mark Andrew Z. (1987), 35 Canadian Criminal Cases (3d) 144.

Good People, Dirty System:
The Young Offenders Act and Organizational Failure

Jim Hackler

Organizational Characteristics That Make Good People Do Poor Work

More than two decades ago, Everett Hughes wrote an influential article entitled "Good People and Dirty Work" (1964). One of the themes in that article was that, when people work with stigmatized clients, such as the handicapped or the insane, some of that stigma "rubs off." In a larger sense, individuals cannot function independently of the organizational setting in which they are found. I would like to expand on these ideas to suggest that various aspects of organizations, the setting, and the nature of the interaction surrounding their activities will, in fact, "rub off" on the well-intentioned people. It is my contention, however, that the juvenile justice system in Canada works badly, despite valiant efforts on the part of many within the system. Part of the problem, it is proposed, is the increased emphasis on legal procedures. Although such procedures are intended to protect juveniles, I argue that they have done more damage than good. The emphasis on proceduralism not only "rubs off," it captures the people involved. They may complain, and at times become frustrated and quit, but frequently they will have difficulty modifying a system that is performing badly. Alternatively, they may become complacent and accept the system as it is.

The picture is not completely dismal, however. Occasionally we see instances where people have been able to overcome some of the deficiencies in the system and accomplish a good deal despite the severe handicaps imposed on them by an extremely inefficient structure. One goal of this chapter, then, is to provide both positive and negative examples of experiences and situations that have been observed.

Readers may well question the methodology that has led to some of these conclusions. Some of my early work in juvenile justice emphasized traditional data-gathering approaches. In Vienna, I utilized questionnaires, which were translated into German and administered to more than 300 people serving in eleven different roles throughout the Viennese juvenile justice system. These data were analysed and presented in one of the longest and driest articles I have ever written (Hackler, Brockman and Luczynska, 1977). In addition to administering the questionnaires, I interviewed many people. These interviews not only answered most of my questions more effectively than did the data analysis, but also moved quickly from my initial questions to greater insights about the system. My questionnaire data permitted the use of statistics but lacked the sensitivity to deal with complex questions.

In recent years I have been relying more heavily on intelligent people who work in the system and have insights that I consider superior to many of the ideas that come out of some of our more formal research. I describe this strategy more thoroughly under the label "the local-wisdom approach" (Hackler, 1983-4).

Although this chapter tries to get its message across with anecdotes rather than formal logic, I have definitely been influenced by those sophisticated scholars who use an organizational approach to the criminal-justice system (e.g., Hagan, 1983), particularly those who have pointed out that informal structures operating throughout the criminal-justice system are quite capable of evading, absorbing or blunting any reforms imposed on them by legislation (Feeley, 1983). The Canadian scene has suffered in attempts to modify a bureaucratic system by passing detailed legislation without trying to gain a better understanding of the informal dynamics of the subsystems within Canadian juvenile justice. Studies of the "court-room work group" (Eisenstein and Jacob, 1977) should have warned us that many of the activities of juvenile justice are extremely difficult to legislate in a predictable way.

It is interesting that we are beginning to recognize that the interaction of technology with the larger world leads to accidents and damage: oil rigs catch fire in the North Sea; CFCs damage the ozone layer; and pollution is leading to the destruction of forests, and so on. What is less obvious is that some of these same calamities also represent organizational failures, the inability of bureaucracies and other institutions in society to interact successfully. When failures are dramatic, such as the burning of an oil-rig or the explosion of a space shuttle, both technological and organizational failures come to light. However, when a juvenile justice system imposes an additional burden on the lives of young people already facing a decreased chance of success, it does not undergo the same scrutiny. In fact, the movement from child-saving to child-blaming has provided a rationale for the continuation of destructive practices (Haveman, 1986). Such practices will probably eventually lead to young people being less successful citizens in the future and contributing as adults to more than their share of child abuse, wife abuse and crime. My more radical colleagues provide scathing criticisms of the system, which are frequently appropriate, based on faults in capitalism. I agree that there are great injustices in society, which require changes at the societal level. In the meantime, some small changes could be introduced relatively easily. My approach is to see if moderate changes in the system could be achieved by using an organizational approach. If we view juvenile justice as a "loosely coupled system," it may be easier to identify areas where change is possible.

Juvenile Justice as a Loosely Coupled System

There are a number of organizational models that can be used to study juvenile justice. John Hagan has utilized the concept of "loosely coupled systems" to study the criminal justice system (Hagan, Alwin and Hewitt, 1979; Hagan, Nagel and Albonetti, 1980). Earlier, Reiss spoke of American criminal justice As a "loosely articulated hierarchy of subsystems" (1971: 114-20). This approach also makes sense for juvenile justice, where different subsystems vary in the tightness or looseness of this coupling (Hagan, 1983: 5). Youth court judges, probation departments, prosecutors' offices and the police are responsive to one another in varying degrees but still maintain considerable independence.

It is quite possible that there are many advantages in having loosely coupled rather than tightly coupled systems, but the Young Offenders Act was introduced without taking into account the realities of such a system. According to Peter Solomon, the behaviour of professionals, such as the police and crown attorneys, derives as much from occupational organizational influences as from the influence of the law and the rules that are supposed to define their roles (1983: 5). In addition, the law and the rules provide these actors not only with constraints, but with resources that enable them to achieve their own goals and justify their actions. The argument I wish to make here is that this loosely coupled system has satisfied the needs and goals of some components of the system while, in fact, damaging juveniles. Furthermore, I will argue that this does not have to be the case. The juvenile justice system in France is also a loosely coupled system but has been adapted to serve the society more effectively.

How does the Young Offenders Act fit into this picture? It is also the product of "loosely coupled systems," but because of the agreement that was finally produced in Parliament, some people assume that it produced a consensus.

The Myth of Agreement in the Young Offenders Act

Prior to the 1984 Young Offenders Act, several attempts to draft new legislation met with failure. The new legislation was long and involved, and entailed many compromises. Those who worked so hard on drafting this legislation sincerely believed that they had achieved something positive because they were able to satisfy a variety of conflicting interest groups and organizations. In this respect, the law succeeded. However, the result is that the YOA sends confusing messages.

Maria Los writes that the new legislation did not reject the treatment philosophy outright in favour of the "just desserts" model (1987: 26). In fact, the law was designed to satisfy a number of influential groups who were not in agreement. In her study of the media during this period, Los points out that the different parts of the country were also preoccupied with different concerns. For example, the press in Quebec was primarily inter- ested in the province's legislation, which preceded the federal law. The result was concealed messages in the legislation that were contradicted by statements presented more openly. In practice, the YOA had led to much proceduralism and inefficient patterns of behaviour that reflect concern of the different components of the system. For example, the YOA has been a boon for young lawyers needing to gain court-room experience; however, this may not have been in the interest of young offenders. According to Los, other concerned groups, such as adolescents, parents, social workers and researchers, had little chance to express their opinions (1987: 3). The law was the product of "paper" not "people" specialists.

In this chapter, it is not my goal to argue for revisions in the law. It is regrettable that the legislation was drafted without taking into account the flexibility and ingenuity displayed by people who work in these systems, and with fear rather than appreciation of the extensive variability that exists in the system. At present it is more reasonable to accept this legislation as a given. A simpler system that did not try to plug so many loopholes would have enabled the realties of loosely coupled systems to operate by utilizing the considerable talent that we see at the local level. But it is also important to point out that the Young Offenders Act is not the primary culprit. Under the Juvenile Delinquents Act, we had similar problems. Some parts of the system worked out ingenious and effective ways of coping with the problems. At other times, the needs of powerful players in the system were favoured over the needs of the juveniles and society. This situation has also arisen under the Young Offenders Act, but now it takes more skill and ingenuity to overcome some of the procedural requirements.

Let us now turn to three models of juvenile justice as a way of organizing some other arguments.

The Welfare, Legal and Negotiated Models of Juvenile Justice

It has been argued that the Juvenile Delinquents Act reflected a welfare model of juvenile justice, whereas the Young Offenders Act shifted to a legalistic model. Since this debate is well known, I shall not elaborate, but suggest instead that a "negotiated" model, which might describe juvenile justice in France, could be seen to have certain advantages.

Under the French system, a juvenile can be recorded and released or sent to the *procureur*, who is similar to our prosecutor. The police can hold a juvenile overnight, but most cases are seen by the *procureur* and sent on to the judge the same day. The *procureur* can screen out the case or send it to the *juge des enfants*. While the *procureur* might recommend that an offender be held in secure custody, only the judge can actually approve such a placement. When a juvenile is confined, it is in a juvenile wing of an adult prison. Such detentions are rare, with the result that very few juveniles are in custody in France relative to the numbers in Canada (Hackler *et al.*, 1987).

Most of the time, the judge handles cases informally in the office. However, if a trial is called for, the judge must follow certain formal procedures, including ensuring that a defence attorney is present. If the judge does not use the formal trial, the juvenile cannot be incarcerated. No punitive measure can be used. The juvenile can be assigned to supervision by a correctional social worker (an *educateur*) but if the juvenile resists being supervised, being placed in a closed institution is not an alternative. When the judge decides not to use the formal court, the emphasis turns to meeting the needs of the juvenile. The judge does not make a decision as much as negotiate options and services. A very wide range of services, including residential facilities, is available. Being placed in a residence is not a sentence. If a juvenile leaves a facility, the judge cannot threaten him or her with prison. During my first visits to France, I was suspicious about judges being so persuasive without using punishment; but, as time went on, I began to understand that most of the judges felt that juveniles could not be helped unless they participated in the decision making. This philosophy and its consequences are developed in another paper (Hackler, 1988).

Not only does the judge negotiate with juveniles, he also negotiates with residences. While some facilities operated by the government are obliged to accept juveniles, the majority are private and are free to accept or reject clients. However, most of the facilities are run by benevolent agencies that are dependent on clients and the concomitant funding for their support. Thus, these facilities must be sensitive to the judge's request. The judge can convince them to take a share of difficult cases.

Both North American and French judges are concerned about juveniles; however, the French judge is more effective because of his flexibility and knowledge of the case. After giving up his or her power to punish by using a trial, the French judge still has a great deal of influence as well as extensive information about the juvenile. Judges also have at least one social worker with whom they work closely. Unlike our judges, those in France even talk to people on the telephone about their cases.

By contrast, Canadian judges work hard to remain ignorant about their cases before deciding on guilt or innocence. Let us explore how this practice makes our system work badly.

Keeping Judges Ignorant

Under the former JDA, it was true that judges could abuse their power as they performed their welfare role. They could "lock up children for their own good." The French have avoided this dilemma by not providing the judge with punitive powers unless a formal trial is held. By contrast, the Canadian system seems eager to have trials for even the most trivial offences. During trials, we feel it is important to separate guilt from sentencing. Before finding a child guilty, judges must remain ignorant of family background and a whole variety of circumstances that are deemed irrelevant to judging guilt for a particular offence. Once finding the child guilty, which we do in the vast majority of cases, the judge must suddenly become well-informed, feverishly reading through pre-disposition reports that have been prepared anticipating a guilty finding. Or the judge can adjourn the case until enough information has been gathered. French judges and French juveniles find such a situation ludicrous. To them, and to me, it is obvious that background factors are relevant to the question of guilt. An anecdote may help explain this view.

A boy had run away from an open facility, and his Canadian judge had a rule that anyone leaving a non-custodial setting would spend six weeks in a custodial setting. While this reasoning makes a good deal of sense to many judges, I later learned that this boy was being beaten by larger boys in the non-custodial residence. In the court room, with other boys waiting in the audience, the defendant was not about to tell the whole story. Nor was the judge going to be on the phone talking to others who understood the situation better. Since the residence was fifty miles away, the psychologist at the facility could not spend half a day at court on the chance possibility that his information would be used. Certainly, a Canadian judge could not call up someone involved in the case and get information. Given our tendency to keep judges ignorant, many of them are trapped by their own informal rules. Otherwise sensitive judges say they wish to make an example of those juveniles who "do not follow orders." That anyone who leaves open custody automatically gets closed custody is a rule used by many judges. It makes sense according the justice model but defeats any attempt to understand the roots of a problem. It also limits the options that can be used.

In France, juveniles cannot be placed in custody for breaking an administrative rule. As a French judge said, "Leaving a residence without permission is not a crime. We lock up juveniles only for committing crimes." In another interview, a judge said, "Sometimes the kids make better decisions than we do."

Although most Canadian judges realize that many of their decisions are unwise, most of them feel that even their stupid decisions should be obeyed. Our mentality insists that it would be terrible if authority were not obeyed, even when that authority makes a poor decision. Therefore, we sometimes punish youths for disobeying administrative decisions more severely than for committing crimes.

In another Canadian case, the boy had been picked up on a Friday evening and held in detention until Monday morning. He was charged with missing appointments with his probation officer, not seeking work and not living with the family to whom he had been assigned. The crown attorney presented the case from the paperwork she had in front of her. However, no probation officer appeared, and there was some confusion as to which probation officer was currently handling the case. The boy's employer had not arrived. (Would having an employer be relevant to the charge of not seeking work?) The boy was staying at home, and his mother was in the court room, but evidently he was supposed to be staying in another home. There seemed to be some confusion about all three charges. Asked how he pleaded, the boy was confused, but pleaded guilty. The duty counsel was also confused. At that point, the judge accepted the guilty plea and adjourned the case until Thursday, when he would decide on the sentence on the basis of a pre-disposition report. In the meantime, the boy would go back to the detention centre. No thought was given to the possibility that this dangerous criminal could go home with his mother. The mother tried to speak, but the judge cut her off, saying that she would be able to speak on Thursday, at the disposition hearing.

During the break, the distraught mother approached the prosecutor, saying, "I know my boy is a brat, but he shouldn't be shit on like that." After further discussion, the prosecutor agreed to raise the matter with the judge when he returned to the court room. When the judge returned, and the prosecutor pointed out that the mother would like to say something about the case, the judge simply repeated that the boy had pleaded guilty and the mother would have adequate time to provide information at the time of sentencing. When the mother stomped out of the court room, the judge hurled threats of contempt of court at her as she disappeared through the doors.

In this case, a minor offender had two sessions in detention. It is most unlikely that he or his mother will have much faith in the justice, efficiency or intelligence of the system. But even with skilled people handling such cases, structural barriers prevent an intelligent response.

First, we insist that juveniles plead guilty or not guilty. They cannot tell their story in their own way. They must conform to the rituals. Second, the prosecutor usually has limited information. The French *procureur* refers a case to the judge because it merits attention, but the Canadian prosecutor is already arguing that the juvenile is guilty. Third, the judge is inhibited about exploring confusing situations or discussing topics outside of their proper sequence. These conditions frequently make a mockery of the youth court as a setting for the sensitive handling of complex problems. Fourth, once we have botched a situation, it is harder to correct it. A judge cannot call up a detention centre and say that he made a mistake and that the mother will come by and pick up the kid. By contrast, French judges are more goal- than ritual-oriented.

Now it is possible that if any of the actors in this loosely coupled system had displayed more skill, the situation might have been handled more smoothly; however, the organization of the system and the laws are also to blame. For example, any decision made by a French judge must be reviewed immediately by the *procureur*. If the *procureur* disagrees, there is an appeal. Admittedly, such appeals are rare, but the *procureur's* role is to represent the interests of the public and provide a check on the judge.

The reader may have also noticed one other point in the case of this dangerous criminal who might have been missing appointments with his probation officer, who might not have been looking for work and who was improperly living in the home of his concerned mother. Obviously, such a dangerous character could not be left to roam the streets before appearing in court, but why was the warrant served late on Friday? He would then have to stay in custody over the weekend. If a probation officer wants to give a juvenile a "taste of the cells," the timing of a warrant can be crucial. In this case, good communications between the probation officer and the police might have increased the likelihood that a warrant would be served on a Friday. But we have strayed somewhat from the question of keeping judges ignorant.

In my interview, I sometimes ask the judge to comment on the following hypothetical situation. A girl has been rejected by her parents and is staying in a non-custodial facility on a charge of theft. The disposition was used, not because of the theft, which the judge and probation officers thought was minor, but because the parents would not accept the girl. After several months, relations with the parents had improved and the girl was to return home. However, she has contracted gonorrhea and the social workers are afraid to tell the parents, feeling it would lead to another rejection. They would like to extend her stay in the residence until the girl can get medical treatment; the girl might not carry out this treatment if she stays at home. The dilemma is that, if this reasoning is explained in court, the parents might be shocked and whatever progress has been made towards reconciliation might be destroyed. My question to the judge is: would you talk to a social worker about such a case in private before the courtroom hearing? All the judges agreed that this would be improper.

Saying Too Much in Court

While keeping judges ignorant is part of the problem, another aspect of it involved revealing too much. In one situation, a girl learned in court for the first time that she had been adopted. It was a traumatic experience for the girl, and it created pandemonium in court. In a legalistic court, information that is shared is screened according to rules of law, not according to the impact on human beings. Since youth courts convict eighty to ninety per cent of defendants, is our emphasis on the right concerns?

Another danger is having professionals testify in court if they have been striving to develop rapport with the juveniles (Lebel, 1981). While it is important to provide the judge with useful information, how much should a psychologist or social worker tell in open court? Will divulging information damage rapport with the client and make the counsellor less effective in the future?

I am fully aware of the dangers of discussing cases in advance and pre-judging them before the hearing, but the above situations illustrate our unwillingness to assume that judges often deal with sensitive issues. We do not trust them. In France, a magistrate is expected to have integrity, to handle extensive information in advance, and still to be able to make equitable judgements in the court room. One might argue that, if the judge recommends that a case go to trial and then sits the case, the cards are stacked against the defendant. Possibly, but I watched one trial where the defence counsel argued that there was some doubt in the evidence, and under such conditions the judge should acquit. The defendant was acquitted. Again we see the ability of magistrates to play different roles at different times. But more important is the basic assumption that judges in France should be well informed. Even the juveniles in France thought that our system must be unfair because we permit judges to make decisions without knowing every-thing possible about the case. French juveniles said they preferred to be sentenced by the judge who had followed their situation and misdeeds for years. Later, I will suggest that one might create a new role, that of "social service" judge, which could avoid some of our present difficulties.

Illustrations of Organizational Failure in a Loosely Coupled System

Three anecdotes may help us to understand how loosely coupled systems can function badly. In the first case, a sixteen-year-old girl was in court for trespassing. She and a number of her friends climbed the fence of a community swimming-pool in the middle of the night and went swimming in the nude. This was a small town, and the juveniles were all related or grew up together. It was not clear why this case ended up in court. The judge suspected there was something behind the case but had no luck in getting an adequate explanation in court. The girl was found guilty of trespassing and fined ten dollars. She now has a juvenile record.

When I pursued this case out of court, I discovered that the manager of the swimming pool was the brother of the mayor and was tired of juveniles climbing over the walls during warm summer evenings for a swim. His complaints to the mayor led to a "stake-out," using the majority of the six-man police force. After the juveniles climbed the fence and were frolicking about in the nude, the police sprang their trap and arrested them all.

One can sympathize with the manager of the pool, but is this the best way to utilize the court? Having engaged in such behaviour many decades ago, I suspect that, had I been caught in all my naked glory and been forced to dress under the flashlights of the police, I would not have been a repeat offender. If this loosely coupled system had a better communication network among the police, probation officers and judge, such a case might never have appeared in court. I cannot imagine this type of case appearing in a French juvenile court.

When loose coupling is accompanied by inefficient information flow, different parts of the system may perform ineffectively, with each organization "covering its ass." Perhaps little damage was done in this case, but was it necessary to give a girl a record of delinquency?

The second case involved a girl in court for theft. The parents separated, and the mother and father lived in two different cities. The daughter lived in a small town with a family who treated her like one of their own. She had been in no trouble in the community and had done well in school. However, this fifteen-year-old began to date a twenty-year-old. The family did not approve. When the father heard of the situation, he drove to the small town, picked up his daughter and moved her to his apartment in the larger city. The girl did not like the woman who lived with the father. She stole eleven dollars from her father's wallet to buy a bus ticket back to the small town to return to the family with whom she had been living. The father swore out a warrant for her arrest for theft, and the police picked up the girl, put her in the local detention centre, then brought her to the larger city and housed her in a second detention centre, pending her arrival in juvenile court on a charge of theft. The social worker who looked into the case found it difficult to recommend any specific action.

In court, the girl expressed her desire to return to the small town. The father, who had legal custody, was concerned about the older boyfriend, even though the girl said she was no longer seeing him. The charge of petty theft remained. Duty counsel recommended that the girl plead not guilty, and she did. Therefore, a trial had to be held. But what to do with the girl in the meantime? The judge did not wish to send her back to the detention centre, but the father refused to accept her in his apartment as long as she was pleading not guilty. The session adjourned with the girl being sent back to the detention centre. She turned to the social worker and said, "Why did I plead not guilty?" After a couple of days in detention, the girl came back, pleaded guilty to the theft before a different judge, and was sent home with her father.

I do not know the best way of dealing with family squabbles, but three different stays in detention centres and a criminal record may not be the best way of handling an argument between a father and daughter. We also saw good people doing dirty work: a probation officer, a social worker, and two reluctant judges wishing there were a reasonable way to handle the situation. In France, a judge may have had difficulties as well, but the girl would not have ended up in detention.

The third illustration involved a girl who was accused of stealing a chocolate bar from a store that reported all incidents of shoplifting. The police determined that she had no previous record and recommended her for alternative measures. However, a mistake was made somewhere between the police station and the prosecutor's office, and the girl was summoned to appear in court. There the prosecutor recognized the minor nature of the offence and asked why she had not been placed on alternative measures. Misunderstanding the proceedings, the father and daughter thought the girl had been recommended for the program and left the court. When their absence was noted, the prosecutor insisted, against the judge's preference, that a warrant for arrest be issued. Different parts of this loosely coupled system blamed each other for the mistake, but the girl was finally put in the program and completed it quickly. The prosecutor, however, did not revoke the warrant until almost two weeks later. In the meantime, the girl and her parents suffered a great deal of stress, wondering if and when she would be arrested.

Here was an illustration of "stealing conflicts" from those who are in a better situation to resolve them (Christie, 1977). In this case, the girl's parents were not only concerned but also seemed to be capable of handling the situation. I have argued elsewhere that the YOA has encouraged more stealing of conflicts than in the past (Hackler, 1987). One might argue that, under the Juvenile Delinquents Act, social workers were guilty of being "professional usurpers" of other people's problems. Now they have been joined, or have even been pushed aside, by those with more legal training.

The reader should not assume that the illustrations provided above are particularly rare. Relatively minor cases get bogged down from time to time as our loosely coupled system struggles with all of the rules. Nor would we assume that cases that are run assembly-line fashion through the court are being handled well. Cases that are routinely given communty-service orders or probation may not get the sort of attention that might reveal background problems. From the clients' perspective, sometimes they are relieved, many times they are confused (Wilks, Birnie and Chamberlain, 1979), but rarely do they feel the system has provided them with a valuable service. By contrast, French youngsters frequently feel they have been helped.

Liaisons and Linkages

There is no magic solution for some of the clumsy ways our current system operates, but efforts to build communication bridges between parts of the system may be helpful. In Victoria, juvenile probation officers ride with the juvenile police from time to time. There could be some negative aspects of this interaction. Some probation officers argue their role is quite different, that they should be helping clients rather than emphasizing social control, and that close contact with the police would blur that distinction. While we were walking and riding the beat one night, it was clear the policeman was in charge, even though he was much younger than the probation officer. The officer's "harder" orientation towards juveniles emphasized control of behaviour. I asked the probation officer if the police mentality, which tended to be negative towards most of their clients, might make probation officers less sympathetic. The probation officer agreed that this might be a concern, but an experience at the end of the evening suggested that two professionals can communicate effectively without forgetting that they have distinct roles to play. The policeman dropped the probation officer off at the end of the shift, and while he was driving me home, he commented "Mark does well by his people." It seems that this policeman felt that probation officers should be bleeding hearts and should be helpers rather than controllers. Since he had established good rapport with the probation officer, he would probably be helpful if the probation officer were to ask for assistance regarding a client. Of course, he would tease the probation officer about being a softy and letting these juvenile thugs lead him around by the nose, but that was simply the way you played your role.

While it is not clear if linkages between juvenile probation and the police serve clients more effectively, police departments that have juvenile liaison officers seem to reduce some of the organizational problems in these loosely coupled systems. For example, in New Westminster, BC, one experienced probation officer handles all of the forty to fifty juvenile cases that are active at a given time. One experienced police officer is also responsible for all juveniles. Little goes on in the community that escapes the attention of these two men. Does this help to explain why relatively few cases end up in the New Westminster youth court? Are problems addressed in a more effective way before there is a need for a court appearance?

Two other illustrations of linkage creation are provided by the Burnaby and Richmond RCMP detachments in British Columbia. The Burnaby unit created a special counseling program, the Burnaby Youth Services program. The Richmond unit brought two social workers into the police department. The specific nature of these services is not the concern of this chapter, but the creation of communication networks that link the police with other agencies and community resources may be one way of helping loosely coupled systems to operate more effectively.

Variability and Flexibility

Juvenile justice in Canada displays a great deal of variability but not necessarily flexibility; that is, the organization of juvenile justice inevitably varies from place to place, because these loosely coupled structures will be connected in different ways. This situation could lead to flexibility, but the constraints created by legislation sometimes lead to illogical practices. For example, how does one detain a juvenile overnight in smaller communities? Large cities have regular detention facilities, but in smaller communities the police may travel long distances to place juveniles in appropriate places. Sometimes, police units try to create a small holding facility that would be adequate for a juvenile detained for a few hours in the police station. If it is 3:00 a.m. and the youth is to appear in court at 9:00 a.m., a long trip to a detention centre has clear disadvantages.

When the YOA was first implemented, detention was one of the areas of concern mentioned by police departments. Since then there has been an accommodation, and it would be interesting to see how innovative local agencies have been. Obviously, some rules are needed concerning detention, but one of the weaknesses of the Young Offenders Act is that it attempts to treat local systems as if they were quite uniform. The detention situation is only one of many where it is impossible to anticipate all the factors that will be relevant and to draft detailed rules that take all such factors into account.

This attempt to legislate variability becomes a farce when one notes that, in Ontario, different types of courts are maintained for those under age sixteen and those age sixteen and seventeen. Such was not the intent of the YOA. My argument is that good legislation would permit flexibility.

Unlike many who feel that uniformity is part of providing justice, I would argue that this variability may, in fact, enable local systems to adapt, to be flexible and to serve their clients more effectively. The French system has built in a certain amount of flexibility. For example, in the French system the school for magistrates trains people who will serve as *procureurs* and judges, at either the adult or the juvenile level. A magistrate can also be a *juge d'instruction*, an investigating judge. These magistrates look for different positions that are open throughout the country, and occasionally move from one role to the other. Since the pay is the same, they base their career decisions on a variety of other factors. The important fact is that judges are aware of the distinct roles to be played in the system and, with each new role, integrity must be a requisite within the system.

A striking illustration of this type of flexibility was displayed in Vienna when I arrived in court and saw one of the judges playing the role of defence lawyer. Naturally, I was surprised; when I inquired afterwards, I learned that a woman defendant had travelled some distance to Vienna for the hearing, but her defence lawyer had not appeared. Since members of the Viennese judiciary sit as judges for some cases but perform investigations before recommending that other cases go to trial, a judge had reviewed this women's case in advance. At the last moment, he told her that he was very familiar with the case, having done the investigation, and if her lawyer did not arrive, he would act as her defence. This seems somewhat incredible to North Americans, but the response of the Austrian judge who was presiding over the hearing was that this was the best defence he had heard all year. In other words, the role must be played with integrity, but people can play different roles.

In France, the magistrates have the same status, even though they are playing different roles. In North America, we are concerned if the judge is too "chummy" with the prosecutor, but in France, co-operation does not obscure the fact that the different roles are designed to be a check on each other. In one sense, our hierarchy, with a judge on top but not necessarily well tuned to the system, can lead to arrogance and arbitrariness. In many of my discussions with judges, I have suggested that it might be healthy if judges were to act as duty counsel one day a month. In addition, they might be permitted to defend an occasional case instead of sending youth on to legal aid. The judges were amused, and none of them took the suggestion seriously.

Let me provide an illustration of variability without flexibility. A trial was to begin at a certain time, but the defence attorney was not there. The prosecutor had no other cases that could be presented at the time, and the judge was annoyed because things were not ready to go. He ordered the prosecutor to find the defence attorney (which she had been trying to do). Meanwhile the judge adjourned the case for fifteen minutes. After fifteen minutes, the judge returned to the court room and waited impatiently, because the prosecutor was not there. When she hurried into the court room, explaining that she had still not been able to reach the defence attorney, the judge was angry and berated the prosecutor. From the standpoint of loosely coupled systems, this judge did not understand the way these agencies interact.

A judge may insist that everyone perform according to a set schedule; however, anyone who has observed court rooms in operation is aware that there are many last-minute changes, with witnesses not appearing, charges being withdrawn and defence counsel not appearing. Lawyers give lower priority to defending juveniles than to defending adults. Frequently, a lawyer can find himself or herself with a time conflict between adult and juvenile court.

While some defence lawyers can be negligent about their juvenile cases, the point is that last-minute changes are a normal part of courtroom operation. Let me describe the court room in a western city that displayed considerable skill in responding to the normal chaos that characterizes any youth or family court.

This court has several court rooms, several judges and several additional occasional judges. However, the scheduling of cases was in the hands of the clerks and prosecutors. The judges have learned to allow time for a variety of informal processes to operate. For example, during one case, the judge wanted some more information before proceeding. It was possible that a probation officer could provide that information. Instead of adjourning the case until a different day, the judge simply adjourned temporarily. In this system, personnel from the sheriff's office control the flow of cases into the court and have an effective communication network with the outside world. Therefore, while one of the sheriff's officers was looking for the liaison probation officer, the clerk and prosecutor were moving on to another case.

Frequently, many activities are being pursued at the same time. Sometimes another judge will come in with a different case, sometimes with a different clerk and different prosecutor. There are also times when the court-room action takes the case to a certain stage where an informal resolution is possible. Some perceptive judges will adjourn the case temporarily while the people involved see if they can work something out informally.

After I had observed this court room for a while, it was obvious that the system was adaptable and able to deal with a wide range of situations in a variety of ways. While some courts would attempt to resolve a case in one setting, or adjourn it until a later date, this particular system was able to use several techniques, such as temporary adjournments, more effectively. Judges learned to adapt to the system by staying in their offices until they were called. At times there was much scurrying around behind the scenes, with the judges occasionally involved in the informal dynamics, but the effective linkages between the different players in the system seemed to result in more effective resolution of problems. This court seemed less trapped by procedures and more able to adapt to the needs of clients. Instead of being aloof and isolated, as they are in many courts, judges were frequently a resource, giving advice outside the court room. There seemed to be less pressure to render a decision in awkward cases. Other justice professionals might become involved with problem resolution, with the judge deliberately stepping back until progress had been made.

Another court displayed the same type of flexibility during an incest case, which had many typical characteristics: the mother had difficulty believing that the father could behave in this way, the two young girls had difficulty talking about it in court. One girl refused to testify in court but was willing to talk to the judge privately. The judge took the stenographer and the girl to his office and took her testimony in private. It is not clear to me how such testimony could be used, but the judge was trying to understand the situation.

The defence attorney played a unique role in that he was trying to look after the interests of the family and not simply trying to get the father acquitted. The defence counsel questioned his client extensively, while the prosecutor remained silent. The judge adjourned the case at a certain stage, and, during the break, a number of things happened. For example, Social Services took the girls into custody. When the trial resumed, the mother now accepted the awful reality. One of the questions of concern to the judge was what would happen, as the family was preparing to move into a new home. As the proceeding reached a point where the reality was clear, but solutions were not, the judge adjourned the trial without attempting to render a verdict or bring the proceedings to a conclusion. He directed the defence attorney, who spoke the language of the immigrant father, to stay with the case and remain in touch with the prosecutor.

Notice that the judge used the trial to bring the problem to the surface. However, aside from simply punishing the father, it was not clear how to resolve other issues. The defence counsel was clearly in a key position to expedite solutions. The prosecutor also stepped back from the case to await further developments. A less-skilled judge might have attempted to force a conclusion to the case that same day.

While it is difficult to link lack of flexibility with the Young Offenders Act, my impression is that the type of communication that encourages the adaptability and flexibility displayed in the above case has been replaced by greater attention to rituals and procedures, as illustrated by the legal objection to adjourning cases *sine die*.

The Unfortunate Loss of Adjourned *Sine Die*

Since the passage of the Young Offenders Act, judges have been unable to adjourn cases *sine die*, that is, to adjourn the case without making a decision. This procedure was used very effectively in Winnipeg in the period prior to the YOA, particularly for first time offenders. A typical situation would involve a first time offender facing the prospect of being found guilty. The judge might stop the proceedings, adjourn the case *sine die*, and point out to the juvenile that, if he or she got into trouble again, this case could be reopened and the judge would render a verdict and decide on a sentence. Psychologically, the juvenile had been to the edge of the cliff, but at the last moment had been allowed to step back. There was no criminal record. If the offender stayed out of trouble, he or she would not receive the formal label "delinquent."

In my discussion of this matter with the clerk of the Ottawa court, who had just been clearing out many juvenile files, he could not remember any of the cases that had been adjourned *sine die* ever being returned to court. Unfortunately, our system prefers neatness. None of this wishy-washy business of adjourned *sine die*. If the kid is guilty, let us be sure to brand him or her. People with this sort of mentality would not have appreciated some strategies used by a Nova Scotia judge. A first offender might have found the judge hesitant about rendering a guilty verdict. Instead, the judge might suggest to the defendant that she or he talk to the person sitting in the court room who arranges a variety of community-service projects while the case was adjourned for a month. The next month the youth would return and explain to the judge that she or he had helped to paint an elderly person's house. The judge may decide not to make a decision for another month. Two months later the youth would return and describe another worthwhile community activity. The judge, in turn, would dismiss the charges. The youth had no criminal record. Of course, the legalists would argue that the juvenile had been punished without having been found guilty. True, but from the standpoint of the defendant, that seems to be a clear advantage. Adjourned *sine die*, an intelligent option, has been lost as a means to satisfy procedural neatness.

The Auditor Versus the Contingency Model

Assuming that variability will continue in our system, how does one also encourage the flexibility that might maximize the returns? Assuming diversity, what administrative policies would best expedite the operation of juvenile-justice systems? One could argue that upper-level administrators would serve the long-term goal of juvenile justice by offering help to local judges, probation officers, and administrators as to how they might deal with particular issues. We refer to this as the contingency model. By providing intelligent options, perhaps by passing on information as to how other local units are dealing with particular problems, upper-level decision makers could expedite the work of the courts and juvenile-service agencies. Unfortunately, administrative policies for providing help from above are frequently less common than those emphasizing directives from above. This latter is the auditor model.

The YOA implicitly supports an "auditor model" for court administration, with an emphasis on monitoring and controlling activities in the various jurisdictions (Gallas, 1976). The goal of the auditor model is to achieve uniformity, but this model assumes that the actors at the line level in the juvenile justice system need to be controlled. A contrasting argument is that the conditions affecting juvenile courts vary from place to place and are influenced by the context of the situation. Because of this diversity, the auditor model is inadequate and is understandably resisted at the local level.

The system might do much better under a "contingency model," which emphasizes the ability to adapt and would take advantage of the intelligent personnel who currently administer the system at the grass-roots level. This does not imply neglect or overlooking deficiencies, but it does recognize the reality that those who staff the courts and front-line services are usually just as talented as those at other levels in the bureaucracy or those who draft the legislation, and, in addition, probably have a better understanding of the problems in the local community. Under the contingency model, upper-level administrators would attempt to expedite the innovative procedures developed by local units and provide information regarding alternative practices elsewhere. This would increase the options available to local problem-solvers.

In France, the contingency model is explicitly recognized. Judges have much flexibility, as long as they are helping the juvenile. If they are punishing, they must adhere to careful procedures. The contingency model seems to characterize the prosecutors who organized and controlled the timing of court activities. In other places, the auditor model seems to be the accepted way of working, with the people at the line level resisting in order to maintain their autonomy. Young clients frequently get hurt while various players struggle for power under the auditor model. I would argue that an auditor model does not work well in a loosely coupled system.

Another illustration of the lack of flexibility in our system is provided by a boy who had spent five months in a group home as part of a six-month sentence. He was doing well in school; his family was located in another town and did not seem to be well equipped to provide an appropriate environment for him. The workers in the group home were trying to work out some sort of strategy for when he finished his six-month sentence. The French judge who was visiting the group home with me asked why the boy could not continue to stay in the group home. It was explained to him that the group home was only for boys serving sentences and that juveniles had to leave when their sentences were finished, even if they had made a good adjustment and were doing well in school. The French judge was puzzled; in France, the judge has the authority to adapt the system to the needs of the juveniles. In fairness, we see this type of flexibility in our system at times. Creating a few beds for social-service youths in a facility for "delinquents" is one illustration. However, I would argue that encouraging line workers to be innovative is relatively rare in our system.

The last illustration of the loss of flexibility under the YOA that I will present here is the formalization of procedures in the docket court.

The Docket Court

As the youth court now resembles the adult court, we see the growth of the impersonal docket court. This court is where many of the minors cases pleading guilty are dealt with summarily. More difficult cases and those pleading not guilty establish dates for later hearings. But let us focus on some of the minor cases that are handled routinely with a lecture and perhaps a short community-service order. Given the impersonal nature of the setting and the fact that the judge usually has little information on the case, beyond the offence, there is little search into the conditions that might have led to this offence.

By contrast, the French judge talks to the juvenile in the office. Parents may or may not be there. The juvenile presents his or her story and the judge can explore questions involving the family. There may be another visit with the parents involved. If a juvenile is hesitant about talking with the parents present, the judge will excuse the parents while he talks to the juvenile privately. The goal is for the judge to become well informed about the situation as soon as possible. Notice that if the case is deemed serious enough to appear in court, the same judge will preside over the trial. From the standpoint of the juveniles in France, this makes sense. They want to be judged by someone who really understands their situation. When I tried to explain how we try to keep the judge from knowing these background factors before rendering a verdict, the response was that our system would seem woefully inadequate to address the needs of young offenders.

To conclude this section, I would suggest that the extensive variability that characterizes our system has lost some of its adaptive qualities: 1) because the YOA has unsuccessfully tried to reduce that variability; and 2) because an auditor model usually prevails. Many well-meaning people hoped that uniform procedures would provide a better defence for juveniles. In the next section, I argue that this wish has not been realized.

The Pretence of Defence

While observing a trial in Austria, I noticed that the defence attorney did a very poor job when he concluded his case. He simply gave the normal "weeping and wailing" approach, which typifies the level of defence in many of our juvenile cases. However, the Austrian *Staatsanwalt* (prosecutor) rose after the defence was finished and questioned the juvenile again, this time bringing out a number of issues that were more appropriate for the defence. I was surprised, and spoke with the prosecutor afterwards, saying that it appeared that he had provided the defence as well as the prosecution. His response was "Of course. The defence did a poor job, and it was my obligation to bring all of the facts out so that the judge could come to an intelligent decision. I understand that in your country you have an adversary model, where the two different sides try to win. Aren't you people interested in the truth? In justice?"

Up until that time, I had taken the adversarial model for granted. Since then, I have developed some grave reservations about the adequacy of the adversarial system in juvenile justice. For most of the cases appearing in youth court, the problem of guilt or innocence is not the major dilemma. Prosecutors are not interested in convicting juveniles where there is some doubt, but there is frequently a dilemma in knowing what to do with the juvenile in a constructive manner. When a defence lawyer does the "weep and wail" routine, it is usually before a judge who is desperately looking for any constructive alternative. Pleas to be gentle are unhelpful, and, in the youth court, lawyers rarely develop a plan that would help a juvenile.

Although defence lawyers are supposed to be representing the client, there are times when one has reason to doubt this is so. In once case, where a boy wished to plead guilty, the lawyer convinced the boy to go to trial. After losing the case (the boy was sent to a group home, where he made reasonable progress), his lawyer continued to appeal the case. Toward the end of the boy's sentence, after he had made a good adjustment to school and his outlook seemed promising, the lawyer was still appealing the original conviction. The major disruptions for the boy during his rehabilitation were those caused by the appeals, which pulled the boy out of school so he could appear in court.

One might well ask if the use of defence counsel has hindered rather than helped the juveniles. Prior to the YOA, I watched one court case where experienced prosecutors were regularly used, but defence attorneys rarely appeared. I have argued elsewhere that the prosecutors are more inclined to "do the defence" as well when there is no defence lawyer present (Hackler, 1984). However, when a defence lawyer is present, and does a poor job, the prosecutor is less inclined to fill in the gaps. To do so would imply criticism of a colleague. In general, I felt that youths were better defended when there was only a prosecutor who was well informed.

In a loosely coupled system, the defence counsels are another component who have needs to be met, and these needs may be different from those of the juveniles. With more lawyers being provided to juveniles by legal aid, one is beginning to see the legal-aid system being pressured by lawyers to provide them with work. Is it the goal of legal aid to provide work for lawyers or to provide service for clients? Some of the lawyers act as if the former were the case.

In fairness, in those jurisdictions that have more experienced defence attorneys, those who become somewhat specialized in youth-court cases may offer better services. In Montreal, for example, there seem to be more lawyers with a specific interest in juvenile work. I was able to watch a number of attorneys who provided a vigorous defence when they thought a youth was inappropriately charged; but when guilt was not really the question, they concentrated their efforts on the type of disposition the prosecutor was willing to recommend.

Eddie Greenspan, a well-known Toronto lawyer, argues that an advocate should look ahead for the client's interests. In one case, he acted for a lad who had committed a number of break-and-enter offences. The boy was on drugs, and his parents were fed up with him (Greenspan, 1982). Greenspan worked with the parents to get the boy into a rehabilitation centre. Because of numerous upsetting incidents at the centre caused by his client, Greenspan kept adjourning the case, and after one year and three months, when things were finally going well for his client (the lad had cured his drug problem and restructured his life), they pleaded guilty before a judge, who quite coincidentally happened to be a director of the rehabilitation centre (1982: 206-7). The lad got probation.

Greenspan calls this "constructive delay," and while defence counsels are vilified for delaying trials, Greenspan points out that, if the lad he was defending had pleaded guilty soon after his arrest, abandoned by his parents, a drug user, with twenty-one charges and no prospects or hopes, he would have received a stiff term of incarceration.

I would agree that the above case demonstrates a success, but a flexible system might permit more such adjournments based on a shared communication system without the need for a high-powered lawyer.

The Use of a Public Defender

While Greenspan provided an illustration of "constructive delay," many of the delays in youth court create hardships for juveniles and their families. Parents sometimes make considerable sacrifices to get to court only to face a five-minute hearing and an adjournment. In his book *The Process is the Punishment: Handling Cases in a Lower Criminal Court*, Malcolm Feeley suggests that going through the youth-court procedures could be more traumatic than the sentence (1979). Some of this delay might be avoided if we utilized a public-defender system. At present, we use a duty-counsel system, which provides legal advice to a juvenile at first appearance; if the juvenile decides to go to trial, the duty counsel steps aside while the juvenile finds a defence lawyer.

While visiting the juvenile court in Oakland, California, I was told by the prosecutors that public defenders seemed to be more effective than other defence lawyers. If public defenders felt that a juvenile was being railroaded by the system, they put up an extremely vigorous defence. Their familiarity with the system gave them an advantage over less-experienced defence counsel. By contrast, guilt was rarely the major issue, and the public defender, having more knowledge of and contacts with those who could provide services, was able to negotiate more rapidly and effectively for recommended dispositions that would be of assistance to the client. If this is called plea bargaining, so be it.

In arguing on behalf of a public defender, one should note that research in the 1960s and 1970s provided a somewhat negative image of both defence lawyers in general and public defenders in particular (Blumberg, 1967; Casper, 1971; McIntyre, 1987: 2). Later research, however, provides a much more adequate assessment of the public defender (Brantingham and Burns, 1981; McIntyre, 1987: 45-8). It seems they are just as effective as private lawyers, especially for those of low status and with less serious charges.

In many cases public defenders have entered this position with a certain amount of zeal, but after a while their morale drops. Others do not see how they could get much satisfaction out of constantly defending those whom some consider to be "scum." In addition, public defenders get little appreciation from their clients. In the youth court, however, conditions might be different. The enthusiasm that brings a lawyer to this role might lead to more satisfaction. Although it sounds like a radical idea, why could we not have crown attorneys and public defenders who can interchange roles? In reality, we have people who have worked as prosecutors who have been, or will be, defence lawyers. If a Viennese judge can act as a defence counsel, why should not our crown attorneys play that role occasionally? In fact, would it not be interesting to have our judges defend a few cases each month? They might get a different perspective on the way the system operates.

At present, public defenders tend to get discouraged and leave the job. However, we could create a body of legally trained civic servants who performed the tasks of prosecutors, defenders and judges, and who moved among these roles the way people move about in other bureaucracies, such as the way professors move into administrative roles and back again into scholarly tasks. Our system creates a gap in terms of salary and prestige between judges and prosecutors and public defenders. For obvious political reasons, it is unlikely that we can alter the present system for appointing judges. However, in the youth and family courts, particularly, would not the roles of prosecutor and public defender be equally important? An attractive career pattern for such legally trained civil servants might improve the quality of justice. In fact, requiring experience as a prosecutor and public defender might be a logical prerequisite for anyone becoming a family court judge.

Let us now ask if the use of public defenders might modify another problem that may have increased since the introduction of the YOA: taking the conflict out of the hands of those most concerned and cutting youths out of the discussion of their problems.

Cutting Youths Out of the Dialogue

Allison Morris and Henri Giller have pointed out that when legal representatives are involved, the possibility of foreclosing direct dialogue between the bench and the defendant is all the greater (1987: 173). This point was rather obvious in many of the Canadian hearings I observed. A lively discussion ensued among judge, prosecutor and defence counsel while the defendant and parents were left to one side, wondering what it was all about. In some situations the defendant sits next to the defence lawyer, which allows the possibility of private communication. In other situations, the defendant is physically placed at the extreme far side of the court room. I heard a number of legally trained persons in youth court state their preference for a situation that leaves the defendant over to one side of the court room so that the professionals can get on with business at hand without being bothered by the defendant. In England, Morris and Giller (1987: 173) suggest, current practices may provide the appearance rather than the reality of due process. This seems to be an appropriate comment for Canada as well.

One of the goals of the Young Offenders Act is to be sure that juveniles understand their rights,. Previous work has shown that juveniles did not understand the process very well under the JDA (Smith, 1985; Wilks, Birnie and Chamberlain, 1979). My impression is that young people are more confused today. However, it is not clear who provides the best information. In one American study, probation officers claim that they, not police or attorneys, are the primary source of juveniles' understanding of their rights. However, the juveniles said it was the lawyer who provided this information (Lawrence, 1983-4). We do not have a comparable study in Canada.

One could argue that, even though every juvenile tried in France must have a defence lawyer, that defence is usually based on a brief preparation shortly before the trial. The difference is that such a defence is less crucial because of the infrequency of trials and the length of sentences, usually a few weeks. Normally, the French judge spends little time on the child's rights, unless the case goes to trial. Usually, the judge brushes this aspect aside. In one sense, the charges are dismissed immediately. There is nothing to defend, so judge and youth can concentrate on effective new steps.

Recommendations for Change

In a chapter on minor crime and the courts, Peter Solomon concludes that the court is a very expensive and unsatisfactory place to deal with crimes that are not very serious (1983: Chapter 5). One could extend that idea to the youth court. While there are some serious cases that justify the formal procedures of the court, the vast majority of cases are of a minor nature, often reflecting underlying problems of a family or personal nature. The court is an inefficient place in which to deal with these social issues. In this regard, the French judge has a considerable advantage. In France, the court room is simply not used for problem-solving. Instead, the court is used when other alternatives have failed. Before suggesting a strategy that might be compatible with our present system, let me provide one more anecdote that illustrates the problem-solving orientation of the French judge, which is so lacking in our system.

The setting was a small facility for temporary care. A fourteen-year-old girl was in conflict with her mother, who wanted her to continue in school. The girl wished to take a course in hair-styling. The stepfather was sympathetic toward the girl, but felt that he should not interfere. The girl ran away from home, stole some food and ended up before the judge. The judge simply swept the crime aside and turned immediately to the problem behind it. Since the girl did not want to go home and the mother did not want her, the judge made arrangements for the girl to stay in the facility. However, the judge and social workers were trying to get the girl to go back home and go along with the mother to a greater degree. If the girl had been sixteen, the judge might have been more sympathetic to the girl being on her own, but as she was fourteen, both social worker and judge were encouraging a family reconciliation. The judge did not pontificate and then issue an edict for everyone to obey. Instead, he accommodated the key actors in the situation without taking the conflict out of their hands (Hackler, 1987). If a reconciliation developed with the parents, the girl would go home. There would be no court hearing, no formal proceedings. If the girl was later dissatisfied at home, she might come to see the judge again, since in France the judge is viewed as a source of help, unlike in North America, where most youngsters have a different view of judges.

It is important to emphasize that French judges have no advantage in compassion or training over their Canadian counterparts. However, the structure of the Canadian court puts an unreasonable demand on our judges. They must render a decision. Somehow they are supposed to bring closure to what is frequently an ongoing and messy situation. This response is frequently unsatisfactory. The French judge, with advice from the youth and others, is willing to try many alternatives.

Although I was originally skeptical about the effectiveness of judges under such circumstances, I soon learned that juveniles spoke of "my judge." Judges were responsible for specific geographical areas, thus enabling the juvenile to establish a relationship with a single judge. In one case, a juvenile appeared at court asking to see "his" judge because he had left the residence where he was staying. However, as the judge was away for a few days, the boy talked with social workers, prosecutors, and others, but he wanted to tell his story to his judge and to no one else. In North America, it is unlikely that the system would respond to a runaway in such a tolerant manner, but in this situation arrangements were made for the boy to stay in another facility until the judge returned.

Even though I use some aspects of the French system to provide ideas for change, I am also aware of weaknesses. For example, while many French delinquents are of Arab background, I saw no magistrates from that culture. By contrast, in Oakland, California, the two judges were black, and blacks were well represented among prosecutors, probation officers and so on. In other words, minority-group offenders in Oakland have more successful role models than do the French minority-group offenders. But this chapter is not designed to provide a balanced view of French juvenile justice or French society. The point is that, in French society, one with faults like ours and with people with frailties like ours, a structure has been created that serves young people more effectively. I believe it is possible to capture some of the advantages of the French system through the creation of the role of "social-service judge."

The Social-Service Judge

In a formal court room, judges are restricted in the amount of problem-solving they can do. There are constraints on the information they can utilize prior to deciding on guilt. Once guilt has been determined, there are also other limitations in terms of exploring helpful alternatives. A social-service judge would be one operating in a non-punitive setting. Referrals could come from prosecutors, police, welfare, probation, school and so on. For example, a prosecutor might prefer to avoid formal processing but, because of other potential problems facing the youth, have someone explore the situation further. While direct referrals to other agencies are possible, someone like a judge may be in a position to consider a wider range of possibilities.

Instead of demanding an appearance at a set time, the judge might talk with the youth by phone first. Should the meeting be with parents or not? Should the parents and youth talk to the judge separately? The judge would make it clear that he or she has no punitive powers while acting as a social-service judge. In addition, the judge might be disqualified from hearing any future case involving the youth. Without punitive powers, a judge could even permit the youth to talk about actual crimes or anything of relevant concern.

The goal would be to see if there were any services that would be helpful. For example, if the family were temporarily in disarray, a child might stay in a group home. Public or private agencies, or volunteer services, could be considered. Note that all participation would be voluntary. Failure to take part would not be an offence. While judges might be persuasive, they could not require compliance.

Naturally, the judge would need help from others to provide the actual services and thus would have people in social service, probation, the police or volunteer agencies who could respond. Again, these services might normally be available, but a judge might be effective in seeing that a young person is not overlooked.

These services could become expensive, although probably less expensive than services committed to youths who become wards of the province. While a pilot project might be done through informal co-operation, eventually legislation might be needed to authorize the judge to guarantee payment for these services. In one sense, could we provide all of the help that is at present available to a child without having to make the young person a ward of the province? Instead of requiring that a juvenile be treated after being found guilty of an offence or found to be neglected, can we offer help under conditions where the youth can have more of a say? There is some evidence that having a voice in decisions makes people more willing participants. The goal would be to involve the youth in the process. The extent of involvement of the parents may depend on circumstances and the assessment of the judge.

There are two principles that would be central to this endeavour. First, the youth would be able to turn to someone who has a certain amount of clout. Parents and youths can be sloughed off; agencies might discourage a client, but it would be more difficult for them to slough off a determined judge. Second, agency personnel change from time to time, creating the possibility of discontinuity for the youth or family. Under a system where we were not stuck with formal lines of jurisdiction, the person actively helping the youth might be able to stay in contact for a longer period of time. Whether that person was a probation officer, social worker or policeman would not matter, because no one has any formal power — only persuasion, with a judge as expediter. Obviously, a pilot project would lead to a variety of efforts that would change over time as the judges experimented with different situations.

Conclusion

This chapter has argued that Canada has permitted a clumsy and insensitive juvenile justice system to evolve. Well-meaning people have attempted to correct many weaknesses with detailed legislation, but these efforts have failed. At the same time, we see illustrations of ingenuity at different levels in the system in attempting to adapt the bureaucracy to the child. Those efforts can be rewarded by modifying minor aspects of the system. The types of adaptations will vary from place to place, and one must always be alert to abuses.

A specific recommendation for change would be a public defender in juvenile justice. Such a role might advantageously alternate from time to time with the role of prosecutor. A second recommendation would be the creation of a social-service judge. In a helping role, this person would have all the power available to the judge in the court room without the power to punish or restrict the liberty of young people. At present we have good people doing dirty work in a clumsy system. It is possible to utilize the talent and goodwill of these people more effectively.

Acknowledgement

The author would like to acknowledge support from the Ministry of the Solicitor General of Canada through their Contributions Grant; the Social Sciences and Humanities Research Council of Canada; and the Exchange of Researchers Program, National Research Council and the Government of France.

References

Blumberg, A.S. 1967. "The Practice of Law as a Confidence Game: Organization Cooptation of a Profession." *Law and Society Review* 1: 15-39.

Brantingham, P. and P. Burns. 1981. *The Burnaby, B.C. Experimental Public Defender Project: An Evaluation Report*. Ottawa: Department of Justice.

Casper, J. 1971. "Did You Have a Lawyer When you Went to Court? No, I had a Public Defender." *Yale Review of Law and Social Action* 1: 4-9.

Christie, N. 1977. "Conflicts as Property." *British Journal of Criminology* 17: 1-26.

Eisenstein and H. Jacob. 1977. *Felony Justice*. Boston: Little, Brown and Co.

Feeley, M. 1979. *The Process is the Punishment: Handling Cases in a Lower Criminal Court*. New York: Russel Sage.

Feeley, M. 1983. *Court Reform on Trial: Why Simple Solutions Fail*. New York: Basic Books.

Gallas, J. 1976. "The Conventional Wisdom of State Court Administration: A Critical Assessment of an Alternative Approach." *The Justice System Journal* 2: 35-55.

Greenspan, E. 1982. "The Role of the Defence Lawyer in Sentencing" in Boydell, C.L. and I.A. Connidis (eds.), *The Canadian Criminal Justice System*, Toronto: Holt, Rinehart and Winston.

Hackler, J. 1983-4. "Interpreting Meaning in Juvenile Court: The Use of Local Wisdom." *Juvenile and Family Court Journal* 24: 71-82.

Hackler, J. 1984. "Canada" in Klein, M. (ed.), *Western Systems of Juvenile Justice*, Beverly Hills: Sage.

Hackler, J. 1987. "Stealing Conflicts in Juvenile Justice: Contrasting France and Canada." *Canadian Journal of Law and Society* 2: 141-51.

Hackler, J. 1988. "Practicing in France what Americans Have Preached: The Response of French Judges to Juveniles." *Crime and Delinquency* 34: 467-85.

Hackler, J., J. Brockman and E. Luczynska. 1977. "The Comparison of Role Inter-relationships in the Juvenile Courts: Vienna and Boston." *International Journal of Criminology and Penology* 5: 367-97.

Hackler, J. C. Fringon Garapon and K. Knight. 1987. "Locking up Juveniles in Canada: Some Comparisons with France." *Canadian Public Policy* 13: 477-89.

Hagan, J. 1983. *Victims Before the Law*. Toronto: Butterworths.

Hagan, J., D. Alwin and J. Hewitt. 1979. "Ceremonial Justice: Crime and Punishment in a Loosely Coupled System." *Social Forces* 58: 506-27.

Hagan, J., I. Nagel and C. Albonetti. 1980. "The Differential Sentencing of White Collar Offenders in Ten Federal District Courts." *American Sociological Review* 45: 802-20.

Haveman, P. 1986. "From Child Saving to Child Blaming: The Political Economy of the Young Offenders Act, 1908-1984" in Brickey, S. and E. Comack (eds.), *The Social Basis of Law*. Toronto: Garamond Press.

Hughes, E. 1964. "Good People and Dirty Work" in Becker, H. (ed.), *The Other Side*. New York: Free Press.

Lawrence, R. 1983-4. "The Role of Legal Counsel in Juveniles' Understanding of their Rights." *Juvenile and Family Court Journal* 34: 49-58.

Lebel, B. 1981. "Expertise et déontologie." *Canadian Journal of Criminology* 23: 203-5.

Los, M. 1987. "La loi sur les jeunes contrevenants et les masse-media." *Criminologie* 20: 7-33.

McIntyre, L. 1987. *The Public Defender*. Chicago: University of Chicago Press.

Reiss, A. 1971. "Systematic Observation of Natural Social Phenomenon" in Costner, H. (ed.), *Sociological Methodology*, San Francisco: Jossey Bass.

Smith, T. 1985. "Law Talk: Juveniles' Understanding of Legal Language." *Journal of Criminal Justice* 113; 339-53.

Solomon, P. 1983. *Criminal Justice Policy; from Research to Reform*. Toronto: Butterworths.

Wilks, C., L. Birnie and C. Chamberlain. 1979. "The Expectations of Children and Their Families Regarding Juvenile Court." Family Court Clinic, Toronto (mimeo).

Dispositions as Indicators of Conflicting Social Purposes Under the JDA and YOA

Alan W. Leschied and Peter G. Jaffe

Much has been made of the transgressions of civil rights encountered by youths and their families under the Juvenile Delinquents Act (JDA). It is important, therefore, in the context of rather negative reviews of the JDA, to remember that the original theoretical underpinning of the act was not so much to mete out justice to young persons as it was to "heal" the sufferings that young persons had experienced leading to their commission of an offence and judgement of being delinquent. The original "child-savers" wanted to do nothing less than rescue young persons from the families and social conditions that promoted the evils that had befallen Canada's young people of the day. The assumption was that young persons became delinquent as a response to poor parenting or economic and social disadvantages. Therefore, the sole purpose of the JDA was to take delinquents "in a state of need" and provide for those needs through some form of state-mandated intervention. Hence, as is well known to the general readership in juvenile justice in Canada, judges held a free hand in placing young persons in a range of facilities, with the intent of correcting past wrongs. Hence, the focus for disposition was not so much the offence as it was the offender. Young persons presented to the court with a rather minor offence could potentially be placed in training school if the court felt that such intervention was justified, based on the young person's being judged in need of specific guidance and direction. The judge was allowed an extremely liberal interpretation of the best interests ethic (section 20(5)) under this statute regarding disposition, and was not weighted down by complexities of civil-rights and courtroom procedure.

A considerable amount of attention has been focused on the abridgment of civil rights within this ethic of social purpose under the direction of the juvenile court (Bala and Clarke, 1981; Leon, 1977). Little attention was paid to proportionate sentencing based on the offence, and even less emphasis was placed on standardization of sentencing across jurisdictions. The statute gave considerable liberties to individual judges, providing for individual interpretations of the best interests ethic.

Few people today would agree in favour of the extent of intrusiveness allowed under the JDA. Recent authors (Leon, 1977, Grant, 1984) are correct in their estimation that society was well overdue for a revamping of the social purpose and obligation to provide state care for young persons under the JDA. Society simply could not support a system that produced results from training-schools stays that could reduce reoffending by only one-third (Lambert and Birkenmeyer, 1972).

Civil libertarians railed against the JDA specifically because of the lack of proportionality in sentencing based on the nature of the offence. As well, they objected to the court's power to order committal to training school indefinitely — or to retain some authority over the offender until his or her twenty-first birthday. The extent of discretion used by non-judicial officials in recommitting young persons to training school was considered abusive. The lack of determinacy specifying length of time in training schools or group homes also opened the way for abuses to occur. Essentially, except for province-wide monitoring by such systems as training-school advisory boards, non-judicial officials governing the JDA-based juvenile justice system were largely unmonitored and unevaluated. While one article suggested that the JDA-based system was not working well in keeping young people out of trouble (Lambert and Birkenmeyer, 1972), there is only minimal evidence of the impact of the JDA in keeping young persons out of difficulty. Though there are specific cases frequently cited to underscore the abuse of legal rights for young persons under the *parens patriae* system (Bala and Clarke, 1981), there is not a great deal of information that would lead to empirical findings regarding the extent of the abuse. Rather, the fact of potential abuse in individual case studies was sufficient to raise concerns with civil libertarians and others.

There is some evidence to suggest that prior to the proclamation of the YOA, some provincial jurisdictions had attempted to restrict the use of training schools under dispositions through amending provincial law, while establishing policies that provided a clear message to the court with guidelines respecting sentencing. For example, in Ontario in 1977, there was a repeal of section 8 of the Ontario Training Schools Act, which meant that young persons could not longer be committed to training school for offences that could not be prosecuted through the court had they been committed by an adult (Grant, 1984). This section spoke directly to the concerns regarding the placement of young persons charged with truancy, and specifically females who had come to court at the behest of parents who were concerned about their inability to manage their child. Data indicate that, in 1973, committals to training school under section 8 of the Ontario Training Schools Act accounted for almost half (42.5 per cent) of all committals made. By 1975, the provincial policy had directed courts to consider alternatives to dispositions regarding training school with this delinquent group, and the relative percentage dropped to 16.1 per cent (Birkenmeyer and Polonski, 1976). Notably, committals to training school for females following the repeal of section 8 in 1977 were reduced from thirty per cent in the early 1970s to fourteen per cent in 1981-2 (Ontario Ministry of Community and Social Services, 1977). During the 1970s and early 1980s, Ontario also reduced the total number of training schools from thirteen to seven, and the bed capacity by two-thirds. In Ontario, the closure of training schools and shifts in policy from institutionalization to community-based programming encouraged the development of a specialized group of foster homes as well as specialized treatment programs in children's mental-health centres (Leschied and Thomas, 1985). There is little doubt that these policy shifts from Ontario, dating from the mid-1970s, were in part the result of anticipation of the more rights-oriented YOA. It is also evident that other provinces were showing signs of parallel development in provincial legislation through the reduction of institutionalized care to community-based care for juvenile delinquents, as was reflected, for example, in Quebec's Youth Protection Act.

The Young Offenders Act, as has been well established in both numerous reviews and case law, is not child-welfare legislation (Bala, 1986). Whereas the JDA based its social purpose on the provision of guidance and direction for youths judged to be out of control in both their families and their communities, the YOA emphasizes young persons' responsibility and accountability within a legal framework.

Specific to dispositions, this shift in emphasis allowed for four important developments: (1) the standardization of dispositions across jurisdictions; (2) provisions for determinant sentencing; (3) the prohibition of committals to child-welfare agencies; and (4) the prohibition of committal to treatment centres without the consent of the parents, young persons and the facility to which the referral was being made.

Table 1 summarizes the dispositions made available under the JDA and the YOA.

Table 1. Dispositions Made Available Under Juvenile Delinquents Act and Young Offenders Act.

	Juvenile Delinquents Act	Young Offenders Act
Discharge	Suspend final disposition (s. 20(1)(a))	Allows for absolute discharge following finding of guilt (s. 20(1)(a))
Delays in proceedings	Adjournment allowed for occasional court reappearance (s. 20(1)(b))	Judge must dispose of matter at hand; cannot arbitrarily delay proceedings
Fines	Imposition of fines to a maximum of $25 (s. 20(1)(c)); judge may also order that parent/guardian pay fine if considered opinion suggests that parent/guardian was a contributor directly or indirectly in the commission of the offence (s. 22(1))	Imposition of fines to a maximum of $1000 to be levied directly against the young person (s. 20(1)(b))
Probation	Young person placed in custody of a probation officer or designate (s. 20(1)(d))	Young person placed on probation for a period not to exceed two years (s. 20(1)(j))
Committal to child-welfare authority	Youth committed to the charge of any children's aid society as designated under provincial legislation (s. 20(1)(b))	No provision allowed for child-welfare committal
Institutionalized care	Youth committed to a training school for unspecified length of time; when released can be recommitted at the discretion of the probation officer and superintendent of the industrial school	Young person committed to custody to be served continuously or intermittently for a specified period to a maximum of three years (s. 20(k)(i),(iii)); judge to determine if custody to be served in secure or open facility (s. 24(2))
Treatment	Treatment placements not specified in act but typically made a term of probation not requiring consent of the young person	Under (s. 20(1)(i)), judge may order youth to be detained for treatment for specified length of time with conditions set forth under s. 22(1), which requires consent of the parents, youth and treatment facility
Restitution	Not specified under the act; could be made a term of probation	Section 20(1)(d)(e)(f) allows the court to order the youth make personal or financial restitution to victims
Community service order	Not specified under the act; could be made as a term of probation	Allows for judge to order under s. 20(1)(g) the youth to provide community service with the restriction that, under s. 21(8) such service can be completed in 240 hours

It has been argued (see e.g., Leschied and Jaffe, 1986, 1987) that the basis for the YOA's emphasis in dispositions is partly a recognition of the need to protect the civil rights of young persons (Bala and McConville, 1985); partly a response to the pessimism expressed in reviews of the literature reflecting the ineffectiveness of treatment programs for juveniles (Shamsie, 1981); and partly a belief that dispositions under the JDA were "too soft." In many respects, the liberal agenda of encouraging state intervention on behalf of children and youths has been discouraged, and, offsetting this, an increasing emphasis on the conservative agenda of "getting tough" with youth crime, balanced by the protection of civil liberties, has been given pre-eminence (Leschied and Gendreau, 1986).

The disposition summary in section 20 of the YOA outlines the possible courses of action the youth-court judge can take in consequencing youth crime. These range from less serious interventions, such as restitution, a community-service order or a fine to the more onerous dispositions of open and secure custody. All dispositions are determinant in their length and specific in their nature. For example, the type of custody — open or secure — and length is specified by a youth-court judge, though the specific location of custody is left to the provincial director.

It would appear that the disposition section of the YOA manifests the belief expressed in the first principle (s. 3(1), which indicates that youths will be held accountable and responsible. The sanctions outlined in section 20 are made in the context of proportionate sentencing based on the seriousness of the charge and are meant to have a specific deterrent effect on subsequent behaviour of the young offender. Though there have been attempts by judges to use young-offender dispositions as a general deterrence, these expressions have been overturned by higher courts. Specific deterrence has been considered the more appropriate sentencing policy.

The specific nature of what constitutes the disposition is left to the individual provinces to determine. For example, what might constitute open custody in one province may not correspond to open custody in another province. Hence, the nature of programming and the degree of intrusiveness of programming are not determined by the federal statute. In some respects, the lack of specificity has left open the exact nature and intent of the sanctions outlined in section 20. For example, since section 22 requires the youth to consent to treatment, many jurisdictions have noted this exclusion from treatment by the consent section as dictating the need for an absence of treatment in custodial dispositions where the youth does not have the option of withholding consent. In other words, if treatment were to be allowed in open- or secure-custody facilities, then there would not have been the exclusion under section 22 to allow young persons to exempt themselves from treatment by withholding or withdrawing their consent. Therefore, the nature of custody is left to each provincial jurisdiction to determine on its own, though there have been cases where the definition of 'open custody' has been considered too intrusive to fit the definition of what constitutes an open facility.

There are some data to suggest that individual youth-court judges have interpreted the declaration of principle pertinent to sentencing as encouraging incarceration. Data from a study by Hanscomb (1988) suggest that three-quarters of family-court judges in Ontario who responded to a survey on dispositions felt there was a greater emphasis on punishment/accountability; one in five judges noted the shift to increasing incapacitation; and almost half (forty-two per cent) felt this reflected a trend toward general deterrence. Two notable quotes from judges, who maintained anonymity in this study, share beliefs that one hears routinely in the YOA system. The first judge notes: "I hope that I haven't changed; the system is forcing more punishment! I predicted that more kids would be jailed under the YOA rather than less as promised. I was right! Incarceration has been up an astounding amount." The second judge commented: "I don't like to but I must give rehabilitation less emphasis under the YOA."

Additional data from Manitoba suggest that there has been an increasing emphasis on open custody (Manitoba Community Services, 1986). Alberta judges are reportedly concerned that, with a de-emphasis on treatment, custodial facilities are becoming nothing more than "warehouses" (Gabor, Greene and McCormick, 1986). These findings seem to have been met with some surprise by YOA scholars who felt that one of the encouraging aspects of the YOA was the move toward deinstitutionalization. It is therefore ironic that data from Ontario with respect to committals to training schools under the JDA suggest that, prior to the YOA, there was a decrease in the number of youths placed in training school, only to have a consequent increase in committal rates once the YOA was proclaimed (Ontario Ministry of Community and Social Services, 1977; Leschied and Jaffe, 1987).

Tables 2 and 3 summarize disposition data from a JDA year (1981-2) and YOA year (1986-7). The provincial data illustrated are extracted from figures compiled through the Canadian Centre for Justice Statistics. Notably, under the YOA, approximately thirty-one per cent of dispositions have been for custody, whereas training school committals were only thirteen per cent under the JDA. Some judges have suggested that open custody is used in many cases where, were the child-welfare option still available, youths would be placed in group or foster homes. One could debate the different environments and mandates of foster homes relative to those of the average YOA open-custody placement. Even so, if child-welfare committals are combined with the training-school committals in the JDA data, committals to custody under the YOA are still almost twice as frequent. Another datum of note is the extremely low rate of treatment orders made. Table 4 summarizes committals under subsection 20 (1) (i) for 1984-7. During that period, the number of treatment orders made across seven provinces was slightly more than seventy-five.

Table 2. Dispositions Under the Juvenile Delinquents Act, 1981-2.

Type of Disposition	Percentage
Suspended/Adjourned	13.1
Reprimand	3.4
Fine/Restitution	28.7
Probation	32.2
Child-welfare order	5.1
Training school	12.6
Other	4.9

Note: Includes provinces of Alberta, Saskatchewan, Manitoba, Quebec, New Brunswick, Nova Scotia and Newfoundland; N = 72,818 delinquencies.

Source: Canadian Centre for Justice Statistics.

Table 3. Dispositions Under the Young Offenders Act, 1986-7.

Type of Disposition	Percentage
Absolute discharge	3.2
Fine/Restitution	12.9
Community service order	6.5
Probation supervision	45.1
Open custody	14.9
Secure custody	16.2
Treatment order	0.1
Other	1.0

Note: Includes periods of reporting data to Statistics Canada by provinces of Alberta, Saskatchewan, Manitoba, Quebec, New Brunswick, Nova Scotia and Newfoundland; N = 73,866 delinquencies.

Source: Canadian Centre for Justice Statistics.

Table 4. Treatment Orders Made Under Section 20(1)(i) of the Young Offenders Act, 1984-5.

Year	Number of Orders Made
1984/5	89
1985/6	58
1986/7	80

Note: Includes provinces of Alberta, Saskatchewan, Manitoba, Quebec, New Brunswick, Nova Scotia and Newfoundland; N = 73,866 delinquencies.

Source: Canadian Centre for Justice Statistics

It has been reported (see e.g., Leschied and Jaffe, 1986, 1987) that judges have utilized the community-service-order option and probation frequently, and have encouraged the use of custody. As previously reported, section 20 dispositions with respect to treatment have been largely ignored.

Two reasons would seem to account for the low rates of use of the treatment disposition. The first relates to the interpretation by judges of the YOA as being largely criminal justice legislation and, indeed, as others have commented, not child-welfare legislation. Second, the fact that the civil-rights aspects of the legislation require consent by the young person excludes many young persons who, though perhaps in need of treatment intervention, may not have the insight and foresight to make a decision allowing for placement in a treatment centre (Leschied and Jaffe, 1986). An elaboration of reasons for the low rates of consent for committals under section 20(2) is found elsewhere (Leschied and Hyatt, 1986).

Once again, a comparison of Tables 2 and 3 makes it apparent that the wishes of the legislators in revisiting juvenile justice law, making penalties more harsh, have been actualized. Committals to custody have been few in number. As commented upon by Reid and Reitsma-Street (1984), it is quite apparent, as expressed through the disposition section, that the YOA is emphasizing crime control to the exclusion of child-welfare and treatment concerns.

Summary

Juvenile justice legislation expresses the state's belief that crime by young persons needs to be controlled: the dispositions available under this legislation express the philosophy and intent of the legislation. The YOA has marked a significant shift away from child-welfare/treatment intervention to accountability and responsibility with specific deterrence to individual crime. The obvious question at this point, posed not only by legislators but more importantly by the public, is whether or not the sanctions allowed under the YOA are sufficient and of the nature that will have the desired effect of controlling youth crime.

The debate with respect to effectiveness in controlling crime has a long history. Martinson (1974) focused this debate by stating, in a rather inflammatory article, that nothing worked when it came to intervention, and the least we can do as a society is to sanction those who break laws and hope that sufficient punishment will provide a deterrence to subsequent crime. This rather scathing review by Martinson has been rebuked by many, most notably Palmer (1978) and Gendreau and Ross (1979, 1987). The debate rages on. The recent review of the rehabilitative literature by Gendreau and Ross (1987) suggests, from a positive view, that human behaviour can be changed. This review would seem to give sufficient encouragement to those who want to see a more liberalized view of the nature of interventions specific under sentencing/dispositional practices. However encouraging the literature is, actual practices in sentencing and policies within justice seem not to follow it. Specific to the YOA, recent data produced through the Centre for Criminal Justice Statistics would suggest that offence rates by persons of young-offender age have shown a steady increase since 1984. This has occurred at a time when Canada, except for the province of Quebec, has seen a coincidental decrease in the adolescent population. Does this suggest that the policies specific to the YOA have failed? It is difficult to conclude at this point that an increased crime rate in young persons can be tied to any specific policy. More controlled studies need to be carried out in order to address this very important issue. One such study that has been carried out by the authors has examined the recidivism rates of a more disturbed group of young offenders who appeared in youth court in southwestern Ontario. These data suggest that the deterrence-focused dispositions of the YOA seem not to have the same effect of reducing crime as did the treatment disposition within the JDA (Leschied, Austin and Jaffe, 1988). Further research needs to be reported to examine this very critical issue. What can be stated thus far with respect to dispositions under the YOA is that, in their nature and practice, YOA dispositions seem to be following the legislation's intent, as evidenced in the increased rates of custody and emphasis on more accountability provisions with respect to sentencing, and individual-restitution programs, as evidenced in community-service orders. The decrease in emphasis on rehabilitation/treatment is also evidenced in the extremely low numbers of youths committed under subsection 20(2) pursuant to treatment disposition. Hence, the principles of due process and accountability in the act seem to be expressed in the current available data. Data reflecting on implementation of child-welfare and special-needs principles appear invisible.

There is some recent evidence to suggest that some judges are becoming frustrated at the inflexibility of the YOA sentencing process. A recent as yet unreported case of one judge in an urban southwest Ontario jurisdiction committed a thirteen-year-old female to a period of secure custody not in response to the serious nature of the crime she committed — a "breach of probation" — but out of concern for the fact that the girl had been involved in street prostitution and her history included many serious risk factors for subsequent disturbance, such as sexual abuse.

The court, in passing disposition, noted the reality that teenage prostitution was not a criminal issue but rather a "life-style" concern. The court was quite conscious of contravening the YOA concept of having the limitation to intrusiveness commensurate with the nature of the offence. The judge in question invited the defence to appeal his decision, which indeed occurred, and the disposition was overturned.

It is difficult at this point to estimate the degree of discordance between what people view as the desired social purpose in young-offender policy and the realities manifest in YOA practice.

Social purpose in the JDA reflected the intense belief that the state played a vital role in recognizing and assisting young persons who were seen as committing crimes not out of a sense of "badness" but largely out of social mistreatment. This belief has given way to a young-offender system that views young persons as needing court advocates to mitigate largely against the uninvited intrusion of the state (Bala and McConville, 1985) and to see behaviour and motivation rectified through punishment rather than treatment. In the United States, Shireman and Reamer (1986) have noted this evolution reflected in the following cogent passage:

> The perceptible move away from the forgiving views of the child savers is not entirely inappropriate. Today we are far less naive about the nature of juvenile crime and ways of responding to it than we were at the turn of the century. Solicitous care, nurturance, and affection are not enough to alter the ways of many contemporary offenders. Sophisticated treatment, trained professionals, adequate facilities, and an emphasis on due process are essential

> ingredients in any reasoned effort to confront the modern-day variety of juvenile crime. The relative simplicity and paternalism of the child saving days are now obsolete. Yet, in our pursuit of updated measures to handle today's offenders, we seem to have lost a particular virtue of the child savers. No matter what one believes about the motives of the principals of that movement — whether or not one accepts the cynical assessments of that era — the optimism and faith in youths that moved the child savers now has largely evaporated. (170-1)

Have Canadians let their 'optimism and faith in youth...evaporate'? It is clear that a review of JDA and YOA dispositions marks a significant shift in how Canadians are dealing with youthful crime. However, this shift suggests a dramatic paradox. In an effort to provide civil rights and due process for young offenders and save them from the unfettered paternalism of JDA judges, a worse consequence may have resulted. The increase in custodial sentences and decreased access to rehabilitative services may suggest more process but less meaningful outcomes for young offenders. One hopes that a new generation of child-savers and civil libertarians can become stronger allies in creating a balance in the Canadian juvenile justice system.

References

Bala, N.M. 1986. "The Young Offenders Act: A New Era in Juvenile Justice" in Landau, B. (ed.), *Children's Rights in the Practice of Family Law*. Toronto: Carswell.

Bala, N.M. and K.L. Clarke. 1981. *The Child and the Law*. Toronto: McGraw-Hill Ryerson.

Bala, N.M. and B.J. McConville. 1985. "Children's Rights: For Us Against Treatment." *Canada's Mental Health* 33(4):2-5.

Birkenmeyer, A.C. and M. Polonski. 1976. *Trends in Training School Admissions: 1967-1975*. Toronto: Ministry of Correctional Services.

Gabor, P. and P. McCormick. 1986. "The Young Offenders Act: The Alberta Court Experience in the First Year." *Canadian Journal of Family Law* 5(2):301-319.

Gendreau, P.G. and R.R. Ross. 1979. "Effective Correctional Treatment: Bibliotherapy for Cynics." *Crime and Delinquency* 25(4):463-89.

Gendreau. P.G. and R.R. Ross. 1987. "Revivification of Rehabilitation: Evidence from the 1980s." *Justice Quarterly* 4(3):349-408.

Grant, T. 1984. "The 'Incorrigible' Juvenile: History and Prerequisites of Reform in Ontario." *Canadian Journal of Family Law* 4(3):293-318.

Hanscomb, D.K. 1988. "The Dynamics of Disposition in Youth Court." Unpublished

Research Report, University of Toronto.

Lambert, L.R. and A.C. Birkenmeyer. 1972. *An Assessment of the Classification System for Placement of Wards in Training Schools: Factors Related to Classification and Community Adjustment.* Ministry of Correctional Services Research Report. Toronto: Ontario Ministry of Correctional Services.

Leon, J.S. 1977. "The Development of Canadian Juvenile Justice: A Background for Reform." *Osgoode Hall Law Journal* 15(1):71-106.

Leschied, A.W. and P. Gendreau. 1986. "The Declining Role of Rehabilitation in Canadian Juvenile Justice: Implications of Underlying Theory in the Young Offenders Act." *Canadian Journal of Criminology* 28(3):315-22.

Leschied, A.W. and C.H. Hyatt. 1986. "Perspective: Section 22(1), Consent to Treatment Order Under the Young Offenders Act." *Canadian Journal of Criminology* 28(1):69-78.

Leschied, A.W. and P.G. Jaffe. 1986. "Implications of the Consent to Treatment Section of the Younger Offenders Act: A Case Study." *Canadian Psychology* 27(3):312-13.

Leschied, A.W. and P.G. Jaffe. 1987. "Impact of the Young Offenders Act on Court Dispositions: A Comparative Analysis." *Canadian Journal of Criminology* 29(4):421-30.

Leschied, A.W. and K.E. Thomas. 1985. "Effective Residential Programming for "Hard-to-Serve" Delinquent Youth." *Canadian Journal of Criminology* 27:161-77.

Leschied, A.W., G.A. Austin and P.G. Jaffe. 1988. "Impact of the Young Offenders Act on Recidivism of Special Needs Youth: Clinical and Policy Implications." *Canadian Journal of Behavioural Science* 20(3):322-31.

Manitoba Community Services. 1986. *Young Offenders Act: The Second Year.* Winnipeg.

Martinson, R. 1974. "What Works! Questions and Answers About Prison Reform." *The Public Interest* 35:22-54.

Ontario Ministry of Community and Social Services. 1977. *Operational Review of Observational and Detention Homes. Report One: Where We Are.* Toronto.

Palmer, T. 1978. *Correctional Intervention and Research: Current Issues and Future Prospects.* Lexington, MA: Heath.

R. v. Theresa C. Judgement unreported. (Ontario Provinvial Court — Family Division, County of Waterloo), Campbell J.

Reid, S.A. and M. Reitsma-Street. 1984. "Assumptions and Implications of New Canadian Legislation for Young Offenders." *Canadian Criminology Forum* 7:1-9.

Shamsie, S.J. 1981. "Anti-Social Youth: Our Treatments Do Not Work — Where Do We Go From Here?" *Canadian Journal of Psychiatry* 26: 357-6s4.

Shireman, C.H. and F.G. Reamer. 1986. *Rehabilitating Juvenile Justice.* New York: Columbia University Press.

Patterns of Discrimination:
Aboriginal Justice in Canada

Catharine Crow

It is generally acknowledged that the Canadian criminal justice system has major flaws with respect to its application to Canada's Aboriginal groups. The problems experienced by Aboriginal Canadians have historically been evidenced by their disproportionately high rates of criminality and incarceration. This situation has occasionally focused political attention onto the over-representation of Aboriginal people in the criminal justice system, and over the past fifty years many attempts have been made to develop programs to alleviate the problem. However, the situation today is essentially the same; Aboriginal peoples are still over-represented in criminal justice statistics, and the solutions that have been attempted have been largely unsuccessful in stemming their flow into the system. Many people have argued that this lack of success is largely because the programs have been "band-aid" solutions which have not reduced the conflicts which Aboriginals face within the system, nor have they substantially addressed the root causes of Aboriginal crime.

One of the major reasons why the attempts to address the problem have been unsuccessful is that the philosophical underpinnings of the Canadian criminal justice system are alien to aboriginal people. In this respect, James C. MacPherson, Dean of Osgoode Hall Law School, argues that:

> The principal reason for this crushing failure [re: Canadian criminal justice system] is the fundamentally different world view between European Canadians and Aboriginal peoples with respect to such elemental issues as the substantive content of justice and the process for achieving justice.[1]

There is little doubt that cultural conflicts have led to a great deal of misunderstanding between Aboriginal peoples and the Canadian criminal justice system. This misunderstanding has led to overt and covert discrimination, which in turn has resulted in the abuse of discretion and ultimately to miscarriages of justice. Blame has been placed at all levels from line police officers to high-level officials and politicians, and attempts to resolve the problems constitute an ongoing process. Unfortunately, the efforts do not really address the heart of the issue, and Canadian authorities appear to be continuing a trial and error intervention strategy which is almost certainly doomed to failure.

Canada's Aboriginal people are well aware of these issues and have become increasingly vocal in their demands for change. In the past decade, attempts have been made to make policing and the court process more sensitive to the needs of Aboriginal peoples. Aboriginal police forces have been established based on the Amerindian model.[2] Aboriginal constables have also been recruited by mainstream police forces, e.g. the RCMP and OPP, and the courts have attempted to integrate Aboriginal values into the judicial aspect of criminal justice. However, despite these well intentioned efforts, Aboriginal people still make up the single largest ethnic group processed through the system. In 1991, about twelve per cent of the inmate population in federal correctional institutions (housing offenders sentenced to terms of two or more years) were Aboriginal. The inmate population in provincial institutions (housing offenders with terms of less than two years) was fifteen per cent Aboriginal. Considering the fact that Aboriginals represent only 3.6 per cent of the overall Canadian population, these figures are alarming.[3]

A.C. Hamilton and C.M. Sinclair, in the *Report of the Aboriginal Justice Inquiry* (AJI Report), found that Aboriginals were more likely to be charged with multiple offences and were over twice as likely to be incarcerated upon conviction than were non-natives (twenty-five per cent of Aboriginals received sentences of incarceration compared to ten per cent for non-Aboriginals).[4] They also found that Aboriginal offenders were denied bail and held in custody pending trial more frequently than non-Aboriginal defendants. The magnitude of the problem is exacerbated by the fact that Aboriginal defendants were more likely to plead guilty (sixty per cent of the cases compared with fifty per cent for non-Aboriginals), often because they did not fully understand the process.[5] These figures can be placed into perspective when one realizes that, although Aboriginal people have crime rates 1.8 times the national crime rate, their offences are heavily concentrated in the more minor offences such as theft under $1000 and public mischief. Further, their violent crime rate, while 3.5 times the national average, is predominately alcohol-related and concentrated in the category of family violence. These aspects of their criminality suggest that it is related to such structural factors as poverty, frustration and the inability of existing social institutions adequately to serve the needs of Aboriginal people.

The intent of this article is to conduct separate discussions of institutionalized racism and culture conflict as possible causes of the over-representation of Aboriginal people in the Canadian criminal justice system. This will be followed by a consideration of community-based policing and autonomous court systems as possible solutions to the problem. The article will conclude with a brief discussion of some of the conditions which need to be met before an autonomous Aboriginal justice system would be viable.

Institutionalized Racism as a Source of Conflict

It is not surprising that both the Canadian government and Aboriginal organizations are gravely concerned. The problem, however, is a complex one and is not limited to the over-representation of Aboriginal people in correctional institutions. In broader terms, it involves the institutionalized racism which characterizes many institutions and which is difficult to detect because it is not always overt. Indeed, a major problem is that the racism has become so ingrained in the operating patterns of criminal justice agencies that it is beyond the awareness of those who practice it. Over time, it is possible that discriminatory conduct becomes so subtle that officers and citizens no longer notice that their conduct displays prejudice and discrimination. Thus, it is not only difficult to detect, but it is also difficult to prove and almost impossible to eradicate without changing the entire way in which the agency operates. Three recent cases illustrate this point and have brought the injustices experienced by Aboriginals to the forefront of the Canadian social conscience. These case involve the death of J.J. Harper, the murder of Helen Betty Osborne and the wrongful incarceration of Donald Marshall.

The shooting of J.J. Harper is a clear example of how racist stereotypes can become institutionalized in the minds of those who are closeted in an atmosphere of racism. Harper, a senior official in a Manitoba Aboriginal organization, was stopped on a Winnipeg street by Constable Robert Cross who was searching for two suspected car thieves. Several factors suggest that Harper was confronted by police specifically because he was Aboriginal. First, it is obvious that he did not bear any physical resemblance to the descriptions of the suspect which were broadcast by the police.[6] Second, evidence was uncovered to suggest that Cross was aware that the suspected car thieves had already been taken into custody by other officers when he stopped Harper.

> Cross for one reason or another, ignored other particulars of the description of the suspect, seizing on the word "native". He stopped the first Aboriginal person he saw, even though that person was a poor match for the description in other respects and a suspect had already been caught.... Racial stereotyping motivated the conduct of Cross. He stopped a "native" person walking peaceably along a sidewalk merely because the suspect he was seeking was native.[7]

These factors underline the point that many police officers hold the view that all Aboriginal people are alike, and are probably guilty of something and thus should be randomly questioned on the basis of a generalized suspicion. The day following Harper's death, the police department exonerated Cross despite a multitude of unanswered questions and discrepancies. Although Cross maintained that Harper had been shot when he attempted to grab his (Cross') service revolver, the fact that the Winnipeg Police failed to check the conflicting evidence before exonerating Cross suggests that they felt that the death of an Aboriginal leader did not warrant an extensive investigation. Although Robert Cross is no longer on active duty with the Winnipeg Police, he has never faced criminal or internal disciplinary charges for his role in Harper's death.

The case of Helen Betty Osborne illustrates how community indifference can interact with racist attitudes held by the police. The racist atmosphere in this case was broadly based in the community, such that the unsolved rape and murder of a young Aboriginal woman failed to illicit much public concern.[8] Helen Betty Osborne was abducted and brutally murdered near The Pas, Manitoba in November of 1971. She was a nineteen-year-old high school student originally from the Norway House Indian Reserve. Lee Colgan, Frank Houghton, Dwayne Johnston and Norman Manger forced Osborne into their car and assaulted her. Despite her screams and attempts to escape, Osborne was taken to a cabin belonging to Houghton's parents at Clearwater Lake. After being stripped, she was viciously beaten, and stabbed more than fifty times with a screwdriver. Her face was smashed beyond recognition. Her body was then dragged into the bush and her clothes were hidden.

The Royal Canadian Mounted Police investigators concluded that the four young men were involved in the death within seven months of the murder. Many people in the town of The Pas also learned the identity of those responsible within a very short time after the murder but chose to do nothing about it. Indeed, it became common knowledge in the town that the four men had committed the murder but "...because Osborne was an Aboriginal person, the townspeople considered the murder unimportant."[9] The RCMP failed to lay charges in the murder and it was not until sixteen years later that Johnston and Houghton were charged. Colgan and Manger were never charged, and ultimately only Houghton was convicted.

In their investigation of Osborne's death, the Aboriginal Justice Inquiry concluded that racism played a large role in both the community's apathy to the situation and in the lack of police interest demonstrated by the sixteen year delay in bringing the case to trial. Although the RCMP claimed that they had lacked sufficient evidence to charge the men, their lack of interest is evidenced by the fact that they simply dropped their investigation when the suspects refused to talk to them. This was clearly preposterous, since suspects frequently refuse to co-operate with the police and this rarely stops a professional police force from pursuing a murder investigation. It is significant that, when media and political pressure finally forced the reopening of the case sixteen years later, they were able to get a conviction on even less evidence than they had in 1971, since one of the key witnesses had died.

The RCMP's lack of interest in pursuing the case is further evidenced by their failure to lay lesser charges against the other suspects, a practice which is routinely used by police forces as insurance against a possible acquittal on the main charges. The behavior of the RCMP is paralleled by that of the public, many of whom heard the four men bragging about the murder and could have precipitated an early end to the case. Unfortunately, the community was also unco-operative and uninterested.[10] These events demonstrate all too clearly that the RCMP allowed their behaviour to be influenced by the racist stereotyping that existed within the community they patrolled.[11] As Hamilton and Sinclair noted in the *AJI Report:*

> It is clear that Betty Osborne would not have been killed if she had not been Aboriginal. The four men who took her to her death from the streets of The Pas that night had gone looking for an Aboriginal girl with whom to "party". They found Betty Osborne. When she refused to party she was driven out of town

and murdered. Those who abducted her showed a total lack of regard for her person or her rights as an individual. Those who stood by while the physical assault took place, while sexual advances were made and while she was being beaten to death showed their own racism, sexism and indifference. Those who knew the story and remained silent must share their guilt.[12]

Donald Marshall, Jr. was another aboriginal person who learned how easily racism and racist stereotypes can lead to misfortune. Marshall spent eleven years in prison for the 1971 murder of Sandy Seale in Sydney, Nova Scotia. Marshall maintained his innocence throughout the eleven years and pressed his friends to keep searching for the real murderer of his friend Sandy Seale. The problem started when Marshall and Seale went for a walk in Wentworth Park in Sydney on the night of May 28, 1971. While in the park Marshall and Seale got into an argument with Roy Ebsary and Jimmy MacNeil who were also in the park. Ebsary, having been mugged in the past, drew a knife and stabbed Seale in the stomach and slashed Marshall on the left forearm. Frightened, Marshall fled and MacNeil and Ebsary left the park to go home. Seale was found by a couple on their way home from a local dance, and Marshall returned to the scene, accompanied by a youth named Maynard Chant whom he had met on a street across from the park. Police and an ambulance were called and Seale was taken to hospital where he died.

Initially, Marshall was not a suspect in the case. He was taken to hospital by the police, where he received stitches to close his wound. He gave a brief description of the assailants to the police and was then allowed to go home.[13] It was after this point that racism began to play a role in the proceedings of the case. Marshall spent all of the following Saturday and most of Sunday at the police station assisting the police. On one of his trips back to the Membertou Reserve where he lived, Marshall repeated his story to an acquaintance named John Pratico. Later, when questioned by police, both Pratico and Chant later stated that they had actually been at the scene when the murder took place.[14] The first statements taken from Pratico and Chant tended to corroborate Marshall's account of the incident. These statements, however, were not used in the prosecution's case, and apparently were not known to the defence. John MacIntyre, Chief of Detectives for the Sydney police, became convinced that Marshall was the murderer, and coerced both Chant and Pratico into changing their stories and giving statements implicating Donald Marshall.[15] Although the two statements contained a number of mutually contradictory assertions, and there was no other evidence on which to base a charge, MacIntyre presented these "facts" to the Crown Prosecutor, Donald C. MacNeil, and was authorized to obtain a warrant for Marshall on a charge of second degree murder. The murder weapon was never found and no evidence of motive for the stabbing was ever offered.[16]

On November 2, 1971 Marshall was tried before a judge and jury, and convicted on the basis of the eyewitness testimony of these teenagers. He was sentenced to life in prison and taken to Dorchester Penitentiary in New Brunswick.[17] However, within a few days of the conviction, Jimmy MacNeil informed the police that he had been in the park with Ebsary on the night of the stabbing, and named Ebsary as Sandy Seale's assailant. A brief RCMP investigation of MacNeil's allegations discounted his claim and Marshall's conviction was sustained on appeal in late November 1971.[18]

Marshall continued to maintain his innocence and another investigation was finally commenced in 1982 after Marshall had learned the name of the real murderer from a friend. This time the RCMP determined that Chant and Pratico had given perjured testimony at Marshall's trial under pressure from Detective MacIntyre. Following this investigation, Marshall was exonerated and charges were brought instead against Ebsary.[19] The interesting aspect of this chain of events is that he was sentenced to only three years in prison, which the Nova Scotia Court of Appeal reduced to one year in 1986. This lenient treatment of a white adult stands in stark contrast to the life sentence handed down to Marshall when he was a juvenile.[20]

Cultural Values as a Source of Conflict

The above three cases clearly illustrate the effect that racist attitudes can exert on the administration of justice. However, although racism plays a significant role in the treatment of Aboriginal peoples in the justice system, the problem is more complicated than simple bigotry on the part of Euro-Canadians. The cultural conflict that sparks racism also contributes to a more basic misunderstanding between Aboriginal people and the mainstream Euro-Canadian culture. It also fosters misunderstanding and mistrust of mainstream Canadian social institutions (including the criminal justice system) by Aboriginals. Although many aboriginal people no longer live in a traditional lifestyle, their residual cultural values create misunderstandings, and often lead to conflicts because the Eurocentric system of laws is philosophically incompatible with Aboriginal values. Some of these inherent philosophical differences between aboriginal peoples and our Euro-Canadian justice system were summarized and presented by James Dumont in a paper presented to the Royal Commission on Aboriginal peoples.[21] Essentially, Aboriginal cultures view crime as a disruption of community harmony, which necessitates that harmony be restored between *both* the offender and the community. This contrasts drastically with the Euro-Canadian assumption that crimes are transgressions of commonly held norms, and require punishment and/or treatment to prevent future anti-social behavior. A more detailed outline of the major points of disagreement between the two views of justice is contained in Figure 1.

Figure 1. Zones of Conflict in the Justice Arena.

Aboriginal Approach to Justice	Eurocentric Approach to Justice
• regular teaching of community values by elders and others who are respected in the community;	• everyone under obligation to obey set laws as determined by superior state authorities;
• warning and counselling of particular offenders by leaders or by councils representing the community as whole;	• society reserves the right to protect itself from individuals who threaten to harm its members or its property;
• mediation and negotiation by elders, community members, and clan leaders, aimed at resolving disputes and reconciling offenders with the victims of the misconduct;	• retributive punishment: justice requires that a man should suffer because of and in proportion to, his moral wrong-doing. Punishment is set by legislation; judgement is imposed;
• payment of compensation by offenders (or their clan) to the victims or victims' kin, even in cases as serious as murder;	• the perpetrator is the object of sentencing; retributive incarceration and rehabilitation are means to deter and punish offenders;
• in court, a front that appears silent uncommunicative, unresponsive and withdrawn — based on the desire to maintain personal dignity and dignity. This is often interpreted as insolence and an unco-operative attitude;	• expected behaviour in court: defendant must give appearance of being willing to confront his/her situation and voice admittance to error and show remorse and willingness to change; must express desired motivation for change;
• reluctance to testify for or against others or him/herself, based on a general avoidance of confrontation and imposition of opinion or testimony;	• obligated to testify and defend oneself in order to get at the facts based on an adversarial mode of dealing with legal challenges;
• often pleads guilty on the basis of honesty or non-confrontational acquiesence.	• expected to plead not guilty on basis that one is innocent until proven guilty.

Because these two justice ideologies and modes of social control differ to such a large degree, it has been argued that the white philosophy of "policing" is at least partially responsible for the mistrust and prejudice which characterizes interactions between the two cultures. Aboriginal people inevitably view Euro-Canadian policing as the imposition of authority from above and thus instinctively mistrust it. In the *Aboriginal Justice Inquiry Report*, Hamilton and Sinclair argued that the major objective of their recommendations was "...to foster the establishment of effective Aboriginal police forces, staffed with officers who will be sensitive to Aboriginal people, and to improve the manner in which non-aboriginal forces serve Aboriginal people." They further argued that it was essential to adopt a community policing approach which would provide services that are culturally appropriate and committed to justice for Aboriginal people within their own cultural framework.[22]

Community-Based Policing in Aboriginal Communities

Community-based policing views the police as agents of social regulation and control by the community, rather than by external, independent police forces. It recognizes the necessity to deal with crime and social control issues in a community context. Many people suggest that the application of this approach to the policing of Aboriginal people would help avert relationships characterized by mutual hostility and distrust. It is axiomatic that good relations between any two differing groups depend first and foremost on good lines of communication and mutual understanding. In this respect, it is argued that community-based policing initiatives would increase understanding, communication and interaction between the two cultures, and thus help decrease conflict based on misunderstandings and communication breakdowns. In addition, a thorough understanding of each other's values and concerns, which can only be obtained through appropriate and adequate cultural training and/or immersion programs (for non-Aboriginal police officers and Aboriginal police officers from other locations) could also assist in reducing levels of conflict. However, not all Aboriginal people believe that the problems can be resolved simply by increasing the numbers of Aboriginal police officers. According to several Aboriginal leaders consulted by the Law Reform Commission of Canada,

> the indigenization of mainstream police forces is not a desirable goal, if all it means is that Aboriginal people will be enforcing "White" law.[23]

An Aboriginal RCMP constable working out of Williams Lake, British Columbia expressed similar sentiments:

> [I get] the feeling that although many in my community respect me, there were also a large number who feel I'm nothing more than "a white man in red skin" and therefore am worthy of less respect.[24]

Thus, although the majority of the recommendations for the alleviation of police/Aboriginal tensions tend to support the concept of Aboriginal officers policing aboriginal communities, it cannot be considered a "miracle cure" which would eliminate Aboriginal over-representation in the criminal justice system. At present, there are a number of community-based policing initiatives in progress, some of which have been studied in relative detail by researchers. These studies have determined that while many in the non-Aboriginal community see the police as a symbol of public protection, this view is often not shared in many Aboriginal communities. Not only do Aboriginal people feel the mainstream police forces are uninterested in their problems, many also feel that the presence of police is a threat to their community.[25] Although this is most true of mainstream police forces, it often extends to community-based Amerindian police as well. In addition, Amerindian police forces exhibit other problems, which detract from their effectiveness.

Recent research has produced mixed evaluations regarding the effectiveness of the Amerindian model of policing. A 1990 study by Auger revealed that although the majority of Aboriginal citizens thought that problems should be dealt with within the community rather than be referred to the outside police or courts, only half the community felt comfortable calling the Amerindian police when trouble arose. At the same time, they also felt that the community leaders were not successful in getting people to stop causing trouble. In addition, the Amerindian police also received significant numbers of "service calls" regarding such non-police related tasks as delivering pension cheques, which detracted from their effectiveness.[26] Auger's research also appeared to contradict the conventional assumption that Aboriginal police officers would be more likely to resolve problems informally, using cultural norms as a guide. In his study of three communities within the jurisdiction of the Clear Lake OPP Detachment, he found that constables from the Clear Lake OPP Detachment were more likely to use their discretion *not* to lay charges than Amerindian officers in Castle Dame and Deep River. Although these results are inconclusive, they certainly raise questions about the assumption of culturally sensitive policing.[27]

Mary Hyde, on the other hand, paints a different picture. In a study of

Amerindian police in Quebec, Hyde found that Amerindian police forces alleviated at least some of the tensions between whites and Aboriginal people.

> Amerindian police play an important role in service provision; they respond to a variety of service calls, keep law and order and perform the function of crisis intervention.[28]

Hyde does, however, qualify the positive aspects of the Amerindian policing model by pointing out that the benefits that accrue through improved police services must be weighed carefully against the potential for over-policing and the possible use of police for services that could better be provided by other agencies. However, she does not adequately address the negative perceptions many natives have of Amerindian police as second rate police forces. This is particularly true of Aboriginal arms of mainstream police forces, such as the (now disbanded) RCMP Special Constable Program (which can be considered an Amerindian police for the purposes of this discussion). It was a common complaint of Aboriginal RCMP constables that they were often seen as an extension of the white arm of the law and accorded even less respect than white RCMP officers. However, the RCMP practice of regularly transferring constables contributed to the isolation of the Special Constables and to their lack of respect. In recognition of this problem, Hyde refers to Aboriginal-controlled Amerindian policing as a "positive" first step in a wider shift toward greater autonomy for Aboriginal communities.[29]

Thus, community-based Amerindian policing initiatives do resolve some of the problems associated with Aboriginal over-representation within the system. However, it cannot be assumed that they will eliminate all the problems faced in the equitable delivery of justice. The problems that exist incorporate numerous social issues which the police, regardless of their ethnicity, are unequipped to handle effectively. These social problems (both cultural and economic) accentuate the effect of conventional law and law enforcement in creating inequitable treatment for aboriginal people. Indeed, at least one researcher has argued that the over-representation of Aboriginal people in the criminal justice system is not entirely due to discrimination by the police. In a 1992 publication, S. Zimmerman argued that empirical evidence about the extent to which the police are responsible for Aboriginal over-representation in the criminal justice system is at best unreliable.[30] Instead, he suggested that their high rate of involvement may be a reflection of their low socio-economic status, which creates a visible minority that is targeted by police.[31] Thus, he argued, over-surveillance of low socio-economic groups is the deciding factor, and racism is an indirect factor which contributes to their low socio-economic status.

In the final analysis, community-based policing may address some of the "cultural" issues surrounding Aboriginal involvement in the criminal justice system; however, culture is only one facet of the equation. Before any substantial conclusions can be made regarding formal initiatives, the overall success of programs now in existence must be established. The hiring of greater numbers of Aboriginal police officers might well reduce the numbers of Aboriginal offenders, but only if they are truly committed to Aboriginal values. Aboriginal peoples do not simply require Aboriginal representation on police forces, but rather they also require Aboriginal police officers who are capable and sensitive to the needs of Aboriginal communities, and not just "white officers with red skins."

Aboriginal Community-based Courts

Many Aboriginal leaders have suggested that replacing white functionaries with Aboriginal ones will not solve the problems plaguing the criminal justice system. They argue that the conflicts will not disappear until Aboriginal people are able to establish their own autonomous justice systems based on tribal customs rather than Eurocentric laws. While once deemed too radical to be accorded serious consideration, this suggestion is increasingly supported by white officials and politicians, white-dominated commissions and even the judiciary. The Royal Commission on the Donald Marshall, Jr. prosecution determined that the justice system had failed Marshall at every point, from his arrest and conviction until his acquittal by the Supreme Court of Nova Scotia, and that his Aboriginal status contributed to his mistreatment within the system. It was for this reason that the Commission recommended that the Micmac of Nova Scotia should examine, as a long-term goal, the possibility of instituting an autonomous tribal justice system based on indigenous concepts of justice. It further suggested that this approach should be implemented on a community-by-community basis, according to the needs and aspirations of community members.[32]

The Aboriginal Justice Inquiry was in full agreement. In their words it was felt that:

Federal and provincial governments should

recognize the right of Aboriginal people to establish their own justice systems as part of their inherent right to self-government. It is also recommended that these governments assist Aboriginal people to establish Aboriginal justice systems according to the wishes of the communities; and

Aboriginal communities be entitled to enact their own criminal, civil and family laws and have those laws enforced by their own justice systems. If they wish, they should also have the right to adopt any federal or provincial law and to apply or enforce that as well.[33]

The recommendation to establish community-based courts has received a great deal of support from both Aboriginals and the Euro-Canadian actors within the criminal justice system. There are two main reasons for this sweeping support. The actors presently working in the system welcome any proposal which would eliminate the need to fly into remote communities, where they are pressed to clear a court docket quickly so that they can fly off to the next community. In addition, many of the problems that arise with respect to circuit courts could be eliminated if the courts were community-based and did not need to rely on appropriate weather conditions and/or mechanical good will. Aboriginal communities also welcome any proposal which would accord them the ability to control their own communities and deal with deviance and crime in their own culturally appropriate fashion. Community-based courts would not only alleviate the cultural conflicts that Aboriginals find within the system, but would also place responsibility for social control in their own hands.

There are approximately 400 aboriginal justice projects currently operating across the country. These projects were created both to ease the administrative difficulties presented by remote communities, and also to improve cultural sensitivity to Aboriginal issues.[34] The tribal courts suggested in the *Aboriginal Justice Inquiry Report* are only one possible solution to the problems faced with respect to courts. In this respect, Canada can rely on the experience of the U.S. justice system, where approximately 145 American Indian tribes have some type of functioning autonomous court system.[35] There are three basic forms used in the United States:[36]

(1) Traditional Courts. These exist with the original jurisdiction

established by traditional tribal laws, restricted only by express federal legislation. Their orientation is to administer customary laws as supplemented by explicit tribal enactments.

(2)   Courts of Indian Offenses. These courts are regulated by the Code of Federal Regulations and their jurisdiction is limited by the terms of those regulations to minor crimes and a narrow range of civil matters. Most of the laws which are applied and the structure of the courts are established by the federal government.

(3)   Tribal Courts: These courts are governed solely by tribal constitutions and tribal codes passed pursuant to the Indian Reorganization Act and any other express federal legislation.

The Indian tribal courts in the United States have jurisdiction over their own tribal members and any other Indians who may be present within the tribal territory. Thus, any Indian who commits an offence within the Flathead Reservation is subject to the jurisdiction of the police and courts of the Flathead Tribe. However, a non-Indian who commits the same offence is subject to the jurisdiction of the State police and the State courts. This has caused Canadian First Nations observers who have studied the American Indian tribal justice system to criticize the issue of jurisdiction based on racial distinctions. It is their contention that differentiation based on race is both too complicated (i.e. how would they deal with Métis in Canada) and an undesirable way of enforcing laws because of its racist implications.[37] Instead, they argue that jurisdiction should be absolute, based on territory and apply equally to all people regardless of race. Although this approach would certainly have its advantages, it would also obviate any possible claim for aboriginal jurisdiction over aboriginal people who commit crimes off reservations. In such cases, the principle of territoriality would presumably mandate that the Aboriginal offenders would fall under the jurisdiction of the mainstream criminal justice system.

In Canada, our closest approximation of tribal court systems can be found in Akwesasne, Quebec. In essence, the Akwesasne tribal court establishes its own code of behaviour and administers its own laws. Although such a system is considered ideal by many Aboriginal leaders, its widespread application would almost certainly require amendments to Canada's Constitution. A temporary solution, suggested by the Aboriginal Justice Inquiry, would involve adapting present court systems to incorporate peacemakers or other Aboriginal participation. The role of the peacemaker is based on the principles in Alternative Dispute Resolution, a system which replaces the adversarial court process with a conciliatory method of dispute settlement. The Aboriginal Justice Inquiry saw the role of the peacemaker as being different from that of a judge. While a judge's role is to listen to admissible evidence, render a verdict and impose sentence when there is a conviction, the peacemaker's goal is the maintenance of stability within the community. In cases where there is an admission of fault, the peacemaker can try to rectify the harm by determining the issues that led to the inappropriate action, and finding a remedy to the situation through consultations with those involved.[38]

A peacemaker system has operated since 1984 in Ste. Teresa Point, a northern Manitoba community on an island in Lake Winnipeg. In this community, a case committee, made up of two elders, two other adults and two youths, reviews charges against young offenders and decides how these charges should be handled. The peacemaker options include directing the accused to the tribal youth court, to alternative measures hearings, or to meetings with the chief and council. Alternately, they have the option of referring young offenders to the Manitoba Youth Court system.[39] The peacemaker process here involves a meeting with the accused, his/her parents and an elder to iron out minor disputes. (The tribal court does not handle cases involving rape, murder and other violent crimes; these are dealt with in Manitoba Provincial Court.) The response to the program to date has been exceedingly favourable:

> The result [of the program] is a significant reduction in crime within the entire community.... the whole community takes responsibility for its youthful offenders.[40]

Cpl. Craig MacLaughton, the officer in charge of the Garden Hill RCMP detachment, agreed with this assessment, noting that in his two years of service in the area, only one case had been transferred to provincial youth court.[41]

The sentencing circle, a similar program found in Saskatchewan, deals primarily with adult offenders. To qualify for consideration by the sentencing circle, offenders must meet several criteria. The offender must:

(1)   be eligible for either a suspended sentence, an intermittent sentence or a short term of imprisonment (less than two years) coupled with a probation order;

(2)   be genuinely contrite;

(3)   be supported in his/her request for a sentencing circle by the community in which he/she lived; and

(4)   be honestly interested in turning his or her life around.[42]

In a sentencing circle, all the interested parties, including friends and family of the offender, the victim, band elders and other community residents sit in a circle with the judge, the prosecutor and defence counsel. All members discuss and participate in the sentencing of the offender.[43]

The Oji-Cree community at the Sandy Lake reserve in northwestern Ontario operates in a similar, albeit more structured, manner. The judge, his clerk and three reporters sit at one side of a square of tables, the three elders and an interpreter sit at an adjacent side. The defence lawyers, offenders and their families sit at the side across from the judge, together with probation officers and anyone else who may wish to address the court. The final section is occupied by the Crown Attorneys and the police officers involved in the case.

The elders bring to the court their knowledge of the accused and his or her family circumstances. Often the elders will meet with the accused, the victim and both their families in advance of the court proceedings; and the court will adjourn cases, if necessary, to allow the elders to complete their investigation.[44] The goals are to understand all factors involved in the accused's actions, and to establish a method of healing or teaching which will restore the balance between and within the individual and the community.

The involvement of the judge is often seen as making a crucial difference. The judge's presence lends importance and significance to the Aboriginal justice initiative and empowers the community process. The judge shares power with the community, and thus better enables it to deal with conflict.[45] It is for this reason that the Northwest Territories Community Justice of the Peace Program established at Fort McPherson chose to utilize Justices of the Peace chosen from their communities, rather than relying solely on a Council of Elders.

Fort McPherson is an example of a community-based court which evolved from an existing circuit court. Following some initial meetings between the circuit court judge, Judge Bruser, and some interested members of the community, a justice committee was formed. This justice committee, composed of a broad spectrum of people, including elders, began to attend circuit court to advise on the dispositions of offenders from their community. Before the circuit court arrived in the community each month, the justice committee was provided with a docket of the offenders who were to appear before the territorial court. The committee would then decide which, if any, of the matters before the court they wished to make representations on. Many communities have since appointed their own presiding Justice of the Peace who comes from the community and who understands what will work and what will not. In this fashion, the people were gradually able to obviate the need for circuit courts.[46]

Although the Fort Macpherson project appears to be working satisfactorily, it has two major problems. The primary one centres on the need to recruit Justices of the Peace who are willing to judge people from their own communities. The independent "judging" role ascribed to Justices of the Peace runs counter to the Aboriginal practice of relying on a consensual framework which deflects responsibility for the decisions onto the community as a whole. Similarly, the strong community support networks sometimes mandate that responsibility for offences is also reflected onto the community as a whole rather than onto a specific individual (the offender). The other problem faced is one in which all institutions face, namely, the lack of financial resources.[47]

The above discussion indicates that Aboriginal tribal courts appear viable, either with or without the assistance and/or guidelines of the Euro-Canadian system. The courts described here operate with varying success in the United States and to some extent in Quebec and Canada's Northwest Territories. In large urban areas, where it is likely that full community courts are not feasible, the peacemaker systems appear to represent a viable option. It is apparent, however, that for such a system to meet the needs of Aboriginal people, substantial changes must be made to the existing court system. The possible alternatives include both the complete structural changes recommended by the Aboriginal Justice Inquiry and the less sweeping changes suggested by The Royal Commission on the Donald Marshall Prosecution. Regardless of the options chosen, it is evident that the Aboriginal community-based courts and peacemaker systems are working to the satisfaction of the Euro-Canadians as well as the Aboriginals. As has often been mentioned, each Aboriginal community is different, not only culturally, but also physically. This in itself demands something other than "the standard" mode of justice. Circuit courts are at best dysfunctional, providing little more than illusion of justice. This leads to a feeling of futility which was expressed by almost every individual interviewed with regard to this outdated mode of justice delivery.

The only arguments against Aboriginal community-based courts focus on the political instability that exists in some communities. Not all Aboriginal communities have the strength and cohesion to support a legitimate community-based program. Superintendent George Watt of the Thompson, Manitoba RCMP Detachment voiced this concern both in relation to policing and the courts. He indicated that many reserves in northern Manitoba are already policed by the chiefs and band constables, and that they are generally given a great deal of autonomy.[48] Despite this, the crime rates and the rates of incarceration are still disproportionately high, when compared to the white population in Northern Manitoba. In addition, the political structure of the reserve itself can lead to a misadministration of justice:

> ...corruption within reserve settings in Manitoba runs rampant often to the point of "gang wars" between family blood lines.... the chief is elected and uses his power for the benefit of his family and supporters. Often this filters through to violence.[49]

Judge Murray Howell expressed the same point in his criticisms of the *Aboriginal Justice Inquiry Report* recommendations:

> The politics that exists on reserves...[leads] to family feuds, a "Hatfield and McCoy" scenario, this could make justice a joke, depending on who's in power.[50]

It is therefore important that the dynamics of the community be evaluated before community-based justice is established in its entirety. Carol LaPrairie agrees:

> The limited community-based work that has been undertaken has either theorized broadly about crime in different communities, has narrowly focused on police findings, without a corresponding analysis of community life, or provided comparative crime data but again without reference to the community context.[51]

This concern is very real and could render justice void; however, it appears to be an exception rather than a rule. Generally, elders seem eager to establish their own court system for the benefit of their citizens and are confident that their judgmental impartiality would remain intact.

Conclusions

The issue of Aboriginal justice is a complex one that cannot be addressed lightly. Aboriginal communities are as diverse as the Aboriginal peoples themselves and must therefore be treated with respect for their individuality. Broad assumptions of what is best or most appropriate for Aboriginal justice must be considered with extreme caution. The issues discussed in this articles regarding the police and the courts have made this evident. Aboriginal self-determination has been raised as a possible solution by Hamilton, Sinclair and others on several occasions. However, one must remember that not all Aboriginal communities are starting at the same point on the developmental scale. Many reserves face abject poverty, social and political instability and isolation which would put them at a distinct disadvantage and perhaps doom them to failure. Such failure at this point in time might well force them back into a relationship of even greater dependence. A greater understanding of Aboriginal cultures, in combination with greater Aboriginal representation within the controlling institutions of our society, seems to be the most reasonable path to follow at this point in time. This is not to abdicate any future goals of Aboriginal self-determination, as complete self-determination for Aboriginal peoples must remain the ultimate goal. However, until all communities are equally prepared to proceed, sweeping policies should be avoided.

Endnotes

1   James C. MacPherson "Report from the Round Table Rapporteur," Aboriginal in *Peoples and the Justice System* (Ottawa: Ministry of Supply and Services Canada, 1991), p. 4.

2   It should be noted that in the United States, writers often distinguish between community-based and Amerindian police forces. Amerindian police forces are staffed by Aboriginal persons and are controlled directly by Aboriginal Bands. Community police forces are staffed by Aboriginal persons but are largely controlled by outside forces. However, this distinction is rarely used in Canada and the term "Amerindian" police will be used to denote all tribally affiliated police forces which police reservations exclusively. Thus, any tribal police force can be assumed to be an Amerindian police force, whereas the use of the terms RCMP or OPP, even in conjunction with the adjective "Aboriginal," will refer to mainstream police forces.

3   Curt Griffiths and S.N. Verdun Jones, *Canadian Criminal Justice* (Toronto: Butterworths, 1993), p. 633-43.

4   Perhaps most startling, twenty per cent of Aboriginal females received sentences of incarceration for their offences compared to four per cent of the non-Aboriginal population. While part of the explanation for this discrepancy may be that Aboriginal women commit more serious crimes than non-Aboriginal women, it is also likely that Aboriginal women don't benefit as much from judicial paternalism as non-Aboriginal women.

5   A.C. Hamilton and C.M. Sinclair, *Report of the Aboriginal Justice Inquiry of Manitoba: The Justice System and Aboriginal People*, Vol.I (Winnipeg: Province of Manitoba, 1991) pp. 87-88.

6   In fact, the differences could not have been greater. Harper was overweight and in his mid-forties, whereas the suspects were described as "slim" teenagers.

7   *Ibid.*, p. 94.

8   In comparison, the public outcry over the abduction and murder of Christine French in Ontario serves to illustrate the levels of concern over a similar incident involving a white woman.

9   *Ibid.*, p. 3.

10   *Ibid.*, p. 3.

11   *Ibid.*, p. 8.

12   *Ibid.*, p. 98.

13   Michael Harris, *Justice Denied: The Law Versus Donald Marshall* (Toronto: Totem Books, 1986), p. 41-51.

14   Ibid., pp. 57-67.

15   In fairness to Detective MacIntyre, part of his reason for disbelieving Chant and Pratico's original statements was the discrepancies between their stories. These discrepancies occurred because neither man had been present at the crime and they were basing their statements on separate accounts given to them by Marshall. MacIntyre however, was unaware of this at the time. However, there was also considerable evidence indicating that Detective MacIntyre, may have influenced the testimony of Chant and Pratico based on his previous experience with Marshall. Marshall was known as a troublemaker who frequented the park on a regular basis, often begging or threatening individuals for money. This, in conjunction with the community's view of the Natives being drunkards, may have led MacIntyre to assume Marshall's guilt despite the limited evidence.

16   *Ibid.*, pp. 94-95.

17   *Ibid.*, p. 129.

18   *Ibid.*, pp. 234-240.

19   *Ibid.*, pp. 309-344.

20   Royal Commission on the Donald Marshall, Jr., Prosecution, *Findings and Recommendations*, Vol.1 (Halifax: Province of Nova Scotia, 1989), p. 1.

21   James Dumont, "Justice and Aboriginal People" in *Aboriginal Peoples and the Justice System* (Ottawa: Minister of Supply and Services Canada, 1993), p.66.

22   Robert Depew, "Policing Native Communities: Some Principles and Issues in Organizational Theory," *Canadian Journal of Criminology*, July/October 1992, p. 252.

23   S. Zimmerman, "The Revolving Door of Despair: Aboriginal Involvement in the Criminal Justice System" *UBC Law Review* (Special Edition, 1992), p. 375.

24   Interview with an Aboriginal RCMP Constable, Williams Lake, British Columbia, December 1992.

25   Robert Silverman and M. Nielsen, *Aboriginal Peoples and Canadian Criminal Justice* (Toronto: Butterworths, 1992), p. 104.

26   D. Auger *et al.*, "Crime and Control in three Nishanwabe-Aski Nation Communities," *Canadian Journal of Criminology*, Vol 34 (1992), p. 331-335.

27   *Ibid.*

28   Mary Hyde, "Servicing Indian Reserves: The Amerindian Police," *Canadian Journal of Criminology*, Vol 34 (1992), p. 383.

29   *Ibid.*, p. 383.

30   *Op. cit..*

31   *Op. cit.*, pp. 471-475.

32   Royal Commission on the Donald Marshall, Jr. Prosecution, pp. 71-75.

33   Hamilton and Sinclair, *Op. cit.*, pp. 734-735.

34   Mary Ellen Turpel, *Aboriginal Peoples and the Justice System: Report of the National Round Table on Aboriginal Justice Issues* (Ottawa: Ministry of Supply and Services Canada, 1993), p. 179.

35   "Native American Tribal Court Profiles" in Hamilton and Sinclair, *op. cit.*, p. 275.

36   *Ibid.*, p. 276.

37   Leonard Mandamin, "Aboriginal Justice Systems: Relationships" in *Aboriginal Peoples and the Justice System,* p. 297.

38   Hamilton and Sinclair, *op. cit.*, p. 374.

39   *Winnipeg Free Press*, Monday, 16 August 1993, p. B3.

40   Interview with Justice A. Hamilton, Winnipeg, Manitoba, 16 August,1993.

41   *Winnipeg Free Press*, Monday, 16 August 1993, p. B3.

42   *R. v. Cheekinew,* Sask. Q.B., Grotsky J. (Mar.2/93), cited in *The Lawyers Weekly*, 15 October 1993, p. 16.

43   *Ibid.*

44   Rupert Ross, "Dancing with a Ghost" in *Exploring Indian Reality* (Markham: Octopus Publishing, 1992), p. 6.

45   Mandamin, *op. cit.*, p. 286.

46   At this point approximately forty per cent of the Justices of the Peace are Aboriginal. As well, approximately forty per cent of these Aboriginal Justices of the Peace are women.

47   *Ibid.*, p. 389.

48   Interview with Superintendent George Watt, RCMP, Thompson, Manitoba, 20 August 1993.

49   Interview with Dr. Charlie Ferguson, Native Health Care and Abuse Coordinator, Winnipeg, Manitoba, 15 August 1993. Dr. Ferguson is also a police expert on sexual child abuse, having serviced Northern Manitoba reserves for approximately twenty years.

50   Interview with Judge Howell, Provincial Court Judge servicing the Northern Manitoba Circuit, Thompson, Manitoba, 25 August 1993.

51   Carol LaPrairie, "Who Owns the Problem? Crime and Disorder in James Bay Cree Communities," *Canadian Journal of Criminology*, Vol 34 (1992), p. 421.

Policing Native Communities:
Some Principles and Issues in Organizational Theory*

Robert Depew[1]

In this paper, the organizational demands of the Native policing environment are examined to analyze their effects on Native policing arrangements and the constraints and linkages that govern innovation and reform at the levels of policy and program development. It is argued that, as environmental conditions vary and change, current methods of organizing and delivering Native police services will become increasingly problematic. Some of the key principles and issues that underlie policing models are discussed and examined in the Native context. It is concluded that a community-based approach to policing is a promising strategy that may uniquely serve the interests and requirements of particular Native communities.

Introduction

The ethnological record reveals important differences in the ways in which Natives and non-Natives have conceptualized and institutionalized the police and policing (Finkler, 1976; Humphrey, 1942; Smith, 1975; Van den Steenhoven, 1959; Van Dyke and Jamont, 1980; Wachtel, 1983). A variety of environmental forces, however, can affect traditional Native and conventional non-Native concepts and practices and create a need to modify or change approaches to policing. Therefore, we are not committed, *a priori*, to any specific historical or cultural definition of the organization and delivery of police services to Canadian communities, Native or non-Native. It will become increasingly apparent that Native policing relates to situationally-specific definitions of social regulation and control. These definitions in turn have important implications for the ways in which the police can and should be organized for service delivery to Native communities.

Institutional Constraints on Native Policing

Conventional Non-Native Policing

In contemporary Canadian society, the organization of conventional police services is consistent with an "urban" criminal justice system which is generally designed to prosecute, punish and deter offenders. Accordingly, police organizations are dominated by a crime control model aimed at detecting offences, apprehending criminals and laying charges. The needs and characteristics of the criminal justice and legal system are further reflected in the police agency's frequently adversarial style of intervention and investigative functions, rapid response requirements and internal discipline and management control (Murphy and Muir, 1984: 170-171). This is given effect by a paramilitary bureaucracy which directs and constrains personnel behaviour and information flow according to principles of rank, hierarchical authority and conformity to rules. A specialized division of labour assigns routine policing tasks to institutional roles. The incumbents who play these roles have their responsibilities, obedience and loyalty to superiors in particular and to the police agency in general clearly defined and emphasized for them by the institution. While some benefits may be derived from these principles of organization, the crime-control model of policing has been the subject of increasing criticism that draws attention to its limitations, particularly under changing social conditions and other environmental demands.

In general, the limitations stem from the conventional police organization's narrow emphasis on, and commitment to, the crime fighting and law enforcement role. There is no question that these functions are important aspects of a police agency's mandate. But they tend to be over-emphasized by police administrators at the expense of the more frequently exercised functions of crime prevention, law and order maintenance and routine service delivery such as social assistance, referral and public education (Loree, 1984: 21, Table 2; Murphy and Muir, 1984).

Traditional Native Policing

Traditionally, Native people of Canada organized their lives in a variety of small scale communities where sustained interaction occurred in both informal and formal settings. Each community's culture and social structure reflected a wide range of community concepts of order which provided the foundation for a multitude of institutions and mechanisms of social control similar in scale and function to those of other pre-urban societies. While conducive to high levels of social integration and interdependence, Native cultural and social configurations do not imply an overly harmonious picture of group life which, as the ethnographic record suggests, was not immune to social and political tension or disruption. Put another way, members of traditional Native communities do transgress the moral and social order, at least on occasion, thereby incurring disapprobation on the part of relatives, friends and neighbours. This is a significant point since it draws attention to a fundamental difference between Native and conventional non-Native approaches to policing. Native policing may be observed to operate in a context of reciprocal constraints that are derived from a variety of social relationships and, therefore, it is shaped and directed by the interests of the wider community. The obvious theoretical implication here is that non-urban, traditional Native communities are structured in such a way that community responses to crime and deviance are likely to take precedence over those of a formal, centralized police agency, at least in certain circumstances.

Most Native communities in Canada, including Indian reserves, have small populations and are widely distributed throughout rural and remote locations. Historical and ethnographic documentation, as well as other comparative research (Schwartz, 1954), indicates that small-scale Native settlements may be more likely than complex urban communities to develop effective informal social control mechanisms and institutions and police themselves on the basis of their own social resources. *But it cannot be assumed,* a priori, *that traditional, informal or pre-urban responses to crime and deviance are fully operational among Canada's Native communities.* Processes of modernization have reached out to and influenced even the most remote Native communities (Finkler, 1983; Rasing, 1988) and have placed questions of Native policing within a broader context of social, cultural, economic, demographic and political change. More importantly, Native communities are diverse along all these dimensions. As a result, the place of the community in contemporary approaches to policing, and the status of police agencies assigned the task of policing them, must be carefully considered from first principles.

All forms of policing, Native and non-Native, are subject to changing environmental demands and pressures. However, the key in coming to grips with this issue lies not in the search for an ideal programmatic approach to Native (or non-Native) policing but in identifying those principles of police organization and service delivery that facilitate adaptation to fluctuation and diversity. Politically, support for innovation and reform in the nature of police organizations and the method of their service delivery may not be immediately forthcoming where vested interests in the *status quo* are at stake. However, the demand for change is likely to be substantial among those communities seeking to redefine their relationship to the criminal justice system. This is clearly one of the most striking characteristics of current Native political engagement with non-Native authorities and institutions. As a planned approach to these issues, community-based policing models are worthy of consideration.

Community-Based Models of Policing

As a conception, philosophy and strategy of police organization and service delivery, community-based policing represents a significant departure from conventional crime control models of policing. In general, community-based policing advocates a closer association between the police and the community by structuring their mutual involvement in policing according to a number of key principles.

Principles of Community-Based Policing

1) Responsibility and Accountability for Policing

Unlike the crime control model of policing which encourages independent decision-making and policy formulation by the police department, community-based policing promotes co-operation and mutual participation in the policing process where policy, and administrative and operational decisions are influenced by and negotiated with the local community. As a result, the community is encouraged to play a more active and influential role in the management and delivery of police services.

2) Policing Objectives and Goals

Given its general orientation to substantive problem solving in the community, community-based policing operates under a broad, socially-defined mandate to control c\rime, maintain peace, order and security in the community and to perform other service functions that enhance the quality of life in the community and help to preserve its integrity.

3)   The Nature and Scope of Police Roles

Studies of non-Native policing indicate that police roles are constantly forced into variable and changing circumstances which place demands on their redefinition. A wide variety of tasks and services consistently relate public demands for service and public definitions and expectations of the police to actual police activities. "On the basis of these findings, police work emerges as being diverse in nature, complex in task assignment and reactively structured" (Murphy and Muir, 1984: 122). While crime control is seen by the public as the most important police function (Murphy and Muir, 1984: 123), a narrow definition of police roles that focuses exclusively on crime control and law enforcement ignores the fact that most police work involves other tasks and functions. Significantly, these fall within normative definitions of police roles that are shared by the public and many police officers alike (Murphy and Muir, 1984). Thus, insofar as a community-based approach to policing acknowledges the diverse nature of police activities, it provides for the legitimation of the police role as multi-purpose. This is especially important where the objectives of policing are broad and socially defined, since a multi-purpose role can accommodate the necessary flexibility in police functions required to exercise them. Similarly, a multi-purpose role is more adaptable where social conditions and service demands are constantly changing.

4)   Interdependency and Responsibility for Policing

Community-based policing models see the police as agents of social regulation and control by the community in contrast to conventional policing models that encourage regulation and control of the community by external, independent police forces. By operating with and through the community, community-based policing is not only more likely to consolidate its position and standing in the community but may be able to mobilize more effectively the policing resources of the community itself, such as informal sanctions and alternative forms of institutional intervention. This prospect is critical, especially in view of increasing environmental pressures and changing social demands on police organizations and service delivery.

5)   Reactive and Proactive Policing as Principles of Police Service Delivery

Conventional police departments tend to regard more passive policing strategies as a central and necessary element in the organization of service delivery. While the reactive mode of service delivery is both desirable and realistic under certain unanticipated crisis situations, it may be inadequate, inefficient and ineffective if it becomes the exclusive organizing principle for the delivery of police services.

As an alternative to exclusively reactive styles of policing and police service delivery, community-based policing models introduce a significant measure of planning and anticipatory exercise into policing which provide the foundation for a proactive police role in the community. In order to address more effectively the nature and scope of community policing problems, community-based policing encourages the development and implementation of long-term preventive policing strategies and programs. As response options, these should be aimed at broader policing issues in the community that, while not immediately apparent, provide the origin and context of more visible and particular policing problems. Under most conventional organizational forms, the police are usually limited to dealing with the particular symptoms of crime and disorder as they appear on a daily basis and are rarely involved in exploring and addressing their patterns and causes.

Community-based policing recognizes the necessity to deal directly and indirectly with crime and issues of social disorder in a community context. Accordingly, the police should retain the capability for effective incident response but at the same time broaden and develop the range of response options open to themselves and the community. These response options include proactive policing activities that encourage alternative forms of institutional participation in the policing process and community programs and services that enhance public responsibility and credit for the resolution of community policing problems.

The Relevance of Community-Based Policing Concepts to the Policing of Native Communities

In recent years, debate over the social role or mandate of the police and their underlying philosophy has compared the benefits of community-based approaches to those of more conventional crime control models. In general, the debate has focused on the question of which role model best fits contemporary policing. This issue is not merely of academic interest. From alternative role definitions flow different organizational structures and objectives, social responsibilities and policing priorities that affect the status and operation of the police in society. Proponents of community-based policing have challenged crime control conceptions of the police by arguing that narrow, crime-fighting definitions of the police role are not always consistent with the realities of police work. As a result, they have urged a redefinition of police roles that can accommodate a wider range of policing functions and objectives more consistent with the actual duties and activities, as well as public definitions and expectations of the police. In order to strengthen the argument, proponents of community-based policing have drawn particular attention to the economic issues involved. As Murphy and Muir (1984: 107) argue, the question is whether community-based policing can more effectively and efficiently allocate scarce policing resources to alternative policing objectives and goals that are increasingly being recognized as socially determined.

While the debate has generated an extensive literature with important implications for policing in Canada, few theoretical arguments and little empirical research may be found that deal specifically with the case of native policing. This oversight raises an obvious question. What relevance does the promotion of community-based policing have for the policing of Native communities? More specifically, do the same arguments advanced for the place of community-based policing models in non-Native communities apply to Native communities, and if so, with what force? Alternatively, how do the conditions of Native policing facilitate or inhibit the development and implementation of community-based policing strategies in Native communities?

The Case for Community-Based Policing in Native Communities

Political Considerations

In its review of current Native policing arrangements, the Federal Task Force has emphasized the political and practical necessity for Natives to assume greater control over the delivery of policing services to their communities. There is a need, therefore, to develop and establish appropriate native governing structures at the community level which can support and sustain new policing arrangements (Task Force Report, 1990: 11-21). A significant vehicle for achieving this end is the negotiation of community-based Indian self-government which may lead to new legislative or other arrangements in the area of justice administration in general, and policing in particular. The achievement of Indian self-government would lay the foundation for a greater measure of Native political autonomy and internal control in the policing enterprise. Furthermore, policing goals, objectives, strategies and methods would likely be defined more directly in community and Native terms. Depending on the scale and function of new Native government arrangements, policing models that localize decision-making, responsibility and accountability for policing at the community level may provide an attractive alternative to external, centralized police agencies. Where the political or economic status of Native communities do not imply the self-government formula (Weaver, 1984: 219), a much greater effort may be required to lay the necessary foundations of community-based approaches to Native policing. It must be recognized, however, that even in the case of those Native communities currently involved in self-government initiatives, there exist uneven capacities and opportunities to articulate policing preferences or to influence policy and decision-making in the direction of innovation and reform.

An especially difficult issue to resolve in this context is the question of political responsibility for the police and police accountability to the community. This is not a problem unique to Native communities. Generally in Canada:

> The scope of police authority to act independently of political or ministerial control must be defined. Related to that there are a number of questions to be answered such as: who sets general policy for public police forces in Canada; which police decisions require approval from an appropriate civilian body or from higher authority; and which civilian has, or ought to have, the right or duty to oversee the police and at what level should this control be exercised? (Murphy and Muir, 1984: 39).

The unique political evolution of Native communities in Canada suggests that these questions are likely to come under close scrutiny by all interested jurisdictions and prove difficult to resolve, at least in the short term. In the meantime, they may stimulate new community tasks that require innovative forms of political consultation, leadership and public involvement. Much may be gained by allowing the nature and status of political institutions to be addressed by developments at the community level. Indeed, this would appear to be one of the main challenges and promises of negotiating new Native self-government arrangements that provide scope for local policing.

Economic Imperatives

Only recently have the long term implications of economic changes been felt at the level of police program planning and funding in Canada. Global patterns of economic decline are reflected in the general policy of financial restraint that Canadian governments at different levels are now attempting to practice (Task Force Report, 1990: 5-7, 11, 17-21). Since financial resources are becoming seriously out of step with program require-ments, both current and projected, decisions must be made that address this discrepancy. In the case of Native police programs, there is a tendency to place such decision-making within a broader context of constitutional, legal and political considerations which define relations between federal, provin-cial and Native governments (Task Force Report, 1990: 9-11). Historically, the "solution" to the problem of increased costs has been that of cost-shar-ing between governments. But there is little indication that various govern-ments will be in a position to participate in required or increasing levels of cost-sharing (Murphy and Muir, 1984: 46; Task Force Report, 1990: 5).

Governments' practice of shifting program dollars under variable politi-cal circumstances and priority scales seems to be reflected in the apparent instability and deficits in federal and provincial funding for certain Native police programs (Depew, 1986: 50, 63, 65, 67; Task Force Report, 1990: 5-6). Yet, despite current and projected financial difficulties, native policing continues to grow in size and cost (Task Force Report, 1990: 5-6, 46). More importantly, both per capita expenditures and the growth in expendi-tures for Native policing generally exceed those for Canadian regional and national figures.

In general, Native policing is more expensive than non-Native policing because there are more police per capita policing areas with significant con-centrations of Native people than areas in which the Native population is considerably less (Havermann, Couse, Foster and Matonovich, 1984: 22). Nevertheless, the Native public requests and professional consultants and government officials recommend more police personnel for Native policing programs (Depew, 1986: 40-66; Task Force Report, 1990: 20). Inevitably, costs will be pushed to even higher levels.

The issue needs to be re-emphasized. Fiscal or economic strategies that require more police and more expenses may be unrealistic for the con-tinuation and further development of Native police programs in Canada. Therefore, alternatives to conventional policing must be found which signifi-cantly reduce or minimize government reliance on economic solutions to the problems of Native police programming. This demands a shift in perspective on the status of the organization and delivery of Native police services. Specifically at issue is the relationship between the organization and methods of police service delivery and the purposes for which the police are, can or should be employed in Native policing situations. This requires a closer examination of what is known about these situations.

Police Service in Native Communities

There are several characteristics of the available data on police work in Native communities and with Native people in general which suggest that the crime control model does not offer a very promising or practical approach to policing, and may even be an impediment to improvements in police services for Natives. In general, the data may be interpreted in terms of the following concerns:

(1)   variation and change in local policing circumstances;
(2)   police emphasis on crime control/law enforcement;
(3)   contingent or narrow definitions of police roles;
(4)   community dependency on the police; and
(5)   cross-cultural policing and indigenization.

The available evidence indicates that there is a serious discrepancy between current police emphasis on crime control and the range of policing problems to be addressed in Native communities (Clark, 1989; Depew, 1986; FSIN Study, 1984; LaPrairie, 1987, 1988). For example, in some rural reserve communities, Natives experience relatively low or decreasing rates of serious crime while problems of social disorder tend to predominate. In other reserve communities, relatively high or increasing rates of violent or property crimes may be observed, accompanied by variable demands for general service or crisis intervention. Significantly, the types of crimes committed by natives may also be linked to the types of communities in which they occur (LaPrairie, 1988). There is also evidence to suggest that Native communities may be more susceptible than non-Native communities to the disruptions and dislocations of rapid social change. Indeed, local variation and change in Native policing circumstances and problems can occur at an astonishing rate (Finkler, 1976, 1981, 1982, 1984; Rasing, 1988).

The "crimes" committed by Natives require some clarification. At this point research findings indicate that the character of Native deviance fluctuates between minor offences and more violent crimes, while their frequency of occurrence depends on variations in such factors as gender, ethnicity, age, jurisdiction and institutional infrastructures. However, an especially significant finding in the available literature indicates that Native involvement in the criminal justice system may be disproportionately alcohol-related. This possibility has very important implications for the kinds of policing problems faced by many Native communities.

Defined as a social issue, the role of alcohol abuse in the perpetration of Native "crime" suggests that such acts may be more a result of social disorder than of criminal intent. If this is the case, it follows that to interpret much of Native "crime" which comes to the attention of the criminal justice system as exclusively criminal in nature is to misunderstand the nature of much Native "criminality." More importantly, to persist with the application of criminal justice mechanisms that are largely punitive in response to Native "crime" may result in the miscarriage of social justice.

This brief digression was necessary in order to point out that practitioners of the crime control model will find it increasingly difficult to provide an integrity between the model's emphasis on the control of crime through law enforcement and cases where the principal policing problems, needs and priorities are focused on social issues. One major conclusion, therefore, is immediately apparent: similar to most non-Native communities, many Native communities appear to require police services that are based on much broader and socially-oriented police roles and functions. The main difference in their requirements at this level is, perhaps, mainly one of degree: there seems to be a more pressing need for law and order maintenance in Native communities (and, in particular, Indian reserves) taken as a whole, than in non-Native communities. This difference may be related to the higher degree of social disorganization and underdevelopment in Native communities which, historically, have been politically and economically induced (Gerber, 1979; Kellough, 1980; LaPrairie, 1987, 1988).[2]

The structures and constraints of the crime control model tend to promote adversarial policing roles. In a Native context, this style of policing has a significant impact on the nature of Native involvement in the criminal justice system. For example, Bienvenue and Latif (1974) have drawn attention to the high arrest rates experienced by Natives. At the time of their study, Natives comprised three per cent of the Winnipeg urban population but accounted for twenty-seven per cent of all male arrests and seventy per cent of all female arrests in Winnipeg. Apparently, police over-surveillance of highly visible urban Natives contributed significantly to patterns of disproportionate Native arrests. Native complaints heard by the Alberta Board of

Review also suggest that Natives in rural environments are subject to unnecessary involvement with the police due to the over-policing of Native individuals and communities (Alberta Board of Review, 1978). These and other imbalances in Native/police relations may not only reflect cross-cultural tensions between (non-Native) police and a Native public (Smith, 1975) but also the definitional constraints on the role of police officers who perform their duties in terms of the crime control model.

These constraints are even more apparent in view of a recent study of law enforcement on Indian reserves in Saskatchewan which links the incidence of occurrences and actual crime to the percentage of time spent by the police on Indian reserves and neighbouring communities (FSIN Study, 1984).[3]

Analysis of the data shows that while police spent only 17.3 per cent of their total time on Indian reserves, 12.99 per cent of all occurrences and 30.19 per cent of all actual crimes recorded by the police took place on the reserves. Confronted with a discrepancy between occurrence/crime ratios of two to one and seven to one for reserve and neighbouring communities, respectively, the authors of the study offer two tentative explanations for it.

First, given the poor response time and the reportedly poor relations between the Indian community and the detachment, it may be that the Indian communities only request the police to attend serious matters. Secondly, it may be that the police spend little time on reserves unless it is absolutely necessary (FSIN Study, 1984).

Other, equally plausible explanations could be advanced to account for this "anomaly."[4] However, the explanations offered by the study invite further analysis for reasons not pursued by its authors. If the first explanation is valid, it would appear that current police services for some reserves in Saskatchewan are under-utilized. If either or both explanations are significant, it should follow that police practice by non-Native police agencies (in this case, the R.C.M.P.) tends to foster or reinforce a narrow definition of police roles and functions among some of Saskatchewan's Native communities. Or the organization of the police may promote crime-fighting and law enforcement at the expense of other response options. In either case, the data suggest that crime-control definitions of policing are inconsistent with Native definitions and expectations of police work in their communities. As a result, they may unjustifiably exclude a broader, social definition of policing and force natives to under-utilize potentially more comprehensive police services. When such policing conditions prevail, working definitions of the police often fail to surface and address the full range of Native policing needs and preferences at the community level. This situation has the unfortunate consequence of restricting both our knowledge of the Nature and scope of policing problems and requirements in Native communities, and our ability to respond to these issues with the right types of policing services.

Our ability to provide the right types of police services and responses to Native communities partly depends on how the police organization understands and responds to community needs. At one level, the concern is with the nature of police/community interdependence in the policing process. For many Native communities, interdependence is problematic under the crime control model. As implied above, police withdrawal from the Native community, physically and/or socially, or the limiting of contact with the Native community to the point of crisis intervention and crime-fighting (Finkler, 1976: 73; Lambert, 1978; Loree, 1984) severely restricts the potential for interdependency. But without voluntary public support from the Native community concerned, the moral and legitimate status of police agencies policing Natives is weakened to the extent that there is often very little opportunity for the police effectively to mobilize community resources to the common pursuit of social order and control. Beyond this point, Native "acceptance" of the police may ultimately rest on force and coercion. Under these and similar circumstances, we can expect what Smith (1975: 68) calls "hostile dependency" to provide a less than satisfactory basis for articulation.

The general failure adequately to articulate police service delivery with Native needs and requirements has been interpreted by some government officials and other professionals not so much on the basis of any organizational deficiencies of the crime control model, but more in terms of assumed cross-cultural constraints in policing culturally diverse Native communities. Accordingly, the federal policy to indigenize the crime control model has led to the proliferation of special Native police programs where Native police officers are assumed and expected to provide "culturally sensitive" and, therefore, improved police services to Native communities (Task Force Report, 1990). But Native police officers are as constrained and directed by their pre-defined roles as non-Native police officers (Van Dyke and Jamont, 1980). Unfortunately, the role structure provides little scope for an effective partnership in community policing. Under these conditions, it is unlikely that the individual police officer will be in a position to mobilize a wider range of potentially significant policing resources in the community for the purposes of problem definition, identification and resolution. It is not surprising, therefore, that there exists no convincing evidence that indigenized police forces have improved police service delivery to Native communities or significantly reduced Native crime and deviance (Depew, 1986).

There is another fundamental inconsistency to indigenization when it is brought to bear on the realities of the Native policing environment. The underlying assumption is that Native criminality and deviance are a function of culture conflict with the existing non-Native criminal justice system, including the police. "Culturally-sensitive" policing is thought to bridge culture differences and, therefore, minimize Native conflict with this system. Under this approach, Native policing problems tend to be viewed in constant or fixed cultural terms. But police response options then can hardly be expected to deal with variation and change in Native crime and deviance, especially within a specific culture area. It follows that factors other than culture differences play a role in precipitating and shaping the genesis of Native involvement in the criminal justice system. Significantly, there are no studies which clearly demonstrate that culture differences are a key factor in the production and reproduction of Native "criminality." It is, perhaps, for these and other reasons that indigenization of the police is often socially and politically problematic (Brass, 1979; Native Counselling Services of Alberta, 1980; Parnell, 1979; Van Dyke and Jamont, 1980).

Notwithstanding the possibility of more limited and isolated positive effects of "culturally sensitive" policing, it bears repeating and emphasizing that community-based policing models are intended as systemic responses to policing issues. The model defines its objectives and priorities not on the basis of assumed cross-cultural differences and constraints but in relation to policing problems that may be traced to a variety of demographic, economic, political, and cultural exigencies of social life in contemporary Native communities. Nor is it the intention of community-based policing to recreate the forms and methods of policing practised by Native cultures in precontact or pre-urban times. Despite the validity and tenacity of many Native cultures in Canada, changes in environmental conditions strongly suggest that strictly traditional forms of Native policing may be inadequate, insufficient or inappropriate in dealing with new and changing patterns of Native crime and deviance. This does not mean, however, that we should ignore the ways in which Native communities assume and assert local authority and control. The point at issue is to capture principles of community involvement in the policing enterprise which may also reflect unique community configurations with distinctive cultural and historical roots and characteristics. Thus, far from advocating an extreme cultural relativism or legal pluralism that entails separate justice systems for Native groups (Jackson, 1988; Keon-Cohen, 1981; Jayewardene, 1979/80), a community-based model of policing assumes a comprehensive approach to community planning which takes into consideration community-level political and economic development to ensure stability and coherence in local social organization and an appropriate legislative framework to sustain inter-governmental co-operation, co-ordination, and support for new Native policing arrangements.

Summary and Conclusions

While critical comment on the status of the crime control model of policing in Native communities is limited, it is becoming increasingly evident that, despite programmatic amendments and concessions, the crime control model of policing frequently fails to define policing arrangements in terms that are acceptable or beneficial to many Natives and their communities. Consequently, there is an increasing danger that the standardization of Native policing under the crime control model will be to the detriment of Native communities which are subject to a variety of complex and changing environmental conditions.

As a conceptual model dedicated to the improvement of Native police services as well as the general relationship between Natives and the criminal justice system, community-based policing has been discussed as a policing strategy that may uniquely serve the interests of particular Native communities. Since its principles of organization are flexible and pragmatically oriented, community-based policing is more likely than the crime control approach to reflect the social, political, economic and cultural conditions of a wide range of Native communities. In addition, its principles of organization seem cross-culturally valid and independent of the resolution of broader constitutional and legislative issues affecting aboriginal rights. The practical concern, therefore, becomes one of maintaining a significant level of consistency with more general federal and provincial policy and legal considerations. This presupposes, of course, that governments will have the necessary political will to embrace the development and implementation of more generalizable, practical and adequate policing models for native people in Canada.

Endnotes

*   Reprinted by permission of the *Canadian Journal of Criminology* 34 (33-4: 461-478). Copyright by the Canadian Criminal Justice Association.

1   The author is a senior official with the Department of Indian Affairs and Northern Development; however, the views expressed herein are not necessarily the Department's.

2   An apt illustration of this thesis is LaPrairie's (1987) study of Native women's involvement in the criminal justice system. Situating the genesis of crime within the broader context of political economy and structured inequality, she analyses the historical changes that have taken place in the structure of role relationships among women and men in Native communities. Integral to her argument is the assumption that many Native communities manifest caricatures of previous kinship structures that were first deformed by the fur trade and then disfigured by the market system. Drawing on certain insights of role and learning theory, LaPrairie traces the social and psychological implications of these historical transformations to crime patterns among Native women and men.

3   Unfortunately, the report does not describe the composition of the population in neighbouring off-reserve communities. It may be assumed, however, that the reserve populations are mainly, if not entirely, Native or Indian.

4   The first explanation suggested in the report is, perhaps, difficult to reconcile with the fact that the largest proportion of Native Criminal Code offences that come to the attention of the criminal justice system in Saskatchewan are of a less serious nature. The second explanation might be more compelling if expressed in a slightly different way in the light of comparative evidence. If Natives in general, and reserve Indians in particular, are notably vulnerable to arrests and charges by the police (Alberta Board of Review, 1978; Bienvenue and Latif, 1974) or they are known and/or unsuccessful "criminals" (Finkler, 1976; Hylton, 1982) the police would, it seems, require considerably less time to investigate and assess occurrences or crimes.

5   In a study of Native policing in Alberta, Saskatchewan and Manitoba, Loree (1984: 21) estimates that routine service calls are second only to alcohol-related incidents in terms of the most frequent context of official contact between Natives and police cited by the police. Significantly, Criminal Code and serious offences occupied a small percentage of the total time spent by police officers surveyed, during official contact with Natives.

References

Alberta Board of Review. 1978. *Provincial Courts. Native People in the Administration of Justice in the Provincial Courts of Alberta.* Edmonton: Attorney General of Alberta.

Bienvenue, R.M. and A.H. Latif. 1974. "Arrest, Dispositions and Recidivism: A Comparison of Indians and Whites." *Canadian Journal of Criminology and Corrections* 16:105-116.

Brass, Oliver, I. 1979. *Crees and Crime: A Cross-Cultural Study.* Regina: University of Regina.

Clark, Scott. 1989. *The Mi'kmaq and Criminal Justice in Nova Scotia.* Halifax: Royal Commission on the Donald Marshall, Jr., Prosecution.

Depew, Robert C. 1986. *Native Policing in Canada: A Review of Current Issues.* Ottawa: Ministry of the Solicitor General of Canada.

Finkler, Harold W. 1976. *Inuit and the Administration of Criminal Justice in the Northwest Territories: The Case of Frobisher Bay.* Ottawa: Indian and Northern Affairs.

Finkler, Harold W. 1981. *The Baffin Correctional Centre.: A Review of Current Programs and Alternatives*. Ottawa: Indian and Northern Affairs.

Finkler, Harold W. 1982. "Corrections in the Northwest Territories 1967-1981, With a Focus on the Incarceration of Inuit Offenders." *Canadian Legal Aid Bulletin* 5:27-38.

Finkler, Harold W. 1983. "Violence and the Administration of Justice: A Focus on Inuit Communities in Northern Canada." *Third World Law Journal* 4:123-150.

Finkler, Harold W. 1984. "Inuit and the Criminal Justice System: Future Strategies for Socio-Legal Control and Prevention." Paper presented to the Fourth Inuit Studies Conference, Montreal.

FSIN Study. 1984. "Joint Canada-Saskatchewan-FSIN Studies of Certain Aspects of the Justice System As They Relate to Indians in Saskatchewan." Ottawa: Ministry of the Solicitor General of Canada.

Gerber, Linda M. 1979. "The Development of Canadian Indian Communities: A Two-dimensional Typology Reflecting Strategies of Adaptation to the Modern World." *Canadian Review of Sociology and Anthropology* 16: 404-24.

Havermann, Paul, Keith Couse, Lori Foster and Rae Matonovich. 1984. *Law and Order for Canada's Indigenous People*. Ottawa: Ministry of the Solicitor General of Canada.

Humphrey, N.D. 1942. " Police and Tribal Welfare in Plains Indian Culture." *Journal of Criminal Law and Criminology* 33:147-161.

Hylton, John H. 1982. "The Native Offender in Saskatchewan: Some Implications for Crime Prevention Programming." *Canadian Journal of Criminology* 24:121-131.

Jackson, Michael. 1988. *Locking Up Natives in Canada. A Report of the Committee of the Canadian Bar Association on Imprisonment and Release*. Ottawa: Canadian Bar Association.

Jayewardene, C.H.S. 1979/80. "Policing the Indian." *Crime and/et Justice* 718:42-47.

Kellough, Gail. 1980. "From Colonialism to Economic Imperialism: The Experience of the Canadian Indian" in Harp, John and John Hofley (eds.), *Inequality in Canada*. Toronto: Prentice Hall.

Keon-Cohen, B.A. 1981. "Native Justice in Australia, Canada and the U.S.A.: A Comparative Analysis." *Monash University Law Review* 7:250-325.

Lambert, C. 1978. *Research Priorities in Northern Labrador*. Montreal: McGill University.

LaPrairie, Carol P. 1987. "Native Women and Crime: A Theoretical Model." *Canadian Journal of Native Studies* 7: 121-137.

LaPrairie, Carol P. 1988. "Community Types, Crime and Police Services on Canadian Indian Reserves." *Journal of Research in Crime and Delinquency* 25:375-391.

Loree, Donald J. 1984. *Policing Native Communities*. Ottawa: Canadian Police College.

Murphy, Chris and Graham Muir. 1984. *Community-Based Policing: A Review of the Critical Issues*. Ottawa: Ministry of the Solicitor General of Canada.

Native Counselling Services of Alberta. 1980. *Policing on Reserves: A Review of Current Programs and Alternatives*. Edmonton.

Parnell, T. 1979. *We Mean No Harm: Yukon Indian-Police Relations. A Preliminary Survey of Attitudes*. Whitehorse: Yukon Association of Non-Status Indian.

Rasing, Wim. 1988. *Legal Anthropological Study of Legal Pluralism in Igloolik, Northwest Territories, Canada*. Ottawa: Department of Indian Affairs and Northern Development.

Schwartz, R.D. 1954. "Social Factors in the Development of Legal Control: A Case Study of Two Israeli Settlements." *The Yale Law Journal* 63: 471-491.

Smith, Derek G. 1975. *Natives and Outsiders: Pluralism in the Mackenzie River Delta, Northwest Territories.* Ottawa: Department of Indian Affairs and Northern Development.

Task Force Report. 1990. *Indian Policing Policy Review.* Ottawa: Department of Indian Affairs and Northern Development.

Van den Steenhoven, Geert. 1959. *Legal Concepts Among the Netsilik Eskimo of Pelly Bay.* Ottawa: Northern Co-ordination and Research Centre.

Van Dyke, Edward W. and K.C. Jamont. 1980. *Through Indian Eyes: Perspectives of Indian Constable on the 3b Program in "F" Division.* Regina: Native Policing Section, Royal Canadian Mounted Police.

Wachtel, David. 1983. "The Effects of Traditionalism on the Navajo Police Officer." *Police Studies* 57-62.

Weaver, Sally. 1984. "A Commentary on the Penner Report." *Canadian Public Policy* X: 215-221.

The Role of Sentencing in the Over-representation of Aboriginal People in Correctional Institutions

Carol LaPrairie

Introduction

For the past two decades, virtually everything written and discussed in the area of Aboriginal people and the criminal justice system has used as its starting point the over-representation of Aboriginal people as inmates in federal, provincial and territorial correctional institutions. Rarely, however, has there been any concerted attempt to analyze this issue in any systematic way.[1] There are assumptions that sentencing accounts for a significant part of the problem, but the relationship between sentencing and over-representation has not been explored systematically. The politicization of criminal justice issues within the agendas of land claims, self-government and constitutional matters has created the prevailing discourse. The lack of attention to the issue in the academic criminology world has permitted continuation of the political rhetoric. This article seeks to address some of the outstanding questions by focusing on sentencing and examining the over-representation phenomenon within the context of criminal justice processing at two critical points, i.e., police and judicial decision making.

1. The Meaning of Over-representation

Over-representation has been used to describe the percentage of Aboriginal people in federal, provincial and territorial correctional institutions as compared to their percentage in the general population.[2] For example, Aboriginal people comprise approximately 1.5-2 per cent of the Canadian population but make up approximately eight to ten per cent of the federal correctional institutional population and considerably more in provincial and territorial institutions, particularly in northwest Ontario and the western provinces, although the exact percentages are unclear.[3] It is apparent, that for certain Aboriginal groups such as women and juveniles, the rates may be even more extreme (La Prairie, 1987).

Reliance on the standard of Aboriginal population ratios, i.e., inmate versus general populations, has obscured other ways of understanding over-representation. For example, if one changed the standard to Aboriginal and non-Aboriginal *age distributions* in the general population, the "over-representation" picture might look quite different. Higher birth rates and lower life expectancy suggest a relatively large Aboriginal fourteen- to twenty-year-old age group. The Aboriginal percentage of this group is higher than the Aboriginal percentage of the general population. This is also the group with the highest participation rate in the criminal justice system; so it would not be surprising to see high Aboriginal representation among offenders from this age group. Whether this group would be disproportionately represented is another question. One of the few researchers to address the age distribution issue analyzed the characteristics of a large cohort of Aboriginal and non-Aboriginal inmates in B.C. and concluded that:

> The distribution of age for the offender population, for example, seems to have a greater correspondence with the native population at large than it does with the general population at large. The increased number of native offenders may prove to partially be a function of the age distribution within the general native population (Muirhead, 1981).[4]

Similarly, if one follows the theoretical approach of the critical criminologists and uses class (based on socio-economic level) as the standard and predictor of who goes to jail, Aboriginal people may well be statistically *under*-represented. Given the same economic reality, non-Aboriginal offence rates would no doubt be much higher. There are, then, different ways to look at the over-representation issue and relying solely on population ratios may limit the analysis.

2. The Causes of Over-representation

Simply put, there are three competing but not mutually exclusive explanations for the disproportionate representation of Aboriginal people in correctional institutions. These are:

(1)   differential treatment by the criminal justice system (i.e., something different is happening to Aboriginal people than to non-Aboriginal people in their contact with the criminal justice system, at police, charging, prosecution, sentencing and parole decision-making points);

(2)   differential commission of crime (i.e., Aboriginal people are committing more crime as they have "non-racial attributes placing them at risk for criminal behaviour" (Bonta, 1989: 49). These attributes could be related to socio-economic marginality and, concomitantly, alcohol abuse); and

(3)   differential offence patterns (i.e., Aboriginal people commit crimes that are more detectable (more serious and/or more visible) that those committed by non-Aboriginal people).

These explanations are self-explanatory and there is little need to discuss them further. There is, however, a need to provide a context within which to locate them. The issues of incidence of crime and offence patterns of Aboriginal people have been largely ignored in discussions of over-representation. The willingness to focus on criminal justice processing serves a number of agendas, not the least of which is political, in both Aboriginal and non-Aboriginal terms. For Aboriginal political goals of self-government, it directs attention to the need for a "parallel" system of justice if the system of the majority group can be shown to be irrelevant or unsatisfactory to the indigenous minority; for non-Aboriginal, dominant interests, it allows attention to focus on the criminal justice system rather than on disparities in society, the solution to which would be economic restructuring.

Attention to incidence of crime or offence patterns would require an examination of fundamental social structure and economic disparity. This paper is an attempt to demonstrate how fragile the criminal justice processing explanation is and to argue the need for the criminal justice system to redirect the issue to where it more properly belongs — in the social, political and economic spheres. The first step in this process is to examine the state of research knowledge in the sentencing of Aboriginal people.

Differential Criminal Justice Processing

Decision making is inherent to each component of criminal justice processing but the most critical points, i.e., police charging and sentencing, are usually targeted in discussions of Aboriginal over-representation, even though there is often inconsistent or uneven information about the nature and scope of this involvement.

1. Police Decision Making

Considerable anecdotal data exist with regard to police/Aboriginal contacts and police decision making, but few empirical data have been collected because of methodological difficulties in participant observation research. In addition, examining practices in one jurisdiction would not necessarily allow the generalization of findings. Reserve policing varies from band constables to band police force to general police services, rural policing varies from RCMP to provincial police forces, and municipal policing varies from RCMP to provincial forces to municipal forces. As a result, it is difficult to explicitly point to differential police charging and arrests as the basis for the disproportionate incarceration rates. However, Bienvenue and Latif in their study of arrests in Winnipeg showed a disproportion of Aboriginals and attributed it to the over-surveillance of Aboriginal people by police (Bienvenue and Latif, 1974).

Although empirical data are lacking, assumptions about the existence of differential, racist charging practices abound.[5] The acceptance of these assumptions has led to the implementation of initiatives designed to reduce the cultural conflict between Aboriginal people and police. These include cross-cultural training and the indigenization of policing, i.e., the addition of Aboriginal people as special constables to forces such as the RCMP and the Ontario Provincial Police.

Police decision making in criminal justice processing remains the most critical information gap in accounting for the disproportionate presence of Aboriginal people in the system. It is essential to know if Aboriginal people receive different police treatment from non-Aboriginals. For example, are they being differentially arrested and charged? Are they over-policed (i.e., the "more police more crime" syndrome)? Are they investigated differently (i.e., more or less comprehensively)? Are there differences between and among types of police forces (e.g., urban/rural) in their contacts with Aboriginal people? And is there geographic variation in police response to Aboriginal people? The above questions raise the need to understand better the exact nature and scope of the problems that face Aboriginal people in their contacts with police. This is not to minimize the seriousness of the issue of over-representation but to reiterate concern about the use of rhetoric in the absence of knowledge.

2. Judicial Decision Making (Sentencing)

The most critical and controversial area of criminal justice processing of Aboriginal people is sentencing. There is considerable rhetoric about overt racism and unwarranted disparity in the conviction and sentencing of Aboriginal people. In one of the most recent and widely reported papers, *Locking Up Natives in Canada* published under the auspices of the Special Committee on Imprisonment and Release of the Canadian Bar Association, Michael Jackson states that "one reason why Native inmates are disproportionately represented in the prison populations is that too many of them are being unnecessarily sentenced to terms of imprisonment" (Jackson, 1988: 212). No data are presented to support the implication that racial bias leads to imprisonment. In a similar way, Morse and Lock support the view of Aboriginal offenders that "virtually the entire justice system as a system...is biased against native people." (Morse and Lock, 1988: 48), and appear to base this belief, at least in part, on Aboriginal inmates' perceptions that they receive harsher sentences than do non-Aboriginals. The Morse and Lock study does not compare Aboriginal inmate perceptions with those of a non-Aboriginal control group of inmates, and Jackson gives no data to support his claim. These are examples of the limited methodologies and levels of analysis which have prevailed to date. In order to examine the sentencing of Aboriginal offenders, it is necessary to identify the sentencing issues. For purposes of this paper these are:

(1)   Unwarranted disparity in dispositions — are Aboriginal people incarcerated for offences for which non-Aboriginal offenders receive non-carceral sentences, controlling for seriousness of offence, prior record and other legally relevant variables?

(2)   Unwarranted disparity in sentence length — do Aboriginal offenders receive longer sentences (of incarceration, probation and community service orders) than non-Aboriginal offenders, controlling for seriousness of offence and prior record?

To date, there have been few empirical attempts to address these questions. This may be changing. Recent research by Scott Clark (1989), sponsored by the Federal Department of Justice, and the draft terms of reference for the proposed Task Force on the Criminal Justice System and Its Impact on Indian and Métis People in Alberta[6] (Alberta Task Force, 1989) suggest that research activity in this area may increase significantly.

Clark's review of sentencing literature and empirical research in Aboriginal criminal justice (Clark, 1989) provides no conclusive evidence to support or reject the existence of unwarranted disparity or overt racial bias in the sentencing of Aboriginal people. He points out that the lack of a solid empirical base has inhibited any real understanding of whether bias exists in the conviction and sentencing of Aboriginal accused. It is clear from Clark's account that there have been few attempts in Canada to examine the sentencing of Aboriginal people within the standard "individual-processual" theoretical approach much less the broader "structural-contextual" approach envisioned by Hagan and Bumiller (1983). The former approach explains sentencing in the context of legal and extra-legal factors; the latter in the social, economic and political context. The utility of the emphasis on criminal justice processing as the cause of over-representation explains the reluctance to promote a more fundamental context for sentencing.

a)Unwarranted Disparity in Dispositions

Two of the first Canadian attempts to examine the issue of disparity in dispositions were undertaken by Dubienski and Skelly (1970), using Winnipeg arrest data, and by John Hagan (1977), using a sample of incarcerated offenders and a sample of offenders for whom pre-sentence reports had been written. Hagan's 1977 work followed his earlier research on factors affecting judicial decision making where he found that judicial reliance on a law and order model of society explained more variance in sentencing than did race (Hagan, 1974). Dubienski and Skelly found relatively fair treatment of Indian accused except in the area of regulatory offences where fines were disproportionately imposed.

This was a form of discrimination because the Indian group was less able to pay fines. Hagan's 1977 research revealed more severe sentencing of Aboriginal people in rural areas; he attributed this to the lack of bureaucratization in courts resulting in greater discretion in the criminal justice system.

Contrary to Hagan's urban/rural court findings were those of Boldt *et al.* (1983: 269) in the Yukon where no evidence of harsher or more lenient sentencing was revealed, and legal factors (particularly prior record) explained sentence variance. In addressing the concern that Aboriginal people are less likely to receive probation to the same degree as do non-Aboriginal offenders, the Research Group's study for the Correctional Sentences Project using national data on custodial, fine default and probation admissions is informative (The Research Group, 1987). For the year 1984-85, for the jurisdiction where data were available, the highest number of *custodial* admissions for Aboriginal offenders were for murder, aggravated assault and manslaughter. The lowest number of custodial admissions for Aboriginal offenders for the same period were for extortion. The highest number of *fine default* admissions for Aboriginal offenders were for public mischief and obstruct justice; the lowest for trafficking in drugs. The highest number of *probation breach* admissions were for aggravated assault and possession of stolen property under $1000; whereas the lowest was for theft of credit cards.

Aggregating the data (although limited because all jurisdictions are not represented) is useful in challenging the belief that Aboriginal people receive probation for serious offences less often than do non-Aboriginal people. Variations by province and territory or by race of victim may exist; but the fact that the number of probation admissions for a serious offence such as aggravated assault is higher for the Aboriginal than the non-Aboriginal accused might suggest less prejudicial treatment than is generally supposed. Moyer's research on comparative dispositions for Aboriginal and non-Aboriginal people accused of homicide provides some interesting findings (Moyer, 1987). The Canadian Centre for Justice Statistics, Homicide Project provided Native and non-Native victim, suspect and court procedure data for the period 1962-1984. However, from 1962-73, only murder offences are included; from 1974, murder, manslaughter and infanticide offences are included.

Moyer's analysis revealed that Natives were less likely to be convicted of first or second degree murder and more likely to be convicted of manslaughter than were non-Natives — 76.3 per cent and 73.7 per cent of Native men and women respectively as compared to 45.6 per cent and 56.4 per cent non-Native; only 4.0 per cent of Native men were convicted of first degree murder as compared to 13.5 per cent of non-Native men; one-half as many Native suspects were convicted of second degree murder as were non-Native. It is important to keep in mind that Moyer's data did not include information on victims and alcohol involvement so the application of the findings is limited.

A recent study in B.C., under the auspices of the Legal Service Society, examined the effect of sentencing practices in summary conviction courts for the single charge offences of common assault and theft under $1,000, for a nine-month period in 1988. The sample consisted of Legal Services Society cases — a total of 1,7222 of which 409 involved common assault and 1,363 theft under the value of $1000. Aboriginal people comprised 29.3 per cent of the common assault cases and 21.0 per cent of the theft under cases. In general, the findings showed that:

> ...individuals of Native ancestry with prior criminal convictions were acquitted less frequently and found guilty more often [of theft under $1,000 category only] than non-Native individuals in similar circumstances. Individuals of Native ancestry free of prior criminal convictions are granted stay of proceedings more frequently, and found guilty less often than individuals of non-Native ancestry. Single, unemployed individuals of Native ancestry residing off-reserve were sentenced to jail time more often than those of non-Native ancestry [or than those of Native ancestry living on reserve, seems to be the assumption in the paper although it is not specified]. (Lewis, 1989: 15).[7]

The study included variables such as education, sex, age, employment and residency (on/off reserve); but the relationship of these factors to sentence outcome for the Aboriginal and non-Aboriginal groups is unclear, except a previously noted for employment and residency. More sophisticated analysis using regression or other techniques with large sample sizes would be necessary to clarify the effect of these variables.

Taken together these findings provide no definite answers to the question of racial bias or unwarranted disparity in the sentencing of Aboriginal people, but highlight some of the contradictions that exist.

b) Disparity in Sentence Lengths

Better data on sentence lengths for Aboriginal and non-Aboriginal accused allow for a more focused discussion on whether unwarranted disparity exists. Early work by Schmeiser (1974), Hagan (1974) and Hylton (1981) concluded that the shorter sentence lengths given Aboriginal accused reflected the fact that they received custodial sentences for the less serious offences. The issue of disparity in disposition is still unclear but recent work suggests that Aboriginal accused may be receiving shorter sentence lengths even when controlling for type of offence. Missing from the analysis are the effects of socio-economic and cultural factors upon judicial decision making.

The findings from Moyer's homicide data are interesting and raise questions for further research (Moyer, 1987). About one-half of the non-Aboriginal persons convicted of homicide received life sentences as compared to one-fifth of the Aboriginal persons; nearly fifty per cent of the Aboriginal accused received periods of detention less than five years as compared to less than twenty-five per cent of the non-Aboriginal group. The sentences for Aboriginal women were particularly light as twenty-nine per cent were placed on probation or given a suspended sentence as compared to only ten per cent of the non-Aboriginal women (Clark, 1989: 24). Although Moyer was unable to present the findings in terms of offence category by sentence length, her findings suggest that aboriginal homicide offenders receive less severe sentences than do non-aboriginals for the same offence categories. Again, it should be stressed that data on alcohol involvement and race of victim were not available for consideration in the analysis.

The research by Canfield and Drinnan (1981), using five years of federal admissions data from 1976-1980, shows disparity in sentence length which favours Aboriginal accused.[8] When examining offence type by sentence length, the Native groups almost consistently received shorter sentences than did the non-Native groups for the same offences. For example, 55.1 per cent of the Natives received sentences of four years or less for attempted murder as compared to 23.2 per cent of non-Natives; 34.4 per cent of the Natives received sentences of six years or more as compared to 60.2 per cent of the non-Natives. For manslaughter the figures were 43.4 per cent (Native) and 22.2 per cent (non-Native) for sentences of four years or less, and 26.7 per cent and 51.3 per cent respectively for six years or more. Similar disparities were found for break and enter, theft, assault, robbery and sexual offences as well. In general, these findings were supported in a later study by Moyer et al. (1985) using 1981-82 data.

The Moyer et al. research examined sentence length by offence type for Aboriginal and non-Aboriginal admissions to federal, provincial and territorial correctional institutions. Admissions to the provincial and territorial institutions revealed few differences between the two groups in terms of sentence lengths for Criminal Code and provincial/territorial offences (Moyer et al., 1985). However, Correctional Services Canada data showed

Aboriginal sentenced admissions to be generally shorter than non-Aboriginal sentences admissions in 1982.

The most recent research on sentence lengths (Bonta, 1989) found no significant difference between average sentence lengths for Native compared to non-Native offenders even after controlling for criminal history.

Discussion

The data concerning the role of judicial discretion in causing the alleged statistical over-representation of Aboriginal people in correctional institutions remain contradictory and unclear. On the one hand, there are suggestions of unwarranted disparity recurring throughout the Aboriginal criminal justice literature and in media reports emanating from the three inquiries presently under way in Canada.[9] In addition, where there appears to be some empirical basis to the allegations of disparate sentencing in terms of sentence type, the contributing factors range widely from rural court procedures, as suggested by Hagan (1977: 597), to the over-imprisonment for minor offences explanation put forward by Dubienski and Skelly (1970). More comprehensive data are required, however, on sentencing patterns for both Aboriginal and non-Aboriginal offenders for a range of offences controlling for legal and extra-legal factors as much as possible in order to determine whether unwarranted disparity in sentence types causes disproportionate incarceration of Aboriginal persons. It is quite clear that more Aboriginal people in Canada are in correctional institutions than would be expected given their numbers in the general population (if that is even the most appropriate standard to be using, as discussed earlier). The exact role of sentencing in creating over-representation is still unknown.

Sentence length data, however, tell a different story. Canadian data are limited, but they suggest the possibility of shorter sentences for Aboriginal offenders for some offences. There are some international data which parallel the Canadian findings. Recent and relatively comprehensive data from Australia show shorter sentence lengths for Aborigines for virtually all offence categories. Using 1984 aggregated average sentence length data (excluding Queensland where ethnicity is not recorded), the author found that:

> In only two significant categories are the Aboriginal average sentences grater than the equivalent for non-Aboriginals — despite the gross disparities in prior imprisonment records.

Even though 81.1 per cent of Aboriginal prisoners have previously been in prison under sentence, compared with only 57.5 per cent of non-Aboriginal prisoners, the average sentence for Aboriginal prisoners is only 42.6 months compared with 74.9 months for non-Aboriginals. This cannot be entirely attributed to the different types of offences committed by Aboriginals since the sentencing disparity is roughly consistent across the whole range of offences (Walker, 1987: 111).

The Australian findings contradict what is generally known about sentencing decision-making from the available Canadian research, i.e., seriousness of offence and prior record are the most significant variables. If shorter sentence lengths for Aboriginal offenders are confirmed in future research, it will be necessary to determine if judges rely more on incarceration when Aboriginal offenders cannot meet the criteria for probation but balance incarceration decisions with shorter sentence lengths. There may be important consequences to such a practice. For example, does the combination of incarceration and shorter sentence length result in higher recidivism rates and longer prior records? Do longer records make incarceration more likely in the event of a subsequent conviction?

Hogarth (1971) examined sentencing decisions with respect to Aboriginal people. More recently, a study by Patricia Brantingham, Daniel Beavon and Paul Brantingham (1982) analysed sentencing decisions for 2,000 legally aided cases (not necessarily Aboriginal people) initiated in two Canadian communities. We can derive from these studies the message that research into the sentencing of Aboriginal people must account for factors (cultural, historical, political, social, economic and geographic) that have created a particular identity and environment for Aboriginal groups in Canada. The complexities that result with respect to who appears in the criminal justice system and how they are perceived by decision-makers may require different theoretical and methodological approaches than those normally adopted by researchers. Indeed, the need to take a broader view has been identified by Hagan who suggests that "consensus and conflict theories do not provide sufficient attention to the structural relationships that emerge from a joining of organizational and political forces in the direction of criminal justice operations" (Hagan, 1989).

The findings of Brantingham et al.[10] question some of the "sacred cows" in the Aboriginal over-representation discourse. For example, is it valid to state generally that Aboriginal people plead guilty more often and are more likely to be sentenced to periods of incarceration as a result of so pleading? Similarly, can it generally be said that Aboriginal people suffer more adverse effects in their dealings with the criminal justice system because they have legal representation rather than lawyers from the private bar? The Brantingham *et al.* findings suggest the need for comparative research to determine if their findings based on research in non-Aboriginal communities apply to an Aboriginal sample.

It is clear that understanding the sentencing of Aboriginal offenders is like trying to complete a jigsaw puzzle without all the pieces. Even where data are available, they often raise more questions than answers. Perhaps what is required at this point is the presentation of three possible explanations, i.e., overt racism, systematic discrimination and/or preferential treatment, as a way of identifying the parameters for further exploration.

Racism, Systematic Discrimination or Preferential Treatment?

As previously discussed, accusations by Aboriginal people and others of overt racism in the criminal justice system have played an important role in the "over-representation" discourse to date. The fact that solid data on the relationship between criminal justice processing and the over-representation of Aboriginal people as inmates in correctional institutions are limited at best does not inhibit the widespread use of this explanation. Perhaps the adoption of this perspective fulfills both real and perceived (i.e., symbolic) needs in ways that other explanations could not accomplish — the illuminating of contemporary Aboriginal life as marginalized, resulting from the historical processes of colonization, dislocation from homelands and erosion of traditional activities. This position also supports certain political agendas (such as self-government development) that require the treatment of Aboriginal people by dominant systems to be such that Aboriginal-specific systems would be the only logical solution to the "problem."

That is not to say that no racism exists in the criminal justice system. Anecdotal material suggests that racism (both real and perceived) is a major concern to Aboriginal people and warrants attention by those charged with criminal justice policy responsibilities. A commitment to research, which examines race as an explanation for disparities in criminal justice processing, is required (Zatz, 1987). In the absence of sound empirical data, one is left to speculate about the anomalies identified above.

If Aboriginal people are indeed at greater risk of incarceration than non-Aboriginal accused for the same offences, explaining this phenomenon solely in racism terms may be simplistic and misleading with respect to finding real and long-lasting solutions to the over-representation problem. Some theorists have recently raised the issue of systemic discrimination as a means of accounting for disparity in sentencing dispositions (Archibald, 1989; Clark, 1989; LaPrairie, 1988). It would undoubtedly be useful to explore this approach later.

Systemic Discrimination or Preferential Treatment?

In short, systemic discrimination as defined by Archibald, Clark and others points to the significance of "treating unequals equally"; that is, applying the same criteria to all offenders in disposition considerations. This phenomenon may have more adverse consequences for Aboriginal accused if, for example, judges make disposition decisions and/or probation officers make recommendations regarding dispositions based on the presence or absence of certain structural factors such as employment, education or family and community supports. As researchers such as Petersillia (1985) have noted in analyzing the criminal justice processing of blacks in the U.S., the granting of probation is based on certain risk factors, in part, and that providing the court with more complete background information may prejudice judges against granting probation. The recognition that Aboriginal people reside at the lowest socio-economic level in Canadian society and that perceptions of marginality may affect judicial decision-making should not be ignored in understanding and explaining the phenomenon of differential sentencing.

Archibald, in his discussion of systemic discrimination in sentencing, suggests that a social responsibility model of crime causality, which locates crime in social and economic marginality and inequality, should be taken into account at sentencing (Archibald, 1989). Adopting such an approach implies institutionalizing the practice of "treating unequals equally" to reduce the impact of social and economic disparities between groups. If some of the findings indicating less severe sentences for Aboriginal accused are verified in further research, this may be evidence that some judges are aware of the realities facing Aboriginal people in everyday life and that this is reflected in length of sentences. In short, there may be some evidence of "treating unequals equally." What remains a greater problem for the criminal justice system is the "overuse" of incarceration for Aboriginal people when criteria for existing options for sentencing cannot be met.

Sentencing Reform

Existing data, although limited and incomplete, would suggest the disproportionate sentencing of Aboriginal people to periods of incarceration in the absence of other sentencing options. This situation makes one of the most compelling arguments for sentencing reform. Nowhere else is the use of the criminal justice system to address a major social and economic problem so potentially problematic as it is in relation to Aboriginal people. It is this group which appears to be incarcerated for less serious offences because its members do not qualify for probation, and few options but incarceration are available to judges. Their deprived socio-economic situation acts against Aboriginal people at sentencing and against communities in the development and maintenance of community-based alternatives. The geographic location of the majority of reserves makes access to universal sentencing alternatives difficult and often impossible.

The sentencing of Aboriginal people to shorter periods of incarceration as a way of "balancing" harsher dispositions has a long-term revolving door effect in addition to the short-term unpleasantness of being put in jail. Over time, the revolving door syndrome creates a large group of Aboriginal people with long records of incarceration which act against them in subsequent court appearances.

Clearly, if many Aboriginal people are incarcerated for relatively minor offences (an issue for provincial institutions only, as federal inmates are in for more serious offences) for which few options are available, it is imperative to examine other avenues for dealing with the problems they present. The social and economic marginality of Aboriginal people in Canadian society is the fundamental problem and their involvement in the criminal justice system as offenders is a vivid testimonial to it. The criminal justice system is not a vehicle for social restructuring; neither should it be a storage receptacle for social problems. The criminal justice system could divert those to be handled outside it, and develop alternatives to incarceration for those who require handling within it. Incarceration should be used only as a last resort.

The social disintegration, economic deprivation and geographic location of the majority of reserves (resulting from colonization, cultural dislocation and marginalization) often present a poor prognosis for the implementation and maintenance of community-based diversion and/or sentencing options. Criminal justice policy and program decision makers must be committed to developing, evaluating and institutionalizing justice programs, where required and feasible. This is necessary to ensure that community-based criminal justice initiatives become entrenched and do not suffer the "here today, gone tomorrow" syndrome of so many activities in Aboriginal communities dependent on outside funding. Creative planning and commitment is also required in urban areas to provide alternatives to imprisonment.

Adequate training of community-based workers and monitoring and assistance from provincial professionals have been identified by Clark as integral to the success and stability of programs (Clark, 1989). Serious consideration must also be given to the "access" problem, i.e., Aboriginal people being excluded from universal alternative programs because of where they live. Perhaps the most critical element is the necessity for criminal justice programs to reflect the real needs in reserve, rural and urban communities as well as the ability of the communities to develop and sustain them.

Endnotes

1   One of the few exceptions is the work by James Bonta (1989), where risk assessment scales were administered to Native and non-Native inmates in three northern Ontario jails and the issue of over-representation was related to criminal justice processing.

2   Over-representation figures emerge from information collected routinely on admissions to correctional institutions and are based on self-identification. Because information is collected routinely only at the corrections admission level, it is the one consistent source of data.

3   Normally, admission data are used to describe the over-representation phenomenon. However, the difficulty with admissions to provincial institutions is that it can count the same person more than once, if an individual is serving numerous short sentences over a two-year period. As well, it has been suggested that in some provinces fine defaulters, upon sentence to a correctional institution, are admitted to the institution and immediately released to fine option programs. What this means is that they could appear in admissions data but are not serving actual custodial time.

4   Statistics Canada data on the age distribution of the B.C. Native population in 1981 show the under-twenty Native group to be 50.18 per cent as compared to 29.83 per cent for the non-Native group.

5   *Kainai News*, 23 June 1989, 4, 11. While only one reference is provided here, there is an abundance of material which refers to the racial nature of police decision making. The assumption of overt racism on the part of police was very much at the root of the three inquiries into the treatment of Aboriginal people by the criminal justice system — the Donald Marshall, Manitoba and Alberta (Blood Reserve) inquiries. In a recent presentation to the Western Judicial Conference, June 24-29, 1989, Brian Throne of the First Nations of South Island Tribal Council stated that non-Indian policing is "filled with subtle and sometimes blatant racial prejudice" (Western Judicial Education Centre, 1989).

6   The term which refers specifically to the sentencing disparity research issue is as follows: "determine whether and to what extent differences exist in sentencing practices as (sic) between Indian and Métis people."

7   Aboriginal participation rates are difficult to interpret in the offence categories because it is not necessarily a random sample, as the Legal Services Society was established to provide assistance to groups with special needs, in this case Aboriginal people. The analysis also limits findings, for example, number and type of prior convictions are important factors in sentencing dispositions; single variables were analyzed in relation to sentence outcome for the Aboriginal and non-Aboriginal groups rather than looking at them in combination, so that it is impossible to determine how much explanatory value each variable has. Finally, there is no information provided for sentence lengths.

8   Sentence lengths were calculated by the author from the tables provided.

9   Royal Commission on the Donald Marshall, Jr., Prosecution, the Manitoba Public Inquiry into the Administration of Justice and Aboriginal People and the Alberta Public Inquiry into Policing on the Blood Reserve.

10   Case facts, aggravating and mitigating circumstances and prior record were most strongly related to sentence type decision making. Entering a guilty plea, although statistically significant, was weakly related to sentence type — guilty pleas were associated with higher probation and lower fine rates, but were not associated with incarceration rates. Individuals represented by a public defender received fewer jail sentences than private counsel clients. Sentence length decisions were strongly associated with prior record, use of weapons and length of criminal career.

References

Alberta Task Force. 1989. *Terms of Reference: Task Force on the Criminal Justice System and Its Impact on the Indian and Métis People of Alberta.* Alberta: Ministry of the Attorney General, Alberta.

Archibald, Bruce P. 1989. "Sentencing and Visible Minorities: Equality and Affirmative Action in the Criminal Justice System." Paper presented at the Sentencing Now and in the Future Conference, 3-4 March, Halifax, Nova Scotia.

Bienvenue, Rita M. and A.H. Latif. 1974. "Arrests, Disposition and Recidivism: A Comparison of Indians and Whites." *Canadian Journal of Criminology* 16: 105-16.

Boldt, Edward, Larry Hursh, Stuart Johnson and Wayne Taylor. 1983. "Presentence Reports and the Incarceration of Natives." *Canadian Journal of Criminology* 25:-269-76.

Bonta, James. 1989. "Native Inmates: Institutional Response, Risk and Needs." *Canadian Journal of Criminology* 31: 49-61.

Brantingham, Patricia, Daniel Beavon and Paul Brantingham. 1982. *Analysis of Sentencing Disparity in Two Canadian Communities.* Ottawa: Department of Justice, Canada.

Canfield, Carolyn and Linda Drinnan. 1981. *Comparative Statistics: Native and Non-Native Federal Inmates — A Five-Year History.* Ottawa: Ministry of the Solicitor General.

Clark, Scott. 1989. *Sentencing Patterns and Sentencing Options Relating to Aboriginal Offenders.* Ottawa: Department of Justice, Canada.

Dubienski, Ian and Stephen Skelly. 1970. "Analysis of Arrests for the Year 1969 in the City of Winnipeg with Particular Reference to Arrests of Persons of Indian Descent." Unpublished.

Hagan, John. 1974. "Criminal Justice and Native People: A Study of Incarceration in a Canadian Province." *Canadian Review of Sociology and Anthropology* Special Issue: 220-36.

Hagan, John. 1977. "Criminal Justice in Rural and Northern Communities: A Study of the Bureaucratization of Justice." *Social Forces* 55: 597-612.

Hagan, John. 1989. "Why Is There So Little Criminal Justice Theory? Neglected Macro- and Micro-Level Link Between Organization and Power." *Journal of Research in Crime and Delinquency* 26: 116-35.

Hogarth, John. 1971. *Sentencing as a Human Process.* Toronto: University of Toronto Press.

Hylton, John. 1981. "Locking up Indians in Saskatchewan: Some Recent Findings." *Canadian Ethnic Studies* 13: 144-51.

Jackson, Michael. 1988. *Locking Up Natives in Canada: A Report of the Special Committee of the Canadian Bar Association on Imprisonment.* Ottawa: Canadian Bar Association.

LaPrairie, Carol. 1987. "Native Women and Crime: A Theoretical Model." *Canadian Journal of Native Studies* 1: 121-37.

LaPrairie, Carol. 1988. "Aboriginal Youth and the YOA" in Hudson, Joe, Joe Hornick and B. Burrows (eds.), *Justice and the Young Offender in Canada.* Toronto: Wall and Thompson.

Lewis, Dave. 1989. "An Exploratory Study into Sentencing Practices in Summary Convictions Court in British Columbia." Vancouver: Legal Services Society, Vancouver, British Columbia.

Morse, Brad and Linda Lock. 1988. *Native Offenders' Perceptions of the Criminal Justice System.* Research Reports of the Canadian Sentencing Commission. Ottawa; Department of Justice Canada.

Moyer, Sharon. 1987. *Homicides Involving Adult Suspects 1962-1984: A Comparison of Natives and non-Natives.* Ottawa: Ministry of the Solicitor General.

Moyer, Sharon, Brenda Billingsley, Faigie Kopelman and Carol LaPrairie. 1985. *Native and Non-Native Admissions to Federal, Provincial and Territorial Correctional Institutions.* Ottawa: Ministry of the Solicitor General.

Muirhead, Greg. 1981. *An Analysis of Native Over-representation in Correctional Institutions in B.C.* Vancouver, B.C.: Ministry of the Attorney General.

Petersillia, Joan. 1985. "Racial Disparities in the Criminal Justice System: A Summary." *Crime and Delinquency* 31: 15-34.

Research Group, The. 1987. *Research Reports on Sentencing. Reports of the Correctional Sentences Project.* Ottawa: Department of Justice Canada.

Schmeiser, Douglas. 1974. *The Native Offender and the Law.* Ottawa: Law Reform Commission of Canada.

Walker, John. 1987. "Prison Cells with Revolving Doors: A Judicial or Societal Problem?" in Hazelhurst, Kaylean (ed.), *Ivory Scales: Black Australia and the Law.* Canberra: Australian Institute of Criminology.

Western Judicial Education Centre. 1989. *Introduction to Aboriginal Law. The Western Workshop Proceedings.* 24-29 June. Vancouver, British Columbia.

Zatz, Marjorie S. 1987. "The Changing Forms of Racial/Ethnic Biases in Sentencing." *Journal of Research in Crime and Delinquency* 24: 69-92.

FROM BIG HOUSE TO BIG BROTHER:
CONFINEMENT IN THE FUTURE

IAN M. GOMME

> ...The poster with the enormous face gazed
> from the wall. It was one of those pictures
> which are so contrived that the eyes follow you
> about when you move. BIG BROTHER IS
> WATCHING YOU, the caption beneath it ran
> (George Orwell, *Nineteen Eighty-Four*).[1]

Introduction

The big houses[2] are full to overflowing. Canada's jails and prisons are generally filled to capacity or, depending upon the season, stretched beyond their limits (Canadian Centre for Justice Statistics, 1991a). By comparison, penal facilities in the United States are holding convicted criminals in numbers far in excess of what their designs humanely and safely permit (Inciardi, 1987). The big houses are expensive to build and to maintain and they cost a king's ransom to operate and to staff. For Canada in 1990-91, the bills for operating the corrections system were $862 million federally and $938 million provincially for a grand total slightly in excess of $1.8 billion. Over the five year period from 1986-87 to 1990-91, there was an increase of twenty-six per cent in government operating costs. The increase in the single year from 1989-90 to 1990-91 was eight per cent.[3] For provincial corrections in 1990-91, the operation of custodial services accounted for eighty-two per cent of costs. In comparison, community corrections programs[4] generated about eleven per cent of the operating expenditures. During 1990-91, the average daily cost of housing an inmate in a provincial institution was $114.76. Staff salaries accounted for seventy-five per cent of the total provincial expenditures (Canadian Centre for Justice Statistics, 1991a).

When it comes to financing corrections, taxpayers tend to subscribe to the "principle of less eligibility." The less eligibility postulate holds that persons convicted of crimes ought to benefit less from society's bounties than the worst-off of law-abiding citizens. Those who have broken society's laws should experience more pain and deprivation than any of those who have adhered to the rules. Given the pain and deprivation routinely endured by the law-abiding poverty-stricken and homeless across North America, the principle of less eligibility does not bode well for those convicted of criminal offences. At any rate, the maintenance and expansion of high quality corrections facilities and programs are unpopular targets for the expenditure of tax dollars. The reluctance to expend scarce resources to ensure that law-breakers are contained under any more than the most minimal of conditions is especially true at times when the standards of essential services to the law-abiding such as education and health care appear threatened.

From all appearances, North Americans find themselves on the horns of a rather thorny dilemma. On one hand, official data indicate that crime is rising. On the other hand, government revenues are severely stretched. Violent crime increased fifty-six per cent over the decade from 1980 to 1990. The rate for violent offences rose from 947 per 100,000 in 1989 to 1,013 per 100,000 in 1990 for a single year increase of seven per cent. Nationally, property crime also increased seven per cent from 1989 to 1990. The 1990 national rate for the Criminal Code category "other crimes" was thirty-one per cent higher than the 1980 rate and eight per cent above the 1989 rate (Canadian Centre for Justice Statistics, 1991b).[5]

By no means have reported increases in crime escaped the public eye. The General Social Survey conducted by Statistics Canada in 1988 showed that twenty-five per cent of all Canadians felt unsafe walking alone in their own neighbourhoods at night. For women, the percentage rose to forty per cent. The survey also revealed that the majority of Canadians (sixty-five per cent) believes that sentences handed down by the criminal courts are insufficiently severe. Significantly, older Canadians (over the age of twenty-five) and Canadians in higher income brackets are among those most likely to express concern over the soft sanctions meted out by Canadian courts.

At the same time as they have experienced the problems associated with rising levels of crime, Canadians are faced with tough economic times brought on by a troubled global economy. Canadians, and Americans for that matter, must cope with growing budget deficits, with increasing corporate disinvestment, with rising unemployment rates, with shrinking tax bases and with the mushrooming costs of social services. Significant expansion of prison systems in an effort to deal with apparent rises in crime across North

America would cost Canadian and especially American governments millions upon millions of dollars. Plainly speaking, citizens want a more punitive system to address increasing crime but they and their governments are reluctant to foot the bill for it. Alternatives, less expensive but nonetheless punitive, would appear to be the order of the day.

While 1984 may be fading into memory, Big Brother most certainly is not. More than alive and well, he continues to leap from the pages of science fiction into the realm of everyday life. In the progression toward a presumably better world, captains of technological wizardry continue to transform yesterday's fantasies into today's reality with a dizzying array of machinery in a host of disparate contexts. The crime control industry has by no means been left untouched by the high-tech revolution. Ever more highly specialized and increasingly sophisticated equipment continues to be introduced in the campaign to win the war against crime as it unfolds in the brave new world of the next century.

It is becoming increasingly common to employ state of the art technological devices and procedures in the pursuit, apprehension, conviction and containment of society's outlaws. The impacts of modern scientific developments on the control of crime have been enormous. The automobile, the shortwave radio and finger printing were early technological developments that transformed the face of crime control during the early decades of the twentieth century. By the 1990s, the use of high powered technology has become routine and taken for granted. The radar trap and the breathalyzer have enabled traffic officers to catch and convict speeders and impaired drivers with much improved efficiency. On the less mundane level, police with electronic bugs listen in on the private conversations of organized crime figures (Rhodes, 1984). They use video cameras to build cases against participants in "indecent" sexual exchanges in public rest rooms (Desroches, 1990). Forensic experts gather physical evidence at the scenes of murders and later accused persons are convicted in part because fibres found under the victim's fingernails match the textiles used to manufacture a garment worn by the accused. Scientists use semen samples taken from sexual assault victims to construct genetic profiles of rapists. The genetic prints can subsequently be used to confirm whether or not an accused person is the attacker (Zonderman, 1990).

The use of technology is not confined solely to detection, apprehension and conviction. It is also making its mark in the area of penology. Various jurisdictions in North America are now using or considering the use of electronic monitors. These devices are highly sophisticated miniature radio transmitters attached to an offender's wrist, ankle or neck. The transmitter monitors the detainee's presence in a given location, thereby restricting his or her geographical mobility. Should a detainee move beyond a specified range, a signal is triggered alerting authorities who then investigate to determine whether or not a breach has occurred (Friel and Vaughn, 1986). In essence, electronic monitoring is a means of detecting curfew violation.

Our analysis of the movement toward electronic monitoring begins with a discussion of the context in which the need for an intermediate sentencing option has arisen in the United States. Transformations in the field of corrections south of the border have historically affected the nature and pace of innovation in Canadian correctional policy. Developments in the United States are by no means irrelevant to the evolution of corrections initiatives north of the 49th parallel and this fact makes it necessary for us to consider carefully American conditions and circumstances. The policies adopted by Canada with respect to electronic monitoring will be in part a consequence of the outcomes of the American experience.

Following a discussion of intermediate sentencing, the history of electronic monitoring is documented and the operation of the most popular of the active and passive systems is described. The advantages articulated by electronic monitoring's proponents are catalogued and the applications of this technology in Canada to date are outlined. The problems that arise from the implementation of electronic monitoring are examined in some detail. The paper concludes with an assessment of the prospects and implications associated with the application and deployment of this technology in the future.

The Need for an Intermediate Sentence

The recent growth in enthusiasm surrounding electronic monitoring has arisen out of the fact that the sentencing options available to courts over the last few decades have been bi-polar in nature (Currie, 1985). Either those convicted have been sentenced to unnecessarily lengthy prison terms or, in the public eye especially, they have been effectively "let off easy" through their relegation to non-custodial community-based corrections programs with low intensity supervision. Community-based corrections are alternatives to incarceration that reflect the conviction that rehabilitation and reintegration can be more effectively achieved in the community as opposed to the institutional context (Ekstedt and Griffiths, 1988). The objectives of community corrections programs are to divert people out of the corrections system entirely, to provide offenders with temporary relief from the pains of imprisonment and to reduce the period of an offender's incarceration. Probation and parole are two well-known traditional community corrections strategies.[6] In the 1960s and 1970s, new programs were added and expanded (Menzies, 1986). Among these initiatives were diversion, community service orders, and restitution.[7]

The bi-polar extremes represented by imprisonment on one hand and by community corrections on the other have fuelled desires for a penal sanction that falls somewhere between the two ends of the continuum. Home confinement with intensive supervision, supplied either through frequent face-to-face checks or through electronic monitoring, is a non-custodial measure with a very high degree of supervision that on the face of it would appear to assure considerable security. Compared to traditional non-custodial community corrections, house arrest is a more intrusive means of controlling detainees. On the other hand, home confinement is less intrusive than imprisonment. For these reasons, house arrest in conjunction with the intensive supervision afforded by electronic monitoring is considered an intermediate or mid-range sentence (Berry and Matthews, 1989).

Several factors warrant consideration in understanding the popularity of the movement toward home confinement with electronic monitoring. Prisons in Canada are filled to, and occasionally beyond, their capacities. In the United States, however, they are packed to the proverbial rafters. Overcrowding is a very serious problem that, for a number of reasons, became particularly acute during the 1970s and early 1980s. It was during these years that the baby boomers reached the critical age for participation in violent and property crime.[8] It was also during this period that the creation and enforcement of laws prohibiting the use, trafficking and smuggling of psychoactive illicit drugs took on the epic proportions of an all-out war. Enormous numbers of people are currently in jail in the United States for criminal activity related to the manufacture, distribution, sale or purchase of prohibited substances (Inciardi, 1986). Concern over the illicit drug trade and growing fears of violent and property crime have merged to fuel the development and implementation of a more punitive set of correctional policies. These policies were, first, to make imprisonment a mandatory sentence for an expanded list of crimes, second, to increase the probability that convicted offenders would indeed be incarcerated, third, to stiffen jail sentences by lengthening prison terms and fourth, to reduce or eliminate the early release of prisoners by restricting parole or abolishing it altogether (Friel and Vaughn, 1986). To say the least, these tactics have fused to mushroom the numbers of offenders behind bars in American penal facilities. Furthermore, many of these measures were implemented during a period of fiscal turmoil, government spending restraint and the general political conservatism of the Reagan years.

Between 1980 and 1988, the corrections population in the United States increased ninety per cent (Maxfield and Baumer, 1990). State expenditures on corrections did not keep pace with the need for more facilities and as a result massive overcrowding has occurred in many jurisdictions. Indeed, in several states, prisoners have successfully undertaken class action litigation against the government claiming that overcrowded conditions represent cruel and unusual treatment. In some cases, entire states have been placed under court order to reduce prison populations one way or another by simply turning offenders loose, by expanding community corrections programs, or by developing other viable alternatives (Vaughn, 1987). Indeed, a United States court in 1980 declared the entire Texas prison system unconstitutional. Moreover, the decision was upheld upon its appeal in 1982 (Inciardi, 1987).

Community-based corrections arose as a partial solution to a combination of problems associated first with incarceration and later with prison crowding. Prison reformers have always been cognizant of the potential evils of imprisonment. Among the more serious of these perils are subcultural socialization into a life of crime and the material and physical victimization suffered by relatively powerless inmates at the hands of their more powerful comrades (Sykes, 1958). For reasons such as these, reformers have sought to limit the prison experience in terms of who is jailed in the first place and for how long. Diverting offenders out of the prison system altogether and providing early release to those who have remained satisfactory institutional citizens throughout their sentences are not initiatives that have enjoyed universal popularity, however.[9] In conservative political times especially, non-custodial programs are seen as soft and their effectiveness in rehabilitating offenders is considered suspect. There is, in short, a certain disillusionment with community-based corrections initiatives (Friel and Vaughn, 1986) and there is a desire to replace them with stronger medicine (Berry, 1985).

In sum, apparent rises in crime rates, growing fear of crime among citizens and disillusionment with the rehabilitative potential first of prisons and more recently of community corrections programs have combined with an air of general political conservatism to increase the public's desire for an ever more punitive regimen of criminal sanctions. One of the most tangible results of the shift toward greater punitiveness, especially in the United States, has been institutional overcrowding. In some states more than others, crowding itself has been profoundly exacerbated by crippling economic constraints.

Three fundamental questions emerge in this context. First, how can society contain as many of its burgeoning numbers of undesirables as possible? Second, how can this containment be accomplished while preserving the legal and constitutional rights of prisoners? Third, how can the dual and frequently conflicting objectives of crime control on one hand and the preservation of due process on the other be met as economically as possible? The answers are found with a crime fighting super-hero and a Harvard psychologist. To their stories, we now turn.

Spiderman and Dr. Schwitzgebel

The solution came to a district court judge in Albuquerque, New Mexico in 1977 in what is one of the most unusual accounts in the field of crime control. According to the story, Judge Jack Love was reading a comic at the time of his remarkable flash of insight. The hero of the piece, Spiderman, had confronted an especially ingenious villain who had placed around the super-hero's wrist an electronic device that allowed the black-guard to monitor the web-slinging crime-fighter's every move. Keeping tabs on Spiderman's whereabouts proved to be a distinct advantage for the villainous scoundrel bent on the perpetration of a series of dastardly deeds. The enterprising judge was struck by the possibilities for the creation of a similar device, but one that would turn the tables by allowing champions of truth and justice to monitor the whereabouts of those embodying the forces of evil.

Love approached a variety of computer manufacturers with his idea for the design of a mechanism that would enable law enforcement agents to verify electronically the location of a given convicted offender at a specified point in time. He was unable to interest the communications industry initially, but the employee of one corporation, Michael Goss, eventually left his employer to develop the product through his own company newly formed for just this purpose. In April of 1983, Judge Love became the first to sentence an offender to electronically monitored house arrest. The detainee, a probation violator, was sentenced to home confinement and required to wear the GOSSlink device for the duration of a month (Fox, 1987).

Judge Love's idea for the practical development of an electronic monitoring device was not the first, however. These honours go to a Harvard psychologist, Ralph K. Schwitzgebel, who in the early 1960s foresaw the utility of an electronic device capable of tracking wearers' locations, transmitting back information about their conditions, communicating with them and perhaps even modifying their behaviours. The prototype of such a device, not surprisingly referred to as "Dr. Schwitzgebel's Machine," was created and tested in the mid-1960s.

In the initial experiments, Dr. Schwitzgebel strapped his machine onto his research subjects and turned them loose. The prototype device consisted of a transmitter and battery pack weighing in excess of one kilogram and capable of emitting a signal that could be picked up by a receiver located within a quarter mile range. The information from the receiver was fed into a missile tracking device and the subject's location was displayed on a computer screen (Schwitzgebel, 1969).

The results of these early experiments were greeted with considerable enthusiasm as Dr. Schwitzgebel and his colleagues contemplated the modifications to the technology that they thought might be possible in the future. They speculated that the device could be adapted to gather and transmit data on a subject's physiological condition (pulse, blood alcohol level, brainwaves) and, through a listening device, on the content of his or her conversations. Researchers also foresaw the potential for incorporating into the contrivance the means whereby stimuli could be administered to subjects from afar. Dr. Schwitzgebel patented his machine in 1969 (Fox, 1987).

The potential applications to corrections of more refined versions of his device were by no means lost on the good doctor. Noting the limitations of custodial restraint, Schwitzgebel advocated the use of more humane noncustodial measures wherein offenders could remain in the community and yet still be closely controlled through the intensive supervision afforded by his technological marvel. The claims for the potential utility of the machine were by no means modest. First, future models would provide a continuous record of the offender's location throughout his or her sentence. Second, because future offending would be detected by the machine, it would reduce recidivism by serving as a deterrent. Third, by tracking the offender's whereabouts the device would also discourage both commiseration with undesirables and the hatching of new nefarious plots in the company of other known criminals.

But the possibilities did not stop there. Schwitzgebel mused that the day might come when science would catalogue the physiological precursors to a criminal act. When this occurred, he speculated that it would be possible to use the machine first to identify the crime-related physiological changes occurring in the offender immediately prior to his or her law breaking, second, to transmit this information back to the base station, and third, to intervene from the base station with an appropriately noxious stimulus

(Schwitzgebel, 1970).

The good doctor's musings aside, we proceed with an examination of the monitoring systems that have been developed in the wake of the pioneering efforts of Judge Love and his associate Michael Goss in the early 1980s.

The Device

The devices currently being used in electronic monitoring programs in North America, thanks to micro-chip technology, are considerably more compact and lighter than Dr. Schwitzgebel's one kilogram prototype. Despite the existence of the technologies that could offer the level of surveillance Schwitzgebel envisaged, the extent of supervision afforded by contemporary monitoring systems is in practice much less. Monitors in use neither track offenders over extended distances nor do they gather and transmit data on the wearer's conversations and physiological conditions. The devices most certainly do not permit the application from afar of noxious anti-crime stimuli.

Contemporary monitoring systems can be either active or passive in their functioning. Active systems consist of three parts — a transmitter worn by the offender, a receiver-dialler located in the detainee's home and a central monitoring computer connected via the phone line to the receiver-dialler. With active systems, controllees wear a miniature battery-operated radio transmitter that weighs about 110 grams and is shock resistant, waterproof, and provides indication when power is running low. The monitor is usually attached to offenders' ankles or wrists by means of a tamper-proof strap. Under normal conditions, the transmitter broadcasts radio signals to the receiver-dialler at regular intervals ranging from several seconds to a few minutes. The electrically powered receiver-dialler detects radio impulses from the transmitter worn by the offender, automatically dials the central computer, and reports over the phone line the status of the signal. Should the wearer move outside the sixty or so metre range beyond which the signal can be picked up by the receiver-dialler, a violation will be recorded. The severing or stretching of the transmitter strap breaks a circuit and also signals a violation.

Through messages sent from the receiver-dialler, the central computer records the existence of the signal, its loss, and if lost, the time of its subsequent return. The computer compares the times of signal receipt against the offender's curfew schedule and records discrepancies. The computer also keeps track of phone disconnections, power failures and any equipment tampering in the offender's home. Printed reports generated by the central computer are reviewed on a regular basis by corrections personnel who investigate any apparent violations of curfew conditions.

Most modern electronic monitoring systems are relatively free of major technical problems. Nonetheless, some conditions do occasionally interfere with the transmission of signals. Radio interference can be a problem as can the creation of dead space in the wearer's home. Sleeping in certain positions and walking behind major metal appliances such as furnaces, freezers and shower stalls can disrupt transmission and indicate a violation where none has occurred. Some offenders have complained about chafing and skin irritation caused by the transmitter strap (Fox, 1987; McCarthy, 1987; Blomberg *et al.*, 1987).

Passive systems differ from their active counterparts in that with passive monitoring it is the corrections office that initiates contact. On this dimension, passive monitoring resembles regular probation wherein corrections authorities check on offenders at various points in time. As with active systems, the connection is usually made by phone. Offenders are automatically dialled during periods when they are required to be home but the exact times of the calls are randomized in order that detainees will not know precisely when to expect them. When contacted, offenders must reply to a series of inquiries. They are asked to respond with their names, with the time of day and with answers to random questions. Their verbal acknowledgements facilitate manual or mechanical voice confirmation. Some state of the art systems are fully automated and make use of voice verification boxes (Erwin, 1989). As with active systems, controllees wear watch-sized sealed modules. The circuitry of these monitors contains a code unique to the individual offender. When called upon to do so, controllees must insert the module into a verifier that signals their presence to the central computer via the phone lines.

The passive system is rather more simple to operate than the active system and the chances of false violation signals are smaller. The major disadvantage of this particular system is that it usually involves making calls to offenders during their curfews. Calling controllees in the evenings and on the weekends presents few problems. However, it is necessary for obvious reasons to contact detainees at various times during the middle of the night. For offenders, being awakened at three in the morning can be both disruptive and annoying. Nonetheless, advocates maintain that being called at home in the dead of the night is better than being awakened at the same time in prison with a flashlight check (Fox, 1987; McCarthy, 1987; Friel and Vaughn, 1986).

Another passive system in limited use does not require a phone connection. With this system, a corrections officer patrols designated areas in a vehicle equipped with a special radio receiver capable of picking up signals from the wrist or ankle module worn by a controllee. The officer drives to within about a block of where an offender is supposed to be located and checks that he or she is present. This system is particularly useful in monitoring an offender's presence at a treatment session, at school or at work (Vaughn, 1987).

Whether active or passive, the central monitoring computer station is usually staffed only for the standard eight-hour work day. Records of a controllee's presence or absence during the evenings, at night and on weekends are reviewed by corrections personnel when they come to work and indications of violations are pursued at that time. Some programs have telephone answering machines available in order that offenders can call to explain the reasons for apparent after hours violations. The delay in investigation is justified by noting that those who are eligible for enrolment in electronic monitoring programs have committed very minor offences and do not represent a danger to the community. Face-to-face inspections represent a component of some passive monitoring programs. As with regular probation and parole, officers responsible for electronic monitoring with both active and passive techniques exercise considerable discretion in recommending incarceration for violators. Penalties for absconding typically involve being charged with the theft of the transmitter and being required to serve the original sentence behind bars (Fox, 1987; Nellis, 1991; Friel and Vaughn, 1986).

Uses and Offender Types

Electronic monitoring is designed for use either at the "front end" or at the "back door" of the corrections system as a means of limiting the size of the population behind bars (Walker, 1990; Nellis, 1991). The initiative involves placing those who would otherwise be incarcerated in non-custodial programs with more intensive supervision than is provided by less intrusive community corrections programs such as probation or parole. The goal is to reduce the numbers imprisoned without sacrificing the safety and protection of the public that is provided through incarceration. The heightened security afforded by the electronic monitoring of home confinement makes it an intermediate sentence falling between imprisonment on one hand and diversion, probation, community service and parole on the other (McCarthy, 1987).

Electronic monitoring can be used at the front end of the correctional system in two ways. First, home confinement with electronic monitoring is employed as a condition of probation for some of those low risk offenders who have committed minor offences but who nonetheless are destined to be incarcerated. Second, electronic monitoring can be used to place under house arrest some of those being held on remand in municipal lock-ups.[10] The number of people held on remand in the United States is increasing making local jails, the most dilapidated confinement facilities in the American system, even more crowded than in the past. Furthermore, accused persons held under these less than desirable conditions are just that — accused. Many so confined are never found guilty of an offence (Berry and Matthews, 1989). In Canada in 1990-91, the provinces recorded over 92,000 remand admissions. The average count of those held on remand at any one time during the year was 4711. In Canada, most people on remand (seventy-one per cent) are released within a week. Fewer than ten per cent are held more than a month (Canadian Centre for Justice Statistics, 1991a). At the back door, house arrest with electronic monitoring is presumably intended to provide early release to a broader range of correctional clientele than would normally meet the requirements for ordinary parole.

To be eligible for electronic monitoring, offenders must be classified as low risk. Low risk offenders are those who have committed relatively minor property offences such as petty theft, break and enter and fraud. Another quality that defines detainees as low risk involves their having few if any prior criminal convictions and generally being of "good character." Typically, candidates for the program must have a home, possess a phone and be able to pay, in full or in part, for the rental of the monitoring equipment (McCarthy, 1987; Friel and Vaughn, 1986; Berry and Matthews, 1989). In many jurisdictions, the rule in this regard is "No home and no phone, no program" (Vaughn, 1987).

The time served under home confinement with electronic monitoring often ranges from three to four times as long as the mandated period of incarceration. Therefore, a jail sentence of two months could translate into six to eight months of electronically monitored house arrest (Fox, 1987).

One of the offences for which electronic monitor has proved a popular option is impaired driving (Schmidt and Curtis, 1987). Across Canada and the United States, drunk driving statutes increasingly make mandatory, especially for repeat offenders, some period of incarceration. In some jurisdictions, compulsory jail time has placed a considerable strain on facilities that are already overburdened. Another reason for the popularity of this option for drunk drivers is that so many of those convicted of this offence are ideal candidates for success in the program. In comparison to those convicted of many other offences, impaired drivers are older, better educated, more affluent, more mature and have families (Baumer *et al.*, 1990). These same traits, incidentally, are possessed by many of those contained in another offender group considered a prime candidate for electronic monitoring — those convicted of white collar crime.

Advantages of Electronic Monitoring

The catalogue of positive outcomes that its advocates attribute to electronic monitoring is similar to the list put forward by proponents of community-based corrections more generally with one important addition — the luxury of the added level of security. First and foremost, home confinement with electronic monitoring is touted as an effective means of limiting the size of burgeoning jail and prison populations. Furthermore, since the offenders involved have committed relatively minor offences, the level of security is considered sufficient to meet the citizenry's demand both for public safety and for punitiveness. The privilege of being monitored as opposed to jailed is easily revoked should a particular controllee violate the conditions of the program. Finally, because electronic monitoring is typically offered as a condition of release, its use does not require special legislation (Fox, 1987).

Proponents maintain that while it is more expensive than traditional community corrections programs, home confinement with electronic monitoring is much less expensive than incarceration. The primary reason for the lower cost is that electronic monitoring is considerably less labour intensive (Schmidt and Curtis, 1987). The technology eliminates the need for the large numbers of custodial personnel essential for the operation of prison facilities.

Like other forms of community-based corrections, house arrest with electronic monitoring provides a means by which those convicted of comparatively minor offences can avoid the deleterious impacts of life behind bars. Criminologists have long observed that prisons provide a pivotal training ground wherein an initiate can learn from his or her more seasoned colleagues the skills and motivations conducive to more serious offending (Thomas and Peterson, 1977). Therefore, they argue, it is better to reduce as much as possible the extent to which young first time offenders are exposed to the subculture of more hardened criminals.

Containing offenders in their own homes also avoids two other problems central to the prison experience. First, advocates maintain that those kept out of jail, whether they are awaiting trial or whether they have already been convicted, experience less in the way of negative social stigma (Berry and Matthews, 1989). There is evidence that those who are held on remand awaiting trial are more likely to be found guilty of their offences and to experience harsher sanctions upon conviction than those who are not held in custody prior to trial (Berry, 1985). Research also indicates that ex-inmates are discriminated against in a variety of ways when they attempt to resume the straight life upon release. Jobs are more difficult to find and housing is harder to come by (Kratcoski and Walker, 1984).

Second, doing time behind bars is intended to represent punishment through the deprivation of liberty. The pains of imprisonment actually experienced, however, are routinely in excess of those engendered by captivity alone. Prisons are settings where physical violence and sexual assaults are matters of routine. The strong prey on the weak and in prisons the most vulnerable are often first time offenders jailed for comparatively minor crimes (Jayewardene and Doherty, 1985). Confinement of such offenders in non-institutional contexts is considered far more humane in that it protects them against personal victimization (McCarthy, 1987).

Advocates maintain that home confinement facilitates rehabilitation and reintegration into society because it allows offenders to participate in treatment programs, to attend school and to hold a job (Nellis, 1991). It also permits those who are employed to continue to work thereby supporting their families and paying taxes (Clarkson and Weakland, 1991; Schumacher, 1987). Furthermore, by ensuring that curfews are observed, electronic monitoring reduces crime. For all intents and purposes, the program effectively incapacitates controllees because they are isolated from fellow miscreants and they are kept away from high risk locations such as street corners, pool halls and bars during prime crime times such as evenings and weekends (Nellis, 1991).

Finally, proponents point out that house arrest with electronic monitoring is extremely flexible. It is an ideal strategy for dealing with the special needs of detainees who are disabled, who require specialized medical treatment or psychological counselling and, in the case of women, who are pregnant. Perhaps the major problem facing the prison system in the 1990s, particularly in the United States, is a large scale outbreak of full blown AIDS among the institutionalized population. Electronic monitoring is seen as one means by which the special requirements of this inmate group may be more effectively and more humanely met while simultaneously maintaining surveillance and control (Berry and Matthews, 1989).

The second point about flexibility concerns the pairing of electronic monitoring with other correctional strategies. Electronic monitoring can be used alone or in concert with other programs. It can also be tailored to provide security at different times of the day as required. Electronic monitoring can be twinned with incarceration in such a way that the offender is institutionalized at some times and confined in the home at others. Electronic monitoring can be applied at different stages in the processing of prisoners from pre-trial through parole and it can be administered by a variety of different agencies in both the public and the private spheres (Berry and Matthews, 1989).

Electronic Monitoring in Practice

Electronic monitoring is well on the road to becoming the latest fashion on the corrections scene (Fox, 1987). While programs are most numerous in the United States, they are also being implemented or seriously considered in the United Kingdom, Australia and Canada. Program evaluation reports issued by the jurisdictions in which home confinement with electronic monitoring has been undertaken have by and large cast the program in a favourable light (Schmidt and Curtis, 1987).

In the United States in 1988, estimates of electronically monitored controllees numbered between 3,000 and 4,000 (Ball *et al.*, 1988). By 1990, the number of detainees was estimated at about 7,000 (Nellis, 1991). Approximately forty states have implemented the strategy (Renzema, 1989). More than a half a dozen companies in that nation are currently manufacturing and distributing the necessary hardware under such trade names as "Supervisor" and "On Guard" (Griffiths and Verdun-Jones, 1989). While the idea of electronic monitoring has been aggressively marketed and has been greeted with enthusiasm by politicians and corrections personnel eager to diminish prison crowding and to cut costs, there has been very little in the way of rigorous and independent empirical research investigating the implementation and operation of these programs and evaluating their success (Berry and Matthews, 1989).

Given that eligibility for electronic monitoring to date has been for the most part confined to less serious offenders, it seems likely that in Canada the technique is most appropriate for those facing incarceration in provincial institutions. Provincial facilities, with a few exceptions, hold offenders convicted of crimes for which the maximum sentence is less than two years. Of those contained in provincially operated prisons across the country, seventy-four per cent have been convicted of Criminal Code offences. This figure includes impaired driving offences. Seventeen per cent of inmates have been convicted of violating provincial statutes. The majority of these convictions are alcohol related. Eight percent of prisoners have broken federal laws and the lion's share of these violations are drug related. Only one per cent of those incarcerated in provincial institutions have been jailed for infractions of municipal bylaws.

There are 162 provincial facilities in operation from coast to coast with a total regular bed space of 18,537. Over the five years prior to 1990-91, the average provincial inmate population has increased fourteen per cent to its current level of 17,944. In addition to this figure, there were on average approximately 2,400 provincial inmates who were "on register" but not in custody at the time of the enumeration upon which these figures are based. The median sentence length on admission to provincial facilities in 1990-91 was thirty-one days. By comparison, the equivalent figure for inmates incarcerated in federal facilities was just under four years. The differences in these medians reflect the fact that the offences qualifying an offender for federal prison tend to be much more serious.

Sentenced inmates admitted to provincial custody are typically twenty-eight-year-old males. Twenty seven per cent of all admissions are for fine default. Provincial facilities on average run at ninety-seven per cent of capacity but do experience problems of overcrowding due to seasonal variations in intake (Canadian Centre for Justice Statistics, 1991a).

The Canadian experience with electronic monitoring is quite limited. In 1983, the Corrections Service of Canada and several of the provinces undertook feasibility studies and designed experimental electronic monitoring programs. In 1987, the Corrections Service of Canada abandoned its plans to test electronic monitoring on a trial basis citing as its reason the threat of legal action from concerned civil liberties groups (Griffiths and Verdun-Jones, 1989).

The only province to proceed with electronic monitoring trials is British Columbia. In 1987, the British Columbia Corrections Branch implemented a nine-month program involving the house arrest with electronic surveillance of twenty-five offenders serving intermittent sentences, many of which were for impaired driving. Meeting several conditions were necessary for a participant's inclusion. Participation could not undermine the intent of the offender's sentence. Public safety had to be assured. Candidates were required either to hold a job or to be attending an educational institution. The monitoring system employed was active as opposed to passive and participation in the program was entirely voluntary. An evaluation centred upon the following dimensions: cost, safety, the effect on offenders and members of their families, the type of offender most suited to participation and the reactions of the public, the professional corrections community and various interest groups (Solicitor General of Canada, 1987). The evaluation deemed the program a success (Griffiths and Verdun-Jones, 1989).

A report in 1989 on a twelve-month project undertaken by the Vancouver Court Adult Probation Office emphasizes the success of electronic monitoring and underlines the enthusiasm for this corrections strategy. According to the report, the twelve-month test program involved ninety-two violent offenders anticipating sentences of ninety days or less and who were considered likely to serve their time intermittently. The assessment indicated that electronic monitoring worked well with all but one participant. The evaluation report stated that "the cases accounted for 1533 days of EMS residential confinement or the equivalent of 4.2 jail beds per day on an annualized basis." Based upon these results, program assessors estimate that the demand for beds for those sentenced to ninety days or less can be reduced by eleven per cent province-wide. The report recommends that all defendants potentially sentenced to intermittent terms be screened to determine their suitability for electronic monitoring (Neville, 1989).

An Evaluation of Electronic Monitoring

Electronic monitoring has four fundamental and interconnected goals: 1) to reduce the population in custody; 2) to reduce the costs of corrections that are generated by custodial sentences; 3) to provide humane punishment while promoting rehabilitation and reintegration; and 4) to maintain the security and the safety of the public. The ability of electronically monitored house arrest to meet successfully each of these objectives appears highly suspect. In the absence of rigorous program evaluations, the extent to which goals are attained cannot be definitively discerned. Nonetheless, there is justification for scepticism on logical, historical and empirical grounds. The concern over the rapid proliferation of these programs in the absence of independent, meticulous and methodologically sound research is well founded. In this section, we assess the extent to which each of the stated aims of electronic monitoring are (or can be) achieved.

1. Reduction of the Population in Custody

Recent years have been characterized by economic recession, political conservatism, ever increasing concerns about apparent rises in crime, growing desires for punitiveness in corrections and heightening perceptions of an inefficient criminal justice system gone soft on hardened criminals. Among other developments, rehabilitation has increasingly come to be seen as a goal beyond the capability of prisons to provide. Rehabilitative programs are being scaled down or eliminated in favour of a purely punishment oriented approach to more serious offenders (Ekstedt and Griffiths, 1988). Disenchantment with the rehabilitative potential of community corrections is also mounting (Friel and Vaughn, 1986).

In keeping with trends toward greater punitiveness, it is conceivable that the intermediate sentence of electronic monitoring will be used not as an alternative to incarceration but rather as a tougher alternative to other less intrusive forms of community corrections. Those convicted of minor offences who might formerly have been either released altogether or channelled into existing non-custodial programs may well be sentenced to house arrest with electronic monitoring largely because the more restrictive and secure option is available. Evidence suggests that there would be little in the way of return on the added insurance, however. Because candidates for these programs are low risk minor offenders in the first place, non-custodial low intensity supervision programs such as probation, community service orders, and parole are successful in approximately eighty-five per cent of cases (Berry and Matthews, 1989; Muncie, 1990; Griffiths and Verdun-Jones, 1989).

It must be remembered as well that electronic monitoring does not successfully contain all controllees. In the United States, despite comparatively stringent eligibility requirements, failure rates run between ten per cent and twenty per cent on average (Berry and Matthews, 1989). Where serious violations occur, the non-custodial sentence is revoked and jail sentences are invoked. As the numbers of electronically monitored offenders grow, the numbers of violations warranting incarceration will increase commensurately.

It is unlikely that electronic monitoring can significantly reduce the numbers of persons incarcerated unless more serious personal and property offenders are made eligible in reasonably large numbers. Inclusion of higher risk offenders in electronic monitoring programs, however, increases the likelihood of security breaches. More serious offenders with less desirable socio-biographical attributes are more likely to abscond and to re-offend

(Schmidt and Curtis, 1987). Higher failure rates necessitate efforts to recapture those who abscond. If those who escape also re-offend, police forces are called upon to devote their time and their resources to deal effectively with the new crimes committed (N.E.E., 1990). The public's confidence in the corrections system would hardly be bolstered if higher risk offenders on electronic monitoring were to breach security in anything resembling large numbers (Schmidt and Curtis, 1987). In addition, higher failure rates and the eventual return of offenders to prison would limit any overall reductions in numbers produced by electronic monitoring.

The lessons of history should not be ignored. During the 1960s and the 1970s, community corrections were substantially expanded as an alternative to incarceration. Their stated purposes have an all too familiar ring. Their aims were to reduce the numbers of offenders imprisoned, to offer a more humane alternative to incarceration, to promote rehabilitation and reintegration and to lower corrections costs. Evidence suggests that the numbers in community corrections programs increased as predicted. However, the numbers incarcerated did not decrease (Chan and Ericson, 1981). Indeed, the numbers behind bars also grew (Hylton, 1982). On the whole, more people found themselves under the supervision and control of the state than had been the case before these alternatives to incarceration were expanded (Blomberg, 1987; Lowman and Menzies, 1986). What was in theory intended as a substitute for incarceration was in practice transformed into a supplement to incarceration (Rothman, 1980).

Should history come close to repeating itself, a new intermediate sanction program confined to non-serious offenders with acceptable socio-biographic traits will simply expand the social control net. With added numbers of minor offenders on electronic monitoring, space may be created to expand the ranks of those eligible for less intrusive measures such as probation. The danger is that increasing numbers of non-serious offenders will be "netted" while at the same time serious offenders will continue to be incarcerated at the previous rate.

2. Cost Cutting

If in practice electronic monitoring is confined to low risk offenders and added as insurance to the less intrusive community corrections provisions already in existence, overall costs cannot help but increase since electronic monitoring is more expensive than other forms of non-custodial supervision (Fox, 1987). American data suggest that this danger is real. In some programs, it is estimated that at least twenty-five per cent of those currently being monitored electronically were probably not destined for prison (Berry and Matthews, 1989). Presumably these offenders should have qualified for non-custodial options with less intensive surveillance.

Where violations result in revocations, the cost of imprisonment is simply deferred. The state must ultimately assume financial responsibility not only for offenders' electronic monitoring but for their jail terms as well, since these offenders eventually wind up serving their time behind bars after all. For offenders who abscond, expenditures are incurred for their initial monitoring, for their re-apprehension, re-trying and re-sentencing, for damage to or loss of monitoring equipment and for their eventual incarceration (Fox, 1987). Where those who abscond commit additional offences, the cost of these new crimes must also be added to the tally. The failure rate for low risk offenders on electronic monitoring ranges between ten per cent and twenty per cent on average. If higher risk offenders are eventually included in these programs, failure rates and associated costs will grow commensurately.

The costs engendered by program failures are rather difficult to determine with precision and they are seldom calculated when the economic advantages of electronic monitoring are being assessed (McCarthy, 1987). Typically, the degree of benefit is measured by comparing the average daily cost of an offender's incarceration with the average daily cost of maintaining a controllee under house arrest with electronic supervision. Using this simple formula, most estimates suggest that the expense of electronic monitoring is between thirty-three per cent (Ball et al., 1988) and forty-five per cent (Fox, 1987) of the costs of incarceration. The comparison is misleading, however, because the electronically monitored are low risk offenders and consequently would cost less than the average dollar sum for incarceration. Moreover, if one day in prison translates into more than one day of electronically monitored house arrest, the savings decline substantially (Berry and Matthews, 1989). For example, if one day in prison translates into three or four days of home confinement with electronic monitoring, the latter could become more expensive than the former.

Cutting the costs of corrections by a simple reduction in the numbers confined in institutions is not as straightforward an undertaking as it might seem at first glance. First, if only the excess "crowd" were eliminated, no meaningful staffing reductions could be realized because institutions would still be operating at or near capacity (Vaughn, 1987). Second, it is estimated that about eighty-five per cent of institutional costs are fixed (Berry and Matthews, 1989). The lion's share of operating expenses are devoted to staff salaries (seventy-five per cent in Canadian provincial institutions (Canadian Centre for Justice Statistics, 1991a)) and certain minimum staffing requirements are necessary for these institutions to function regardless of the numbers incarcerated. Researchers estimate that the inmate population would have to be cut by fifty per cent before significant staff cuts could be made and the associated savings realized (Berry and Matthews, 1989). It seems unlikely that a reduction of that magnitude would be feasible. Third, observers note the historical tendency for any available corrections space to be filled by one means or another (Inciardi, 1987). For these reasons, it seems improbable that meaningful savings can be achieved by limiting institutional populations and cutting costs through the expansion of electronic monitoring.

3. Humanity, Rehabilitation and Justice

Some observers have suggested that the cost savings from electronic monitoring are far from the most important consideration (Nellis, 1991; McCarthy, 1987; Vaughn, 1989). They suggest that home confinement with electronic monitoring is superior to incarceration because it is more humane and because it increases the likelihood of rehabilitation.

The humaneness of electronic monitoring can be challenged on a number of dimensions. Confinement, whether in an institution or in one's own home, represents a deprivation of liberty. North American jurisprudence views deprivation of liberty as a serious sanction to be used only as a last resort. More restrictive measures should not be the preferred option if less restrictive measures are equally effective. If, however, electronic monitoring is added to community corrections options as insurance, punishment will become more punitive than necessary (Fox, 1987; Berry, 1985). Where the duration of time in confinement is increased two, three or four times by virtue of the fact that people are being detained in their homes as opposed to in jail, the time for which liberty is deprived is dramatically extended (Berry and Matthews, 1989). Furthermore, few jurisdictions have guidelines in place to govern the application of electronic monitoring at the sentencing stage. This lack of direction may well exacerbate sentencing disparity (Fox, 1987; Berry and Matthews, 1989).

Home confinement for obvious reasons frequently involves offenders' families and where this is the case a number of problems can arise. First, a family can be stigmatized as it becomes common knowledge that one of its members is a state detainee. Second, a home containing a monitored

offender is subject to ongoing intrusion around the clock by corrections officials. Such invasions of privacy can be stressful for the kin of detainees
who, after all, have themselves not been convicted of an offence (Friel and
Vaughn, 1986). Third, being cooped up at home for lengthy periods of
time may result in offenders suffering varying degrees of cabin fever (Friel
and Vaughn, 1986). Life in close quarters for lengthy periods under less
than ideal conditions can easily create friction within the home (Nellis,
1991). Fourth, families may have contributed to the offender's problems
with the law in the first place. Dysfunctional families can be criminogenic.
Finally, the offender's kin may aid and abet such licentious diversions as
alcohol consumption and illicit drug use.

Another point of contention regarding the humaneness of electronic
monitoring concerns the issues of consent and privacy (Blomberg *et al.*,
1987). The question raised about consent pertains to whether or not it is
freely volunteered or, given the threat of jail as an alternative, whether or
not it is coerced. The other issue is the extent to which the intrusive supervision entailed in electronic monitoring represents an undue invasion of privacy. The very few American test cases to date are instructive. The courts
would appear to consider as unfounded concerns about coerced consent
and invasion of privacy. Rather, they view electronic monitoring as less of
an infringement of human rights than the alternative of incarceration (Del
Carmen and Vaughn, 1986). Nonetheless, should a case be made in future
that the alternative being replaced by electronic monitoring is not incarceration but rather that the alternative being replaced is a less intrusive form of
community corrections, the courts might well take a different view. Among
the legal rights that might be at issue under such circumstances would be
freedom of speech and association as well as protection from unreasonable
search and seizure, from self incrimination and from cruel and unusual punishment (U.S. Bureau of Justice Assistance, 1989).

The degree to which electronic monitoring facilitates rehabilitation has
also been questioned. First, rehabilitation entails the development of trusting
and supportive relationships between controllees and community corrections counsellors. The surveillance and control functions served by the electronic monitoring device are not conducive to the development of these
sorts of bonds (Fox, 1987).

Second, to the extent that electronic monitoring is fully automated, personal contact between offenders and trained personnel is greatly curtailed.
Some critics have pointed out that to be economically viable and cost effective it may prove necessary for very large numbers of electronically monitored controllees to comprise the caseload of a single corrections officer

(Fox, 1987). If electronic monitoring is widely available but limited to use with low risk offenders convicted of non-serious crimes, the likelihood that electronic monitoring will be overused is by no means farfetched. Should electronic monitoring services be privatized, the tendency for abuse may be further exacerbated. It is by no means inconceivable that market forces might fuel an expansion in the numbers of "clients" especially given the importance to profits of economies of scale (Nellis, 1991).

Third, compared to less secure community corrections initiatives such as probation and parole, levels of community contact are less. Living under house arrest diminishes normal socialization and erodes the re-integrative functions promoted by the nurturing of strong ties to the community (Fox, 1987; Berry and Matthews, 1989). Finally, because the devices cannot be removed and are often visible, there is concern that wearers will experience stigmatization when they are at work, at school, in treatment or in a public place (Fox, 1987). The visibility of the device is a problem that more frequently confronts women because of their feminine attire. Women's dresses do not conceal ankles with nearly the effectiveness of men's pants (Vaughn, 1987). One observer goes so far as to suggest that for many monitored females the device may become the equivalent of an electronic scarlet letter (Friel and Vaughn, 1986).

The justice of electronic monitoring programs has been challenged on the equity dimension. To be eligible for electronic monitoring requires, at the very least, a home and a phone. "No home and no phone, no program." Sometimes admission to the program also requires the ability to pay both for equipment rentals and for administration fees. Each of these requirements necessitates some degree of material well-being. Those without resources can be denied the right to participate (Berry, 1985). Programs that allow the more affluent to avoid institutionalization while relegating the poor to imprisonment are inequitable and discriminatory.

At present, the most suitable candidates for electronic monitoring are those convicted of minor offences for which traditional community corrections programs cannot be used because the minor offences have attached to them mandatory jail terms. The classic example in this regard is a repeat conviction for impaired driving. With respect to impaired driving, however, it is worth remembering that the rationale for the mandatory jail term was to demonstrate to the offender and to the public at large the seriousness of this crime. Confining convicted drunk drivers at home with electronic monitoring mitigates the gravity of the offence because house arrest is perceived as a soft sanction. This is particularly true where offenders come from the middle or upper classes. According to critics, house arrest as a punishment trivializes the crime and in so doing defeats the original purpose of the law (Fox, 1987).

4. Protection of the Public

Existing electronic monitoring programs contain low risk offenders. Since the risk to the community posed by controllees who violate their curfews is negligible, the reaction time separating violation from response can stretch from several hours to a couple of days. Most monitoring stations operate only during standard working times — eight hours per day five days per week. If higher risk offenders are placed in electronic monitoring programs, maintenance of security will demand immediate responses. Immediate responses in turn will necessitate the staffing of facilities around the clock seven days a week. Failure to do so might place the citizenry at some risk and it would certainly undermine public confidence in the program (Schmidt and Curtis, 1987). Nevertheless, even an immediate response would be insufficient to protect the public if a serious offender were to violate a curfew and be at large in the community. The inability to guarantee such a high level of protection will likely be sufficient to preclude the inclusion in electronic monitoring programs of higher risk offenders who have committed truly serious crimes.

Conclusions

Electronic monitoring has four fundamental and interconnected goals: a) to reduce the population in custody, b) to decrease the costs of corrections that are generated by custodial sentences, c) to provide humane punishment with the potential for rehabilitation and reintegration and d) to maintain the security and the safety of the public. There are several points that require emphasis in evaluating the extent to which electronic monitoring meets its specified objectives. These points concern the nature of the offence and the eligibility requirements that make the intermediate sentence a judicious option.

First, for electronic monitoring to be an acceptable alternative to incarceration, the offence must be comparatively minor and worthy only of a short jail term. Many existing electronic monitoring programs automatically exclude from participation offenders who have been convicted of violent offences such as common assault, wife battering, child abuse, sexual assault and other sex offences. Many programs also rule out the participation of offenders who have committed serious property offences (judged by the value of loss created by the theft or fraud). Also excluded are those guilty of drug offences such as trafficking and smuggling (Palm Beach County, 1987; Fox, 1987; Nellis, 1991; Friel and Vaughn, 1986; Berry and Matthews, 1989). With these exclusions, the offences rendering someone eligible for electronic monitoring are pared down to minor property crimes such as break and enter, to white collar crimes such as fraud and income tax evasion where dollar amounts are relatively low and to impaired driving offences. It is not an insignificant point that convictions for impaired driving and for tax evasion have mandatory sentences attached to them. People convicted must go to jail.

Second, to qualify for electronic monitoring instead of incarceration, offenders must meet certain eligibility requirements in addition to having committed only minor offences. They must, in short, possess the requisite socio-biographical traits. Typically, they must be of good character, they must not be drug addicted, they must have a home and a phone, they must have a job or be going to school, and they must have no prior record for serious criminality. If they have minor criminal records, offenders must have no history of absconding (Fox, 1987; Nellis, 1991; Solicitor General of Canada, 1987).

Third, offenders placed upon electronic monitoring must be destined for incarceration. They must, therefore, be ineligible for less intrusive community corrections programs such as probation and parole. Herein lies the proverbial Shakespearean rub. Home confinement with electronic monitoring is an intermediate sentence falling between incarceration on one hand and a non-custodial option with low intensity supervision on the other. As an intermediate sanction, proponents claim that it has many of the advantages of less intrusive non-custodial corrections programs along with the added benefit of heightened security. Presumably, the intermediate sentence is tailored for the intermediate offender. It is designed for those whose law breaking is sufficiently non-serious that incarceration is essential neither as punishment nor as protection for the public. On the other hand, offenders receiving intermediate sentences must be ineligible for existing less intrusive community corrections programs such as probation and parole either because of the seriousness of their offences or because they possess certain socio-biographical attributes that designate them as high risk candidates for escape and re-offending.

Given current eligibility requirements, the line separating the offender who requires the intermediate level of security afforded by electronic monitoring from the offender who requires the maximum level of security afforded by imprisonment is reasonably clear. Those who have committed serious crime and whose socio-biographical traits indicate high risk of escape and re-offending go to jail. Alternatively, offenders who have committed compara-tively non-serious crimes and whose socio-biographical characteristics are considered low risk are confined at home under electronic surveillance.

Not nearly so clear, however, is the line that separates the non-serious and low risk offender who nonetheless requires electronic monitoring from the non-serious and low risk offender who qualifies for less intrusive mea-sures such as probation and parole. Except for minor offences with manda-tory jail sentences, it is difficult to imagine that persons with the characteris-tics necessary to qualify for electronic monitoring would not also qualify for non-custodial measures with less intensive supervision. In other words, the qualifications for electronic monitoring (non-serious offence, employment, a home etc.) and for other less intrusive forms of community corrections are essentially the same. It seems all too likely that if the application of electron-ic monitoring extends much beyond offenders convicted of minor crimes with mandatory jail sentences (impaired driving) that it will become in prac-tice not an alternative to incarceration as claimed but an alternative to non-custodial sanctions involving less intensive and less intrusive supervision. Sentencing judges must keep an extremely sharp eye to ensure that they avoid misclassification and inconsistency.

Electronic monitoring as a substitute for or condition of probation or parole is problematic on several dimensions. First, such applications repre-sent an escalation of penalties in cases where those placed on electronic monitors do indeed qualify for less punitive non-custodial sentences with low intensity supervision. Second, there is considerable danger that more people will become enmeshed in the criminal justice net as the use of this intermediate sanction expands. Greater numbers of offenders will be accommodated in non-custodial sentences with various levels of supervision. Third, given the stringency of the eligibility requirements for non-custodial sentencing (minor offences and good character), it will be impossible to reduce prison populations to any meaningful extent. Too few of those presently in jail meet the conditions. With crime rates, especially violent crime, reportedly on the rise, it seems reasonable to assume that there will be no shortage in the near future of candidates for incarceration. It seems more reasonable to expect that electronic monitoring on a larger scale will expand the scope of state control by escalating penalties and by increasing the size of the pool of non-custodial controllees. At the same time, the number of offenders incarcerated will remain constant or continue to rise. Such a widening of the net would of course also drive up the overall costs of corrections.

The invention and refinement of electronic monitoring equipment is accelerating at a rapid pace while the legal standards governing the application of these technologies lag behind. The development and proliferation of electronic monitoring systems provides yet another example of corrections policy being implemented either in the absence of sound research or in the face of solid data suggesting that its virtues are at best overstated and at worst non-existent. Despite uncertainty regarding the efficacy of this control strategy, enthusiastic advocates remain undeterred. Proponents continue to call not only for the continued use of the technology but for the exploration and development of its potential promise for controlling a broader range of client groups and for intruding further into the lives of those monitored (Erwin, 1989).

As a number of critics have pointed out, community corrections generally and electronic monitoring and surveillance in particular represent a decentralization of state control and an expansion of penal space (Muncie, 1990; Cohen, 1979). The potential for the abuse of electronic monitoring and surveillance techniques is considerable and caution is warranted. Today's practices may substantially influence the legal standards governing tomorrow's applications and tomorrow's applications will be executed with increasingly accurate, powerful and intrusive equipment. Even now, the Japanese, who themselves have neither a major crime problem nor any interest in using electronic monitoring domestically, are developing for the export market camera systems specially designed for installation in offenders' homes (Nellis, 1991). Big Brother may be watching soon.

Endnotes

1   George Orwell's *Nineteen Eighty-Four* was published in June of 1949. Its images of doublethink, the Thought Police, the all seeing, all hearing telescreen, the Party and of course, Big Brother have made "1984" the classic fictional exemplar of the evils associated with political authoritarianism, state control and the total domination and indoctrination of the individual.

2   "The big house" is a slang term used to refer to such old, large and infamous American prisons as Alcatraz, San Quentin and Sing Sing. The term was immortalized through its use in early gangster films starring the likes of Humphrey Bogart, George Raft, Edward G. Robinson and Paul Muni.

3   These percentage increases are computed on the basis of constant dollars.

4   Community-based corrections are non-custodial programs situated in the community. Operated both by the Correctional Service of Canada and by the provinces and territories, they are intended to serve as alternatives to imprisonment. Their principal goals are to promote offender rehabilitation and, for offenders who have been

incarcerated, to facilitate reintegration into society.

5   Crimes of violence consist of six categories of offences — homicide, attempted murder, assault, sexual offences, robbery and abduction. Property crime also consists of six categories — breaking and entering, motor vehicle theft, theft of $1000 and under, theft over $1000, possession of stolen goods and fraud. Drinking and driving offences include impaired operation of a motor vehicle, vessel, or aircraft (i) impaired driving with over 80 mgs., ii) impaired driving causing bodily harm or iii) impaired driving causing death, and failure or refusal to provide a breath or blood sample. The "other crimes" category includes all offences within the Criminal Code that are neither violent nor property crimes.

6   Probation is a type of court disposition that is served in the community under conditions of supervision. A probation order may be issued in conjunction with a suspended sentence, conditional sentence or fine. In most but not all cases, probation is a substitute for a jail term. Parole, on the other hand, is a form of early release from custody. An inmate who is considered eligible may be released, at a time considered appropriate by a parole board, to serve the balance of a sentence in the community subject to supervision and stated conditions. Most inmates are ineligible for parole until they have served one third of their sentences. Paroles from federal institutions fall under the jurisdiction of the National Parole Board. Provinces have the option of establishing parole boards to oversee early release from provincial facilities. At present, only Quebec, Ontario and British Columbia have established parole boards (Ekstedt and Griffiths, 1988).

7   Diversion is a mechanism through which accused persons who are charged with minor crimes and who do not have long criminal records are "diverted" out of the criminal justice system into an appropriate resource program. Normally, alleged offenders are given the choice of either participating in the resource program or facing prosecution on the charge. A community service order is usually granted as a condition of probation. It requires offenders to perform community services for an individual or non-profit organization in lieu of serving time in jail. Attempts are often made to have offenders perform services for the victims of their criminal activities. Restitution is a program available to those on probation wherein the offender agrees partially or fully to compensate the victim for damages.

8   The most crime-prone age group for property and violent offences contains those in their late teens and early twenties. In circumstances where this age category represents the largest age cohort in the population, it is not surprising that crime rates increase. Birth rates in the post-war years from 1948 until 1960 were unusually high. A person born in 1954 (the mid point of the range) was twenty one, a prime crime age, in 1975. The same person in 1990 was thirty-six, an age at which involvement in violent and property crime is much less likely. A factor such as society's age structure is a significant consideration in understanding the production and distribution of criminal activity.

9   Mandatory supervision is a form of early release based upon earned remission. Eligibility requirements dictate that inmates serve two thirds of their sentences. Released inmates are supervised in the community for the duration of their sentences. Failure rates have been higher for mandatory supervision than for parole primarily because parole requires the meeting of criteria beyond good institutional behaviour. Mandatory supervision, because it is administered by the National Parole Board, has often been confused with parole. The media frequently report that offenders out on parole have committed crimes when in fact these offenders have been released on mandatory supervision. Dissatisfaction with this program has

resulted in the National Parole Board being given (in 1986) the power to deny mandatory supervision to an offender who it considers might pose a threat to the community.

10   Accused persons confined on remand are people who have been charged with offences but not convicted. They are held in jail as opposed to being released on their own recognizance or on bail either because the court believes that they will not appear for trial or because it fears that they will tamper with or intimidate witnesses for the prosecution.

References

Ball, R., C. Huff, and R. Lilly. 1988. *House Arrest and Correctional Policy.* Beverly Hills: Sage.

Baumer, T.L., R. Mendelsohn, and C. Rhine. 1990. *Final Report: The Electronic Monitoring of Non-Violent Convict Felons: An Experiment in Home Detention.* Indianapolis, IN: School of Public and Environmental Affairs, Indiana University.

Berry, B. 1985. "Electronic Jails: A New Criminal Justice Concern." *Justice Quarterly* 2: 1-24.

Berry, B. and R. Matthews. 1989. "Electronic Monitoring and House Arrest: Making the Right Connections" in Matthews, R. (ed.), *Privatizing Criminal Justice.* Beverly Hills: Sage.

Blomberg, T.G. 1987. "Criminal Justice Reform and Social Control: Are We Becoming a Minimum Security Society?" in Lowman, J., R.J. Menzies and T.S. Palys (eds.),. *Transcarceration: Essays in the Sociology of Social Control.* Aldershot, U.K.: Gower Publishers.

Blomberg, T.G., G.P. Waldo, and L.C. Burcoff. 1987. "Home Confinement and Electronic Surveillance" in McCarthy, B.R. (ed.), *Intermediate Punishments: Intensive Supervision, Home Confinement and Electronic Surveillance.* Monsey, New York: Criminal Justice Press.

Canadian Centre for Justice Statistics. 1991a. *Adult Correctional Services in Canada 1990-91.* Ottawa: Supply and Services.

Canadian Centre for Justice Statistics. 1991b. *Canadian Crime Statistics 1990.* Ottawa: Supply and Services.

Chan, J.B.L. and R.V. Ericson. 1981. *Decarceration and the Economy of Penal Reform.* Toronto: Centre of Criminology, University of Toronto.

Clarkson, J.S. and J.J. Weakland. 1991. "A Transitional Aftercare Model for Juveniles: Adapting Electronic Monitoring and Home Confinement." *Journal of Offender Monitoring* 4: 1-15.

Cohen, S. 1979. "The Punitive City: Notes on the Dispersal of Social Control." *Contemporary Crises* 3: 339-363.

Currie, E. 1985. *Confronting Crime: An American Challenge.* New York: Pantheon.

Del Carman, R. and J. Vaughn. 1986. "Legal Issues in the Use of Electronic Surveillance in Probation." *Federal Probation* 50: 60-69.

Desroches, F.J. 1990. "Tearoom Trade: A Research Update." *Qualitative Sociology* 13: 39-61.

Ekstedt, John W. and Curt T. Griffiths. 1988. *Corrections in Canada: Policy and Practice.* 2nd. ed. Toronto: Butterworths.

Erwin, B.S. 1989. *Intensive Probation Supervision with an Electronic Monitoring Option.* Atlanta, GA.: Georgia Department of Corrections.

Fox, Richard G. 1987. "Dr. Schwitzgebel's Machine Revisited: Electronic Monitoring of Offenders." *Australian and New Zealand Journal of Criminology* 20: 131-147.

Friel, C.M. and J.B. Vaughn. 1986. "A Consumer's Guide to the Electronic Monitoring of Probationers." *Federal Probation* 50: 3-14.

Griffiths, Curt T. and Simon N. Verdun-Jones. 1989. *Canadian Criminal Justice.* Toronto: Butterworths.

Hylton, J.H. 1982. "Rhetoric and Reality: A Critical Appraisal of Community Corrections Programs." *Crime and Delinquency* 28: 341-373.

Inciardi, J.A. 1986. *The War on Drugs: Heroin, Cocaine, and Public Policy.* Mountainview, CA.: Mayfield.

Inciardi, J.A. 1987. *Criminal Justice.* 2nd. ed. New York: Harcourt Brace Jovanovich.

Jayewardene, C.H. and D. Doherty. 1985. "Individual Violence in Canadian Penitentiaries." *Canadian Journal of Criminology* 27: 429-439.

Kratcoski, P. and D. Walker. 1984. *Criminal Justice in America: Processes and Issues.* New York: Random House.

Lilly, J.R., R.A. Ball, and J. Wright. 1987. "Home Incarceration with Electronic Monitoring in Kenton County, Kentucky: An Evaluation" in McCarthy, B.R (ed.), *Intermediate Punishments: Intensive Supervision, Home Confinement and Electronic Surveillance.* Monsey, New York: Criminal Justice Press.

Lowman, J. and R.J. Menzies. 1986. "Out of the Fiscal Shadow: Carceral Trends in Canada and the United States." *Crime and Social Justice* 26: 95-115.

Maxfield, M.G. and T. Baumer. 1990. "Home Detention with Electronic Monitoring: Comparing Pre-trial and Post-conviction Programs." *Crime and Delinquency* 36: 521-536.

McCarthy, B.R. 1987. "Introduction" in McCarthy, B.R. (ed.), *Intermediate Punishments: Intensive Supervision, Home Confinement and Electronic Surveillance.* Monsey, New York: Criminal Justice Press.

Menzies, K. 1986. "The Rapid Spread of Community Service Orders in Ontario." *Canadian Journal of Criminology* 28: 157-169.

Muncie, J. 1990. "A Prisoner in My Own Home: The Politics and Practice of Electronic Monitoring." *Probation Journal* 37: 72-77.

N.E.E. Corrections Research and Planning Unit. 1990. *Home Office Research and Statistics Department Research Bulletin* 29: 28-31. London: British Home Office.

Nellis, M. 1991. "The Electronic Monitoring of Offenders in England and Wales." *British Journal of Criminology* 31.

Neville, Linda. 1989. *Electronic Monitoring Systems for Offender Supervision: Pilot Project and Evaluation.* Ottawa, Canada: Corrections Branch, Minister of the Solicitor General.

Orwell, G. 1949. *Nineteen Eighty-Four.* London: Secker and Warburg.

Palm Beach County, Florida Sheriff's Department. 1987. "Palm Beach County's In-House Arrest Work Release Program" in McCarthy, B.R. (ed.), *Intermediate*

Punishments: Intensive Supervision, Home Confinement and Electronic Surveillance. Monsey, New York: Criminal Justice Press.

Renzema, M. 1989. "Annual Monitoring Census: Progress Report." *Journal of Offender Monitoring* 2: 20-21.

Rhodes, R.P. 1984. *Organized Crime: Crime Control Vs. Civil Liberties.* New York: Random House.

Rothman, D. 1980. *Conscience and Convenience: The Asylum and Its Alternatives in Progressive America.* Toronto: Little Brown and Co.

Samaha, J. 1988. *Criminal Justice.* New York: West Publishing.

Schmidt, A.K. and C.E. Curtis. 1987. "Electronic Monitors" in McCarthy, B.R. (ed.), *Intermediate Punishments: Intensive Supervision, Home Confinement and Electronic Surveillance.* Monsey, New York: Criminal Justice Press.

Schumacher, M. 1987. *Supervised Electronic Confinement Pilot Program.* Santa Ana, CA.: Orange County Probation Department.

Schwitzgebel, R.K. 1969. "Issues in the Use of an Electronic Rehabilitation System with Chronic Recidivists." *Law and Society Review* 3: 597-611.

Schwitzgebel, R.K. 1970. "Behavioural Electronics Could Empty the World's Prisons." *The Futurist* 4: 59-62.

Scull, A.T. 1977. *Decarceration: Community Treatment and the Deviant — A Radical View.* Englewood Cliffs, N.J.: Prentice Hall.

Scull, A.T. 1983. "Community Corrections: Panacea, Progress, or Pretence?" in Abel, R.A. (ed.), *The Politics of Informal Justice: The American Experience.* New York: Academic Press.

Smith, M.E. 1984. "Will the Real Alternatives Please Stand Up?" *New York University Review of Law and Social Change* 12: 171-197.

Solicitor General of Canada. 1987. "Electronic Surveillance: Turning Homes into Jails." *Liaison* 13-10: 4-8.

Sykes, G.M. 1958. *Society of Captives: A Study of Maximum Security Institutions.* Princeton, N.J.: Princeton University Press.

Thomas, C.W. and D.M. Peterson. 1977. *Prison Organization and Inmate Subcultures.* Indianapolis, IN.: Bobbs Merrill.

United States Bureau of Justice Assistance. 1989. *Electronic Monitoring in Intensive Probation and Parole Programs.* Washington, D.C.: United States Bureau of Justice Assistance.

Vaughn, J.B. 1987. "Planning for Change: The Use of Electronic Monitoring as a Correctional Alternative" in McCarthy, B.R. (ed.), *Intermediate Punishments: Intensive Supervision, Home Confinement and Electronic Surveillance.* Monsey, New York: Criminal Justice Press.

Vaughn, J.B. 1989. "A Survey of Juvenile Electronic Monitoring and Home Confinement Programs." *Juvenile and Family Court Journal* 40: 1-36.

Walker, J.L. 1990. "Sharing the Credit, Sharing the Blame: Managing Political Risks in Electronically Monitored House Arrest." *Federal Probation* 54: 16-20.

Zonderman, Jon. 1990. *Beyond the Crime Lab: The New Science of Investigation.* New York: John Wiley and Sons.

A Restorative Lens

Howard Zehr

As I was thinking about writing this article, I took time out to go to court. An eighteen-year-old boy, my neighbour, is scheduled to be sentenced. He has pleaded guilty to molesting the young girl next door. Her mother has asked for my help. She doesn't want him to go to prison where he might become a victim himself, but she wants the behaviour to stop. "If it were anyone else," she tells me, "I would want to string him up. But Ted just needs help."

Ted has bothered children before, including one of my daughters.

"I'm going to continue this sentencing until a later date," says the judge. "Frankly, I don't know what to do. Howard, maybe you can help."

Where does one start in this sort of case? I begin by framing the issues in a conventional way. He's broken the law. What does the law require? What will the court accept? What should the court do with him? Then I remember what I've been writing, and my framework begins to shift.

The framework: it makes a difference. How do we interpret what has happened? What factors are relevant? What responses are possible and appropriate?

The lens we look through determines how we frame both the problem and the "solution." That lens is the focus of this article.

I have been involved in photography for many years. One of the lessons I have learned is how profoundly the lens I look through affects the outcome. My choice of lens determines in what circumstances I can work and how I see. If I choose a "slow" lens with a small maximum aperture, the image will be dim and good quality photographs may be hard to obtain under low light levels.

The focal length of the lens also makes a difference. A wide-angle lens is highly inclusive. It incorporates within the frame a multitude of subjects, but it does so at the cost of a certain distortion. Objects which are nearer become large, leaving objects in the background small. Also, the shapes of objects at the corners of the frame are altered. Circles become ellipses.

A telephoto lens is more selective. The scope of its vision is narrower, incorporating fewer objects within the frame. It too "distorts," but in a different way than a wide-angle lens. With a telephoto lens, objects are larger but distances are compressed. Objects appear closer to the camera — and closer to one another — than they are to the naked eye.

The choice of lens, then, affects what is in the picture. It also determines the relationships and proportions of the elements included. Similarly, the lens we use to examine crime and justice affects what we include as relevant variables, what we consider their relative importance to be, and what we consider proper outcomes.

We view crime through a retributive lens. The "criminal justice" process which uses that lens fails to meet many of the needs of either victim or offender. The process neglects victims while failing to meet its expressed goals of holding offenders accountable and deterring crime.

Such failures have led to the widespread sense of crisis today. An array of reforms have been attempted. The fads of today such as electronic monitoring and intensive supervision are simply the most recent of a long line of "solutions." Yet this system has shown itself remarkably resistant to significant improvement, absorbing and subverting efforts at reform. A French proverb seems true: "The more things change, the more they remain the same."

The reason for such failure, I am arguing, lies in our choice of lens: that is, in the assumptions we make about crime and justice. These assumptions, which govern our responses to wrongdoing, are in fact out of step with the experience of crime. Furthermore, they are out of step with our Christian roots and even with much of our own history in the West. To find our way out of this maze, we will have to look beyond alternative punishments, and even beyond alternatives to punishment. We will have to look to alternative ways of viewing both problem and solution. Professor Kay Harris, a specialist in sentencing, has reminded us that it is a matter of alternate values, not of alternate technologies of punishment.[1]

Our failures are negative signposts which identify a need for change, but there are positive signposts which point a direction. The experiences and needs of victims and offenders indicate some of the concerns we must address. The biblical tradition offers some principles.

Our historical experience and more recent "experimental plots" suggest possible approaches. Perhaps these signposts can serve as elements for a new lens.

A new lens, perhaps, but a new paradigm as well? A paradigm is more than a vision or a proposal. It requires well-articulated theory, combined with a consistent grammar and a "physics" of application—and some degree of consensus. It need not solve all problems, but it must solve the most pressing ones and must point a direction. I doubt that we are there yet.

More realistic at this stage are alternative visions, rooted in both principle and experience, which can help to guide our search for solutions to the present crisis. We can adopt a different lens, even though it cannot as yet be a full-fledged paradigm. Such visions can help give direction to what must be a shared journey of experimentation and exploration.

In this search, we are seeking a vision of what the standard ought to be, what is normative, not what would be a realistic response in all situations. The current lens builds upon the unusual, the bizarre. It makes procedures for such cases normative for "ordinary" offences. Some offenders are so inherently dangerous that they need to be restrained. Someone must make that decision, guided by rules and careful safeguards. Some offences are so heinous that they require special handling. But these special cases should not set the norm. Our approach, then, should be to identify what crime means and what normally ought to happen when it does, while recognizing the need for certain exceptions. For now, then, we will not preoccupy ourselves with whether our vision can encompass all situations. Rather we will try to envision what ought to be the norm.

One way to start this exploration is to take crime down from its high plane of abstraction. This means understanding it as we experience it: as injury and as a violation of people and of relationships. Justice ought, then, to focus on repairing, on making things right.

In that case, the two contrasting lenses might be sketched like this:

Retributive Justice
Crime is a violation of the state, defined by lawbreaking and guilt. Justice determines blame and administers pain in a contest between the offender and the state directed by systematic rules.

Restorative Justice
Crime is a violation of people and relationships. It creates obligations to make things right. Justice involves the victim, the offender and the community in a search for solutions which promote repair, reconciliation and reassurance.

Crime: Violation of People and Relationships

I pointed out that people often experience even minor property crimes as an attack on the self. Victims feel personally violated, even when the direct harm is only to property. The shalom vision* reminds us that this material level is important to a sense of well-being.

But the shalom vision also reminds us that crime represents a violation of human relationships. Crime affects our sense of trust, resulting in feelings of suspicion, of estrangement, sometimes of racism. Frequently it creates walls between friends, loved ones, relatives and neighbours. Crime affects our relationships with those around us.

Crime also represents a ruptured relationship between the victim and offender. Even if they had no previous relationship, the crime creates a relationship.

And that relationship is usually hostile. Left unresolved, that hostile relationship in turn affects the well-being of victim and offender.

Crime represents an injury to the victim but it may also involve injury to the offender. Much crime grows out of injury. Many offenders have experienced abuse as children. Many lack the skills and training that make meaningful jobs and lives possible. Many seek ways to feel validated and empowered. For many, crime is a way of crying for help and asserting their personhood. They do harm in part because of harm done to them. Often they are then further harmed in the "justice" process. This dimension grows in part out of larger distributive justice issues. It also is an integral part of the shalom vision.

Crime, then, is at its core a violation of a person by another person, a person who himself or herself may be wounded. It is a violation of the just relationship that should exist between individuals. There is also a larger social dimension to crime. Indeed, the effects of crime ripple out, touching many others. Society too has a stake in the outcome and a role to play. Still, these public dimensions should not be the starting point. Crime is not first an offence against society, much less against the state. Crime is first an offence against people, and it is here that we should start.

This interpersonal dimension of crime reminds us that crime involves conflict.[2] Indeed, several European scholars working toward a new lens for viewing crime have urged us to define crime as a form of conflict. After all,

---

*   Editor's Note: "Shalom" is a biblical concept which usually is taken to mean that God intended humankind to live in peace and material/physical security. In secular terms, it can be defined as the belief that physical and material well being are essential to psychological or emotional happiness.

crime creates interpersonal conflict and sometimes it grows out of conflict. Certainly crime is related to other harms and conflicts in society. Properly approached, many such conflictual situations can be opportunities for learning and growth whether or not one defines them as crimes.

Marie Marshall Fortune has warned that to label crime *conflict* can be misleading and dangerous.[3] In situations of domestic violence, for example, we have too often defined violent acts with serious consequences as simply an outgrowth of conflict. This has tended to mute responsibility for behaviour by blaming the victim. It also assumes that violence is simply an escalation of conflict. Violence is not, Fortune reminds us, simply an escalation of conflict. It is categorically different. It is one thing to have a difference of opinion and to argue. It is quite another to attack another physically.

Because of its interpersonal dimensions, crime obviously involves conflict. To equate it with conflict, however, may be misleading and may obscure some important dimensions.

What about the term *crime?* Some would have us avoid the term altogether. Crime is a result of a legal system which makes arbitrary distinctions between various harms and conflicts. It is an artificial construct which throws into one basket a variety of unrelated behaviours and experiences. It separates them from other harms and violations and thereby obscures the real meaning of the experience.

Because of this, Dutch criminologist and lawyer Louk Hulsman has suggested the term *problematic situations.*[4] That term helpfully reminds us of the connection between "crimes" and other types of harms and conflicts. It also suggests the learning possibilities that are inherent in such situations. But *problematic situations* feels vague and, for serious harms, may seem to minimize the dimensions of the hurt. Certainly it is difficult to imagine "problematic situations" taking the place of "crime" in ordinary discussion!

An alternate term would be helpful, but so far I have not found an acceptable replacement. So for now I'll stick to *crime,* keeping in mind its inadequacies.

Crime involves injuries which need healing. Those injuries represent four basic dimensions of harm:

(1)   to the victim;
(2)   to interpersonal relationships;
(3)   to the offender; and
(4)   to the community.

The retributive lens focuses primarily on the latter, social dimensions. It does so in a way that makes *community* abstract and impersonal. Retributive justice defines the state as victim, defines wrongful behaviour as violation of rules, and sees the relationship between victim and offender as irrelevant. *Crimes,* then, are categorically different from other types of wrongs.

A restorative lens identifies people as victims and recognizes the centrality of the interpersonal dimensions. Offences are defined as personal harms and interpersonal relationships. Crime is a violation of people and of relationships.

Understandings of Crime

Retributive Lens	**Restorative Lens**
Crime defined by violation of rules (i.e., broken rules)	Crime defined by harm to people and relationships (i.e., broken relationships)
Harms defined abstractly	Harms defined concretely
Crime seen as categorically different from other harms and conflicts	Crime recognized as related to other harms and conflicts
State as victim	People and relationships as victims
State and offender seen as primary parties	Victim and offender seen as primary parties
Victims' needs and rights ignored	Victims' needs and rights central
Interpersonal dimensions irrelevant	Interpersonal dimensions central
Conflictual nature of crime obscured	Conflictual nature of crime recognized
Wounds of offender peripheral	Wounds of offender important
Offence defined in technical, legal terms	Offence understood in full context: moral, social, economic, political

So far we've limited most of our discussion to the harms and conflicts that we usually label as crimes. Such a narrow focus, however, does not satisfy the vision of how people ought to live together in a state of shalom, of right relationship. Behaviours we call crime violate such relationships, but so do a variety of other harms, including acts of injustice and oppression by the powerful against the powerless. Thus we need to view injustice holistically, without artificial lines between crimes and other injustices. We must include the whole continuum of harms, in which crimes merge into other harms and conflicts between individuals that we normally term *civil*. These injustices join with injustices of power and wealth, and such structural injustices in turn breed more injustice.

Restoration: The Goal

If crime is injury, what is justice? If crime harms people, justice should be a search to make things right to and between people. When a wrong occurs, the central question ought not to be, "What should be done to the offender?" or "What does the offender deserve?" Instead, the primary question ought to be, "What can be done to make things right?"

Instead of defining justice as retribution, we will define justice as restoration. If crime is injury, justice will repair injuries and promote healing. Acts of restoration — not further harm — will counterbalance the harm of crime. We cannot guarantee full recovery, of course, but true justice would aim to provide a context in which the process can begin.

If the harm of crime has four dimensions, reparative energies ought to address these dimensions. The first goal of justice, then, ought to be restitution and healing for victims.

Healing for victims does not imply that one can or should forget or minimize the violation. Rather, it implies a sense of recovery, a degree of closure. The violated should again begin to feel as if life makes some sense and that they are safe and in control. The violator should be encouraged to change. He or she should receive freedom to begin life anew. Healing encompasses a sense of recovery and a hope for the future.

Healing of the relationship between victim and offender should be a second major concern of justice. The victim-offender reconciliation movement has identified this goal as reconciliation.

Reconciliation implies full repentance and forgiveness. It involves establishing a positive relationship between the victim and offender. The Victim-Offender Reconciliation Program (VORP) experience suggests that this is possible. Yet it would be unrealistic to expect reconciliation to occur in all cases. In many cases, nothing like reconciliation will be accomplished. In other cases, a satisfactory relationship may be worked out that does not imply intimacy or complete trust. In no way should participants feel coerced toward reconciliation. Ron Kraybill, former director of Mennonite Conciliation Service, has reminded us that reconciliation has a rhythm and dynamic of its own. Even if we consciously want reconciliation, our emotions may go a different direction.

> To the brain's concern with what *ought* to be,
> the heart responds with what is. The head *can*
> set a direction for the heart, but the heart must
> arrive at its own pace. Heart reconciliation is a
> cycle with stages along the way.[5]

According to Ron Claassen, director of the VORP in Fresno, California, we must see reconciliation as a continuum.[6] On the one end is outright hostility. On the other is the restoration or creation of a strong, positive relationship. When a crime occurs, the relationship is usually at the hostile end of the scale. Left unaddressed, the relationship usually remains there or even moves toward deeper hostility. The aim of justice, then, ought to be to move the relationship toward reconciliation. Such healing of relationships, even if only partial, is an important step toward healing for individuals. Justice cannot guarantee or force reconciliation, but it ought to provide opportunities for such reconciliation to occur.

I have been involved in VORP cases where little progress toward a reconciled relationship seems to have occurred. Having met to discuss the offence and its resolution, victim and offender remained hostile. Yet the nature of their hostility had changed. No longer were they mad at an abstraction, at a stereotype of a victim or offender. They were now mad at a concrete person. Even that represents some improvement.

Offenders too need healing. They must be accountable for their behaviour, of course. They cannot be "let off the hook." Yet this accountability can itself be a step toward change and healing. And their other needs must receive attention.

The community also needs healing. Crime undermines a community's sense of wholeness, and that injury needs to be addressed.

The experience of justice is a basic human need. Without such an experience, healing and reconciliation are difficult or even impossible. Justice is a precondition for closure.

A full sense of justice may, of course, be rare. However, even "approximate justice" can help.[7] Even a partial experience can lay the groundwork which is necessary for a sense of recovery and closure. For example, when an offender has not been identified, or refuses to take responsibility, the community can play a role in providing an experience of justice. They can truly hear and value victims, agreeing that what happened was wrong and listening and attending to their needs. Approximate justice is better than no justice and aids the process of healing.

How should we envision justice? The blindfolded goddess with balance in hand symbolizes well the impersonal, process-oriented nature of the contemporary paradigm. What is our alternative?

One possibility is to image justice as healing a wound. My colleague Dave Worth, responding to a draft of this chapter spelled out this image well:

> New tissue must grow to fill the space where the old was torn away. The proper conditions and nutrients must be present to allow the new to grow. There must be safety and cleanliness and time. Sometimes there is a scar, and sometimes there is impairment. But when it is healed we can move and function and grow. And through our experience of wounding and healing, we can have some understanding of the conditions which brought about that wound and the conditions which brought about that healing. [Then] we can work to change the former and to offer the latter to others who are wounded.

Wilma Derksen, whose daughter was brutally murdered, has suggested still another metaphor which I find even more hopeful. Crime creates an emptiness, so justice is filling a hole.[8]

The restorative approach to justice shows that true justice must often be transformative justice.[9] To make things right, it may be necessary not merely to return to situations and people to their original condition, but to go beyond. In cases of wife abuse, for example, it is not enough to make amends for the damages. True justice cannot occur unless people and relationships are transformed into something that is healthy so the injury does not recur. Justice may mean moving in a new direction rather than returning to the situation of the past.

Justice may involve more than filling a hole and leveling it off. The hole may be needed to be heaped up until it overflows. Again Dave Worth summarized this image of justice better than I can.

> That is perhaps the essence of reconciliation: something new has happened between two people. Not something based on the way it was in the past, but on the way it should be. Reconciliation is really a forward-looking approach to the problem.

> [Overflowing] is what justice is about. It is not the level-over-the-top kind of legalistic approach to justice that we are talking about.

We are not talking about the scales of justice.
We are talking about a situation where true justice has occurred which has made a new thing
come to pass. A thing which leaves people not
lower, not just equal, but full and overflowing
so they can go out and spread justice to others
around them. Perhaps the problem with the
present legalistic approach to justice is that it
doesn't heap people up so they have no justice
left to give others.

Justice Begins with Needs

Justice which aims to fill and overflow must begin by identifying and
seeking to meet human needs. With crime, the starting point must be the
needs of those violated. When a crime occurs (regardless of whether an
"offender" is identified) the first questions ought to be, "Who has been
harmed?" "How have they been harmed?" "What are their needs?" Such
an approach would, of course, be far from that of retributive justice which
first asks, "Who did it?" "What should be done to them?" — and then rarely
moves beyond that point.

Victims have a variety of needs which must be met if one is to experience even approximate justice. In many cases, the first and most pressing
needs are for support and a sense of safety.

Soon after that, however, come a variety of other needs. Victims need
someone to listen to them. They must have opportunities to tell their story
and to vent their feelings, perhaps over and over. They must tell their truth.
And they need others to suffer with them, to lament with them the evil that
has been done.

Somewhere in the process, victims need to feel vindicated. They need
to know that what happened to them was wrong and undeserved and that
others recognize this as wrong. They need to know that something has
been done to correct the wrong and to reduce the chances of its recurrence. They want to hear others acknowledge their pain and validate their
experience.

The language of truth-telling, lament, and vindication may sometimes
be harsh and angry. We must accept that and truly hear it. Only then can
people move beyond. Mort MacCallum-Paterson has concluded that crime
victims' cries of anguish often sound angry and vengeful, but they are not
necessarily demands for community action. As one murder victim's father
said to Paterson, "We may sound as if we're asking for the death penalty.

We really aren't ... but what else can we say?" Paterson observes,

> What else can we say? That's the point. There
> are no words more ultimate than a blood-cry as
> a way of expressing the grief, the pain and the
> rage of the survivors of murder victims.
> Whether or not those words become active
> strategizing toward the goal of executing the
> murderer requires another move. It requires a
> further decision. Lament as such does not con-
> tain the decision, but...lament does contain the
> language. It takes the form of a curse. In effect,
> it is a prayer that God will damn that one who
> took the life of the victim.[10]

Retribution may be one form of vindication, but so also is restitution. In an important little book entitled *Mending Hurts,* John Lampen of Northern Ireland notes that restitution is at least as basic a human response as is retribution.[11]

Restitution represents recovery of losses, but its real importance is symbolic. Restitution implies an acknowledgment of the wrong and a statement of responsibility. Making right is itself a form of vindication, a form which may promote healing better than retribution.

Retribution often leaves a legacy of hatred. Perhaps it is more satisfying as an experience of justice than no justice at all, but it does little to address hostilities. Such hostilities can impede healing. That is the beauty of forgiveness. By addressing hostilities, it allows both the victim and the offender to take control of their own lives. Like reconciliation, however, forgiveness is not easy and cannot be forced. For many an experience of justice is a necessary precondition for forgiveness to occur. For some, forgiveness will not seem possible.

Both retribution and restitution have to do with righting an imbalance. While both retribution and restoration have symbolic importance, however, restitution is a more concrete way to restore equity. Also, retribution seeks to right the balance by lowering the offender to the level to which the victim has been reduced. It tries to defeat the wrongdoer, annulling his or her claim to superiority and confirming the victim's sense of worth. Restitution, on the other hand, seeks to raise the victim to his or her previous level. It recognizes his or her moral worth and acknowledges the role of the offender and possibilities for repentance. It thereby acknowledges the moral worth of the offender as well.[12]

Most of us assume that retribution is high on victims' agendas. Recent surveys of victims, however, suggest a different picture. Victims are often open to nonincarcerative, reparative sentences — more frequently, in fact, than is the public.[13]

Moreover, they often rank rehabilitation for the offender as an important value. Help for the offender, after all, is one way of addressing the problem of safety and the prevention of future wrongs.

Victims also need to be empowered. Justice cannot simply be done to and for them. They must feel needed and listened to in the process. Since one dimension of the wrong was that they were robbed of power, one dimension of justice is to return power to them. At minimum, this means they must be a key in determining what their needs are, how they should be met and when they should be addressed. But victims should have some role in the overall process.

Victims need reassurance, reparation, vindication, empowerment, but they especially need to find meaning. Remember Ignatieff's insight: justice provides a framework for meaning. Victims need to find answers to questions about what happened, why, and what is being done about it. They need to address the six questions which provide steps to recovery.* Only the victims themselves can answer some of these questions, although it may be that we can help them in their search. However, some of these questions are questions of fact. Who did it, why, what kind of person are they, what is being done about it? At minimum, justice should provide such information.

Thus victims often seek vindication. This vindication includes denunciation of the wrong, lament, truth telling, deprivatization and deminimization. They seek equity, including reparation, reconciliation and forgiveness. They sense a need for empowerment, including participation and safety. Another need is reassurance, including support, "suffering with," safety, clarification of responsibility and prevention. And they have a need for meaning, including information, fairness, answers and a sense of proportion.

---

*   Editor's Note: Charles Finley has suggested that the answers to six basic questions are necessary to promote healing. These are:

> (1)   What happened?
> (2)   Why did it happen to me?
> (3)   Why did I act as I did at the time?
> (4)   Why have I acted as I have since that time?
> (5)   What if it happens again?
> (6)   What does this mean for me and for my outlook?

Charles Finley, (1983) "Catastrophe: An Overview of Family Relations," Chapter 1 of Charles Finley and Hamilton McCubbin, *Stress and the Family*. (New York: Brunner/Mozel).

Victims feel violated by crime, and these violations generate needs. Communities feel violated as well, however, and they have needs too. Since one cannot ignore the public dimensions of crime, the justice process in many cases cannot be fully private. The community, too, wants reassurance that what happened was wrong, that something is being done about it, and that steps are being taken to discourage its recurrence. Here too information can be important as it can help to reduce stereotypes and unfounded fears. Here too restitution can play an important role by providing a symbol of the restoration of wholeness. In fact, the role of symbolism is important. Crime undermines the sense of wholeness in a community. For a community, reparation often requires some sort of symbolic action that contains elements of denunciation of the offence, vindication, reassurance and repair.

The public dimensions of crime are important, therefore, but they should not be the starting point. Also, the community needs to be challenged in some of its assumptions about crime. One of these assumptions is that full order and safety is possible, at least within the framework of a free society.

At a recent fund-raising party for the organization which operates our local VORP, I sat across a picnic table from a well-to-do young man. A spectacular storm was approaching, and everyone else had abandoned us for the safety of the house. As we sat watching the storm, he asked about the organization to which he had just contributed, and that led to a discussion of justice. He told me with considerable candor of his own internal struggle with the question. He had known since childhood a man who was a perpetual thief. Part of him was concerned about that friend's rehabilitation and well-being. On the other hand, he saw himself as conservative and felt that the thief deserved harsh punishment. "Sometimes," he said, "I think we should do what Iran does — cut off an arm, punish severely. Then we'd be safe." "Perhaps," I replied, "but would you want to live here then?"

Order and freedom are two opposites on a continuum. Complete freedom, at least in the sense of freedom to do whatever we wish without formal or informal controls, would likely be chaotic and unsafe, a Hobbesian world. Complete order, on the other hand, even if it were obtainable, would come at the price of freedom. If harsh punishment were to deter crime, for instance, it would have to be swift and sure. The price? We would have to be willing to make mistakes and to give arbitrary power to central authorities — a power which would surely be misused. Most of us would not wish to live in such a world. So we find ourselves moving back and forth somewhere in the middle of that continuum, seeking to balance freedom and order. The conservatives among us find themselves closer to the order end, the liberals closer to the freedom end.

There is yet another error in usual assumptions about freedom and order. Most of the time we think of order as rules and penalties, formal controls. We forget, however, that throughout history order has been maintained by informal controls — by belief systems, by social pressures and obligations, by the rewards of conforming. This is true also in our own everyday lives. To assume that order derives simply from laws and punishment is to overlook what holds society together.

The point in all this is that we cannot live in complete safety and retain other values which we hold dear. At the same time, our freedom is also at risk when we do not call people to account when their attempt to exercise their will infringes on the freedom of others.

Crime Creates Obligations

A discussion of needs quickly leads to questions of responsibility and liability. Violations create obligations.

The primary obligation, of course, is on the part of the one who has caused the violation. When someone wrongs another, he or she has an obligation to make things right. This is what justice should be about. It means encouraging offenders to understand and acknowledge the harm they have done and then taking steps, even if incomplete or symbolic, to make that wrong right. Making right is central to justice.

Making right is not a marginal, optional activity. It is an obligation. Ideally, the justice process can help offenders to acknowledge and assume their responsibilities willingly. This can happen. It often does in the VORP process. More often, however, persons accept this responsibility reluctantly at first. Many offenders are reluctant to make themselves vulnerable by trying to understand the consequences of their action. After all, they have built up edifices of stereotypes and rationalizations to protect themselves against exactly this kind of information. Many are reluctant to take on the responsibility to make right. In many ways taking one's punishment is easier. While it may hurt for a time, it involves no responsibility and no threat to rationalizations and stereotypes. Offenders often need strong encouragement or even coercion to accept their obligations.

The VORP movement in North America and in England has discussed this often. Obviously this acceptance of responsibility is better when voluntary. Obviously too, coercion can be abused. Still, in principle I do not object to the requirement that offenders must assume their responsibilities. After all, if someone harms someone else, he or she has created a debt, an obligation. The offender should recognize that and willingly accept responsibilities. The justice process should encourage that.

However, persons often will not willingly assume their responsibilities. One of the reasons many offenders get into trouble is a lack of certain kinds of responsibility. One cannot overcome such irresponsibility quickly. What society can say to offenders, then, is simple: "You have done wrong by violating someone. You have an obligation to make that wrong right. You may choose to do so willingly, and we will allow you to be involved in figuring out how that should be done. If you do not choose to accept this responsibility, however, we will have to decide for you what needs to be done and will require you to do it."

One can require offenders to accept the obligation to make right. One can strongly encourage them to take fuller responsibility by facing their victims. However, one cannot and must not force them to do so. And one certainly should not coerce victims to participate! Forced encounters are unlikely to be good for either offender or victim, and may well backfire. We can require offenders to make right, but they cannot be fully responsible without some degree of voluntarism. One purpose of both punishment and reparation is to send messages. The utilitarian aim of punishment is to say to offenders, "Do not commit offences because they are against the law." "Those who do wrong deserve to get hurt." Reparation or restitution seeks to send a different message. "Don't commit offences because it harms someone. Those who harm others will have to make it right." The message of our actions does not always sink in, as British author Martin Wright has noted. But when it does, we need to make sure it is the right message.[14]

Regarding the need to send a message that crime is wrong, Wright also observes:

> We can denounce crime more constructively by doing things for the victim (and requiring the offenders to do so), rather than against the offender.[15]

Crime creates a debt to make right, and that debt remains regardless of whether forgiveness happens. When we offend, we cannot assume that because we have experienced forgiveness from God or even from the one wronged no other obligation remains. Nevertheless, it is also true that victims may choose to forgive even the concrete obligation that is owed. Rarely is an offender able to make up completely for what both the victim and the offender have lost. Herman Bianchi has noted that crime creates a liability, and that forgiveness is about removing the liability for that which cannot be restored.

Insofar as it is possible, offenders should make amends. However, in many cases there are considerable delays before offenders are identified. Often offenders are never identified at all. Also, many of the needs which the victim and the community have as a result of crime are beyond the means of offenders to set right. And offenders have needs as well. This is society's responsibility: to attend to the needs to which individuals alone cannot attend. Certain obligations on the part of the community are thus also generated by crime.

Offenders Have Needs Too

Restoratively, justice is done not because it is deserved but because it is needed. Although in a retributive or just desserts model offenders may not "deserve" to have their own needs given priority, society's self-interest dictates that these needs be part of a just response. Identifying and addressing offenders' needs is a key element of restorative justice.

In the story with which I opened this article, Ted needs to receive treatment. The legal system interprets his behaviour as "sexual molestation." This behaviour is part of a larger pattern of inadequacy and dysfunction. Left unattended, it will only get worse. Part of the treatment needed involves helping Ted recognize the impact of his actions on his young victim.

Offenders have many needs, of course. They need to have their stereotypes and rationalizations — their "mis-attributions" — about the victim and the event challenged. They may need to learn to be more responsible. They may need to develop employment and interpersonal skills. They often need emotional support. They may need to learn to channel anger and frustration in more appropriate ways. They may need help to develop a positive and healthy self-image. And they often need help in dealing with guilt. Like victims, unless such needs are met, closure is impossible.

In the aftermath of crime, victim's needs form the starting point for restorative justice. But one must not neglect offender and community needs.

A Matter of Accountability

Needs and responsibilities — it's a matter of accountability. When harm is done, offenders need to be accountable, and in ways that represent natural consequences of their actions. This accountability means understanding and acknowledging the harm and taking steps to make things right.

There is a third, intermediate dimension of accountability by offenders: to share in the responsibility for deciding what needs to be done. Judge Challeen speaks of responsible sentencing.[16]

Since offenders' behaviour often reflects irresponsibility, simply to tell them what is going to happen lets them off the hook, encouraging further irresponsibility. In his court, therefore, he tells offenders the dimensions they must address. Then he tells them to come back with a proposal on how they expect to meet these requirements and how the sentence will be monitored and enforced. VORP works at this by having offenders negotiate and agree to restitution.

In a new "juvenile reparations" experiment operated by The Center for Community Justice here in Indiana, young offenders must come to our program before the "sentence" is decided. There they are encouraged to understand that their behavior does harm (1) to the victim (2) to the community and (3) to themselves. The staff works with them to help them propose a "sentence" which addresses all three. Through VORP, for example, they may learn of victims' needs and make restitution. Through community service they may seek to repay the community. Through tutoring, art therapy or other activities they will address some of their own needs. It is not yet clear how successful this experiment will be, but the point is this: accountability should empower and encourage responsibility. And it should take seriously all three levels of obligation: victim, community and offender.

Offenders must be held accountable, but so too must society. Society must be accountable to victims, helping to identify and meet their needs. Likewise, the larger community must attend to the needs of offenders, seeking not simply to restore but to transform. Accountability is multidimensional and transformational.

Understandings of Accountability

Retributive Lens	Restorative Lens
Wrongs create guilt	Wrongs create liabilities and obligations
Guilt absolute, either/or	Degrees of responsibility
Guilt indelible	Guilt removable through repentance and reparation
Debt is abstract	Debt is concrete
Debt is paid by taking punishment	Debt paid by making right

Retributive Lens (cont'd.)	**Restorative Lens (cont'd.)**
"Debt" owed to society in the abstract	Debt owed to victim first
Accountability as taking one's "medicine"	Accountability as taking responsibility
Assumes behaviour chosen freely	Recognizes difference between potential and actual realization of human freedom
Free will or social determinism	Recognizes role of social context as choices without denying personal responsibility

The Process Must Empower and Inform

Judges and lawyers often assume that what people want most is to win their cases. But recent studies show that the process matters a great deal, and that the criminal justice process often does not feel much like justice. Not only *what happens* but also *how it is decided* is important.[17]

Justice has to be lived, not simply done by others and reported to us. When someone simply informs us that justice has been done and that we should now go home (as victims) or to jail (as offenders), we do not experience that as justice. Justice which is actually lived, experienced, may not always be pleasant. But we will know that it has happened because we have lived it rather than having it done for us. Not simply justice, but the *experience* of justice must occur.

The first step in restorative justice is to meet immediate needs, particularly those of the victim. Following that, restorative justice should seek to identify larger needs and obligations. In identifying these needs and obligations, the process should, insofar as possible, put power and responsibility in the hands of those directly involved: the victim and offender. It should also leave room for community involvement. Second, it should address the victim-offender relationship by facilitating interaction and the exchange of information about the events, about each other, and about each other's needs. Third, it should focus on problem-solving, addressing not only present needs but future intentions.

I have already spoken of the importance of participation for both victim and offender. For victims, disempowerment is a core element of the violation. Empowerment is crucial to recovery and justice. For offenders, irresponsibility and a sense of disempowerment may have been some of the bricks on the road to the offence. Only by participating in the "solution" can they move toward responsibility and closure.

The community has a role to play here too. Part of the tragedy of modern society is our tendency to turn over our problems to experts. That is our tendency with regard to health, education and child-raising. And it certainly applies to the harms and conflicts we call crime. In doing that, we lose the power and ability to solve our own problems. Even worse, we give up opportunities to learn and grow from these situations. Restorative responses must recognize that the community has a role to play in the search for justice.

An important part of justice is the exchange of information — about each other, about the facts of the offence, about needs. Victims want answers to their questions about what happened, why it happened, and who did this thing. Offenders need to understand what they have done and to whom. Faces should take the place of stereotypes. Misattributions need to be challenged. The exchange of such information is crucial, and ideally it can occur through direct interaction. In that context, the question of what to do about what has happened in the past and what is to happen in the future can be addressed. Such outcomes need to be registered in the form of agreements and settlements which are measurable and monitored.

Mediation between victim and offender is one approach to justice which meets these criteria. Victim-offender mediation empowers participants, challenges misattributions, provides for an exchange of information and encourages actions aimed at making right. Through the use of community mediators, it provides for community participation. Mediation is fully compatible with a restorative approach to justice.

Mediation assumes certain preconditions, however. Safety must be assured. Participants must receive the emotional support which they need and must be willing to participate. Trained mediators are essential. The timing must be right.

When such preconditions are met, mediation must be conducted appropriately and must address key issues. Mark Umbreit has pointed to the importance of an "empowering" style of mediation rather than one in which the mediator imposes his or her agenda and personality, either directly or through manipulation.[18]

One must not bypass the exchange of information and expression of feelings on the road to agreements. Ron Claassen teaches his VORP mediators that, for mediation to be complete, three questions must be satisfactorily answered:

First, has the injustice been recognized and acknowledged? Has the offender owned up to and accepted responsibility for his acts? Have victims' questions been answered? Has the offender had a chance to explain what has been going on in his life?

Second, has there been agreement on what needs to be done to restore equity as far as possible? Third, have future intentions been addressed? Does the offender plan to do it again? Is the victim feeling safe? Is there provision for follow-up and for the monitoring of agreements?

Claassen summaries the three categories as confession, restitution and reprentance.[19]

But mediation is not always appropriate. The fear may be too great, even with support and assurances of safety. Power imbalances between parties may be too pronounced and impossible to overcome. The victim or the offender may be unwilling. The offence may be too heinous or the suffering too severe. One of the parties may be emotionally unstable. Direct contact between victim and offender can be extremely helpful, but justice cannot depend only on such direct interaction.

There are, in such cases, a variety of other ways to proceed which keep interaction and exchange of information in focus. The use of surrogate victims, pioneered by programs in Canada and England, is one example. Here offenders meet with victims other than their own as a step toward assuming responsibility and sharing information. This can be particularly helpful in emotionally-charged situations such as sexual offenses or where cases remain unsolved.[20]

Most sexual abuse therapy treats victims and offenders separately, in isolation. It provides little recognition or ways to work at the abuse of trust involved in the offence. It offers few avenues for closure. Little attention is given to how the events of the offence are perceived or to misattributions about the event or the individuals.

"Victim-sensitive sex offender therapy" developed by therapist Walter Berea is different.[21] This therapeutic approach has three stages. The first is the "communication switchboard" stage. Here the therapist makes contact with the probation officer, previous therapists and, perhaps most unusually, with the victim. Contact with the victim provides more complete information about the events, lets the victim know that the offender is in therapy and allows the therapist to inquire whether the victim's needs are being met.

In the second stage of therapy misattributions about the victim are challenged. The offender is helped to acknowledge responsibility and to understand the consequences of his behaviour. During this time, he writes a letter of apology to the victim. For the victim, this stage provides a lime to make sure that he does not take fault or blame on himself.

The third and final stage of this therapy has a reconciliation focus. Options include actually receiving the letter of apology which the offender has written, a face-to-face meeting or a "no-contact" contract with the offender for the future. The choice is the victim's. Such an approach takes seriously the harm and the interpersonal dimensions of the offence as well as the needs of both victim and offender.

"Genesee justice — crafted with pride in New York State." So reads the logo of a program operated by the sheriff's department in Batavia, New York. Concerned about overuse of the jail and about victims' needs, this program was designed specifically for cases of serious violence: manslaughter, assault and homicide. When such an offence occurs, immediate and intensive aid is offered to victims and survivors. The support offered is holistic. It concentrates not simply on their legal needs, but on emotional and spiritual needs.

Staff persons walk through the victimization experience with victims. In the process they help them in providing full information to the "system" about their experience. During that process, victims are allowed some involvement in decisions such as bail and even sentencing, for example through a victim-offender encounter. Given all that support and participation, victims' wishes often turn out to be surprisingly creative and redemptive. At minimum, their needs are addressed and the various dimensions of the harm are recognized.

The ideals of direct victim-offender interaction and empowerment cannot always be fully attained. Some third-party decisions are inescapable. Cases with important implications for the community cannot simply be left up to victim and offender. There must also be some sort of community oversight. But these cases need not set the norm for how we view and respond to crime. Even in such cases, we need to keep before us a vision of what crime really is and what really should happen.

Justice Involves Rituals

Our legal system makes much of ritual. Indeed, trials are to a large extent ritual, drama, theatre. But we usually ignore the most important needs for ritual. One of these points of need is when an offence has occurred. This is where the ritual of lament, stated so eloquently in the

Psalms, is appropriate. "Genesee justice" has recognized this need by facilitating religious services of lament and healing for those who are interested.

But as justice is done — whether complete or approximate — we also need rituals of closure. Louk Hulsman has called these "rituals of re-ordering." They may be important for both victim and offender. Such rituals provide an arena in which the church could play a particularly important role.

Is There a Place for Punishment?

I have argued that punishment should not be the focus of justice. But is there room in a restorative concept for some forms of punishment? Certainly options such as restitution will be understood by some as punishment, albeit a more deserved and logical punishment. In one major study of VORP, for example, offenders described their outcomes as punishment but viewed them more positively than traditional punishment. Perhaps punitive language arose due to a lack of alternate terminology (although some did use the language of "making right" to describe justice). However, accepting responsibility is painful and will of necessity be understood in part as punishment. Similarly, isolation of those who are dangerous, even under the best of conditions, is painful.

The real question, then, is not whether persons will experience some elements of restorative justice as punishment, but whether punishment *intended as punishment* has a place. Christie has argued that if pain — intended as pain — is used, it should at least be used without an ulterior purpose.[22] Pain should be applied simply as punishment, not as a way of reaching some other goal such as rehabilitation or social control. Perhaps punishment cannot be eliminated entirely from a restorative approach, but it should not be normative and its uses and purposes should be carefully prescribed.

When we as a society punish, we must do so in a context that is just and deserving. Punishment must be viewed as fair and legitimate, Ignatieff notes, because we cannot experience justice unless it provides a framework of meanings that make sense of experience. For punishment to seem fair, outcome and process need to relate to the original wrong. However, the societal context must also be viewed as fair, and this raises larger questions of social, economic and political justice.

If there is room for punishment in a restorative approach, its place would not be central. It would need to be applied under conditions which controlled and reduced the level of pain and in a context where restoration and healing are the goals. Perhaps there are possibilities for "restorative punishment." Having said that, however, I hasten to add that possibilities for destructive punishment are much more plentiful.

Two Lenses

Earlier I summarized briefly the retributive and restorative lenses. These two perspectives can be formulated in somewhat longer form. According to retributive justice: (1) crime violates the state and its laws; (2) justice focuses on establishing guilt (3) so that doses of pain can be measured out; (4) justice is sought through a conflict between adversaries (5) in which offender is pitted against state; (6) rules and intentions outweigh outcomes. One side wins and the other loses. According to restorative justice: (1) crime violates people and relationships; (2) justice aims to identify needs and obligations (3) so that things can be made right; (4) justice encourages dialogue and mutual agreement, (5) gives victims and offenders central roles and (6) is judged by the extent to which responsibilities are assumed, needs are met and healing (of individuals and relationships) is encouraged. Justice which seeks first to meet needs and to make right looks quite different from justice which has blame and pain at its core. The following chart attempts to contrast some characteristics and implications of the two concepts of justice.

Understandings of Justice

Retributive Lens	**Restorative Lens**
Blame-fixing central	Problem-solving central
Focus on past	Focus on future
Needs secondary	Needs primary
Battle model; adversarial	Dialogue normative
Emphasizes differences	Searches for commonalities
Imposition of pain considered normative	Restoration and reparation considered normative

Retributive Lens (cont'd.)	**Restorative Lens (cont'd.)**
One social injury added to another	Emphasis on repair and social injuries
Harm by offender balanced by harm to offender	Harm by offender balanced by making right
Focus on offender; victim ignored	Victims' needs central
State and offender are key elements	Victim and offender are key elements
Victims lack information	Information provided to victims
Restitution rare	Restitution normal
Victims' "truth" secondary	Victims given chance to "tell their truth"
Victims' suffering ignored	Victims' suffering lamented and acknowledged
Action from state to offender; offender passive	Offender given role in solution
State monopoly on response to wrongdoing	Victim, offender and community roles recognized
Offender has no responsibility for resolution	Offender has responsibility in resolution
Outcomes encourage offender irresponsibility	Responsible behaviour encouraged
Rituals of personal denunciation and exclusion	Rituals of lament and reordering
Offender denounced	Harmful act denounced
Offender's ties to community weakened	Offender's integration into community increased
Offender seen in fragments, offence being definitional	Offender viewed holistically
Sense of balance through retribution	Sense of balance through restitution
Balance righted by lowering offender	Balance righted by raising both victim and offender
Justice tested by intent and process	Justice tested by its "fruits"
Justice as right rules	Justice as right relationships
Victim-offender relationships ignored	Victim-offender relationships central
Process alienates	Process aims at reconciliation
Response based on offender's past behaviour	Response based on consequences of offender's behaviour
Repentance and forgiveness discouraged	Repentance and forgiveness encouraged
Proxy professions are the key actors	Victim and offender central; professional help available
Competitive, individualistic values encouraged	Mutuality and co-operation encouraged
Ignores social, economic, and moral context of behavior	Total context relevant
Assumes win-lose outcomes	Makes possible win-win outcomes

Retributive justice, restorative justice. The world looks quite differently through these two lenses. Retributive justice, we have. It may not do what needs to be done, or even what its practitioners claim it does, but it "works" in the sense that we know how to carry it out. What about the more elusive perspective that I've called restorative justice? Where do we go from here?

Endnotes

1   See M. Kay Harris, "Strategies, Values and the Emerging Generation of Alternatives to Incarceration," *New York University Review of Law and Social Change*, XII, No. 1 (1983-4), 141-170, and "Observations of a 'Friend of the Court' on the Future of Probation and Parole," *Federal Probation*, LI, No. 4 (December, 1987), pp. 12-21.

2   See, e.g., Louk Hulsman's work, cited above. See also John R. Blad, Hans van Mastrigt and Niels A. Uldriks, (eds.), *The Criminal Justice System as a Social Problem: An Abolitionist Perspective* (Rotterdam, Netherlands: Erasmus Universiteit, 1987).

3   Marshall Fortune raised this concern in a consultation on restorative justice and "tough cases" held in Guelph, Ontario, in 1986.

4   Cf. "Critical Criminology and rthe Concept of Crime," *Contemporary Crises: Law, Crime and Social Policy*, 10 (1986), pp. 63-80.

5   Ron Kraybill, "From Head to Heart: The Cycle of Reconciliation," *Mennonite Conciliation Service Conciliation Quarterly*, 7, No. 4 (Fall, 1988), p. 2.

6   Ron Claassen and Howard Zehr, *VORP Organizing: A Foundation in the Church* (Elkhart, Indiana: Mennonite Central Committee, 1988), p. 5.

7   Marie Marshall Fortune suggested this terminology at the Guelph consultation. Cf. Fortune, "Making Justice: Sources of Healing for Incest Survivors," *Working Together*, Summer, 1987, p. 5; and "Justice-Making in the Aftermath of Woman-Battering," *Domestic Violence on Trial*, ed. Daniel Sonkin (New York: Springer Publishers, 1987), pp. 237-248.

8   Wilma Derksen, "Have You Seen Candace?" (working title), manuscript in preparation for publication.

9   I am indebted to Marie Marshall for this term.

10 Morton MacCallum-Paterson, "Blood Cries: Lament, Wrath and the Mercy of God," *Touchstone*, May, 1987, p. 19.

11 John Lampen, *Mending Hurts* (London: Quaker Home Service, 1987), p. 57.

12 Cf. Jeffrie G. Murphy and Jean Hampton, *Forgiveness and Mercy* (Cambridge, England: Cambridge University Press, 1988).

13 See, for example, Russ Immarigeon, "Surveys Reveal Broad Support for Alternative Sentencing," *National Prison Project Journal*, No. 9 (Fall, 1986), pp. 1-4.

14 "Mediation," (FIRM) 5, No. 2 (March, 1989), p. 7.

15 Martin Wright, "From Retribution to Restoration: A New Model for Criminal Justice," *New Life: The Prison Service Chaplaincy Review*, 5 (1988), p. 49.

16   Dennis A. Challeen, *Making It Right: A Common Sense Approach to Crime* (Aberdeen, South Dakota: Mielius and Peterson Publishing, 1986).

17   See "Mediation," June, 1988; and Martin Wright, *Making Good: Prisons, Punishment and Beyond* (London: Burnett Books, 1982), pp. 246ff.

18   Mark Umbreit, *Victim Understanding of Fairness: Burglary Victims in Victim Offender Mediation* (Minneapolis: Minnesota Citizens Council on Crime and Justice, 1988), pp. 25ff.

19   Claassen and Zehr, *VORP Organizing*, pp. 24-25.

20   See, for example, Gilles Launay and Peter Murray, "Victim/Offender Groups," *Mediation and Criminal Justice*, ed. Wright and Galaway, pp. 113-131.

21   Walter H. Bera, "A Three Stage Sex Offender/Victim Reconciliation Model with a Systemic and Attributional Analysis." Unpublished paper prepared for the Task Force on Restorative Justice, October 30 through November 2, 1986, Guelph, Ontario.

22   See works previously cited.

Copyright Acknowledgements